Londinium:
A Biography

Londinium:
A Biography

Roman London from its Origins to the Fifth Century

Richard Hingley

Illustrations by Christina Unwin

BLOOMSBURY ACADEMIC
LONDON • NEW YORK • OXFORD • NEW DELHI • SYDNEY

BLOOMSBURY ACADEMIC
Bloomsbury Publishing Plc
50 Bedford Square, London, WC1B 3DP, UK
1385 Broadway, New York, NY 10018, USA
29 Earlsfort Terrace, Dublin 2, Ireland

BLOOMSBURY, BLOOMSBURY ACADEMIC and the Diana logo are trademarks of
Bloomsbury Publishing Plc

First published in Great Britain 2018
Reprinted 2018, 2019 (twice), 2021, 2023

Copyright © Richard Hingley, 2018

Library of Congress Cataloging-in-Publication Data
Names: Hingley, Richard, author. | Unwin, Christina, illustrator.
Title: Londinium : a biography : Roman London from its origin to the fifth century /
Richard Hingley ; illustrations by Christina Unwin.
Other titles: Roman London from its origin to the fifth century
Description: London, UK ; New York, NY : Bloomsbury Academic, 2018. |
Includes bibliographical references and index.
Identifiers: LCCN 2017055424 | ISBN 9781350047303(hardback) | ISBN 9781350047297 (pbk.) |
ISBN 9781350047327 (ePDF) | ISBN 9781350047310 (eBook)
Subjects: LCSH: London (England)–History–To 1500. | London (England)–Antiquities, Roman. |
Great Britain–History–Roman period, 55 B.C.-449 A.D.
Classification: LCC DA677.1 .H56 2018 | DDC936.2/12–dc23
LC record available at https://lccn.loc.gov/2017055424

ISBN: HB: 978-1-3500-4730-3
PB: 978-1-3500-4729-7
ePDF: 978-1-3500-4732-7
eBook: 978-1-3500-4731-0

Typeset by RefineCatch Limited, Bungay, Suffolk
Printed and bound in Great Britain

To find out more about our authors and books visit www.bloomsbury.com and sign up for our newsletters.

This book is dedicated to
the antiquaries and archaeologists
of Roman London
and especially to
Ralph Merrifield
(1913–1995)

CONTENTS

LIST OF ILLUSTRATIONS

PREFACE

This book is an exploration of Roman London that brings together evidence from the surveys, excavations and analyses conducted by the many archaeologists who have worked on the materials from this ancient urban centre. One of my inspirations for writing this book was Ralph Merrifield's handwritten dedication in a copy of the 1983 edition of his book *Roman London*, presented to Christina Unwin, an archaeologist and illustrator at the Museum of London at the time and now my partner. Christina contributed line-drawings to Ralph's book and has also produced all the maps and plans for this volume.

Building on earlier perspectives upon Roman London, this book draws upon the vast quantities of information that have been generated by archaeological investigations. I have to say that I did not fully anticipate the scale of the task involved in writing this book, although I maintain that it is vital for archaeologists once again to produce synthetic publications that address the details of the materials derived from ongoing excavations. I should make it clear that it is not possible to write a full history of Roman London that assesses all the important aspects of the urban settlement, since much of the data has not been fully processed and published. Instead, the aim of this book is to provide a synthesis of some of the most important information for Londinium and to present new perspectives consciously chosen to stimulate debate. Since my research interests extend from the beginning of the Iron Age to the Early Anglo-Saxon period, it is natural for me to explore across traditional chronological boundaries used in previous accounts of London.

I particularly wish to thank Christina Unwin for her excellent work on the illustrations and for her consistent help with the editing and production of this volume. Nick Bateman encouraged me to pursue this initiative at an early stage and I am very grateful to him for his discussion of aspects of Roman London and for his comments on the entire text of the book. Peter Rowsome, James Gerrard and Jenny Hall also helped me to set this research in context at an early stage in the writing. Anthony Birley and Roger Tomlin read through the entire text and I am particularly grateful for their attention to detail and guidance concerning Latin terms and the meanings of some complex linguistic concepts. Peter Marsden provided insightful and detailed comments on the important excavations he has undertaken in Roman London and I am grateful for his permission to use his photographs. Jenny Proctor and Victoria Ridgeway provided advice and access to a number of unpublished reports produced by Pre-Construct Archaeology; I am grateful to Victoria for permission to use the photograph of the Tabbard Square temple inscription. Rebecca Redfern made a considerable contribution to the sections of the book that address the dead of Londinium and I am particularly grateful for her extensive and helpful comments based on her highly innovative work at the Museum of London. Mike Fulford made several really useful observations about early Roman London. Colin Haselgrove and Tom Moore provided insightful comments on the Iron Age landscape.

The comments of five anonymous referees, appointed by Bloomsbury Academic, on the first draft of this book, helped me to refine the arguments I have used in discussion. I wish to thank the editors and staff at Bloomsbury for their help and guidance.

The picture research for this book was greatly facilitated by Andy Chopping, Head of Photography at MOLA, and by Richard Dabb, Picture Library Researcher, and the Museum of London. My grateful thanks to the following: Faber & Faber and Farrar, Straus & Giroux for the extract from 'Bog Queen' by Seamus Heaney; Peter Ackroyd for the quotation from *London Under* (2012); Cooking Vinyl for the extract from the lyrics of 'Defending Ancient Springs' by Jackie Leven; and Verso Books for the quotation from Jean Baudrilliard's *Passwords* (2003).

Durham University provided a grant that funded preparation of the maps and plans that form a vital part of this publication and also allowed me two terms of research leave specifically for the writing of this book.

Richard Hingley
Shincliffe
County Durham

Introduction

In the deep discovery of the Subterranean world, a shallow part
would satisfy some Enquirers.

THOMAS BROWNE 1658: 1

Setting the scene

This book explores the evidence for Roman London, which was the most substantial urban settlement of Roman Britain.[1] It may have been made a colony during the second century and probably served as the provincial capital for much of the Roman period, but definitive evidence for its urban status is lacking. The study of its remains commenced during the seventeenth century and, since the middle of the nineteenth century, excavation and research has been conducted on a substantial scale. Following the destruction of much of the city's urban infrastructure during the bombing raids of the Second World War, extensive excavations were carried out. The substantial scale of London's development as a financial centre since the 1980s has led to major campaigns of excavation and post-excavation work. As a result, it is often stated that Londinium is one of the most extensively excavated of the cities of the Roman Empire.[2] The popular journals *British Archaeology* and *Current Archaeology* regularly feature significant new discoveries made during urban development, while major discoveries are also featured in the national media. Regular items in *London Archaeologist* also provide a survey of recent discoveries. Highlights have included the discovery of the amphitheatre (1988), the discovery and excavation of the temple site at Tabard Square in Southwark (2002–3) and the recent uncovering of a substantial number of writing tablets at the Bloomberg site, close to the Walbrook river (2012–14). Significant new discoveries are made almost every year. This book demonstrates the considerable significance of the archaeological work that has been conducted and the vital role of this research in establishing the early history of London, providing a general review of a complex and substantial body of information.

As a result of this highly important archaeological work, a large number of publications have assessed aspects of Roman London's urban infrastructure, its people and the classes of objects recovered from excavation.[3] The Roman gallery in the Museum of London communicates the evidence in an accessible way for both Londoners and visitors. There is an excellent map and an app, 'Londinium', for smart phones.[4] Peter Rowsome has commented that 'We know a lot about Roman London but some interesting research still remains to be done.'[5] James Gerrard has observed in his study of late Roman London that 'Nothing could be further from the truth' than to suggest that few 'big questions' remain to be answered.[6] In many areas opinions are strongly divided regarding the archaeology of Londinium.

Yet, as I started to write this book, the last full synthesis of the evidence was published in 2000 and the most thorough account dates from 1991.[7] There is no more up to date academic synthesis than these of information from Roman London.[8] Archaeological work since the mid-1990s has entirely transformed the comprehension of London's Roman past as a result of the very substantial scale of excavation work,[9] particularly with regard to the characters and lives of its occupants and the later history of Londinium. It is very difficult, however, for scholars, students and the public to appreciate this material. Although some attempts at synthesis have been produced, these articles address only certain aspects of the archaeological record. Perhaps the quantity of new information is, in itself, preventing synthesis by constraining the production of new ideas and original thought.

In addition, research frameworks for London's Roman archaeology have been viewed as conservative and traditional.[10] Although crucially important studies of particular aspects of Roman London have been published since 2000, many of these reflect the gradual transform-ations of earlier interpretations.[11] This may help to explain the relatively few references to London in the 2001 *Archaeological Agenda* for Roman Britain and in the recent *Handbook of Roman Britain*.[12] Since the mid-1990s the agenda for Roman studies has been deeply transformed by the development of more critical and nuanced accounts of Roman Britain and the Roman Empire.[13] These approaches often appear to have had little impact on research focused on London.[14] It is true that a number of useful accounts of aspects of the information have placed the evidence from Roman London in a broader geographical and theoretical context, but much remains to be achieved. The development of new understandings of the character of Londinium in this book builds upon the foundation of all the excellent archaeological research that has been undertaken over several generations. Working to place this material in a broader intellectual and geographical focus can help to make the published research of truly international significance.

This book aims to assess Roman London in the context of the province and the empire. The motivation is, in part, to provide a set of contrasting research perspectives that aim to recast comprehension in a different light. This book is also intended to provide an accessible introduction for students to the main themes alongside a detailed body of references. This is not an assessment of Londinium's environs but the book explores activities occurring at and slightly beyond its margins.[15] These include areas of settlement and burial (Shadwell, Old Ford and St Martin-in-the-Fields), but not the broader landscapes that surrounded Roman London and supplied it with resources.

Research perspectives

Part of the purpose of this study is to emphasize the considerable significance of the archaeological research that has been undertaken in London since the 1950s and how this information can be used to provide new understanding.[16] I seek to provide a biography of Roman London, building upon other biographical works, including my own earlier writings.[17] This book develops this critical angle through a detailed assessment of past observations, but the amount of published literature prevents the full implementation of a critical assessment.

Although this book explores the evidence for the economy, industry, trade, status and urban infrastructure, the narrative takes a different perspective from past accounts.[18] In looking at how power, status, gender and identity are reflected through the materiality of the evolving urban landscape, the ritual and religious context in which these activities occurred is also addressed. It explores the evidence for the multiple functions of Londinium in the context of the meanings of places through time.[19] The rituals and religious beliefs of the people who populated Roman London should not be separated from aspects such as status, power, economy and industry. Drawing deeply on the seminal research of Ralph Merrifield, among others, this book addresses the idea that ritual, power and everyday life are unlikely always to have represented entirely separate fields of experience.[20] It investigates the plural landscapes and waterscapes of Londinium with regard to the different ritual practices they encompassed, including everyday rituals and more public forms of religious activity.[21] In particular, it focuses upon the concept that places within the urban landscape were inherited,[22] that the history and meanings of particular places within the urban landscapes were built upon earlier associations derived from the recent and ancient past.[23]

The numerous cult places of Iron Age Britain would have been in the open, including hilltops, dense woodlands, springs, rivers and brooks. Many beliefs are also reflected in the landscapes and waterscapes of Roman Britain, and rituals were conducted and offerings made to the spirits who inhabited particular places. Archaeological discoveries indicate activities that provide information about the spirits that once inhabited these places. Spirits, or genii, were believed to inhabit the Roman world as guardians of particular places who needed to be placated. Small models of gods and goddesses are frequently found throughout Londinium.[24] Offerings were also made at certain times in the life history of everyday structures and places and, indeed, foundation deposits and termination deposits are not uncommon in wells and houses across Londinium. It is most important to address how rituals drew upon a wide range of actions and concepts that aimed to set these practices apart from everyday routines.[25] Rituals extended from the local and informal and ephemeral to the highly-organized and monumental, forming a continuum of practices that were not entirely set apart from other aspects of life.[26] The perspectives explored in this book suggest that it is vitally important to focus on the ritual meaning of actions in everyday contexts and public spaces across Roman London.[27] In this regard, water and the control of water appears to have formed a vital aspect of its ritual and economic significance. As Veronica Strang has observed, water in the landscape is invariably encoded with the powers of life and death.[28] We shall see that this observation is deeply relevant to the interpretation of the archaeological discoveries that have been made when the deeply-buried remains of Roman London have been disturbed by modern development.[29]

Two particular themes that are explored in detail are (i) defining place though bounding, draining, consolidating and building; and (ii) the peopling of place, addressing the evidence for the populations in London and their transforming traditions of life. The first theme builds on research that has addressed the ritual and symbolic creation of the urban spaces. The materiality of the urban settlement and how the creation of place transformed the meanings inherent in the landscapes that were incorporated are extensively explored. New places were created through the establishment of Londinium, their meanings as transforming terrains, waterscapes, structures and places drawing upon the past history of the particular locations. The meanings of the dry, waterlogged and wet places that made up this extensive urban area were dramatically changed, perhaps reflecting the earlier history of the significance of place.

Envisaging the people of Roman London may be approached through the extensive research that has been undertaken on the physical remains of their bodies, but also by drawing upon evidence for practices such as literacy, naming and lifestyles.[30] In this way we can populate the urban landscapes of the Roman world. This book interprets ways of life by drawing deeply on the important work undertaken by the Museum of London. This theme also addresses the interface between current conceptions of ancestry, origin and muticulturalism and the evidence provided through research.[31] This is becoming central to changing interpretations of Roman Britain, reflecting the social and cultural issues of our own time.[32]

This book is divided into nine chapters showing how the town was developed through time and a final chapter that summarizes the arguments. As such, it primarily emphasizes the making and bounding of Londinium during the period of its construction, occupation and eventual (partial) abandonment.

Qualifications

A number of issues are fundamental to the approach taken in this book. First, the urban context in which the modern excavations have been undertaken means that the available information for buildings, streets and urban plans is almost always extremely fragmentary. Over the decades, archaeologists have attempted to build up a comprehensive picture of the development of Londinium, culminating in the production of the informative map of Roman London produced by the Museum of London in 2011. The app mentioned above provides a site-by-site account of the individual archaeological features that can be used by visitors exploring London today. It is not simple, however, for a visitor to understand the physical form of the urban landscape and waterscape, or the development and eventual abandonment of Londinium.[33] Only fragments of the buildings, street systems and cemeteries have been excavated (see Fig. 0.1), while only a very

FIG. 0.1 Archaeologists from the Museum of London excavate the remains of the walls and mosaic floors of a late Roman building at 1 Poultry in 1994.

FIG. 0.2 The line of the arena wall of the amphitheatre, excavated in 1992–9, is marked by dark slates set into the patterned pavement of Guildhall Yard. This view looks eastwards towards Guildhall Art Gallery, below which the eastern entrance of the amphitheatre is displayed.

few physical traces remain visible in the modern city (see Fig. 0.2). In addition, the terrain and waterscapes have been changed a great deal over the past 2,000 years.

Second, the scale of the excavations has resulted in the publication of many highly important articles and monographs.[34] This book will not address the history of excavation and discovery of archaeological remains, but a short summary of the major finds and excavations will help to set the available material in context.[35] The first significant stage of antiquarian research was marked by the work of Sir Christopher Wren and John Conyers during the late seventeenth and eighteenth centuries, recording the burials and kilns found during the rebuilding of St Paul's Cathedral.[36] During the eighteenth century, few records were kept of disturbed archaeological deposits, although mosaic floors were illustrated, including the elaborate design from Leadenhall Street.[37] Major archaeological discoveries were being made during the 1830s and 1840s as a result of the improvement of the sewers and the building of London Bridge.[38] The antiquary Charles Roach Smith produced an extensive record of the Roman remains uncovered by this work and established a collection of the finds which was later acquired by the British Museum.[39] In 1848 a suite of impressive heated rooms was found at the new Coal Exchange in Lower Thames Street (now known as the Billingsgate bathhouse).[40] The large mosaic floor uncovered at Bucklersbury in 1869 generated great public interest (Figure 0.3).[41]

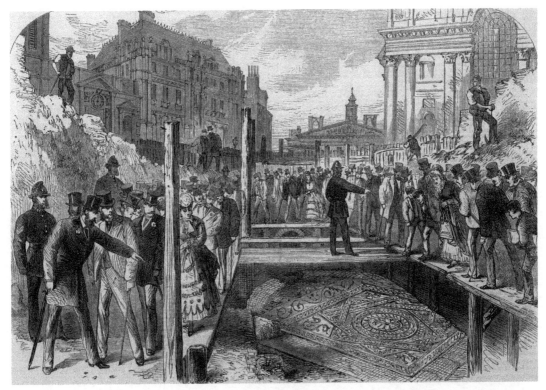

FIG. 0.3 The Bucklersbury mosaic, the 'Roman Pavement found in the Poultry, near the Mansion Houses'. Illustration from the *Illustrated London News*, volume LIV (1540, 1541), 29 May 1869, p. 545.

The discovery of the well-preserved ship in the Thames muds at County Hall in 1910 also helped to publicize the Roman past,[42] but excavations of structures in advance of development remained rare. The Guildhall Museum and the London Museum developed collections of Roman objects from London during the late nineteenth and early twentieth centuries.[43]

Bomb damage during the Second World War resulted in a substantial programme of excavation in advance of urban reconstruction work.[44] Significant discoveries made by Professor W. F. Grimes between 1946 and 1968 included the fort at Cripplegate and the well-preserved temple of Mithras.[45] Peter Marsden conducted significant excavations on the sites of the 'governor's palace' during the 1960s and early 1970s, Huggin Hill bathhouse in 1964 and 1969, and the Blackfriars ship in 1962–3.[46] The establishment of the Museum of London's Department of Urban Archaeology (DUA), a full-time archaeological field unit, in the early 1970s focused attention on the city's Roman past, and from this the current archaeological provisions developed.[47] The Museum of London Archaeological Service (MOLAS) was established in 1992 and this has become the largest archaeological contractor working in London.[48] This archaeological unit became Museum of London Archaeology (MOLA) in 2008. A number of other commercial archaeological units also operate in London.[49] Many of the important excavation reports published in the past fifteen years have been produced by MOLA, but knowledge of Londinium has developed as a result of excavations throughout the city.[50] This work has often been disparate, uncovering only limited areas of buildings and urban landscapes, but it has provided vitally important information about the chronology and topography of Roman London.

These excavations have made certain aspects of Londinium extremely well known. For example, we now have a detailed understanding of the houses belonging to some of the less wealthy people, considerable knowledge of the objects that they possessed and some information on aspects of their lifestyles. We also know a good deal about the location and chronology of 'public' buildings.[51] This knowledge is often extremely fragmentary, but it is also extensive. Londinium is the best-known Roman town in Britain and one of the most studied urban centres of the empire.

Owing to the limited areas of excavation and the destruction by later development of the buried deposits, the task of writing this book may be compared to assembling a massive jigsaw puzzle with up to 95 per cent of the pieces missing. In reality, this process has been far more complex, since these landscapes and waterscapes were in constant transition through time. As a result, instead of one picture there is a constantly transforming set of images for Roman London over almost four centuries. The uncertainties of archaeological dating techniques means that it has often been possible to give only broad dates to individual phases of buildings. This has been used to split the sequence of activities on individual sites into the scheme adopted in the nine chapters.[52]

Londinium has been explored so extensively that this book can only provide a partial impression based mainly on published accounts or those in the public domain.[53] Some aspects have been fully interpreted and detailed recent studies are available for some classes of material.[54] In addition, much could be achieved by the increased use of GIS to plot and analyse the distribution of both artefacts and structures.[55] This book draws upon the available information and recent discussions to highlight themes that draw aspects of the archaeology of Londinium together.

Some events in the early history of Roman London help to explain the chronological span of Chapters 1 to 9 in this book. The extensive burnt deposits that are thought to mark the destruction of Londinium by Boudica in AD 60 and the widespread fire that occurred during the AD 120s or 130s help to divide periods of construction, but there are some doubts about the extent to which either of these events entirely destroyed Roman London. Information for elements of Roman London has been placed into a chronological framework, usually following the arguments of the excavators and finds specialists who have undertaken the most recent work.[56] Much of the material derived from Londinium is not, however, very closely dated and this means that some items cannot be incorporated into the chapters. In addition, the dating of many finds and sites is open to detailed discussion. Many events and activities that cannot be ignored are not closely dated and are placed where they seem to fit best; for example, the building of the landward section of the Roman wall, which has been dated to different times between the AD 120s and later third centuries, is included in Chapter 8. Evidently, this building programme will have had a substantial impact on life in Roman London, but it is not closely dated.

The names used for Roman sites in this book mainly relate to the modern City of London, since we have no certain knowledge of the names used by Londinium's inhabitants for particular areas and features. A lead sheet of unknown purpose was found in 1984 during excavation at Billingsgate Lorry Park and has an inscription which includes the words '*Vico Iovio*', meaning 'Jupiter's Village'.[57] This is likely to record the name of an unknown place, perhaps in Britain,[58] although it is also possible that it records the name of a 'ward' of Londinium.[59] A jug found in 1912 has an inscription '*Londini ad fanum Isidis*', meaning 'At the temple of Isis, London'.[60] The 'addresses' on the Bloomberg writing tablets do not refer, however, to places but to the names of people.[61] For example, Writing Tablet 14 contains the statement 'You will give [this] to Junius the cooper, opposite [the house of] Catullus'.[62] We do know the names of some gods and spirits that were worshipped within this landscape and the names of a number of Londinium's inhabitants. Occasionally, we can place individuals in particular parts of the urban landscape, particularly through burial monuments and occasionally as a result of dedications. Those names given by the people of Roman London to buildings, streets, rivers, streams and wetlands are unfortunately, however, likely to remain unknown.

The Guildhall Museum and, from 1972, the Museum of London have allocated site names and site codes to the numerous excavations based on the present topography of the city. Individual sites are referred to by these names (e.g. 'Bloomberg'); the site code (e.g. 'BZY10') is given alongside the main published references (e.g. 'Tomlin 2016') in the relevant endnote.[63]

Justification

This book is likely to frustrate a number of archaeologists who specialize in the archaeology of Roman London since they will probably see the arguments as based on incomplete information. However complex this information may be, archaeologists really need to produce new syntheses. Specialist work is vitally important but the results of such research need to be placed in a broader context by looking more widely. The approach in this book is to look across the boundaries between some of the chronological, methodological and theoretical categories into which the archaeological information has been placed in order to explore research directions that draw upon both the surviving materials themselves and past ideas.

1

Rites of Passage on the Thames
in the Iron Age

and I rose from the dark,
hacked bone, skull-ware,
frayed stitches, tufts,
small gleams on the bank.

SEAMUS HEANEY 1990: 68

Introduction

There is no evidence for a nucleated settlement in the London area prior to the Roman conquest of south-eastern Britain. Many of the southern Roman urban settlements of the province of Britannia were preceded by Late Iron Age 'oppida' which came to form local centres of power in the Roman period due to the cooperation of native elites with the Roman administration.[1] Londinium was apparently an exception to this rule. It has often been argued that it was developed in a liminal space at the boundary between a number of the distinct Late Iron Age coin distributions and approximately midway between the *oppida* that are supposed to represent the power-centres of these peoples (see Fig. 1.1).[2] Nevertheless, the landscape across which Roman London was to be built had particular significance, indicated by the Iron Age metalwork that has been found in the River Thames between Battersea and the City.[3]

An academic fixation with the centrality of power in Late Iron Age Britain has led to the idea that the area in which Londinium was to develop was largely unoccupied and insignificant prior to the arrival of the Roman army in AD 43. Relatively little Middle to Late Iron Age material has been found during the archaeological excavations in and around the City. Nevertheless, richly elaborate items of Iron Age metalwork have been discovered in the River Thames and the claim for the Roman foundation of Londinium may have obscured evidence for continuity between the Iron Age and Roman uses of land and water.[4]

Thinking about the potential of this location for Late Iron Age activity is made problematic by the dominant concept of London as a Roman foundation.[5] The existence of a strong tradition of research means that the available evidence has been placed in an unchallenged chronological sequence. Most Roman towns across the south-east of the province of Britannia originated before the Roman conquest. The local populations of these places are likely to have obtained the support of the Roman administration during the conquest period in order to encourage

FIG. 1.1 Britain in the Late Iron Age, with the main regional coin distributions, selected *oppida* and the location of Londinium.

urbanization projects within the *civitates* of the south of the province.[6] The Roman colony of Camulodunum (Colchester) was an official establishment but a substantial '*oppidum*' had preceded the fortress and colony at this site.[7] This had been the main power-base from which armed opposition to Rome was organized in AD 43. The Roman towns that developed at Verulamium (St Alban's), Calleva (Silchester), Durovernum (Canterbury) and Noviomagus Regnorum (Chichester) all appear to have been preceded by Late Iron Age *oppida*.[8]

These tribal centres are thought to have formed the dominant political places within the Late Iron Age landscape of south-eastern Britain, the political and religious centres of 'kingdoms'. *Oppida* are generally defined by characteristics such as substantial linear dykes enclosing a territory, nucleated settlement, high status burials, imported high-quality goods from the continent (including pottery, amphorae and metalwork) and the production of a local series of coins.[9] Many of the southern British *oppida* developed into towns in the decades following AD 43. Archaeologists have therefore expected to find evidence for concentrations of Late Iron Age high-status activities at central places, although the activities that defined many of the *oppida* were dispersed across extensive territories. The presence of Roman towns has also sometimes been used to identify the locations of *oppida* even when many of the other distinctive characteristics have not been identified.

The absence of such evidence underlying London has led to the idea that this location had little significance at this time.[10] The linear earthwork known as Grim's Dyke (close to Oxhey and Brockley Hill to the north-west of London) is possibly partly Late Iron Age in date, but comparatively little is known of its significance, dating and context.[11] No nucleated settlement or high-status burials have been found. Imported continental material and high-status goods have not been identified in the archaeological deposits below the modern City.[12] Although Iron Age coins, including potin coins, have been found on the gravel terraces of west London, these are not sufficient to indicate the location of an *oppidum*.[13] Indeed, it has been suggested that at this time the London area was on the periphery of the zone of continental imports, high-status burials and *oppida* development.[14]

This provides too definitive an impression of the complex nature of power.[15] The nature of the Late Iron Age is undergoing a fundamental review that may throw new light on the foundation of Londinium. Tom Moore has argued against the concept that distinct 'tribal' groupings were based in clear territorial units.[16] He has proposed that the idea of 'tribes' has been projected backwards in time from the more centralized system of *civitates* that characterized the Roman political organization of southern Britannia. Places of power during the Late Iron Age are likely to have reflected a more fluid cultural system of changing alliances. In this context, the power centres that we refer to as '*oppida*' appear only to have developed in the decades prior to the Roman invasion and then continued to be elaborated following the settlement of the province. Moore has argued that these *oppida* developed as meeting places, which were later elaborated through the creation of monuments that projected the political power and status of the dominant families in a region.[17] It has been assumed that there were only a few 'royal sites' or capitals during the Late Iron Age, although the evidence increasingly suggests that there were multiple places of ritual and social significance throughout the landscape. Without certain 'signals' such as dykes and rich burials, these places are often unrecognized or misinterpreted.[18]

Many of these *oppida* were in areas of the landscape that were sparsely occupied during the period preceding their initial development.[19] It is possible that these places coalesced in marginal locations because they constituted new locales for creating and developing power. After the initial conquest of AD 43 it would have been in the interests of the Roman government of

Britannia to support these developments in particular territories since the administration of the province was based on local government. The terrain of Londinium was intersected by river courses and streams and was a waterscape as much as a landscape. It may have constituted a neutral area in which the Roman urban centre developed in a manner that was independent of pre-existing power-relations, reflecting developments that were occurring a few decades earlier at Calleva, Verulamium and Camulodunum.

In this chapter it is suggested that there is considerably greater evidence for Middle and Late Iron Age activity in particular parts of the Roman urban area than has previously been supposed.[20] This is not to dismiss the trading and administrative significance of the location at which early Roman London was to develop, but it emphasizes that past events rarely have one simple explanation. This chapter will suggest that the significance of this area as a place to meet and to dispose of the dead may have contributed to the location of Londinium and its development during early Roman times. It may be suggested that during the Iron Age the banks of the Thames and the islands in the river constituted the interface between the territories of the living and the dead, explaining why human remains and metalwork came to be deposited in the Thames.

Medieval foundation myths

The idea that Londinium was founded in the early Roman period was developed to dismiss the medieval origin myth suggesting that it was founded many centuries before the Romans came to Britain.[21] According to a medieval myth of origin, London was founded several hundred years before the Romans arrived in Britain and its encircling walls were constructed by King Lud. This legendary tale is derived from the allegedly traditional story composed by Geoffrey of Monmouth (*HKB* i: 17) that a group of Trojans commanded by Brutus founded 'Troia Nova' ('New Troy'), later known as Trinovantium.[22] Geoffrey also claimed that, at a later date, King Lud, the brother of Cassivelaunus, surrounded his capital with lofty walls and towers and renamed it Kaerlud, or 'Lud's city', later known as 'London'. Geoffrey stated that Lud 'ordered the citizens to construct their homes and buildings there in such a style that no other city in the most far-flung of kingdoms could boast of palaces more fair' (*HKB* iii: 20). Geoffrey also related that when Lud died, his body was buried in this city, near a gateway named after him in British as Porthlud, called in Saxon 'Ludgate'.

During the reign of Queen Elizabeth I, John Stow included a summary of this myth in his *Survay of London* (1598),[23] although he also noted that Julius Caesar's commentary on Britain was 'of farre better credit' than that of Geoffrey of Monmouth.[24] Stow repeated Geoffrey's suggestion that Ludgate was named after King Lud but also provided some details about the medieval gateway, which included statues of Lud and other ancient mythical figures. He noted that the gateway was rebuilt in 1586 with new figures of Lud and 'others' on its east side and a contemporary image of the Queen, Elizabeth, on the west.[25] Stow also discussed another medieval gateway called Billingsgate and cast doubt on Geoffrey of Monmouth's suggestion (*HKB* iii: 10) that this was first constructed by a British king called Beline (Belinus) several centuries before the Roman conquest.

Prior to the late seventeenth century, little was known of the origins of London, but Stow used the comments of Tacitus to challenge Londinium's mythical history. Stow mentioned the writings of Tacitus to record that at the time of revolt of AD 62 (now believed to have taken place in AD 60 or 61) Londinium was not a colony, but was 'most famous for the great multitude of marchantes, provision, and intercourse'. Stow also wrote that London, like other Roman towns in Britain, appeared to have been walled in stone and he made a few additional comments about earlier discoveries of Roman antiquities. Although Geoffrey of Monmouth's fables concerning the origins of London have persisted into modern times, from the early seventeenth century most scholars paid greater attention to the observations of the writer Tacitus and to the growing information about the buried Roman deposits uncovered in London by building works. The next significant stage in antiquarian research was marked by the work of Sir Christopher Wren during the late seventeenth and eighteenth centuries. It was to take centuries of antiquarian and historical research to finally dismiss the ideas embodied in this mythical history and the claim that Lud and Belinus were historical figures.

Pre-Roman London

The substantial research into the archaeology of London has created a far better understanding of the prehistoric landscape that lies under the modern city. The available evidence from the area that became overlain by Roman London, both to the north and south of the Thames, indicates that there was little occupation and settlement during the period immediately prior to the Roman conquest.[26] By contrast, a larger quantity of evidence exists for occupation and agriculture earlier in prehistory, particularly during the Late Bronze Age. The substantial evidence for Late Bronze Age and Early Iron occupation contrasts with the particularly scarce Middle and Late Iron Age activity across this landscape.[27] Although some sites have been located in the outer areas of the modern city, these are generally little known, and little material has been found beneath Londinium itself. The quantity of information is, however, increasing.

Landscapes and waterscapes

In discussing the etymology of the name Londinium, Richard Coates has suggested that it may have originated from an Old European language stratum and was a compound name of two elements.[28] He has reconstructed an early form that may have the meaning 'river notable for boats', 'river which requires swimming, as opposed to fording, to cross it', or perhaps 'river which characteristically floods'.[29] Coates has suggested that the name might have originally been applied to the Thames at London during later prehistoric times and that it subsequently was taken as the name of the Roman settlement.[30] The terrain over which Londinium was to be built was transected by the River Thames and its network of tributaries, making this landscape a challenging area to urbanize (see Fig. 1.2).[31] The considerable archaeological research into the course and nature of some of these waterways and the environmental evidence has provided information about these pre-Roman and Roman landscapes and waterscapes.[32]

Today only the Thames is visible in London's modern urban landscape, since the other rivers and streams have been canalized and buried under the modern city. The Thames was far wider before the Roman period, with less well-defined banks, tidal floodplains and several islands near its south bank in the area of modern Southwark and also further to the west and east. Information has been collected from environmental analysis of river deposits to assess the changing location of the River Thames tidal head through time. By the Late Bronze Age the river was consistently tidal as far upstream as Thorney Island.[33] There appears to have been a downstream migration of the tidal head in the Roman period, which is generally used to explain the disuse of the final

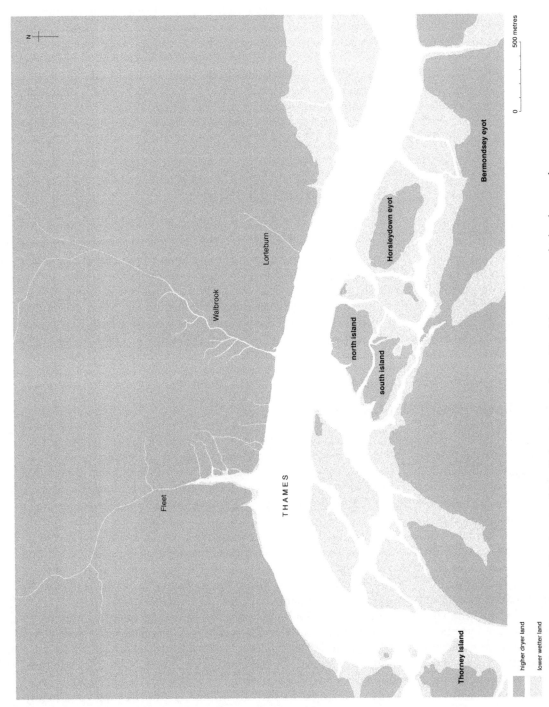

FIG. 1.2 Riverscape and landscape of Londinium in around AD 43, with streams and islands named.

waterfront works in the mid-third century,[34] although it appears to have moved upstream again during the late Roman and Early Saxon periods.[35] Roman Londinium and the Middle Saxon settlement of Lundenwic may both have been located around the head of the tidal reach.[36]

To the north of the Thames, Londinium was eventually to develop across three hills between watercourses. The westernmost spread of Roman London was defined by the River Fleet which was fed by additional tributaries from its east side.[37] Just to the east another series of streams was canalized in Roman times to form the 'western stream' later incorporated into the urban area.[38] The centre of Roman London was transected by the Walbrook which was fed by several streams in its upper reaches,[39] where the land formed a 'natural amphitheatre'.[40] The eastern boundary of early Londinium was marked by another watercourse, the Lorteburn, flowing south-westwards to the Thames.[41] The hills of London were composed of brickearth overlying gravel terraces. The underlying interface between the gravels and the London Clay forms a natural spring line, which suggests that springs of fresh water will have been common across this area. Along the north bank of the Thames, substantial works were undertaken, from the mid-first century AD to the mid-third century, to develop a series of waterfront installations to supplement the natural slope of the riverbank and to provide harbour facilities.

To the south, Londinium was gradually built across the two main islands in the river, generally referred to in archaeological publications as the 'north island' and the 'south island', and there were also a number of smaller islands (eyots). All the islands in the Thames were subject to regular tidal flooding, but the building of waterfront revetments and the dumping of material during the Roman period gradually filled in some of the channels, particularly between the north and the south island and between the latter and the south bank of the river.

The available environmental evidence from this landscape, particularly from the waterlogged deposits of the Walbrook, suggests that woodland had not been entirely cleared by the Late Iron Age and that there had been a regeneration of tree growth after the large-scale clearance during the Middle Bronze Age.[42] Detailed work on pollen from the recent excavations at 1 Poultry, just west of the Walbrook, suggests that the Iron Age landscape here was uncultivated wasteland or rough pasture with scattered trees.[43] Work at the 'governor's palace' has revealed a pre-Roman marsh that probably covered the north bank of the Thames close to its confluence with the Walbrook.[44] The environmental evidence from this location indicates that the Walbrook was clean and slow moving before the Roman invasion. There are other indications of a moderately swampy or marshy riverside beside the Thames and in its tributary valleys, but evidence also exists to indicate that there was open grassland and that wheat, barley, oats and rye were being cultivated across the area that was to become Londinium.[45] This arable cultivation within the vicinity of the area that was to become Roman London may indicate that at least some parts of the landscape were not as underused as has sometimes been surmised.[46]

The current evidence suggests that the drier areas between the river valleys north of the Thames were sparsely settled during the decades prior to the Roman conquest.[47] The small-scale nature of many of the excavations in London may have prevented the discovery of more extensive evidence for Iron Age activity, but enough work has been undertaken to indicate that there was no substantial or nucleated Late Iron Age settlement under the City of London. Roman and later activity across the area of the present city has removed substantial areas of the pre-Roman ground surface but elsewhere in London there are deposits built up by activities during the Roman period.[48] It is here that prehistoric deposits would have been protected from later disturbance. Iron Age activity has been located on the 'north island' and on some of the other eyots in the Thames at Southwark, including the Horselydown and Bermondsey eyots.

Islands, rivers and rites of passage

There were many islands in the Thames before it was canalized and drained, including in the reaches of the rivers that flow through London; the role of these islands and eyots is a particularly significant issue.[49] Richard Bradley has explored the deposition of human remains and metalwork items, particularly weapons, in the River Thames during the Bronze Age and Iron Age.[50] This forms part of a broader tradition which extends to much of eastern Britain and the Low Countries.[51] Bradley and Ken Gordon have commented that it is 'tempting to suggest that some of the finds from the Thames were deposited during rites of passage to another world' during a period when it seems that people were not usually buried.[52] A large quantity of human remains and metalwork found in the Thames may have been associated with the disposal of the dead, perhaps focused upon the islands and banks of the river.[53]

Around 150 human cranial remains have been recorded from the Thames and its tributaries,[54] although many others will have been lost without detailed records being made.[55] Radiocarbon dating of the cranial remains of twenty-four individuals from the Thames and its tributaries has shown that they were mainly Late Neolithic, Bronze Age and Iron Age people, with a number from the Roman and later periods.[56] Recent research has indicated that many of these cranial remains exhibit both healed and unhealed injuries inflicted with weapons.[57] The general scarcity of crania from the Thames dated to the Roman period suggests that the natural or cultural factors that led them to be deposited in the river during prehistory had come to an end.[58]

Items of metalwork discovered in the Thames close to the later site of Londinium include artefacts such as the Battersea and Wandsworth shields and the Waterloo Bridge helmet (see Fig. 1.3).[59] These are visually impressive objects from an established tradition of the deposition of later prehistoric weapons in the river.[60]

Recent evidence from two excavations in southern Britain may help to place the human bone and metalwork from the Thames in context, emphasizing the significance of rivers and islands in rites of passage. The excavations at Eton Rowing Course (Berkshire) in the Thames Valley have provided direct evidence that bodies were deliberately deposited on the edges of islands in the Thames during later prehistory to enable the remains to be removed by the river currents.[61] A recent excavation directed by Christopher Evans in the Cambridgeshire Fenlands has explored an island in a braided river channel of the Great Ouse at the western end of the Godwin Ridge, where an Iron Age settlement and a substantial embankment were associated with large quantities of pottery, animal bone and some human bone, formed by 'ridge-end rituals'.[62] Evans has drawn on the evidence for the deposition of cranial remains in the Thames to support the idea that corpses were exposed to river water on river banks at Godwin Ridge.[63]

Plentiful information for Bronze Age activity on the islands and eyots of Southwark includes ard marks from cultivation and finds that are likely to indicate occupations.[64] For the Iron Age, when the tidal reach was higher, there is less data for occupation, and deposits of this date may have been lost as a result of river erosion.[65] The environmental evidence suggests that the islands and southern riverbank of the Thames around Southwark were low-lying marsh with some evidence for grassland and deciduous woodland.[66] A deposit of river clay over natural gravels has been found in several places, suggesting that these islands were flooded during the Late Iron Age or early Roman periods.[67] The evidence for periodic flooding indicates that any activities at these places may have been seasonal.[68]

Figures 1.4 and 1.5 show finds dating to the Middle and Late Iron Age in relation to the river courses as they were around the time of the Roman conquest.[69] Considering the human remains from Eton Rowing Course and Godwin Ridge, it may be assumed that the pottery and scattered

FIG. 1.3 This bronze ceremonial helmet and covering for a leather or wooden shield were found in the River Thames. The helmet was found near Waterloo Bridge some time prior to June 1866 and the shield covering was found near Battersea in 1857. Both have been decorated in the curvilinear La Tène style.

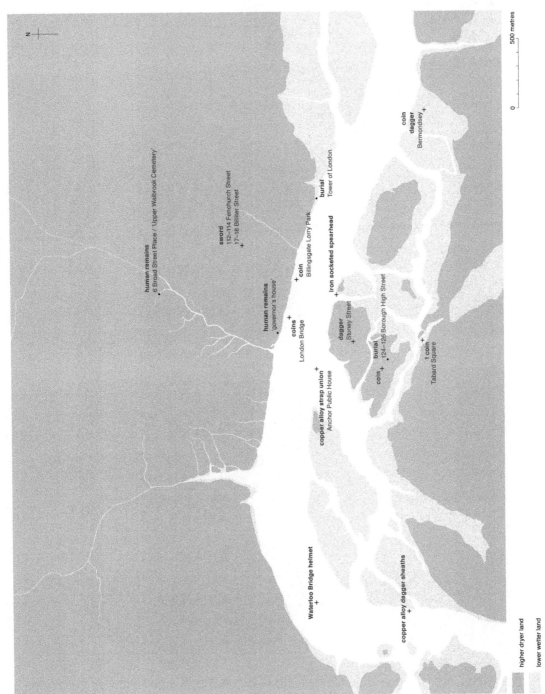

higher dryer land

lower wetter land

FIG. 1.4 Iron Age human remains and metalwork finds in the area of Londinium.

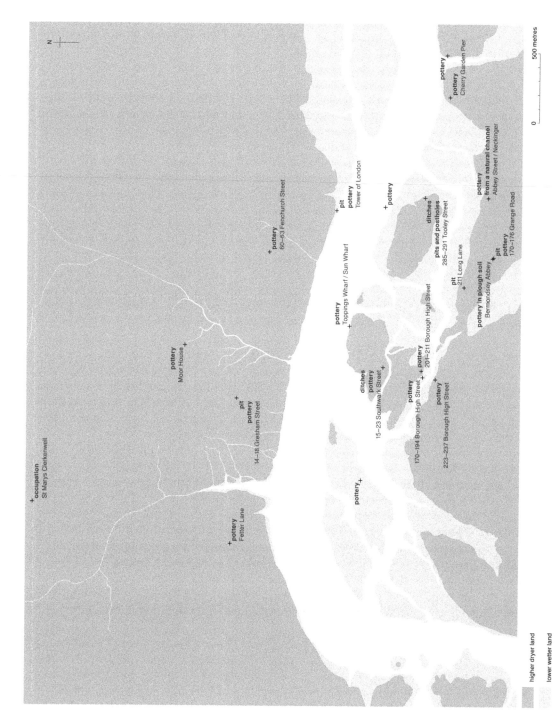

FIG. 1.5 Middle and Late Iron Age pottery and archaeological features in the area of Londinium.

features on the Southwark islands were associated with the exposure of corpses to the water of the river. The braided nature of the Thames around Southwark may have constituted a particularly appropriate context for rites of passage that used the tidal flow to erode the corpses.

Some Iron Age metal items found in the Thames in the vicinity of Roman London may have been offerings left with the dead. The tidal flow may have carried these items away, moving them either upstream or downstream depending on the currents. One of the most impressive finds from this section of the Thames is the 'Waterloo Bridge Helmet', recovered near this bridge some time prior to June 1866.[70] An Iron Age dagger was found in 'Stoney-street' on the north island in March 1865, apparently closely associated with two Roman pottery urns and an iron object that was interpreted as a small gladiatorial trident.[71] H. Syer Cuming noted that these 'relics were exhumed together at the same time and place', although no further details of the context is given.[72] The dagger had an anthropomorphic hilt, although it may have been deposited centuries after its production and in a Roman context.[73] A Late Iron Age strap union was found on the Thames foreshore in 1971, halfway down the shore in front of the Anchor Public House.[74] An Early Iron Age dagger and a Late Iron Age coin were found downstream close to Chambers Wharf, Bermondsey.[75] The three swords from the Thames at London listed in Ian Stead's corpus of Iron Age swords and daggers may also have derived from this part of the river.[76]

Human remains from Iron Age contexts are, however, strikingly rare. An inhumation found at 120–4 and 124–6 Borough High Street on the south island was probably of a mature man whose grave was later sealed by a layer of sandy loam containing Roman pottery, which was in turn sealed by the earliest levels of construction of the main north–south road, and the burial, therefore, pre-dates around AD 50.[77] This individual is usually argued to have been buried during the Iron Age.[78] The body was laid into a broad, flat-bottomed scoop in the sand and no trace of a coffin was found and there were no grave offerings.[79] Martin Dean and Michael Hammerson have noted that the body was laid on its back with its arms and legs spread against the side of the grave and the position of the skull suggested that the head had originally been supported, perhaps on the sloping edge of the grave.[80] The body appears to have been complete although the position of the skull suggests that perhaps it was left exposed in this shallow scoop of a grave. The burial was placed on low-lying ground at the head of a small inlet on the south-east side of Guy's Channel.[81]

A few Late Iron Age sherds from other sites on the south island may relate to the earliest phases of Roman activity alongside the main north–south road rather than to the Iron Age.[82] On the north island, archaeological features including ditches, postholes and gullies have been uncovered at 15–23 Southwark Street.[83] The information appears to indicate settlement, perhaps including a small semicircular building and drainage gullies, although comparatively little detailed information was obtained. The pottery has been dated to the Middle Iron Age, but may also include Late Iron Age wares.[84] A deposit of sandy soils on this site contained pottery and may have been the result of the flooding of the nearby stream.[85] At Toppings Wharf and Sun Wharf several sherds of probable Iron Age pottery were found in the uppermost stratum of sand in the river gravels.[86]

Excavations on the western part of Bermondsey eyot at Bermondsey Abbey produced a substantial quantity of Later Bronze Age and Early Iron Age pottery and Late Iron Age and Roman pottery from unstratified contexts.[87] Another excavation slightly further to the south-east revealed a large pit containing a substantial assemblage of Late Iron Age pottery, including a wide-mouthed, everted rim jar and a beaker.[88] Louise Rayner has argued that the three largely complete vessels from this pit are likely to pre-date AD 50.[89] Pottery that may date to the Late Iron Age or earliest Roman period has also been found at several others sites on Bermondsey eyot,[90] indicating activities prior to the conquest. Evidence has been found for Late Iron Age activity at several excavations on Horselydown eyot, including pits, postholes and perhaps an oven,[91] which Jim Leary has suggested represents occupation and agriculture on the higher ground to the north of the island.[92]

In the western part of the island formed by the Godwin Ridge (Cambridgeshire) there was some evidence for settlement that was partly defined by the Iron Age embankment, including traces of a house and an enclosure.[93] Evans has argued that these structures were not substantial enough to explain the production of the large amount of Iron Age material from the excavations and there was only a limited amount of agricultural land available which suggests that this was not an agricultural settlement.[94] This may indicate that the Godwin Ridge island was used for rituals that included the deposition of rubbish and the disposal of corpses. Numerous human skeletal elements, including the parts of seven skulls, were found during the excavation, mostly from close to the embankment on the north-west part of the island.[95] It is possible that the Southwark islands and eyots were also seasonally occupied and used for comparable rites of passage.

Other islands in the Thames around London may have been used for comparable purposes. A particularly large number of Iron Age metalwork items, including swords, daggers and scabbards, have been recorded from the Chelsea Reach of the Thames around 4 kilometres upstream from Roman London.[96] These objects were found significantly close to the highest point of the Thames reached by the tide during the Bronze Age and the Iron Age.[97] The Battersea location of many of these finds was recoded by H. Syer Cuming, who noted that 'numerous human crania . . . mingled with weapons of *bronze* and *iron*' were located 'during a period of several months, certainly extended from December 1854 until October 1855'.[98] Cuming remarked that the skulls and weapons 'were scattered from the Middlesex shore to about the middle of the river, where the greater quantity were found'.[99] They included the Battersea shield which is usually dated to the Early or Middle Iron Age.[100] Four additional swords and a scabbard have been recorded by Ian Stead from the Battersea reach of the Thames,[101] possibly including some of the examples mentioned by Cuming.

The depositing of metalwork and crania at Battersea may have been associated with an eyot. Mike Morley has reconstructed a relict river channel called the Battersea Channel which formerly defined two eyots close to the findspot of the Battersea shield.[102] Excavation at the Royal College of Art just south of Battersea Bridge located activity at the northwestern corner of the northern eyot.[103] Pits and gullies contained pottery dating around 400 BC to AD 40–50, while animal bones and clay daub were also found. Excavations further upstream from Battersea at Snowy Fielder Waye in Isleworth have revealed evidence for Late Bronze Age, Early and Middle Iron Age activity on a former island, uncovering pottery, gullies and pits, including a single cremation burial and three fragments of unburnt human bone.[104]

Although there is little direct evidence for the exposure of the dead on the Southwark islands, this practice would help to account for the discovery of items of Iron Age metalwork in the Thames.

The north and south banks

Activity north of the Thames may also have been related to the disposal of the dead. Excavations at the Inmost Ward of the Tower of London uncovered twenty-one fragments of Iron Age pottery from pre-Roman river silts and a pit.[105] The grave of a young male was found cut through the backfilled remains of the pit, possibly in an early Roman context.[106] Geoffrey Parnell has noted that this grave seemed barely deep enough to have contained the body. Evidence was found to suggest that the edges of the grave had been subject to river erosion and this area of the river bank may have been a marsh at this time. The burial was covered by a layer of sand and gravel probably deposited by flooding that included a human leg bone.[107] At the 'governor's palace' the left humerus bone of an infant was found in the top layer of the marsh in association with some Roman artefacts.[108]

Some disarticulated human remains from at least three adults were recovered from pre-Roman palaeochannels at the 'Upper Walbrook Cemetery'.[109] Many corpses were buried or deposited on the edges of a tributary of the Walbrook at this burial ground during the late first to third centuries AD and were subsequently disturbed by river water. In the excavation report it has been argued that the bone from the pre-Roman contexts 'is clearly intrusive'.[110] It has also been argued that this particular mode of burial was brought to Londinium from elsewhere in southern Britain or the continent.[111] It is possible, however, that the exposure of the dead to running water at the 'Upper Walbrook Cemetery' was derived from a tradition that was already being followed on the banks and islands of the Thames during the Iron Age.

Few of the human remains from the upper Walbrook have been radiocarbon-dated and, although six bone fragments may all date to the Roman period, one date centred on the Late Iron Age.[112] It will be important to date human bones and the deposits that contain them from future excavations in order to consider whether some of these remains were deposited during the Iron Age. This book pays particular regard to the human remains from wetland contexts of Roman date across London, in order to assess the potential continuity of depositional practice.[113]

A few Iron Age sherds were found in the upper Walbrook Valley at Moor House.[114] Two complete urns found in Fetter Lane in 1892 may have been uncovered during the building of the Public Records Office.[115] It has been suggested that they contained cremation burials since they were found complete and may date to before AD 43. An 'Early Iron Age' sword with a bronze handle was found during excavations in 1872, close to the junction of Fenchurch Street and Billiter Street.[116] Vaughan Birbeck and Jörn Schuster have observed that the dating of this item is open to question, although they have noted that fragments of two or three Late Iron Age pots were found in buried soil during excavations at 60–3 Fenchurch Street.[117] A pit associated with Late Iron Age pottery and worked flint was found during excavations at 14–18 Gresham Street.[118]

This sparse scattering of sites suggests that the area north of the Thames may have been settled by Middle and Late Iron Age communities that did not use the landscape in a particularly intensive way. Indeed, the marginal context of the location may help to explain the wealth of metalwork items from the Thames that marked it as a boundary place. At the Augustinian Nunnery of St Mary's, Clerkenwell, excavations have produced evidence for potential Middle and Late Iron Age settlement across quite an extensive area.[119] The features included pits, scoops, postholes and gullies and Late Iron Age ceramics and fragments of daub indicate that there was a settlement at this location. It is likely that there were comparable sites in close proximity to where Roman London was to develop and that these remain to be found.

There is a notable scarcity of material from the south bank of the Thames. A single sherd of Late Iron Age pottery was found 223–37 Borough High Street,[120] while the excavations at Tabard Square have produced small quantities of Late Iron Age or early Roman pottery, although this area was probably not settled until the AD 70s.[121] A single potin coin of the Cantii was also found, although this may have been brought to the site during the Roman period.[122] Even though extensive excavations have been undertaken in this area, it is remarkable that so little material has been found in contrast to the extensive information on the islands and eyots in Southwark.[123]

A meeting place on the boundary

The finds from the Thames indicate that the site of Londinium formed a significant meeting place, although activity at this location was not accompanied by any substantial settlement or the construction of linear earthworks or buildings. Although there is no evidence either in or around London during the Late Iron Age for high-status burials, nucleated settlement or coin production, the items of metalwork from the river emphasize the ritual significance of this waterscape. As it has not been possible to place an exact date on many of these items, they are mostly argued on art historical grounds to have been made during the Early and Middle Iron Age. Practices related to the disposal of the dead, however, may not have changed very quickly and the general absence of Late Iron Age burials and imported pottery in the immediate vicinity of London may have little relevance; archaeologists have tended to apply simplistic interpretations to the processes through which polities became more centralized.

Chris Thomas has considered the evidence for the point at which the Roman army crossed the Thames during the conquest of AD 43.[124] Cassius Dio wrote an account of the initial phases of the conquest of southern Britain, including details of the crossing of the Thames. Dio (lx: 20.1–3) stated that after an initial battle

> ... the Britons retreated to the River Thames in the area where it empties into the Ocean and at flood-tide forms a lake. They crossed it without difficulty, as they had accurate knowledge of the firm ground and the places where movement was possible. But the Romans in attempting to follow them went astray in the area. However, the Germans again swam across, and another group crossed some way up-stream by a bridge. Then they attacked the barbarians from several sides at once and cut down many of them. But they pursued the rest somewhat incautiously and fell into marshes from which it was difficult to extricate themselves and they lost a large number of men.[125]

Dio noted that the Romans used what is usually translated from the Greek to mean a 'bridge' to cross the river.[126] It has been argued that it is far from clear that the technology to bridge the Thames would have existed in pre-Roman times,[127] although the discovery of the Bronze Age and Iron Age timber structures at Eton Rowing Course suggest that Iron Age people were able to bridge the river.[128]

Considering the evidence for the tidal head of the Thames and if Dio's account is correct, the point at which the Britons and the Romans crossed the Thames in AD 43 may have been between Westminster and Battersea, just west of the future site of Londinium.[129] It is worth considering whether the two main islands in the river at Southwark constituted a fording point during pre-Roman times.[130] Excavations south of the river in Southwark indicate that the land was crossed with several watercourses and very heavily waterlogged, making it difficult for people to move through this area before the substantial drainage that commenced during the AD 50s.[131] People were clearly coming to the islands and eyots in the Thames during the Iron Age, however, and it is likely that they had a detailed knowledge of the waters and tides of the Thames between Hammersmith and Southwark. The discovery of the Iron Age bridges at Eton Rowing Course raises the possibility that the islands in the Thames at Southwark were accessed by bridges prior to AD 43. The place where fresh river water met the salt sea was a significant location and was chosen for the site of Londinium.[132]

The significance of the London area in the immediately pre-Roman period might have related to an established crossing of the River Thames.[133] Metalled Late Iron Age roads have not yet been located across southern Britain, although many of the Roman roads may have formalized earlier routes. Roads eventually connected Londinium to the urban centres of Camulodunum, Verulamium and Calleva, presumably replacing earlier routes. The London area might have been crossed by several tracks or roads during the Late Iron Age, one of which possibly crossed the River Thames where Londinium was to be built.[134] Access to the Thames for trade and transport was also important. Continental imports of pottery and other goods found at Late Iron Age sites to the west of London were probably shipped along the Thames. It is unclear how this river traffic might have been managed.[135] The Iron Age features and finds on the islands and eyots of the Thames may be the last traces of the settlements from which the river was monitored and controlled. Archaeological excavations have only rarely located features that produce groups of specifically Late Iron Age material.[136] This may suggest that Londinium was planned and founded at a time when imported pottery became widely available, probably during the final years of the AD 40s (see below). There is currently an assumption that such pottery was not imported to London before the Roman conquest and that it begins to occur in archaeological contexts as a result of the establishment of the port and urban centre during the late AD 40s or early 50s (see below).[137] Many of the imported fine wares from early deposits cannot be very precisely dated and therefore some assemblages with imports that have been dated to the late 40s or early 50s might even have been disposed of prior to AD 43.[138] It is also possible that the pottery known as 'Highgate Ware', commonly found in early Roman deposits in London, might have begun to be produced before AD 43.[139] If so, the extent of occupation during the Late Iron Age may have been rather more extensive.

Summary

The argument for the significance of pre-Roman London is not an attempt to establish another origin myth but to focus attention on the complex context in which the early Roman urban development occurred. That the landscapes and waterscapes of this area of the Thames Valley had particular significance in pre-Roman times means that the early development of Londinium may be compared more closely to the histories of other urban centres in southern Britain and Gaul during Late Iron Age and early Roman times. This significance challenges the division that is drawn between ritual and mundane activities in past accounts of Londinium's origins. The ritual and religious importance of the riverside influenced the urban development, creating a religious as much as a political and economic foundation.

Many actions conducted during the Roman campaigns across Britain in the AD 40s were in response to the political geography of Late Iron Age Britain. The Romans did not campaign and conquer a landscape that was a blank political canvas. Perhaps the establishment of a settlement to either side of the River Thames and the construction of a bridge during the AD 50s or 60s symbolized the way in which Rome had imposed its domination on this terrain and waterscape, subverting yet also building upon the area's significance as a place of transition, a meeting place and a ritual landscape. If so, this may reflect contemporary developments at Camulodunum, where the fortress and colony were built within the territory of the *oppidum*. To establish whether London was a highly significant and / or a marginal landscape in pre-Roman times will take additional excavation and careful research.

2

A Place of Trade:

Londinium from AD 45 to AD 60

A spot of sacred ground retains its sanctity over many centuries.
PETER ACKROYD, 2012, 22

Introduction

This chapter will explore the initial establishment of Roman London, which appears to have commenced a few years after the Roman conquest of south-eastern Britain. How Londinium was laid out and the early foundation of the port will be explored, addressing the evidence for the River Thames crossing and for the activities that cleared the land and created a terrain across which the roads and buildings were constructed (see Fig. 2.1). These actions are associated with the growing physical and symbolic control of the urban community over the landscapes and waterscapes during the early phases of the establishment of Roman London. One of the main events was the construction of the two main roads, which have been referred to as the 'main north–south road' and 'main east–west road', along which the urban centre was to develop.[1] The establishment of a wharf (Waterfront 1) on the north bank of the Thames also comprised a significant programme of work.

Whether Londinium was an official imperial foundation or developed as a result of decisions made by settlers from overseas and Britain to establish themselves at this location is a strongly debated issue.[2] It is likely that this debate will continue due to the entrenchment of both sides. These two concepts should not, however, be viewed as mutually exclusive explanations. An urban council may have been founded after the conquest which cooperated with the Roman administration and the army to develop the infrastructure.[3] There is, however, very little direct evidence either for a military or an official contribution to the foundation of Roman London prior to AD 60. Londinium may have been founded by a community of traders who wished to exploit the potential of the location of the port. The position taken in this book is that, although the available evidence for the Roman military and members of the administration in Londinium throughout its history cannot be dismissed, this does not establish that Roman London was primarily a military foundation or, indeed, that most of the important building activities were carried out by the military. More nuanced accounts of Roman urbanism are required that allow for complex origins.[4]

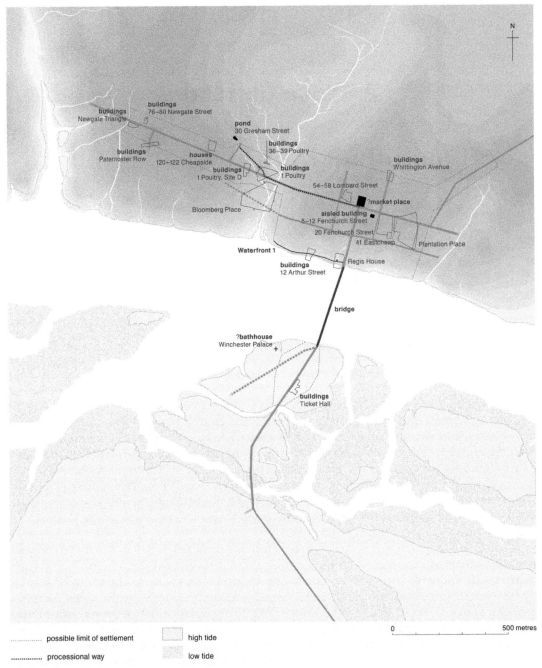

FIG. 2.1 The occupation of Londinium in around AD 47–60.

Londinium was certainly the most extensive and highly populated urban centre in the province of Britannia prior to its destruction in AD 60.[5] Hedley Swain and Tim Williams have used some complex and well-informed arguments to suggest that Roman London at this time was home to around 9,300 people.[6] This must have been the largest population to have lived permanently in a single settlement in Britain prior to the middle of the first century AD. The scale of the activities required to create this urban settlement during the decade and a half following the invasion is highly impressive.

The discussion of this initial urban development will address some of the evidence for the construction of housing, industry and shops on the north and south banks of the River Thames. The establishment of a public centre, or marketplace, on the high ground on Cornhill will be explored, together with recent information for the initial development of the peripheral areas of Londinium just west of the Walbrook and south of the Thames in Southwark. The information from archaeological sites at these locations usually has been employed to argue for the considerable economic significance of early Roman London, with an emphasis placed on the importation of goods to the port from overseas and the scale of the industrial and economic development of early Roman London. I shall address these themes and explore the available information for the people, including those from Britain and overseas, who came to settle here. This chapter will also explore the symbolic and ritual associations of the occupation and control of this developing urban arena, involving the colonization of land, waterlogged areas and watercourses. A discussion of the creation of urban space will address the information for the making of early Londinium through the practices of digging ditches, building up of land for occupation, road construction, the creation of a waterfront and marketplaces, and the placing of human remains at the margins of the occupied landscape.

Establishing Londinium

When the Roman army invaded southern Britain in AD 43, there was little contemporary occupation across the area that was to become Londinium. Nevertheless, this location may have been an important place during the Iron Age. Much of the landscape had long been cleared of trees and was at least partly under cultivation. Pre-Roman London was as much a waterscape as a landscape; rivers, streams and wetlands dominated the terrain of the people who lived within it and travelled through it, with dryer islands and areas of land between. Boats and ferries carrying people and goods would have been important in such an environment. Human cranial remains and metalwork found in the Thames indicate the importance of these wet areas in pre-Roman times. Whatever the significance of the waterscapes in this location prior to the Roman conquest, it became the core of the urban centre as Londinium began to be developed during the latter part of the AD 40s. The evidence is not adequate to distinguish exactly when Londinium originated, although the earliest detailed dating evidence indicates that the main east–west road at the western periphery of the new urban centre was laid out and built around AD 47.[7]

The development of early Londinium was clearly closely linked to the significance of its riverside location as a port for the importation and exportation of produce. The author Tacitus (*Ann.*: 14, 33.1) mentions Londinium during the uprising of Boudica, recording that, although not distinguished by the name of a colony, it was extremely well known because of the large number of merchants who frequented it and the great quantity of merchandise that passed through it.[8] For centuries this has been taken to suggest that Roman London originated on a new site exploiting the opportunities for trade, possibly as a 'settlement of Roman citizens' of a type well known in the eastern empire.[9] This would suggest a foundation that was intended to make a financial profit for traders deriving from outside the province of Britannia. The information from the writing tablets at Bloomberg indicates that there were traders in Londinium prior to AD 60.[10] It is possible that by the late AD 40s Londinium had its own urban organization and officials providing the resources and contacts necessary for the extensive landscaping works on both sides of the Thames. It is also likely that the Roman state and army had a direct role in the foundation of Londinium, possibly assisting an officially-organized urban council with these activities.[11]

'Waterfront 1' and the bridge over the Thames

The construction of Waterfront 1 may have begun in AD 52 and has been viewed as a coordinated building programme along a considerable length of the north bank of the Thames. In a key publication, Trevor Brigham has defined seven successive waterfronts dating from the mid-first to the mid-third century,[12] marked as 'Waterfront 1 to 7' on the Museum of London's map of Roman London.[13] As there is no very thorough and up-to-date study of these riverside port facilities, the information for the successive phases of the waterfronts must be collated from separate monographs and interim reports.[14] Some of the information derived from excavations carried out since 1990 may indicate that the waterfronts developed in a more piecemeal manner than is suggested by the Museum of London map. The first phase of riverfront facilities was constructed on the bank of the Thames during the late AD 40s or early 50s.[15] Early Roman deposits from sites excavated in London have yielded large quantities of imported pottery and evidence for imported foodstuffs consumed by the population. This information, in itself, demonstrates the location of a port at which traded goods had been loaded and unloaded.

The evidence for the dating and structure of 'Waterfront 1' has been derived from excavations undertaken at Regis House.[16] A timber wharf, probably constructed in AD 52, straightened the line of the riverbank, providing a terrace for the loading and unloading of cargo from boats. Prior to this, boats presumably remained moored in the deeper part of the river channel and were loaded and unloaded by the crews of smaller vessels that could be drawn up onto the foreshore. Posts driven into the riverbank just outside the timber wharf may have been for mooring the larger vessels.[17] Evidence for Waterfront 1 has also been found at 12 Arthur Street, where a post-and-plank revetment was dated by tree-ring analysis to AD 55–6.[18] Several hundred metres further upstream at Suffolk House, two oak piles may have represented a jetty constructed in the 50s or 60s, although there was no clear indication of Waterfront 1.[19] It has recently been suggested that at this date the timber waterfront was constructed as far west as the Salvation Army International Headquarters,[20] although further excavation would be required to confirm the early waterfront upstream from 12 Arthur Street. This suggests that Waterfront 1 was built along the riverbank between Regis House in the east and to the Walbrook in the west, although its construction may not have been a particularly coordinated operation.[21]

On the south bank and the islands of the River Thames there is no evidence that quaysides and wharfs were constructed at this early date, although a gravel flood bank protecting the north island at Toppings Wharf may have been built prior to AD 60.[22] It has sometimes been suggested that the Romans bridged the Thames soon after the conquest, but there is no clear evidence to support this. The initial timber bridge across the river (Bridge 1) may have been constructed during the late AD 40s or early 50s, perhaps in association with the building of Waterfront 1 at Regis House, but it could certainly also have been built during the early AD 60s.[23] The exact dating of this first bridge is unclear as it has not been possible to excavate its foundations.[24] Trevor Brigham has suggested that Bridge 1 was constructed by the army in order to shorten the journey time between the ports of Richborough and Dover and the military frontier of the northern and western periphery of the province.[25]

Even if there was a bridge at this early date, it will not have provided the only means of crossing the river.[26] Ferries probably crossed the Thames during pre-Roman times and boats would have been rowed and sailed both across and along the Thames throughout the Roman period. The bridge connected networks of road transport but did not necessarily provide the best means of transport, and travel by boat remained important for the transportation of goods during the entire history of Londinium. The Thames and its tributary rivers formed a convenient network for travel across Roman London and there may have been a toll point on the bridge. Prior to the construction of the Waterfront 1, Roman merchants would have had considerable difficulties in unloading goods from ships in the Thames to the foreshore. Some merchants may have preferred not to use the wharves since it is probable that charges were levied on the loading and unloading of cargoes. Jetties projecting into the river for mooring boats were probably common from this early phase of urban development along both riverbanks and also on the Thames islands. The possible remains of jetties have been found at 12 Arthur Street on the north bank and on the south island in the Thames.[27] Jetties may have continued to have been maintained along sections of the riverfront beyond the timber waterfronts.[28]

Building the main roads

The initial phases of the development of Roman London required substantial groundwork in order to establish a land- and waterscape that could support urban living.[29] Londinium became the location at which several Roman roads joined. Although it is not clear exactly when these roads were built, some important new information has arisen from recent excavations on both sides of the Thames. This river was far wider in AD 43 than it is today, encompassing islands and eyots with gently sloping banks. Major operations in Roman and later times radically changed this terrain, shoring up the northern and southern banks of the Thames, draining and raising low-lying areas and filling in the sub-riverine channels across Southwark.

On the north bank of the Thames, the 'main north–south road' extended from the lowest tidal point at which the Thames could be crossed. This road ran up the riverbank to an area of higher land on Cornhill, where the early civic centre was developed. At this point, the road formed a T-junction with the 'main east–west road' that extended westward towards Calleva.[30] It is from the roadside ditch of this east–west road that the earliest date has been obtained for construction work related to the establishment of Roman London, several hundred metres west of Cornhill at 1 Poultry. Tree-ring analysis has suggested that a wooden drain underlying the main east–west road was constructed in AD 47–8.[31] The construction of the main east–west road across the Walbrook and westward involved landscaping and drainage work on a substantial scale.[32] The road crossed the valley of the Walbrook at the highest point of the tidal reach and the gradient of the riverbanks at this point probably required the construction of a bridge. Some tree clearance was required in addition to substantial engineering works in order to drain the area and raise the level of the road above the waterlogged landscape of the middle Walbrook. The road consisted of compact metalling laid to a width of 8 metres on a bed of sand and clayey silts, with drains running underneath.[33]

Excavations at Bloomberg have revealed the timber pile foundations of a second east–west road that crossed the Walbrook further to the south.[34] Human remains were found close by and in an interim discussion the excavation director Sadie Watson has suggested that these constituted a foundation offering.[35] Other roads north of the Thames pre-dated AD 60. The land between the Walbrook and the Lorteburn rivers was accessed by roads that divided the area up into a number of insulae.[36] Several of these roads to the north and south of the main east–west road clearly pre-dated the Boudican uprising. Ermine Street probably ran from east of the market area northwards out of Londinium,[37] while another road ran north-eastward toward Colchester.[38] Minor roads and alleys were laid out within the insulae.[39]

The south bank of the Thames featured several islands in the area of modern Southwark forming part of a river system characterized by shifting river channels, the formation of creeks and varying patterns of deposition and erosion.[40] The building of the main north–south road across these islands and up on to the south riverbank commenced during the early years of the AD 50s and was accompanied by very extensive drainage, dumping and landscaping.[41] This road construction work, together with major draining and landscaping, was a highly significant undertaking that included the laying of timber foundations for the road in poorly drained locations. The road was built as a low sand-and-gravel bank between 6 and 7 metres wide and is likely to have required the bridging of the Borough Channel between the south island and the south bank of the Thames.[42] If the bridge that linked the north bank of the Thames with the north island was also constructed at this time, bridges would have provided a dry land corridor for transport between the south and the north bank of the river up to Cornhill. A second road, running south-westwards from a junction at the northern limit of the north island, may have been constructed around AD 55,[43] although fully convincing evidence for this dating has yet to be obtained.[44] Perhaps this road provided access to an early bathhouse at Winchester Palace.

Lacey Wallace has recently argued that the main east–west and north–south roads were laid out before the establishment of Londinium was planned.[45] The evidence from 1 Poultry suggests that the buildings post-dated the first construction of the main east–west road and a comparable sequence has been argued for Southwark. The difficulty in dating the initial phases of occupation across London, however, means that this can be no more than conjecture since it is likely that the first buildings may have been ephemeral structures that have not have survived due to later activities. It is also unclear from the evidence whether the east–west and north–south roads were built in a single coordinated operation. It is possible that a campaign of work was undertaken during the late AD 40s and early AD 50s to lay out the initial roads, construct Waterfront 1 and build the first bridge across the Thames. These developments may have constituted part of a plan to establish a port and urban centre at this location.

Wallace has discussed the scant information for how the road building was organized and financed, suggesting that this could have involved the tribal authorities, the military or the state.[46] The labour could have been provided by Roman soldiers or by conscripted labourers. The considerable variation in the construction, width and drainage methods used for these roads suggest that road building was not centrally coordinated. The army did not always operate in a thoroughly coordinated manner, however, and the variability in road construction provides no direct evidence for who was responsible for planning and developing the roads. Perhaps the governor or procurator was establishing an urban authority to fund and organize the initial development of the settlement and port and the army assisted.

An early marketplace and civic amenities

Previous accounts have portrayed early Roman London as a place of low-key urban character.[47] The excavations of the roads and the waterfront, however, have produced evidence to suggest an ambitious urban programme. It is thought that the core of Londinium was established early on the high ground at Cornhill in close proximity to the junction of the two main roads.[48] Excavations have explored this area and some ideas have emerged about its potential public role, which may have been significant from early Roman times.[49] Unfortunately, the detailed understanding of the structure and chronology of the buildings and properties is constrained by the limited extent of the excavations and also by the damaged nature of the early deposits which have been eroded and truncated by substantial later activities.

A gravelled surface, extending at least 33 metres east–west and 40 metres north–south, was constructed just north of the junction of the main roads.[50] This was probably where the early market area of Londinium was located and a forum building may have been planned for this location from the earliest phase, although it was not actually constructed for another twenty or thirty years. The gravel area was resurfaced several times before the surrounding buildings were burned down, probably during AD 60. The laying and maintenance of this large area would have required considerable resources and it is likely to have been the early administrative centre in addition to providing a central location for trading.[51] Martin Pitts has suggested that the early fine ware assemblage at Londinium is similar to that found in early military sites and that this is also consistent with the idea that the city was settled by a migrant civilian community.[52]

It has been argued that the building of the first forum in the AD 70s occurred when Londinium's urban charter had been granted.[53] The urban council may, however, have been established at an earlier date, perhaps during the late 40s. The presence of a forum need not necessarily have been fundamental to the status of an urban centre that was still under construction. Tacitus mentions that Verulamium was a *municipium* before the Boudican uprising and the first forum there does not appear to have been built until later. John Wacher has suggested that an enclosure in the centre of Verulamium may have served as a forum during the 50s.[54] The gravelled area at Cornhill could have served much the same purpose for the population of Londinium prior to the Boudican uprising. The urban council of Londinium may have required a significant length of time to organize the resources required to build a forum.

The second significant phase of the development of this marketplace at Londinium comprised three buildings aligned east–west. The southernmost building is best known and has been interpreted as a substantial timber-and-earth structure measuring 57 metres long and 14 metres wide,[55] with a portico or veranda facing southwards onto the main east–west street and possibly with a tiled roof.[56] Fragments of decorated wall plaster from the interior wall faces were found.[57] The easternmost room contained a quantity of charred grain, which may indicate that it was a shop or store supplying the urban population.[58]

A small fragment of an iron water-pipe collar was found on the road frontage immediately south of the southern building, indicating that a wooden water–pipe was laid along the street front of the main east–west road.[59] The natural springs would have been exploited as water sources by the occupants of Londinium but piped water at this particular location suggests that an aqueduct had been constructed to supply water to the core area of Roman London. This may also indicate that there were public fountains, or that water was being supplied directly to properties.[60] The two buildings to the north are far less well known, since it was not possible to excavate these on any scale. The central building produced painted plaster from its early phases, which illustrates a certain level of ostentation.[61] All three buildings may have been associated with the marketplace and, as the pottery assemblage included a large quantity of imported wares and locally-made vessels inspired by them, this may have been a commercial area.[62] A significant number of samian (*terra sigillata*) inkwells in early contexts may indicate that records of market trading were being kept.[63]

Just south of these buildings, an aisled hall at 5–12 Fenchurch Street had been built on a site with earlier occupation.[64] Although this building was originally thought to have dated to the second century, a recent reassessment has suggested that it pre-dated the Boudican uprising. It was constructed with stone walls and had decorative pilasters along its roadside northern wall and a latrine was located immediately to the west. This building may be compared to the market halls at Viroconium (Wroxeter) and Verulamium.[65] Lacey Wallace has proposed, however, that it might have served as a public hall that had been commissioned and was maintained by a member of the urban elite or by the urban council for the purpose of communal gatherings and displays of status.[66] Since aisled halls were common in the countryside of Roman Britain,[67] it is also possible that this is a high-status urban house, perhaps built by a Briton, situated at the core of early Roman London.

The gravel area and the evidence for piped water suggest that a considerable investment was being made.[68] It is also significant that two of the buildings just east of the gravelled area had painted wall plaster, since evidence for this Mediterranean innovation is rare in early urban contexts across Britannia. It is likely that these developments were funded and organized by an association of people who were settling in the nascent settlement in order to exploit the port.

There may have been a bathhouse in Southwark at this early date, since imported building stone and box-flue tiles have been found on the south of the river, suggesting at least one substantial stone building was located on the north or south island between AD 50 and 75–80.[69] The bathhouse may have been at Winchester Palace on the north-west of the north island, where very large quantities of building materials were reused as levelling before the initial occupation which may have occurred around AD 60.[70] It has been suggested that a bathhouse may have been located close to Plantation Place, just south-east of the marketplace,[71] although the excavated evidence does not necessarily support this idea.[72]

The people and status of early Londinium

The founding of Londinium has been explained in two distinct ways, either that it was established by the Roman army or that an urban authority was solely responsible. Roman London may in fact have been established by an urban council supported by the provincial administration and the army.

Military and civil roles

The idea that London originated as a military fort or camp has led generations of archaeologists to look for Roman military fortifications during developer-funded excavations. Other Roman towns in Britain, including the *civitas* capitals of Isca (Exeter) and Viroconium (Wroxeter), did originate as military fortresses (see Fig. 2.2). The absence of evidence for a Late Iron Age *oppidum* at London has often been taken to indicate that the Roman army played a vital role in the development of Londinium. One reason for supposing a military involvement is provided by the extensive drainage, landscaping, road laying and other building operations that were required. It is sometimes supposed that only the military, under the orders of the governor, possessed the skills required to conduct such large-scale construction.[73]

The presence of the Roman military is indicated by the discovery of items of military metalwork.[74] Military items have been uncovered in pre-Boudican layers at the archaeological

FIG. 2.2 Roman urban centres and frontier works in Britannia.

sites at 1 Poultry, Bloomberg and in Southwark. The sites at 1 Poultry and Borough High Street have produced armour, studs and a couple of spears and brooches, but many of these were fragmentary and from dumped deposits.[75] They may have become incorporated in dumped material rather than having been incidentally lost, suggesting that they were intended for recycling for their metal content. Evidence for metal production is common in the early deposits, and military items formed part of larger collections of waste metal for recycling. At Bloomberg six military artefacts were uncovered from contexts dating to AD 47 to 63.[76] Angela Wardle has noted that these finds occur sporadically in the pre-Boudican contexts and that the disturbed character of the stratigraphy casts doubt on their contexts and dating, indicating that they may have derived from the building and occupation of the post-Boudican fort.[77]

These finds imply that members of the military travelled to Londinium or were in residence but it does not necessarily indicate that Roman London had any official military status or role. The evidence of the infantry helmet from the Thames has also been particularly prominent in debates about the early history of London,[78] but this item may have belonged to a visiting soldier. Soldiers on leave from active service may have visited the facilities of Londinium while others may have been stationed there to obtain supplies from the port or to take part in building operations. The early phases of civic construction could have involved military engineers and other soldiers. Certainly the building of a bridge across the Thames may have required the involvement of military engineers. The building of the main east–west and north–south roads could also have been undertaken by, or with the support of, the Roman army. The military units stationed across the south of Britain during the initial conquest period were moved away to the north and west by around AD 50. At least some sections of the main north–south road south of the Thames had not been built by this time, but military engineers could have remained to help complete the work that had begun prior to AD 50 or to train others who continued the construction.

An alternative explanation for the foundation of Londinium is that this work was conducted under the supervision of an urban council which determined the lines of the roads, organized the division of properties and arranged for the extensive landscaping, drainage and construction that this difficult site required. Military skills may have been available to the civil administration through the redeployment of soldiers, and veterans may also have assisted the urban authority in the construction of Londinium's infrastructure.[79] At Calleva and Verulamium the development of the early road system and the first phases of building construction were probably organized by the ruling families of the native community.[80] At Londinium, early development was a more extensive and demanding operation than at these two tribal centres, raising the issue of whether the civic authority would have been able to organize and carry out works on such a scale. Roman London appears to have developed on the boundaries of several *civitates*, suggesting that it is unlikely that the leading families of a pre-Roman political group controlled the construction of these works.

We should not, however, underestimate the abilities and resources of the people who came to settle in this Thames-side location. The traders are likely to have come from Gaul and other parts of the empire and there is good evidence for the impressive scale of trade during Londinium's early years.[81] Wealthy traders may have had the resources and contacts to commission architects and builders from other parts of the empire. Across the Mediterranean and southern Gaul, cities were developing with well-ordered urban facilities during the early first century AD.[82] The early buildings constructed in London were relatively simple, although there may have been bathhouses. The resources of the civic council were necessarily mainly directed into drainage, landscaping and the building of bridges, with other people building the first houses and shops.

Settlers from other areas of the empire may have founded an urban council possessing the resources and influence to plan, landscape and build across this extensive area within a decade of the conquest. The excavations at 12 Arthur Street and 5–12 Fenchurch Street suggest that there may also have been a few more luxurious houses (see below).

The significance of the port to the Roman government of Britain, combined with the long-term association of the army with Londinium, however, could well indicate that the state played a significant role in establishing Roman London. Archaeologists have often regarded the civil authorities and the army in Britannia as two completely separate areas of provincial life that had little or no contact with one another. In reality soldiers will often have interacted with civilians, and the army certainly played a significant role in the subsequent history of Londinium.

The people

The practice of the recording of names in stone inscriptions and on wooden writing tablets has provided extensive information for people living in and visiting Londinium.[83] Important new insights into the founding of Roman London have emerged from the excavations at Bloomberg on the east side of the Walbrook.[84] Over 400 writing tablets have produced significant information about the population of Londinium during the period from around AD 57 to AD 90.[85] They refer to the names of 92 individuals, including Roman citizens, freedmen and slaves, although all are male. The tablets that were found in pre-Boudican contexts were brought from another area of Londinium and dumped as landfill at this riverside location when banks, ditches and gullies were constructed.[86] Twelve tablets were deposited prior to AD 60 and seven contained legible text.[87]

Individuals named Metellus and Gratus were recorded on two tablets.[88] One incomplete tablet, recording no personal names but sent from one businessman to another, refers to the enemies of the recipient, 'boasting through the whole market [forum] that you have lent them money'.[89] This may be a reference to the market area on Cornhill or to another commercial area in Londinium, although it could equally well refer to the market of another urban centre to which both businessmen belonged.[90] A tablet from Tibullus, the freedman of Venustus, dated 8 January AD 57, was a formal acknowledgement that he owed a trader called Gratus, the freedman of Spurius, a debt of 105 denarii in respect of 'merchandise that has been sold and delivered'.[91]

Roger Tomlin has suggested that Gratus and Tibullus may have been involved in business on their own account, although it is more likely that they were acting for their patrons who had freed them from slavery;[92] he has argued that Spurius was a Roman citizen, while Venustus probably was not.[93] Slaves and freedmen could have made up a high proportion of the population of early Londinium, although the writing tablets do not provide detailed information about whether these freedmen and patrons were living there or visiting. They do, however, help to confirm Tacitus' description (Ann.: 14, 33.1) of the large number of merchants who frequented Londinium and the great quantity of merchandise that was traded there.[94] These tablets do not record military personnel or administrative officials, possibly indicating that Roman London had no particular official role.[95]

We have very few other names for the early occupants and there is little to indicate where they may have originated from.[96] A copper-alloy label or name-tag was found in a pre-AD 60 context at Paternoster Row, belonged to Vitalis, son of Similis.[97] He was probably an auxiliary soldier from the Lower Rhineland, possibly from Cologne, and the label may have been attached to his military equipment. It has been suggested that Vitalis may have participated in the building of the main east–west road, but he could equally have been visiting or had retired to live in

Londinium. It is likely that soldiers were present throughout the history of Roman London, providing the context for the exchange of ideas between military and civilians.[98] A senior Roman officer who visited London during the crisis of AD 60 was the provincial governor Suetonius Paulinus. A name stamp ('C ALBVCI') on an early amphora made of Sugar Loaf Court ware from Ironmonger Lane in London indicates that the potter was called Gaius Albucius.[99] It has been suggested that he may have migrated to Londinium from the pottery at Gueugnon in southern Burgundy (France).[100]

The roundhouses revealed at several sites are likely to indicate that people came to live in Londinium from other parts of Britain, while the aisled house at 5–12 Fenchurch Street also has parallels in south-eastern Britain during the Roman period. The evidence for fragmentation rites involving human bones on several sites will be considered in subsequent chapters and may also indicate the British origins of some of the population, since such activities were common during the Iron Age.[101]

The most reliable method of identifying the physical remains of people who came to settle is the stable isotope analysis of teeth from inhumations,[102] although the results of such work for London mainly relate to burials of a later date. A person who was buried in a wooden coffin at Harper Road, well beyond the south boundary of the settlement on higher ground, was found in an extended position and accompanied by an array of grave goods, some interpreted as 'indigenous' and others as 'Roman' (see Fig. 2.3).[103] These included a mirror, a toilet set, a

FIG. 2.3 The burial excavated at Harper Road in Southwark in the late 1970s was that of a person who died around AD 50–70.

neck-ring, a flagon, two samian dishes and pig bones. The flagon and samian vessels suggest that the burial may date to before AD 65.[104] The neck-ring resembles a number of arm–rings and torcs from Hertfordshire and East Anglia, while the two-piece toilet set has an Iron Age pedigree.[105] The aDNA analysis indicates that this person had brown eyes and dark hair and, although the style of burial and the skeletal anatomy was indicative of a female, the chromosomes were male (XY).[106] Stable isotope analysis has suggested that he or she was probably born in Britain, although a maternal ancestor may have travelled from eastern Europe or further afield. It is likely that this person came from a British family who buried her on the periphery of early Londinium.[107] This burial was probably an indigenous response to the rapid changes occurring in south-eastern Britain in the first century AD.[108]

The evidence for the considerable quantity of imported goods also suggests that the population was highly cosmopolitan. New types of buildings and styles of living suggest that many of them were incomers. Ceramic lamps are particularly common from certain early Roman sites in Britain.[109] Usually found at military sites, the large number of lamps from Camulodunum reflects its roles as a fortress and subsequently as a colony. It has been suggested that the large number of lamps in pre-Boudican contexts may relate to the metropolitan, official and trading functions of Londinium and the cosmopolitan nature of the population.[110] Peoples across Britain adopted continental methods of lighting for interior spaces, one of several innovations that demonstrate changing lifestyles.

Roman fashions of dress and behaviour, including bathing, quickly replaced traditional ways of bodily cleaning and grooming. The evidence from pre-Boudican Londinium suggests that bathing was an important aspect of urban life from the beginning and it appears likely that future work will locate an early bathhouse north of the Thames. Any well-connected settler from the continent would have required such facilities since bathing was a key aspect of the Mediterranean lifestyle that was soon taken up in Britain after the conquest.[111] This style of bathing also required articles such as oil flasks and strigils (to remove the oil), items that are common in early Roman deposits across London.[112]

Another innovation was the practice of writing, using waxed wooden tablets, iron styluses and samian pottery inkwells.[113] Writing tablets have been recovered from the early Roman deposits at Bloomberg, while pre-Boudican deposits at 1 Poultry included several styluses, two writing tablets with illegible script and a lead inkwell.[114] The Latin language soon became widespread in the north-western areas of the Roman Empire where there had been no tradition of writing. Early evidence for writing in Latin need not always indicate incomers to the province, since some of the Late Iron Age coins had adopted legends in Latin, but it is unlikely that literacy was widespread before the invasion.[115]

Marking the place

Although this landscape appears to have been sparsely settled during the Iron Age, the tidal head of the Thames may have been a place where people met and disposed of their dead, as well as affording a crossing point over the river. The construction of the port, the roads and the bridge facilitated this assembly of people. Many wetland resources of this landscape – rivers, streams, springs and damp areas – may have been undeveloped when the first settlers came into this area. The land had been largely cleared, with trees surviving in places. Arable agriculture does not appear to have been particularly widespread and the water in the tributaries of the Thames was clean and easily drinkable.

From the second century there is a wealth of evidence for the building of temples, but there is less evidence for religion and ritual during Londinium's early years. This reflects the efforts of the early settlers to establish the infrastructure – the roads, property boundaries and houses – although it does not indicate that their religious beliefs were insignificant, since everyday life in ancient times was imbued with ritual. The pre-Roman finds from the Thames suggest that the landscapes and waterscapes of Londinium had significance and we shall see that Roman-period finds in wetland deposits indicate the continuing ritual importance of water-filled features and waterscapes.[116] Many wet areas and waterways across this Roman urban landscape received items that suggest that ancestors and spirits were venerated.

The creation of the infrastructure deeply marked and altered its landscape and waterscape through the construction of waterfronts, roads and bridges. These elements controlled the flow of water and linked isolated areas together into a single communication network. In addition, the forming of the urban landscape was based on the draining of wet areas, attempts to control river flow, and the clearing, consolidation and landscaping of this terrain.[117] Sustained projects of earthmoving and draining were required to create places where people could live, produce industrial goods and trade. In the classical mind, water and land had associations with divine spirits, and economic and ritual considerations are likely to have been interconnected while undertaking groundwork and constructing roads and buildings. The substantial changes that reworked the landscapes and waterscapes are likely to have required acts of propitiation to spirits of land and water across the whole area. It is important to consider the practices of canalizing and defining watercourses and the draining and raising of the ground that characterized the occupation of early Londinium. The establishment of roads, waterfronts and boundaries and the creation of firm dry land to build upon also required offerings to the gods and spirits of place. The prevailing focus by archaeologists on the economic development of early Roman London should not exclude the consideration of locating ritual practices.

At 1 Poultry and in Southwark the draining and building up of the ground were vital operations due to the waterlogged and uneven nature of the terrain. At 1 Poultry, initial dumps of peaty gravel were laid down in preparation for the construction of the main east–west road.[118] One of these gravel dumps, which filled the channel of a tributary stream of the Walbrook, was marked on the surface with a small area of striations possibly made by ploughing and approximately aligned with the Walbrook to the east.[119] Hill and Rowsome were able to date this activity to an early phase prior to the construction of the main east–west road. This ploughing may have been connected with the clearing of the route of the road.[120] The area of 1 Poultry appears not to have been first settled until after the construction of the road, and the ploughing may have constituted both a practical attempt to clear land and a ritual practice defining occupied ground at the periphery of urban space.

From early in the growth of Londinium, the dumping operations to build up the landscape used materials containing domestic waste such as plant food, animal bones and large quantities of pottery. The pottery was often in good condition with conjoining sherds. Julian Hill and Peter Rowsome have argued that some of this material was domestic waste derived from areas of settlement at some distance from 1 Poultry, especially since much of it appears to pre-date housebuilding at this location.[121] The subsequent creation of house platforms, during the early AD 50s, also involved similar material and in many areas of early Londinium this was the case where the level of the ground surface was built up.[122]

The dumped material and the possible evidence for cultivation at 1 Poultry are interpreted by the excavators in pragmatic terms as evidence for the preparation of the land to support the main east–west road and for the building work that followed, but other complementary interpretations are possible. John G. Evans has explored Roman deposits close to a river crossing in the valley of the River Test in Hampshire and has argued that pottery and tile in these deposits relate to 'entexturing the land'.[123] He has also suggested that midden material played a significant role in Roman society as a way of symbolizing the identity of the local community at particular places of transition. The spreading of midden material over fields can enhance the fertility of the soil, and ploughing is crucial for crop production.[124] The use of cultural material and soil to establish well-drained level areas at 1 Poultry may not have been related to agricultural fertility since the site was subsequently built upon, although Hill and Rowsome point out that a short period of cultivation may have taken place.[125] It is unlikely that dumping and landscaping were perceived in entirely pragmatic terms. The sparsely settled landscape of pre-Roman London was consolidated to enculture and modify it in order to establish lines of communication and to provide level and well-drained areas for occupation.[126]

Early Roman dumped deposits at sites north of the Thames and in Southwark often contained considerable quantities of domestic material.[127] In the excavation reports, this material is explored in detail for potential dating evidence provided by the pottery and other artefacts and also for an indication of the range of items and foods available to Londinium's occupants. Materials may have been dumped in contexts where land was being colonized, requiring offerings to propitiate gods and spirits in the face of these dramatic alterations to terrains and waterscapes. Critical debates have characterized the discussion of the significance of the cultural material that was dumped both in and around the streams flowing into the Walbrook from the middle of the first century AD.[128] Practices involving the deposition of cultural material disposed may also have drawn upon its symbolic significance in recycling it to make physical claims to land and to provide offerings to spirits of place. Such activities characterized the occupation of Londinium throughout its history and are discussed extensively below.

Pits with interesting and unusual deposits are also very common across Roman London and the burial of parts of animals at various sites may constitute offerings.[129] Particular ritual acts in Londinium may have marked the creation and abandonment of individual buildings and structures.[130]

Occupying the landscape

The buildings close to the gravel surface at Cornhill were built of timber-and-earth and, although some of them had tiled roofs, others were thatched. These are typical of the early urban buildings across London and the other towns of Roman Britain.[131] Stone buildings in urban centres are very rare in such early contexts in Britain, since the dominant building tradition was to use timber and earth in construction.[132] Some of the early buildings of Londinium had tiled roofs, which suggests that tile kilns were established to supply the demand for construction and maintenance.[133] It is now known that a scatter of houses with stone foundations may pre-date the Boudican destruction of Roman London.

The recent publication of the evidence from the excavations at 1 Poultry and at the Borough High Street Ticket Hall in Southwark provides detailed information about the houses and industrial premises of early Londinium, indicating the wealth and dynamism of its population. The construction of the main east–west and north–south roads probably pre-dated the initial development of properties alongside each thoroughfare by several years. At these sites drainage and engineering works required to construct the major roads assisted with the process of raising and draining the terrain, enabling the development of properties in close proximity to the roads.

These excavations also indicate the scale and significance of the early development and serve to challenge earlier interpretations of Londinium's limited early significance. They provide a vivid insight into the scale of the urban developments that were occurring in areas that are likely to have been peripheral to the main core of the urban centre.

North of the Thames

At 1 Poultry the construction of the main east–west road has been approximately dated by tree-ring analysis to AD 47–8.[134] The settlement that developed at and around 1 Poultry to either side of the main east–west road constituted part of a ribbon development that ran from the Walbrook westwards almost as far as the River Fleet, although the buildings may not have been continuous along the entire road frontage by AD 60.[135] As 1 Poultry is some way west of the junction of the two main roads on Cornhill, a substantial area of the north bank of the Thames was laid out with streets during the late 40s and 50s.

After the road had been built at 1 Poultry, quarry pits were dug to create materials for the building of houses and material was dumped that included substantial quantities of artefacts.[136] Settlement during the period from AD 53 to 60 was very intensive, with the creation of a narrow urban area alongside the main road and two side roads constructed to the north.[137] Dominic Perring has suggested that the early road joining the main east–west road at 1 Poultry (Road 2) was initially constructed during the AD 50s to provide access to a sacred area that included the pond at 30 Gresham Street.[138] A series of buildings comprising the amphitheatre, the Cheapside bathhouse and several temples was to develop close to this pond.

A sequence of timber-and-earth buildings was built on plots at 1 Poultry that were established through the levelling of considerable quantities of dumped material, including rectangular houses and one round building built of woven stakes and daub at 'Site D'.[139] The vast majority of the houses of early Roman London were rectangular in plan. These so-called 'strip-buildings' were often set end-on to the street frontage and usually consisted of a shop at the front and a living area to the rear.[140] Comparable strip-buildings have been found in urban contexts across the empire, suggesting that many in Londinium were built by settlers from overseas although others may have been built by Britons who were adopting continental styles of architecture. The roundhouses may have been lived in by British families, since Iron Age houses in southern Britain were often round in plan and such buildings were rare on the continent. The roundhouse from Site D was a wattle building around 5 metres in diameter and located approximately 20 metres south of the main east–west road frontage. This building was used at the most for five years before being replaced by a series of rectangular timber-and-earth buildings prior to the Boudican uprising.[141]

Roundhouses have also been found at other early Roman sites in London.[142] On the western periphery of Londinium at 76–80 Newgate Street, a small circular building was one of the first structures to be constructed.[143] Slightly later, also before AD 60, three small round wattle-and-daub structures where built behind a rectangular building.[144] The roundhouse may have constituted a fairly common type of building in early Londinium, although these were replaced by new rectangular styles of architecture.[145] The people who lived in them may have been Britons,[146] although it has also been suggested that some structures in Londinium were outhouses.[147] Roundhouses were common in rural contexts during the Roman period across Britain and at least some may have been occupied by Britons who came to London to exploit the new opportunities for trade.[148]

The discovery of finds incorporated in burned deposits associated with the Boudican destruction from the extensive excavations at 1 Poultry allowed the excavators to interpret the function of several of the rectangular houses (see Fig. 2.4). 'Building 23' had four rooms and was defined as a shop on the basis of a substantial quantity of well-preserved samian pottery and a large amount of burnt spices, indicating the marketing of imported pottery and other luxury goods for Londinium's population.[149] 'Building 11' was identified as a tavern or eating-house on the basis of deposits both within and around the structure containing evidence for imported food such as olives, grapes and almonds.[150] Large quantities of amphorae suggested the drinking of wine. This property also included a latrine. The excavation of 'Building 13' produced evidence for the storage of grain prior to its destruction, indicating that supplies of cereals were abandoned when Londinium was evacuated.[151] 'Building 12' contained several rooms and evidence was found for painted wall plaster, predominantly white but with decoration in black or red, pink and green.[152] The buildings at and around 1 Poultry were used for domestic occupation and commerce; there was no clear evidence for industrial production until later in the sequence.[153] This peripheral part of Londinium was developing as a thriving market area prior to AD 60.

The pottery assemblage from the pre-Boudican deposits at 1 Poultry has been described by Louise Rayner as 'highly Romanized' and included imported wares, especially amphorae and samian.[154] The high percentage of imported vessels demonstrates Londinium's significance as a port to which goods such as pottery and foodstuffs were being brought over from the continent. Samian imports at this time formed between around 11 per cent and 37 per cent of the pottery assemblage (as calculated by the number of estimated vessel equivalents).[155] Londinium imported a high percentage of samian throughout the first and early second centuries in relation to other British urban sites, presumably reflecting its status, the nature of its population and its role as a port.[156] The building identified as a pottery shop at 1 Poultry stocked fine wares imported from central Gaul and the Rhone Valley.[157] The pre-Boudican waterlogged deposits also produced spices, fruits and nuts from human fecal matter.[158] The evidence from these vitally important excavations has provided a glimpse into the lives of early Londoners that may be representative for the majority of families living across early Londinium on both sides of the River Thames. Claudian coins which were struck between around AD 41 and 65 were also common at 1 Poultry, indicating the early commencement of residential and commercial activity.[159]

At 36–9 Poultry, around 30 metres north of 1 Poultry, two phases of building pre-dated the Boudican uprising.[160] The buildings were located just to the north of the main east–west road and several timber-and-earth structures were partially uncovered during the excavation. To the south the first buildings at Bloomberg were post-Boudican.[161]

The full extent of settlement west of the Walbrook prior to AD 60 is unclear.[162] Further west, just north of the main east–west road, two timber-and-earth buildings at 120–2 Cheapside may have pre-dated the Boudican uprising, and the heavily burnt remains of one of these suggest that it was engulfed by the conflagration.[163] The publication of several small excavations undertaken further to the west around Paternoster Square has provided information for an area south of the main east–west road.[164] The buildings on the two sites occupied by AD 60, at Paternoster Row and Newgate Triangle, are broadly comparable to those at 1 Poultry.[165] At Newgate Triangle, the buildings were constructed immediately south of the main east–west road, while at Paternoster Row a secondary road was constructed running to the south from the main east–west road with houses to either side. Imported fine wares were very common at Newgate Triangle and Paternoster Row, demonstrating that the occupants had access to a comparable range of pottery to those living at 1 Poultry.[166]

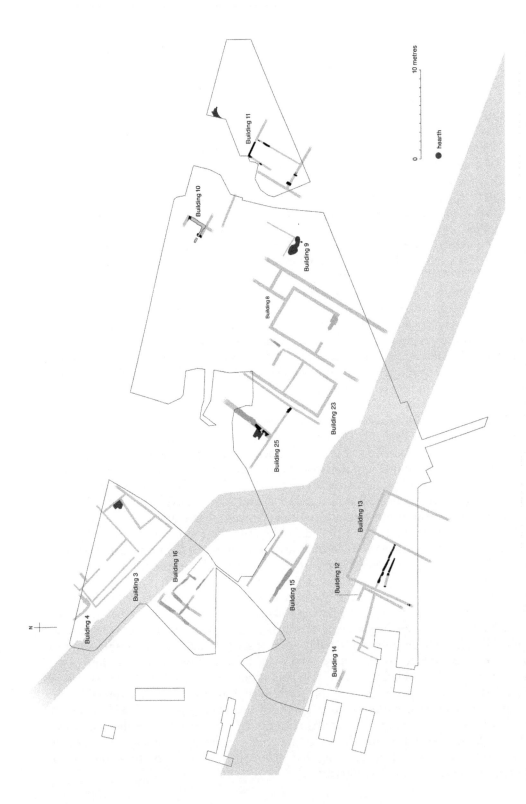

FIG. 2.4 The buildings at 1 Poultry in around AD 60 with buildings numbered. The nature of the excavations at this site mean that substantial areas of these buildings are conjectural and the excavated areas will not have recovered all the archaeological features across this excavation area. The plan gives an idea of the size, character and distribution of these buildings.

It is likely that the northern edge of Londinium lay just beyond the market area on Cornhill. At Whittington Avenue a north–south road was constructed and houses had been burned down, probably during the Boudican revolt.[167] At Leadenhall Court excavations uncovered ditches, a quarry and cremation burials but no evidence for settlement prior to AD 60.[168] Recent excavations south-east of the gravel area on Cornhill has uncovered evidence for intensive occupation at 20 Fenchurch Street in the decade prior to the burning of Londinium, including two distinct building phases.[169] The survival of archaeological deposits was patchy but the initial features included postholes and quarry pits which were swiftly followed by the construction of rectangular timber-and-earth buildings built in different ways. Traces of two roads running north–south were also recovered. At 41 Eastcheap earth-and-timber buildings were burned around the time of the Boudican uprising.[170] At Plantation Place two phases of timber-and-earth buildings were associated with roads, including a section of the main east–west road.[171] In the second phase of building, the site appears to have been intensively occupied with at least seventeen closely-packed buildings of different shape and size. A large fragment of infantry cuirass armour was found in a dump of material in an early context.[172]

The area immediately behind Waterfront 1 on the north bank of the Thames was developed for occupation and trade prior to AD 60. At 12 Arthur Street the riverbank was soon landscaped and traces of a substantial building were uncovered.[173] Built on timber piles, the building had a stone or clay wall, little of which survived, including part of an apse which suggests that it was a bathhouse or private house.[174] Levelling and consolidation dumps at 12 Arthur Street from a later wharf ('Waterfront 2'), built in front of Waterfront 1 during the early AD 60s, contained substantial quantities of building material that probably derived from this early building, including roofing tiles, bricks and some wall plaster.[175] At Regis House some traces of early timber buildings were found behind the waterfront which may have pre-dated AD 60.[176]

South of the Thames

Across the Thames in Southwark, the extent and location of the settlement was limited to the higher ground above the watercourses and floodplains. On the north island, rectangular timber-and-daub houses were built along the main north–south road. In the most extensively excavated area, at Borough High Street Ticket Hall, referred to below as the 'Ticket Hall site', eight buildings were revealed, with side streets allowing access to the areas behind the main street frontage.[177] Quantities of high-quality imported pottery were found and the remains of charred plants, including lentils, which were probably imported from the Mediterranean. One building was thought to have been a granary, indicated by the evidence for charred wheat and barley found on the remains of a burnt timber floor.[178] Another was interpreted as a blacksmith's shop from the quantity of hammerscale that covered the floor.[179] The limited area of excavation suggested that this long rectangular building, which was constructed of timber and earth with a brickearth base, went out of use some time before the Boudican uprising.[180] Quantities of roofing tile in the burnt layers sealing these deposits indicate that at least some of these buildings had tiled roofs.[181] Just to the north at Joiner Street, a large quantity of ceramic moulds demonstrate that copper–alloy objects, perhaps a statue or large vessel, had been produced at this location.[182] The public areas of early Roman London would have been installed with bronze statues of the emperors Claudius and Nero.

This densely settled area of the north island is likely to have been part of a ribbon development along both sides of the main north–south road.[183] The spread of settlement at AD 60 has been reconstructed according to the extent of the fire debris that is thought to derive from the destruction of Londinium, but it is possible that Southwark was not burned entirely. The burnt deposits do not appear to extend much beyond the frontages of the road and are mainly restricted to the north island,[184] with a scattering of sites at the north of the south island. It is possible that the occupied area was restricted to the corridor of the main north–south road on the north island, with some possible additional development at Winchester Palace,[185] where there may have been a bathhouse.[186] A change in the alignment of two successive sets of buildings at the Courage Brewery site may suggest that the earlier phase pre-dated AD 60, but no evidence of burning at this date was found.[187]

Owing to limited excavation, the detailed development of Londinium at this time is unclear. The extent of the settlement has been mapped several times, but the quality of evidence for most of the area of early Roman London is far lower than that obtained from around 1 Poultry and at the Ticket Hall site. At 1 Poultry and Paternoster Square side roads had been constructed to enable the development of further properties on both sides of the main east–west road. At the Ticket Hall site and on Cornhill paved alleys between some of the buildings allowed access to the back yards of the properties. It is not yet clear how much of Londinium had been laid out with a network of side roads by AD 60.

Marking the boundaries

The boundaries of Roman cities were often defined by ritual acts that may have included the sacrifice of animals and the construction of temples and shrines.[188] Other activities, such as industry, feasting and the disposal of the dead, may have usually been located at the margins of Roman cities.[189]

Digging ditches

In supporting the military claim for the foundation of Londinium, Perring has considered that two ditches with double v-shaped profiles constituted part of the outline of a substantial conquest-period 'camp'.[190] The ditch section at 7–11 Bishopsgate pre-dated a late first-century road, but could only be dated to between around AD 43–70.[191] Four ditches, closely aligned north–south, were cut into the natural gravel at another recently-excavated site just east of the Walbrook, the two earliest of which had 'v-cut' profiles.[192] Perring has suggested that two of these ditches constituted the western perimeter of a Roman fortress, fort or camp constructed in AD 43.[193] An alternative suggestion is that it constituted the western limits of the earliest phases of Londinium.[194] A third explanation is that the eastern ditch might have been associated with the Late Iron Age activities.[195]

The v-shaped nature of the ditches is not, in itself, enough to suggest a Roman date for their construction or that they were excavated by the army.[196] It is only possible to differentiate military and civil boundary ditches through extensive excavation.[197] The substantial v-shaped ditches found on additional sites in first-century contexts in London may be early civic boundary ditches or drainage features.[198] Some of these ditches could indicate separate attempts to define civic boundaries or distinct areas within the growing urban centre. Early Roman Verulamium was characterized by a series of distinct ditched enclosures lying to either side of the river.[199] This may also have been the case during the first phases of Londinium and it is difficult to determine its exact extent throughout the first and second centuries. Many activities in the marginal areas, as exemplified by the deposition of human remains, may have been intended to reinforce ill-defined boundaries across the riverine landscape of Londinium.

Industry

By AD 60, Londinium was already a significant centre for trade, serving a resident community while providing a market for people from elsewhere. The ironsmith's shop at the Ticket Hall site was one of many metalworking facilities since iron, as well as copper-alloy and lead, would have been required in substantial quantities (see Fig. 2.5).[200] The early Roman burial from beyond the southern edge of Londinium at Harper Road contained the bones of a person who had come into contact with a high level of lead during her life, possibly as a result of drinking water supplied by lead pipes or of living in close proximity to metalworking or other related processes.[201] That this woman was probably born in Britain indicates that her exposure to lead may have occurred during her time in Londinium.

The large quantity of tile incorporated in early Roman deposits suggests that kilns will have been operating near Roman London, although this material will also have been imported from production sites across south-eastern Britain.[202] Distorted and discarded tile 'wasters' found in pre-Boudican contexts close to Paternoster Row suggest that kilns had been close by.[203] At Sugar Loaf Court (14 Garlick Hill), pottery production was underway prior to AD 60, indicated by the large quantities of wasters.[204] An oxidized, light-coloured pottery known as 'Sugar Loaf Court ware' was produced from the local clays. The wasters were found associated with timber buildings and are likely to have constituted dumped material from kilns although none were located. This pottery was sold locally since it is very common on pre-Boudican sites across the area of Londinium north of the Thames.[205] Forms produced in this fabric included a range of locally-made amphorae, but it is not clear what these were intended to store.[206] Potters were probably drawn to the market in Roman London before AD 60 when at 60–3 Fenchurch pottery production may also have begun.[207]

Mortuary landscapes

Archaeologists have tried to define Londinium's spatial limits according to where the dead were buried. This approach is based on the idea that the dead should not have been interred within the boundaries of cities,[208] and Roman law did indeed require this practice to be followed.[209] In subsequent chapters it will be seen that a marginal mortuary terrain surrounded Londinium, but that these zones may not always have been entirely beyond the boundaries of the areas of the living.[210] This marginal mortuary landscape included many locations at which dead bodies and pieces of human bone were deposited.[211]

It will be seen below that the burial of human remains formed part of a range of practices marking the boundaries of the urban community. These early boundary-creating activities contrast with later Londinium, when discrete cemeteries developed at locations beyond the boundary. Boundary practices involving the fragmentation of human remains nevertheless continued into the second and third centuries, suggesting that different groups of Londinium's population treated dead members of their community in their own way. The evidence from first-century Londinium may also indicate a lack of centralized control over burial. The gradual expansion of the settlement incorporated existing burial grounds that sometimes continued to be used by the people living in the vicinity.

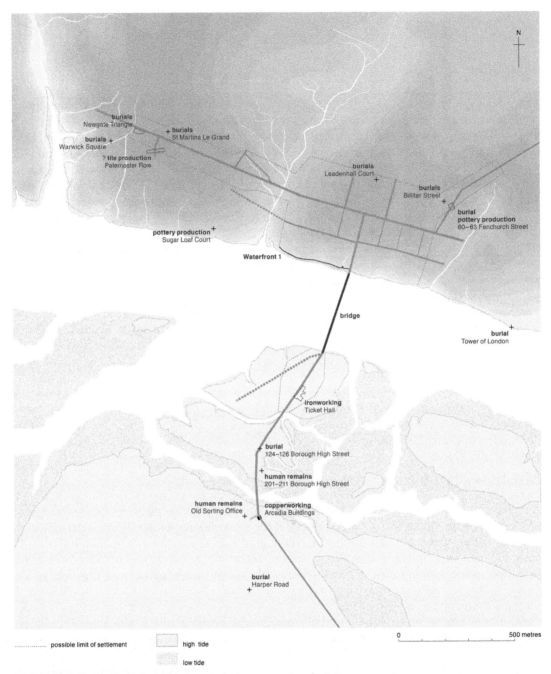

FIG. 2.5 Industry, burials and human remains across Londinium.

The usual method of disposing of the dead during the first to second centuries in Roman Britain was thought to have involved the cremation of the body and placing the incinerated remains in a container put in a hole in the ground.[212] From the second century, inhumation is thought to have been a more common burial practice and it appears to have become the dominant rite over much of the province by the late third century. The supposed prevalence of cremation rites would suggest that the discovery of early inhumation burials should be a rare occurrence in London and would also suggest that fragments of unburnt bone from contexts dated to the first and second centuries require some explanation.[213] Recent discoveries have demonstrated, however, that the general change from cremation to inhumation from the second to fourth centuries in London is far less well defined than was formerly assumed.[214] Early cremation cemeteries have been identified to the west, north and east of Londinium,[215] although a number of early inhumation burials have also been located and it has become increasingly clear that cremation also continued throughout the Roman period.[216]

At least three first-century cremation cemeteries are indicated by burials that have been found close to St Paul's Cathedral, Warwick Square and St Martins-le-Grand.[217] At least six individual cremations placed in pottery urns were found during early excavations close to St Martins-le-Grand,[218] while at Warwick Square at least eight cremations were uncovered in 1881 and a further two in 1966–8.[219] The cemetery close to St Paul's may have been established later in the first century, although there is very little available detailed information about these burials since they were uncovered during the seventeenth century.[220]

Some of these cremations may have dated to before AD 60.[221] A cremation burial of a male of around thirty years old from Warwick Square was placed with a coin of Claudius in a vase of grey fine-grained porphyritic igneous rock (see Fig. 2.6).[222] This high-shoulder urn with a pair of loop handles and a pedestal foot has almost certainly been carved from basalt derived from the Haddadin flow in northern Egypt.[223] Simona Perna has recorded that forty comparable urns have been found in wealthy tombs in the Roman Empire.[224] She has observed that there is a close connection between such porphyry and also alabaster cinerary urns and the imperial family, including their various dependants. The London urn may have been buried with a wealthy individual with a particular connection to Egypt.[225] The coin of Claudius was struck between AD 41 and 50 and was relatively unworn, suggesting a pre-Boudican date for the burial.[226] In close proximity to this stone urn a cylindrical lead canister depicting the sun god Sol driving his four-horse chariot was found containing a glass jar of burnt bones.[227] This type of container has rarely been found in Britain and the small hilltop Warwick Square cemetery may have been a private burial ground.[228] Another cremation excavated nearby during the 1960s dated to the later first century, indicating that this cemetery was in use over a long period that probably spanned the events of AD 60.[229]

John Shepherd has suggested that houses were built between these three cemeteries.[230] The extent of Londinium in AD 60, however, suggests that the burial grounds may have been initially established at the margins of early Roman London and that settlement then expanded to fill the areas between.

A small cemetery to the north of Londinium has been excavated at Leadenhall Court, where the location of a cluster of five cremation burials may suggest that the top of Cornhill lay beyond the urban boundary at this time.[231] This cemetery could post-date AD 60 but pre-dated renewed activity which was associated with a coin of AD 64.[232] Quentin Waddington uncovered several cremation burials at the junction of Fenchurch Street and Billiter Street in 1925–6.[233] These were not closely dated although the area in which they lay was incorporated within the expanding settlement during the later first century. Several of these burials were within cists of

FIG. 2.6 This first-century stone urn was cut on a lathe from porphyry and finished to a high polish. Found at Warwick Square in 1881, it contained the cremated remains of a man of around thirty years of age.

oak planks, while one was deposited within a Spanish amphora.[234] The evidence from the cemeteries at Leadenhall, Warwick Square, St Martins-le-Grand and Fenchurch Street / Billiter Street may suggest that cremation burials in early Roman London were deposited in small clusters in plots to the rear of houses.[235]

Inhumations also occurred in early Roman contexts and the burial from Harper Road was interred in a grave with a number of burial offerings. There is evidence that corpses were also placed in ditches on the urban margins of Londinium, representing a practice common during the Iron Age and Roman periods across southern Britain.[236]

During the excavations at 60–3 Fenchurch Street, several ditches of mid-first-century date were uncovered, one of which contained the partially-preserved inhumation of a mature adult.[237] This burial was highly disturbed in post-Roman times but Jacqueline McKinley has suggested that it had been exposed to the elements at the time it was deposited, since the body had lost its upper and lower limbs and the bones were fairly weathered.[238] The cranial remains of a young woman had been placed on the pelvis of this body and this may relate to a practice that is well attested later in the history of London when heads were removed from bodies and placed in positions close to the legs.[239] This inhumation may have been exposed at the edge of the early cremation cemetery located by Waddington in the vicinity of Fenchurch Street and Billiter Street.

The excavations at Newgate Triangle to the west of Londinium have located the inhumations of two young men.[240] These were placed in a ditch, apparently without coffins or shrouds. The skull of one individual had become disarticulated, although it is not clear whether this had occurred in antiquity.[241] The ditch may have pre-dated the main east–west road and buildings that were built on the south side and burned down in AD 60.[242]

These three inhumation burials may support the argument that the definition of inhumation and cremation as two entirely distinct funerary practices is too simplistic. There is some evidence for a 'two-stage' funerary process in Iron Age and early Roman Britain, including the initial exposure of the body and the subsequent cremation of selected remains.[243] Two-stage funerary practices may have been carried out widely across south-eastern Britain and perhaps in northern Gaul.[244] Because this type of funerary rite was conducted over a protracted period, it could have been used as a rite of passage that transformed the deceased from their membership of the living community to their new role as a commemorated ancestor.[245] Perhaps the inhumations from 60–3 Fenchurch Street and Newgate Triangle represented the first stages of burial rites that were initially intended to end in the cremation of the bodies.

The numerous finds of cranial remains and other bones from archaeological features and watercourses across London suggests that parts of bodies were removed during the process of exposure.[246] Particular bones appear to have been valued as items that were kept and deposited in special locations during fragmentation rites, particularly on the margin of Londinium.[247] Human remains, including crania and long bones, are common in wet and waterlogged contexts of the first and second centuries, including roadside ditches, pits and wells.[248] Most of the accurately dated human cranial remains from excavated contexts across London post-date the Boudican uprising and are fully discussed in subsequent chapters. At 201–11 Borough High Street in Southwark, two complete 'Neronian' pottery vessels (dating to around AD 55–70) were found close to the cranial remains of a woman in a drainage ditch that ran parallel to the main north–south road just at the southern edge of the south island.[249] The upper levels of this ditch was filled with layers of water-laid sand, and samples from the vegetation contained mollusks and beetles that favour open water habitats, suggesting that this site was a waterlogged location on the edge of the early settlement.[250]

Mark Beasley has suggested that human bones found in first- and second-century contexts at the Old Sorting Office on the south bank of the River Thames were the result of fragmentation rites during which they may either have been taken from corpses exposed to the elements at the periphery of Londinium or removed from inhumation burials after the bodies had undergone a period of decay.[251] Early activities included the digging of two phases of ditches marking the south edge of the settled area and a range of associated features including additional ditches, pits, a line of postholes and three wells. One of the more substantial ditches contained pottery which has been thought to pre-date AD 60 and there were two disarticulated human femur bones in the lower deposits of the fill.[252] This ditch was probably constructed to drain the surrounding area and so these human remains were deposited in a wet context. Two of the wells also produced substantial parts of almost complete pottery vessels.[253] Beasley has noted the significance of complete or near complete pots in Roman contexts in London and other sites in Britain, including the temple site at Uley (Gloucestershire) together with evidence for the ritual 'killing' of pots by making holes in their sides after they had been fired.[254] Beasley has suggested that the large number of complete and near complete pots from the wells at the Old Sorting Office were deposited as part of ritual activities.[255]

These varied burial rites may illustrate the mixed ethnic and cultural origins of the population and also the survival of Iron Age traditions of exposure.

Summary

The initial development of Londinium clearly exploited the potential of its location on the Thames for the creation of a port, while the large quantity of early imports introduced into Roman London after around AD 50 indicates the scale of trade.[256] The core of the settlement appears to have been on Cornhill, where excavation has indicated that an early marketplace was associated with substantial buildings. The shop and inn at 1 Poultry indicates that trading was not restricted to the core area and there were presumably a large number of shops and workshops across Londinium.[257] The area of settlement to the west, between the rivers Walbrook and Fleet, and that to the south in Southwark, were less rigidly planned and may have been sub-urban in character. The fast rate of the development of Roman London could simply have outstripped the ability of the urban authorities to control the laying-out of side roads and properties in these areas. The cores of many Roman urban centres in Britain include rectangular building plots characterized by roads, while other less formal types of urban settlement are often defined by roads and building plots that are less rigidly laid out.[258] It is likely, however, that the development of these outlying areas were also under official control.

The population of early Roman London will have been ethnically mixed. The range and quantity of artefacts indicates a variety of settlers from overseas, including a potter from southern Burgundy and a soldier perhaps from the lower Rhineland or Cologne. The names of several traders are recorded on the Bloomberg tablets, although the identity of other early settlers is unclear. The discovery of roundhouses and the aDNA analysis of the Harper Road burial suggest that people with family origins in Britain were living in early Roman London. The recent publication of excavation work at the 1 Poultry and Ticket Hall sites indicates the scale of the engineering works that were required to construct the roads and to lay out and build houses and public facilities. The initial investment in London may have focused on providing fundamental aspects of civic infrastructure and on obtaining artefacts from sources in Continental Europe. The pottery shop at 1 Poultry selling fine wares and spices imported from Europe demonstrates the buying power of the resident population and of those who visited Londinium to exploit the shops and the market. The shop and inn demonstrate the presence of people with money in this marginal area at this early date. At least three granaries have been located from the limited areas that have been excavated, indicating that the population of early Londinium may have had to import grain from some distance.

These endeavours to found an impressive urban centre were thwarted by the Boudican uprising. Londinium may have been the most important urban centre in Roman Britain at this time, as indicated by the evidence for some elaborate domestic housing and developments on and around Cornhill and in Southwark. The early buildings were relatively simple timber structures, but there are also hints of more impressive buildings constructed both north and south of the Thames. Certainly, Boudica and her followers regarded Londinium as sufficiently important to destroy it after they had sacked the colony at Camulodunum.

3

Boudica and Londinium in AD 60

now i'm back
i've known the rain that stings
now i'm back
i've seen the pain of kings
now i'm back
defending ancient springs

JACKIE LEVEN 2000

Introduction

This brief chapter assesses the evidence for the destruction of early Londinium, exploring the historical context of the burning of the settlement by Boudica's followers. Much of the urban infrastructure that was being developed on both sides of the River Thames was destroyed at this time, although some part of Roman London may have survived. A thick burnt layer derived from this destruction has been found sealing many of the early archaeological deposits. It was not long before Londinium was re-established, however, and new structures were built often in relation to the roads and boundaries set out during the initial establishment of Roman London. This suggests that there was a good degree of continuity in both the population and in the planning of the settlement. The majority of the people may have had time to escape before the arrival of Boudica's forces and may have returned soon after the uprising was suppressed to resume their lives and to reconstruct Londinium.

Londinium became caught up in the events of Boudica's uprising either in the year AD 60 or 61.[1] The chronology of these events is not well enough established to be certain about their date or details. They will not be discussed here, and information about their background may be read elsewhere.[2] Boudica was the wife of Prasutagus, a king who was cooperative with the Roman administration. He ruled over the Iceni, a tribe who lived in the area of present-day northern East Anglia. Prasutagus may have made an alliance with Rome during the initial phases of the invasion of AD 43. According to the writings of two classical authors – Tacitus and Cassius Dio – Boudica led an uprising against Roman rule after her husband's death as a result of abuses against herself, her family and her people. Her forces included people from tribes across south-eastern Britannia and we are told that she sacked three places – Camulodunum, Londinium and Verulamium.

In the context of the use of the Thames to dispose of the dead during the Iron Age, it is interesting that Tacitus (*Ann.*: 14.32) described portents at the beginning of the rebellion:

[A]t the mouth of the Thames a phantom settlement had been seen in ruins. A blood-red colour in the sea, too, and shapes like human corpses left by the ebb tide, were interpreted hopefully by the Britons – and with terror by the settlers.[3]

Tacitus related that the Roman commander Suetonius Paulinus returned in haste from campaigning in north Wales and considered whether to make a stand and engage the Britons at Londinium. He eventually decided to sacrifice the settlement in order to save the province as a whole (*Ann.*: 14.34). Tacitus further notes that:

Unmoved by lamentations and appeals, Suetonius gave the signal for departure. The inhabitants were allowed to accompany him. But those who stayed because they were women, or old, or attached to the place, were slaughtered by the enemy.

After the destruction of Londinium, Boudica's forces advanced to attack and burn Verulamium. After the Roman army had eventually destroyed them, the province of Britannia was re-established, including substantial new works at Londinium from the early AD 60s.

Burnt deposits

The writings of Tacitus contain significant information about the early history of Londinium, including its importance as a place for trade and merchandise. It is very difficult, however, to find archaeological evidence to support the events of the uprising of Boudica as it was described by Tacitus.[4] The only convincing evidence comprises the burnt deposits dating to around AD 60 that have been found in the urban stratigraphy of Camulodunum, Londinium and Verulamium. Since the early twentieth century archaeologists working in London have found evidence for the uprising in the form of a thick dark layer of burning close to the base of the Roman deposits.[5] Work over the past twenty years has shown that this layer is very extensive and seals many of the archaeological layers connected with the initial phases of the development of Londinium.[6]

The extensive burnt deposits found on sites of this date have helped archaeologists to establish the extent of the early settlement. We have seen that the main building techniques incorporated large quantities of earth and timber and such structures would have burned very readily, the fire spreading from one to the next.[7] The destruction deposits seal archaeological layers associated with artefacts that date to around AD 55–70. The published results of excavations in Southwark and at 1 Poultry have explored the evidence for the destruction of these areas in some detail.

Many of the excavated early sites across Londinium have not produced substantial quantities of finds. This has been taken to suggest that the population had time to clear their possessions before the settlement was sacked.[8] At Camulodunum, by contrast, the extensive evidence for destruction includes many artefacts associated with the life of the occupants of the colony.[9] At 1 Poultry, fire debris was recorded across most of the excavated areas and later landscaping probably accounts for its absence in places.[10] A large quantity of burnt samian was found in situ in 'Building 23', which may have been a pottery shop.[11] This could have been 'pottery stock' for sale which has been compared to those from two shops in Camulodunum that were burned by Boudica's followers.[12] This pottery from 'Building 23' is the first convincing evidence that the shop owners in Londinium may not have been expecting the events of AD 60. Occasionally other buildings across Londinium were burned without having first been cleared of their stock and goods.[13]

The samian pottery was found in the burnt deposits of the building itself and in the fire debris that overlay it.[14] This large quantity of pottery comprised four main types, decorated samian from La Graufesenque in France, central Gaulish glazed wares, Pompeian red ware dishes and lids and Rhone Valley oxidized-ware mortaria. Some of this material was in deposits clearly connected with the pre-Boudican use of the building but other sherds had been redeposited in dumps derived from the building debris. In the pottery report, it is argued that all this material derived from the pottery shop but it is also noted that some of the assemblage may have dated to around AD 70, including some of the decorated samian and a local type of pottery called 'Highgate Wood C ware'.[15] Decorated samian can be dated quite closely and some of the pottery from 'Building 23' is likely to have been produced rather later than AD 60.[16] Highgate Wood was a pottery production site about 10 kilometres to the north of Londinium. The first production of Highgate Wood C ware is usually considered to date to later in the first century.[17] The evidence from 1 Poultry suggests, however, that this pottery was available in Londinium prior to the Boudican uprising.[18]

Martin Millett has examined the stock from the two pottery shops at Camulodunum and another possible shop from St Albans, pointing out that the samian pottery might be expected to be 'much newer' than the pottery found in normal archaeological deposits, since the pottery stocks from these shops were destroyed before they entered into general circulation.[19] Pottery shops would have often included newer and more up-to-date forms and wares than those expected to be found in the discarded refuse more usually studied by archaeologists. If the London shop was burned down in AD 60, the pottery may not all derive from the original stock, since some of the finds came from deposits that had been disturbed by activity dating to the redevelopment of the site.[20] It is also possible that 'Building 23' was burned down up to a decade later than the uprising. At 1 Poultry Site D the burnt deposits also contained Highgate Wood B/C ware that are usually dated to around AD 60–70.[21]

A comparable burnt layer has been located on sites north of the Thames, indicating the extent of Londinium in AD 60. At 36–9 Poultry, just north of 1 Poultry, some early buildings appeared to have been burned by the same conflagration.[22] At 120–2 Cheapside, a building was probably destroyed in this fire.[23] At Newgate Street there was a heavily burned horizon of probable Boudican date that included the remains of buildings.[24] To the east of Londinium the burnt deposits of a ribbon development of buildings flanked a road running north-eastwards toward Colchester. Evidence was also found for contemporary burning at 20 Fenchurch Street, Plantation Place and 41 Eastcheap, just to the south-east of the early market square.[25]

Recent excavation and analysis of sites on the western periphery of Londinium have suggested that parts of this area may not have been destroyed by fire at this time,[26] although this evidence is far from conclusive. At Newgate Triangle, three of the rectangular buildings south of the main east–west road were burned, but at least one ('Building 7') may have escaped the conflagration.[27] Provisional dating of a group of roundhouses at 10 Gresham Street has suggested that some of these buildings were in use before AD 53.[28] Since no evidence was found at this site for Boudican destruction, it was suspected that these roundhouses had been deliberately left unburned.[29] The final post-excavation work for this site has suggested, however, that the roundhouses were constructed after the uprising.[30] An interim report on Bloomberg has suggested that pre-Boudican buildings were not burned,[31] although the more recent assessment of evidence has indicated that this area had not been built up by AD 60.[32] The evidence supports the idea that the area of Londinium to the north of the river was fairly thoroughly destroyed in AD 60–1.

The excavated sequence appears to suggest Boudican destruction at sites in Southwark.[33] Boudica's followers could have crossed the bridge (Bridge 1) to set fire to the houses south of the Thames.[34] The timber bridge may have been damaged or destroyed at this time and subsequently mended or repaired in the early AD 60s.[35] Convincing evidence for the fire has been found from excavations undertaken in 1995 at the Ticket Hall site.[36] The eight houses and buildings east of the main north–south road and another building on the west side had been burned. Fire swept through these buildings, leaving a layer of scorched and burnt brickearth, burnt daub, timber and charcoal.[37] This layer contained considerable quantities of burnt ceramic building material and was from 0.5 to 30 cm thick. It was visible across the entire site, except where it had been disturbed by later activity. Many of the timber features of the buildings, such as posts and floors, were burned in situ. These buildings may have been razed to the ground, possibly either during the destruction of this part of Londinium or during the subsequent rebuilding operations. As at 1 Poultry, the widespread reworking of destruction deposits makes it necessary to be cautious about assigning an exact date and character to these contexts. They may include evidence for activities that were occurring a few years after the burning in order to prepare the ground for new buildings.[38]

The evidence for the burnt deposit is mainly limited to the north island of Southwark, with a scattering of sites on the south island. Burnt deposits such as those at 1 Poultry and Borough High Street have long been regarded as an indication of the extent of the urban centre at AD 60. An absence of burnt deposits has usually been interpreted as indicating a lack of building before this date, although this is based on the assumption that the entire settlement was burned. Careful analysis of pottery from sites where there has been no clear evidence for burning has suggested that the south island was also settled around AD 60.[39] There may also have been a bathhouse at Winchester Palace. Further excavation across Southwark is required before it will be possible to be definitive about the extent of the destruction of this area of Londinium.

Since some of the buildings in the southern parts of Londinium may not have been burned, further excavation and research will be required to assess the full extent and nature of the destruction that engulfed the settlement. Some of the buildings in the peripheral areas that are currently dated to around AD 70 may actually have been built prior to AD 60, since it is possible that they might not have been burned. Indeed, the absence of burning and the presence of Highgate Wood C ware have sometimes been used to date deposits to after AD 60.[40] The recent evidence from 1 Poultry, 36–9 Poultry and Newgate Triangle could suggest that this pottery type was introduced prior to the uprising, or the extensive burning on these sites must post-date AD 60.[41]

As the two examples of 1 Poultry and Southwark have indicated, very careful excavation and detailed finds analysis are required to develop a convincing case for the dating of archaeological deposits. Even when such work is undertaken meticulously, difficult questions remain about the extent, chronology and significance of burnt deposits. Many fires will have broken out during the history of Roman London since most buildings included highly flammable materials; fire was vital for warmth, for lighting and for industrial processes.

Looting, mayhem and the restoration of the natural order

Perring has reconsidered the old idea that the human remains, including hundreds of 'skulls' from the Walbrook, were victims of either the uprising or of the Roman reprisals that took place in its aftermath.[42] He has suggested that it is 'entirely credible' that victims of Roman justice would have been left on 'gruesome display' on the margins of Londinium.[43] This emphasizes the violence of the event, but a detailed study of the finds appears to contradict this.[44] Perring has argued that most of the datable skulls from Roman deposits come from post-Boudican construction layers.[45] A cranium was deposited in a pit with a waterlogged fill at Watling Court, apparently pre-dating building work from around AD 70–95.[46] Other cranial remains from excavated contexts may date to the AD 60s and 70s. One was found associated with the skeletons of two dogs in a well at 119–21 Cannon Street, just east of the Walbrook Valley, where a date in the AD 60s could be indicated by associated 'Neronian' pottery.[47] The human cranial remains from the roadside ditch at 201–11 Borough High Street in Southwark may date to the pre-Boudican or immediately post-Boudican periods.[48]

The fuller assessment of human cranial remains from Londinium in this book suggests, however, that the few examples from contexts that might date to the AD 60s or 70s are part of a long-term tradition spanning the period from the middle of the first century to the late second century.[49] The acts of deposition may have related to the exposure of corpses and to the manipulation of pieces of human bodies, a rite that appears to have been commonly conducted on the margins of Londinium for well over a century.[50] The classical accounts of the uprising certainly refer to violent reprisals against the Britons, although there is no particular reason to suggest that these occurred at Londinium, since the rebels were not necessarily among the population.

It is likely that any valuable items left behind will have been looted by Boudica's followers. It is possible that a good deal of material wealth was removed before the attack and the occupants may have returned later to retrieve other possessions. The stock of samian pottery from the 1 Poultry shop could have been too large to carry away quickly, while the grain from Cornhill, 1 Poultry and Southwark could have been considered of insufficient value. The centre of Londinium is likely to have been well furnished with bronze statues of emperors and gods throughout the Roman period and there were probably statues of Claudius and Nero on display. Bronze statues of gods and emperors that stood in the public areas of early Londinium were probably hacked to pieces by Boudica's followers if they had not been hidden or removed.[51]

A left hand and forearm of an early Roman bronze statue, just over life size, was found at 30 Gresham Street.[52] It was recovered from the top of a series of water-laid sediments within a large pond that may have been formed during quarrying of brickearth and gravel and that was not completely filled in until the second century.[53] Ceramics from the sediments surrounding the arm are dated to around AD 60–70.[54] The arm is presumed to have been part of a statue of a god that had stood in a public place, although a detailed study of its date and form might suggest that it was an imperial portrait.[55] If this was a statue of the emperor Claudius or of his successor Nero, it may have been destroyed during the uprising.[56] The deposition of the bronze statue fragments from 30 Gresham Street in a watery context may have followed a tradition of the ritual associations of water that was widespread across north-western Europe during the Iron Age and Roman periods.[57]

Miles Russell and Harry Manley have suggested that the badly damaged head of a marble statue found in 1906 during urban development at Great East Street, London, may also have come from a statue of Nero that was destroyed at the time of the Boudican rebellion.[58] The context of discovery was not recorded but the head was found in an area of Islington just over 2 kilometres north of Londinium. There has been very little archaeological investigation in the vicinity. The marble head may have been looted and dumped in a significant location beyond the edge of the settlement.

The potential ritual role of the Iron Age landscape may be considered in association with the burning and large-scale destruction of Londinium. It has been observed that the uprising occurred at the significant time when the governor Suetonius Paulinus was attempting the conquest of the island of Mona (Anglesey) despite resistance encouraged by Druids. Miranda Aldhouse-Green has used Tacitus' writings to suggest that this action was a direct cause of the Boudican uprising,[59] although this is uncertain. It has usually been assumed that Boudica's followers attacked Camulodunum, Londinium and Verulamium as symbols of Roman oppression. These acts of burning and destruction were intended to destroy the urban infrastructure that had accrued at these three particularly important locations.

Summary

The destruction of Londinium provides a vital source of evidence for archaeologists who are researching the early history of the urban settlement, but there are concerns about associating archaeological evidence too closely with the uprising. The detailed work that has been undertaken on the pottery incorporated within the deposits on several of the most carefully excavated sites has raised questions about the exact date at which the episodes of burning had occurred. The extent and scale of the evidence for burning does seem to indicate that Boudica's followers had burned Londinium to the north and south of the Thames. The general scarcity of objects from the burnt deposits could suggest that many occupants had time to escape the attack with many of their possessions. It is not possible, however, to provide a more detailed interpretation of the nature of Londinium's destruction and even the evidence for the extent of the burning of buildings needs to be considered with caution as some buildings may not have been destroyed by fire.

Further excavations based on a more questioning approach could result in a new understanding of the extent and nature of the burning of Londinium. More evidence may be found that buildings were not destroyed or that completely burned structures were soon replaced. At the Ticket Hall site in Southwark the destroyed smithy was replaced after the fire by a new building with a similar function.[60] The site of the early market square at the centre of Roman London was later occupied by the first forum and basilica, the routes of the early roads on both banks of the Thames were re-established, while some properties, such as those at Newgate Triangle, may have been rebuilt by the original occupants when they returned after the uprising.

4

Re-establishing Urban Order
from AD 60 to 70

Introduction

It has been supposed that the destruction of Londinium resulted in the temporary abandonment of the settlement and that the roads, properties and public areas were not restored for a decade or longer.[1] Substantial evidence has now been found for the swift re-establishment of port facilities and urban infrastructure that demonstrates that there was an official will to refound Londinium without much delay (see Fig. 4.1).[2] From around AD 62 substantial works were undertaken to build a riverside quay on the north bank of the Thames. About the same time a fortification, probably a Roman fort, was built just to the south-east of the earlier market area and a new supply of fresh water was established with the construction of at least one substantial well west of the Walbrook, while the imperial procurator Julius Classicianus was commemorated with an imposing monument. Recently discovered writing tablets from Bloomberg have indicated the presence of traders and military men, demonstrating the strategic significance of the port.

Gaius Julius Alpinus Classicianus

Evidence for official activity includes the burial monument of the procurator Gaius Julius Alpinus Classicianus.[3] Classicianus' monument probably stood in an early Roman cemetery just beyond the eastern margin of the early urban settlement. The three surviving fragments had been incorporated into one of the fourth-century bastions on the Roman wall.[4] The significance of this fine burial monument may have resulted in its survival until the mid-fourth century, when the bastions were built.[5] The inscription states that it was set up by Classicianus' widow, Julia Pacata, daughter of Indus.[6] We know from Tacitus (*Ann.*: 14.38) that Classicianus was appointed procurator soon after the outbreak of Boudica's uprising, probably in AD 60–1. Tacitus also mentions that Classicianus had an argument with the provincial governor, Suetonius Paulinus. A procurator is unlikely to have been appointed for more than four years, which suggests that the monument dated to between AD 61 and 65.[7]

Classicianus probably came from Gallia to Londinium and was of equestrian rank, but since the text from the inscription is incomplete, we know little about his life or death. The monument displayed Classicianus' authority and wealth since the style of the lettering and sculptural detail

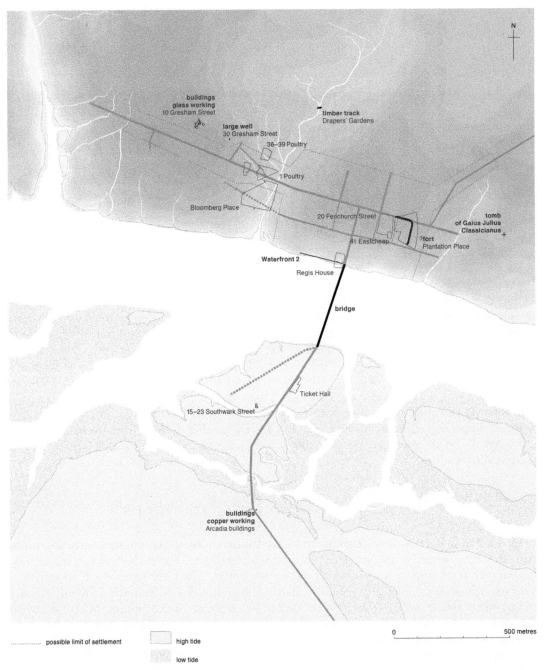

FIG. 4.1 Londinium in AD 61–70.

compare well with high quality sculpture from elsewhere in the empire.[8] It is not clear why the procurator was buried in Londinium, but the location of his monument will have emphasized the significance of the port and settlement to the government of the province.[9] The procurator was responsible for the financial administration of Britannia and was involved in the re-establishment of order across the province during the early 60s, presumably operating from his base at Londinium.[10] Tacitus' account of the destruction of AD 60 suggested that the merchants settled at Londinium will have left with their possessions and Classicianus may have established his centre of operations here with the intention of encouraging them to return in order to finance the rebuilding of the urban settlement and port. Classicianus may have had sympathy with the Gallic settlers from his homeland, in the immediate aftermath of the uprising.[11] The writing tablets from Bloomberg have provided significant information supporting the strategic importance of Londinium.

Textual evidence for the re-establishment of Londinium

At Bloomberg the pre-Boudican banks and ditches silted up for a brief time before they were replaced by new enclosures.[12] These enclosures have been closely dated to between AD 60–1 and 62 and seven wooden writing tablets have been found in closely-dated associated contexts. As in the case of many others from Bloomberg, these tablets were brought to the site from another part of Londinium along with material that was dumped to build up the ground surface.[13] The only tablet with legible text, dated 21 October AD 62, recorded the names of two Roman citizens, Marcus Rennius Venustus, who had contracted Gaius Valerius Proculus to 'bring from Verulamio [Verulamium] by the Ides of November [13 November], 20 loads of provisions at a transport charge of one one-quarter *denarius* for each' (see Fig. 4.2).[14] Although this text was damaged, it indicates that the delivery was to arrive at Londinium,[15] providing clear evidence for the rapid recovery of both urban centres.[16] Tomlin has observed that the terms of the contract suggest that this was quite a small consignment of goods, of unknown character, probably only requiring a single waggon.[17]

One writing tablet from another context dated to a day in the final months of AD 64, recording that Florentinus, the slave of Sextus Cassius, was writing on the order of his master to say that he had received two payments in respect of a farm.[18] This letter of receipt was contemporary with another letter in which Aticus refers to a specific sum of money held by a partner.[19] Evidently Londinium was quickly recovering its role as centre of trade.

Tacitus has commented (*Ann.* 14.38) that the garrison of the province was reinforced with 2,000 legionaries, eight auxiliary cohorts and 1,000 cavalry from Germany. The waterfront in Londinium was probably the disembarkation point for these forces who were campaigning to recover the province from the Britons.[20] The military significance of Londinium is emphasized by three tablets probably dating from the AD 60s. One mentions a fort in the territory of the Iceni, possibly called Epocuria, that could have been associated with the movement of soldiers during the suppression of hostilities.[21] Another mentions 'Classicus', prefect of the Sixth Cohort of Nervians, and Tomlin has suggested that this officer may be identified with the well-known Julius Classicus, possibly promoted by the provincial procurator Julius Classicianus, who was later to lead a cavalry unit during the Batavian uprising of AD 70.[22] This tablet was found in the same context as another naming Rogatus 'the Lingonian'.[23] The Lingones were a tribe in Upper Germany and Rogatus may have been a soldier in a newly-recruited auxiliary cohort from this community that had been sent to Britain, or even to Londinium itself.[24] A third tablet dated to

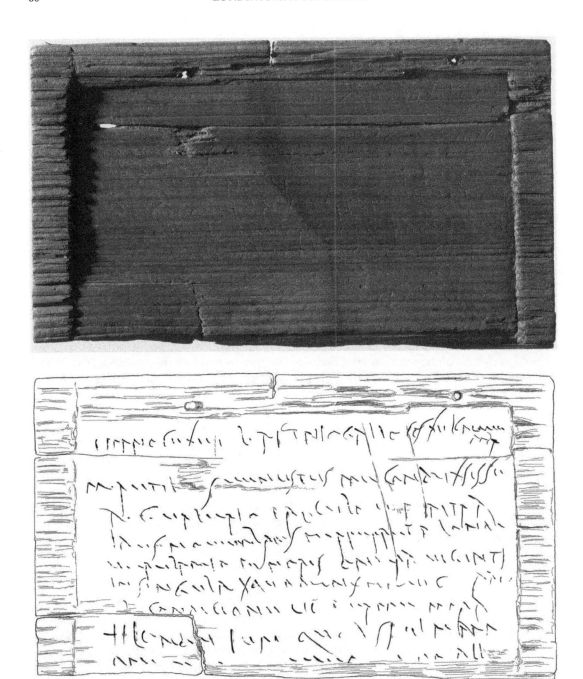

FIG. 4.2 Writing Tablet 45 from the Bloomberg site, which dates to 21 October AD 62.

AD 67 seems to have been a legal document initiated by a soldier or veteran of the First Cohort of Vangiones, from a German *civitas* that also supplied auxiliary soldiers to the army.[25] The three cohorts identified by these tablets were all recruited from *civitates* in the Rhineland areas of the empire; the Lingones and the Vangiones were partly mounted units, recalling Tacitus' comments about the cavalry units sent to Britain.[26] Tomlin has suggested that some of these soldiers were stationed at the Plantation Place fort.[27]

The fort at Plantation Place

Excavations at Plantation Place, just to the south-east of the early civic centre, have located what has been interpreted as the north-east corner of a Roman fort dating to immediately after AD 61.[28] It has been suggested that this was established as a sign of Rome's determination to reconstruct the shattered settlement, although the dates given for the construction and occupation of this defended enclosure ranges from around AD 63–85.[29] The construction of the fort has been dated to the period AD 61–70 and a strong case has been made by the excavators to associate it with the post-Boudican reconstruction of Londinium in around AD 63.[30]

The fortification comprised a double ditch system protecting a turf-fronted, timber-laced mud-brick rampart (see Fig. 4.3).[31] It may have covered an area of around one hectare, although only the north-east section of the enclosure has been excavated and its exact extent is unclear.[32]

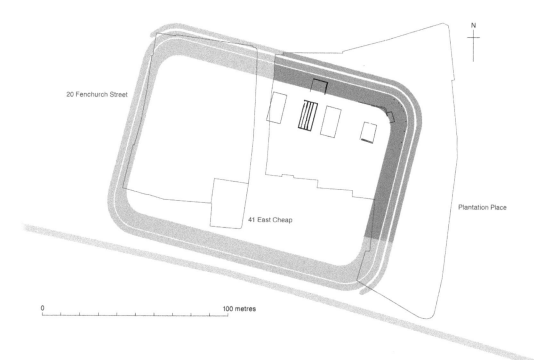

FIG. 4.3 The first-century Roman fort at Plantation Place. The western and southern extent of the supposed fort is shown as planned by the excavators but no definitive evidence was found for the defensive boundaries during the excavations at 20 Fenchurch Street.

No entrances were found but this could be a consequence of the limited area that was available for excavation.[33] The fort, as reconstructed by the excavators, is far smaller than the second-century fort at Cripplegate.[34] Dominating a strategic point of high ground, the fortification was close to the major road junction and the early marketplace above the bridgehead.[35] Its northern ditches cut through the main east–west road of early Londinium and it is unclear why this road was put out of use.[36] This fortified enclosure overlay timber buildings which are thought to have been burned during the Boudican uprising and the rampart itself contained charred timbers and burnt mud bricks that were reused from destroyed buildings.[37]

Inside the fortification there was a granary, a latrine, a cookhouse and a road running around the inside of the rampart, although no barrack blocks were revealed.[38] Finds that indicate high-status buildings included tesserae of various colours and hypocaust tiles,[39] although these could have been brought to the site from elsewhere. The military character of these remains is indicated by the defences, the internal buildings and finds made during the excavations.[40] The pottery assemblage and the collection of military finds support the presence of Roman soldiers. The percentage of amphorae sherds in the pottery assemblage is considerably larger than on other contemporary sites across Londinium,[41] and there were nearly fifty military artefacts, including armour, military dress and horse gear.[42]

The excavation at 20 Fenchurch Street has sampled an area that should coincide with the north-west of this fortification and has produced evidence for buildings and roads but no definitive indication of the fort.[43] The pre-Boudican buildings were replaced with a range of similar timber-and-earth buildings and a stone building which were built immediately following the Boudican uprising.[44] A building in the north of the site produced some evidence that it was used for metalworking.[45] The only items of distinctly military character from the excavation at 20 Fenchurch Street are some fragments of armour.[46] Although these remains were fragmentary they do not appear to indicate the type of planned interior characteristic of a fort. The excavations at 41 Eastcheap explored part of the interior of the proposed fort and produced no distinctively military artefacts.[47]

The absence of barrack blocks may indicate that the military units were living in leather tents;[48] they may then have been swiftly redeployed to serve in other parts of the province. It is also possible that the fort was constructed by the military for civil use as a fortified enclosure.[49] The population of Londinium is likely to have included retired Roman soldiers and their presence may have given the urban community a sense of security in the aftermath of the uprising of AD 60. The evidence indicates that the Plantation Place fortification remained serviceable until around AD 85.[50] It could have been largely unoccupied for much of this time and was perhaps maintained for emergency use.[51]

Starting to build Waterfront 2

In the aftermath of the uprising, a sustained programme of quay building (Waterfront 2) commenced on the north bank of the Thames downstream of the bridge over the Thames.[52] An earlier timber bridge (Bridge 1) in the same location may have been repaired during the early 60s, although evidence for both the initial construction and the rebuilding of this structure is very limited.[53]

Replacing the simple timber revetment (Waterfront 1) constructed during the AD 50s, Waterfront 2 was extended further to the east and west during the later first century. This development was replaced by Waterfront 3, possibly around AD 120. The scale of the work undertaken to establish Waterfront 2 demonstrates the Roman administration's determination to re-establish Londinium as a major port, a decision that appears to have been made within three years of the suppression of the uprising.[54] Excavations at Regis House in 1996, close to London Bridge, uncovered evidence for this waterfront,[55] including a tree-ring date indicating that timber was felled for this construction in AD 63.[56] This quay-building was the start of an operation that took at least three decades to complete along the Thames, both upstream and downstream of the bridging point.[57]

It has been suggested that Waterfront 2 was built in sections of around 120–130 metres in length, beginning in AD 63–4 with the section immediately upstream of the bridge that has been sampled at Regis House.[58] Here a substantial quay, 2 meters high, was constructed in front of the line of the earlier waterfront. This quay had a solid front framework of squared oak beams retained by side and back timbers that formed a series of boxes that were infilled with soil containing pottery, metal objects and other artefacts.[59] Finds from the infill of the waterfront at Regis House that may indicate that the military were involved included strips of scale armour (*lorica squamata*) and leather tent fragments.[60] A stamp or brand that reads '. . . IRAECAVG . . .' had been impressed twice into an axe-hewn end of the timber incorporated into the quay, perhaps by an engineer from a Thracian military unit.[61]

It has been suggested that the scale of these waterfront works from the later first to the third century indicates that the work was undertaken by the *classis Britannica*, the British fleet. Gustav Milne has suggested that the involvement of the *classis Britannica* is indicated by their comparable works in building the port facilities at Dubris (Dover, Kent) which were also constructed and maintained from the mid to later first century to the third.[62] It has yet to be clearly demonstrated, however, that soldiers would have been directly involved for a period of thirty years or more in constructing these port facilities. Perhaps military engineers from the fleet helped to plan and construct the initial phases of this work and trained others, including retired soldiers, to continue these operations. Alternatively, the waterfront may have been initially planned by the *classis Britannica*, but then the urban council quickly took over the building and maintenance of the port works, perhaps with occasional military or official support.

The urban water supply

Water was supplied to the inhabitants of Londinium from a network of springs and wells.[63] Major works commenced during the early AD 60s to supply a significant quantity of water to one particular location. To the west of the Walbrook at 30 Gresham Street, just to the south-west of the site of the later amphitheatre, excavations in 2001 located three substantial timber-lined wells dating to the first and early second centuries.[64] The area they are located in was defined by roads possibly laid out in the AD 70s and also included the Cheapside bathhouse.[65] Perring has suggested that the construction of the first well in AD 63 was part of the highly organized plan to reconstruct the infrastructure at this early date, an operation that would have produced enough water for several thousand people.[66] The substantial quantity of clean water that could be produced from this well may have supplied a bathhouse or the extensive area of the new settlement that was to be built west of the Walbrook.[67] The well was a massive structure that included a bucket-chain water-lifting system of wooden water boxes. Its construction has been dated by tree-ring analysis to AD 63 and it was abandoned after about ten years, perhaps as a result of the failure of its wooden structure.[68] The other two wells, one of which also had a water-lifting system, were constructed during the late first and early second centuries.[69] The excavators have suggested that the spatial planning of Londinium allowed for this area to be left fairly free of buildings to maintain the freshness of the water supply.[70]

Although the Cheapside bathhouse is very poorly dated, it is probable that the civic authorities may have planned its construction during the early 60s, in an otherwise undeveloped part of early Roman London. It appears unlikely that an urban settlement of the scale and importance of Londinium would have been left without a public bathhouse for a decade following its destruction, especially since there could have been a bathhouse in Southwark prior to AD 60. One possibility is that the construction of the first well at 30 Gresham Street was the beginning of a programme of works that was intended to include a bathhouse but that this plan took a decade or more to complete. This well may also have supplied water while the surrounding areas were developed for housing.

Occupation

Following the destruction of the Boudican uprising the houses and shops were generally not immediately rebuilt,[71] although there is some evidence for building during the early AD 60s on several sites. It has been observed that the rebuilding of Londinium did not commence on any scale for about a decade,[72] but it is now thought that this apparent delay could at least partly relate to the disruption in the supply of pottery to the port.

The dating of archaeological deposits has depended mainly on the analysis of the pottery they contain. Tree-ring analysis has also contributed to the dating of structures, such as the initial works to Waterfront 2 and the construction of the first well at 30 Gresham Street.[73] It is clear that Londinium must have been at least partly resettled early in the AD 60s since construction activities such as those on the waterfront indicated that there was a resident population. The Bloomberg writing tablets indicate that traders and military personnel were visiting or living in London during the early AD 60s. At this time the people of Londinium, including soldiers, may have lived in temporary accommodation that has left little trace in the archaeological record. Some of the fullest information for how people were living has come from the excavations around 1 Poultry and from the Ticket Hall site in Southwark.

At 1 Poultry the pre-Boudican surface of the main east–west road and the side road to the north were sealed by a layer of sand and silt, perhaps indicating that there was a period of poor maintenance or abandonment immediately following the Boudican destruction.[74] Nevertheless, a timber-lined reservoir was constructed adjacent to the side road, dated by tree-ring analysis to the years immediately following the uprising.[75] A tree-ring date of AD 62–3 could indicate that comparable work was undertaken to provide a drain for the road on the neighbouring site slightly further to the west.[76] These drainage features were probably connected with repairs to the road network. The full-scale rebuilding of houses across this area may not have commenced until around AD 70. Just north of 1 Poultry, at 36–9 Poultry, there was some reoccupation around AD 65 with the construction of a short-lived timber-and-earth building to the south-east of the site.[77] A more substantial replanning of this area included the construction of a road and several new buildings around AD 70.

At the Ticket Hall site, on the north island in Southwark, some destruction deposits associated with the remains of buildings appear to have been cleared around AD 61.[78] Just after this time beside the main north–south road some timber buildings were constructed, including what appears from the evidence of animal bone to have been a butcher's shop. In about AD 70 a more substantial phase of reconstruction was carried out across this area.[79]

Although people were returning to Londinium and rebuilding it in some areas during the decade after the destruction, excavations at 10 Gresham Street have produced evidence of a more intensive sequence of occupation (see Fig. 4.4).[80] A cluster of thirteen small round or oval timber-built houses and one rectangular building were constructed during the AD 60s just beyond the margins of the ruined settlement, possibly surrounded by a ditch and comparable to the enclosed settlements of the Iron Age.[81] The rectangular timber building was identified as a workshop and the authors of the excavation report have argued that the ground plan may indicate that the people came from elsewhere in Britain and had adopted a Roman style of building.[82]

The rectangular building, or 'workshop', featured two hearths that had been used for the manufacturing of glass beads.[83] These included incomplete beads, waste fragments and raw material in the form of vessel glass, rods and threads. These plain annular beads, blue melon bead and single eye bead were presumably among those intended to be sold at a market in Londinium.[84] The 'pre-Roman style' used to manufacture these glass beads may suggest that they were made by and for Britons,[85] although it may be preferable not to draw too distinct a division between Iron Age and Roman styles of bead manufacture.[86] Hearths and occupation deposits in one of the roundhouses indicate that people were living in at least some of these buildings. The circular buildings may have been temporary houses erected by itinerant workers who came to the site on a regular basis.[87] Alternatively, they could indicate that enslaved Britons were undertaking the work of reconstructing Londinium under military supervision; perhaps the glassworking was a sideline.[88] Additional sites with comparable buildings may be found on the margins of Boudican London during future excavations.[89]

Other signs of occupation and activity occurred at the margins of the earlier settlement. At Drapers' Gardens in the upper Walbook Valley, a timber structure has been tree-ring dated to AD 62.[90] The exact role and significance of this structure and its associated deposits was unclear, but it was possibly part of a trackway running close to the northern edge of Londinium for at least 66 metres, associated with a ditch and channel.[91] To the north, four timber boxes were excavated, three of which contained the remains of infants interpreted by the excavators as having had ritual connotations.[92] Infant burials have occasionally been found within the occupied area of Roman London, but these particular examples were buried on the periphery.

The area of Southwark occupied by AD 60 may have been restricted to the road frontages on the north island.[93] On the south side of the north island ditches and pits at 15–23 Southwark Street may, however, represent the remains of timber-and-earth buildings constructed between AD 60 and the early 70s on a previously unoccupied site.[94] This occurred just north of the Southwark Street Channel, which was probably being filled in around this time.[95] Several metal items that are likely to have been connected with the Roman army were found in association with these early structures, although there was no clear evidence for buildings of military character.[96] Louise Rayner's analysis of pottery from Southwark that probably pre-dated AD 70, however, indicates that a more extensive area was settled at this time, including occupation on the south island and on the main south bank of the Thames.[97] It is possible that this indicates that this southern area was not occupied prior to Boudica's uprising but that people were settling on the southern margins of Londinium during the early AD 60s.

South of the Thames at Arcadia Buildings evidence was found for copperworking including several hearths, one of which may have been a bowl furnace, associated with a timber building.[98] Deposits containing Iron Age style crucibles suggest that craftspeople from Britain were working here between AD 50 and 70.[99] The limited area that has been excavated could constitute part of a substantial industrial complex at the junction of the main north–south road (Watling Street) and Stane Street.

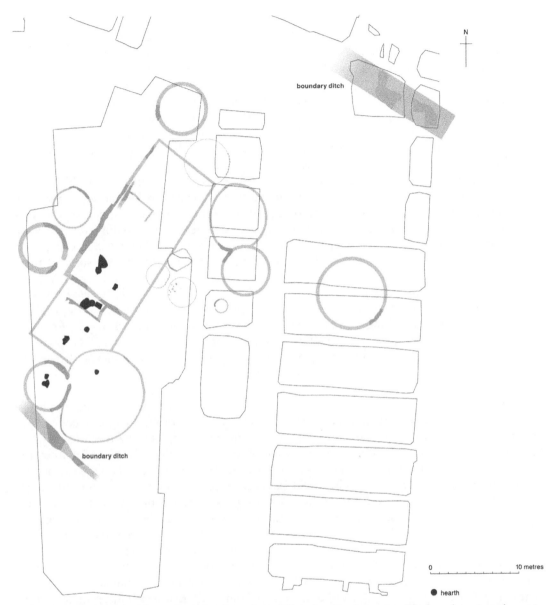

FIG. 4.4 The early buildings at 10 Gresham Street. The plan has been simplified to show just the main outlines of the houses reconstructed in the excavation report, the hearths in these buildings and the ditch sections of what is interpreted as an enclosure that surrounds these buildings.

Summary

Mapping the areas of occupation and activity makes it clear that many building activities during the AD 60s took place beyond the margins of the earlier occupation; presumably the ruins of the early settlement were being cleared and prepared for reoccupation during this decade. It is clear from the Bloomberg writing tablets that trade was central to the recovery of Londinium from at least the autumn of AD 62. These tablets also show that Roman military personnel were present in Roman London and support the identification of the enclosure at Plantation Place as a transhipment centre for soldiers on their way to areas of the province to the north of the Thames. Military finds are also common from other sites across London, including Bloomberg, Regis House and 1 Poultry.[100] All this information supports the idea that the Roman military were present, but some of the items could have been retained by retired soldiers who came to settle with the intention that they could be mustered should troubled times return.[101] The presence of the procurator also indicates the administrative and financial importance of Londinium at this time. The evidence for administrative and military personnel after AD 60 suggests the growing strategic importance of the port and urban settlement within the province of Britannia.

5

Londinium from AD 70 to AD 120

The intention of the conquering race has been, whilst firmly holding the dominions of which they have become possessed, to interfere as little as possible with the natives so long as they were content to submit quietly to the demands of their conquerors.

BERTRAM WINDLE 1897: 11

Introduction

This chapter will address the evidence for the fifty years after AD 70. The re-establishment of Londinium and the nature of the infrastructure, buildings, economy and creation of terrain and waterscapes until around AD 120 will be explored. During the decades after AD 70, a major phase of urban renewal involved the construction of monumental buildings, including the first forum and basilica, bathhouses and temples. Housing, shops and industrial premises were constructed over an extensive urban area and the available information indicates that there were dramatic differences between the inhabitants of Londinium in terms of wealth. The limits of Roman London remained poorly defined physically but they were marked by activities and practices such as the deposition of human remains in marginal mortuary terrains, connected acts of feasting and the development of industries.

The people and status of Londinium

The complex social differentiation of the urban community is demonstrated by the texts on writing tablets and tombstones. There is some evidence to support the presence of the provincial governor and the procurator in Londinium, and wealthy traders, industrial workers and slaves were living and working in Roman London.

Mark Hassall has argued that the permanent office of the governor's staff was based at Londinium.[1] Although there is no definitive evidence for this,[2] the names of officials recorded in stone inscriptions and on writing tablets provide strong support for the idea that Londinium had a significant role in the administration of the province of Britannia.[3] The presence of imperial officials, however, did not necessarily imply that London was the permanent base of the provincial governor or the procurator. Administrative officials and military units embarked and disembarked at the port which demonstrated Londinium's administrative, military and economic significance.[4]

Evidence from four of the writing tablets found at Bloomberg from contexts dating to AD 60–80 provide details that may indicate that the provincial governor was based in Londinium.[5] An incomplete text dated 22 October AD 76 constituted the preamble to a preliminary judgement of a legal case between Litugenus and Magunus by a judge whose authority had been delegated by the emperor Vespasian.[6] Tomlin has suggested that this judge may have been appointed by the provincial governor or his deputy rather than by the elected magistrates of the community. Another tablet names Rusticus, who may have been one of the governor's bodyguards (*singularis*).[7] Tomlin has noted that two additional writing tablets from this site appear to refer to imperial officials.[8]

One of the letters from the Roman fort of Vindolanda (Northumberland) may refer to the provincial governor's groom as resident in London.[9] A centurion from the First Cohort of Tungrians was for a time on duty in Londinium, as mentioned in the strength report found in a first-century ditch at Vindolanda.[10] Mark Hassall has argued that a detachment of forty-six troops that are mentioned in the same report may have served under this centurion, supporting the idea that the governor's headquarters was in London.[11]

A fragmentary stone relief carving from the burial monument of a legionary soldier which was originally sited on the northern margins of Londinium was found built into one of the fourth-century bastions on the Roman wall at Camomile Street (Bastion 10) in 1876.[12] Mike Bishop has argued that on stylistic grounds this was an unusual burial monument that dated from the later first century, although the inscription that recorded the soldier's name, place of origin or role has not survived.[13] Bishop has suggested that this soldier might have been a *beneficiarius consularis* ('a beneficiary of the consular governor'), a legionary soldier attached to the governor's clerical staff.[14] Hassall has assessed the role of such individuals and has suggested that they may have been concerned with the supplies to the legions.[15] The tombstone of Celsus, a *speculator*, or military policeman, of the Second Legion Augusta probably dates from the first half of the second century and was set up by three of his colleagues to the west of Roman London.[16] Hassall has argued that the presence of these four military *speculatores* in Londinium was significant since such officers were few and they may have been serving on the provincial governor's staff.[17] It is possible, however, that they were visitors to London and were not actually based there.

A waxed writing tablet found at 1 Poultry was inscribed with a deed of sale referring to a Gallic female slave called Fortunata.[18] It also recorded that Fortunata had been bought by Vegetus who was the 'assistant slave of Montanus the slave of the August Emperor and sometimes assistant slave of Iucundus'.[19] Although Vegetus was himself the slave of an imperial slave, he was probably an official of some importance, since imperial slaves and freedmen were on the staff of the emperor's house and managed his estates.[20] The Bloomberg tablets show that slaves and freedmen were conducting financial affairs for their masters and patrons; perhaps Vegetus was working in this capacity for the procurator.[21] Tomlin has argued that Vegetus' wealth is indicated by the fact that he was able to afford 600 *denarii*, a sum equivalent to two years' salary for a legionary soldier, to purchase Fortunata.[22] That Vegetus, an imperial slave, had such resources at his disposal is an indication of the complex identities within Roman society.[23] The writing tablet records that Fortunata was sold to Vegetus by Albicianus and, although we do not know where the sale occurred, it may have been at Londinium.[24] The purchasing of Fortunata by an individual who was named as the slave of a slave exemplifies the elaborate social structure of the Roman Empire.

A tombstone found on Ludgate Hill that had originally been set up to the west of Londinium was dedicated to Claudia Martina by her widower, Anencletus. The style and character of the inscription suggests that the tombstone dates from the early to mid-second century.[25] The term attached to Anencletus' name, *provinc[ialis]*, means 'slave of the province' although the exact sense of this word is unclear.[26] Anencletus may have been a slave of the council with a responsibility for maintaining the imperial cult,[27] or the term may indicate that he was born in the province.[28] He may have been a slave of the provincial council, which would support the idea that Londinium played an important administrative role in the province.[29]

The burial of Julius Classicianus to the east of Londinium in the early AD 60s shows that the procurator was based there at this early date.[30] A writing tablet, found either in or close to the Walbrook, was marked with an official stamp indicating that it was issued by the 'procurators' of the province of Britannia.[31] The tablet itself was illegible and may have been sent from elsewhere in Britannia and its date is unclear. The procuratorial tiles found in Londinium may also indicate the involvement of the procurator in London.

The interpretation of the enclosure at Plantation Place as a fort would support the suggestion that soldiers were stationed at Londinium, and Roman military equipment has been found across London in contexts dating from the second half of the first century AD.[32] The most specific references to members of the Roman military in the Bloomberg writing tablets are in texts dating from the AD 60s, although some of the tablets that mention army personnel may date from the AD 70s or 80s.[33] A military diploma from 'Building D' at Watling Court indicates that a soldier had retired to Londinium during the later first or early second century, although it is not certain that he had necessarily been based there.[34] Some tombstones and other documents also indicate soldiers.[35] A tombstone found in 1776 in Church Lane in Whitechapel, probably dating from the late first or early second century, names Julius Valens, soldier of the Twentieth Legion, Valeria Victrix, who had been buried to the east of Londinium.[36] Another tombstone of similar date, found in 1961 in High Holborn to the west of Londinium, names Gaius Pomponius Valens, a tribune of a legion from Victricensis (the colony of Camulodunum at Colchester, Essex).[37]

Although the information from inscriptions is biased towards more wealthy individuals it is not restricted to military personnel and imperial officials. An ornate tombstone found on Tower Hill in 1852 names Aulus Alfidius Olussa, a Roman citizen born in Athens.[38] The formula of the inscription on his tombstone suggests that he was buried in the first century, probably in the same cemetery in which Classicianus' ornate memorial stood.[39] The marble slab from a funerary monument was found reused as packing for a later burial in the Hooper Street area of the 'eastern cemetery'.[40] Probably dating from the late first century, it named the deceased as Lucius Pompeius Licetus from Arretium in Etruria (modern Arezzo in Italy).

Texts from writing tablets indicate that Londinium was an important economic centre for trade and commerce at this time.[41] Those involved in trade and industry were often slaves or freedmen of patrons who may not have lived in or around London. Slaves were numerous in Londinium, as they were throughout the Roman Empire, although they may only be located through sources such as writing tablets. Fortunata the slave, attested on the writing tablet from 1 Poultry, was 'by nationality' from a people called the Diablintes of northern Gaul; this tablet states that she was transferred in good health and warranted not to be liable to wander or run away.[42] Although Vegetus, who purchased Fortunata, may have been wealthy, life for the majority of slaves would have been short and unpleasant.[43] Another writing tablet from the Walbrook contained a business letter instructing the recipient to 'turn that girl into cash'.[44] There is no other direct information for the less privileged women of Londinium.[45] Industry and commerce were conducted by people with fewer resources in Roman society. Some of their names have survived, such as the potters who produced the wares at 20–8 Moorgate in the Walbrook Valley.[46]

Objects found in archaeological excavations can show how ways of life changed. The writing tablets and the inscriptions on pots and other personal possessions indicate that many people were experienced in the practice of writing in Latin, and samian pottery inkwells have been widely found on both sides of the Thames.[47] The construction of two public bathhouses shows that Mediterranean bathing habits had been adopted. Britons living in Londinium are difficult to identify since their ways of life had changed under the influence of Roman rule.[48] A few names on inscriptions from London have recognizably Celtic language elements that may indicate a British ethnic origin, although it is also possible that these people may have been settlers from the continent.[49] The Bloomberg writing tablets have recorded ten examples of 'Celtic' names, including Atigniomarus and Namatobogius, although these men may have been expatriates from other Celtic-speaking areas such as Gaul and Noricum.[50] Britons will quickly have adopted Roman identities and names.

Several roundhouses pre-date the Boudican uprising and those at 10 Gresham Street were dismantled by AD 70, although a single house at Toppings Wharf and Fennings Wharf was used into the second century (see below). The production of glass beads at 10 Gresham Street and the copperworking at Arcadia Buildings were based on Iron Age technologies, but traditional domestic ways of life swiftly disappeared as different types of houses, pottery and other possessions spread with the establishment of Londinium. The treatment of human remains may indicate the presence of Britons within the urban community since it is possible that some of the practices using human remains to mark the boundaries of early Roman London were based on the ways that the land and water were used during the Iron Age.[51]

Monumentalizing the landscape

During the decades after AD 70 there is extensive evidence for the construction of public buildings, including the first forum-basilica, the amphitheatre, temples and at least one bathhouse (see Fig. 5.1).[52]

Public and private buildings

The analysis of the development of Londinium has tended to be dominated by the consideration of buildings as either 'private' or 'public'. In connection with this it has been assumed that private buildings were domestic houses owned by individual families while public buildings were accessible to parts or all of the community at particular times. The fragmentary nature of the remains uncovered by archaeologists across London presents a significant problem for the interpretation of the buildings and the people who occupied and used them. Although a general distinction will be maintained between grander and more elaborate buildings on the one hand and simpler domestic residences, present categories of public and private are not relevant for these structures.[53] The spaces that the construction of these buildings helped to create were used to establish and articulate hierarchical relationships between the occupants of Londinium.

The 'public' buildings include the two successive forum-basilica complexes, bathhouses, temples, the amphitheatre, at least one 'palace' and a building that has been interpreted as a 'mansio'.[54] The many less substantial timber-and-earth and stone buildings located by more recent excavations were houses, shops and industrial premises. No clear distinction can be drawn, however, between public and private buildings across the Roman Empire. Since rank

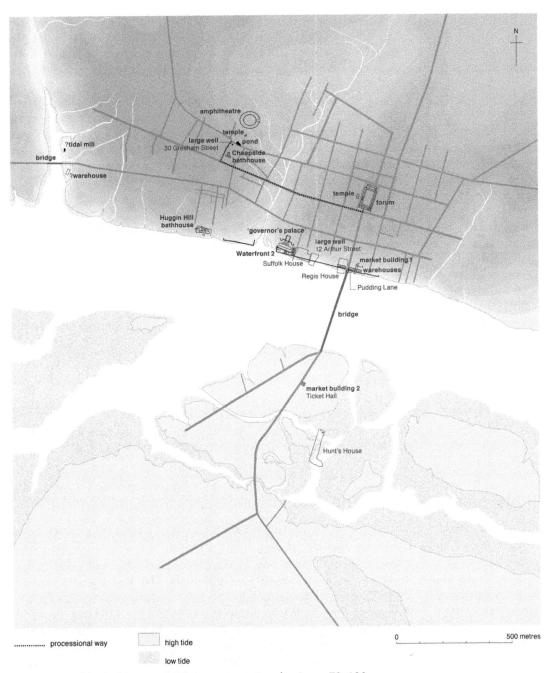

FIG. 5.1 Public buildings and infrastructure in London in AD 70–120.

was indicated and reinforced by social patronage, the houses of the wealthy were essentially also public places.[55] Andrew Wallace-Hadrill has observed that 'the pattern of Roman social life admitted numerous and subtle grades of relative privacy'.[56] This illustrates the extension of the practice of patronage to people of varying status, allowing the creation of spaces for patrons of different rank to receive their clients and to exercise and materialize their social standing.[57] Archaeological research has shown that increasingly ornate houses were constructed across Londinium during the first three centuries of its development, buildings that often featured mosaic floors, underfloor heating and ornate wall plaster in their reception rooms. Evidence has also been found for the less wealthy and fortunate inhabitants and it is important to keep in mind that most of the population will have been tenants, freedmen and slaves of the wealthier individuals who have often been the subject of the main focus of archaeological study.[58]

Other monumental buildings are difficult to interpret in terms of their private or public roles. The degree to which people were able to use the bathing facilities would depend on who had funded the construction and use of the building and also on the motivation behind acts of sponsorship.[59] Bathing was an important occasion for displaying rank and status and, although some substantial bathhouses were built during the later first to third centuries, other examples were small in scale and may have been intended only for the use of single families and their friends.[60] There are other bathhouses in London that have only been sampled by excavation and for which information is very limited.[61] Other types of buildings, such as the forum, amphitheatre and temples, were spaces for social display, making and showing social distinctions through entering and leaving buildings by particular ways and being permitted access to certain rooms and areas.

Across the Roman Empire urbanism was usually driven by competition between the urban elites of particular cities, resulting in the competitive financing of the construction of monumental buildings.[62] The lack of evidence for funding of public buildings by members of Londinium's urban elite has generally been used to suggest that there was not enough wealth or desire to plan and finance the more substantial and ornate buildings. It has often been thought that the governor, procurator and the army must have been involved in planning and executing building programmes on this scale. There is some information that there was official involvement in the construction of some of Londinium's monumental buildings during the late first and early second centuries, since they incorporated tiles that identified the procurator.[63] It has often been argued that these procuratorial tiles indicate the involvement of the provincial administration in building projects undertaken from around AD 80–120, including the Huggin Hill bathhouse, the 'governor's palace' and the amphitheatre.[64] This, in turn, has been taken to support the idea that all the buildings in which these tiles were incorporated had official functions. Examples of these stamped tiles have also been found on sites that are unlikely to have been part of an official building programme and it is likely that the production of the tiles rather than their use in building projects was controlled by the procurator.[65]

Only a single building, probably dated to the late second century, has provided direct evidence for official input in the form of inscriptions that name soldiers or imperial officials.[66] There is little evidence to suggest that the monumental buildings were financed by the urban elite, although this is likely to be a consequence of the scarcity of stone inscriptions and the fragmentary condition of many of the surviving examples.[67] Monumental buildings that may have been privately funded include temples of the late second and third centuries and a building that may have been a market hall at Pudding Lane.[68]

These inscriptions recording the names of the individuals who paid for the construction of buildings show that these wealthy inhabitants originated from other provinces of the Roman

Empire. Many aspects of the urban infrastructure were probably planned and constructed by an urban council established before the Boudican uprising and recreated in its aftermath. The creation of Londinium was probably a joint and cooperative venture between the urban authorities and the Roman administration.

Two of the most impressive monumental buildings that were constructed during the late first and second centuries were the 'governor's palace' on the north bank of the Thames and 'mansio' in Southwark. These were much larger and more ornate than the contemporary domestic buildings and have usually been interpreted as official structures. Building in stone during the first and early second centuries has been thought to have been only for publicly-funded structures, leading to the circular argument that any substantial stone buildings must have had a public or official function. Most domestic buildings across first-century Londinium were constructed of timber and earth, but there is growing evidence for more impressively built houses dating to the early Roman period.[69] The 'governor's palace' and the 'mansio' may therefore have been constructed for wealthy Londoners. Compared to other towns in Britannia, the early houses were particularly impressive and ornate and many may have belonged to merchants from other areas of the empire.

The first forum and a temple

The most significant of the early public buildings, usually identified as a forum-basilica, was constructed on the cleared gravel surface on Cornhill (see Fig. 5.2). The plan of the early forum has been reconstructed from excavations which have sampled parts of its extensive layout.[70] It featured four building ranges surrounding a courtyard, with a basilica to the north and an entrance to the south.[71] The foundations were laid with flint and external buttresses probably supported columns. The southern entrance fronted onto the main east–west road. Traces have been found of another entrance in the west wing that gave access to a small building that was probably a temple. Roads may have been laid to the east of the forum.[72]

Despite the poor preservation of the remains, Marsden was able to summarize the evidence and make some important observations.[73] The basilica was an impressive building that was intended to dominate its landscape, since its floor consisted of an artificial platform raised about 1 metre above its surroundings.[74] The width of its walls at ground level suggested that the nave supported a clerestory to admit light.[75] This was probably where the urban council met and its records were kept. The central courtyard extended in front of the basilica to the south and was divided into two, with the northern section at a higher level, possibly providing a panoramic view of the Thames.[76]

The courtyard may have been used as a marketplace and also for meetings. The west, south and east ranges of the forum each comprised a narrow range of rooms. The remains of six brick-built piers have been excavated in the courtyard area outside the south range and others may have lined the courtyard outside the west and east ranges.[77] This inner portico was a later phase of the first forum.[78] The forum would have been furnished with bronze statues of emperors and gods although few traces of such items have been found, perhaps because they were melted down for the value of their metal which was recast into new objects. The arm fragment from a monumental bronze statue of an emperor or god was found during the excavation of the pond at 30 Gresham Street, an early example that pre-dates the building of the first forum,[79] while additional bronze statue fragments found in London are of second-century and later date.[80]

The foundations of the building identified as a small classical temple were excavated in 1934–5 (see Fig. 5.3).[81] These were comparable in construction and use of material to those of

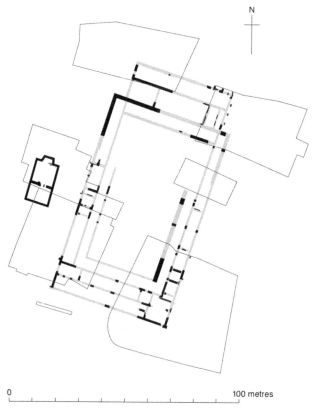

N

0   100 metres

FIG. 5.2 The early forum and the classical temple to the west. Excavated areas are shown and excavated features are shown in black.

the forum-basilica, leading to the assumption that these structures were constructed as part of the same building programme. The temple comprised a *cella* (central room) with an angular apse to the north and a southern entrance that may have been a portico with two columns, accessed by a flight of steps. Little evidence survived for the superstructure. The temple appears to have been surrounded by a gravel surface and a temenos (sacred enclosure).

The exact date of the building of the forum and temple is uncertain. They were probably built after AD 71 and possibly as late as AD 85,[82] but the preferred date is the middle years of the AD 70s.[83] This means that the London forum was approximately contemporary with the far larger and perhaps grander forum at Verulamium dated to AD 79 or 81.[84] The limited evidence for the dating and character of both forums makes it difficult to compare them, although the difference in their sizes may indicate the relative status of Verulamium and Londinium during the AD 70s. These buildings are the earliest forum complexes in Britannia but are approximately contemporary with the timber building interpreted as a forum-basilica at Calleva (Silchester).[85]

Excavations at the south-east corner of Londinium's forum indicate that there may have been at least one phase of rebuilding prior to its demolition.[86] This forum was replaced by a far more substantial building during the early second century, perhaps suggesting that it was soon considered to be insufficiently impressive. The new forum took at least thirty years to complete, involving some replanning of the urban centre.[87]

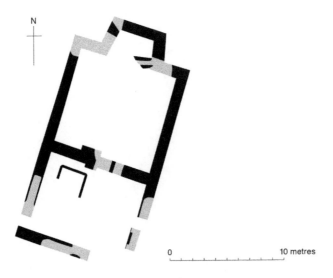

FIG. 5.3 Details of the early Roman temple to the west of the forum.

The amphitheatre

The amphitheatre was constructed to the west of the Walbrook at the edge of Londinium.[88] The Walbrook and its tributaries have long been thought of as a ritual landscape as a result of the discoveries in this area of human remains, artefacts interpreted as 'offerings' and the location of several temples. It has been suggested that the substantial pond at 30 Gresham Street formed an early focus for the development of a ritual landscape (or temple zone) including the amphitheatre and other buildings.[89] The amphitheatre may have constituted one element within a series of buildings and landscape features west of the Walbrook that was tied into a cycle of rituals that built upon the significance of this area in the headlands of the River Walbrook.[90]

The earliest activities on the site of the amphitheatre involved the digging of a series of brickearth quarries and scattered pits during the AD 50s.[91] A ditch was excavated during the period from around AD 50–75, probably in order to channel one of the tributaries of the Walbrook from west to east. The eastern entranceway to the amphitheatre was later constructed along the line of this channel. The area was stripped of topsoil around AD 70 and a substantial timber amphitheatre was built to exploit the local topography of an area of low ground crossed by two tributaries of the Walbrook.[92] This building has been reconstructed from limited excavations as an oval amphitheatre with east and west entrances, perhaps accommodating an audience of around 7,000 people.[93] Tree-ring dating of timbers from the eastern entrance suggested that construction was underway in AD 74.[94]

One of the significant features of the amphitheatre was the control of the flow of water within the structure. During the first timber phase, the earlier river channel at the eastern side was infilled and no evidence was found for the construction of a drain under the eastern entrance.[95] The arena was constructed by digging out at least a 2-metre depth of soil, reused in the surrounding banking, and its edge was defined by a timber palisade.[96] Much of this 'bank' was terraced into the natural slope of the shallow valley into which the structure was built, but the exact line and form of the outer wall of the amphitheatre was unclear.[97] Postholes to the south of the entrance may have formed an animal pen that was constructed at this time.[98] Although a timber-lined water tank and drain were constructed immediately inside the timber threshold of the eastern entrance,[99] the excavators argued that the absence of a drain to remove the water from the arena to the east would have resulted in the flooding of the entrance area, unless the water was removed manually.[100] The arena may therefore have been a wet area during the amphitheatre's first decades. Modifications were made, possibly just after AD 91, when a wooden drain with a timber-lined silt trap was constructed to channel water from the arena and out under the eastern entrance (see Fig. 5.4).[101] This early amphitheatre was dismantled and completely rebuilt during the early second century, probably around AD 120.

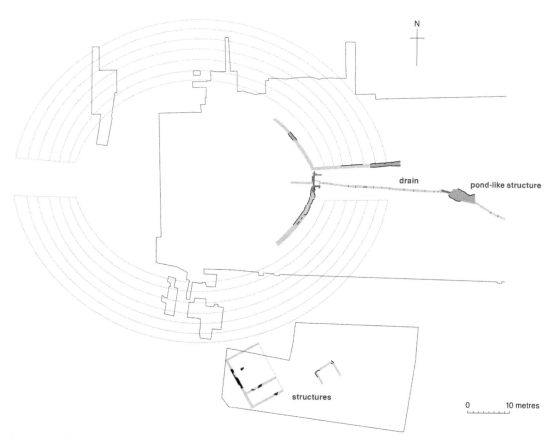

FIG. 5.4 The amphitheatre around AD 91 to AD 125, showing the pond in which glassworking waste and evidence for feasting was found.

In the report of the excavations, the possible military origins of this structure are set against the idea that it might have been established by the urban council.[102] Tony Wilmott has discussed the amphitheatres of Britain and suggested that the successive Londinium examples were more comparable to the legionary structures at Chester and Caerleon than to those at the *civitas* capitals.[103] Many of the amphitheatres in Britannia occur on urban sites, where they are not at all closely connected with evidence for Roman soldiers. This may support the idea that the London amphitheatre was commissioned and constructed by an urban authority rather than by the military. The amphitheatre is likely to have served the cosmopolitan community of peoples derived from across the empire, including retired soldiers.

The possibility that the control of water at the amphitheatre had a ritual purpose is supported by evidence from a broadly comparable building at Marcham (Oxfordshire), where a 'theatre' has been excavated just east of a substantial Roman temple complex.[104] The temple buildings were constructed inside a temenos at some distance to the west. The construction of the theatre involved the excavation of the arena into a shallow valley and the stone enclosing wall was constructed to incorporate a spring with a drain to carry water away under the banking to the south. There were entrances through the banking on the eastern and western sides and a timber stage may have been constructed to the north where the banking was less evident. Constructed by terracing the sides of the stream channel, the topographical situation of this theatre was comparable to Londinium's amphitheatre.[105] The Marcham theatre and the Londinium amphitheatre were both built within landscapes that required the careful drainage of their arenas.

Water was also carefully manipulated and controlled within these structures.[106] At Marcham a range of bronze, glass and iron objects were found close to the drain that ran south out of the arena and have been interpreted as indicating ritual activity.[107] The tributary of the Walbrook flowing through the London amphitheatre may have originated at a spring line about 200 metres to the north,[108] although the excavation was mainly confined to the eastern area of the amphitheatre and did not trace the course of the stream further to the west.[109] The drain under the eastern entrance in the amphitheatre was modified and replaced on several occasions and significant activities occurred along its alignment. For example, a dump of pottery, glass and other material relating to feasting and glass manufacture dating to the early second century was found in a 'pond-like' feature that had formed over the drain, just outside the eastern entrance.[110] A small building constructed over the site of this pond-type feature during the third century contained finds that may suggest ritual activity.

The apparently simple sequence of construction recorded for the amphitheatre may actually have been more complex, since the excavations have only sampled part of the structure and the remains were heavily truncated by later activity. At the Roman colony of Augusta Raurica (Augst, Switzerland), parts of the theatre or amphitheatre are well preserved and have been studied in detail, indicating a complex sequence of development.[111] Augusta Raurica was a highly impressive and monumental city and there is little to indicate that the Londinium amphitheatre had been comparable in scale or complexity, but the sequence at Augst does show that theatres and amphitheatres could progress through successive transformations from what is perceived as one ideal form to another.[112] At Augst it has been argued that the temple and theatre complex was associated with the imperial cult.[113] The numerous theatre buildings at temple sites across Gaul and Britain served more local cults and the available information from Londinium does not indicate that the amphitheatre was directly connected with emperor worship.

Although Londinium's amphitheatre has been only partly excavated, the remains were fairly well preserved and it is possible that the structure may have had a complex sequence of rebuilding.[114] The timber amphitheatre was replaced by a stone and timber structure during the second century and there is additional evidence for later alterations before it became disused in the fourth century. The current understanding of this sequence may, however, underplay the complexity of the development of this building.

The amphitheatre and a temple zone

Bateman has provided a stimulating review of the evidence for ritual activity associated with the amphitheatre and has suggested that it constituted part of a 'temple zone'.[115] He has interpreted the amphitheatre as a 'liminal space' that was woven into the existing patterns of cultural and religious life in Londinium.[116] Bateman has suggested that amphitheatres were liminal spaces that symbolized and 'safely contained' the boundaries between life and death.[117] It is suggested in this book that the upper Walbrook Valley was an area in which the dead were exposed to running waters and the amphitheatre may have been constructed on the margins of this mortuary landscape. This idea differs from more conventional interpretations of amphitheatres as staging places for gladiatorial combat and venues for the creation of imperial order,[118] and it is highly likely that such structures would have served more than a single function.[119] Too much emphasis has been placed on classifying 'spectacle buildings' (amphitheatres, theatres and semi-amphitheatres) into distinct classes when they may have been used for a range of complementary purposes.[120]

The limited information for religious activities at the amphitheatre includes a small inscribed lead curse naming Diana, found in the infilling of a late Roman drain, and two temple buildings just to the south.[121] One was a large stone building partially excavated at 30 Gresham Street, aligned south-west to north-east on an *opus signinum* pier base surrounded by sheets of Purbeck marble.[122] This building is interpreted as a late first- or second-century temple, with the walls of the *cella* enclosed by a colonnade. It has been suggested that it did not survive the 'Hadrianic fire' of the AD 120s and that some of the fragments of substantial masonry and marble incorporated into the later stone phase of the amphitheatre may have come from this building.[123]

The evidence for this early temple raises the possibility that the southern banking of the timber amphitheatre was lowered to provide a view of the temple for people in the northern seating area. This may have been the location of an entrance during the second-century stone-built phase of the amphitheatre, but this area is not well understood. Another small temple with an inner *cella* and surrounding portico was subsequently constructed slightly to the east of the earlier temple.[124] These two temple buildings appear to have been aligned radially with regard to the curve of the amphitheatre and may have formed part of a religious precinct immediately to the south.

Just to the south, a fragment of a bronze statue was found in a layer pre-dating AD 70 in the pond at 30 Gresham Street.[125] It may have derived from the statue of an emperor or god that could originally have stood in the area of the civic centre, but its deposition parallels rituals associated with other watery places across London. This large pond, measured around 20 by 10 metres, was aligned roughly east–west and may have been formed during quarrying of brickearth and gravel and was not completely filled in until the second century.[126] Excavations at 20–30 Gresham Street revealed human burials along with redeposited and disarticulated bones from ponds, streams, pits, demolition surfaces and a road surface.[127] This suggests that a small cemetery was located close to the site on which the amphitheatre was constructed and that Londinium gradually grew to surround this site. Other nearby springs and ponds included the 'water reservoir' excavated some way to the west-north-west at 10 Gresham Street.[128]

The results from the excavation at the major Roman temple complex of Vagniacis (Springhead, Kent) may help to provide a context for the area around Londinium's amphitheatre.[129] The Springhead complex included temples, shrines and ritual structures dating from the late first to the end of the third century AD. It developed into an extensive settlement with a primarily religious focus with a landing place on the river for small boats. Perhaps the construction of temples close to the spring at Vagniacis was paralleled in Londinium by the development of the temple zone in an area of the Walbrook Valley with a pre-existing significance.[130]

The evidence from other broadly contemporary sites in Britain, Gaul and Germany, where temples have been found in close association to theatres or amphitheatres, may help to interpret the fragmentary evidence from Londinium. Small theatres, or 'semi-amphitheatres', are common across northern and central Gaul and are usually closely associated with temples.[131] The construction of theatres at religious places across Britain and Gaul probably related to the assembly of communities to celebrate local cults, including annual festivals.[132] At sites such as Marcham the theatres would not have served a resident community since they were part of a religious complex in a rural location.[133] These complexes of temples associated with theatres may have been developed where there was a tradition of large-scale meetings that eventually led to the construction of buildings to supplement the shrines and meeting places.[134]

There is no evidence for occupation or significant building work in Londinium in the vicinity of the amphitheatre before around AD 70, although people may already have been meeting here, perhaps around the pond at 30 Gresham Street.[135] Since the population of Londinium is unlikely to have been larger than around 30,000, the potential size of the audience at the amphitheatre (7,000) may suggest that it was an assembly place for people from both Roman London and the countryside.[136] The temple zone may have monumentalized a location that was already an important meeting place during the earlier first century AD.

A processional way

The building of the amphitheatre during the early AD 70s may have been connected with the construction of the bathhouse at Cheapside and with the establishment of the temple immediately south of the amphitheatre. All these structures were built within a low-lying area around the sources of several tributaries of the River Walbrook. The pond at 30 Gresham Street lay approximately midway between the amphitheatre and the Cheapside bathhouse.[137]

The development of the urban landscape of Verulamium and Camulodunum may indicate how early landscape features and public buildings in Londinium were linked together.[138] John Creighton has argued that a processional way was established in Verulamium during the early to mid-first century AD in order to link an early enclosure on the site of the later forum ('St Michael's enclosure') to an early bathhouse in Insula XIX, across a causeway that crossed the river and continuing up to the high-status burial enclosure at Folly Lane.[139] At Gosbecks, close to the Roman colony of Camulodunum, a cult may have focused on the worship of a pre-Roman leader at the temple and theatre, probably linked to processions beginning at the forum of the neighbouring colony.[140]

At Londinium a processional way may have led from the forum to the temple zone around the amphitheatre.[141] Passing to the right, through the southern entrance of the forum-basilica, a procession would have passed westward along the main east–west road and past the small classical temple on the right. The procession would have followed the road across a bridge over the Walbrook close to 1 Poultry. The early road that led from the main east–west road at

1 Poultry may have been built during the AD 50s to provide access to a sacred area that included the pond at 30 Gresham Street.[142] At a later date, an alternative route to this place might have continued along the main east–west road and then turned right to arrive at the Cheapside bathhouse just south of the pond and the substantial wells at 30 Gresham Street.[143]

The construction of the Cheapside bathhouse has usually been dated to the AD 70s, although the evidence for its building and abandonment is extremely limited.[144] Other public buildings such as the amphitheatre were being constructed during the 70s,[145] although the bathhouse could have been built as late as AD 120.[146] The bathhouse was a moderately substantial building with flint and mortar foundations and contained a suite of rooms that would have been used from south to north: a *frigidarium*, a *tepidarium* and a *caldarium* (see Fig. 5.5 a).[147] No objects were found that help date this first phase of construction. Extensive modifications were made in a second building phase;[148] these also could not be closely dated but one sherd of late first- or early-second-century pottery was found in a deposit associated with this construction.[149] Minor alterations were carried out in a third phase and the bathhouse was probably demolished by the late second or early third century.[150] A substantial timber-lined tank situated just to the north-east of the bathhouse was the main source of water.[151]

Rowsome has suggested that as this bathhouse was close to one of the main streets of Londinium it was ideally placed to constitute a *balneum*, or commercial bath building, associated with an inn.[152] This inn may be represented by the fragmentary remains of buildings uncovered in close proximity to the bathhouse.[153] The bathing place may have been connected with the ritual activities at a temple immediately to the north.[154] From the bathhouse it would then have been only a short walk to the temple area and the amphitheatre beyond. The early amphitheatre is thought to have had eastern and western entrances only but the later stone-built phase could have had a main entrance to the south for access to the temple area.

Prestigious Thames-side developments

During the later first century a monumental building was constructed to the east side of the Walbrook river mouth. This may have been the beginning of a concerted attempt to monumentalize the riverfront that continued into the second century. There may have been other monumental buildings along the riverbank but excavations here have been limited. An extensive building that has been interpreted as the 'governor's palace' was constructed east of the Walbrook behind the newly established timber wharf (Waterfront 2), while to the west a substantial and impressive bathhouse was constructed at Huggin Hill.[155] These buildings linked together by their location were part of an impressive urban façade behind the waterfront and upstream of the major port facilities. It was not possible to access the entire length of riverfront in Roman times and in order to travel between these buildings it would have been necessary to take a boat or to walk or ride into the urban area to the north.

The building that is usually identified as the 'governor's palace' (or *praetorium*) consisted of the walls and other structural features that were excavated below and to the east of the site now occupied by Cannon Street Station (see Fig. 5.6). Archaeologists worked on this site from 1961 to 1972 and the excavation report published by Marsden emphasized the scale, position and quality of the buildings thought to have been built between AD 80 and 100.[156] Marsden argued that the scale and character of the building complex indicates that this was the palace of the provincial governor.[157] He also interpreted the limited goldworking as evidence of state-controlled activity,[158] although this is no longer thought to be the case. As a result, the modern

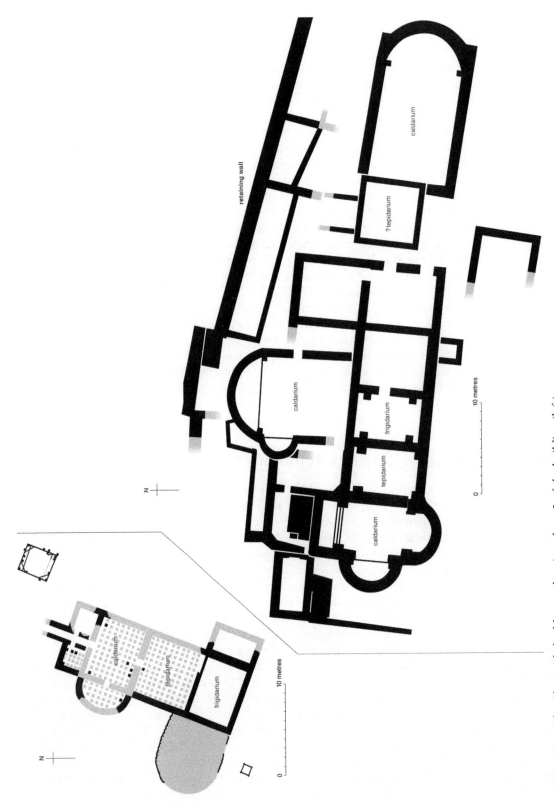

FIG. 5.5 a The Cheapside bathhouse showing phase 2 of the building (left).
b The Huggin Hill bathhouse (right).

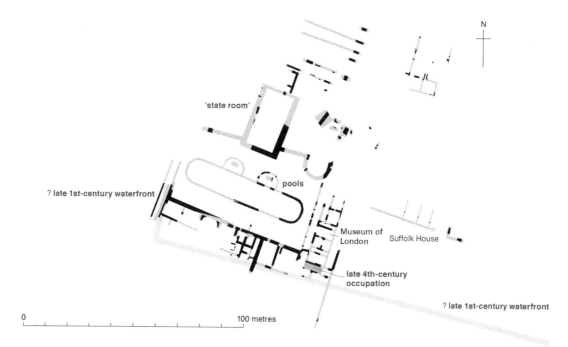

FIG. 5.6 The 'governor's palace' in the late first century. The position of the second waterfront to the south of the palace has not been closely defined as a result of excavation and has been projected on this figure from the Museum of London map (2011). The features shown at Suffolk House to the east of the supposed palace are those that date to the late first century; some elements of the 'palace' will date to the second century or later. It has not been possible to show excavation trenches on this plan. The late fourth-century occupation at the palace (referred to in Chapter 9) is also marked.

building constructed on this site in the late 1990s was named 'Governor's House'.[159] Subsequent discussions have challenged Marsden's suggestion that the main building complex of the 'palace' was a coordinated whole and have questioned whether there was any connection between this building and the provincial governor.[160]

The information from the archaeological investigations during 1961 to 1972 was limited by the excavation conditions.[161] The foundations of the 'palace' indicate that there was a high degree of planning, with a massive northern terrace wall that incorporated a substantial hall (the 'state room') with a hypocaust and a monumental open courtyard complex with pools and a range of rooms on the south and east sides.[162] Marsden located a 'Garden-Court' at the centre of the site with a 'Great Pool', which had a smaller apsidal-shaped pool to one side.[163] Subsequent exploration has revealed further walls close to this location, indicating that there may have been three pools adjoining the larger one that constituted an ornate garden area.[164] Ornamental pools are also known at villas in Britain.[165]

Around these monumental elements Marsden has reconstructed three building ranges that were modified over time. Parts of the east and south ranges were revealed, but the remains of the supposed west range are under Cannon Street Station.[166] Later additions to the complex included the construction of rooms including a hypocaust in the south wing interpreted by Marsden as a bath suite.[167] Many of the mosaics were contemporary with the initial construction of the building, although these were mainly indicated by loose tesserae or were recorded during the seventeenth and nineteenth centuries.[168] Many of these tessellated floors displayed simple designs but they covered hundreds of square metres and their installation would have required a group of skilled craftspeople.[169]

Later excavation has suggested that the west and south ranges were not located exactly where Marsden suggested since a late first-century quay was apparently constructed here, around AD 80.[170] Milne has argued that inconsistencies with the alignment and construction of the parts of the building reconstructed as a courtyard house by Marsden suggested that a series of different properties were built at this site.[171] Trevor Brigham, however, has argued that the evidence summarized by Marsden indicates that this was a very substantial building complex,[172] while the ornate pools may have been associated with grand residential buildings including the 'state room' in the north range. Despite much criticism of the idea that this building complex was the governor's palace, there is sufficient evidence to suggest a very substantial complex of monumental buildings of a scale and character to suggest that this was either an official residence or a major administrative complex.

Part of a monumental inscription found in 1850 at Nicholas Lane to the north-east of Cannon Street included a dedication to the *numen* (divinity) of the emperor made by the province of Britannia.[173] Although the centre for emperor worship was at Camulodunum, it is possible that a second temple dedicated to the emperor was situated close to or at the 'palace' complex. It has been suggested that the excavated northern part of this complex may have been the podium of a major temple or a bathhouse.[174] Tiles found with procuratorial stamps could indicate that the 'palace' was the residence of the procurator rather than the governor.[175] Yet another possibility is that this was the home of a wealthy Londoner with no particular official status. Evidently, the doubts about the character, function and date of the 'governor's palace' will only be resolved if further excavations can reveal more of the plan and sequence of these buildings.

To the west of the Walbrook, the Huggin Hill bathhouse has been excavated on three occasions (see Fig. 5.5 b).[176] This was the largest bathing establishment yet revealed in Londinium and may have served as the main bathhouse,[177] although it was not as substantial as contemporary urban bathhouses elsewhere in the empire.[178] Located in a prominent riverside location, just upstream of the port, the bathhouse was a symbol of Londinium's status and significance that could be viewed from the River Thames.[179] The building was constructed on an impressive series of terraces cut into the hillside in a previously unoccupied area probably during the AD 70s. In its primary phase the bathhouse consisted of a range of five rooms comparable to the broadly contemporary bath building at Calleva.[180] The building was constructed on a larger scale than the bathhouse at Cheapside. The Huggin Hill bathhouse underwent changes and additions, probably as a result of the increased demand on the facilities, although it had gone out of use and was being demolished by the later second century.[181] This could have been the result of an increase in the number of other bathing facilities built within Londinium, although the only other excavated bathhouse that may have been in use at this time is the one at Cheapside.

It is unclear whether the substantial bathhouse at Huggin Hill was planned and built with the support of the provincial government or by a civic authority.[182] The cost of the initial construction, the substantial alterations to extend the building and facilities and the expense of operating and maintaining the bathhouse must have been quite considerable, since a continuous supply of fuel and material would have been required. The wealth invested in some of the houses built during the later first century suggests that the building and running of a bathhouse was affordable for the residents of Londinium. Other urban bathhouses could have been built before this time in Britain and, indeed, there may have been one in Southwark prior to the Boudican uprising. Early bathhouses may also have been constructed at Verulamium during the AD 50s and at Calleva by the late AD 60s.[183] Bathing in a Mediterranean style was important to the people of these urban settlements.

The Thames bridge, the waterfront and market buildings

The early bridge across the Thames (Bridge 1) is thought to have been replaced, probably in the AD 80s or early AD 90s (Bridge 2).[184] The only evidence for this structure is a timber bridge abutment at Pudding Lane on the north bank of the Thames.[185] It has been suggested that this was a temporary construction which may date to around AD 85–90.[186] The abutment was buried beneath the infill of a new quay or revetment around AD 120. Around the same time a more substantial bridge (Bridge 3) was constructed just to the east.[187] This may have been built with stone and tile piers and timber decking that could be maintained and replaced. The information for Bridge 3 is entirely derived from the material found in the Thames during the construction of the present London Bridge in the nineteenth century.[188] The warehouses upstream at Regis House indicates that the arches of Bridges 1 to 3 were large enough to allow the passage of cargo ships.[189]

The bridging of the Thames was probably accompanied by acts of ritual, since comparable building works across the Roman world often required acts of propitiation.[190] The Roman finds discovered in the bed of the Thames during the nineteenth century included items that were votive offerings as well as building materials mainly deriving from Bridge 3.[191] The large number of offerings deposited at the approximate centre point of the line of this bridge included the head of a marble statue, a javelin point and many coins. These items date from the late first to the fourth century and Michael Rhodes has suggested that they may have originally been placed in shrines located along the bridge. Some of the coins were of late first-century date, showing that the ritual activities associated with the bridges commenced early.[192] Lead 'curse tablets' found on the north bank of the river close to the bridge include one inscribed 'Metunus', probably referring to Neptune,[193] which may indicate that there was a shrine either on or close to the bridge. Perhaps travelling over the bridge required an offering to water gods at a shrine and either a coin or object was thrown into the river. The sculptures of river gods and water spirits found in later contexts in London hint at the religious significance of the river and other watery areas.

The construction of Waterfront 2 commenced just west of this bridge. Downstream from the bridge the north bank of the river was defined by timber piles and revetments for at least a further twenty years.[194] It has been suggested that, by around AD 90, three further sections of the waterfront had been completed, downstream from the bridge, including the works at Pudding Lane and to either side of the Walbrook where it flowed into the Thames.[195] This waterfront was constructed partly to extend the amount of space available for building along the riverside with a series of level terraces.[196]

At Regis House, springs and small streams were accessed for domestic use or directed through the timber wharf into the river. Buildings were constructed on the waterfront from the early AD 60s,[197] including a warehouse block of stone, tile and timber. This was divided into at least six two-storey bays, facing onto a wharf that was 4.5 metres wide.[198] One room, which had been used as a glass workshop, containing several successive furnaces and a large quantity of glassworking waste.[199] The burial of a baby was found beneath the floor.[200] A hoard of three lead ingots, derived from the lead mines in Somerset, was found in another room.[201] The name of the emperor Vespasian (AD 69–79) was moulded in relief on these ingots which were deposited

FIG. 5.7 The later first-century timber wharf between Fish Street Hill and Pudding Lane was in use between around AD 80 and 100. The drainage gully between the two projecting timbers was probably added in the second century.

beneath the room's earthen floor. The lead ingots may indicate that the procurator was resident in Londinium, since lead mining was controlled by the Roman state, as indicated by the emperor's name stamp. Roman metalwork hoards often seem to have been deposited as ritual offerings and so this hoard may have been linked with some key rite in the construction or reconstruction of the warehouse.[202]

Later in the first century the port facilities just downstream from the Roman bridge were developed with the building of Waterfront 2 at Pudding Lane and Miles Lane (see Fig. 5.7).[203] Two stone buildings with tile roofs and wooden floors were built at Pudding Lane behind the waterfront.[204] Broadly comparable to the buildings excavated at Regis House, they indicate that the waterfront on each side of the bridge was lined with warehouses. No finds were made to indicate the purpose of these buildings, but they may have been warehouses connected with trading at the port. Upstream from Regis House evidence of the waterfront was found at 12 Arthur Street, although it was not possible to date the structure closely.[205] Slightly further to the west, at Suffolk House, clear evidence for the waterfront was also located,[206] dated by tree-ring analysis to around AD 84.[207] Waterfront 2 may have continued for some distance to the west along the Thames river frontage, since excavations at the Salvation Army site have produced possible evidence for the wharf and part of a warehouse, although these were not closely dated.[208] Traces of a substantial timber building were found within this continuation of the waterfront works.[209] At 12 Arthur Street, on the quayside substantial houses were built of stone and there was evidence for a hypocaust.[210] This residential area, including high-status buildings at 12 Arthur Street, Miles Lane and Suffolk House, may have comprised the houses of merchants sited upstream of the warehouses to either side of the bridge.[211]

The restoration of the riverfront at Regis House early in the second century has been assumed to have been part of the refurbishment of Waterfront 2 rather than constituting the construction of an entirely new wharfside.[212] These alterations have been dated by tree-ring analysis to around AD 102. This revetment consisted of a substantial mortised breastwork which supported a series of posts with plank cladding to the rear. The vast quantity of oyster shells dumped in the infilling of the wharf and the absence of substantial quantities of other domestic material has been taken to suggest that there was a significant processing industry situated nearby that supplied more than local demand. Some additions and alterations were also made to the warehouses on the wharf at this time. The discovery of a substantial quantity of samian pottery dated to around AD 125–30 indicates that a pottery shop was located on the wharfside.

Although the large amount of samian pottery in archaeological contexts of the first and early second centuries indicates the continuing significance of the port, the importation of this material is also likely to reflect the culture and identity of the people of Londinium.[213] Quantities of ornamental stonework from London were also brought though the port, including materials sourced from Britain, Gaul, Greece, Turkey and Italy.[214]

Nick Holder has analysed the distribution and frequency of selected inscribed objects found in different areas of the waterfront.[215] He has defined three zones on the northern bank of the Thames: the wharf west of the Walbrook; the area between the Walbrook and the bridge; and east of the bridge. The distribution of inscribed amphorae, pottery, lead labels, ingots, tiles and leather indicate that the objects may have been imported by boats from the Thames. Few inscribed objects were found west of the Walbrook except tiles, which Holder interprets as indicating that this was where the stone and tiles that were used in the construction of Londinium were unloaded. Fewer inscribed tiles were discovered in the area between the Walbrook and the bridge but there were more inscribed amphorae and pottery vessels. Holder has suggested that the warehouses immediately west of the bridgehead constituted the port area where luxury pottery and produce carried in amphorae were brought ashore. A concentration of lead labels found east of the bridge were probably originally attached to bales or boxes of goods and this may suggest that a range of products was imported through a customs house.[216]

A substantial market hall (Market Building 1) may have been situated just east of the bridge. The south-east corner of this stone building was located during excavations in 1979 to the north-east of the junction of Pudding Lane and Monument Street and has been dated by Milne to the early second century.[217] This may have been a covered market that extended beyond the line of Monument Street and was on the same alignment as the warehouses to the south. The building could have contained the mosaic uncovered in Monument Street in 1887 that displayed a dedicatory inscription recording that a private individual provided funding either for the mosaic or for the building itself.[218] It is attested that merchants and boat owners financed the building of market halls at the Roman port of Ostia in Italy, and the Monument Street mosaic may be an example of a comparable practice in Londinium. This potential market building showed no sign of the burning that engulfed other buildings in the vicinity during the AD 120s.[219]

The development of port facilities was not restricted to the area close to the bridge on the north bank of the Thames. Further west, the River Fleet was tidal in its lower reaches and excavations have located two small eyots near its eastern bank.[220] On the downstream side of the southern eyot a substantial jetty and a warehouse were constructed where wheat was unloaded and stored. The eyot to the north was probably used for processing wheat, as the remains of a possible tidal mill have been found here. Both eyots were abandoned around the end of the second century, by which time tidal regression appears to have made river transport to the mouth of the Fleet untenable.[221]

Works were also conducted in Southwark to consolidate and straighten the south bank of the Thames and the waterfronts on the island in the river between around AD 60 and 80,[222] although there is no evidence for a massive timber wharf comparable to that constructed on the north bank of the Thames. The infilling of river channels in Southwark at this time gradually reclaimed land from the river.[223] Waterfront revetments were constructed in Guy's Channel, at Courage Brewery and at Guy's Hospital on the east edge of the south island.[224] The degree to which these efforts to establish waterfront installations across Southwark were coordinated is, however, unclear.

Another market building (Market Building 2) may have been located on the north island in the Thames at Southwark, at the Ticket Hall site.[225] Fragmentary evidence has been uncovered of a substantial building with stone and tile foundations which had a frontage at least 14 metres long on the east side of the main north–south road, interpreted as a market hall that served the area of Roman London south of the Thames. This building was initially constructed during the late first century and around AD 120 a covered walkway was built along the roadside to the south.[226] It is evident that several markets were established across Londinium to supplement the shops along the main street frontages such as those at 1 Poultry.

Occupation

The earlier roads were restored during the AD 60s and new roads were added around AD 70 when the forum and amphitheatre were constructed.[227] There appears to have been a plan to expand the urban boundary to the east at this time with the establishment of the cemetery almost 500 metres east of the Plantation Place fort.[228] Further roads were constructed during the early second century in the Walbrook Valley.[229] It is likely that the urban council was responsible for the construction and maintenance of these roads.

House construction was very extensive from the AD 70s to around AD 120, indicating the scale and pace of urban development on both sides of the Thames (see Fig. 5.8). By around AD 75 Londinium covered a larger area than before its destruction in AD 60, and by AD 120 it had expanded still further with a population of potentially around 26,000.[230] This would suggest that there had been a substantial increase in the population after AD 60.[231]

The expansion of the AD 70s and 80s was based on the clearing and raising of the land, the canalization of streams and rivers, the re-establishment of the road system and the building of new houses and other properties across Roman London. In places this development seems to have been piecemeal in nature, but the scale of the operation across the urban area to the north and south of the Thames indicates that there was at least a degree of centralized planning by an urban council. There is no direct evidence for the nature of the ownership of land at this time, although a writing tablet found in the Walbrook in 1986 and dating from AD 118 records legal details of the ownership of a wood in the *civitas* of the Cantiaci (Kent).[232] Tomlin has argued that this provides evidence for a judicial authority and a secretariat to record legal decisions in early second-century London.[233] This single tablet suggests that centralized records of the ownership of land may have been kept somewhere in Londinium, but no additional information has yet been found. Land across Britannia will have been owned by individuals or by the emperor himself and much of this is likely to have been rented out to tenants.[234] Many of the houses established during the later decades of the first century continued to be elaborated and occupied up to the time of the 'Hadrianic fire', indicating continuity of occupation.

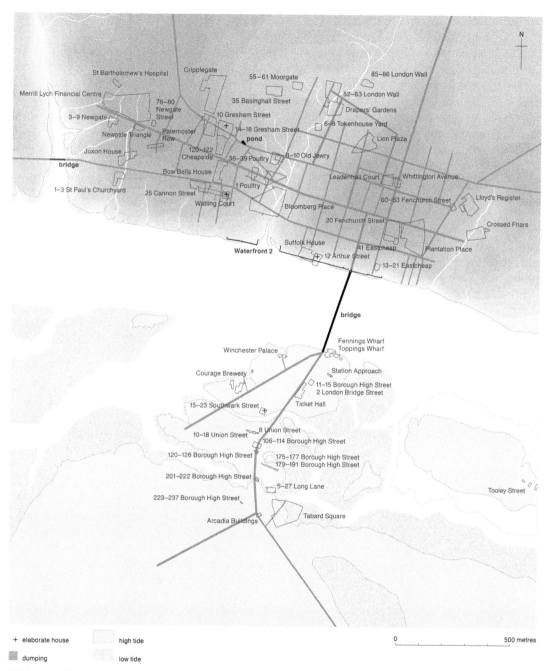

FIG. 5.8 Houses in Londinium around AD 70–120, showing the extent of excavated areas referred to in the text.

Most of the houses that were built from AD 60 to 120 were constructed in timber and earth, the dominant building tradition in early Londinium.[235] Recent excavations indicate, however, that houses were also built of stone during the later first and early second century. Carrie Cowan has discussed the idea that the concept of a 'masonry' house is not as simple as has sometimes been suggested, since many may often have only had stone foundations and timberwork walls above.[236] The poor condition of preservation of many of the houses excavated in London sometimes makes it difficult to distinguish whether particular houses were built entirely of stone or whether they only had stone foundations. The width and scale of the stone foundations of certain buildings has been considered by the excavator to indicate that buildings had substantial stone walls above the foundation level. The function of the building may have influenced its construction since industrial and commercial premises such as bakeries could have required fire-proofing.

Some impressive houses were constructed, such as those at Watling Court, one of which may have been a courtyard building. Equally imposing houses were built at 14–18 Gresham Street and 12 Arthur Street, although their remains have been mostly destroyed by later activity and only partly excavated. The early stone buildings across Londinium, marked as 'elaborate houses' on Fig. 5.8, may suggest that the 'governor's palace' and 15–23 Southwark Street (the 'mansio') in Southwark were the particularly substantial and elaborate homes of wealthy Londoners.

Other buildings, mostly of timber-and-earth construction, included shops and industrial premises such as those at 1 Poultry, 76–80 Newgate Street and Leadenhall Court. The considerable differences in scale and opulence of these structures demonstrates the differences in status and wealth of the occupants of Londinium.

West of the Walbrook

The fullest evidence comes from 1 Poultry.[237] We have seen that the rebuilding of houses and shops may not have occurred on any scale for up to a decade after the Boudican fire, but a range of new buildings connected with a re-established road system had been constructed by around AD 70. The evidence from across the area indicates that new buildings were constructed during the AD 70s and continued to be occupied and reconstructed until the AD 120s. Around AD 90–100 a fire damaged several buildings, but the roads, drains and property boundaries were maintained and rebuilt.[238] These deposits were, in turn, sealed by a fire horizon which excavators have termed the 'Hadrianic fire'.[239] Building techniques used for the construction of shops and houses at 1 Poultry were broadly comparable to the pre-Boudican buildings, mainly involving timber and earth, but one building had stone foundations of a type that has often been thought to be unusual in first-century Londinium.[240] This may have been a bakery or a cookhouse, indicated by the ovens and evidence for food preparation.[241] Another building had at least one sophisticated room with walls finished with painted plaster and floors laid with timber boards or finished as beaten earth.[242] In a further building a quantity of slag from ironworking and some evidence of copper-alloy working were found.[243]

A substantial timber cistern of uncertain function was discovered at 1 Poultry, dating from around AD 70–90. It was associated with cobbled surfaces that included one thousand fragments of lava rotary quernstone that had been imported from Mayen in Germany and many of which were worn when they were deposited in the surface.[244] Excavations at Bloomberg just to the east of the cistern have revealed the substantial foundations of an industrial complex that was probably a watermill, including parts of cogs, pulleys and a lantern gear.[245] Previous discoveries of millstones at other sites in the Walbrook Valley suggest that there may have been several watermills in operation.[246]

The restoration and establishment of these properties at 1 Poultry during the later first century was accompanied by the large-scale dumping of domestic materials.[247] This activity had commenced before the Boudican fire and continued throughout the first and early second centuries, contributing to the infilling of the western slopes of the Walbrook Valley and creating building platforms above the level of the river. This formed part of a substantial programme of work across the middle and upper reaches of the Walbrook Valley involving the revetment of riverbanks and the reclamation of marshy ground through the dumping of clay and gravel that often included cultural material.[248] These activities contributed to the drainage of the valley and eventually enabled the building of roads, houses and industrial premises across a substantial area during the later first and early second century. The sites at 1 Poultry are close to where the main east–west road crossed the Walbrook. This was one of the first areas of the Walbrook Valley to have been substantially developed. The dumped material making up the land over which this occurred contained considerable quantities of pottery and many metal objects often still usable when they were deposited.

The significance of these acts of dumping including cultural material across the Walbrook Valley has been the subject of considerable discussion. Merrifield interpreted this material, which is found within the watercourses and on the riverbanks, as the deposition of cultural material for reasons of ritual.[249] It has been suggested above that this may have been an activity intended to enculture the land, although other archaeologists have argued that these actions constituted the mundane redeposition of rubbish to build up the banks of watercourses and the surrounding ground surface.[250] The extensive deposits of this type located by the excavations at and around 1 Poultry have enabled a detailed assessment to be made of their origin and character.[251] Large quantities of imported samian were present, along with a variety of other finds that included brooches, keys, pins and a comb, several of which were complete.[252] In the excavation report it has been suggested that there is little about these finds to support the idea of the ritual deposition of significant artefacts in or around the Walbrook, although it is also noted that superstition and religious practice permeated everyday life in the classical past.[253] The ritual interpretation for certain classes of these artefacts nevertheless continues to be supported by some commentators.[254] The idea that this practice constituted rubbish disposal that was intended to raise the ground level to enable the construction of new buildings does not in any way preclude the argument that it was also linked to the intention of enculturing the land.

It has been argued that the changes that were being made to control water and establish dry land across London may have required acts of propitiation addressed to the water spirits of the locality. Material that has been perceived as rubbish may also have served to construct and establish ownership and control and to domesticate the land, in addition to representing offerings to the spirits of place. Acts of construction that drew upon cultural material, such as the building of the waterfronts on the north bank of the Thames and the establishment of areas for living across the Walbrook Valley and the waterscapes across Southwark that were being modified for habitation, need not be interpreted entirely in simply practical terms. Some areas of the Walbrook may have been regularly flooded during their periods of occupation.[255] Since rituals related to water were common in Roman-period contexts across the empire,[256] offerings are to be expected.

The building work in the area of 1 Poultry was part of a broader scheme of development west of the Walbrook, perhaps indicating planning of the urban area during the AD 70s that coincided with the construction of other buildings such as the amphitheatre, the Cheapside bathhouse and possibly the first forum.[257] The existing roads and properties of the former ribbon-development alongside the main east–west road were restored and new roads and buildings were constructed across an extensive area to both north and south. The character of this extensive and ambitious new development has been revealed through excavation. At 36–9 Poultry just to the north of 1 Poultry, a road was laid out running south-south-west to north-north-east across the site of earlier housing and several timber-and-earth buildings were constructed.[258] As at 1 Poultry, these properties were destroyed by fire around AD 90–100. Some houses with stone foundations and one fitted with a plain tessellated floor replaced the previous buildings during the early second century. At 8–10 Old Jewry, two timber houses were built along the south side of a road during the late first century AD, one of which was associated with finds indicating the smithing of iron.[259]

At Bloomberg a sequence of buildings were constructed east of the Walbrook, and later to the west, in a low-lying area.[260] The swift sequence of construction, clearing and rebuilding is likely to be indicative of trading on a large scale and the necessity of improving the drainage of this low-lying area.[261] The waterlogging of the deposits has resulted in the preservation of vast quantities of organic finds.[262] Building construction was associated with substantial dumping of amounts of material to raise the ground level that incorporated many writing tablets.[263] Two simple timber-and-earth buildings were constructed east of the Walbrook between around AD 62 and AD 70 on top of such dumped deposits; there were three writing tablets associated with the occupation of 'Building 1'.[264] These buildings were then sealed by further dumping. Two or three timber-and-earth buildings were constructed along a new road that ran east–west north of Bloomberg.[265] Around AD 80, building platforms of dumped material were laid for three timber-and-earth buildings;[266] nineteen writing tablets were recovered from the trampled earth floor of 'Building 9'.[267] These buildings were replaced again toward the end of the century.[268] Additional buildings to the south were less well preserved and less fully excavated.[269] Terracing and building construction was also carried out at Bloomberg to the west of the Walbrook during the later first century AD.[270]

At Watling Court, about halfway between the Cheapside and Huggin Hill bathhouses, drainage and development commenced during the AD 70s, although there may have been occupation here before the Boudican uprising.[271] One of the several large pits, the result of probable quarrying connected with the building of nearby houses, contained human cranial remains.[272] Subsequently this land was levelled and a range of timber-and-earth houses was built in several phases prior to AD 120 (see Fig. 5.9).[273] Some of these substantial and impressive houses were partly stone-built and were floored with mosaics that dated from the later first century AD. These indicate the wealth and international connections of their occupants.[274]

The excavated parts of one building, which had stone foundations and brick-earth walls, may have formed the northern wing of a substantial courtyard building.[275] Measuring around 28 metres long by 11 metres wide, it contained at least eleven rooms with connecting passages and with a verandah on the north side probably added towards the end of the building's sequence of use around AD 120.[276] Five of the rooms had mosaic floors, while the other rooms were floored with mortar or beaten earth. This house was built around its reception rooms in a manner comparable to some of the late first-century villas of southern Britain.[277] David Neal and Stephen Cosh have suggested that the mosaics from this house may be the earliest currently known from London; they discussed two fragmentary mosaic floors designed in a style seen at Ostia (Italy) and Reims (France), but that has been rarely found in Britain.[278] Another black-and-white mosaic had an elaborate scroll issuing from a stylized vessel.[279] The largest and best decorated of the rooms may have faced the entrance to the building across a courtyard.[280]

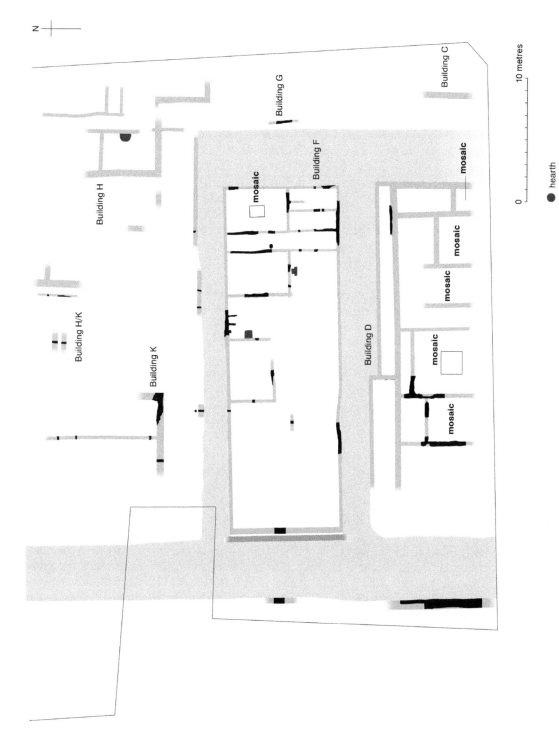

FIG. 5.9 Houses at Watling Court around AD 70 to 120.

Just to the north another building at Watling Court was constructed slightly later as a timber-and-earth rectangular house.[281] The entire plan of ten rooms, one of which had a very worn mosaic floor depicting an arched structure, was recovered.[282] The mosaics in these buildings indicate that lavishly decorated reception rooms provided spaces for hospitality and clientage relationships.[283] Another large building, or group of buildings to the north of the site, was equally elaborate, incorporating stone foundations and dating from the late first and early second centuries.[284] These fragmentary foundations may have belonged to another winged or courtyard building. The walls of several buildings were decorated with painted wall plaster.[285]

These impressive houses at Watling Court appear to have been destroyed in the 'Hadrianic fire' of the AD 120s. In the house with the five mosaics, two fragments of a bronze military diploma dating from AD 98–108 were found.[286] This document granted citizenship and marriage rights to an auxiliary soldier after retirement. One of the witnesses to this grant was called Quintus Pompeius Homerus, although the name of the retired soldier has not survived. Perring has suggested that this diploma was kept in this building and that it identified the head of the family that resided here.[287] Since the document was likely to have been a decade old when the building was destroyed, Perring has suggested that the house at this time may have been owned by the retired soldier or by his heir. He has proposed that this house, which was built sometime before the issuing of the diploma, might have been constructed for a soldier in the employment of the provincial governor who later retired to Londinium. There is no clear evidence, however, for the governor in London at this time; it is also possible that a soldier serving in the province of Britannia retired to its most cosmopolitan urban centre. Indeed, the diploma may have been issued to a Briton who had joined the Roman army as an auxiliary soldier, served overseas and finally retired to live in Londinium.[288]

Just west of Watling Court at 25 Cannon Street, fragmentary evidence for a stone-built house dating from to the late first century has been uncovered which was preceded by timber-and-earth buildings.[289] Despite the extensive evidence for the expansion of the boundaries of the urban settlement to the north and west, detailed excavation is demonstrating that this process of urban development was not always characterized by an increasing density of housing. At Bow Bells House, around AD 60–70, some insubstantial timber-framed houses associated with the digging of pits and quarries were built in the open areas just south of the main east–west road and also along Watling Street to the south of the site.[290] After a period of perhaps thirty or forty years, there appears to have been a substantial decrease in domestic activity and construction.[291] The archaeological deposits were badly disturbed and some buildings continued to be constructed and occupied during the second century,[292] although this appears to have been an area of Londinium that was sparsely inhabited.[293] At least part of this site became an open area, a situation that may have been common across Roman London since gardens and open areas were probably common.[294] Owning a garden was a status symbol in Roman society and market gardens were cultivated on the outskirts of cities or in less built-up areas.[295] There is some limited evidence for gardens and gardening across Londinium, but it is currently not possible to determine the variable make-up of the urban landscape in terms of the location of these open spaces.[296]

At 120–2 Cheapside, new timber-and-earth buildings replaced those thought to have been destroyed in AD 60.[297] One building dated to the late first or early second centuries and was floored with a mosaic the design of which has parallels at Leadenhall Street in London and at Fishbourne.[298] Immediately to the north at 14–18 Gresham Street a road was laid and buildings were constructed during the late first century, including a substantial stone building ('Building 27') that was installed with a hypocaust and a mosaic and had walls decorated with painted plaster.[299] Sadie Watson has suggested that this house was comparable in scale and significance to contemporary buildings at Watling Court. Although very fragmentary, the ground plan could suggest that it may have consisted of a house with two ranges of rooms with a corridor between. This building was in use for a short time before it was demolished and replaced by a timber-and-earth building.[300] Evidence for ironworking was found slightly to the west alongside the road associated with a temporary shelter or small industrial structure.[301] Fire deposits across the south of the site may have been connected with the 'Hadrianic fire', although their exact date was unclear.[302]

The roundhouses and workshop at 10 Gresham Street were dismantled around AD 70 and a north–south road was constructed with side roads or alleys, and a systematically planned area of housing was established, particularly east of the road.[303] Evidence for timber-framed and stone-built houses, mostly of strip design, was limited as a result of the nature of the excavation and the damage caused by later activity. There was no clear evidence that the occupants of these houses were particularly wealthy and they may be representative of the majority of houses across Londinium at this time.[304] One of the houses was more substantial and could have been a courtyard house that was probably constructed during the AD 130s.[305]

There were a number of developments at the Paternoster Square sites.[306] At Newgate Triangle one house appears to have survived the Boudican destruction, while new strip-buildings of timber and earth were built around a decade after this event.[307] The continuity in the location of these houses appears to indicate that the pre-Boudican property boundaries were respected during the redevelopment.[308] The intensity of occupation at Newgate Triangle appears to have increased during the early second century.[309] The information from these excavations has also suggested that there was more substantial redevelopment south of the main east–west road at Paternoster Row and Juxton House.[310] At Paternoster Row, a building with quantities of slag and a vitrified hearth lining was probably a smithy.[311] At Juxton House, the area may not have been as intensively settled and some evidence was found for tile production.

The area to the south has not been extensively excavated, although timber-and-earth buildings were uncovered at 1–3 St Paul's Churchyard.[312] One building, constructed during the late first century, was burned down in the early second century before being replaced with a similar structure. The other building was built during the early second century.

At 76–80 Newgate Street, north of the main east–west road, a sequence of buildings was constructed around AD 70–120 on a site that had been previously occupied (see Fig. 5.10).[313] The two best-defined houses were strip-buildings with wattle-and-daub walls, each of which had several rooms.[314] They fronted onto a road to the south where the larger rooms may have been used for the production of goods that were sold at the shop front, while the smaller rooms at the rear were probably residential.[315] These buildings may have been commercial and industrial strip-houses, while those at Watling Court are interpreted as town houses owned by wealthier individuals.[316]

The occupied area of Londinium was extended further west at this time along the main east–west road with several buildings located close to two stream channels at the Merrill Lynch Financial Centre at Newgate.[317] This area may have been subject to occasional flooding and the streams were canalized at an early date. The buildings were comparable to other strip-buildings recorded at sites with structures of the same date to the east. Excavations at 3–9 Newgate Street and at St Bartholomew's Hospital located evidence for buildings dating from the late first to mid-second centuries.[318] At the former site, three phases of timber buildings were constructed just south of the main east–west road.

Other parts of Londinium were also being developed. To the north, in the area of Cripplegate, settlement commenced sometime after the Boudican uprising.[319] Around the site that was later

FIG. 5.10 Houses with brickearth hearths and sills that originally supported timber walls were excavated at 76–80 Newgate Street in 1975–9. This view towards the north-east shows the central part of Building K which was dated to around AD 100–120.

to be developed as a Roman fort, the first buildings were constructed around AD 70–120 and there was some evidence for industrial activities.[320] Initially, fence lines were connected with several kilns or ovens and at a slightly later date the area was built over with timber-and-earth houses, including one that probably had stone foundations comparable to the early buildings at Watling Court.[321]

The upper Walbrook Valley

When the amphitheatre was constructed during the AD 70s, much of the Walbrook Valley to the east and north appears to have been at the limits of urban development.[322] The streams and wet areas of the upper and middle valley were drained and colonized during the later first and second centuries.[323] The development of this area was a large-scale venture which may have been undertaken with the particular intention of establishing an industrial landscape.[324] A good deal of evidence has been derived from deposits dumped into the stream as a by-product of industrial activities, although it is not clear that these were necessarily operating on a substantial scale.[325]

The tributaries of the Walbrook provided a reliable water supply for industry, despite regular flooding.[326] Evidence for the drainage of the valley, the building up of the land surface and the construction of roads and buildings has been found on several sites. There is also substantial evidence for the dumping of industrial waste from the later first century onwards, comprising a range of deposits derived from the production of metal, pottery, glass and leather.[327] As this programme of drainage and colonization did not prevent flooding, this area probably remained marginal in urban terms.[328] Industrial production may therefore have been conducted on a seasonal basis. This may have provided a context for the deposition of human skulls in the tributary streams of the Walbrook during the second century.

Archaeological sites excavated across the upper Walbrook Valley prior to 1990 have produced substantial evidence for the draining of land and the revetting of streams with timber during the late first and early second centuries.[329] This colonization included the construction of three roads that ran approximately north–south and may date from around AD 120, although there are traces of earlier roads in this area.[330] Two recent excavations have produced evidence for early activities. At Drapers' Gardens, from the AD 70s, the ground level was raised through the large-scale dumping of material before a road and houses were constructed during the period around AD 120.[331] At 6–8 Tokenhouse Yard, drainage work and the dumping of material was associated with evidence for the construction of fences and box drains suggesting that buildings were constructed here during the later first century.[332] A large quantity of leather fragments from sandals and shoes were found here along with a small quantity of shoemaking waste.[333] At 52–63 London Wall, at the northern edge of the expanding settlement, there was clear evidence for drainage work and the construction of a road and buildings, although the evidence for industrial activity appears less certain.[334] Traces of two successive timber-and-earth buildings were found at 85–6 London Wall, dating to the late first and second centuries.[335]

Some sites with evidence for industrial production may also have included domestic houses. At 35 Basinghall Street, timber-and-earth buildings were first constructed around AD 110 or 120, after the area was cleared and levelled.[336] At 55–61 Moorgate, several timber-and-clay buildings were constructed during the late first century and rebuilt during the second century and one was associated with glassworking.[337]

East of the Walbrook

To the north-east of the Walbrook Valley, at Lion Plaza, evidence was found for a timber-and-earth house that probably dated from the period after the 'Boudican fire', while evidence was also found for two timber-and-earth houses dating from around AD 75–120.[338] At Leadenhall Court, timber houses were constructed across the area of the pre-Boudican cremation cemetery, just to the north of the first forum.[339] In the early phase, three small timber-and-earth one-roomed houses were built.[340] A sequence of building phases was followed by the area being cleared for the construction of the second forum-basilica complex, which may have commenced around AD 100.[341] The buildings, which were closely spaced along a road frontage to the west, were mostly of strip plan, although one was more complex with a range of rooms, while the backyards contained pits and wells.[342] To the east of the new forum-basilica, at 1–7 Whittington Avenue, timber-and-earth houses with tile roofs were constructed around AD 70 and were occupied into the second century.[343]

The area of the early 'fort' was cleared around AD 85 and new houses were built.[344] At Plantation Place the east–west road that had been overlain by the northern defences of the fort was reinstated and widened.[345] A north–south road and timber-and-earth buildings, including some substantial examples, were constructed across the site.[346] Installed with painted wall plaster and tessellated floors, some of these buildings were comparable to the well-appointed houses at Watling Court.[347] Significant quantities of waste from the manufacture of glass vessels in late first-century contexts suggest that there was a glassworking workshop at or close to the site.[348] At 20 Fenchurch Street the site was intensively developed, with the construction of timber-and-earth buildings during the late first century and stone-built houses during the early second century.[349] At 41 Eastcheap a sequence of timber-and-earth buildings, one of which may have had stone-built foundations, had been heavily truncated by later building activity.[350]

Around 400 metres east of the forum, at Lloyd's Register, buildings were constructed during the later first and early second centuries in an area that may have been used for agricultural activities.[351] These fragmentary remains included a structure that may have been a timber roundhouse, rectangular timber-and-earth buildings and others that were possibly stone-built and there was also evidence of painted wall plaster.[352] More substantial stone buildings were constructed during the early second century or slightly later.[353] At 60–3 Fenchurch Street several phases of timber strip-buildings were constructed during the later first century and evidence found for pottery production, copper-alloy working and ironworking.[354] At Crossed Friars two widely spaced ditches apparently dating from the later first century may represent field boundaries at the edge of Roman London.[355] There may have been more extensive occupation beyond the traces of a single timber-and-earth building which was found at this location.

The waterfront

Timber buildings dating to the AD 70s were built close to the waterfront at 13–21 Eastcheap.[356] These were replaced by early second-century buildings which were probably constructed of timber-and-earth. A substantial rubbish deposit at this location, composed principally of oyster shells, indicates that oysters were sold and consumed nearby.[357] At 12 Arthur Street impressive houses were constructed between AD 70 and 80 in a similar structure and style to the example at Watling Court and were possibly the residences of merchants.[358] Their substantial stone foundations may indicate that they had multi-storey elevations with tiled roofs, and evidence was found for underfloor heating systems, painted plaster and glass windows in dumped deposits behind the waterfront.[359] Pottery from these dumped deposits mostly dated from before AD 120, although some may have been made as late as AD 140.[360] A large well fitted with a water-lifting device probably dating to AD 61–97 may have been used to supply the local buildings with water for heated baths or ornamental water features.[361]

Immediately to the west at Suffolk House, Marsden uncovered fragments of the plan of a substantial courtyard house, often known as the 'townhouse', which he has suggested might have been the home of a provincial official connected with the governor.[362] Brigham summarized the results of further excavations of this building and has shown that this courtyard house may have been constructed during the second quarter of the second century.[363] It was preceded by at least two other buildings on stone foundations.[364] Limited evidence for goldworking was located in one of these early buildings ('Building 2'), matching the evidence from the 'palace' site and dating to the late first and early second centuries. Brigham has suggested that the construction of the 'palace' may have forced the goldworkers to move to workshops at Suffolk House.[365] From both sites were found crucibles for melting gold, crucibles for testing metal content and gold dust, representing the stages of this precious-metal processing.[366] Gold-mining in the Roman Empire was controlled by the state but the extraction and processing of gold was not necessarily undertaken by state officials. This evidence indicates that jewellers were living and working in this part of Londinium.

South of the Thames

Settlement expanded beyond the area occupied prior to AD 60. Timber-and-earth buildings have been excavated, but there is also evidence for more substantial stone-built buildings. The buildings at 15–23 Southwark Street and the dumps containing building material at Winchester Palace and Courage Brewery suggests that there were several elaborate stone buildings on the western parts of the north island during the late first century. The building at 15–23 Southwark Street may have been a high-status residence and other buildings could have been public or private bathhouses.

At 15–23 Southwark Street, timber-and-earth buildings probably built during the AD 70s were replaced by at least two buildings that may have formed part of a substantial stone-built complex.[367] According to tree-ring dating this was partly constructed around AD 74.[368] This building was probably arranged around an east-facing courtyard that measured approximately 50 by 30 metres.[369] Some interior spaces were decorated with painted wall plaster in different colours.[370] During the early second century this structure was replaced by a more elaborate building with hypocausts and mosaics and walls finished with imported veneers.[371]

Carrie Cowan has argued that the buildings may have functioned as a mansio that was built during the late first century and regularly rebuilt and modified until the late third to early fourth centuries.[372] A mansio was an official inn connected with imperial transport along the roads of the empire. One of the main reasons for the identification of this building as a mansio was the apparent scarcity of evidence for substantial stone-built townhouses in Londinium and other towns in Britain dating from the later first century.[373] The more recent evidence for elaborate stone houses from sites such as 14–18 Gresham Street and 12 Arthur Street suggests that the building at 15–23 Southwark Street constituted a substantial and lavish townhouse belonging to a wealthy Londoner.[374]

The excavations close to Winchester Palace have indicated that additional side roads were constructed on the north island. Small timber-and-earth buildings constructed during the AD 60s were replaced by a timber building with several rooms and another structure to the south-east.[375] These excavations also uncovered a very large quantity of painted wall plaster which had been used in the consolidation of the Thames waterfront that probably had not been moved very far from its original source, suggesting that there had been a substantial building in the vicinity.[376] The pottery associated with the wall plaster was dated to around AD 70–80.[377] The road system at this site was altered during the late first or early second centuries and two further buildings were constructed with stone foundations, one with a rectangular plan and one with circular layout. They may both have been used as granaries, although the circular building could alternatively have been a roundhouse.[378] Constructed in around AD 80, both structures were demolished during the early second century.[379] Traces of other buildings were found in the immediate vicinity, indicating that this area was densely built up.

On the west of the north island a significant ironworking complex developed at Courage Brewery and, just to the south-west of Winchester Palace, evidence was found for box-flue tiles, ceramic tesserae and bricks that could indicate that there had been a substantial stone building in the vicinity.[380] Other buildings at Courage Brewery included at least one that may have been constructed in stone.[381] At the Ticket Hall site a row of shops was excavated alongside the main north–south road, including the market hall, a small blacksmith's workshop and a building identified on the basis of the discovery of a large quantity of animal bone as a butcher's shop.[382] At 11–15 Borough High Street / 2 London Bridge Street, timber-and-earth buildings were associated with evidence for copper production.[383]

At the north of the island, just east of the bridge over the Thames, buildings were constructed at Toppings Wharf and Fennings Wharf during the late first century.[384] One was a substantial roundhouse of wattle-and-daub construction around 10 metres in diameter which may have survived into the early second century.[385] This suggests that traditional buildings were surviving at the edge of Londinium. Evidence for the working of iron and bronze was also found in this building. Several other rectangular timber-and-earth buildings were located close by. Excavations at Station Approach produced evidence for a large stone building constructed shortly after AD 70 that may have been a warehouse, even though it was about 100 metres inland from the quayside.[386] It had four rooms and contained a very large quantity of amphorae fragments, mostly of late first-century date, leading to suggestions that the pottery may have been used as redeposited material to raise the floor level.[387]

On the south island, new timber buildings were constructed close to the main north–south road.[388] At 120–4 and 124–6 Borough High Street, buildings to either side of the road were associated with hearths and industrial waste that may indicate iron smithing and copper-alloy working.[389] The excavations at 8 Union Street, 106–14 Borough High Street and 201–11 Borough High Street have also produced evidence for timber-and-earth buildings dating from the late first and early second centuries.[390] At 10–18 Union Street the two timber-and-earth structures had tiled roofs and walls finished with painted plaster, suggesting that they were residential buildings.[391] At 5–27 Long Lane, land reclamation on the south side of the south island commenced during the late first century AD when a timber-and-earth building with a beaten earth floor was constructed.[392]

At 175–7 and 179–91 Borough High Street a substantial amount of material was being dumped to build up the ground surface at the edge of the island from the later first to third centuries.[393] Wardle has noted that many of the glass vessels from these dumps were complete or nearly complete when they had been deposited, including drinking vessels, tableware, bowls and decorated flasks and jugs for serving liquids.[394] Pottery vessels from these dumped deposits were often largely complete and included miniature jars found often in ritual contexts.[395] This material is difficult to interpret, since it is not clear why complete pottery and glass vessels were included and some of the metal objects from these deposits were also still serviceable.[396] The deposits dated to the late first and early second centuries also contained large amounts of building material, including imported marble inlays, bricks, tiles and water-pipes that may have derived from a bathhouse close to this site.[397] Alternatively, the building debris may have formed part of a long-term tradition of bringing materials to the south island for recycling.

Excavations have produced a limited amount of information for Horselydown eyot and Bermondsey eyot. These low-lying islands were separated from the urban landscape by river channels and were subject to flooding throughout the Roman period. On the east side of Horselydown eyot, rubbish pits indicate that Late Iron Age activities continued for some time after the Roman conquest.[398] The information from Bermondsey eyot also suggests that there could have been some settled occupation during the Roman period as a higher ridge of ground may have been occupied by farmers who were cultivating the surrounding land.[399] The evidence from the limited excavations across this area does not suggest that this occupation was part of the main urban settlement, however, and both eyots may have been used seasonally.

Occupation also developed on the southern bank of the Thames south of the Borough Channel where the main north–south road divided. The western branch has been named Stane Street and the eastern branch Watling Street. Houses and industrial premises were being built close to the junction of these two roads. At Tabard Square a major phase of work to build up the ground surface alongside the course of a stream included timber-piled foundations just east of Watling Street, possibly during the AD 70s.[400] A cluster of timber-and-earth buildings was built around AD 80 on each side of a road that crossed the infilled stream channel.[401] The buildings were fairly simple and standard in character but the discovery of painted wall plaster, a gold chain and high-quality glass suggest that the inhabitants possessed a certain level of wealth.[402] At 223–37 Borough High Street, evidence was found for a small timber-and-earth building dating to the late first century.[403] Other buildings have been located further east at Arcadia Buildings, probably the focus for the industrial activity.

Marking the boundaries

There is little evidence to suggest that Londinium was defined by a single coordinated series of boundary earthworks before the late second century. The marginal areas of Roman London were the focus for particular practices such as industry, feasting and burial. It is likely that these activities helped to mark the ill-defined boundaries of an expanding settlement. Many activities involving the deposition of human body parts are connected in that they often appear associated with waterlogged and wet places close to the edge of the urban landscape, including pits, wells and ditches. Materials left over from the feasting activities were deposited in wet or waterlogged contexts, including ditches, hollows and wells. There may, however, have been no particular connection between the location of major industries on the margins of the settlement and feasting or mortuary practices involving human remains.

Digging ditches

Attempts have been made to define a clear circuit of urban defences from the ditches excavated on archaeological sites around the periphery of early Londinium. It has been suggested that certain excavated ditch sections represent lines of urban demarcation and that they may be evidence for several distinct circuits of enclosing works.[404] The colonies and some of the *civitas* capitals of Britannia acquired entire or partial defensive circuits during the first century, although the walls surrounding certain urban centres may often not have been simple and continuous.[405] Evidence that there was any coordinated boundary circuit at London prior to the construction of the Roman wall is far from convincing.

Guy Hunt has identified a set of boundary features to the north-east of Londinium that could have formed part of an urban boundary during the late first and early second centuries which was abandoned prior to the construction of the Roman wall (see Fig. 5.11).[406] Several ditch sections have been excavated at Baltic House, 9 Northumberland Avenue and 8–14 Cooper's Row / 1 America Square.[407] As Hunt has pointed out, these boundary works vary in the number of ditches and in the nature of their construction at each site.[408] He has suggested that this urban boundary may not have been built as a coordinated structure by a single authority but that it could have been established by property owners who were delimiting their lands, presumably following the instructions of a central urban authority. It is possible that the urban boundary was made up of different types of features which so far have only been located in certain places. There was a road junction just beyond the location of this early urban boundary in the location where the 'cemetery road' ran from the Colchester road eastwards towards Shadwell.[409]

The absence of definitive evidence for clearly-marked and well-maintained physical boundaries may be compared with other urban centres across Britannia. While the colonies of the province

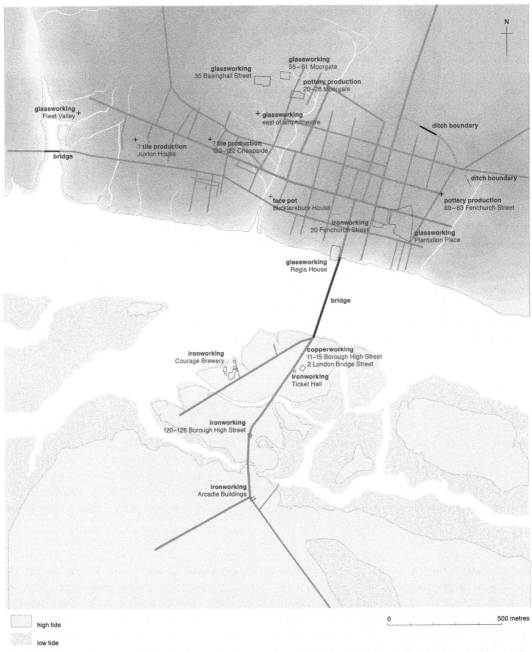

FIG. 5.11 A potential northwestern boundary to the early city and the distribution of industry by AD 70–120.

probably all had coherently-defined defensive circuits by the late first century,[410] the margins of other towns may have remained ill defined until the late second and early third centuries.[411]

Industry

Industrial production was mainly localized in nature and evidence for fairly large-scale industries is limited.[412] At 1 Poultry, evidence has been found for the working of iron and copper-alloy associated with buildings that had a commercial function. At other sites across Londinium small-scale metalworking industries and activities involving other forms of craft production were common.[413] A small glass workshop was located in one of the warehouses behind Waterfront 2 at Regis House,[414] while evidence was also found for glassworking close to the eastern edge of Roman London at Plantation Place.[415] Many of these small ventures may have been family businesses. James Drummond-Murray and Peter Thompson have suggested that there may have been a lengthy sequence of ironworking at the Ticket Hall site on the north island.[416] A smith was based here before the Boudican uprising and a small rectangular structure was erected about 15 metres to the north-east during the late first century. This building, which contained two metalworking hearths, survived well into the second century, suggesting a continuity in the management of this industry at this establishment over a lengthy period.[417]

Other industries were often located at the periphery of settlements, such as pottery and tile production, glassworking and metalworking.[418] A location on the urban margins for such activities was viewed as appropriate in order to keep fumes and fire hazards away from the main areas of the settlement. Leatherworking also produced unpleasant and unhealthy by-products. These industrial processes transformed raw materials into finished products and some present-day societies continue to view them as magical or dangerous procedures to be undertaken at some distance from the homes of the living.[419]

It has long been thought that there was a pottery industry in the western area of Londinium close to several early cemeteries. Roman kilns were found at two locations during the building of St Paul's Cathedral in the 1670s and 1680s. A circular kiln was found below the west end of the cathedral, with pottery and moulds used to make vessels decorated with figures of men, lions and the leaves of trees.[420] In 1677 four kilns that may have been used for firing pottery were discovered enclosed within a single structure, arranged to face the centre.[421] Marsden has excavated a single kiln that may have been used for firing pottery at Paternoster Square.[422] More recent excavations have failed to find any substantial evidence for pottery production in this part of London.[423] Large quantities of over-fired tiles (wasters) have been found at the sites excavated around Paternoster Square, especially from Juxton House, suggesting that tiles were being fired just to the north-west of the location of St Paul's at the western periphery of early Londinium.[424] Some of these wasters were found in pre-Boudican deposits, but the majority of the finds came from later first-century contexts.[425] The scale of this industry is unclear and it has been suggested that much of the evidence was removed by urban development during the 1960s.

Around 300 metres to the east, at 120–2 Cheapside, many tile wasters, including tiles with procuratorial stamps, were found in association with a group of domestic buildings.[426] Ian Betts has noted the large number of over- and under-fired *tegula* and *imbrex* roofing tiles and suggested that a tilery may have been established close to this site to supply roofing material for the Cheapside bathhouse and other public buildings.[427] Such procuratorial tiles occur quite widely across Londinium on both sides of the river and it was formerly believed that they may have been made at Brockley Hill in Greater London.[428] Perhaps a group of workmen had been relocated from Brockley Hill to Londinium to produce tiles. The distance between Juxton House and 120–2 Cheapside suggests at least two distinct areas of tile production during the second half of the first century.

Much of the pottery marketed and used in Londinium during this period was imported from kilns at Highgate Wood (Greater London), Alice Holt (Surrey) and in the Verulamium region.[429] Within Londinium, pottery was manufactured at Sugar Loaf Court prior to the Boudican uprising. A second pottery industry is indicated by the large quantities of wasters found at the east margin of Roman London at 60–3 Fenchurch Street.[430] Here a variety of different types of pots were being made during the first century and it is quite possible that production commenced prior to the Boudican uprising.[431] The wasters mainly came from early features dating from AD 50–75 and represent a type of pottery that has not previously been identified but that is similar to other ceramics in use in London at this time.[432] Several timber-and-earth buildings were contemporary with this activity, although no pottery kilns were found.[433]

It is notable that at these tile and pottery production sites no kilns have been found. It is possible that the excavations had sampled only the margins of the industrial areas or that all the industrial structures had been removed by later development. More substantial remains were excavated at the pottery production site of 20–8 Moorgate in the upper Walbrook Valley,[434] where operations may have begun around AD 110 and probably ceased around AD 160. A cluster of pottery kilns was associated with a workshop and roads just west of a tributary stream of the Walbrook.

The first phase of activity included the construction of at least three circular pottery kilns between AD 110 and 120 or 140 and a similar number were built in a second phase. The fabrics and forms chosen for their products indicates that the potters had close connections with those at Verulamium who had been supplying much of the Londinium market for the previous fifty years.[435] Among the pottery types produced to supply the local market were mortaria stamped by at least six potters. The mortaria attributed to these Moorgate potters were mainly traded in Londinium and across south-eastern Britannia.[436] No other kilns have been found in the neighbouring areas, indicating that production did not supply more than a small amount of the pottery required by the people of Londinium.

Glassworking evidence was found at 20–8 Moorgate in the form of vessel production waste. Collections of glass as cullet (vessels and other discarded glass collected for recycling) have been excavated at nearby sites, especially at 55–61 Moorgate where glassworking was conducted within a timber building.[437] Several timber-and-clay buildings constructed during the late first century were rebuilt during the second century,[438] one of which produced glass waste and large sections of a tank from a glassworking furnace. Jackie Keily and John Shepherd have argued that this activity dated to the first half of the second century.[439] Other industrial activities included the production of shoes, indicated by a large dump of leather scrap waste across the north of the site.[440] A metalled surface with a timber tank just to the north of this excavation trench included a damaged stone statue of a god, possibly Mercury, which dated from the late first or early second centuries.[441] Earlier work had produced a small votive plaque with a repoussé figure of a mother goddess.[442] These finds suggest that a small temple or shrine had been located at this glassworking site.

Immediately east of the amphitheatre, excavations have also produced evidence for glassworking. A hollow or pond-like depression, which had developed over the robbed drain just outside the timber amphitheatre's eastern entrance, contained glass furnace waste from a workshop and over 58,000 fragments of glass that had presumably been collected for recycling.[443] Recent excavation to the north-north-east of the amphitheatre at 35 Basinghall Street has uncovered another large assemblage of glass waste associated with a workshop, probably dating from the period from around AD 140–70.[444] The evidence from this extensive area of the western tributaries of the Walbrook suggests that broken glass was being collected and reworked on a substantial scale, resulting in deposits of waste at several locations during the early second century,[445] an activity that may have continued until around AD 170.[446] Despite the quantities of glassworking debris that have been found, Marianna Perez-Sala and John Shepherd have suggested that only a small number of workers who may have been itinerant were involved at any one time.[447] It is possible that craftspeople operated the pottery and glassworking industries, making products over the summer months when river flooding was less likely to disrupt production.

To the west of Londinium, on the steep eastern bank of the River Fleet at 19–25 Old Bailey, the landscape was substantially terraced during the later first century and eight glassworking furnaces were constructed before around AD 120.[448] The information from this excavation has yet to be fully published but Perez-Sala and Shepherd have suggested that the late first-century glass industry in London was focused on this location and that it moved during the early second century to the upper Walbrook Valley.[449] This glassworking site was later replaced by a substantial building that may have been a Romano-Celtic temple, hinting at a connection between industry and ritual.[450]

A watching-brief close to Bucklersbury House in the middle Walbrook Valley[451] revealed a large upright face pot standing upon a burnt surface and surrounded and filled with a mass of flint and iron rust.[452] The burnt material such as wooden panelling included several pieces carved with arcading and a ribbed surface moulding, possibly derived from a small early second-century shrine.[453] This ritual deposit or small shrine was possibly connected with metalworking. The 1950s excavations across this area had been restricted in scale and it is probable that other shrines and ritual deposits in the area around the later temple of Mithras have been destroyed.[454]

The evidence for intensive ironworking on the main islands in the Thames in Southwark may suggest that there was a particular concentration of industrial activity across the islands and low lying land. Ironworking at the Ticket Hall site, 11–15 Borough High Street / 2 London Bridge Street and at 120–4 and 124–6 Borough High Street has been noted above. On the western margin of the north island two successive sets of buildings at Courage Brewery were constructed from AD 50–70 to 100, each set within its own building plot.[455] These timber-and-earth structures were comparable with other contemporary buildings throughout Londinium. Two of the excavated areas were clearly being used for metalworking, including iron smithing, which was associated in this early phase with a rectangular timber building dating from the late first century.[456] Pits and hearths north of this building were used for ironworking and it has been suggested that the scale of this activity might have formed the output of four to six workers. Another building just to the east may also have been used for ironworking and it is possible that the members of the two households who were involved in iron production lived and worked in the building at each site. Industry continued here until the mid-fourth century and this may have been the most substantial ironworking site in Londinium.[457]

To the south-east of this metalworking area at Courage Brewery a more substantial building has been excavated, possibly the home of the family who owned the business.[458] This elaborate house, which was maintained from around AD 70 until the third century, may have been fitted with window glass. Metalworking waste, including vitrified furnace lining, iron slag, fuel ash slag and crucible fragments, partly defined the island foreshore on the west and alongside the Southwark Street Channel.[459] The dumping of deposits to build up land surfaces as a means of enculturing the land may be of relevance in this context, since ironworking was a highly symbolic and ritually powerful activity and its material waste could have been viewed as particularly significant.

Evidence was found at Arcadia Buildings for the smithing of iron during the late first century at a site that has produced evidence for early copperworking. Industrial processing continued from the mid-first to the third century.[460]

Feasting

In the Roman world, feasting and festivals were often associated with sacrifices and sacred places such as sanctuaries and temples.[461] Feasts were also often arranged to mark the death of individuals and to commemorate ancestors.[462] The detailed analysis of pottery and other finds in particular archaeological contexts dating from the late first and early second centuries has led to the suggestion that feasts were held in a variety of contexts at the margin of Londinium (see Fig. 5.12). This evidence suggests that people were meeting at the urban edge to take part in feasts that served to create and maintain their status and cultural identities. The limited scope of excavations and the truncation of the archaeological deposits may have fragmented the archaeological evidence in a way that prevents these early examples of feasting from being linked more closely to the celebration of the cult of the dead.[463]

It has been suggested that a processional way ran from the forum to the amphitheatre and temple zone at the boundary of Londinium. The pond-like depression east of the amphitheatre contained evidence for glassworking but also large quantities of pottery, including complete vessels. A number of other contemporary features in this area contained pottery from levelling dumps.[464] Large quantities of animal bones from other features associated with this phase of dumping may also have been associated with feasting.[465] While these materials were brought in to build up the ground surface when the stone amphitheatre was being constructed, the ritual and pragmatic aspects of the dumping of material were probably interconnected. Beth Richardson has suggested that this material is not typical domestic rubbish, since many of the pottery vessels were substantially complete and appear to have been deposited over a short period around AD 100–120.[466]

The assemblage contained many drinking vessels and other pottery forms associated with food consumption.[467] Ceremonies connected with the use of the amphitheatre are suggested by the high proportion of samian pottery decorated with gladiatorial scenes from in and around the pond.[468] One particularly interesting fragmentary vessel from the amphitheatre had a depiction of a bull fight that contains three images of the dead gladiators below the feet of the rampant bull.[469] The pottery and animal bones may have derived from banquets given to the combatants by the individual who funded the games, although it is not clear why this material should be associated with such substantial quantities of glassworking waste.

This feasting may have taken place over a larger area since another cluster of pits around 30 metres from the amphitheatre's eastern entrance had been used to dispose of rubbish that may have derived from banquets including most of a samian bowl depicting a hunting scene.[470] The fragmentary remains of a timber-and-earth building were also found in the same area.

At the north-west boundary of Londinium the new area of settlement established at Merrill Lynch Financial Centre included the fragmentary remains of a structure ('Building 8') about 10 metres north of the main east–west road and between the two steam channels that were being canalized.[471] Finds made in association with this building included pottery and a complete ceramic lamp with the 'maker's name' 'FORTIS' ('brave' or 'strong').[472] In an open area to the

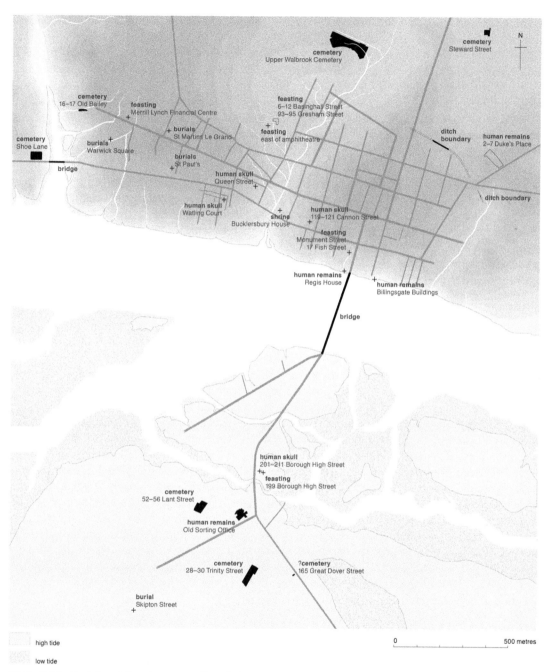

cemetery
Upper Walbrook Cemetery

cemetery
Steward Street

N

cemetery
16–17 Old Bailey

feasting
Merrill Lynch Financial Centre

feasting
6–12 Basinghall Street
93–95 Gresham Street

burials
St Martins Le Grand

feasting
east of amphitheatre

ditch
boundary

human remains
2–7 Duke's Place

cemetery
Shoe Lane

burials
Warwick Square

burials
St Paul's

human skull
Queen Street

ditch boundary

bridge

human skull
Watling Court

shrine
Bucklersbury House

human skull
119–121 Cannon Street

feasting
Monument Street
17 Fish Street

human remains
Regis House

human remains
Billingsgate Buildings

bridge

human skull
201–211 Borough High Street

feasting
199 Borough High Street

cemetery
52–56 Lant Street

human remains
Old Sorting Office

cemetery
28–30 Trinity Street

?cemetery
165 Great Dover Street

burial
Skipton Street

high tide

low tide

0   500 metres

FIG. 5.12 Burial and feasting across Londinium in AD 70–120.

north the excavators uncovered a well possibly connected with this building that contained finds including a pipe-clay figurine of Minerva from which the head had apparently been snapped off prior to its deposition.[473] This well also produced evidence for feasting, including a single sherd of a tazza cup and some glass vessels.[474] The pottery included a large number of flagons and other vessels used in the drinking, serving and storage of liquids. Animal bones had also been deposited in the well, including those from domesticated animals and, rather unusually, of a swan. Jo Lyon has suggested that these items might have been deposited in one episode, perhaps between AD 100 and 110.[475] In this context, the pottery vessels known as tazze are often found associated with lamps in cremation burials and have been interpreted as vessels for burning incense, although a single fragment of such a vessel may not be of significance.[476]

The figurine of Minerva may have been placed in the well as an offering to water deities when it was infilled.[477] This act of deposition may have related to a water cult focusing on the well since Minerva was directly linked to the goddess Sulis at the temple and spring at Aquae Sulis (Bath, north-east Somerset).[478] The well at Merrill Lynch Financial Centre may have been at the location of a feast or series of ceremonies to celebrate a water cult of Minerva, perhaps centred on a small temple or shrine beside the main east–west road and not far from small cemeteries at the north-western margin of Londinium.[479]

A late first-century well just behind the Thames waterfront at 4–12 Monument Street and 17 Fish Street was located just west of the main north–south road and close to a stream that ran into the Thames.[480] It had been filled with fine ceramics, glass and large amounts of bird, fish and mammal bones which it has been suggested may have been brought from a nearby inn or restaurant.[481] This well also contained swan bones which are uncommon in Roman deposits in London.[482] It has been suggested, on the basis of the homogeneous pottery assemblage, that this material represented a single act of deposition made around AD 71–5.[483] A figurine of Minerva, without a head or arms, was found in this well.[484] Only three Roman images of Minerva have been found in London and it is significant that two were deposited in wells containing evidence for early Roman feasting, possibly suggesting that this was connected with water cults.[485]

South of the Thames in Southwark the excavation at 199 Borough High Street produced a large collection of pottery including ten examples of drinking vessels that dated to the late first or early second centuries and had been scratched with ownership inscriptions.[486] Most of these vessels were found in and around a drainage ditch which probably formed a field or property boundary. It has been suggested that the vessels may have been used for communal eating or drinking at a nearby building. The names on the pots suggest that individuals wished to identify their own vessels and so perhaps they took part in the drinking on several occasions.[487] The pottery at this site all pre-dates the mid-second century and includes vessels that may slightly post-date AD 120. It appears to have been deposited over a considerable period of time at a location close to the crossing of the Borough Channel.[488]

Mortuary landscapes

The burial of the dead and the arrangement of human remains were important activities in marking the boundaries of the early settlement. The evidence from the west, south and perhaps the east of Londinium suggests that during the second century the areas in which burials took place were not very well defined. The archaeological information from the urban periphery suggests that mortuary landscapes were delimited by many burial grounds with cremations and inhumations and a range of fragmentation rites. It is difficult to understand burial practice throughout the history of London because the evidence for individual areas has often been poorly recorded and the dating of burials is not always straightforward.[489] Recent excavations have begun to provide a fuller understanding of the location and character of these marginal mortuary terrains. We have seen that, although it has been thought that the usual method of disposing of the dead in Roman Britain during the first and second centuries was by cremation, early inhumation burials were common. The idea that there was a gradual transition from cremation to inhumation is far too simple to account for the wide variety of mortuary practices.

It has usually been thought that the people of Londinium buried their dead outside the margins of the settlement. The four cemeteries along the main roads leading out of Roman London to the west, north, east and south have been said to have originated during the late first and early second centuries and to have continued in use after the walled circuit was constructed during the third and fourth centuries.[490] Recent excavations have shown that this is far too simple an explanation of these complex mortuary terrains. Since the late 1990s archaeologists have focused on defining and interpreting these cemeteries. Some of this new work suggests that the four cemeteries each included several discrete areas of burial that may have been separated by open ground.[491] In addition, the evidence obtained to the west of Londinium has suggested that there was not always a very clear geographical separation between the areas occupied by the living and by the dead.

The information for burial areas to the west of Londinium has been summarized by several accounts,[492] although here the evidence will be approached on the basis that there was no single coherent burial area during the late first and early second centuries (see Fig. 5.13).[493] Burial in

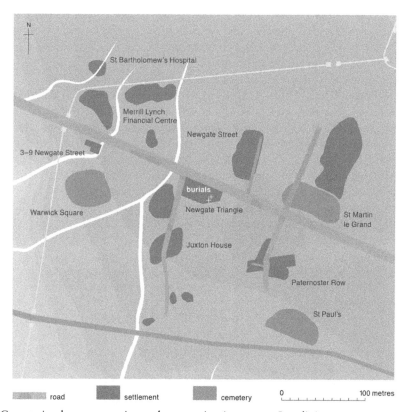

FIG. 5.13 Cemeteries, human remains and occupation in western Londinium.

the western area commenced during the middle of the first century.[494] This part of early Londinium included at least three distinct cemeteries separated by areas of occupation at the site of St Paul's Cathedral, St Martins le Grand and Warwick Square.[495] The small burial ground at Warwick Square included cremations that may have been pre-Boudican and one later first-century burial which comprised the remains of two people placed in an amphora.[496] The fragmentary remains of an inhumation was also found.[497]

Jenny Hall has described this broad scattering of burials at the western margin of early Londinium as a 'non-designated cemetery area',[498] while it has also been suggested that the early urban boundary was some way to the east and therefore excluded these early burials.[499] Perhaps occupation in this western area was sub-urban in character and not subject to the usual rules for the disposal of the dead.[500] An alternative, and perhaps more convincing, explanation is that several early burial grounds were located to the rear of properties and became incorporated into the area of the urban settlement as ribbon-development spread further west along the roads (see Figs 2.5 and 5.8). This may indicate the unplanned early development of the western suburbs.

At 16–17 Old Bailey four fragmentary inhumations and a possible cremation dating to around AD 70–120 lay on the southern fringe of a more extensive burial ground.[501] Quarry and gravel pits probably dug in the late first century were backfilled with material including pottery, and some disarticulated human bones suggested that other burials had been disturbed.[502] This cemetery may have been abandoned during the late first century or early second. Another small cemetery was uncovered in 1927 on the west bank of the River Fleet at Shoe Lane just north of St Bride's Church.[503] Located just north of the road running westwards out of Londinium from Ludgate, it contained eight cremations. The dating of the pottery urns accompanying these burials may indicate the use of this cemetery for a lengthy period of time.[504]

The so-called 'northern cemetery' has also produced cremations and inhumations, including some first-century cremations around Bishopsgate within the later walls, but the information is very limited as a result of the early date of excavation.[505] Early Roman burials were also made in the later cemetery around Spitalfields. At Steward Street, some early Roman inhumations among a scattering of pits and quarries dated from the later first and early second centuries.[506] Other burials have been found at sites close to Spitalfields Market, although these are mainly later in date.[507]

The bones of many people have been found in the Walbrook Valley, washed from cemeteries by the streams that flowed into the Walbrook. The excavation of the 'Upper Walbrook Cemetery', an extensive area of burials just north of Finsbury Circus, has produced evidence that the inhumations were subject to erosion by a stream that had a seasonal flow.[508] Thirteen of these burials probably pre-dated AD 120 and had been cut into the deposits that filled one of the tributaries of the Walbrook. Some of these remains had been disturbed by water action and were very fragmentary. Semi-articulated and separated human bones were recovered from a stream channel east of the site.[509] These may have been body parts from partially or completely eroded graves situated upstream to the west and were found in the upper part of an alluvial deposit directly below the make-up layers for a road, suggesting that partly-fleshed human remains were visible to people visiting the cemetery.[510]

The drainage and colonization of the upper Walbrook commenced during the later first and early second centuries.[511] Excavations in this area have produced a large number of human cranial remains from streams, watercourses, drainage ditches and other archaeological features.[512] Some of these remains may have been deposited during the period from AD 70 to 120, although most of the dated examples came from contexts dated between AD 120 and 200 and may have derived from the 'Upper Walbrook Cemetery' and other burial grounds where corpses were exposed to running waters.

Burials on the eastern margin of Londinium may have commenced as early as the mid-AD 60s. The monument raised to Classicianus was located in the east of Roman London and other tombstones that were reused in later contexts could also date from the first and early second centuries.[513] The burial ground situated around the junction of Billiter Street and Fenchurch Street may have continued to receive burials after AD 60, although this area was also being developed for housing during the second half of the first century.[514]

The excavations at 2–7 Dukes Place have explored an area of the urban boundary just north of the Roman gate at Aldgate and have located a ditch which ran parallel to, but pre-dated, the later Roman wall.[515] The shallow nature of this feature suggested that it did not form an earlier line of defences and that it was a drainage feature. The backfill of the ditch contained pottery dated from around AD 120 and the disturbed remains of two articulated human skeletons.[516] John Maloney has observed that these appeared to have been 'unceremoniously dumped', arousing his suspicions about the circumstances of deposition. These are broadly comparable to the first-century inhumation burials deposited in ditches at Newgate Triangle and 60–3 Fenchurch Street and provide additional evidence for the apparent exposure of corpses in marginal locations.

The most fully excavated area of this eastern mortuary landscape was developed by around AD 70–80 beyond the edge of Londinium in an area defined by earlier field boundaries and quarries and accessed by the 'cemetery road' (see Fig. 5.14).[517] Recent excavations of this 'eastern cemetery' have shown that there were at least 12 hectares with at least two distinct cemeteries with cremation and inhumation burials dating from the late first and early second centuries. The marble funerary inscription of Lucius Pompeius Licetus from Arretium in Italy was sited at this cemetery.[518] A dowel hole in the stone suggests that it was originally mounted on the wall of a mausoleum. The 'cemetery road' ran towards another area of burials around a kilometre east of Roman London at Shadwell where some of the cremation burials may have dated from the late first or early second centuries.

The so-called 'southern cemetery' in Southwark contained cremations and inhumations that have usually been thought to have lain at the boundaries of the expanding urban settlement.[519] It has been argued that it is important to explore the pattern of burials in the 'southern cemetery' by examining their date since the ill-defined nature of burial in this area related to the changing boundaries of the settlement, providing information about the growth and later contraction of the urban area.[520] The locations of the human remains do not necessarily appear, however, to indicate a clear sequence of expansion for the boundaries of the occupied area during the late first and early second centuries.[521]

The main focus for these burial activities was probably on the south bank of the Thames. It is not known if burial and occupation were intermingled at this early date, but the occupation and industry at 223–37 Borough High Street, Arcadia Buildings and Tabard Square suggest that there may have been no very clear distinction here between the areas allocated to the living and the dead.

Excavation at the Old Sorting Office, between the probable line of Stane Street and the river, examined an area of the south margin of Londinium and uncovered a series of ditches that may have divided the settlement area from fields or marginal lands to the south-west.[522] Beasley has suggested that a range of finds from the Old Sorting Office, including the two human long bones from pre-Boudican deposits, indicate ritual activities that marked out the boundaries of the urban settlement.[523] Six of the wells or ritual shafts dated to the later first and early second centuries and some of these contained almost complete pottery vessels.[524] This area was not built over during the late first and early second centuries and it may have constituted the backyards of houses to the north or east.[525]

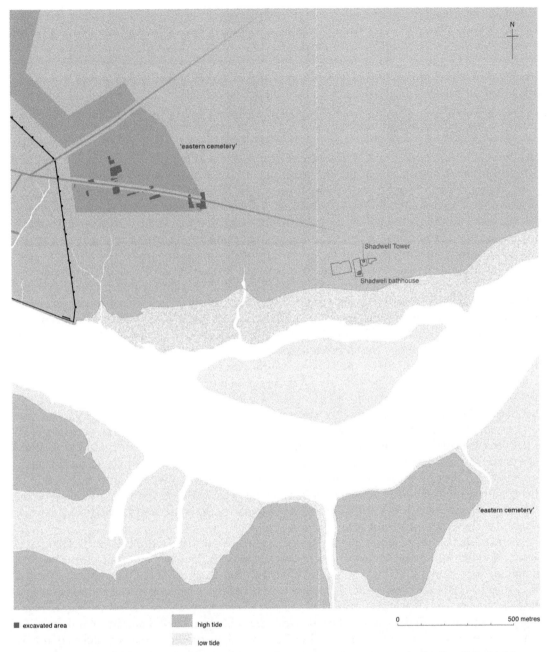

'eastern cemetery'

Shadwell Tower

Shadwell bathhouse

'eastern cemetery'

■ excavated area   high tide   0   500 metres

low tide

FIG. 5.14 The area of eastern Londinium showing the 'eastern cemetery', eastern wall and the bathhouse and 'Tower' at Shadwell. The Shadwell 'Tower' may be a mausoleum dating to the later second century and the Shadwell bathhouse was constructed in the third century. The walls were probably constructed in the late second and early third centuries and the bastions added in the fourth century.

Recent excavations at 52–6 Lant Street have revealed ditches that drained a marshy area and which were filled with deposits containing ceramics and numerous fragments of disarticulated human bone.[526] An alluvial deposit at the western edge of the site suggested that there was marshland on the southern bank of the Borough Channel during the mid to late first century.[527] The cranial remains of two individuals were found close together in the primary fill of a ditch above a fragment of a further skull in its secondary fill,[528] suggesting that certain parts of human bodies were deliberately selected and placed in the ditch with a tripod bowl as an offering. The area at Lant Street may have begun to be used as a cemetery during the later first century, although the excavators have suggested that the number of fragmentary human remains from archaeological contexts indicates that fragmentation rites took place over a substantial part of the southern margin of Londinium.[529] Environmental work has shown that this low-lying marshy land may have been subject to occasional flooding. This suggests that corpses were buried or exposed in locations where they would be eroded during flooding. Fragments of bodies may have been manipulated and deposited in particular contexts. The inhumation burials interred at the north of the Lant Street area during the second century may suggest that a more formally defined cemetery was developed here.

Further south along Watling Street in Southwark the excavation at 165 Great Dover Street located the western roadside ditch and uncovered a single timber building in an area that later became a cemetery.[530] This building may have been a temple or mausoleum, although no burials of this date were found.[531] The burial at Harper Road that was possibly post-Boudican in date indicates that burials may have occurred to the west of this site. Recent excavations at 28–30 Trinity Street have produced evidence for a cemetery that developed from the late second century and also the fragmentary remains of a timber structure that could have been an open colonnade defining part of a rectangular building.[532] This was surrounded by ditches which may have been constructed during the later first century and disused by around AD 120–50.[533]

There appear to have been other burial monuments at the southern edge of Londinium. At Skipton Street, around 800 metres south-west of the junction of Watling Street and Stane Street, an oval pit contained fragments of sculpture, a pottery flagon, a cremated burial and a cattle skull.[534] The sculpture fragments were derived from two objects: a female figure, possibly Venus, pouring water from an urn; and the head of a figure that may have represented a nymph.[535] The context suggests an early second-century date. These sculptures may have been part of grave monuments or a wayside shrine. The widely spaced evidence from Skipton Street, 28–30 Trinity Street and 52–6 Lant Street suggests that there were several early burial grounds south of Londinium, matching the evidence from the western and northern margins. The evidence from across Londinium's margins shows that complex activities were connected with the remains of the dead.

The evidence for fragmentation rites in Southwark may help to explain the discovery of human remains on domestic sites. It is possible that burials and housing areas were not always kept strictly apart, although many burials and bone fragment deposits may pre-date large-scale occupation. These human remains were deposited in their archaeological contexts when people were settling in the area.[536] The cranial remains may have been taken from the exposed or eroded remains of bodies deposited at Londinium's margins.

The cranial remains of a single individual were found in a ditch at 201–11 Borough High Street, just to the north-west of the deposit containing the drinking-vessels inscribed with the names of their owners.[537] The drainage and colonization of the middle Walbrook Valley commenced during the AD 60s, as work at 1 Poultry and Bloomberg has demonstrated, and human remains have been found in several locations. At Watling Court on the western edge of the area, drainage and landscaping began during the late first century and several large pits dug before people settled in the area were filled with deposits; one waterlogged pit contained a human skull without its lower jaw.[538] Nearby, at Aldermary House, 61–2 Queen Street, the cranial remains of a single individual were found in a well that dated from the late first or early second centuries.[539] It is possible that the area around Queen Street was left largely undeveloped and used for pit-digging and the construction of wells, since the local water table was very high and no buildings were located.[540] At 119–21 Cannon Street, at the eastern edge of the middle Walbrook Valley, the earliest recorded feature was a well in the bottom of which a wooden box had been deposited that contained the cranial remains of two humans and two dog skeletons.[541] The fill of the well also included a large number of flagon and amphorae sherds, described in the interim excavation report as 'Neronian'. Dog bones have often been found in contexts identified as special and ritual in Londinium and elsewhere in southern Britain.[542]

Perhaps these offerings were made in contexts where the boundary between the living and the dead required definition. At Billingsgate Buildings skeletal fragments from at least three individuals were found in deposits infilling the waterfront revetment.[543] These deposits contained substantial quantities of finds dating from around AD 80–130. The pieces of arm and shoulder bone may indicate a degree of pre-selection for deposition.[544] At Regis House an adult cranium, body parts and arm and leg bones were found in the make-up of the waterfront (Waterfront 2) and another cranium has been recorded that probably derived from the waterfront works at Upper Thames Street.[545] The deposition of human bones at these sites may indicate that the soils and cultural materials used to infill the waterfront works had been taken from an area where human remains were exposed. Alternatively, fragmentation rites may have been conducted in which selected human remains were removed from burials and reused in practices linked to the management of water flow and the establishment of firm land for trading.

Summary

The development of Londinium from the first to the early second century involved the continuity of some traditions but also considerable changes. The exposure of corpses and fragmentation rites involving human bones on the margin of the settlement began prior to AD 70 and continued into the third century. The location of burial grounds and the distribution of crania suggest that a clear distinction was not always maintained between living areas and those for the disposal of the dead, although most burials were made in the margins.

The dumping of cultural material and soil to build up the ground surface and to establish the river frontages continued throughout this period. These activities may have involved conceptually enculturing the land, as some control was established over the flooding of rivers. Human bones were occasionally deposited as part of the act of building up the land surface, as exemplified by two waterfront contexts. The construction of waterfronts, the bridging of the Thames and the Walbrook, the re-establishment of roads and the construction of monumental buildings and houses were all processes of enculturing, creating the possibilities for urban life across this sacred riverine landscape. Acts of propitiation may sometimes be detected, such as the ritual offerings deposited in the River Thames close to the bridge and the deposition of pipe-clay Minerva figurines in two wells.

The scale of the construction of Londinium at this time is dramatic. It is possible that plans were underway before the Boudican uprising to construct a more substantial port and to expand the area of the settlement so that the destruction brought only a temporary halt to this process.

There is some evidence to suggest that inhabitants who had fled before Londinium's destruction may have returned. Property boundaries were still respected at some sites, the smithy at the Ticket Hall site in Southwark was re-established and the cemetery at Warwick Square apparently continued in use. The cosmopolitan population is reflected in the inscriptions on tombstones and writing tablets, indicating the presence of military men, imperial officials and slaves. A procurator was buried in London during the early AD 60s and the references to Vegetus and Montanus and the four *speculatores* indicate that Londinium was developing as the financial centre of the province.

Roundhouses were evidently uncommon after the AD 70s and either Britons or settlers from overseas may have constructed the simple timber-and-earth houses revealed on many sites. The monumental buildings in the urban centre provided the spaces in which urban competition was acted out. The development of impressive private residences illustrates growing social inequalities and competitiveness. Previous accounts of Roman London have tended to interpret first-century houses as impermanent timber-and-earth structures. Although most domestic buildings were built from these materials, stone was incorporated into the foundations and walls of houses at 10 Gresham Street, Watling Court and Lloyd's Register. The elaborate decorative schemes in the houses at Watling Court and the details of the buildings at 12 Arthur Street and at 15–23 Southwark Street suggest that there were people with wealth and Mediterranean contacts living in Londinium. The 'palace' site at Cannon Street was an even more substantial and impressive building complex that may have been a private or a public structure.

The scale and character of these impressive houses shows that earlier assessments have downplayed the wealth and social standing of some Roman Londoners. Many of the so-called 'public' buildings may have been funded by members of the urban aristocracy, just as they were in other cities across the Roman Empire. The administration and the military were probably involved in such developments but these were not solely inspired and promoted by the procurator or the governor. The development of public buildings shows that Mediterranean styles of living had spread across Londinium, such as access to bathing facilities, the practice of writing in Latin and new ways of preparing and serving food.

6

'Hadrianic Fires', AD 120s and 130s

Introduction

Excavations have found widespread evidence for a second destruction of Londinium during the AD 120s or 130s (see Fig. 6.1). It has been argued that there was one substantial phase of burning in which large parts of Roman London were destroyed, perhaps around AD 125 during the reign of the emperor Hadrian (AD 117–38). The burnt layer resulting from this conflagration has long been interpreted as the second destruction of Londinium, after the fire of the Boudican uprising of AD 60. This 'Hadrianic fire' has provided another convenient time marker that has enabled archaeologists to date phases on individual archaeological sites and to document the extent and nature of Roman London around AD 120. This event has also been used, as we shall see in Chapter 7, to define an apparent decline in the fortune of Londinium. As in the case of the first-century fire, however, it is uncertain how extensive and connected the burnt deposits used to define the 'Hadrianic fire' really were. Since the mid–1980s archaeologists have been trying to determine the character and extent of the fire that may have raged through London at this time. It is unclear whether this was a single event and, if so, how much of London was burned at this time. Areas of the settlement to the north and east and also south of the Thames were not destroyed and there is no information to suggest that the 'public buildings' were burned. This chapter will review current understanding. It is probable that a substantial fire, or fires, destroyed a large part of the western and central areas of Londinium, but other distinct fire events may have become included in this supposed single fire so that its scale and significance have been exaggerated.[1]

The evidence was first identified by Gerald Dunning in the 1940s after the identification of two distinct burnt layers at sites across Londinium representing the 'Boudican' and 'Hadrianic' fires.[2] On the assumption that extensive areas of London had been burned at this time, Dunning was able to date the fire to AD 120–30 on the basis of the samian pottery found at Regis House on the waterfront.[3] Further information to support the idea of the later conflagration was located during the 1980s, in particular at five sites west of the Walbrook.[4] Additional evidence for burning of approximately the same date has been found at sites across London and recent studies of the finds from these contexts has enabled the extent and nature of this supposed event to be examined. The most significant contributions have been Hill and Rowsome's assessment of the evidence for burnt deposits at the sites at and around 1 Poultry and also the work of Lindy Casson, James Drummond-Murray and Anthony Francis on the burnt deposits at 10 Gresham Street.[5] This work suggested that there may have been multiple fires across Londinium during the AD 120s and 130s and that connecting all the burnt deposits that have been found as a single chronological event is probably unrealistic.

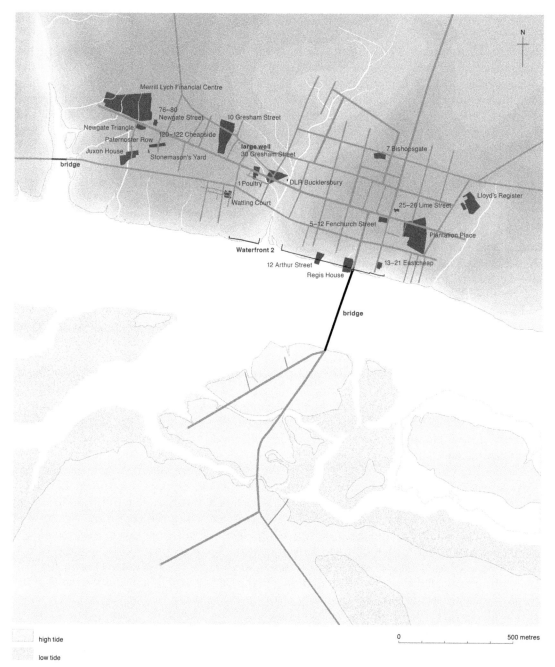

FIG. 6.1 Evidence for the 'Hadrianic fire', showing sites mentioned in the text where there is evidence for burning around AD 120–135.

We have seen that the dominant building tradition during the period prior to the AD 120s was timber-and-earth construction, although buildings with stone foundations or superstructures have also been located. The information from the Boudican destruction of Londinium has demonstrated how easily a settlement built in timber could be destroyed, since extensive evidence for a burnt deposit of this date has been located. Excavated evidence from across Roman London has suggested that localized fires were common during the late first and early second centuries. Domestic life and industrial activities may often have featured the extinguishing of small-scale fires to prevent more extensive damage to properties.

A single fire?

Perhaps the best evidence for the dating of this fire event is the burnt deposit of samian pottery found at Regis House. This material was collected during Dunning's excavation of 1929–31 from a long narrow building with its southern gable end facing the waterfront.[6] Piled against the walls of this building was a huge dump of building debris around 1.2 metres thick containing at least 600 fragmentary burnt samian vessels dating from around AD 120–5. These were associated with a small number of coarse ware vessels. It has been assumed that the samian pots had been imported to be marketed in Londinium, perhaps at the warehouse in which they were found.[7] Following more recent excavations, Trevor Brigham and Bruce Watson have suggested that the samian was brought from a warehouse close by to be dumped at the site.[8] Extensive deposits have been found deriving from the burning of timber-framed buildings at Regis House on the waterfront, although this information has yet to be fully published.[9] At 12 Arthur Street, the substantial buildings associated with the timber-lined well were burned around AD 120–5, possibly during the 'Hadrianic fire', although the dating evidence here is not entirely conclusive.[10] This supports the idea that the conflagration had spread along the waterfront, since this site lies just west of Regis House. In other parts of Londinium limited evidence indicates that the fire had reached further.

Perring has observed that the evidence for the 'Hadrianic fire' has also been found to the south of the forum along the main east–west street to the far west of Roman London.[11] Excavations at 5–12 Fenchurch Street and 25–6 Lime Street have located burnt deposits dating to this period.[12] At Watling Court much of the superstructure of the high-status houses was burnt, forming a destruction deposit up to 1 metre thick.[13] Finds from this deposit included a military diploma from one building and some fragmentary human remains from another, which were interpreted as having derived from a victim of the fire. Perring has noted that the fire may have spread through the areas of denser housing in this part of Londinium and that none of the public buildings seem to have been burned.[14] Convincing evidence for burning has been found at 76–80 Newgate Street where the strip-buildings were destroyed,[15] supporting Perring's suggestion that the focus of the conflagration was along the main east–west road.

Several other more recent excavations have enabled a further assessment to be made of the extent and nature of the fire events, especially along the main road west of 1 Poultry. There were two distinct periods of burning in and around 1 Poultry: during the period around AD 90–100 and again during the AD 120s.[16] Several buildings at 1 Poultry were burned in around AD 95 but the fire did not destroy buildings across the entire area of excavation.[17] Hill and Rowsome have considered whether this evidence from around AD 120 might indicate separate burning events over a period of time.[18] Based on the close dating of pottery from the 'widespread destruction' at this time across much of the 1 Poultry area, Hill and Rowsome nevertheless argue that there was one substantial conflagration around AD 120–40, although the exact details of the extent and character of this event are lacking. As in the case of the Boudican destruction deposits, much of this material was reworked and redeposited after the fire.[19] Evidence for burning was not located in certain areas at 1 Poultry, although this may have been a result of later disturbance and landscaping. The excavation near 1 Poultry at the Bucklersbury site (Site C) located redeposited material possibly from the destruction of a pottery shop including around 400 sherds from decorated samian vessels, several of which were comparable to those found in the contemporary burnt deposits at Regis House.[20]

At 10 Gresham Street many of the buildings appear to have been damaged or destroyed by fire around or after AD 130, but the information was difficult to assess since much of the evidence was derived from dumped deposits and make-up layers from the rebuilding of the site.[21] A detailed analysis of the finds from the excavated buildings was used, however, to argue for the later dating of the fire, perhaps as late as AD 140.[22] A major fire burned across the south-eastern corner of the site at 120–2 Cheapside during a time which may be connected to the 'Hadrianic fire' events.[23] Some buildings were, however, probably unaffected.[24] At 30 Gresham Street, another substantial well (Well 2) with a bucket-chain was dug around AD 108–9 close to Well 1.[25] The mechanism of this well, which was capable of raising a considerable quantity of water, was destroyed by burning. The water containers and ironwork of the water-raising device had fallen into the well and were heavily burnt and distorted by the heat. The excavators have suggested that the well-house above this well was destroyed by the fire,[26] although the exact dating is unclear. Finds from the primary fill of the well included complete box-flue tiles and *tegula* roofing tiles possibly derived from nearby buildings that had been destroyed at the same time.[27] The Cheapside bathhouse does not appear to have been destroyed by fire and, although this building is poorly dated, it is thought to have remained in use until the later second century; this bathhouse is unlikely to have been the source of the building material found in Well 2 at 30 Gresham Street.[28]

At the sites excavated around Paternoster Square the evidence for burning was inconsistent.[29] At Paternoster Row and Stonemason's Yard Ramp, buildings destroyed at this time were indicated by burnt deposits including in situ fire debris.[30] At Juxton House a building was disused by this time, probably as a result of this fire. Pits were dug into its remains, one of which contained an inverted human cranium and two complete mortaria, placed one inside the other, in its basal fill.[31] At Newgate Triangle, immediately south of the main east–west road, there was only limited evidence for burning and a number of buildings were modified soon after around AD 125.[32] At Merrill Lynch Financial Centre, just north of the main east–west road, evidence for burning has been found as redeposited fire debris in some parts of the site and some buildings went out of use presumably as a result of the fire.[33]

Elsewhere, some relevant information has emerged to suggest that the fire may not have been restricted to the western and central part of the settlement. At 7 Bishopsgate, north of the forum, a building with a cellar was burned containing a substantial assemblage of heavily fire-damaged glass and pottery dating from around AD 125.[34] To the south of the forum, at 13–21 Eastcheap, evidence for burning may indicate the destruction of the buildings during the AD 120s.[35] The site at Plantation Place produced extensive evidence for burning that may have been associated with this fire,[36] although no evidence was located at the neighbouring 20 Fenchurch Street site.[37] The areas of both these sites may have been levelled and rebuilt during the AD 120s or 130s, however, which could support the idea that buildings here were destroyed in this fire.[38] At Lloyd's Register, east of the forum, some evidence was found for limited burning of a similar date at the north of the site, possibly indicating that buildings behind the road frontage were not burned.[39] It is possible that this was another distinct episode of burning in this part of Londinium that was unconnected with the conflagration raging further to the west.

There is no convincing evidence that the fire extended to the northern areas of Roman London or into the headwaters of the Walbrook. The construction of buildings in some areas of the upper Walbrook Valley may not have commenced until the period following AD 125, so these areas would not have been settled at this time, although excavations at the amphitheatre and in an area of domestic settlement at Cripplegate found no evidence for a fire.[40] There is evidence for localized fires in Southwark during the late first and early second centuries, but little evidence for widespread burning during the AD 120s or 130s.[41] Information from sites on both sides of the River Thames has suggested that small-scale fires may have been a frequent occurrence within the predominantly timber-built settlement during the second half of the first and the second centuries AD.

If a single substantial fire did burn across Londinium during the AD 120s or 130s, it is unclear just how extensive and significant this event really was. At Regis House the fire destroyed a shop with a stock of new samian pottery. The human remains from Watling Court and Juxton House may indicate that people were caught up in the conflagration, although the cranial remains from the latter site is a feature of a common tradition of depositing human heads in pits and ditches in early Roman London.

Summary

Recent excavations have carefully assessed the 'Hadrianic fire' and have now suggested that at least one substantial fire engulfed part of the western and central area of Londinium at some time during the AD 120s or early 130s. The full extent and character of this event requires further study. The fort at Cripplegate was constructed soon afterwards and this could suggest that, as in the case of the earlier burning in AD 60, the fire was the result of a deliberate attempt to destroy Londinium after which a military unit was stationed at Londinium to supervise the reconstruction.

The public buildings, however, were apparently not burned at this time. The second phase of the forum was probably still under construction or just completed and there is no evidence to suggest that this focal element of urban life was damaged by fire. The amphitheatre was not burned, although the rebuilding of the timber structure in stone soon after this time may suggest that it had been damaged by fire. The two bathhouses at Cheapside and Huggin Hill were also unaffected by burning. It is unlikely that an attack by rebel forces would have resulted in the large-scale destruction of domestic properties without damaging the public facilities of urban life. It is unclear why a fire that destroyed domestic buildings over such a wide area did not affect the public buildings. There is some evidence for burning close to the forum and the Cheapside bathhouse but the buildings themselves may have remained intact. Fire may have broken out across Londinium on several different occasions at this time. As only domestic properties were apparently affected, there are still important questions to be answered about the 'Hadrianic fire'.

7

Londinium's Peak of Development from AD 125 to AD 200

*Even such as hope to rise again, would not be content with centrall interrment,
or so desperately to place their reliques as to lie beyond discovery,
and in no way to be seen again . . .*

THOMAS BROWNE 1658: 2

Introduction

This chapter will explore Londinium from the time of the 'Hadrianic fire' to the construction of the Roman wall around the end of the century.[1] Themes discussed earlier in this book will be developed to demonstrate the considerable continuity of activities in Londinium during the second century. The waterfront along the north side of the Thames was rebuilt on three occasions and trade continued to be an important urban function. The period from the mid-AD 120s witnessed the construction and completion of some highly impressive buildings, indicating the increasing status of this urban community, while the building of a fort to the north of Londinium clearly shows the continuing participation of the Roman army in urban life. There is clear evidence for the continuation of ritual practices, particularly in the marginal areas. This chapter will address the character of the population and the construction of public building before turning to domestic housing and finally evidence for industry, ritual and burial on the urban margins. It has been suggested that Londinium continued to prosper during the first half of the century, after which there was a considerable reduction in the population during the period from around AD 160,[2] although this may be to overemphasize the decline of Roman London.

The people and status of Londinium

Londinium may have been made a colony during the early second century perhaps reflecting the status of some of its occupants.[3] A small fragment of a monumental inscription in Purbeck 'marble' was found in a context post-dating the Roman period during excavation west of the Huggin Hill bathhouse, possibly deriving from this bathhouse or from another public building in the vicinity.[4] This inscription is well carved and is probably an imperial dedication to Trajan,

Hadrian or Antoninus Pius. A speculative reconstruction by Tomlin of the letters that have survived (MAX ... NIA) has suggested that the dedication may have been made when Londinium was granted the status of a colony.[5] Tomlin has observed that the most likely context for this grant was Hadrian's visit to London in AD 122. The Huggin Hill bathhouse may have no longer been used by this time and the inscription was probably originally displayed on another building in the vicinity that has yet to be identified. Unless a more complete inscription can be found that identifies Londinium as a colony, the debates about its status as an urban community will continue.

After the early second century, evidence for the names and identities of Roman Londoners is far rarer.[6] The marble inscriptions from Winchester Palace refer to legionary soldiers in later second-century Londinium.[7] The Cripplegate fort may have been in use from around AD 120–60 and a stone pine cone finial from the cemetery at 165 Great Dover Street may have derived from the tomb of a senior military man,[8] but military tombstones dating from this period have yet to be identified.[9] The fort indicates the administrative, military and political significance of the port and that London continued to retain an important administrative role. Imperial officials, soldiers, veterans and wealthy tradesmen would have continued to form part of the population.

The inscribed dedication from the temple at Tabard Square provides information for the presence of an important trader, Tiberinius Celerianus, a citizen of the Bellovaci in northern Gaul.[10] He was referred to as *moritix*, a merchant or the leader of a guild or municipal organization. The maintenance of the waterside facilities on both banks of the Thames and the types of imported objects show the importance of the commerce that passed through the port of Londinium, although the quantity of trade seems to have reduced.

The study of human remains from the cemeteries is providing some information about the geographical origins of the population. It is inevitable that the evidence from the inscriptions has overemphasized the number of incomers, perhaps suggesting that Londinium was more cosmopolitan than may actually have been the case.[11] The tombstones and burial inscriptions were mostly carved for wealthy and well-connected members of the urban community, and poorer people are not represented. The excavators of the 'eastern cemetery' particularly tried to assess whether the people buried there had originally come from the London area.[12] Barber and Bowsher have concluded from the location and nature of the cemetery and from the heterogeneity of burial rites and the skeletal characteristics of the deceased that this was largely an 'indigenous Romano-British population'. This does not preclude the idea that certain people had travelled into Londinium from other parts of Britannia or the empire, as the evidence from the inscriptions and writing tablets has indicated.

Attitudes to the mobility of the population of Britannia have recently been changing. There has been an increasing interest in the geographical origins of the people of Roman Britain and in the movement of people from other parts of the empire into Britain. Attention has been focused on the information from inscriptions and other epigraphic sources, while particular grave goods have been interpreted as having origins abroad. New scientific techniques have become available that are able to revolutionize our understanding of human mobility across the empire.[13] The information from inscriptions and the results from recent excavations indicate that the concept of a largely Romano-British population is too simplistic. The evidence for the hybrid nature of burial practices at the cemeteries could, in itself, indicate the mixing of peoples from different areas of the empire in the cosmopolitan urban community.

There is some limited evidence for immigrants derived from the examination of burials from the 52–6 Lant Street cemetery in Southwark.[14] Oxygen stable isotope analysis was successfully conducted on twenty of the burials, including four of the second-century burials. Ancestry analysis was also undertaken on seventeen of the skulls from the burials.[15] Current opinion from the combined analyses indicates that four of these individuals may have originated from North Africa and two from Asia.[16] One of these individuals was buried during the second century, the other three during the fourth. In addition, two skulls buried in an early ditch may have belonged to people with African ancestors.[17]

According to lead stable isotope analysis, a woman who was buried with a neonatal infant from the Great Dover Street cemetery in Southwark may also have travelled from the Mediterranean to Londinium.[18] Evidently further comparable work on inhumation burials has the potential to transform understanding of the character of the population in terms of its geographic and cultural origins. At present, the information may suggest that London's population was highly cosmopolitan, although the potential local origin of some of the people buried in the marginal mortuary terrains that surrounded Londinium should be considered.

Monumental buildings and infrastructure

The vitality of the urban community was expressed by the construction of new buildings (see Fig. 7.1). These included a larger forum, a stone-built amphitheatre, a fort, three phases of waterfront on the north bank of the Thames and substantial new building complexes at the Salvation Army site and at Winchester Palace. Other buildings continued in use, including the Cheapside bathhouse, the 'governor's palace' and two structures that may have been market halls at the Ticket Hall and Pudding Lane sites. The Huggin Hill bathhouse was at least partly demolished during the later second century but evidence of glassworking and metalworking may indicate the later industrial use of its ruins continued into the third century.[19] Building projects undertaken during the second half of the century included the construction of temple buildings to the south of Londinium and perhaps also to the west.

The forum and basilica

A large area of the urban centre was cleared for the construction of the new forum-basilica during the first thirty years of the second century.[20] The forum extended over an area five times larger than the earlier building at around 166 by 167 metres (see Fig. 7.2), the far more substantial building now required to reflect the growing status of Londinium.[21] The new forum was very carefully planned, with the main southern entrance positioned at the head of the north–south road as it ran up from the Thames bridge. The construction involved the dumping of enormous quantities of brickearth, gravel and building material used to raise the level of the building by a metre above ground level.[22] Set impressively above the surrounding settlement, the tall roof of the basilica would have been visible from the River Thames. This was the largest forum in Britannia and the basilica was the largest in the north-west provinces of the empire.[23] The apparently simple architectural form in comparison with other fora at particularly important cities in the Western Empire is presumably partly a consequence of the almost total destruction of the superstructure; it is possible that the building was far more elaborate than the surviving remains suggest.[24]

Excavations on the basilica that constituted the northern range of the forum at Leadenhall Court have suggested that this massive construction project took between twenty and thirty years to complete.[25] The work commenced with the construction of the basilica around

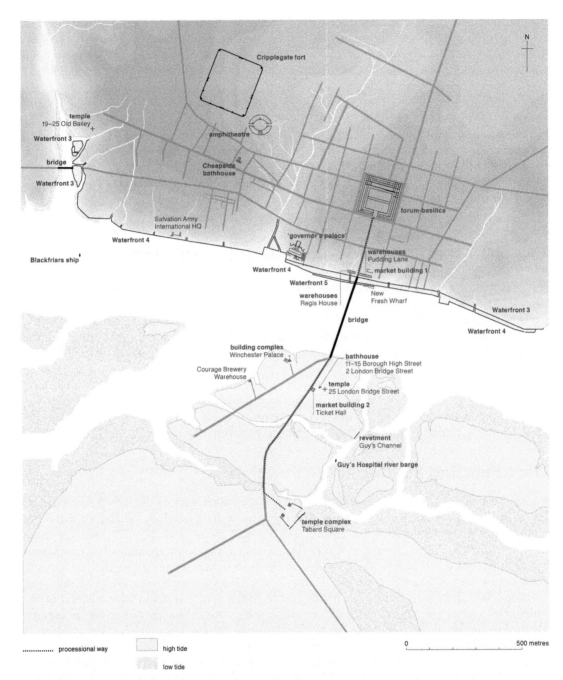

Cripplegate fort

temple
19–25 Old Bailey

Waterfront 3

bridge

Waterfront 3

amphitheatre

Cheapside
bathhouse

Salvation Army
International HQ

Waterfront 4

Blackfriars ship

'governor's palace'

forum-basilica

warehouaes
Pudding Lane

market building 1

Waterfront 4

Waterfront 5

New
Fresh Wharf

Waterfront 3

warehouses
Regis House

Waterfront 4

bridge

building complex
Winchester Palace

bathhouse
11–15 Borough High Street
2 London Bridge Street

Courage Brewery
Warehouse

temple
25 London Bridge Street

market building 2
Ticket Hall

revetment
Guy's Channel

Guy's Hospital river barge

temple complex
Tabard Square

N

.... processional way

high tide

low tide

0   500 metres

FIG. 7.1 Public buildings and infrastructure in AD 120–200.

N

Leadenhall Court

sunken pool
or colonaded
walkway

0   100 metres

FIG. 7.2 The second-century forum and basilica. Excavated features are shown in black.

AD 100–20, followed by the forum's west and east ranges from around AD 120–30.[26] The earlier forum may only have been demolished after the south range of the second forum was built, probably just after AD 130.[27] Around the same time that the ranges of the forum were completed, the basilica was altered with the addition of piers to form a grand colonnaded nave.

Fragmentary evidence has suggested that the internal walls of the basilica were plastered and in some places decorated plaster was found painted with designs such as scrollwork and a robed human figure.[28] The walls were built of grey ragstone with regular courses of tile, while several of the roof tiles were marked with procuratorial stamps.[29] The impressive space of the basilica's nave was flanked by aisles and the east end was built in the form of an apse, probably the most significant part of the building and the tribunal court for the magistrates of Londinium.[30] There may have been an apse at the west end of the nave, but this has not been demonstrated since its position is occupied by the church of St Michael's Cornhill.[31] The width of the nave walls and the presence of buttresses may indicate that the apex of its roof might have been around 25 metres high.[32]

The basilica and forum were arranged around a central courtyard. The west and east ranges initially each comprised two lines of shops or offices with a portico. The main entrance to the forum through the south range was presumably an arched opening. Painted wall plaster has been found in this range, indicating that at least parts of the internal walls of the forum were decorated.[33] Some piers in the south aisle were built upon the pier stumps of the first forum and supported a row of columns or perhaps monuments or statues along the side of the portico.[34] Comparatively little is known about the courtyard.[35]

The new forum appears not to have been constructed with a temple building,[36] although there were commonly altars inside these buildings and there was almost certainly a shrine in the basilica.[37] Statues of emperors and gods will have embellished the internal spaces and the bronze statue of Hadrian, the head of which was found in the Thames close to London Bridge on the Southwark side in 1834, may originally have stood on a pier or in a niche in the forum or the basilica.[38] This statue was hollow-cast and one and a quarter life-size. The head is well preserved, apart from a gash in the hair on the left side and a narrow crack down the left cheek. It had been roughly hacked from the body of the statue and presumably thrown into the river close to the Roman bridge.[39] Jocelyn Toynbee has suggested that the statue may have been set up to commemorate Hadrian's visit to Britain in AD 122 and that it was destroyed and thrown into the Thames by Saxon raiders.[40] Fragments of other bronze statues found in London include fingers and parts of arms that are second century or later in date.[41]

The construction work associated with this forum and basilica included the laying of new roads along its northern side.[42] The northern range of rooms of the basilica, possibly accessed from the street rather than from the courtyard, may have been commercial properties independent from the forum itself.[43] The road in front of these shops was laid out as part of this civic development and excavations have located parts of another building across the road to the north. Within decades of its completion, repairs and reconstructions were made to the basilica as a result of damage caused by subsidence.[44] During the middle of the century, there was a substantial fire within the basilica after which it was thoroughly rebuilt and refurbished, indicating the building's continued use throughout the second century.[45] Little evidence has been recovered from excavations of the maintenance of the three ranges of the forum.[46]

The masonry amphitheatre

The timber amphitheatre was robbed or dismantled around AD 120 and the site cleared.[47] The building was thoroughly reconstructed in stone and timber, probably around AD 125–30 (see Fig. 7.3).[48] The new amphitheatre was located very close to the south-east corner of the fort on Cripplegate, which was constructed around the same time, possibly indicating that these building works were connected. The absence of evidence for an earlier fort connected with the construction of the first phase of the amphitheatre in AD 70, however, undermines this idea.[49] Bateman has argued that the fort and new amphitheatre were constructed at this location because it was largely undeveloped during the late first century. Although it is likely that soldiers were engaged in the construction of the stone amphitheatre and doubtlessly attended events in the arena, the

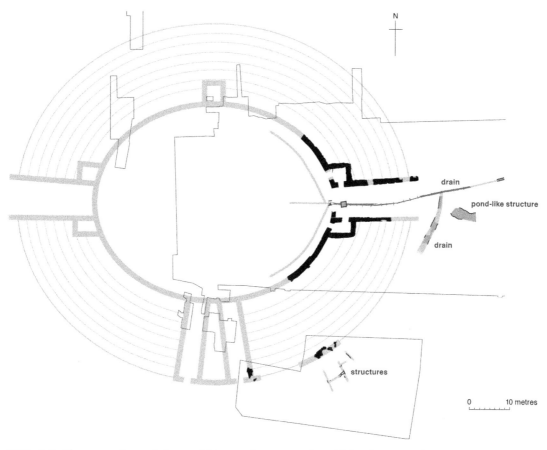

FIG. 7.3 The stone phase of the amphitheatre from around AD 125 to late second century.

military were not necessarily responsible for its planning and construction. It has been estimated that the fort's garrison consisted of around 1,000 men. They would have only partly filled the audience space at the amphitheatre, as the seating capacity was probably for between 7,000 and 10,500 people.[50]

This amphitheatre overlay the earlier timber structure on the same orientation, although it was constructed at a slightly larger scale.[51] The walls defining the arena were built in roughly dressed and squared masonry, overlain by a double brick course and coated with plaster painted with a decorative scheme in green and red on the side facing the open space of the arena. The east entrance had a small stone-built chamber to each side, probably waiting areas for humans or beasts before they entered the arena.[52] A timber-lined drain associated with a silt trap was built below the east entrance, directly above the buried remains of the earlier drain, and an additional perimeter drain was dug around the inside of the arena wall.[53] Limited excavations have located probable traces of an entrance through the south bank of the amphitheatre that may have had an imposing double-portal gateway constituting the main access for spectators. There may also have been an entrance through the north bank.[54] The truncated remains of what may have been the outer stone wall of the banking were located on the south-east but no traces were found at the east entrance.[55] Post pits found in the banking supported a timber seating superstructure.[56]

The east entrance was later modified and a larger-scale renovation of the amphitheatre was undertaken during the late second or early third centuries.[57] Outside the amphitheatre to the south-east, the fragmentary remains were found of small buildings or temporary structures that may have been associated with the provision of refreshments or the maintenance of security during performances in the arena.[58] Further to the south-east, a small building that may have been a Romano-Celtic shrine has been revealed at 54–66 Gresham Street,[59] indicating the sacred nature of the amphitheatre's environs.[60] Scenes of gladiatorial combat depicted on samian pottery vessels from London may indicate the popularity of the events that were staged in the arena, although gladiators may have been rare in Londinium.[61] A woman was buried at the cemetery at 165 Great Dover Street in Southwark with a lamp that was decorated with the popular gladiatorial theme.[62]

A fort on Cripplegate

A substantial stone-built fort was constructed in the north of Londinium around AD 120 (see Fig. 7.4).[63] This major archaeological discovery was made by W. F. Grimes between 1947 and 1968.[64] This fortified enclosure was constructed before the Roman wall and its northern and western defences were later incorporated into the urban circuit. Grimes excavated the west gate, sections of the north and west ramparts, the defensive ditch on the south and east sides, an intramural road on the south and west and parts of two barracks in the southern area of the fort.[65] Further excavation during 1965–6 uncovered parts of the eastern defences of the fort.[66] Excavation during the 1990s uncovered additional evidence for the internal buildings that resulted in a reassessment of the date of the fort's construction and the nature of its occupation.[67]

Evidence has been found for settlement and activities pre-dating the construction of the fort although there is no indication that this was of a military character.[68] It has been suggested that the fort could have been built following the 'Hadrianic fire' in around AD 125,[69] although there is little evidence for the burning of any buildings pre-dating its construction.[70] Samian ware found in the lowest levels of the sequence, including sherds from the fort rampart, may indicate a construction date soon after AD 120.[71] The datable materials from recent excavations may support the idea that the fort was constructed during the third decade of the second century.[72]

This defended enclosure was rectangular in plan and covered around 4.7 hectares, unusually large for an auxiliary fort, with overall dimensions of 220 by 215 metres.[73] This large fort with internal buildings may have accommodated a unit of at least 1,000 men. Although evidence for stables has yet to be found, cavalry and infantry soldiers may have been stationed here. The defences consisted of a narrow stone wall just over 1 metre wide backed by an earthen rampart and fronted by a ditch with a v-shaped section; on the eastern defences this ditch had been recut.[74] There was a curve in the southern section of this ditch where it formed the fort's south-eastern corner. It is possible that there was a second outer ditch, which has been located at the south-western corner of the fort,[75] although this outer ditch was not found during the excavation of the eastern defences.[76] The corners were reinforced with internal towers and two interval towers have been found along the internal line of the fort's wall (see Fig. 7.5).[77]

Part of the impressive west gate was excavated by Grimes and comprised a double portal flanked by towers.[78] The internal buildings are far better understood as a result of the excavations during the 1990s of parts of six barrack blocks, bringing the total to eight blocks that have been

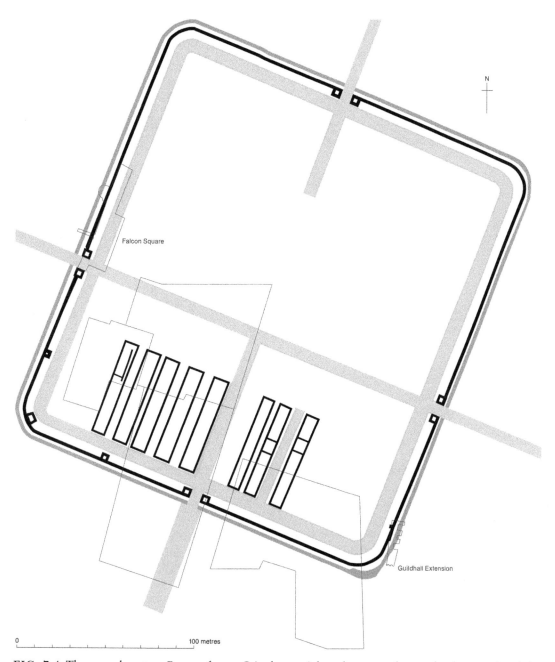

FIG. 7.4 The second-century Roman fort at Cripplegate. Selected excavated areas that have explored the fort are marked including Falcon Square.

FIG. 7.5 View of the south-west corner of Cripplegate fort, showing its wall and corner tower.

partly uncovered.[79] Two types of barrack buildings have been found, one comprising a single row of rooms fronted by a corridor and the other the more usual 'double-row' type.[80] These buildings had stone foundations and tile roofs and two were decorated with painted wall plaster.[81] Although Grimes excavated in the area thought to contain the central headquarters building nothing survived as the cellars of the bombed office buildings were too deep.[82]

All these features support the idea that this fort was broadly comparable to fortifications built throughout the military frontier regions of the Roman Empire. It may have been associated with a series of ditches defining a defensive circuit for Londinium, since evidence for a boundary ditch was located running from the fort's south-west corner toward the west and on the same alignment as the later Roman wall.[83] Interpreting the significance of the fort is difficult due to the lack of epigraphic evidence or documentary information for the military unit that was stationed there.[84] Very few Roman forts of early second-century date are known in the southern and eastern parts of Britannia, since by this time the army had mainly been redeployed to the military frontier regions of the province. Hassall has argued that the Cripplegate fort must have played a particularly important role in the life of Londinium, housing soldiers who served on the governor's staff and as his bodyguard.[85] The governor was the commander-in-chief of the legions and auxiliaries in the province and was accompanied by a guard of infantry and cavalry. Connecting this fort with the governor does not, however, explain why it was built at this particular time. Inscriptions found in London attest to the presence of military personnel although none of these are thought to date from the period of the occupation of the fort. The fortification was demolished after a few decades and was not replaced.

The fort may have been connected to the control of trade and transport with the continent. Londinium and Dubris (Dover) were the two major ports of Britannia during the early second century and were the sites of the only forts of this date known from the south-east. The transport of soldiers and military supplies across the English Channel was controlled by the *classis Britannica*, the Roman fleet that patrolled the seas around Britain. At Dubris two successive forts were constructed by the fleet during the first half of the second century.[86] Excavations of these forts produced large numbers of tiles stamped with CLBR, CL.BR or CLAS BR, referring to the *classis Britannica*.

Such tiles were previously thought to have been restricted to Roman ports on the south-east coast of Britannia and to ironworking sites in the Weald of Kent managed by the fleet, but a few examples have been found at several locations in Southwark.[87] These stamped tiles may originally have derived from a building that was connected with the fleet and were reused in later contexts.[88] A single example came from the site of the Cripplegate fort,[89] although this evidence is far too limited to indicate that the fleet was responsible for its construction. Gustav Milne has suggested, however, that the *classis Britannica* organized the building of the waterfront works in Londinium and Dubris during the later first to early third centuries.[90] The fort at Londinium was constructed with regard to the port facilities on the Thames in a similar location to the port at Dubris on the River Dour.[91]

A very substantial fort connected with the *classis Germanica* was constructed at Alteburg near Colonia Claudia Ara Agrippinensium (Cologne, Germany).[92] Established in the first half of the first century AD, this was abandoned in the late third century. It is likely that warships of the *classis Britannica* will have docked at Londinium's port. A miniature bronze prow of a warship found in the River Thames was inscribed 'AMMILLA AVG FELIX', naming the warship '*Ammilla*'.[93] An intaglio depicting a warship in a comparable style has been found on the Thames foreshore in Southwark, close to Winchester Palace.[94]

The *Castra Praetoria* in Rome constitutes another interesting potential analogy for London's Cripplegate fort.[95] Constructed under the emperor Tiberius at the north-eastern periphery of Rome, this fort housed the *praetorian* and urban cohorts that had previously been billeted at scattered locations across Rome and in surrounding towns. Three sides of the *Castra Praetoria* were incorporated into the Aurelian walls of Rome during the late third century.[96] The parallel of the *Castra Praetoria* might support the idea that the Cripplegate fort was constructed to form the base for the provincial governor's infantry and cavalry forces.[97]

Grimes' excavations have suggested that the Cripplegate fort might have been abandoned when the Roman wall was constructed towards the end of the century. By this time the north and west walls of the fort had been incorporated into the wall.[98] The v-shaped ditch on the south and east was also being infilled, although this does not necessarily indicate that the fort had been abandoned, since the construction of the wall might have removed the need for ditches to the east and south of the fort.[99] The south and east walls of the fort may have remained standing for some time.[100] The more recent excavations have provided some indications that the internal buildings may have been abandoned during the AD 160s, at the end of military occupation at this site.[101]

The waterfronts, trade and shipping

It is possible that, following the burning associated with the 'Hadrianic fire', there was a major rebuilding of the Thames-side wharf, although the information for this waterfront (Waterfront 3) has been derived from very limited excavations.[102] Trevor Brigham has identified

Waterfronts 3 to 5 at sites along the north bank that are though to define three distinct periods during the second century of coordinated construction of successive riverside wharves.[103] The regular rebuilding of the waterfront during the later first and second centuries is thought to have been associated with the requirement for deeper water to accommodate larger ships and the continuing significance of the port, although these timber wharves decayed swiftly and required constant maintenance.[104] The extension of the waterfront further out into the river may also have been a response to tidal regression and the dropping of the level of the river at high tide.[105]

Waterfront 3, which may have been partly constructed to fill a gap in Waterfront 2, extended further eastwards toward the bridge and beyond.[106] This structure is largely buried under the dual carriageway of Lower Thames Street and has only been explored in a few locations but evidence from Billingsgate Buildings and Suffolk House has suggested that it may have been built during the AD 120s.[107] At 12 Arthur Street, the new wharf was constructed around 13 metres south of Waterfront 2, although its structure lay outside the area of excavation.[108] At Pudding Lane this waterfront was constructed around 25 metres south of Waterfront 2, creating a larger space for wharfside buildings to be rebuilt or replaced.[109]

Two successive extensions to the wharfside were constructed during the second century, as the waterfront was built further out into the river.[110] At New Fresh Wharf (St Magnus House), upstream of the Roman bridge and to the south-east of Pudding Lane, a timber-piled embankment was built that may have formed part of Waterfront 4 and is thought to have been constructed towards the middle of the second century.[111] The substantial remains of this phase of the waterfront recorded at Swan Lane most probably dated from after AD 140.[112] At Riverbank House a section of a revetment probably associated with Waterfront 4 has been dated by pottery analysis to around AD 120–60.[113] A dockside building at this site was constructed during the mid-century.[114] Waterfront 5 comprised a post-and-plank revetment constructed 6–7 metres south of the earlier wharf, built towards the end of the century,[115] excavated at several locations including at New Fresh Wharf.[116] The dumped materials behind Waterfront 5 included a large deposit of samian pottery and four fragments of redeposited human bone.[117]

It has been suggested that the rebuilding and replacement of waterfront structures was conducted in a series of coordinated construction phases and that the maintenance of these wharves was controlled by a central authority, possibly the *classis Britannica*, throughout the second century. It is also possible, however, that the work was arranged by the urban council since the waterfront facilities were vital to the trade passing through the port. Goods continued to be loaded and unloaded on the north bank of the Thames throughout the century. The warehouses at Pudding Lane were rebuilt as storage buildings or shops after the 'Hadrianic fire', while to the south a warehouse was replaced.[118] At Regis House the wharfside warehouses were reconstructed and, although little evidence was found for their maintenance during the later second century, this may have been a result of the truncation of these deposits.[119] The maintenance of the lengthy waterfronts indicates that they were not only intended to serve the warehouses immediately to each side of the Thames bridge.

South of the Thames, the first-century waterfronts were extended by the establishment of timber revetments along the riverbank and its channels and material was dumped to raise the level of the ground.[120] The main riverfront of the Thames and also the channels dividing up the occupied areas were reinforced with post-and-wattle structures in an attempt to prevent erosion and flooding of the settlement in Southwark. During the early AD 160s a substantial timber revetment was built at Guy's Channel to define the riverbank. Lucy Wheeler has observed that the topography of the land and water across Southwark would have been 'radically altered' by the end of the second century.[121]

On the north island in Southwark, 200 metres south-west of Winchester Palace, evidence was found at Courage Brewery for a well-preserved timber warehouse situated just beside the river and close to an ironworking site.[122] This building, which has been dated by tree-ring analysis to the winter of AD 152–3, had timber flooring that had been laid below ground level and was particularly well preserved. It provided cool and damp storage, possibly for wines and food, and may have been used for only a short time.[123] The fragmentary remains of other buildings that may have been smaller warehouses have been found throughout Southwark.[124] Although these are not as well organized or substantial as the rows of warehouses to either side of the bridge on the north bank of the Thames, their presence indicates the importance of trade to people living south of the river. The finds made during excavations in Southwark included imported pottery and exotic foodstuffs such as dates and olives.

From around the middle of the century there was a reduction in the quantity of traded goods coming into Londinium through its port.[125] This may have been due to a decrease in the population and the greater number of ports that had been established in Britannia and there was a general decrease in cross-channel commerce at this time. The lower proportion of samian wares in pottery assemblages at particular sites across London presumably indicates the declining quantity of trade being brought through the port.[126] On the sites at and around 1 Poultry, for instance, there was a marked decline in the frequency of imported samian around AD 170–220, when it was becoming far more common to manufacture fine wares in Britain,[127] although imports did not cease. Samian has been found in later deposits across London and substantial quantities had been included in dumped deposits incorporated in the third-century waterfront facilities at New Fresh Wharf.[128] A large percentage of this samian had been fired in kilns in central Gaul and has been dated to around AD 170–80, although some later samian was also recovered.[129]

The samian from Pudding Pan in the Thames estuary, which may have been derived from several shipwrecks, indicates that this type of pottery continued to be imported to Londinium during the later second century.[130] Although the samian from New Fresh Wharf also indicates that samian continued to be imported on a large scale, it is uncertain why such a substantial quantity of unused pottery would have been kept for as long as forty or fifty years before being used as dumped material.[131] Trade through the port on the north bank of the Thames may have remained significant during the later second century and with the maintenance and improvement of the waterfront. Londinium continued to dominate trade networks in eastern Britain,[132] perhaps through a fleet of cargo vessels constructed and based at the waterfront.

A writing tablet found in the Walbrook area at Lothbury was inscribed with a probable description of the construction of ships.[133] The wrecks of two vessels dating from the later second century, from Guy's Hospital and Blackfriars, found in the sand and gravel of the Thames, show the types of vessels that were navigating the Thames and its tributaries. The vessel from Guy's Hospital, discovered in what was once a shallow creek in Southwark, probably worked along the Thames in the locality of Londinium. It was found in 1958, lying in the silted creek of Guy's Channel that ran along the south-east edges of the two main islands.[134] Much of the land to the west had been raised and drained for occupation by the time it was abandoned and an island of marginal and unoccupied ground formed the east side of the Channel. The northern part of the vessel was revealed in 1958 and a small portion of the middle, buried below the modern streets, was revealed during excavations in 2010 and 2011.[135] It was a broad barge-like vessel at least 16 metres long and it is likely that it was only used on the river since the freeboard, or height of the sides above the water line, was very low and was unsuitable for the open sea.[136] It may have been constructed around the middle of the second century and there was considerable evidence for repair. The vessel had been dumped in Guy's Channel towards the end of the century.[137] The Channel was still navigable for small boats during the late second century, but probably only at high tide.[138]

The Blackfriars ship, found at the edge of the Thames opposite Westminster, was a seagoing merchant vessel (see Figs 7.6 and 7.7). It was discovered in 1962 and excavated by Marsden in

FIG. 7.6 Peter Marsden of the Guildhall Museum (foreground) and volunteer Patrick Minns inspect the remains of Blackfriars ship I in 1963.

FIG. 7.7 The Blackfriars ship, docked at the warehouses built to the east of the Thames bridge. Later second century.

1963.[139] It is thought to have sunk in the Thames at some distance from the waterfront, probably during the later second century, while carrying a cargo of building stone that had been quarried near Maidstone in Kent.[140] It may have been constructed during the mid-century,[141] while some pottery associated with the wreck has indicated that the ship sank later that century.[142] A single unfinished millstone was also found in the bow of the ship, possibly from an earlier cargo, although why this was not removed is unclear.[143] This ship is similar in size to other examples of small seagoing vessels.[144] The planks had been infested by marine boring molluscs (ship worm), indicating that the vessel had spent long periods at sea. The flat bottom of the hull is common to a tradition of shipbuilding in the north-western parts of the Roman Empire.[145] It was built with a single mast and its shallow draft would have facilitated beaching on tidal shores for loading and unloading. The trees from which its timbers were cut had probably grown in south-east Britain. The ship may have had a maximum cargo capacity of around 50 tonnes.[146] A very worn coin of Domitian dating from around AD 88–9 was found in the step cut into a floor timber to house a mast, drawing upon a Mediterranean tradition of placing a coin in such contexts.[147] The reverse of the coin which faced upwards depicted Fortuna, goddess of luck, holding a ship's rudder.

High-status buildings on the north bank of the Thames

During the later second century a substantial building complex was constructed to the west of the Huggin Hill bathhouse.[148] These remains were recorded close to the Salvation Army site by archaeologists between the 1840s and 2003, although the interpretation of the results is limited by poor preservation and the small scale of the excavations.[149] Two main building phases have been distinguished, with Period I dating to the second century.[150] Timothy Bradley and Jonathan Butler have argued that the buildings across the large area around the Salvation Army site formed part of a single project.[151] The excavations undertaken in 2001–3 at 99–101 Queen Victoria Street have shown that the earliest building activity did not commence before AD 160s.[152] Culverts dug into the steep hill prior to any building works at this location indicate that this was a particularly difficult area to develop, which remained outside the boundaries of Londinium until the AD 160s.[153]

The remains of the Period I buildings recorded during the 1960s included the substantial stone foundations of two parallel walls, each with a corresponding kink in their alignment, a curving section of wall interpreted as an apse further to the east and a substantial wall higher up the river bank to the north.[154] The scale of these works and the character of their construction suggested that this was an important building complex, although it is not entirely clear that this site included a single complex of buildings. The later excavations have located a western apse, further evidence for the curved section of walling interpreted as the eastern apse, and other walls on different alignments to those recorded previously.[155] This excavation also revealed a timber pile beneath the stone foundation of the eastern 'apse' that provided a tree-ring date of around AD 165.[156] This demonstrates that at least one significant part of this substantial complex of buildings was constructed during the later second century and this is currently the earliest dating evidence for any of the buildings on this site. If there were earlier buildings at the Salvation Army site, their forms and functions have been completely obscured by later development. It has been suggested that some of the large quantities of building material reused in the Period I buildings may have been derived from the Huggin Hill bathhouse, which had become disused by the later second century.[157] Other building materials found during the excavations including some imported marble veneers probably derived from the superstructure of the Period I buildings themselves.[158]

The excavations at 99–101 Queen Victoria Street produced evidence for the substantial modification of these Period I buildings during the subsequent century, including the building of the western apse during the mid-third century.[159] The complexity of this information may suggest that the Period I building works were constructed in at least two distinct phases on different alignments, both post-dating AD 165.[160] The eastern part of the building complex was probably built earlier than the west. The sculptures that were found at the nearby site of Baynard's Castle may have been taken from temples and monuments in the western area at the Salvation Army site.[161] A large quantity of masonry, including the remains of at least two monumental structures and other sculptures, derived from one or more temples dating from the later second or, more probably, the third or fourth centuries.[162] There is no direct evidence, however, to indicate that these temples had been located at the Salvation Army site.[163]

Bradley and Butler have observed that this building complex in its latest phases had east and west apses facing the river in a manner similar to the *praetorium* (governor's palace) at

Colonia Claudia Ara Agrippinensium (Cologne, Germany).[164] The scale of the foundations and polished marble veneers may indicate that it was a palace connected with the governor or the procurator, although it may also have been an opulent private house. The complexity of the surviving information across this site indicates that a large-scale excavation would be required to obtain a more complete picture of the character of these buildings and their sequence of construction.

A monumental building at Winchester Palace

This high-status building was constructed on the north island in Southwark during the AD 120s (see Fig. 7.8).[165] Traces of three distinct 'buildings' have been revealed forming part of a single complex, perhaps located around a courtyard facing north across the Thames towards the 'governor's palace' on the north bank. The lavish and impressive series of structures has been interpreted by Brian Yule as a 'large, perhaps even palatial, building complex' built by the authority of the provincial government.[166] The fragments of two different inscriptions

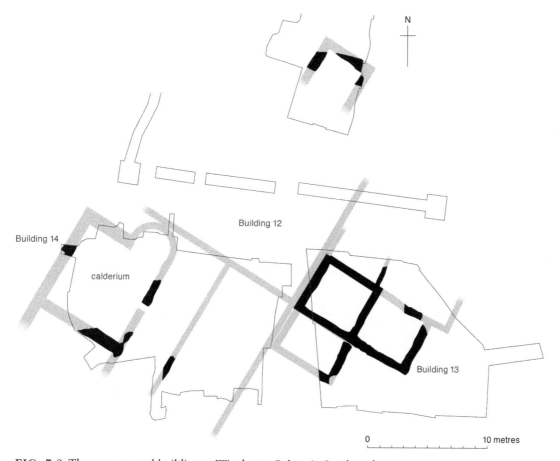

FIG. 7.8 The monumental building at Winchester Palace in Southwark.

recording lists of Roman soldiers supports the idea that the buildings were constructed by or for the provincial administration (see Fig. 7.9). These buildings may have been a palace, a substantial suite of bath buildings and an administrative complex for military and administrative personnel.

The excavated parts included the corner of what was interpreted as the main block of a substantial house,[167] a suite of heated rooms with hypocausts and very high quality internal

FIG. 7.9 The marble inscription recovered from the excavations at Winchester Palace in Southwark in 1983. Probably carved in the late second century, it lists individuals by their cohort, perhaps specialist military men.

decorations that may have been the reception rooms of the north-west range,[168] and part of a large and opulent self-contained bathhouse that contained a *caldarium* with a hypocaust and a heated plunge bath.[169] The building complex was developed in scale and complexity during the second century, since the bathhouse was constructed after around AD 150 and may even have dated from the third century.[170] The substantial character of all these elements indicate that this was an ambitious project that had a high status over a long period of time, especially considering the opulent decoration and fittings of the second-century phases.[171]

The excavation of the reception rooms produced a substantial quantity of painted plaster that had decorated the walls of one of the rooms.[172] A substantial section of plaster from the earliest phase of decoration had fallen face down onto the remains of the hypocaust, possibly from a barrel-vaulted ceiling.[173] The painting depicted an elaborate architectural composition with a cupid holding a plate, described by S. A. Mackenna and Roger Ling as of 'exceptional delicacy and sumptuousness'.[174] A wide variety of colours had been used, including red cinnabar and gold leaf. The closest parallels for this work are from Italy, including from contexts in Rome and Ostia dating from the AD 120s.[175] This painting was later covered over with another scheme that has been dated on art historical grounds to the third century.[176] Although the layout and extent of the bathhouse is unknown,[177] the *caldarium* was similar in size to those at Cheapside and Shadwell and smaller than that at Huggin Hill.[178] Yule has argued that this indicates that the Winchester Palace bathhouse was more than a private structure associated with a high-status residence.[179] Constructed during the late second or early third century, the demolition deposits of this building contained painted wall plaster in several colours and fragments of marble veneer imported from several sources in the eastern Mediterranean, indicating lavish internal decoration.[180]

In the backfill deposits of the *caldarium* stoking pit were found the fragmentary remains of two marble inscriptions.[181] The more complete example on two panels was probably a list of personnel drawn from at least four cohorts of a legion; parts of the names of twenty-three individuals have survived.[182] Although it has been supposed that these inscriptions date to the third century,[183] a more recent detailed study has argued that they date to the later part of the second century.[184] These records help to date the construction of the bathhouse and may indicate that a legionary detachment was brought to Londinium to construct the building.[185]

Two other fragments of inscriptions found close to this site have been used to support an alternative idea that the buildings at Winchester Palace constituted the base for a group of clerical and administrative staff connected with the governor.[186] It is possible, however, that the whole complex was an elaborate civic bathhouse, although it is unclear why the military should have been involved in its construction. Overall, the evidence for the connection of the military with these buildings is very strong and the discovery of inscriptions suggests an official role. There may have been several centres of military activity in Londinium during the second century, since the initial phases of the Winchester Palace complex and the construction of the Cripplegate fort date from around the same time, although the inscriptions might date to just after the abandonment of the fortification.

Temples at the margins

Two temple complexes were constructed on the south bank of the Thames and on the east bank of the Fleet. South of the Thames a cluster of domestic buildings of early second-century date at Tabard Square fell out of use and were cleared during the creation of a religious precinct around

AD 120–60 (see Fig. 7.10).[187] A timber-lined ditch, which may originally have been dug along the line of a watercourse, formed the south-east section of a temenos boundary around the temple.[188] The fill of the ditch contained artefacts such as complete pottery vessels, brooches, leather shoes, seal boxes and coins that dated at least one phase of the ditch to around AD 140–60.[189] One find was a sealed canister containing a fatty substance that has been interpreted as a preparation to be applied to the face or body.[190] This ditch remained as a boundary and focus for occasional acts of the deposition of various materials until the fourth century.[191] Two other ditches were observed during the excavation that may have defined a religious complex to the north-west.[192]

Two temples were built between AD 160 and 200 within the area already defined by the temenos (see Fig. 7.11).[193] Traces of two robbed-out features between the temple buildings may have been the bases for columns.[194] A bronze left foot shod with a sandal, found in a fourth-century context, may have derived from an over-life-sized bronze statue that stood within the temple enclosure.[195] A stone cloven hoof from the site may have formed part of a sculpture of the god Pan.[196] A helmet plume from a copper-alloy figure of Minerva found at Silvester Buildings just west of Tabard Square may also have derived from the temple.[197]

An almost complete marble inscription was carefully placed in a fourth-century pit, with the text facing upward and covered with a tile (see Fig. 7.12).[198] This inscription may originally have been placed as a dedication in the northern temple building and was carefully buried after the temple was dismantled.[199] The Latin inscription translated as 'To the divinities of the emperors

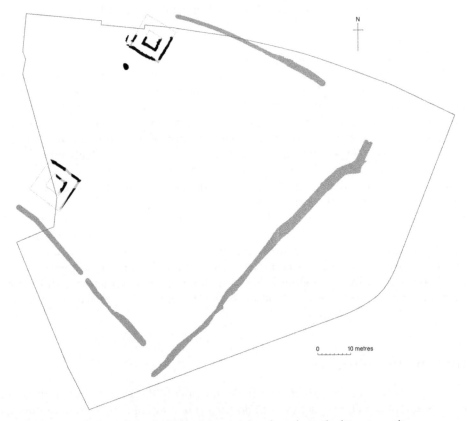

FIG. 7.10 The temple site at Tabard Square, Southwark, in the later second century.

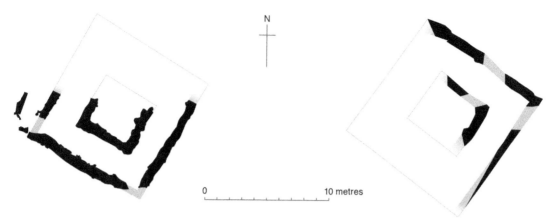

FIG. 7.11 Details of the temple buildings at Tabard Square.

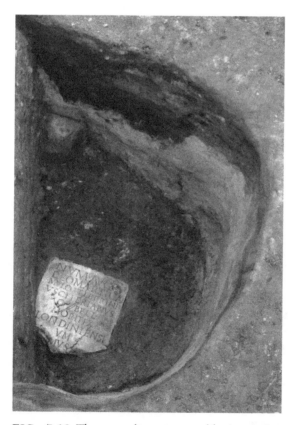

FIG. 7.12 The second-century marble inscription found placed within a fourth-century pit inside the temple precinct at Tabard Square.

and to the god Mars Camulus. Tiberinius Celerianus, a citizen of the Bellovaci, *moritix*, of Londoners the first . . .'.[200] The text, which had been cut with characters that still retained red pigment, had been broken off at the base of the inscription. The term *moritix* may indicate that Celerianus was a trader or the leader of a guild or municipal organization, although the exact meaning is uncertain.[201] The inscription records that the dedication was made to the 'divinities of the emperors' and to the god Mars Camulus. The reference to the divinity of the emperors together with the style of the lettering indicates that the dedication was carved when there were joint rulers of the empire (AD 161–9 or AD 177–80).[202] Mars Camulus was a war god recorded from inscriptions in Gallia Belgica (northern Gaul) and in one case from Britannia. This god was particularly popular in the *civitas* of the Remi, who were the neighbours of the Bellovaci in Gallia Belgica.[203] The term 'Londiniensis' indicates that Celerianus, although a citizen of a Gallic *civitas*, regarded himself as a Londoner. Another very fragmentary inscription carved on marble was found about 2 metres from the dedication slab during the Tabard Square excavations that dated from the later second century and may have constituted an 'official' imperial dedication made by a guild of worshippers or a dedication made to an emperor.[204] It has been suggested that the foundation of this temple was a decision taken at the highest level of authority in Londinium.[205]

The foundations of the two temple buildings were too fragmentary and poorly preserved to indicate in which direction the entrances faced, but if this had been toward the south-east, as is usually the case with temples, they would have looked towards the temenos ditch and along the south bank of the Thames.[206] The waterside revetments alongside Guy's Channel would have made the temple easily accessible from the river and the location of the Guy's Hospital boat in this waterway suggests that it remained navigable during the third century. Alternatively, the temples may have faced north-west towards the river crossing from the south island to the south bank of the Thames and toward the stone statue or memorial referred to above.[207] The addition of several plinths during the third century just to the north-west of the temples may indicate that this was a meeting place. The temples may, therefore, have been orientated towards the crossing of the main north–south road over the Borough Channel, suggesting that this religious complex was the destination of a processional way that began at the forum and led over the bridge over the Thames, and over the two main islands.

Excavations at 25 London Bridge Street have revealed evidence for a Romano-Celtic temple that may have been deliberately built close to this processional way.[208] A column base had been inscribed with a dedication to the god Silvanus made by two probable freedmen of Publius Fabius. This base may have supported a statue of Silvanus, a woodland god associated with hunting.[209] It is possible that the hunter god and some of the other sculptures from the well at Southwark Cathedral originally stood in and around this temple. A high-status masonry building was partly uncovered at 11–15 Borough High Street / 2 London Bridge Street, probably constructed during the early second century.[210] The presence of a circular room may suggest that this was a bathhouse, possibly associated with the temple. Alterations during the second century indicate that the building remained in use, although evidence for later activity was more limited.

This linking of sacred places may have continued 40 kilometres further eastward from Southwark along the line of Watling Street.[211] At Greenwich Park, about 8 kilometres from Southwark, a temple has been found on a hilltop that may have been in use from the first to fourth centuries.[212] Significant finds from this partly-excavated site include a free-standing statue of Diana Venatrix and part of a marble inscription that may have dedicated the site to the divinity of the emperor.[213] Thirty kilometres further to the east there was a Roman temple complex at Vagniacis (Springhead, Kent) where a cluster of religious buildings and burial areas was located at the head of the River Medway, 30 kilometres to the south-east of Londinium.[214]

The fragmentary remains of another building that has been tentatively identified as a temple was found during the 1980s on the east bank of the Fleet river, just south of Watling Street and close to Newgate at 18–25 Old Bailey.[215] With an octagonal plan around 16 metres across, this building was constructed on substantial terracing that had previously been used for glassworking. Ian Haynes has suggested it may have been built soon after AD 200,[216] although Perring has suggested around AD 170.[217] Although little of the wall fabric survived, the plan could be distinguished from the trenches that had been dug to rob the stone. If the identification of this building as a 'Romano-Celtic' temple is correct, it is a particularly large example.[218] The octagonal *cella* may have been surrounded by an ambulatory. Finds associated with the structure suggest that it was constructed in stone, had a tiled roof and internal wall plaster painted in red, white and green. Traces of an ancillary building were found and a pit, adjacent to the outer wall-line of the 'temple', contained human cranial remains which may have formed a foundation deposit. If this building was a temple it may have been associated with the hunter god attested in Londinium and also in the Cotswolds and may have survived until the late third century when it was replaced by another substantial structure.[219]

Occupation

The disruption caused by the 'fire events' of the AD 120s and 130s was followed by the large-scale rebuilding of houses and industrial properties across many areas of Londinium. Dominic Perring has suggested that London was quickly rebuilt during the AD 120s, but then contracted during the period from around AD 160.[220] He has argued that this may have been the result of the 'Antonine Plague' that affected the empire during the AD 160s.[221] This epidemic broke out on several occasions between AD 165 and 189 and spread throughout the entire empire.[222] Perring has argued that the abandonment of certain public buildings and the contraction of evidence for housing across Londinium mainly occurred during the period AD 160–80 and that the construction of new temples around this time was a reaction to the plague to seek the favour of the gods.[223] Londinium might have been deeply affected by the epidemic, although there is currently only one piece of direct evidence. Found in 1989 at Vintry, close to where the Walbrook meets the Thames, a pewter amulet has been inscribed with a charm against the plague in thirty lines of Greek.[224] Tomlin has argued that this was based on the metrical charm circulated by Alexander of Abonuteichos on the Black Sea, which would date the London amulet to around the late AD 160s.[225]

Not all archaeologists agree that there was a decline in population at this time, and Londinium remained a significant urban centre throughout the century.[226] Complex calculations have been used to suggest that the population may actually have increased from a figure of around 26,000 people in AD 100–20 to 30,500 in AD 200.[227] These calculations are acknowledged to be unreliable, however, since the latter figure is based on the extent of the newly erected walled circuit in around AD 200 which may have included some unoccupied areas.

Figure 7.13 shows excavated sites that were continuously occupied during the second century and also those that the excavators have suggested may have been either partially or entirely abandoned by around AD 150–200. This apparently supports Perring's argument that Londinium was partly depopulated, although this information may overemphasize the extent to which the population had declined. This may be due to the small scale of many excavated areas, the regular truncation of late Roman layers by subsequent activity, the expectations of archaeologists that late Roman buildings were built in stone and the possibility that the building techniques for timber-and-earth buildings may have changed during the second century. Londinium remained

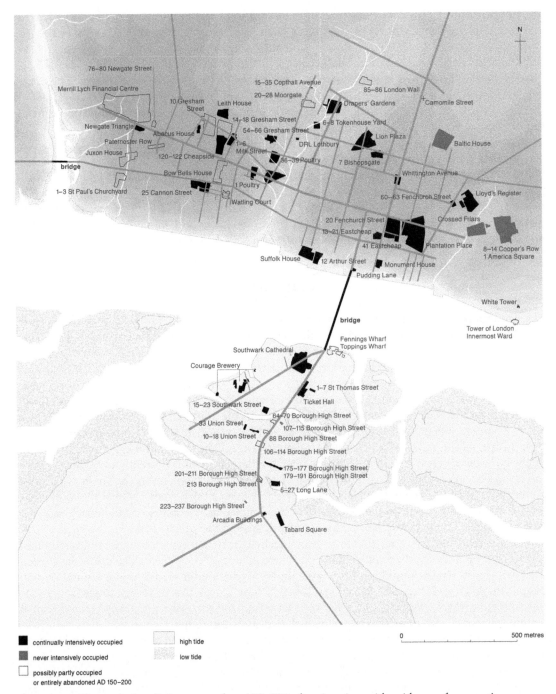

FIG. 7.13 Houses in Londinium around AD 120–200, showing sites with evidence of occupation.

populous and thriving throughout the second century, although the population was likely to have been affected by events such as epidemics.

Arguments for and against depopulation

Dominic Perring and Steve Roskams published a book in 1991 that contained the results of excavations at sites west of the Walbrook Valley.[228] They have argued that Londinium developed rapidly during the later first and early second centuries but that the population declined after the middle of the second century.[229] On several archaeological sites the buildings that replaced structures burned in the AD 120s appeared to form the final phases of Roman construction. Perring has concluded from this that substantial areas of early Londinium were resettled after the extensive burning event of the AD 120s and that London had reached its maximum extent by around AD 150, although it was 'in contraction' from around the middle of the century.[230]

Perring's own excavations at Watling Court have uncovered some fragmentary evidence that new structures replaced the impressive earlier houses that had stood there prior to the 'Hadrianic fire'.[231] The evidence for activity at the site after AD 160 was more limited and the excavation report noted that deposits of this date only survived later truncation in limited parts of the site.[232] At 76–80 Newgate Street, the strip-buildings were rebuilt after the fire and, as the evidence was less complex and more fragmentary than for the preceding period, the excavator has suggested that occupation there was comparatively brief.[233] Some pits and stake holes were later cut into these deposits but there was little to indicate that buildings were constructed after the mid to late second century.[234] The 1–6 Milk Street excavation has produced significant evidence for reoccupation, indicated by building phases dating from just after around AD 120.[235] A narrow timber strip-building fronted onto a street and had a mosaic floor depicting a cantharus, or large two-handled drinking cup.[236] This building was dated to around AD 120–60 and there was little evidence for later buildings.[237]

Doubts were immediately expressed concerning Perring and Roskams' idea for a later second-century urban decline. Yule has argued that later Roman deposits on sites across London have often been truncated by later activities, seriously undermining evidence for building and occupation after the mid-second century.[238] The heavy truncation of deposits post-dating AD 120 that was noted by Perring at Watling Court is common on sites apparently abandoned after the mid-second century. Yule has also suggested that the deposits of 'dark earth', layers of dark-coloured loam, that occur widely in late Roman contexts across London might indicate that later activities such as ploughing had eroded deposits post-dating AD 160.[239] The 'dark earth' located during the excavations of many sites on both sides of the River Thames often seems to mark the end of the Roman layers of stratigraphy. Comparable dark deposits have been found overlying Roman levels in other towns across Britain and on the continent and it has been suggested that 'dark earth' deposits have been recorded on sites where there has been later building and occupation.[240] Such deposits are often thought to have been formed from the reworking of the remains of timber-and-earth buildings and occupation deposits and may have resulted from activities such as cultivation that truncated earlier deposits. It has been recognized that the formation of 'dark earth' may have had multiple causes and that each site must be assessed in detail regarding the character of the latest phases of occupation and also how and when such material was developed.[241] Clearly these deposits are not all related to the abandonment of occupation sites. Robin Symonds and Roberta Tomber have observed that knowledge of the late Roman pottery sequence for London is hindered by a lack of well-stratified sequences and contexts, partly as a result of the truncation of later Roman deposits after around

AD 140.[242] The degree to which distinct ceramic assemblages can be defined has been carefully explored in surviving later Roman contexts.

More recent excavations have revealed evidence to indicate that Londinium continued to be intensively occupied after AD 160. Meticulous attention has been paid to establishing the extent to which later Roman deposits may have been truncated and eroded and also to the formation of 'dark earth'. The excavations at and around 1 Poultry undertaken during the late 1980s and 1990s are of central importance. At these sites, some of the individual properties may have been abandoned, although many houses were rebuilt or replaced from the later second to early fourth centuries.[243]

The types of buildings that archaeologists might expect to find in contexts dating to after the mid-second century are important in assessing the later Roman occupation. It has often been thought that during the third century domestic architecture came to be characterized by larger stone-built houses often with mosaic floors and that the less durable timber-and-earth buildings that were typical of earlier periods were less common.[244] Richard Bluer and Trevor Brigham have remarked, however, that the 'simplistic description of an early Roman timber townscape and a later Roman stone one' requires revision.[245] Masonry houses began to be constructed during the late first and second centuries. There is also increasing evidence for the building of timber-and-earth houses during the second and third centuries, for instance at Lloyd's Register and 1 Poultry.[246] Such buildings continued to be constructed throughout the Roman period in the upper Walbrook Valley and in Southwark. Since timber-and-earth buildings usually leave less substantial archaeological evidence than stone buildings, their remains have probably been preferentially removed by later activities such as cultivation and levelling, which has led to an overestimate to the degree to which stone houses typified late Roman Londinium.

Despite these doubts, Perring has recently argued that the information for the abandonment of sites across western and southern London during the later second century cannot be explained only by the truncation of deposits.[247] The site at 76–80 Newgate Street, for example, was overlain by 'dark earth', but building operations here prior to the mid-second century had involved the uncovering and the reuse of upstanding clay walls.[248] No such evidence for reuse was found following the last of the recorded building phases which dated to the mid-second century. Perring has added the important point that, if occupation had continued at 76–80 Newgate Street, any deep features comparable to those found in the earlier sequence on this site – such as deeper foundations, drainage channels, sumps and timber piles – would have cut into previous deposits and would then have been located during excavation. A few pits were excavated with finds dating from the late second and third centuries at this site,[249] although there was no evidence for the construction, occupation or demolition of buildings. Perring has restated that the absence of such features indicates that this site ceased to be occupied during the second century.

The character of the timber-and-earth buildings built throughout Londinium may, however, have been changing at this time. Mike Fulford has observed that timber buildings dating from the second century and later were very hard to detect during the careful and extensive excavations undertaken at Insula IX in Calleva (Silchester).[250] The results from Calleva may suggest that the late Roman finds (including pottery, coins and small finds) from sites in London with no conclusive evidence for building might have derived from timber buildings that have subsequently been truncated. Most sites in Londinium have been excavated in limited areas and the surviving remains have often been substantially disturbed by the digging of later foundations and cellars.[251] The changes in the construction of timber-and-earth buildings recorded at Calleva may explain the apparent evidence for the abandonment of sites in Londinium.

At sites where occupation continued beyond the middle of the second century, timber buildings may have been constructed in ways that left little structural evidence and this evidence may have been removed by activities that resulted in the formation of 'dark earth'. Deeper features penetrating through earlier deposits, such as wells and pits, may provide important evidence for buildings that have later been removed.[252] Many of the sites across Londinium that Perring suggests were abandoned, including 76–80 Newgate Street, have produced evidence for pits, wells and ditches containing late Roman finds. Wells, pits, foundations and robbed-out trenches containing finds from the later second to fourth centuries warrant particular attention.

Each site requires to be studied individually to build up a more complete picture of the density of occupation across the entire urban area. The available information that is summarized below may suggest a reduction in the density of buildings across Londinium, although many areas continued to be intensely occupied and Londinium probably remained economically buoyant.

West of the Walbrook

The evidence from Watling Court, 76–80 Newgate Street and 1–6 Milk Street may indicate that occupation across the area west of the Walbrook reduced during the second century. Subsequent excavations have provided a fuller picture of where people were living and working to the west of the Walbrook. The western part of Londinium may never have been very intensively settled away from the main road frontages and the decline in occupation density may be an indication of the relative marginality of much of this landscape during the first and early second centuries. This area did not become deserted after AD 160, but houses were built in particular areas within what appears to have been a sparsely settled urban landscape with many open areas, perhaps gardens and agricultural land. It is also probable that truncation of later Roman layers has removed the remains of insubstantial timber houses from excavated sites.

At Bow Bells House there seems to have been a reduction in the density of occupation at an early date.[253] The site was densely built up with housing before AD 100 and the remains of these buildings were covered by a considerable amount of dumped material that appeared to date to around AD 125. Traces of three later buildings were recovered just south of the main east–west road and a stone building was constructed alongside a road further south, although there appears to have been a considerable reduction in the density of building. One of the buildings on the main road was maintained and occupied after AD 160 and possibly until AD 250.[254] This poorly-preserved building was represented by two or three areas of brickearth floor, a beam slot and a single posthole, indicating a comparable situation to the later Roman timber buildings at Calleva.

Further to the west around Paternoster Square, the domestic buildings destroyed by the fire were quickly replaced.[255] Although the buildings with domestic and industrial uses were mainly constructed from timber and earth, limited evidence was found at Juxton House for a substantial house with stone walls ('Building 28').[256] At Newgate Triangle, immediately south of the main east–west road, buildings and evidence of brassmaking associated with two kilns were found.[257] Many of the houses at the five Paternoster Square sites, however, became disused after the middle of the second century,[258] although a poorly-preserved building at Newgate Triangle continued to be occupied.[259] The brickearth floor of this building had been repaired and associated finds dated to the later second or third centuries. The area to the south at Paternoster Square was probably largely abandoned during the later second century and may have been turned over to agriculture.[260] The truncation of the deposits on these sites may, however, have destroyed ephemeral evidence for later buildings.[261] Mosaics were discovered to the south-east of Paternoster Square in 1839–41, 1841 and 1843 that dated from the middle of the second century or later, indicating several substantial late Roman houses in this area.[262] At 1–3 St Paul's Churchyard, excavations indicated that one of two earlier timber-and-earth buildings was reconstructed during the mid-second century but that the other was abandoned and covered by dumped material dating to the third century.[263]

Just north of the main east–west road at the Merrill Lynch Financial Centre, earlier buildings had been destroyed in the fire, but traces of three later buildings were located.[264] Jo Lyon has argued that this area became marginal to the settlement during the later second century and buildings had become disused or had been demolished and cleared in preparation for the construction of the Roman wall.[265] Pits and gullies containing later finds were excavated, but Lyon has argued that it is unlikely that this indicates the presence of later buildings.[266] At a site close to Newgate, which lay within the area of the Merrill Lynch Financial Centre site, the Roman wall was cut through a tiled surface that may have been the floor of an earlier building.[267] The first-century buildings on the north-west periphery of Londinium at St Bartholomew's Hospital had been abandoned by this time and the area became a burial ground during the third century, by which time it lay outside the wall.[268]

At 120–2 Cheapside and 14–18 Gresham Street substantial dumping of waste and rubbish during the second century, including large quantities of building material, filled up earlier features.[269] Apart from some drainage operations, the northern part of the site was largely abandoned, although activities continued south of the site by the main east–west road.[270] These buildings had either been insubstantially constructed or heavily truncated, since only limited traces were found and the quantity of associated pottery was far smaller than for earlier periods.[271] It was unclear to what extent this site continued to be occupied after the middle of the second century, although the truncation of deposits may have removed evidence for later buildings.[272]

The date of the abandonment and destruction of the fort at Cripplegate is unclear but, although several later buildings were constructed on this site, it never appears to have been intensely resettled.[273] It is possible that a cleared area was established immediately south of the fort,[274] although a stone house was built during the late second or early third century at Leith House.[275] Just over 100 metres to the south-south-east of the fort, alongside a road from the south gate, the area of housing at 10 Gresham Street was thoroughly rebuilt and continued to be occupied during the AD 130s and 140s.[276] Traces of around sixteen strip-buildings were revealed and a more substantial and ornate stone-built house was constructed with a reception room with a geometric mosaic floor and a central courtyard.[277] The mosaic had been damaged by later activity but its regular pattern could be fully reconstructed.[278] The detailed discussion of the dating evidence for this substantial house has suggested that it may have been constructed around AD 130. It was destroyed by fire, indicating that the 'Hadrianic fire' or fires may have occurred here at a later date than elsewhere in Londinium.[279] By AD 160 the houses at 10 Gresham Street had been abandoned and the only evidence for later occupation comprised two stone buildings to the north, showing that there was a considerable reduction in the density of building in this area.[280]

Slightly further to the west, at Abacus House, another house was floored with a mosaic of a simple design which Neal and Cosh have suggested may have been the work of a 'jobbing builder'.[281] This building also appears to have been destroyed in a fire and to have been replaced by a third-century building.[282] To the east and south-east of the amphitheatre there is little to indicate that houses were rebuilt after around AD 120, although there was possibly a temple or shrine at 54–66 Gresham Street.[283] This area immediately outside two of the entrances to the amphitheatre may have been used for the marshalling and control of the visiting crowds.[284]

Convincing evidence for continuing intensive occupation to the west of the Walbrook has, however, been found at several sites. At 25 Cannon Street, houses were built and occupied throughout the second and third centuries.[285] The evidence for the period from the AD 120s to the 250s suggests that this site was densely built up with occupation that probably continued into the fourth century.[286] The substantial stone-built houses with utilitarian mosaic floors may indicate that their inhabitants were of moderate status.[287]

The excavators at 1 Poultry have distinguished two succeeding periods, AD 125–70 and AD 170–220.[288] In the earlier period, many of the pre-existing properties were rebuilt and intensively used.[289] Other properties may have been abandoned, although this was not always clear since the later Roman deposits were often truncated by later activity.[290] During the later period many of these properties clearly continued in use with some rebuilding.[291] Hill and Rowsome have suggested that there might have been a reduction in the density of buildings in the areas set back from the road frontages at 1 Poultry, but also that the number of properties along the road frontages did not reduce. The boundaries between properties remained stable from the first to mid- to late-third centuries, suggesting a considerable degree of continuity in the occupation of the site.[292]

Timber buildings continued to be constructed throughout the second and early third centuries on some plots along the main east–west road at 1 Poultry.[293] Occupation also continued throughout this century and beyond at 36–9 Poultry.[294] Some stone-built houses constructed in the later second century were large and imposing buildings, representing an apparent trend across Londinium at this time.[295] The clearest evidence for such buildings in the middle Walbrook Valley has been derived from DLR Lothbury (Site B), dating from around AD 140–80.[296] The ground at this location was terraced and a stone building constructed which covered a substantial area and may, from the size of the foundations, have been several storeys high. It has been suggested that the excavated part of this building formed the north wing of a courtyard house and evidence was found for an underfloor heating system associated with tessellated or mosaic floors and painted wall plaster.[297] Just to the north, a comparable building that had been uncovered in earlier excavations was associated with a hypocaust and a mosaic floor which probably dated from the mid-second century.[298]

Overall, the information from west of the Walbrook indicates that some areas continued to be intensively occupied, while elsewhere people lived in scattered houses. At 1 Poultry and 25 Cannon Street there was no marked reduction in occupation and, although certain areas may have become largely abandoned after around AD 160, the regular occurrence of pits and wells with finds dating to the late second to fourth centuries suggests that people were living on many sites that were previously interpreted as having been deserted. The ephemeral remains of buildings from Bow Bells House and Newgate Triangle may help to demonstrate that later Roman timber-and-earth buildings were often far less substantially constructed than earlier examples and that their traces have often been removed by later activities. It is impossible at the current time to estimate the degree to which the population of this part of Londinium might have reduced during the late second century. Although an extensive area was incorporated into the walled circuit, there were probably many open areas within Roman London and the land west of the Walbrook may have included gardens and open land, even during the late first and early second centuries.

The Walbrook Valley

To the north-east of the amphitheatre, the Walbrook Valley had been drained and partially settled during the late first and early second centuries, with some buildings being abandoned during the later second century. At 20–8 Moorgate, for example, the pottery production site ceased production around AD 160 and the glassworking industry in the Moorgate House area may also have come to an end around this time (see below). At 85–6 London Wall the excavations revealed the timber foundations of buildings that pre-dated the building of the Roman defences.[299] Evidence from other sites has indicated that occupation continued in the upper Walbrook Valley. At 6–8 Tokenhouse Yard a structure that might have been an animal house or byre was built on reclaimed and drained land.[300] Although flooding continued to occur during this century, some pits have been excavated that indicated late second-century occupation.[301] At Drapers' Gardens, excavations have produced convincing evidence for intensive occupation involving timber buildings associated with a road, activity that continued throughout the second century and into the fourth.[302] There was also occupation and activity at 15–35 Copthall Avenue. It has been suggested that industrial activities in the middle Walbrook Valley around Bucklersbury House may have been reduced in scale or had ceased at this time.[303] While some properties appear to have been abandoned across the Walbrook Valley, people were certainly continuing to live and work in this area of Londinium during this period.

East of the Walbrook

To the north of the forum, several small excavations of sites have provided information for intensive occupation throughout the second century. At 7 Bishopsgate, a substantial timber-and-earth building that may have had a courtyard to the north was constructed after around AD 140.[304] At Lion Plaza the earlier timber-and-earth buildings were cleared sometime after AD 120 and new stone houses with mosaic floors and painted plaster were constructed.[305] At Whittington Avenue two substantial buildings were built to replace the earlier houses during the mid-second century.[306] The northern building had ragstone foundations while the southern was of timber-and-earth construction and was installed with tessellated floors, hot air flues and painted plaster. These buildings appear to have fallen out of use by the third century.[307]

At 20 Fenchurch Street, just south-east of the forum, there seems to have been a reduction in occupation during the second century,[308] although the poor preservation of the buildings has limited the degree to which this evidence may be considered conclusive. Robin Wroe-Brown has suggested that the transition to the building of stone houses at this time reduced the need to reconstruct existing properties.[309] A large part of this site remained open and undeveloped, although the area was certainly not abandoned during the century. At Plantation Place a large stone building ('Building 31') was constructed after around AD 150 (see Fig. 7.14).[310] This was heavily disturbed by later activity but was clearly occupied during the late Roman times. It seems initially to have been made up of at least three ranges of rooms, possibly associated with a courtyard at the back.[311] The most notable find was a hoard of 43 gold coins placed inside a small box during the later second century within the make-up deposit adjacent to a wall in a sunken room in the west range.[312] Well-appointed buildings to the north of the main east–west road are also indicated by the discovery during the nineteenth century of mosaic and tessellated floors.[313] At 41 Eastcheap several phases of timber-and-earth buildings were constructed during the second century.[314] At 13–21 Eastcheap two timber-and-earth buildings were constructed after around AD 125 and a more substantial stone building during the second century.[315]

At Lloyd's Register substantial stone-built houses replaced timber-and-earth buildings from the first half of the second century and properties continued to be modified and rebuilt after the

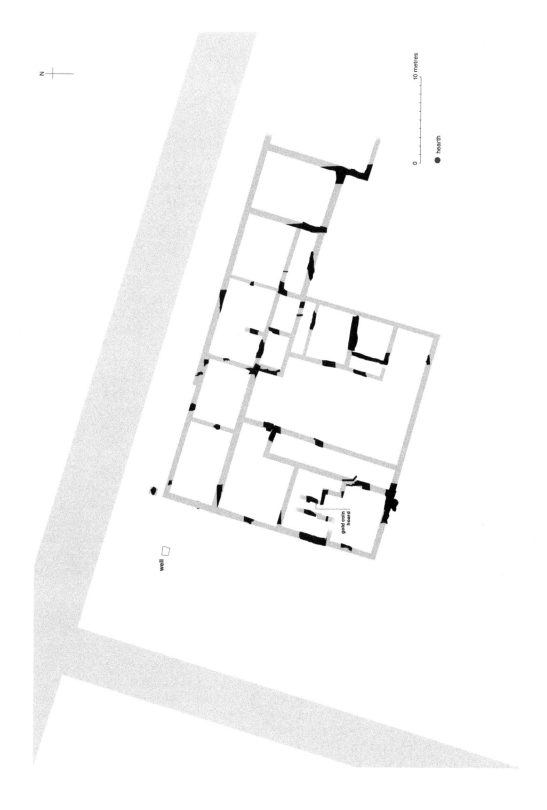

N

well

gold coin
hoard

0　　　　　　10 metres

● hearth

FIG. 7.14 A substantial house of second-century date at Plantation Place.

second century.[316] Timber-and-earth buildings were also occupied during the late second to fourth centuries, although these were poorly preserved.[317] By the late second to early third centuries a large number of buildings including some substantial stone-built properties were crowded together in this small area.[318] The plans and extent of these buildings could not be fully established, although one was interpreted as an aisled hall, possibly with a barrel-vaulted roof which may have been a store or a small market hall.[319] These buildings appear to have been of high status due to their substantial size and the painted wall plaster and fragment of marble inlay that were recovered. Just to the west, at 60–3 Fenchurch Street, buildings were constructed and reconstructed throughout the second century.[320] By the early second century water was being provided to these structures by a system of wooden box pipes along the roadside and evidence for bronze and ironworking was found.[321] During the mid to late second century two substantial stone buildings, one of which contained a tessellated floor, replaced the earlier strip-houses.[322]

In the east and north-east the Roman walls were constructed to enclose areas that were not intensively occupied.[323] At Crossed Friars rubbish pits and drainage gullies dated to the middle of the second century.[324] This area may have been sparsely occupied wetland, but traces of occupation were indicated by a group of three intercutting pits and a well, probably dating from around AD 150–250. The well included eight almost complete vessels, possibly a termination deposit.[325] Excavations at 8–14 Cooper's Row and 1 America Square have produced very little evidence for building or other activities for the entire period of Roman occupation.[326]

At Camomile Street a building may have been truncated by the construction of the Roman wall, as there was a mosaic floor in very close proximity.[327] The excavations at Baltic House have revealed only very limited evidence for Roman buildings, indicating that this area was used for gardening or agriculture.[328] The very truncated remains of a building with a cellar were found and the quantity of building material derived from later features may indicate that the substantial foundations of a stone house had been truncated by subsequent activities.[329] Finds from the cellar suggested that this building may have had a hypocaust and painted wall plaster.[330] Overall the information suggests that a single isolated late Roman house had been built on the east periphery of Londinium in the area that was later incorporated within the walls.

The evidence from Crossed Friars, Baltic House and 8–14 Cooper's Row suggests that certain areas on the urban margins may have been sparsely settled prior to and after the construction of the walls. The incorporation of extensive areas of open land to the north-east within the circuit raises the probability that other undeveloped areas were also included, such as some land west of the Walbrook and in the south-east of Londinium. The inhabitants cultivated garden areas and it is also possible that some land within the boundaries of Roman London was used for agriculture, as has been suggested by the excavation results from Baltic House.

The waterfront

There is good evidence for the maintenance and construction of buildings at this period. To the east, in the Inmost Ward of the Tower of London, two phases of second-century timber buildings were cleared to make space for the wall,[331] although a stone-built house just east of the Tower of London's White Tower was constructed during this century and continued to be occupied during the late Roman period.[332] This building had tessellated floors although much of it lies under the White Tower.[333] It is unclear why this particular building was respected by the builders of the wall while other buildings in the vicinity were demolished.[334]

At Monument House a timber building was constructed sometime after AD 125 and a large stone building during the late second century, or more probably in the early third.[335] This construction work required the substantial terracing of the hill slope above the river. At Pudding Lane the warehouses were maintained and renewed throughout the century, although at Regis House they may have been abandoned. Behind the Pudding Lane warehouses part of a building with stone and tile walls was constructed during the mid-second century ('Building 6').[336] It was altered on several occasions and continued to be used during the succeeding centuries. This winged building faced towards the river, on a terrace above the shops and warehouses that lay immediately in front. Part of the apsidal west wing included a water-tight feature, probably a plunge bath and a latrine.[337] This may have been a small inn, as it was located near the commercial facilities on the quay side.[338] It is also possible that it was a bathhouse associated with a substantial stone house, since comparable buildings dating to the third century have been found at Billingsgate and 1 Poultry.[339] It may also have been a self-contained public bathhouse, the unexcavated eastern part forming a linear suite of rooms comparable to the late first-century bathhouse at Cheapside.[340]

At 12 Arthur Street, further to the west along the waterfront, a building with a hypocaust was rebuilt, probably after AD 120, and some wells and pits were dug.[341] Dan Swift has suggested that this limited evidence for building may be the result of later truncation and that the survival of the dug features may indicate that the shallower remains of buildings of high status have been removed by later activity.[342] A sequence of substantial and apparently high-status buildings were constructed here during the late second or early third centuries. Just to the east of the 'governor's palace' the so-called 'townhouse' (at Suffolk House) was constructed, possibly during the second quarter of the second century.[343] From the limited areas that have been excavated this appears to have been a large courtyard house situated just east of the 'palace' on the waterfront. This building contained painted plaster, at least one mosaic floor, underfloor heating and a fragment of a stone column capital that may have derived from a riverside colonnade.[344] This potential courtyard house may be compared with other buildings from first- and second-century contexts such as the houses at Watling Court, DLR Lothbury and 10 Gresham Street. Since Londinium had impressive international connections and there is good evidence for wealthy merchants here, there were probably many more courtyard houses during the second century. To the east of the 'townhouse' two additional buildings were constructed, although only traces were revealed.[345]

South of the Thames

The evidence from excavations across Southwark has indicated that people continued to occupy the area, although some places may have been abandoned.[346] From around AD 120 additional land was reclaimed as the river level dropped. By this time the topography of the islands and waterways had changed considerably since the earliest Roman settlement. New buildings and structures were particularly common across the northern islands. The waterfront along Guy's Channel was supplemented, suggesting the continued significance of the north island of Southwark.[347] The complex of buildings at 15–23 Southwark Street was modified throughout the second century.[348] A new wing may have replaced the building to the west of the building complex, possibly during the later second century.[349] Tessellated and mosaic floors, imported marble from the Aegean, decorated plaster and hypocausts indicate the high status of this building.[350] Mosaics were installed during the later second and early third centuries.[351]

Excavations at Courage Brewery on the north island have shown that this was a significant ironworking area, with additional evidence for copper-alloy casting. To the south and east of this industrial area, stone houses were constructed that have been interpreted as higher status buildings belonging to wealthy residents.[352] There is no evidence for a decline in the density of buildings at this site after AD 160 and intensive settlement activity and industry continued into the third century.

At Fennings Wharf and Toppings Wharf, just east of the bridge over the Thames, the area that had been intensively occupied during the later first and early second centuries was dug with pits and wells and was less densely inhabited.[353] There was sporadic activity here until the end of the Roman period and the truncation of the later deposits may suggest that this area continued to be occupied. At Southwark Cathedral timber-and-earth buildings were constructed west of the main north–south road around AD 130 and, although the remains were poorly preserved, occupation continued throughout this century.[354] At the Ticket Hall site on the north island a building that may have been a market hall was constructed during the early second century with the addition of a colonnade to the street frontage around AD 120.[355] Several buildings in the vicinity also continued to be occupied and used, including the smithy.[356] The smithy and market hall were abandoned during the later second century. Fragmentary evidence for buildings of late second- or early third-century date was present in the east of the excavated area.[357]

On the south island, timber-and-earth buildings were constructed at several sites during the first half of the second century, although there is little evidence of substantial stone buildings comparable to those on the north island.[358] At 64–70 Borough High Street there was a series of dumped deposits alongside the main north–south road and a timber-and-earth building may have been constructed around AD 120, although there was little evidence of later activity.[359] At 88 Borough High Street there were buildings and pits dating to AD 100–60 and there may have been later occupation, although little survived.[360] At 10–18 Union Street timber-and-earth buildings were occupied and modified during this century.[361] The information from these sites and some other excavated sites on the south island suggests that the area alongside the main north–south road may have been well built-up during the early second century,[362] although there is much less evidence for occupation after around AD 160.[363] At 175–7 and 179–91 Borough High Street, evidence was found for a single timber building of late second-century date with walls decorated internally with painted wall plaster,[364] while buildings at 213 Borough High Street may also have remained in occupation.[365] At 5–27 Long Lane two timber-and-earth buildings were constructed and modified during the second century.[366]

Building debris has been found extensively on the south island. Materials dumped to raise the ground level at 33 Union Street at around AD 120–270 included ceramic pipes, imported marble veneers, painted wall plaster and tesserae.[367] Gerrard has suggested that, in the absence of evidence for a substantial building in the vicinity, the materials at 33 Union Street may have been brought from outside Southwark to be dumped at this location. At 175–7 and 179–91 Borough High Street three wells were located close to the timber building and were filled with considerable quantities of demolition debris including tiles, hypocaust tiles and glass tesserae that may have derived from a bathhouse or other high-status building.[368] Large amounts of building material were dumped in this low-lying area during the late first to second centuries.[369] The dumping of building material appears to have been a long-term activity on the south island as wells here were infilled with considerable quantities during the third century.[370] One possibility is that there were several substantial stone buildings on the south island that were demolished during the second and third centuries and their remains truncated.[371] An alternative is that there was a long tradition of bringing materials from demolished buildings to the south island to be sorted and recycled for reuse elsewhere in Londinium.[372] Some of this material was either not reused and remained in dumps or was used to fill in wells that had been abandoned.

There is only limited evidence that people lived and worked in the area on the south bank of the Thames. At 223–37 Borough High Street a new timber-and-earth building was constructed at this time reusing parts of an earlier building.[373] At least five new buildings were constructed to either side of Watling Street at Arcadia Buildings and may have been associated with industrial activities.[374] The buildings at Tabard Square fell out of use and were cleared during the creation of the religious precinct around AD 120–160.[375] Several new timber-and-earth buildings were constructed in the south-west of this extensive excavated area and may have survived when the temple buildings were built during the late second century.[376]

Urban decline or vitality?

Overall the evidence from north of the Thames has suggested that there may have been a reduction in the density of the built-up area west of the Walbrook but continued intensive occupation elsewhere. Excavations across the east and north-east of Roman London have not produced evidence for intensive settlement at any stage in the occupation and there may have been some extensive unoccupied areas across the urban area throughout its history. It is unclear, however, to what extent changing building traditions combined with the truncation of the later Roman deposits at many sites may have preferentially removed evidence for buildings constructed after the middle of the second century. The small-scale nature of the excavation work has made it very difficult to assess the density of occupation and the distribution of open land across Londinium.

Overall it appears likely that there was a reduction in the density of building and occupation in certain parts of Londinium and this may suggest a general decline in the population from a maximum period of expansion during the early second century. There is a strong possibility, however, that many timber-and-earth buildings have been truncated and the evidence entirely removed. The continued importance and wealth of Londinium during the later Roman period makes it difficult to sustain the argument for a radical reduction in the population. David Neal and Stephen Cosh have observed that the design of the mosaics laid during the late first and second centuries indicate that Londinium was 'vibrant' since they became more diverse and imaginative.[377] They have noted links between mosaicists working in Londinium with those working in Verumlamium and Camulodunum but also that the designs of some of the London mosaics suggest that there were international links between artists. This is indicated by the glass tesserae in several of these floors, a practice that was rare in Roman Britain but paralleled at Cologne and Trier (Germany). London mosaics probably dating from the second century include examples that were very well produced and diverse in design, such as the floor from Birchin Lane depicting a fabulous marine beast and the less professionally laid mosaic from Abacus House in Gutter Lane.[378] The number of temples and other buildings constructed and maintained during the later second century also illustrates the vitality of Londinium.

Marking the boundaries

The possibility that Londinium could have been enclosed by a series of discontinuous ditched boundaries during the late first and second centuries has already been reviewed. The boundaries of early Roman London were marked by the establishment of industries, the burial of entire human bodies, the exposure of the dead, the building of temples and activities that involved feasting. Such practices continued throughout the second century and sometimes were more formalized with the layout of defined burial areas and the construction of mausolea and temples. There were spatial distinctions between areas of burial, religious activity and industry within the urban boundaries.

Industry

Most of the evidence for substantial industries has been found in the upper Walbrook Valley and on the north island in Southwark (see Fig. 7.15). The upper Walbrook Valley constituted a significant industrial landscape that had been drained and developed since the late first century. At 20–8 Moorgate a series of eight kilns produced pottery in the style and form of Verulamium white ware, an industry that may have flourished from around AD 110–60.[379] During the second phase of activity, dated to around AD 140–60, three bottle-shaped kilns were built just east of the workshop which continued to be used and two wells were dug.[380] There is some limited evidence to indicate activity after around AD 160, although pottery production had ceased.[381]

One of the pits at 20–8 Moorgate contained a substantial collection of unused samian pottery mainly from central Gaul and probably dating to around AD 130.[382] The lack of wear on the surviving foot-rings suggests that the pots were kept with care although they were eventually dumped in the pit. Large deposits of unused samian have been found elsewhere in Londinium, but it is unclear why such imported pottery would have been kept at a pottery workshop in an industrial area on the urban margins. The pots may have been 'bench-pieces' from which potters drew inspiration for their own designs.[383] Pits containing deposits associated with ritual activities are common in the Walbrook Valley and it is also possible that this stock of samian was deposited beside the watercourse as an offering.[384]

There was extensive glassworking in the upper Walbrook Valley. Evidence was found for glassmaking at 20–8 Moorgate and at other excavations in the vicinity, including 55–61 Moorgate.[385] At 35 Basinghall Street there was glassworking from around AD 140–70 associated with timber-and-earth buildings.[386] Industrial waste such as broken glass vessels, window glass and furnace fragments were found from glassworking that ceased around AD 160–80,[387] when the site appears to have been abandoned.[388]

At 15–35 Copthall Avenue excavations have revealed evidence for the drainage and canalization of streams, road building and the construction of three timber buildings during the early second century.[389] Hearths were found within one of the buildings which was probably occupied throughout this century. Ironworking may have been conducted and hide offcuts suggest leatherworkers,[390] although much of the potentially industrial material from this site was found in dumped deposits.[391] Excavations at Drapers' Gardens have revealed that timber buildings constructed close to a road were associated with evidence for industrial activities including tanning, butchery, hornworking and gluemaking.[392] At 52–63 London Wall in 1988–9 timber-and-earth buildings were associated with roads and evidence for leatherworking, including leather offcuts and implements.[393]

There was also a focus of industrial activity on Southwark's north island. Five successive phases of metalworking workshops were developed at Courage Brewery during the second century.[394] Two of the buildings that replaced the earlier buildings were very substantial timber workshops associated with pit hearths and other ironworking deposits.[395] Another building, to the east, was probably a metalworking workshop and all these buildings are thought to have accommodated their own group of workers.[396] The workshops were succeeded by other

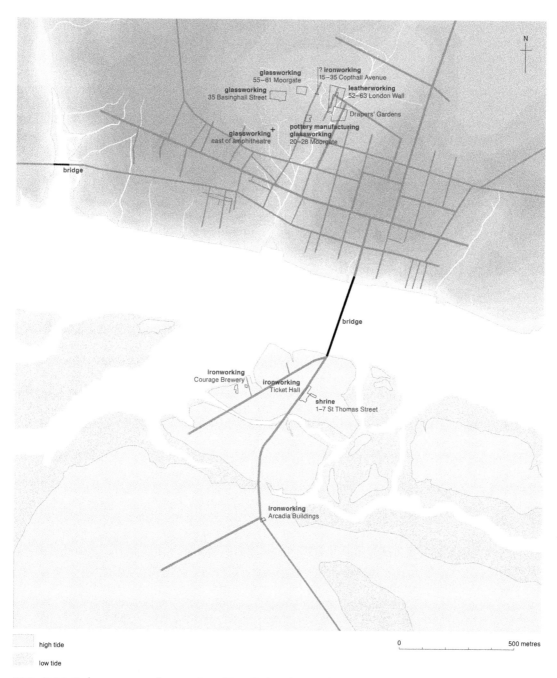

FIG. 7.15 Industry across the margins of Londinium in AD 120–200.

buildings, indicating the substantial scale of this metalworking industry. Meanwhile, the dumping of industrial material on the Thames foreshore continued a tradition established during the first century.[397]

A single family of smiths may have worked at the Ticket Hall site for well over a century, indicating the long period of continuity.[398] Drummond-Murray and Thompson have suggested that a 'smith urn' deposited in a well at 1–7 St Thomas Street, around 20 metres east of the smithy, in a late second-century context, might have constituted an offering made to a smith god.[399] This urn shows a representation of a hammer, tongs and probably a small anvil around its rim and was found associated with dog bones and some building materials.[400] The well was closely associated with two rectangular pits that contained the remains of at least twenty dogs, pottery urns, writing tablets, glass and two gemstones.[401]

At Arcadia Buildings on the south bank of the Thames a number of buildings were associated with metalworking during the first and the third centuries.[402] This suggests that industrial activity may have continued in a location close to burials and temple buildings.

Mortuary landscapes to the north

On the higher ground east of the Walbrook Valley, there were several discrete burial grounds comprising a northern mortuary terrain (see Fig. 7.16). The detailed understanding of the extent and character of this mortuary landscape is constrained by the scarcity of published modern excavations.[403] Jenny Hall's synthesis of the information derived from records of early excavations has suggested that people were buried across this area throughout the Roman period. There was a large number of inhumations and cremations associated with grave goods and also stone sarcophagi and mausolea, although excavations have been rare in modern times. A small area of this extensive burial ground at 201 Bishopsgate produced excavated evidence for several burials interred east of the road known as Ermine Street.[404] Two phases of the cemetery were recorded, including six individuals that may have been buried with grave goods during the second to early third centuries. The earlier burials were close to two poorly preserved small rectangular stone-walled enclosures that may have been mausolea.[405]

Early burials have also been found at Spitalfields Market which was more intensively used during the later Roman period.[406] One of the wells dug at this site, which may have been beyond the limits of the urban boundary, contained a group of complete pottery vessels that may have been an offering to a spirit of place.[407] At Crispin Street thirty-six inhumation burials were found that probably dated from the early second to third century, although there was a scarcity of dating evidence.[408] These inhumations were aligned either east–west or north–south. The head of one had been removed and placed behind the lower back. Ten of the corpses had been interred in coffins, two surrounded with chalk, and a number were accompanied by ceramic vessels. An excavation at Premier Place uncovered thirty-six inhumation burials, although an absence of grave goods made exact dating impossible.[409]

It has been suggested that the human cranial remains found in the upper Walbrook Valley may have derived from the erosion of burials placed alongside or within watercourses (see Fig. 7.17).[410] Many of these cranial remains were found during the nineteenth century.[411] They were often found in watercourses and other water-filled features such as ditches and pits and there has been a lively debate about how these came to be deposited in such contexts.[412] A substantial number of the human cranial remains found during the nineteenth and early twentieth centuries came from the area described by Geoff Marsh and Barbara West as a 'natural amphitheatre', located close to the London Wall and Finsbury Circus.[413] Six radiocarbon dates

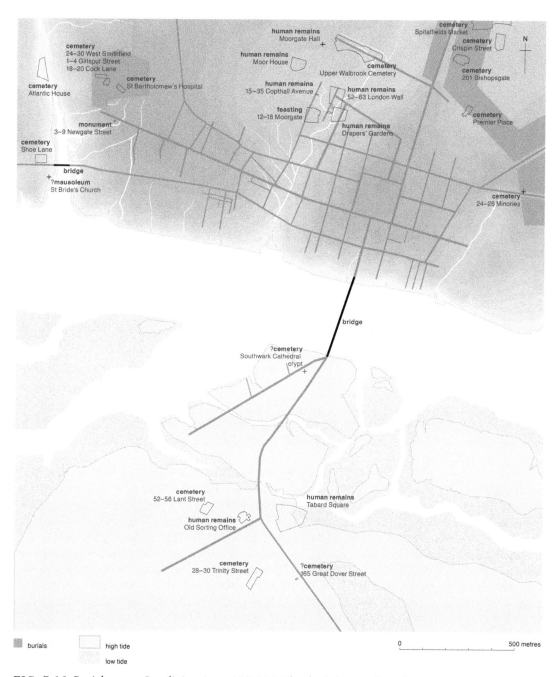

FIG. 7.16 Burials across Londinium in AD 120–200. The shaded areas show the cemetery areas as defined on the Museum of London map (Museum of London 2011).

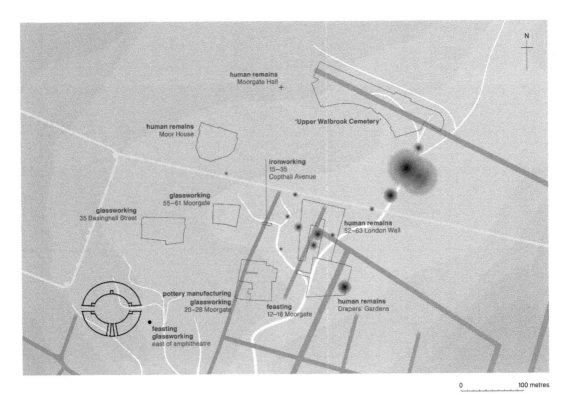

FIG. 7.17 Industry, human remains and feasting in the upper and middle Walbrook Valley.

have been obtained from human bones found in this area, suggesting that they may all have been deposited during the Roman period.[414]

The recent publication of the excavation at the 'Upper Walbrook Cemetery' has cast new light on this topic.[415] Many of the cranial remains found across the upper Walbrook Valley may have been redeposited by water action washing them downstream from their original contexts.[416] Some of the information from other sites in the valley, including 52–63 London Wall, suggests, however, that certain bones were deliberately selected for redeposition in particular watery places.[417]

The Upper Walbrook Cemetery was located just north of Finsbury Circus and was separated from a more extensive burial area further to the east. During the early second century a major east–west ditch was dug to channel the streams running across this area. A road was constructed immediately to its south,[418] possibly a section of the radial road that ran south-eastwards to Ermine Street just north of Bishopsgate and perhaps further beyond the urban boundary.[419] Limited excavation south of the road located other stream courses,[420] suggesting that the road may have constituted a causeway between watercourses. Deposits within and alongside the east–west ditch indicate that the area was an active stream environment with marshy conditions, while seasonal flooding was suggested by the erosion to the road.[421] An intensively-used cemetery developed across this marshland around AD 120–200.[422] The cemetery may have extended further north to the area beyond the major ditch.[423] The main tradition of burial was inhumation and most bodies were interred in an east–west alignment, around a quarter in timber coffins.[424] A single cremation burial and some pits containing pyre debris dating from this century were uncovered, while some of the pottery urns from the ditch may also have been cremation urns for burials that had been entirely eroded.[425] The bodies and their grave goods were buried across an area running approximately east–west, including the road and the major ditch, but most were deposited within the ditch itself.[426] As burials were dug into the road, this route was out of use by the end of the century.[427] The placing of inhumation burials within the ditch resulted in their erosion as a result of water action that may have occurred seasonally.[428] Disturbed and partly rotted human remains were probably visible to visitors to the cemetery.[429] The erosion of burials in the ditch did not lead to the abandonment of the cemetery, suggesting that this watery location was of special significance.[430] Many partially disarticulated bodies were deposited at the southern edge of this ditch; these were regularly covered by floodwater and alluvial deposits. In some areas distinct phases of burial were separated by episodes of water erosion, and disarticulated human bones and burial offerings were also found in the ditch fill.[431] The deposition of human bones in pits cut into the base of the ditch suggests that attempts were made to rebury remains which had been disturbed by the river water, but a substantial quantity of disarticulated bones were not recovered for reburial.[432]

At the eastern and downstream extremity of the excavated site, human cranial remains from twelve individuals were uncovered during observation of the Blomfield Street channel of the Walbrook.[433] These were probably derived from the erosion of burials deposited further west. Natasha Powers has drawn upon forensic studies to argue that crania may often be transported over considerable distances by slow-moving water once they become detached from the body.[434] She has also suggested that the flow of water in the meandering streams of the Walbrook might have led to the movement of human remains and their redeposition in certain places, possibly concentrating certain types of bones in particular locations. The concentrations of disarticulated and semi-articulated bones from the fluvial deposits at the Upper Walbrook Cemetery has led Powers to conclude that the human crania from ditches, pits and archaeological features throughout the Walbrook Valley are derived from further upstream rather than that they represent a cult of the skull.[435]

At Moorgate Hall, to the west of the Upper Walbrook Cemetery, excavated deposits have indicated that the area was a marsh and that a series of east–west ditches, probably for drainage, had been cut.[436] Part of the site had been used for the dumping of domestic and industrial rubbish and a single burial was revealed together with large quantities of disarticulated human bones, suggesting that other burials had been disturbed.

The main concentration of the cranial remains in the Walbrook Valley was found just to the north and north-east of areas of industrial activity, and several sites with evidence of occupation and industry have produced human bones. At Moor House early activities included quarrying and land drainage, while some evidence for occupation was suggested by gravel surfaces, beam-slots and stake holes.[437] The construction of the Roman wall just to the south during the late second century inhibited natural drainage and that eventually led to the formation of an extensive marsh.[438] The Moor House excavations uncovered 107 human skeletal elements from sixty-six archaeological features dating from the first century to the eighteenth, particularly those dating from between AD 160 and 220–50.[439] Male and female bodies were represented by cranial remains of thirteen individuals and other human remains that were mostly long bones. A programme of radiocarbon dating has suggested that all these bones originally derived from first- and second-century contexts.[440] Two bone fragments had been marked by an axe or a cleaver and by a very sharp-bladed implement.[441]

Many of the individual bones at Moor House were found in stream channels and ditches in an area that environmental analysis has demonstrated was prone to regular flooding.[442] Jonathan Butler has suggested that the bones may have been derived from burials that had been deposited beside watercourses and which were subsequently eroded from their depositional context by flooding.[443] It is possible that there was an early inhumation cemetery at or immediately west of Moor House that had been subject to this process.

The largest group of cranial bones from a single excavation was found at 52–63 London Wall in 1988–9,[444] associated with timber-and-earth buildings. Although the site has not been fully published, the extant human bones have been studied by Rebecca Redfern and Heather Bonney.[445] The remains of forty individuals, including thirty-nine partial or complete crania and one right femur, were revealed in an area interpreted by the excavators as industrial. The cranial bones were found in waterlogged pits and drainage channels.[446] The majority of the human remains were deposited between around AD 120 and 160, although some may have been deposited earlier or slightly later.[447] Almost all of these remains were derived from adult males aged between eighteen and thirty-five years, most of whom had received several peri-mortem (at the time of death) multiple blunt-force injuries to the face, mouth and sides of the head.[448] Some males had healed injuries, suggesting that assaults were common in the lives of these men.[449]

There is more evidence for trauma on these bones from 52–63 London Wall than on many other examples recovered from the Walbrook Valley.[450] Most of the human remains from this site were crania, often without the facial bones. The very high frequency of cranial material, together with the high proportion of young males and the evidence for trauma, indicates a selective deposition since fragments of bone from other parts of the skeleton would have been present if they had been washed into the features dug into the ground.[451] There is direct evidence from sculptures that portray warfare during the second century that Roman soldiers indulged in head-hunting on the northern frontiers of the empire.[452] Redfern and Bonney have suggested that acts such as these may have led to the deposition of the cranial remains at 52–63 London Wall, derived from captives who had been brought back to Londinium to be beheaded.[453] Another possibility is that the remains of defeated gladiators who had fought in the amphitheatre were deposited at this marshy site. The corpses of gladiators were often considered to be 'polluted' and so were sometimes placed in rivers and other wet places.[454] Gladiators may, however, have been few in Londinium and these crania may have derived from criminals who had been beheaded at the amphitheatre.[455]

At the industrial site of 15–35 Copthall Avenue the cranial remains of three individuals were found, one in a canalized stream, another embedded in materials derived from a channel fill and the third from a roadside drainage ditch in a context dated to around AD 120–40.[456] At Drapers' Gardens an adult inhumation was without a skull which was probably removed when the channel of the Walbrook was recut.[457] Disarticulated human remains were recovered from twenty-four contexts, fourteen of which included crania or cranial fragments, indicating the preferential selection of skulls.[458] These human remains were deposited in revetment structures, pits and dumped layers.[459]

This information suggests that many of the cranial remains from the upper Walbrook Valley were derived from burial areas where bodies were exposed to running water. This may suggest a broad continuity of the practices of the exposure of bodies to flowing water on the edges of dry land that began during the Iron Age. The Upper Walbrook Cemetery is probably the first of such cemeteries to have been recognized and the human remains from Moor House indicate other likely locations for the exposure of human bodies. These acts of exposure continued into the third century, although the majority of burials at the Upper Walbrook Cemetery and most of the cranial remains from the upper Walbrook Valley date to the second century AD. The information from 52–63 London Wall, however, also indicates that human skulls may often have been selected for special treatment.

At 12–18 Moorgate, just to the west of Drapers' Gardens, a timber-and-earth building that probably dated from the early to mid-second century may have been associated with feasting.[460] This building was poorly preserved but the excavations produced an unusual pottery assemblage of mostly flagons, suggesting the storage and pouring of liquids.[461] Drinking vessels, beakers and cups were also well represented, suggesting that this building, or another close by, may have been a *taberna* (inn) or that feasting ceremonies were held in this marginal location.

Mortuary landscapes to the south

The south bank of the Thames was marked out during the later first and second centuries by religious and ritual practices.[462] There appears to have been little occupation after the later second century in this area which was used for burial and as the focus for a substantial new temple complex dedicated to a god of war at Tabard Square. The concentration of temple buildings and mausolea indicates that this area was a particularly significant sacred landscape.[463]

Disarticulated human bones were found in several contexts at Tabard Square, possibly the result of the particular burial ritual at this site, although most of this material dated from the late first and second centuries and therefore may have pre-dated the construction of the two temple buildings.[464] These bones had been included in dumping and levelling deposits and in the fills of ditches and pits. Some had been gnawed by animals which may suggest that corpses had been exposed in the vicinity.[465] The location of the Old Sorting Office and 52–6 Lant Street sites just to the west of the temple suggests that the manipulation of human bones was occurring over an extensive area.[466]

The excavations at the Old Sorting Office have uncovered fragments of human bones from ditches, wells and pits dug at the edge of the area occupied south of Londinium during the later first and early second centuries.[467] Much of the relevant material has been discussed above, but further important discoveries date to the period from around AD 120–200. Activities generally appear to have reduced, with fewer archaeological features dating to the period after the middle of the century, but a few wells or shafts were constructed or infilled. One of the wells contained the top half of a human skeleton placed head downwards in the upper fills.[468] The legs and torso of an adult male of around twenty-six to forty-five years of age had been truncated by later activity. The bones may have been manipulated after the flesh had decayed but while the skeleton was still articulated.[469] These remains were associated with pottery and the bodies of three adult male dogs which had been thrown in as complete but disarticulated carcasses.[470] Three wells and other pits also dating from this period were found containing complete or near-complete pottery vessels, including those that had been ritually 'killed' by making a hole through the pot wall and painted face pots.[471] Beasley has suggested that some of the deep wells may have originally been dug as ritual shafts rather than to supply water and that the human bones were obtained from bodies exposed outside the boundaries of the habitation area or were from the exposure (or excarnation) of previously buried corpses.[472]

Beasley has argued that these activities reflect the domestic ritual activities of the occupants of Southwark at the margins of the urban settlement. Broadly contemporary shafts have been found at a second-century Roman temple complex to the south-east of the spring at Vagniacis (Springhead).[473] The close association of these burials and the shaft containing the human cranial remains with the temple enclosure at this site may suggest the location of a significant ritual-complex in the vicinity of the Old Sorting Office. There were several shrines and temples at Vagniacis and the same may have been the case in Southwark.

Excavations at 52–6 Lant Street have produced further important information for the treatment of the dead. A group of nine inhumations were deposited north of a boundary ditch, possibly on the southern margin of a substantial cemetery.[474] As the people buried here were not placed in timber coffins they may have been of lower status than other individuals buried in the Southwark area. Their bodies were accompanied by animals and pottery vessels.[475] As most of the evidence for fragmentation rites has been derived from the earlier phase of activities at both 52–6 Lant Street and the Old Sorting Office, the place where fragmentation rites were undertaken may have been relocated further to the south during the second century.

At 28–30 Trinity Street, excavations have uncovered part of an extensive cemetery.[476] It has been suggested that burial in this cemetery did not begin until the late second century at the earliest,[477] but some ditches were dug across this area during the early Roman period in close proximity to the earlier structure that may have been a timber shrine.[478] A ditch aligned north-west to south-east contained pottery dating from between AD 50 and 160 and also some later material, perhaps indicating that it was recut during the third century.[479] A large quantity of disarticulated human bone was recovered from the fill of this ditch, including large pieces that have been described as 'randomly deposited' and three human crania in a line.[480] An almost complete pottery vessel was found in the fill of the ditch containing the cremated remains of a young adult.[481] The main phase of burial in this cemetery may have begun around AD 180,[482] but the evidence suggests that human bones were being manipulated before the main period of burial commenced.[483] The deposition of material in this feature may have ceased by the second quarter of the second century but there was evidently later material in the fill of the ditch.[484]

The burial practices at 28–30 Trinity Street may be compared with the deposition of corpses in the major east–west ditch at the Upper Walbrook Cemetery. Fragments of human bones in drainage ditches have also been found in the earlier phases at 52–6 Lant Street and the Old Sorting Office. These may have derived from the tradition of the exposure of corpses in various ditches and wet places on the north and west margins of Londinium during the first to third centuries.[485] The cluster of three crania in an early feature at 28–30 Trinity Street is reminiscent of the collection of cranial materials at 52–63 London Wall.

Many of the dead in Southwark were interred in graves in more formally-defined cemeteries and from around the middle of the second century mausolea were constructed on the south bank of the Thames. A small unenclosed cemetery was established at 165 Great Dover Street no later than the mid-second century.[486] At least thirty burials of twenty-five inhumations and five cremations and several mausolea and enclosed cemeteries were placed here. A *bustum* burial of an adult female probably dated from just after AD 120.[487] The accompanying grave goods included eight unused ceramic lamps and eight undecorated and deliberately broken tazze, all made during the late first or early second centuries.[488] The deceased may also have been buried with textiles including those woven or embroidered with gold thread.[489] Four of the lamps were undecorated, one depicted a fallen gladiator and three the jackal-headed Egyptian god Anubis.[490] Representations of gladiators on lamps from London are rare, and Anubis, the conveyor of the souls of the dead to the underworld, does not often occur in imagery in Britannia.[491] These grave goods were initially interpreted as indicating that this was the burial of a fallen female gladiator.[492] Bateman has recently proposed that the rites that accompanied this burial interwove different strands of Greek, Egyptian and Latin ritual that related to beliefs in the afterlife and the possibility of resurrection, drawing upon the complex meanings inherent in the activities conducted in the amphitheatre.[493] This woman was buried in an area of Londinium which is distant from the amphitheatre although the reference to gladiators links these two marginal areas. Another Egyptian divinity closely related to Anubis is represented on a first-century flagon from Tooley

Street in Southwark which has an inscription that mentions a temple of Isis.[494] Other artefacts record the veneration of Isis in Londinium, indicating cults related to the afterlife.[495]

The earliest mausoleum at 165 Great Dover Street may have been contemporary with this burial (see Fig. 7.18). A small inner *cella* (chamber) was surrounded by an ambulatory or precinct.[496] The floor of the building did not survive, although a stone-lined well was constructed

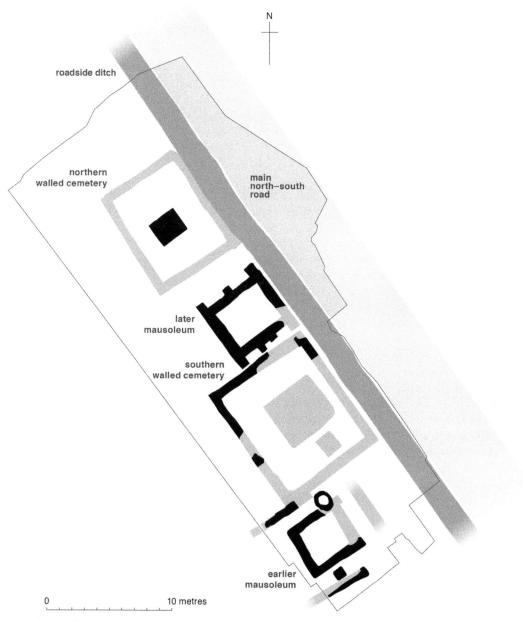

N

roadside ditch

northern
walled cemetery

main
north–south
road

later
mausoleum

southern
walled cemetery

earlier
mausoleum

0   10 metres

FIG. 7.18 The cemetery at Great Dover Street, showing the early mausoleum, two walled cemeteries, the late mausoleum and excavated sections of the main north–south road and roadside ditch.

in the north-east corner. This mausoleum was large enough to contain one or two stone or lead coffins, although no burials were found within the *cella*. Further buildings were constructed during the second and early third centuries.[497] The temple-mausoleum was initially retained although later it was partially robbed. Two small walled cemeteries were established with another mausoleum between them during the later second century.

The southern walled cemetery contained a substantial rectangular foundation, possibly of a mausoleum or a monument ('Structure 1'), and a large robbed foundation may have been the base for a column or cenotaph.[498] An amphora buried in an upright position in this enclosure was probably intended for pouring libations to the dead. Two burials were found within this enclosure. The earlier burial had been almost entirely removed by the cutting of the grave for the second corpse and only fragmentary disarticulated bones remained.[499] The later burial was of an adult male whose skull had been removed and laid on the rib cage after the body had decayed, indicating either that the burial had been left open or that the corpse was partially disinterred after some period of time.[500] Comparable burials in which skulls and other bones have been moved after burial were a common practice across London; examples from the eastern periphery will be discussed below.[501]

The smaller walled cemetery ('Structure 3') contained a stone plinth which may have supported a funerary monument or stone sarcophagus.[502] This enclosure also contained three inhumation burials and at least one of these, the body of an adult woman, had been partially disturbed and some of the bones reburied in antiquity.[503] Between the two walled cemeteries there was a substantial stone structure with stone buttresses ('Structure 2'), probably a free-standing mausoleum.[504] Fragments of tufa may suggest that it had a vaulted ceiling and, although no traces were found, the mausoleum might have housed a free-standing sarcophagus. Sixteen other burials were interred around these structures and this section of Watling Street may have been lined on its western side with high-status tombs and monuments from around the mid-second century until around AD 250.[505] The widely spaced burials in the walled cemeteries may have formed the private plots of wealthy families who lived in Southwark.

Two fragments of sculpture found during the excavations were interpreted as parts of decorative structures that stood over the burials. These included the head of a divinity, probably Neptune or a river god, and a pine cone finial. The finial is representative of pine cones that have often been found in funerary contexts but which are restricted to military contexts in Britain.[506] Tom Blagg has suggested that it might have been associated with the burial of a military officer serving in Londinium. The bearded deity resembles other representations of water deities found in Britain, although it may also portray Pan or Silenus.[507] It is notable that the sculpture of the head is very worn and had been broken off at the neck. The deposition of the head of the water spirit in a roadside ditch just north-east of the larger enclosed cemetery may have been a deliberate act since human cranial remains are often found in such locations.

This cemetery area extended further south-eastwards along Watling Street. At 82–96 Old Kent Road a building that may have been a mausoleum was located in a burial area which was probably established around AD 120.[508] The robbed foundations of this substantial stone structure were comparable in size to the Great Dover Street mausolea. The building was associated with pits containing artefacts that may have been placed in burials, although no human remains were found.[509] Fragments of another mausoleum were found at Leroy Buildings, suggesting there were ornate burial monuments for several hundred meters south-east along Watling Street.[510] Traces of two phases of stone buildings dating from to the first or second centuries were associated with a fragmentary capital that may have derived from a funerary monument.

There may also have been a cemetery on the north island just west of the bridge over the River Thames. Broken statues were found in the fill of a late Roman well excavated in the crypt of Southwark Cathedral.[511] This well was also filled with a considerable quantity of building material including tile, building stone and painted plaster that may have been derived from a mausoleum or temple-mausoleum. Both the sculptures and the building materials were presumably the remains of burial monuments which, with the burials found nearby,[512] may suggest that a well-furnished cemetery was located nearby.[513] The well appears to have been constructed during the third century and was filled with these broken sculptures during the fourth century.[514]

The statues included a hunter god, a genius, a depiction of a female figure reclining on a couch, a small altar and a dolphin's head by the leg of a male figure, probably Neptune or Oceanus. The hunter god, damaged and broken across the waist, equipped with a sword and bow and accompanied by a dog and a stag, may date to the mid-second to mid-third centuries.[515] The genius was probably carved in the second or third centuries.[516] The carving of a reclining woman may have been the lid of a funerary ash chest,[517] but its function is now considered to be unclear.[518] The well-carved Neptune or Oceanus was probably made in a Mediterranean workshop during this century.[519] A fragment of a funerary inscription included the name of the woman who dedicated the burial monument, Matrona, although the name of the deceased did not survive.[520] A fragmentary altar was also found.[521]

The head of the statue of a river god from 165 Great Dover Street, the marble dolphin's head with the male figure from Southwark Cathedral and the fragment of a possible nymph from an early second-century context at Skipton Street show that water spirits were commonly worshipped throughout Southwark.[522] Blagg has observed that stone sculptures of water deities such as Oceanus, Neptune or Tamesis associated with burials may refer to voyages of the spirit of the deceased to the isle of the blessed in the afterlife.[523] These river gods reflected the spiritual significance of the Thames, possibly drawing on the cult of the Tiber and its perceived role in the foundation and growth of the city of Rome.[524] Miniature figures of Venus discovered in large numbers across London also drew upon watery associations by representing the goddess as rising from the sea.[525] These figures were associated with beliefs concerning the afterlife and regeneration.[526] Divinities with watery attributes may have been particularly associated with the low-lying areas of Southwark and the Walbrook Valley,[527] connecting these two marginal mortuary terrains.

Mortuary landscapes to the west

An extensive area of cremation and inhumation burials on the west margin of the urban area was extended outward for a considerable distance west along Watling Street to around Holborn and Smithfield, incorporating burial grounds on the west side of the Fleet river. This 'western cemetery' probably comprised several distinct burial areas, although there have been few modern excavations. To the west of the Fleet, at Atlantic House, in a low-lying area well beyond the urban boundary, there were nineteen inhumations and twenty-nine cremations.[528] Most of these burials dated from the late second to the late third century, while others may have been later. The inhumation burials were mainly orientated north–south and aligned with the river, although some were arranged east–west. Two burials were made in very well preserved timber coffins, one of which contained a food offering and pottery vessels, while a necklace and coins were also found. Other excavations within what may have represented a more coherent 'western cemetery' at St Bartholomew's Hospital have located a few second-century cremations and inhumations but the majority were later in date.[529] Excavations at 24–30 West Smithfield, 18–20 Cock Lane and 1–4 Giltspur Street have revealed around 127 inhumations, although these are yet to be fully published and the dating is unclear.[530]

On the west bank of the Fleet river, just south of the road that ran west from Ludgate, two areas of a Roman tessellated floor were uncovered in 1952–4 and 1993 and are on display in the Crypt Museum of St Bride's Church.[531] The design of red and some yellow tesserae extended at least 5 metres north–south and 4 metres east–west. Traces of the northern wall of the building were also revealed. Painted wall plaster indicated that the walls had been decorated and that this building may have been constructed during the second or third century.[532] Milne has interpreted this building as located in an extramural settlement that had developed alongside the road.[533] It is also possible that it may have been a mausoleum in a suburban cemetery.[534]

At 3–9 Newgate Street, substantial stone foundations were located just south of the main east–west road.[535] A smaller foundation to the north might have supported a series of columns, perhaps a portico fronting on to the road.[536] Pottery found in the construction deposits of this structure has suggested that it was built around AD 140 to 160.[537] These foundations were probably the base of a small temple, a monument or a mausoleum alongside the main road, possibly a tower tomb.[538] No human bone was found,[539] although such a tomb is likely to have contained a sarcophagus from which any burial remains might have been removed when the monument was demolished. This structure was located about 50 metres north of the early cemetery at Warwick Square that produced the remarkable alabaster urn.[540] The monument at 3–9 Newgate Street appears to have survived into the late third century, indicating that it was incorporated into the area of the walled circuit during the late second or early third century.

Mortuary landscapes to the east

Excavations have been more extensive on the eastern margins of Londinium. The 'cemetery road' and some ditches defined burial plots that were being used episodically from the late first or early second century,[541] with burial continuing into the later second century. Cremations and inhumations were made in the main parts of the 'eastern cemetery' over a protracted period of time, perhaps by different families burying their dead in particular plots.[542] Six cases of skull displacement (sometimes called 'decapitation') were found in the burials, one with a pottery vessel of second-century date.[543] The treatment of these corpses may indicate that the skulls in certain inhumation burials had been manipulated during the period from the second to fourth centuries. The moving of skulls to a position over the lower legs of the body may suggest that burial had been delayed for some time or that the burial was opened some time after death and the head moved. One burial contained no skull, possibly indicating that it had been removed after burial.[544] Skulls were also displaced in burials at other Roman cemeteries in Britain, although at the 'eastern cemetery' and 165 Great Dover Street only a small minority of inhumation burials were treated in this way.

A small proportion of the inhumation burials were surrounded with chalk.[545] Although this was mainly a third- and fourth-century practice, in the 'eastern cemetery' it began during this century. A number of comparable burials of late second- or early third-century date have been found at 165 Great Dover Street.[546] The meaning of placing chalk around the body is unclear, although it certainly produced a dramatic visual impact when the bodies were uncovered. Some of the burials in the 'eastern cemetery' had been made in timber coffins and two burials in lead coffins may have dated from the third or fourth century. Offerings placed with the dead and the remains of animals and broken pots and glass vessels from the burial area may indicate that funeral feasts were held or that later feasting events were held in close proximity.[547] Comparable evidence for feasting has been found at the 52–6 Lant Street and at the Atlantic House cemeteries.[548]

In the city of Rome and elsewhere in the empire it was customary for relatives and dependents of the deceased to take part in the ancestral cult, visit tombs and hold funerary banquets as a key performance in the transformation of the dead from a polluted body into a sanctified ancestor.[549] The burial monuments and mausolea around Londinium represent comparable practices linked to the commemoration of dead individuals on the margins of the urban settlement. Several buildings or structures were associated with the burials in the 'eastern cemetery', although these were difficult to interpret and the evidence was taken to indicate that many of the burials may only have been marked by a mound of earth. Four of the cremation burials placed in amphorae were marked by four-post settings which may have formed temporary wooden structures.[550] Other structures were at least partially built of stone and some may have been decorated with painted plaster and sculptures. These were probably funerary monuments or mausolea dating from the second to fourth centuries.[551] Two buildings were found at East Tenter Street / Scarborough Street just north of the 'cemetery road' in a comparable situation to the mausolea at 165 Great Dover Street and the possible mausoleum at 201 Bishopsgate.

In 2013 an excavation uncovered an area of the 'eastern cemetery' at 24–6 Minories and located the 'cemetery road'.[552] Finds from the fill of the ditch north of the road included building material and a very well preserved limestone half-life-size sculpture of an eagle grasping a serpent in its beak.[553] This sculpture was probably part of a funerary monument within the cemetery and has been dated by associated pottery and other finds to the early or mid-second century.[554] The eagle and the serpent was a particularly potent signifier of the supremacy of Rome in the military and religious spheres.[555] The nearby foundation of a stone structure around 3.5 metres across may have formed a mausoleum or burial monument which may have been where the sculpture was originally set up.[556] Evidence from individual sites suggests that mausolea were commonly built for higher-status burials in the cemeteries to the south and east, and perhaps also to the north, of London from the second to the fourth centuries. Mausolea in Londinium were usually located by the sides of the major roads where they left the urban area.

About a kilometre east of Londinium along the 'cemetery road' was the burial area at Shadwell (see Fig. 5.14). The poorly-preserved remains of a substantial structure called the 'Shadwell Tower' were revealed during the 1970s.[557] Although no definitive dating evidence was found, one sherd of pottery incorporated into the structure possibly dates its construction to after AD 150.[558] This large building had foundations of mortared flint measuring around 9 metres square externally, although it is not clear whether it stood more than one storey tall. Nine cremations were found close to the building and the pottery vessels accompanying these burials may have spanned the century.[559] The building was interpreted as a watch tower, although it has now been suggested that it was a late second-century mausoleum.[560]

Summary

The period from around AD 125 to 160 has long been considered to have been a time when Londinium's fortunes were at their peak and that there was a subsequent decline and a revival during the early third century. Evidence from more recent excavations has suggested that there were substantial building operations throughout this century, such as construction of the forum-basilica, monumental building complexes including 'palaces' possibly connected with the governor and the procurator on both banks of the Thames and new temples on the periphery of the urban area. From around AD 120 to 160 the large fort at Cripplegate may have been connected with superintending trade through the port, which continued to play a significant role in the life of the province. Although the level of imports into Londinium from overseas seems to have declined during the course of the second century, the maintenance of the waterfront suggests the continuing importance of the port.

The apparent decline in the density of settlement west of the Walbrook, and perhaps on the south island in Southwark, may indicate that there were fewer people living in particular areas of Londinium, although this did not affect the central significance of London within the province. There is no clear evidence that the governor or the procurator were in residence, although the construction of monumental 'public' buildings and 'palaces' such as the building at the 'governor's palace', at the Salvation Army site and at Winchester Palace indicates the importance of Londinium. More recent excavations have identified substantial buildings that were probably private residences, such as those at 10 Gresham Street, DLR Lothbury and the 'townhouse' just east of the 'governor's palace'.[561] The 'mansio' was probably a slightly earlier example of a comparable building that continued to be elaborated during the second century. These buildings and the mosaics dating to the later second century demonstrate the international connections and wealth of the people of Londinium. The construction of at least one temple at Tabard Square by a trader whose family originated in from Gaul indicates the resources and aspirations of the wealthier members of the population. The mausolea to the south and east of Roman London show that some of the other residents were well connected internationally.

The status and significance of Londinium during the second century is shown by the quality and designs of the mosaic floors that were installed in some high-status buildings. David Neal and Stephen Cosh have argued that the late first- and second-century mosaics indicate that Londinium was vibrant, even though the floors were around half the size of those installed in buildings at Camulodunum, Calleva and Verulamium.[562] The mosaics from Londinium are often poorly preserved but more recent excavation has shown that they were often laid in narrow strip-buildings built in a commercial centre where land was in demand. This may suggest that grand townhouses such as those constructed at Calleva and Verulamium were rare in Londinium. Another possibility is that much of the occupied area of Londinium was so densely built up during the second and third centuries that it was necessary for elaborate townhouses to be built within pre-existing properties.

The people of Londinium continued to develop their boundary practices on the periphery of the settlement throughout this century. Temples and mausolea may have been a familiar sight where cemeteries were established on the margins. There is plentiful evidence for a range of burial practices and activities using the partial remains of human bodies, particularly in the Walbrook Valley and on the south bank of the Thames in Southwark. The evidence from the Upper Walbrook Cemetery indicates that there was a distinct burial custom of placing the corpses in a drainage ditch and the subsequent erosion of the remains by water action. The deposition of corpses in water might well have been customary for the settlers from northern Gaul, since there is extensive evidence for the exposure of the dead across Western Europe during the Iron Age and these practices may have continued into the second century. If the practices of disposing of the dead and manipulating their remains, evident on the margins of Londinium, were derived from Iron Age funerary customs, these may have been more broadly adopted during the Roman period. There is impressive evidence for large-scale industrial production in the marginal areas, including pottery production, glassworking and ironworking. Industries such as tanning and boneworking became common in this period, particularly in the Walbrook Valley. Although much of the materials used by the residents of Londinium presumably continued to be imported through the port and along the road network, the reduction in this trade may have been matched by the rise of local and regional trade.

8

Third-Century Stability

We are able to obtain correct knowledge of the extent of many of the Roman towns in Britain by the durability of their walls ... but Londinium ... has long since liberated herself from mural boundaries.

CHARLES ROACH SMITH 1842, 150

Introduction

This chapter will explore both continuity and change, including the construction and walling of Londinium, the continued use of 'public' buildings, economy and ritual life.[1] The early third century has been identified as the period of the 'restoration of London', following the supposed decline in the development of the urban environment during the second half of the second century.[2] While the population may have reduced during the later second century, however, London remained culturally buoyant and its continuing vitality was expressed by the building of the Roman wall. The construction of new temples, monuments and elaborate houses also indicate that Londinium remained influential and wealthy. The scale of overseas trade reduced and the port on the north bank of the Thames was abandoned, although commercial activities continued and there is plentiful evidence that Londinium continued to play a significant role in the administration of the province.

Until the early third century, Britannia was a single province overseen by a governor who was appointed by the emperor. The province was then subdivided into *Britannia Superior*, and *Britannia Inferior* with its capital at Eburacum (York).[3] Londinium was probably the capital of *Britannia Superior* and the centre of operations for the governors who were high-ranking ex-consuls. By contrast, the governorship of *Britannia Inferior* was an appointment for a senator who had not yet served as a consul.

The people

There is less information for the population than for earlier periods, although emperors, officials and military personnel are well in evidence. Londinium played a key role under the emperor Septimius Severus and his sons Geta and Caracalla. Severus campaigned in Britain from AD 208 to 211 and it has been proposed that a monumental arch may have been constructed to commemorate his presence in London.[4] The fine marble head of Serapis from the Mithraeum was possibly from a statue donated by a wealthy patron during the emperor's visit to Londinium, since Septimius Severus identified himself with this deity.[5] Severus's sons Geta and Caracalla became joint emperors when he died in AD 211, although Geta was murdered by his brother later in the same year.[6] The head of a marble statue that may represent the emperor Geta was reportedly found in the River Thames at London.[7] It had been weathered and had been deliberately mutilated with a chisel and a saw, perhaps after his murder. A youthful Caracalla may be depicted by another sculpture from London.[8]

At the end of the century the emperors Carausius (AD 286–93) and Allectus (AD 293–6) minted coins at London and the latter's defeat by Constantius I in AD 296 was commemorated by the production of a gold medallion with an image of Londinium.[9] Carausius could also have instigated the construction of classical temples at the Salvation Army site on the north bank of the Thames.[10] Carausius and Allectus had established their centre of operations in London.[11]

Other officials in the service of the governor were present in London. The two altars found built into the riverside wall at Baynard's Castle provide relevant information. One altar was inscribed 'In honour of the Divine House, Marcus Martianius Pulcher, senator, imperial propraetorian legate, ordered the restoration of the temple of Isis which had collapsed from . . . age'.[12] This records a previously unknown governor of Britain and is likely to date from the period around AD 221–60.[13] The second was inscribed 'For Jupiter Best and Greatest, Aquilinus, freedman of the emperor, and Mercator and Audax and Graecus, restored [this] [temple] collapsed from age'.[14] Mercator and Audax and Graecus may have been imperial slaves who administered the imperial estates or occupied senior posts in the procurator's office.

Although the direct evidence for military activity at Cripplegate and Winchester Palace appears to date to the second century, some inscriptions of third-century date recorded soldiers. A veteran soldier, Ulpius Silvanus, is named on a relief carving that probably derived from the temple of Mithras in the Walbrook and he may even have been responsible for funding the construction of the building.[15] Since the worship of Mithras was particularly popular among soldiers and traders, this temple also demonstrates that soldiers or veterans were present in Londinium. The tombstone of Flavius Agricola, a centurion of the Sixth Legion Victrix, probably derived from a burial area to the east of Roman London;[16] the tombstone of Vivius Marcianus of the Second Legion Augusta probably stood beyond Londinium to the west.[17] Both of these monuments have previously been dated to the third century since they were set up by the wives of these men.[18]

Although Londinium's port became less used, the pottery from New Fresh Wharf and Shadwell has indicated that samian wares were still imported until at least the AD 230s to 250s.[19] Londinium continued to be a significant port of strategic significance in the late Roman period that enabled some of its occupants to become wealthy. The tombstone of a ten-year-old girl called Marciana, built into a fourth-century bastion on the Roman wall, was probably originally in a burial area to the east of Londinium.[20] This fragmentary tombstone, which had been broken into at least nine pieces, was topped by an altar-like pediment.[21] Below the pediment was an arched niche with a stylized bust of the deceased. The fragmentary inscription recorded that the tombstone had been dedicated by a man who may have been a decurion of a non-British colony.[22] Marciana's father may have been a businessman resident in Londinium when his daughter died.

The survival of timber-and-earth building traditions may indicate that the population included slaves and industrial workers, but there is little direct evidence for their lives. At the Courage Brewery and Drapers' Gardens sites, this traditional approach to building was used for industrial premises. Society became increasingly hierarchical in the late Roman period with large numbers of slaves and poorer tenants.

Public buildings and urban infrastructure

A number of earlier public buildings and structures, including the amphitheatre and the forum, continued to be used and modified while new waterfronts were built on the north bank of the Thames (see Fig. 8.1). Although the riverside port ceased to operate during the mid-third century, trading may have been focused at another port downstream, perhaps at Shadwell. The Roman wall is a signifier of the power and status of Londinium. The landward section was probably constructed during the late second and early third centuries and the riverside wall along the north bank of the Thames has been securely dated to the AD 250s to 270s.[23]

The landward wall

The Roman wall was almost 3 kilometres long and enclosed just over 133 hectares (see Fig. 8.2),[24] by far the largest walled urban centre in Roman Britain.[25] Considering its scale and importance, remarkably little recent work has been undertaken to explore the context and character of this monumental work.[26] The building operation must have had a significant impact upon the urban community since it required landscaping, the clearing of buildings along its course and the quarrying and transportation of substantial quantities of stone to Londinium. The construction of the landward wall was an immense engineering operation that required the levelling of the ground surface and the canalization of streams and watercourses. Although earlier dates have been suggested,[27] this defensive circuit was probably constructed between AD 190 and 225.[28]

It has been suggested that the wall may have been constructed in response to a military emergency.[29] The idea that Londinium was in decline has led to the argument that the wall was built to repel potential attackers.[30] Although the population may have reduced, the evidence for the decline in the status of Londinium remains unconvincing and is contradicted by the large scale and the high quality of the wall's construction. The wall was not initially extended along the riverfront and so it is unlikely that it was primarily defensive since raiders would have been able to travel along the river to gain access to Londinium. An alternative suggestion is that the wall projected the status of the urban community to those approaching Roman London by land and that the open riverfront enabled the continued use and development of the port facilities.[31]

Londinium's impressive stone circuit is broadly comparable to the walls constructed during the first or early second centuries around the three colonies of Camulodunum, Lindum (Lincoln) and Glevum (Gloucester).[32] From the late second and early third centuries, many of the civitas capitals of Britannia were defined by well-constructed ramparts, ditches and walls. These earthwork boundaries were supplemented with stone walls during the third century.[33] The new stone wall clearly indicated a desire to construct a well-defined boundary around the landward approaches to Londinium.

The landward circuit of London's Roman walls incorporated the west and north walls of the second-century fort at Cripplegate.[34] The wall was generally based on trench foundations of puddled clay and packed with flints capped with a layer of ragstone rubble.[35] The tiles incorporated into the wall were probably produced close to Londinium, but the stone and flints were transported by water from quarries close to Maidstone in Kent, 110 kilometres from the port.[36] Peter Marsden has estimated that the defensive walls of Londinium incorporated a volume of ragstone estimated at around 35,000 cubic metres.[37] The wall was carefully constructed on

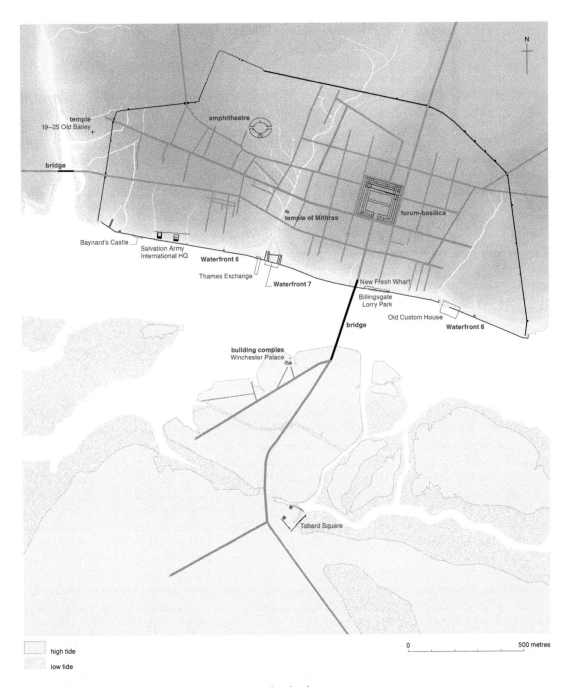

FIG. 8.1 Public buildings and infrastructure in the third century.

FIG. 8.2 The walls of Londinium.

both faces, although it may always have been intended to conceal the inner face behind an internal bank.

The design of the stone wall was particularly uniform, suggesting that it may have been planned and constructed as a single project.[38] The ground level on the external face was marked by a chamfered sandstone plinth and on the internal face by a triple course of horizontally bedded tiles (see Fig. 8.3).[39] The width of the wall just above the plinth varied from between around 2 and 2.6 metres and it became narrower with each of the four tile courses towards the top. The internal and external faces consisted of regular courses of small squared blocks of Kentish ragstone set with rubble and mortar. The original height is unknown, although at two locations it had survived to a tile course around 4 metres above the plinth.[40] It has been assumed that above this level there was a rampart walkway fronted by a crenelated breastwork, although none of this superstructure has survived.[41] Culverts were constructed beneath the wall to channel watercourses and prevent flooding.[42]

There were at least four gateways where the wall crossed the major roads, at Aldgate, Bishopsgate, Newgate and Ludgate. The entrance in the west wall of the disused Cripplegate fort also continued to be accessed and may have been blocked in the medieval period.[43] The Aldersgate gateway has been interpreted as a later feature of the wall,[44] although evidence for a road pre-dating the construction of the wall at this point may suggest that it was an original gateway in this circuit.[45]

FIG. 8.3 Part of the Roman city wall at Trinity Place during its demolition to make way for the Metropolitan District Railway Circle Line.

Detailed information for the gateways is only available for Newgate, where part of the gate's foundations was uncovered during the late nineteenth and early twentieth centuries.[46] This substantial stone gateway probably formed a double carriageway flanked by two towers and was broadly comparable to the west gate of the Cripplegate fort. Details of its construction suggested that the Newgate gateway may have been built prior to the construction of the wall, a situation comparable with Verulamium and Camulodunum where triumphal arches were reused as gateways in the walls.[47] The London wall changes angle at Aldgate and Bishopsgate, suggesting that these gateways may also have been built prior to its construction. Excavations in 1967 and a watching brief in 1998 located traces of stone foundations that may have formed parts of the Aldgate gateway, while the earlier excavation uncovered part of what may have formed a Roman gate tower that projected beyond the line of the wall.[48] The fragmentary foundations of stone structures, possibly parts of the Roman gateway at Ludgate, have been partly revealed by excavations on two occasions.[49] There is evidence that a bridge across the Fleet river may also have been constructed at around the same time.[50] The exact location of the gateway at Bishopsgate has been assumed since there is no excavated evidence.

Towers (or turrets) were built along the inner face of the wall, although it is not known how common these were or at what intervals around the wall circuit they were constructed.[51] These turrets probably housed timber staircases with access to the top of the wall. A well-preserved example at the Central Criminal Court was excavated in 1966 to 1969.[52] Other turrets have been found just to the north of Tower Hill, at Cooper's Row and at 1–6 Aldersgate.[53] The bank inside the wall was not as regularly constructed as the stone circuit.[54] The external ditch had largely been removed by the ditch of the medieval city wall. There is a substantial amount of evidence that earlier buildings were buried under and were truncated by the line of the wall, indicating that the walled circuit did not incorporate all existing areas of occupation.

John Wacher has argued that the construction of defensive works for a Roman town was rarely stopped except for short periods.[55] If this was the case, the building of Londinium's walls may have formed a protracted project that took decades to complete. The only direct information for dating has been derived from the wall's physical relationship to the south-west corner of the Cripplegate fort, where Grimes found evidence to indicate that the fort wall pre-dated the urban circuit. Londinium's wall abutted the fort defences at this point, suggesting that it was constructed after the fort which is thought to date from around the AD 120s.[56]

Grimes found evidence for the thickening of the Cripplegate fort's west and north walls by the addition of a substantial internal wall so that their width approximated to that of the Roman wall.[57] This thickening of the fort wall has been found at several sites and has been interpreted as relating to the programme of works associated with the construction of the landward wall.[58] At Falcon Square a coin of Commodus (AD 183–5) was found in a mortar layer connected with these operations, although it may have been deposited after AD 185 since it has been observed that it was 'well worn'.[59] It is not certain that this thickening was directly connected with the building of the landward wall itself.[60]

Evidence to support this later second-century dating of the construction has been obtained from Dukes Place where a large dump of brickearth, provisionally dated by pottery analysis to around AD 180, was cut by the foundation trench of the wall.[61] Pottery from the bank behind the wall dated to around the same time, indicating the wall was built during or after the later second century since the bank is usually interpreted as having been raised just after the wall.[62] At Aldersgate, just west of the Cripplegate fort, archaeological features cut by the construction of the wall indicated that it was constructed between AD 190 and 225, although dating evidence was sparse.[63] At 42–6 Ludgate Hill and 1–6 Old Bailey, a samian bowl found in the foundation rubble of the wall during excavations in 1982 dated from the mid to late second century.[64]

At the Central Criminal Court site in Newgate Street, 'forger's coins' and pottery were found in what was interpreted as the stairwell of the internal tower on the wall, probably deposited between AD 215 and 225.[65] This has been taken to indicate that the wall had been completed by around AD 225. A much larger assemblage of forger's coins, dating to the second and third centuries, was discovered in the ditch outside the wall at 85–6 London Wall.[66]

Waterfronts and trade

Around the beginning of the century a new quayside was constructed along the north bank of the Thames (Waterfront 6), the final significant installation of waterfront facilities before they were abandoned during the middle of the century.[67] South of the Thames, in Southwark, some limited evidence has been found for the maintenance or reinstatement of the second-century waterfronts, although this work ceased during the early third century.[68] Falling river levels at this time probably resulted in the main port becoming inaccessible, although there will still have been landing stages in and around Londinium. The quantity of trade passing through the port reduced at this time, although Roman London retained a considerable strategic significance during the late third and fourth centuries. As trade declined much of the Britannia's overseas trade in pottery and other goods was replaced by items more locally produced.[69]

Waterfront 6 was constructed around 7 metres south of the previous wharf, a substantial installation that may have extended further along the north bank of the river than its predecessors. The excavations at New Fresh Wharf have provided a detailed understanding of this structure and dating evidence from tree-ring analysis and other sources have suggested that it was built around AD 225 to 245.[70] The new wharf was infilled with dumped material that included a wide variety of objects.[71] Writing tablets and iron styluses from these deposits may have been used by traders on the waterfront. The large quantity of unused but broken samian pottery found at New Fresh Wharf is of particular significance and much of this can be quite closely dated to around AD 170–80, although some was made as late as the AD 230s or 240s.[72] The early date of most of the pottery indicates that it was deposited as part of the establishment of the waterfront after it had been kept for several decades.[73]

Another section of this waterfront has been excavated at the Thames Exchange, just west of the Walbrook.[74] Foreshore deposits had initially built up inside the wharf and an interim report has suggested that this was an openwork timber structure covered with timber decking and supported on timber piles that were not initially infilled with dumped material.[75] A single dendrochronological date has suggested that this was built during the early third century.[76] The waterfront at New Fresh Wharf may also have been built as an openwork structure and the samian found within it may have been dumped over a period of time during the early years of the century.[77] Rhodes has noted that there are several assemblages of unused samian from sites along the riverbank and has suggested that this high quality pottery had been stored in waterfront pottery shops and warehouses and that the large quantities found in the dumped material derived from vessels that had been accidentally broken before sale.[78] Adam Rogers' interpretation, however, emphasizes ritual connections for the deposition of a large quantity of older samian in contexts associated with changes in the waterfront installations.[79]

Just east of the Roman bridge at Billingsgate Lorry Park, Waterfront 6 was reconstructed in around AD 239 to 275 when the other Thames-side wharves were being either abandoned or dismantled.[80] Fragmentary evidence for possible additional third-century works, tentatively named 'Waterfront 7', have been found at the mouth of the Walbrook.[81] Although it is not clear how long this last Roman waterfront may have remained in use,[82] the riverside wall was constructed to complete the circuit of Londinium during the late third century when the waterfront works were out of commission.

The general absence of locally produced wares is distinctive of late Roman pottery in London. In this respect Londinium differs dramatically from Camulodunum, where there was a thriving pottery industry.[83] During the early Roman period, although Londinium had received much of its pottery from Verulamium, there was also a local pottery at Highgate Wood and other small potteries operated within Roman London.[84] Locally-produced pottery is very rare in London assemblages after around AD 200 and most of the pottery was supplied by the industries in Oxfordshire, the Nene Valley and at Alice Holt.[85] Robin Symonds and Roberta Tomber have argued that Londinium was therefore very dependent on the import trade in regional wares and that there was a fluctuating pattern of supply.[86] Much of this imported material was, presumably, brought into Londinium by road.

Other goods may have ceased to have been manufactured in and around Roman London. Sophie Unger has discussed the increased quantity of imported tile in later Roman London and has suggested that an economic downturn in Londinium also led to the collapse of local tile making, with kilns at Harold in Bedfordshire providing much of the supply.[87] Whether the ending of the local supply of pottery and tile indicates a decline in the status of Roman London, however, remains debatable. The scale and character of the private and public buildings suggest that Londinium remained vibrant. The wealth of the inhabitants presumably enabled them to pay the price for pottery and tiles transported from distant sources and the scarcity of evidence for local production might reflect the vibrancy of Londinium rather than its decline. Some late Roman sites across London have produced evidence for pottery imported from the Mediterranean, providing an indication of continuing international trading connections.[88]

Extramural activity at Shadwell

The elaborate sequence of waterfronts on the north bank of the Thames was never built solely as a focus for trade but also as a symbol of the control of river communication and trade through the establishment of the urban community. There may therefore have been more formal port facilities around Londinium after the mid-third century. Important imperial officials and emperors probably disembarked outside the walls and entered through a gate at the bridge-head. Falling river levels may have resulted in a relocation of the port facilities downstream to the extensive extramural area of settlement facilities at Shadwell around 1 kilometre east of Londinium's wall,[89] linked by the 'cemetery road' (see Fig. 5.14). The status and character of the settlement at Shadwell is, however, unclear and port facilities have not been located.[90] Traders may have exploited the creeks and inlets of Southwark, the Thames estuary and the mouth of the River Lea which was navigable at this time. There may have been several 'dispersed ports' in and around Londinium, with markets set up on the foreshores.[91]

A large building, probably a bathhouse, has been excavated at Shadwell (see Fig. 8.4).[92] It has generally been supposed that the 'public' bathhouses of Roman London had been built during the later first and second centuries and that the Cheapside and Huggin Hill bathhouses were

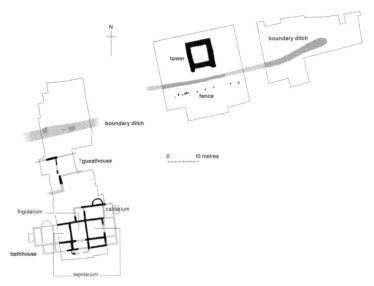

FIG. 8.4 The Shadwell bathhouse, guesthouse and Shadwell Tower. The ground plan of the bathhouse is partly conjectural.

abandoned before the end of the second century. Bathhouses attached to houses in the later second and third centuries had been assumed to have had a more private function than the earlier 'public' bathhouses, although the lavish bathhouse at Winchester Palace may have been a public structure. The building at Shadwell was probably constructed around AD 230–75.[93] Although there is no specific evidence that it was a bathhouse, Gerrard has reviewed some possible explanations for this building, and the interpretation that it was a public bathhouse is preferred.[94] Initially this building had at least ten rooms, including two suites that included warm (*tepidaria*) and hot (*caldaria*) rooms, both entered from a changing or cold room (*frigidarium*) (see Fig. 8.5).[95] It was aligned east–west and had a south entrance close to the conjectured line of the Thames waterfront. A service yard north of the building was bounded on the west, north and presumably to the east by a winged building constructed of timber and earth that may have formed an accommodation block. An excavated area to the west produced traces of buildings contemporary with the construction of the bathhouse.

The excavators have suggested that this bathing complex was too substantial for domestic use and have observed that its topographic location is comparable to the first-century bathhouse at Huggin Hill that was set into a south-facing slope just behind the Thames riverfront.[96] At both sites the baths were facilitated by a constant supply of fresh water due to their positions just below the spring line where the London clay was overlain by Thames terrace gravels. At Shadwell the winged building to the north has been identified as an accommodation block for the patrons of the bath,[97] broadly comparable to the building constructed at the Tabard Square temple complex during the fourth century. It is not clear why a public bathhouse should require accommodation for visitors and one possibility is that the Shadwell buildings formed part of a religious complex that has only been partly excavated. Temples were often associated with bathing facilities since the sequence of ritual activities included the cleaning of the body. Both buildings were subsequently modified into the fourth century, including a major refurbishment of the bathhouse with the addition of new rooms.[98] To the west of the bathhouse at the

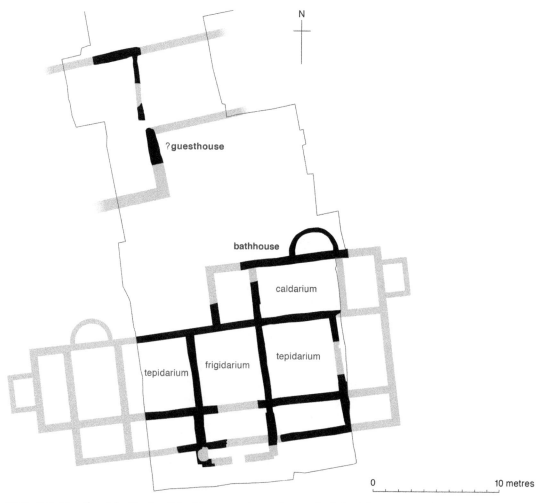

FIG. 8.5 Details of the Shadwell bathhouse and guesthouse. Both buildings were only partially excavated and a second *caldarium* has been proposed to lie to the west of the excavated area.

neighbouring excavations a substantial timber-and-earth building was constructed during the late third century to replace the earlier buildings.[99]

Earlier excavations had located an enigmatic structure known as the 'Shadwell Tower' just to the north-east of the bathhouse site.[100] This building may have been a second-century mausoleum, but the excavators of the bathhouse have suggested that it might have been a water tower to supply the bathhouse.[101] The building was so poorly preserved, however, that it is unlikely that its function, date and character will be determined, although mausolea and temples were associated at several sites in Britain.[102] It is possible that a substantial mausoleum was constructed at this location during the second century that was developed into a temple complex during the third century. There is nothing specific from the excavations of the Shadwell sites to indicate that the bathhouse, guesthouse and mausoleum formed part of a temple complex.[103] The objects from the excavation of the 'Tower' were mostly those usually associated with cemeteries,[104] while those from the bathhouse and guesthouse included bone hairpins, bracelets of shells and copper-alloy and several finger-rings.[105]

It has also been suggested that the 'Shadwell Tower' was a watch tower built by the army at some point during the late Roman period to scan the Thames for boats approaching Londinium.[106] There is no evidence for a military presence or military activity from the excavations of the 'Tower' or from the bathhouse sites and it is now thought unlikely that the building was associated with the army.[107] The excavations of the bathhouse and the 'Tower' have produced significant assemblages of late samian pottery, including some imports dating to around AD 225–50.[108] Bird has observed that late East Gaulish samian imports are usually found at important urban and military sites.[109]

Earlier buildings that continued in use

The urban infrastructure was maintained through this century. The main roads continued in use and, although some side roads were becoming disused, others were constructed. The dates of coins thrown into the Thames near the line of the bridge suggest that it was maintained into the fourth century.[110]

There is limited evidence from the excavations of the second forum and basilica for their continued use. This may indicate that Londinium had overstretched its resources by building such a substantial structure which consequently had a restricted period of use.[111] Structural alterations were made to the basilica, although layers of silt found inside the building may indicate that it had been neglected at certain times.[112] The portico was occupied by iron smelters who could have been reworking the structural fittings or furnishings.[113] The basilica may have been demolished during the early fourth century, although two small parts of the building were left standing. The east, south and west ranges of the forum may have been abandoned and demolished prior to the early fourth century.[114] The evidence for the demolition date of the basilica and the forum is not, however, entirely reliable and does not necessarily indicate that all of the building's functions had ceased during the third century.[115] The fora of some towns of Britain continued to be used as market centres throughout the late Roman period. The buildings interpreted as shops on the north side of the basilica may have continued to trade into the fourth century.[116]

In contrast to the forum, the amphitheatre was regularly renovated and continued in use throughout this century.[117] The arena was resurfaced and excavations of the entranceways on the east and south sides have shown that they were refurbished, indicating that the amphitheatre retained an important role in urban life. A timber-and-earth building just outside the east entrance with decorated wall plaster of a high standard may have been a shop or tavern.[118] This building was located directly over the site of the earlier infilled 'pond' which had produced evidence for feasting and glass production. A fine bone hairpin carved with a helmeted head possibly of Minerva was found associated with the building.[119] The pin was probably of some age when it was deposited and the watery association of Minerva may be a reference to the context of the drains that ran just to the north.

Some substantial second-century buildings that have been interpreted as official in character continued to be rebuilt and elaborated, demonstrating urban wealth and stability. At the Salvation Army site, extensive additions were made to the high-status residence or religious complex, including the building of the western apse.[120] Parts of the 'governor's palace' may have been disused as early as the second century, although comparatively little dating evidence has been recovered. A late Roman building with several rooms was built across the walls of the earlier 'state room', possibly associated with a hypocaust, but very little dating evidence was obtained to indicate when this area became disused.[121] The possible bathhouse in the south range of the 'palace' may have continued in use into the later third century.[122] It is possible that this building complex may have been demolished around the time that the riverside wall was built.[123]

At Winchester Palace the two most thoroughly excavated parts of the building complex were found to have been elaborated and redecorated during the third century.[124] The wing with the reception rooms was refurbished with a suite of heated rooms over hypocausts.[125] Some of the rooms had painted wall plaster and one room was redecorated with a simpler design of a large bowl suspended from strings within a framework of red stripes painted in red and yellow on a white background.[126] Parallels have been suggested for this style in third-century contexts in Rome. The bathhouse may have been constructed during the later second or the early third century.[127] The building complex may have retained an official role during the third century.[128]

The temple at Tabard Square was maintained and respected during the third century.[129] A stone wall ran between the two main temple buildings, dividing the temenos into two areas.[130] Dougie Killock has suggested that an extensive paved area with stone plinths and a monumental column base was laid out west of the northern temple building.[131] A substantial, although poorly preserved, stone building to the south-east of the temenos may have served as a guesthouse.[132] Monuments or statues probably stood around the square, with the two temples facing north-westwards towards the bridge. The temenos ditch to the south-east of the temple also continued to serve as a focus for ritual deposition of objects, including large quantities of pottery.[133]

The building identified as an octagonal temple on the east bank of the Fleet river appears to have been destroyed, possibly by fire, in around AD 270 and was replaced by a stone building with multiple rooms that may have had a courtyard to the east.[134] This was modified with the addition of a hypocaust before being demolished in the first half of the fourth century. Although this building might have been a private house,[135] it would be unusual to construct a house on the site of a temple.

The temple of Mithras

This temple in the middle Walbrook Valley was excavated by Grimes in 1952 and 1954 (see Fig. 8.6).[136] A group of sculptures, including a marble relief of Mithras slaying the bull, had been located in this area in 1889.[137] The temple of Mithras was probably constructed during the

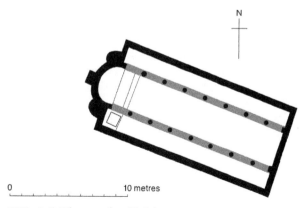

N

0   10 metres

FIG. 8.6 The temple of Mithras.

middle of the third century,[138] although many of the sculptures that it contained have been dated on stylistic grounds to the second century. The worship of Mithras was a mystery cult that spread across the empire during the first to fourth centuries AD.[139] Mystery cults were voluntary associations of devotees marked by initiation rites and characterized by secret knowledge and practices that were intended to result in their salvation. The worship of Mithras became popular with soldiers, merchants and imperial officials in junior clerical grades from the Black Sea to Britain and from the Nile to the Rhine. The temple was probably dedicated by a retired soldier, and those who attended came from the cosmopolitan population of Londinium, although such temples were always built for small groups of worshippers.

The temple was located just to the east of the Walbrook river where there may have been other religious structures that have since been destroyed or remain to be discovered.[140] During the excavation of the Mithraeum a fragment of a stone inscription was found among the Roman debris.[141] This inscription, which could date from the last decade of the late second century or early third, recorded an imperial judicial legate and suggests an earlier temple. There may have been a small religious precinct in this area prior to the construction of the Mithraeum, although the incomplete nature of Grimes' excavations together with the difficult conditions experienced by the excavators mean that the area around the temple of Mithras is poorly known. There may also have been a cult of Bacchus and Sabazios in the vicinity during the third century, alongside other shrines including one devoted to the Dioscuri, Castor and Pollux.[142] Temples to Mithras were often situated in locations with shrines to other gods, as in the case of the Altbachtal at Trier.

It is possible that the temple of Mithras was a free-standing building and it is usually reconstructed in this manner, although additional stone buildings recorded in 1949 may indicate that it constituted the western element in a larger complex.[143] In the port of Ostia (Rome, Italy) several temples to Mithras were attached to houses and other buildings, including shops, baths and houses.[144] The constraints of the area available for the excavation of the London Mithraeum resulted in only the partial excavation of the east of the temple outside the double doors of the entrance (called the 'narthex' by Grimes). This was probably part of an antechamber, a usual feature in such temples, although it may have connected the Mithraeum to a house or other building. The temple was constructed in an area with a high water table, requiring the floor level to be raised on at least eight or nine occasions.[145] This rectangular temple was accessed from the east end and had an apse at its west end, an unusual feature for a mithraeum. The apse contained a raised platform which was the focal area for the cult, supporting a statue of Mithras Tauroctonos, the god slaying a bull inside a cave. The small stone relief depicting this scene found in the Walbrook Valley in 1889 was probably originally installed in this temple.[146] The identification of this building as a temple of Mithras was confirmed by the discovery of a marble head of the god during the excavations.

The interior of the rectangular main room of the temple was divided into three along its length by low sleeper walls supporting seven pairs of columns, with the floor of the aisles at a higher level than that of the nave.[147] A nave and aisles are common features of such temples and are believed to have been used in ceremonies connected with the mysteries of the cult.[148] Only a small group of worshippers would have been able to gather at this temple. The animal bones from the London Mithraeum, interpreted as evidence for feasting and ritual meals, included the remains of chickens, pigs, sheep (or goats) and a few cattle.[149] This may be compared with the complex deposits found in pits dug close to the Mithraeum at Tienen in Belgium which contained the remains of a single large-scale feast, including pottery vessels, glass, metalwork, coins, wall plaster and large quantities of animal bones.[150] During the early fourth century some marble sculptures possibly associated with the cult of Mithras were collected and respectfully buried in and around pits excavated just inside the eastern entrance of the London Mithraeum, beneath the floor (see Fig. 8.7).[151]

The large group of sculptures associated with the Mithraeum from Grimes' excavation and those discovered in 1889 were examined by Toynbee,[152] who compared them to closely dated sculptures found throughout the Mediterranean world, particularly in Italy. This enabled her to classify the London carvings as imported marble of the second century (sculptures 1 to 9), third century (sculpture 10), those that perhaps dated from the third century (sculptures 14–15) and works in British stone of the third century (sculptures 11–13).[153] It is notable that the majority were carved prior to the construction date of the temple and this suggests that an earlier collection of sculptures may have been donated to the worship of Mithras.

The sculptures from Grimes' excavations included the marble heads of Mithras, Minerva and Serapis, a marble sculpture of Mercury seated on a rock and accompanied by a ram, a 'colossal hand' of Mithras slaying the bull and a limestone hand and forearm of Mithras.[154] Toynbee argued that the head of Minerva might have been carved around AD 130 to 190 and the heads of Mithras and Serapis around the AD 180s to 190s,[155] and that all the marble sculptures had been carved in Italian workshops. The well-preserved heads of the three gods had been attached to carved bodies, although these were not found during the excavations.[156] The head of Mithras showed a clean break with the neck, made before it was buried in the pit and possibly with an axe, indicating that it had been deliberately damaged in antiquity.[157] It may be significant that

FIG. 8.7 Fragments of sculptures found during the excavation of the temple of Mithras in 1954.

only one fragment of the body of a statue was found alongside the three heads, suggesting that certain parts of the statues had been specifically selected for burial.[158]

The marble sculptures found in this area of the Walbrook in 1889 may have originally been buried close to the pits that contained the sculptures found in 1954.[159] These included a fragmentary carving of a water deity, a genius and the relief of Mithras slaying the bull.[160] The sculpture of the water deity, which could represent Neptune, comprises the upper part of a reclining figure carved in fine marble and probably dating from the early second century.[161] The genius, from which the head was missing, has been tentatively dated by Toynbee to the middle of the second century.[162] On its left hand the figure holds a cornucopia and next to its left foot is the prow of a ship riding over the waves. These attributes may suggest that the genius is a personification of Londinium, the cornucopia and ship cresting the waves representing the wealth and activities of this busy sea port.[163]

The small votive relief of Mithras slaying the bull has been carved in a style that Toynbee has suggested was British and it has been assumed that it was made at this time.[164] The carving included an inscription that referred to Ulpius Silvanus, a veteran of the Second Augustan legion who had been either enlisted into the army or initiated into the cult of Mithras at Arausio (Orange) in southern Gaul.[165] He may have dedicated the temple at its foundation and could have been resident in or visiting Londinium.[166] Perhaps he also brought the second-century sculptures to Londinium and dedicated them to the temple.[167] A sculpture that probably derived from the temple of Mithras is the damaged limestone relief of Cautopates.[168] A severely damaged relief of a Dioscurus in limestone was found just outside the south wall of the temple and may have derived from a nearby shrine.[169] A fragment of a statue that may have represented Bacchus and another of a Bacchic group found in fourth-century contexts inside the temple were probably carved during the second or third century.[170]

Among the sculptures that have derived from the temple are representations of gods that have also been found during the excavation of other mithraea, suggesting that these divinities were sometimes included in the joint worship, although no other examples of statues of Minerva have been found in such contexts.[171]

A Monumental Arch and a Screen of Gods

The excavation of the riverside wall at Baynard's Castle uncovered fifty-two reused sculptured blocks of stone mainly derived from two monuments, the so-called 'Monumental Arch' and the 'Screen of Gods'.[172] Other stones included two altars that record the restoration of temples.[173] Tom Blagg and Sheila Gibson have reconstructed the Monumental Arch and the Screen of Gods from the sculptural fragments, although there were some uncertainties about their characters.[174] Both the Screen and the Arch were carved from Lincolnshire limestone, although the style of the sculpture and the ornamentation does not indicate that they were carved at the same time or that they stood at the same site.

The Arch has been dated on stylistic grounds to no earlier than the late second century; more probably, it dates to the third century and it has been suggested that it was raised to mark the visit of the emperor Septimius Severus to Britain in AD 208–11.[175] The Screen may have been carved during the second or third century, although this monument is not intrinsically datable.[176] The only direct evidence for the date of the carving of both monuments comes from the location of their remains reused in the construction of the riverside wall, which has been accurately dated at three locations to the AD 250s to 270s by tree-ring analysis.[177] If the two monuments had stood for some time before they were demolished, and their stones were reused in the riverside wall, they may have been carved by the early third century.[178] The third-century context for the reuse of these sculpted stones is not, however, certain. The western section of the riverside wall at Baynard's Castle, into which they had been incorporated, had been constructed very differently from the three excavated sections of the wall that provided the dating evidence for construction in the AD 250s to 270s.[179] The western section may have been reconstructed during the mid-fourth century. The Screen and Arch may therefore have been carved and built during the third or early fourth century.

The Arch has been reconstructed from twenty-nine surviving stones as standing at least 8 metres high and 7.5 metres wide.[180] Blagg has suggested that the character of the decoration was civilian rather than military and the Arch was clearly not triumphal.[181] It may have been a free-standing monument and was perhaps located on one of the main roads or was the gateway through a precinct wall of the forum, public baths or a temple enclosure. On both its broad faces were side niches containing standing figures of divinities, possibly Minerva, Hercules and an unidentified god holding a staff.[182] One of the spandrels of the Arch contained a bust in a roundel that might have represented a sea monster,[183] which is unusual in such a context but might perhaps have related to the importance of the port.[184] Vine scrolls from two-handled wine cups (*canthari*) decorated the two side faces of the monument. Above the archway there was probably an inscription, although the only evidence was provided by a single fragment of one of the cupids that supported the panel.[185] One broad face of the Arch was carved with a frieze of busts of gods and goddesses which may have included Mars, Mercury, Venus, Apollo and probably Luna.[186]

The Screen of Gods was reconstructed from six surviving blocks. It can be paralleled with the Facade of the Four Seasons of the temple at Aquae Sulis (Bath, north-east Somerset).[187] It was around 6 metres long and carved on both broad faces with three pairs of niches containing figures between pilasters.[188] On one face, from left to right, the deities Vulcan and Minerva, probably Mercury and Diana, and an unknown god and Mars were portrayed. On the other face were carved mythological creatures, a bird, a naked woman and possibly a wind god. The Screen may have stood either in an open area or within a building.

Seven other sculpted fragments of stone were found reused in the riverside wall that could not be linked directly with either monument.[189] One of these portrayed four seated female figures, possibly mother goddesses, although such deities are usually represented singly or in threes.[190] Two inscribed altars may have derived from two temples dedicated to Jupiter and to Isis and both had been slightly damaged before or during their incorporation into the wall. One of the altars probably dated from around AD 221–60 and recorded the name of a previously unknown provincial governor.[191]

Charles Hill has noted that the reuse of sculpted stones in the western part of the Baynard's Castle site might suggest that the monuments were originally located further to the west, in the south-western area of Londinium.[192] Comparatively little evidence for Roman occupation has been found in this area,[193] although the building complex at the Salvation Army site may have been where the carved stones were taken from.[194] The clearing of the Period I buildings during the construction of the Period II buildings in AD 293–4 provides a possible context for the demolition of the Arch and Screen and for the incorporation of their sculptures into the riverside wall.[195] If the reused sculpted stones were incorporated into a mid-fourth-century reconstruction of the riverside wall, they may even have been derived from the Period II buildings at the Salvation Army site. Alternatively the stones from the Arch, Screen and the altars may have been transported along the river to Baynard's Castle, having been derived from abandoned and ruined temples throughout Londinium.[196]

The riverside wall

When the riverside wall was constructed along the north bank of the Thames during the later third century the circuit of the wall was completed (see Fig. 8.2).[197] The riverside wall was constructed when the waterfront was no longer maintained, although it is possible that boats could be moored outside the wall at high tide.

The excavations at Baynard's Castle in 1974–6 uncovered the remains of a section of riverside wall 115 metres in length.[198] Constructed of stone with wall courses of tile at intervals, the wall had a brick culvert that channelled a watercourse beneath it and into the Thames.[199] At this point, the wall to the east was constructed over a chalk foundation on timber piles, while on the west it was built of large ragstone blocks rammed directly into the subsoil.[200] A clay bank was raised up against the inner face of the wall, as had been the case with the landward wall, and the absence of evidence for an external ditch was presumably due to the close proximity of the Thames.[201] The analysis of timber piles recovered from the excavation of the eastern section of the riverside wall at Baynard's Castle dated construction to between around AD 255 and 275.[202]

Excavations have revealed sections of the riverside wall at the Tower of London in 1976–7, New Fresh Wharf in 1978, Peter's Hill (Salvation Army site) in 1981 and at Riverbank House in 2006. The results of these excavations suggest that a continuous wall was constructed along the riverfront for 1700 metres. The excavations at the Inmost Ward of the Tower of London revealed evidence that the riverside wall was constructed in two distinct phases.[203] The earlier wall ('Period I') had been reduced to its foundations but was found to have been constructed on a series of timber piles.[204] Tree-ring analysis has suggested that the trees from which these piles were cut were felled in AD 255–70.[205] At New Fresh Wharf a substantial section of the wall had been built on foundations beneath which a raft of chalk and lateral timbers and tile-lined culvert channelled water to the river.[206] The foundations of this wall cut into the dumped material associated with the earlier waterfronts.[207] Tree-ring analysis of the timber piles incorporated in these foundations has provided a date of around AD 255–70.[208] The piles from the foundations of the riverside wall at New Fresh Wharf, the Inmost Ward of the Tower of London and the eastern section of the wall at Baynard's Castle are broadly comparable in date, dating building work to the AD 250s to 270s. Additional information from other excavated sites supports this general dating.[209]

The dating of the piles incorporated into the foundations may imply that the riverside wall was built during a single programme of construction.[210] The foundations of the western section at Baynard's Castle, however, were constructed differently, of large ragstone blocks rammed into the ground. This section incorporated the reused sculptures from the Arch and Screen and altars and may have been constructed at a later date after the foundations of the earlier wall had become unstable.[211] This rebuilding of the wall may have occurred when the civic defences were restored, with the addition of bastions during the mid-fourth century.[212]

Defensive explanations for the building of the riverside wall as a response to political instabilities in the empire have been based on the dating evidence derived from the piles.[213] Postumus, the general commanding the army in the Lower Rhine, had declared himself emperor in opposition to Gallienus in AD 260. He created his own imperial court within the Western Empire, the so-called 'Gallic Empire', which included Britannia.[214] Postumus was assassinated in AD 269 and was succeeded by several shorter-lived Gallic emperors before Aurelian reunited the empire in AD 274. Londinium's riverside wall may have been constructed during this time of insecurity, although the dating evidence from the timber piles is not accurate enough to provide direct support for this historical association.

The port and shipping in the late third century

The riverside wall completed a plan to enclose Londinium with a circuit of stone that took almost one hundred years of building. It also marked the abandonment of the port on the north bank of the Thames after over 200 years of regular reconstruction. This may have resulted from the gradual tidal regression of the River Thames that eventually led to the disuse of the waterside facilities on the north bank,[215] although the quantity of trade with the continent had already been decreasing.[216] The evidence for tidal regression has been derived from the evidence for continuous rebuilding of waterside facilities further out into the river from around AD 50 to the mid-third century.[217] There is also some additional information about changes in sea level from London and other sites across north-western Europe, although the discovery of the 'County Hall ship' at a location upstream from the waterfront suggests that the Thames was still navigable at high tide by larger vessels around AD 300.[218] Marsden has suggested that the ship had been abandoned as a rotting hulk on the marshy bank of the Thames, at a distance from the port and settlement.[219]

This ship was revealed and recoded by officials from London County Council in 1910 at County Hall on the south bank of the Thames, between Westminster Bridge and Hungerford Bridge.[220] It was removed in one piece with a huge wooden crane and was displayed until 1939; the surviving remains are now in storage.[221] Detailed drawings made in 1910 and photographs of the ship in situ show that it was built of oak planks fastened with trenails and occasionally with iron nails.[222] The midship section had survived but both ends of the ship had been lost.

The County Hall ship was carvel-built, a characteristic of ships built in the Mediterranean in Greek and Roman times, but the analysis of the timber has suggested that the vessel was constructed in south-eastern Britain.[223] Unusually, the deck had survived, protected by the alluvium that had been deposited over the collapsed side of the ship. The height of the deck and the absence of any fittings for rowing indicate that the ship was a sailing vessel.[224] Marsden has argued that the shipwright who constructed it was experienced in Mediterranean techniques of shipbuilding. Dendrochronological dates derived from ten samples of oak planking have indicated that the timber may have been cut from trees felled after AD 285 and that the ship was probably built around AD 290 to 300.[225] Repairs to the vessel demonstrate that it had been in use for some time and four late third-century bronze coins found in the bottom of the craft indicate that it may have been abandoned soon after AD 300.[226] When revealed, the vessel was interpreted as a warship and this remains a possibility, although its structure is different from other Roman-period warships or merchantmen found in the Mediterranean and northern Europe. It has also been supposed that this vessel had been sunk during a battle on the Thames in AD 296, but there is no clear evidence to support this suggestion.

Monumental temples on the riverfront

The riverside wall was constructed along the south edge of the Salvation Army site between the AD 250s and 270s and dumped material at Peter's Hill may relate to this building activity.[227] At this time the earlier (Period I) buildings were entirely cleared from across this extensive site and a new series of monumental buildings (Period II) were constructed behind the riverside wall on two or more terraces cut into the hillside for 150 metres along the riverfront (see Fig. 8.8).[228] The Period I buildings on this site have been identified as religious in character, although Blagg has suggested that the demolition of an active temple complex might have been seen as a sacrilegious act.[229] The two massive Period II buildings may have been twinned classical temples,[230] possibly

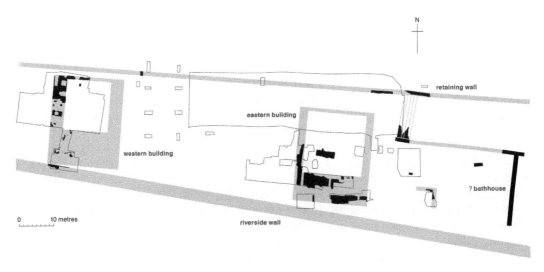

FIG. 8.8 The late third-century 'imperial palace' at the Salvation Army site.

replacements for temples that had been demolished (see Fig. 8.9).[231] They appear to have been substantial stone structures and are larger than other temples discovered in Roman London.

The stone foundations of these Period II buildings were supported by an extensive chalk raft on timber piles.[232] Tree-ring dates from the piles suggest that this building complex was built as a single coordinated project.[233] The substantial nature of these foundations and the width of the walls of the two possible temples suggest that these operations focused upon the construction of a coordinated series of impressive buildings along the riverfront. Owing to the limited areas excavated, poor preservation and the complexity of the archaeology, the character of the individual buildings is unclear.

Tim Williams has discussed the evidence for the building interpreted as the western temple, where the substantial foundations included reused blocks of carved stone and also a greensand block which may have formed a pier or column base.[234] Williams also identified the second comparable building on the east of the site.[235] This eastern building was partially re-excavated by Bradley and Butler and included a stone plinth that may have supported a statue.[236] The remains of both temples were severely damaged by later activities and were difficult to interpret. They were associated with a range of other structures and, although there was little to indicate their plans or character, there was probably a bathhouse in the eastern part of the site.[237] The superstructures of the buildings had been demolished to the foundations, but the general absence of evidence for architectural details from destruction deposits may indicate that the construction work was halted before the walls were built.[238]

The Period II buildings may have been planned by the emperors Carausius and Allectus. Carausius, who had been appointed in AD 286 to rid the channel of barbarian raiders, seized power in Britannia and parts of Gaul.[239] Since Carausius viewed the establishment of his authority as of paramount importance, it is possible that he planned this significant complex of buildings as a monumental statement of his power. Fulford has suggested that Carausius and Allectus had introduced new elements of imperial ideology and that these buildings may have been intended to form a palatial complex with public, administrative and religious functions.[240] It is likely that Carausius and Allectus would also have appointed a praetorian guard, requiring

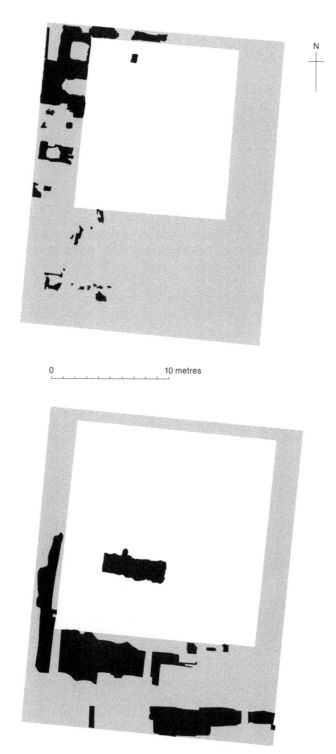

FIG. 8.9 Details of the two probable temple buildings at the Salvation Army site.

accommodation.[241] This would suggest that there were also substantial residential and administrative buildings at the Salvation Army site, only fragments of which have been uncovered.

As most of the dated timbers from the piled foundations were felled and stockpiled in AD 293, the buildings may have been planned by Carausius and the construction continued by Allectus who succeeded him in AD 293 or 294.[242] This historical context may help to explain the apparently unfinished nature of the buildings. Allectus was killed in AD 296 when the emperor Constantius I established control of Britannia. The historical texts explain that the emperor's forces defeated and killed Allectus and finished off the remnants of Allectus' army at Londinium.[243] It is possible that the buildings at the Salvation Army site were under construction until this time. Another possibility is that the Period II buildings were completed and robbed of their stone for the rebuilding of the western section of the riverside wall at Baynard's Castle during the mid-fourth century.

Carausius and Allectus also minted coins at Londinium.[244] The coins of Carausius were initially struck with the mint-mark ML, indicating London, and were issued in gold, silver and base metals. It has been suggested that they were used mainly as gifts to members of the army involved in imperial service.[245] The significance of Londinium is also indicated by a gold medallion minted at Trier and found at Arras, commemorating the recapture of Londinium by Constantius.[246] The reverse of this medallion depicts a war galley and Constantius on horseback being welcomed by a female personification of Londinium (labelled LON) at the gates.[247]

Occupation

During the early part of this century the construction of new and luxurious private houses across Londinium has been interpreted as having represented a 'restoration' that halted a supposed urban decline.[248] It has been argued that late Roman London was typified by opulent and substantial stone houses, often supplied with hypocausts, mosaics and elaborately painted walls. Perring has proposed that there might have been as many as 100 stone houses within the walled area but that the overall density of housing had declined by this time.[249] Subsequent excavations have indicated that stone houses were widespread within late Roman London on both sides of the Thames. It has already been suggested, however, that Londinium remained buoyant throughout the second century and, while it is certainly possible that some areas became abandoned, there is no definitive evidence for urban decline.

The idea that there was a decline in the density of Londinium's settlement during the later second century and the building of isolated and impressive stone houses may have resulted from two connected sources. First, substantial houses have been generally dated to the third and fourth centuries as part of the documentation of an apparent decline in the density of urban housing during the later second century. That some stone houses are now known to pre-date the third century may suggest greater continuity in the wealth of some parts of the population. Second, it has been considered that the timber-and-earth buildings that were common in earlier times generally ceased to be built during the third century when stone houses are supposed to have become common. More recent excavations have clearly indicated, however, that timber-and-earth buildings continued to be constructed after the mid-second century and throughout the history of Londinium.[250] It has already been observed that later truncation may often have preferentially removed evidence for timber-and-earth houses while leaving the evidence for stone structures.[251] The idea of isolated late Roman stone-built houses is probably partly a result of how building techniques have been considered by emphasizing change rather than continuity.

A comparable situation may typify the transition from the early to late Roman periods at other towns in Britain. At Calleva (Silchester), past interpretations have tended to define a decline in the density of occupation in the later Roman period, but recent excavations have uncovered buildings that include timber-and-earth structures, indicating the dense occupation of this urban site throughout the late Roman period.[252] The continued construction of different types of houses at this time at Calleva and Londinium may indicate social inequalities in these urban societies. Timber building traditions continued to be followed for industrial and commercial properties in Southwark and the upper Walbrook Valley and may have been the homes of tenants and slaves. The idea that late Roman Londinium was characterized by scattered stone houses is being replaced as more is discovered about variations in the nature of settlement across Londinium (see Fig. 8.10).

West of the Walbrook

Some buildings at 1 Poultry were rebuilt or extended at this intensively occupied site.[253] Two houses were developed in an elaborate strip form by the addition of rooms to the rear of the timber dwellings that faced onto the main east–west road (see Fig. 8.11).[254] Elaborately fitted and well furnished, these strip-buildings were constructed with a simpler plan than the contemporary winged and courtyard buildings of Londinium. The restricted building plots just north of the main east–west road at 1 Poultry may explain why the strip plan was used at this location.[255] A stone house containing a suite of well-appointed rooms with painted wall plaster was entered through large rooms which led to a pair of heated rooms, and in the fourth century a mosaic floor was laid in this building.[256] Hill and Rowsome have interpreted this as a small but well-appointed bathhouse that accompanied the high-status private residence on the street front.[257]

Immediately to the east a building of timber construction consisted of several rooms, one with a large apsidal end.[258] This building was fitted with two mosaic floors, one described by Neal and Cosh as the work of an 'accomplished contractor',[259] and with high-quality wall plaster. This suite of rooms was probably used for dining or entertainment by wealthy occupants and clients, demonstrating that not all high-status houses in late Roman Londinium were built of stone.[260] Other timber-and-earth buildings continued to be built and modified in close proximity to these impressive houses during the third century and beyond.[261]

Hill and Rowsome have suggested that there may have been a reduction in the density of settlement in this part of Londinium with at least two opulent houses that were developed from a number of earlier properties.[262] Buildings around 1 Poultry were also maintained and modified at this time, indicating a substantial continuity of occupation in this area immediately west of the Walbrook.[263] The impressive Bucklersbury mosaic floor, revealed in 1869, may have dated to the early third century on both stylistic and archaeological grounds.[264] Few traces of stone buildings have been found in the vicinity of this mosaic,[265] suggesting that it may have formed the floor of a timber building along the north side of the main east–west road in a similar manner to the buildings at 1 Poultry.[266]

Excavations at 36–9 Poultry have uncovered pitting and deposits containing late Roman material and at least one substantial stone building was constructed across the course of the road that may have been disused by the end of the third or the beginning of the fourth century.[267] To the north the earlier house at DLR Lothbury (Site B) was modified during the third and into the fourth century.[268] The remains of this building may have formed a substantial courtyard house more than one storey high. The evidence from these sites around 1 Poultry indicates that

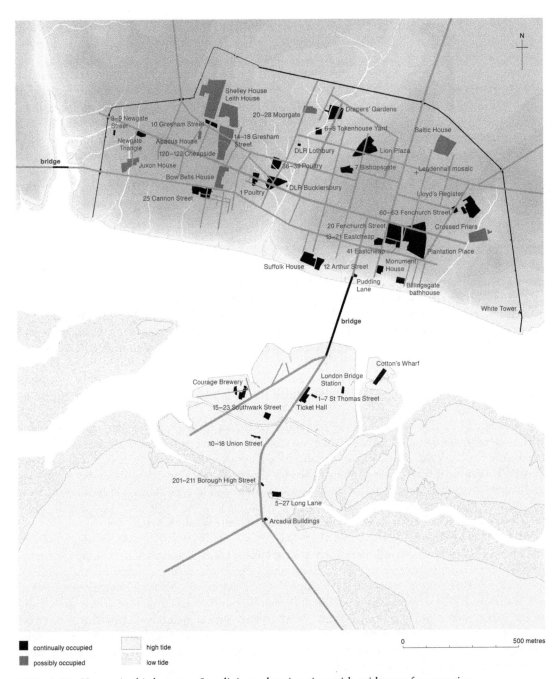

FIG. 8.10 Houses in third-century Londinium, showing sites with evidence of occupation.

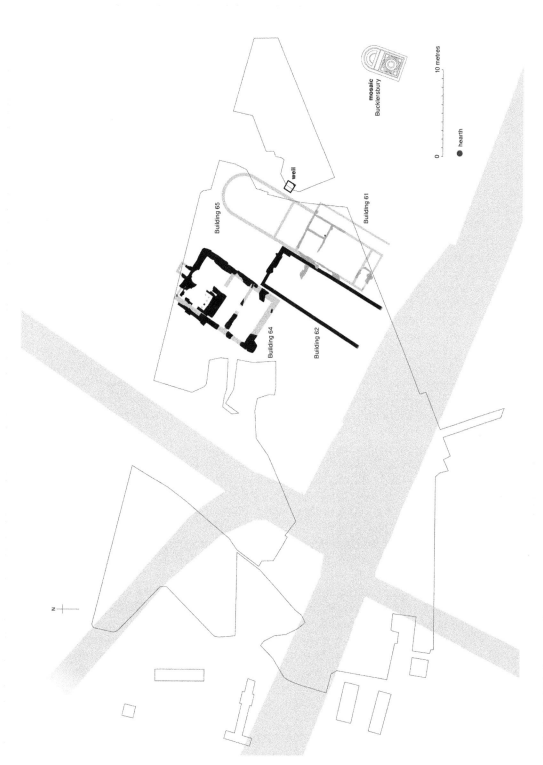

FIG. 8.11 Third-century housing at 1 Poultry, showing 'Building 64' and 'Building 65' and the approximate location at which the mosaic from Bucklersbury House was found in 1869.

there may have been an overall reduction in the number of buildings and an increase in the size and architectural opulence of more scattered houses in this area. Some of these larger houses were at least partly built in timber and earth rather than stone.[269] The remains of the less substantial buildings in the area of 1 Poultry were more difficult to recover and interpret than those of comparably earlier buildings as they were generally less well preserved due to waterlogging and were more truncated.[270]

At 25 Cannon Street the site continued to be intensively occupied throughout the third century, built up with stone buildings that may not have been of particularly high status.[271] A stone mould for the production of pewter plates found in a residual context was probably made after around AD 250, since pewter items in Roman Britain have usually been dated to the period AD 250 to 410.[272] An intensively settled area at 10 Gresham Street was largely abandoned during the second century with evidence for only two later Roman buildings constructed of stone, the better preserved of which was a strip-building.[273] Although substantially built, these houses were less elaborate than the other winged and courtyard houses in Londinium at this period.[274] It is possible that evidence for later Roman buildings might have been removed by truncation from the southern part of this site as some pits were found.[275] At Abacus House, the second-century building with a mosaic had been destroyed in a fire and was succeeded during the third century by a poorly-preserved stone structure or building.[276]

One of the buildings at Bow Bells House was maintained and occupied possibly until AD 250.[277] Pits and a well contained finds dating from the third and fourth centuries, possibly indicating that other later buildings had been truncated by subsequent activities.[278] It is probable that at least part of this site had become open ground by this time. At 120–2 Cheapside and 14–18 Gresham Street there is very little evidence of structural activity after the mid-second century, although dumping was continued and pits were dug, which may indicate that people were still living there.[279] Much of the material from the backfill and the dumping across this area pre-dated the third century, although some of the pottery and coins dated to the third and fourth centuries.

On many other sites later Roman deposits may have been truncated by subsequent activities. Deep features such as pits and wells, containing late Roman finds, have been found where there is no direct evidence of third- and fourth-century buildings. Timber houses may have continued to be built at these sites, although few traces were found. Other sites west of the Walbrook that were apparently largely abandoned at this time but where pits and wells with late Roman objects have been found include 76–80 Newgate Street and the Merrill Lynch Financial Centre site.[280]

The evidence from the sites around Paternoster Square has been interpreted as indicating the former urban land had been cleared for agriculture. At Newgate Triangle the main east–west road remained in use with new roadside drains, and traces of a building ('Building 29') were found that may have dated to the late second or third century.[281] There were small pits dating to the late second and third centuries in this area, although it was not intensively occupied. At Paternoster Row the north–south road became disused and pits were dug to the west that may have been associated with animal husbandry.[282] At Juxton House the scant remains of two timber-and-earth buildings ('Building 30' and 'Building 31') provided no dating evidence, although their occupants could have dumped the rubbish found in the late Roman pits close by.[283] There were certainly some more substantial houses in the western part of Londinium, such as the stone-built house that was constructed during the late third or early fourth century at 3–9 Newgate Street.[284]

The internal buildings of the Cripplegate fort were demolished during the later second century, although the south wall of the fort may have stood for some time. Traces of renewed occupation were uncovered and, even though these deposits were heavily truncated, they included evidence for the resurfacing of one of the roads and for the construction of buildings and fences and the digging of pits.[285] The dating evidence may suggest that activity in this area continued into the mid-fourth century, but there is little to indicate that substantial buildings were constructed.[286]

The upper Walbrook Valley

In the upper Walbrook Valley the site at 15–35 Copthall Avenue appears to have been abandoned during the third century and other sites in close proximity also seem to have been deserted during the second and third centuries.[287] For example, at 20–8 Moorgate, the former pottery production site was used for the dumping of material during the late second to fourth centuries.[288] Pits, gullies, postholes and a hearth may indicate that this area was occupied or that there was industrial activity, while waterlogged deposits suggest that the land was periodically flooded.

People continued to live and work elsewhere in Londinium. The small area excavated at 6–8 Tokenhouse Yard produced evidence for further flooding and also pits and a beamslot which appear to indicate occupation during the third century.[289] At Drapers' Gardens the intensive occupation continued into this century, with existing buildings being rebuilt and new buildings constructed,[290] although the later deposits had been more thoroughly truncated. This site has yet to be fully published but there appears to have been considerable continuity in the form of the small timber buildings constructed from the second century to the fourth. Various industrial activities such as textile working took place here and animals were being slaughtered nearby. This suggests that in this area on the periphery of Londinium small closely-spaced timber houses were built throughout the later Roman period.

East of the Walbrook

To the north of the forum a stone building with a mosaic has been excavated at 7 Bishopsgate.[291] The remains were very heavily cut away by later developments but there were traces of a cellar, stone walls and a fragment of a mosaic of probably third-century date.[292] Immediately to the north-east, at the Lion Plaza site, a substantial stone house was built during late Roman times.[293] This building had been heavily robbed and only fragments of foundations survived to suggest that it had measured at least 30 metres north–south and at least 18 metres east–west, possibly representing a courtyard house.[294] Within this building substantial foundations may have formed the base for an internal tower, although this identification is speculative as a result of very poor preservation.[295] The very fine Leadenhall Street mosaic with a central depiction of Bacchus reclining on a tigress may also have dated to this century, although a later context is also possible (see Fig. 8.12).[296]

To the south-east of the forum, at Plantation Place, the substantial stone house was elaborated during the third century.[297] This house had underfloor heating in at least three rooms and substantial quantities of painted plaster were uncovered. It was probably a lavish courtyard house of a type represented at Calleva and Verulamium.[298] At 20 Fenchurch Street, a single building was found at a site of more intensive earlier occupation.[299] The main feature that survived from this house was a large stone-built cellar that remained in use during the fourth century.[300] Some residual finds suggested that this house, or another building that had been

FIG. 8.12 Reconstruction of the elaborate mosaic found in Leadenhall Street during building work on the premises of the East India Company. The god Bacchus, reclining on the back of a tigress, is surrounded by complex patterns. This mosaic probably dates from the third century.

entirely destroyed, had been fitted with a tessellated floor and painted wall plaster. Robin Wroe-Brown has concluded that there appears to have been a downturn in occupation at 20 Fenchurch Street during the second and third centuries.[301] The evidence for a single substantial building at this site is comparable to the situation across the urban landscape with the construction of more isolated larger stone houses during the late Roman period. It is quite possible, however, that evidence for any timber-and-earth houses had been entirely truncated. At 41 Eastcheap, broadly comparable evidence was found for the construction of a stone building with a cellar; large numbers of tesserae indicated that this house had been floored with a mosaic.[302] At 13–21 Eastcheap, people may still have been living in the earlier building and the large assemblages of early to mid-third century pottery indicated that occupation continued close by.[303]

Further east at the Lloyd's Register site some earlier buildings were modified during the late second and early third centuries.[304] The site was cleared after the mid-third century and it may have been some time before there was another major period of construction, with buildings on a different alignment.[305] These included timber-and-earth buildings and at least two substantial stone buildings, both of which had hypocausts. This site appears to be comparable to 1 Poultry, with substantial stone-built houses constructed alongside timber buildings during the later Roman period. Close by at 60–3 Fenchurch Street, the site had been intensively occupied and rebuilt during the second century with evidence for activity continuing, including the reconstruction of stone buildings and the resurfacing of a road.[306] This site had been heavily truncated by later activity and Vaughan Birbeck and Jörn Schuster have suggested that occupation continued until the mid-third century, although probably not beyond.[307] At Crossed Friars, pits and gullies may indicate the continued use of the area for dumping and perhaps for occupation into the third and fourth centuries.[308]

At Baltic House this sparsely occupied area continued to be used for pit digging and the dumping of waste during the late second to fourth centuries.[309] The dumped building material was derived from nearby demolished buildings although this area was probably mostly open ground; a possible timber building dating from the late second or third century was located.[310]

The Waterfront

In the south-east of the walled area the earlier building close to the White Tower of the Tower of London was occupied and modified throughout the third century.[311] Excavations elsewhere on the waterfront have provided evidence for substantial stone-built houses facing the river. One of the best known later Roman houses in terms of its floor plan is the well-preserved third-century winged house with a brick-built bathhouse that was excavated at Billingsgate in 1968–71 (see Figs 8.13 and 8.14).[312] This building was close to the riverbank in a similar context to the second-century bathhouse at Pudding Lane and both continued to be modified during the third and fourth centuries.[313] The Billingsgate building included three small rooms or chambers that functioned as the *frigidarium* (cold bath), the *tepidarium* (warm bath) and the *caldarium* (hot bath).[314] This small bathhouse was attached to the north range of the house by a passageway. Parts of the north and east ranges of the house were excavated to reveal several tessellated floors, and the east wing of the house was probably originally floored with a mosaic above underfloor heating. This building was developed from two earlier buildings during the early third century.[315] The central location of the bathhouse may suggest that the building served as an inn for travellers; this has also been suggested for the neighbouring bathhouse at Pudding Lane, although it may also have been a private dwelling.[316]

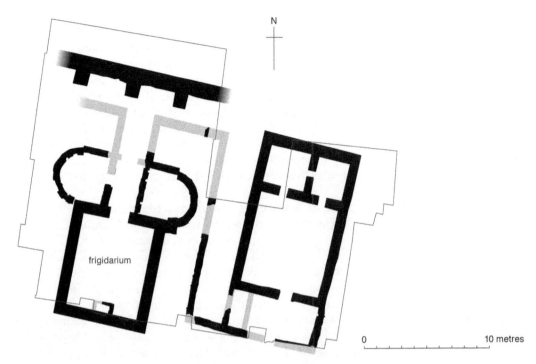

FIG. 8.13 The third-century house with a bathhouse at Billingsgate.

FIG. 8.14 Discovered in 1848, Billingsgate bathhouse was excavated from 1968 to 1971. Built between the wings of a house in the third century, the redeveloped bathhouse was still in use during the latest period of Roman occupation. This photo shows one of the rooms that was heated by a hypocaust.

At Monument House a large stone building was built between around AD 176 and 221.[317] This building was constructed with a large drainage culvert in stone and tile running beneath.[318] The excavated section of the culvert included two silt traps and an access shaft to facilitate its maintenance. Ian Blair has suggested that the size of the culvert may indicate that it led from a public building to the north, possibly the forum-basilica, channelling waste water under the buildings on the river slope and to the Thames.[319] Hygiene and sanitation were addressed by the construction of drains and latrines in densely-populated urban centres such as Londinium.[320] Timber drains have also been found across Londinium, covered with some tile arches where they passed beneath buildings.[321] The culvert at Monument House is the only substantial subterranean Roman drainage system known from Londinium. The excavations produced only limited evidence about the character of the building. A child burial was located buried below one of the floors, a customary treatment of perinatal deaths.[322]

At 12 Arthur Street, at least one high-status building was constructed and partially excavated by Ivor Noël-Hume in 1954–5.[323] The later excavations revealed evidence for three successive stone buildings to the south of the site which may all date from this century. The earliest building comprised at least five rooms, installed with tessellated floors and possibly with mosaics that post-dated AD 180.[324] This building was replaced by a more substantial stone building floored with at least one mosaic dated to around the early third century.[325] Dan Swift has interpreted this building as a substantial house comprising a central gravel courtyard with ranges of rooms on all four sides.[326] A later building replaced this house and, although occupation may have come to an end before the end of the third century, subsequent activities included the digging of pits and dumping of rubbish.[327] The so-called 'townhouse' at Suffolk House close to the 'governor's palace' also continued in use and was modified, as indicated by the pottery found in the demolition deposits.[328]

South of the Thames

It has been suggested that this century was a time of prosperity for at least some of the inhabitants of Southwark.[329] As was the case north of the Thames, many of the timber houses were replaced by stone buildings including large complexes which have been recorded on at least ten sites.[330] On the north island, settlement continued to be intensive; earlier high-status buildings were reconstructed and modified and new elaborate houses constructed. At 15–23 Southwark Street the lavishly decorated second-century buildings continued to be occupied during the early part of the third century and may have been rebuilt and elaborated.[331]

At the Courage Brewery site the ironworking industry continued. A sequence of buildings associated with metalworking hearths replaced the earlier industrial structures and the larger quantity of metalworking waste that was found indicates that production was greater than for the earlier periods.[332] A substantial new workshop and two domestic buildings with tessellated floors were constructed during the later third century.[333] Friederike Hammer has observed that the industrial workshops of the first to fourth centuries at this site were generally built in a less substantial manner than the domestic buildings and that they required regular maintenance and replacement.[334] The domestic buildings at Courage Brewery often had deeper wall slots and may have been built with more skill. The ground plans of several domestic buildings with stone foundations were recorded, the largest of which comprised at least nine rooms possibly with a corridor surrounding a courtyard, a tessellated floor, painted wall plaster and a hypocaust.[335] The remains of this building were heavily truncated, but finds suggest that occupation continued into the fourth century. The workshops at the Courage Brewery site may also have served as domestic dwellings, perhaps indicating that the ironworkers were of lower status than the occupants of other buildings nearby.[336] These workshops may have belonged to the owners of the more substantial houses excavated to the south and east of the industrial area.[337]

At the Ticket Hall site evidence for occupation during the third century had been largely removed and was mainly restricted to pits and 'dark earth' deposits.[338] There was also a long history of metalworking at this site which may have continued into this century.[339] At the eastern edge of the excavated area the fragmentary remains of two or three buildings were recovered, indicated by clay wall foundations, slots and floor timbers.[340] The buildings left only ephemeral traces and most of their remains may have been removed by subsequent truncation. These timber-and-earth buildings are broadly comparable to contemporary buildings from the industrial sites at Courage Brewery and Drapers' Gardens and may be representative of structures that have been truncated across late Roman Londinium. Traces of late Roman stone buildings were found at 1–7 St Thomas Street,[341] while small-scale excavations at London Bridge Station have uncovered a stone building which was probably installed with hypocausts and mosaic floors.[342] At Cotton's Wharf a stone building was located on an islet just east of the north island that had also had hypocausts and mosaic floors.[343]

There is little evidence for late Roman buildings on the south island and it has been suggested that this area may have been depopulated during the later second century. At 10–18 Union Street the corner of a small stone building dating from the third century was associated with a well.[344] At 201–11 Borough High Street on the south edge of the south island excavations revealed part of a stone building with robbed-out walls, back-filled with layers containing red and white mosaic tesserae.[345] At 5–27 Long Lane the two timber-and-earth buildings were modified during the first half of this century and the interior of one had been decorated with painted plaster.[346] These buildings were probably demolished and the site abandoned during the late third century and 'dark earth' subsequently developed across the site.[347]

There appear to have been few domestic buildings on the south bank of the Borough Channel. At Arcadia Buildings there were two phases of activity during the third and early fourth centuries. Industrial activities may have continued at this time, focused on a cluster of brickearth buildings, one of which contained a substantial hearth.[348] During the late third or early fourth century a large building was constructed west of the main north–south road, although industrial activity may have ended by this time.[349] Burials, temples and temple-mausolea stood in the vicinity of the two roads on the south bank of the Thames, but little additional evidence of late Roman occupation has been found. The south island and the main bank of the Thames may have been largely unoccupied during the third century, with just a scattering of industrial and domestic properties.

Marking the boundaries

Mortuary practices, feasting, dumping of cultural materials, industry and religious activities all continued around the margins of Londinium (see Fig. 8.15).

Dumping, feasting and wells in Southwark

The dumping of considerable quantities of building materials, including high-status materials derived from opulent buildings, at several sites on the south island seems to be anomalous in considering the relative absence of evidence for buildings. At 33 Union Street substantial quantities of building materials were dumped across the site that may have been transported to

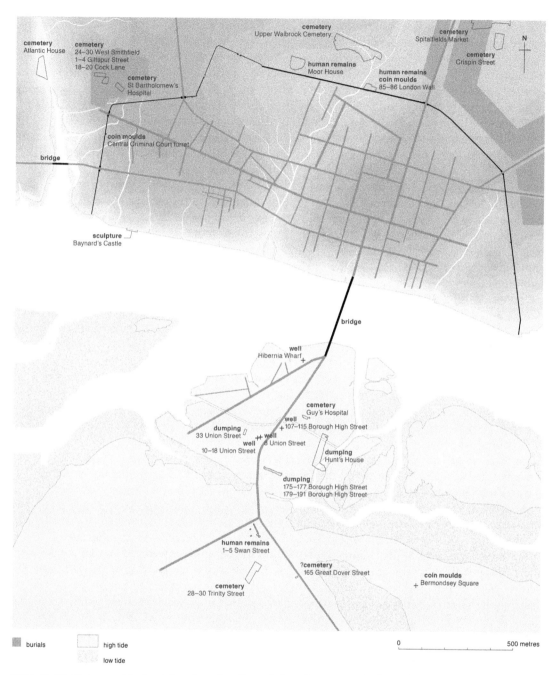

FIG. 8.15 Coin moulds, burials, selected wells and dumping across the boundary areas of Londinium in the third century.

this location from outside Southwark.[350] At Hunt's House material including building debris, pottery and coins continued to be dumped into Guy's Channel into the fourth century.[351] Building materials have been found in other contexts dated to the second and third centuries, including at 175–7 and 179–91 Borough High Street and in three third-century wells.[352] An extensive area of the south island may have been open land used for the recycling of old building material, or the remains of stone buildings may have been truncated.

Three wells on the south island containing significant deposits of material have been dated to the later third century.[353] A square well just to the south-east of the building at the 10–18 Union Street site contained pottery and food waste as did several pits that were located close by.[354] Fiona Seeley and Angela Wardle have described the material from the wells and other features at this site as 'unusual' and 'ritual' in nature.[355] The pottery was deposited in the well around AD 250 to 300 and included vessels that are often thought to have been used in ritual activities, including three tazze and two triple vases.[356] The animal bones were not common food waste, comprising a large quantity of cattle and pig bones, the skull of a red deer and the remains of a dog.[357] The bones of dogs from other wells and pits across Londinium have been interpreted as ritual in character.[358] Just to the east, at 8 Union Street, another well contained material dating from the mid to later third century, including triple vases and unusual animal remains such as two bones from a white tailed eagle and parts of the skulls of two red deer.[359] This well also contained a large quantity of building material including roof and box tiles, evidently derived from a stone building, and slag from a bowl ironworking furnace.[360] There was no evidence for stone buildings in the vicinity.

A third well was uncovered at 107–15 Borough High Street, just east of the main north–south road.[361] No evidence for contemporary buildings was found although there were pits and groups of stake holes that may have been dug during the late third or fourth century.[362] This well contained a substantial amount of building material,[363] evidence for iron smithing and a large group of pottery dating from the second half of the third century.[364] These vessels were burnt and poorly finished and may have been wasters from a pottery production industry of a single vessel form 'Camulodunum 306'. This type of vessel has been found in burial and religious contexts such as at the temple of Mithras and the Tabard Square temple.[365] The animal bones included a particularly large number of dog bones deposited in the well from at least four carcasses.[366]

Seeley and Wardle have observed that the association of ritual vessels with high-status or unusual food waste in these wells may suggest that the dumped materials derive from religious ceremonies.[367] The objects in the well at 107–15 Borough High Street were significantly different from those in the wells at the Union Street sites, but the unusual pottery and animal bones unite them. It is possible that this southern part of Southwark was a relatively open area between the settled areas of the north island and the ritual landscape of temples and burials on the south bank of the Thames. Perhaps the deposits of pottery and animal remains were placed in shafts close to the main north–south road as the result of feasting connected with the movement of people from the forum to the south through the low-lying lands on the south island that were probably still partly surrounded by water, at least at high tide.

A well at Hibernia Wharf, on the north island just to the east of Winchester Palace, was dug on the margins of the occupied area.[368] This well was filled some time during the second half of the third century with a large quantity of pottery and glass vessels, including six drinking vessels. The animal remains, such as pig and deer bones, may represent food waste from a single high-status feast.[369] At Hibernia Wharf the buildings were abandoned by this century. This site is just north of Southwark Cathedral and close to a fourth-century well that contained the sculpted stones that may have been the remains of burial monuments from a cemetery.[370] Perhaps the feasting that was held at Hibernia Wharf was connected with rituals conducted at a nearby cemetery or temple.

It is notable that three of the third-century wells in Southwark contained bones of red deer or roe deer, since remains of these animals are uncommon in Roman contexts in Britain.[371] In Roman society, the keeping of live deer was an elite practice and these animals symbolically transcended the boundary separating wildness from domesticity.[372] Martin Allen has suggested that the hunting of deer provided a means of signifying social inequality in Roman Britain.[373] Perhaps these wells were used to dispose of the remains of religious feasts linked to the creation of status.[374] Three representations of hunter gods have been found in London,[375] including the figure placed in the fourth-century well under Southwark Cathedral that may indicate that divinity and hunting were associated with the islands of Southwark. The other two representations of hunter gods have been found north of the Thames and it has been suggested that there may have been a temple in the Fleet Valley dedicated to this divinity.

Rituals on the walls

Earlier activities that had been undertaken to demarcate the boundaries indicate that the new landward wall had a ritual significance.[376] The surviving sculptural fragments of the Monumental Arch and Screen of Gods may have been selected for reuse in the riverside wall at Baynard's Castle, during either the late third or fourth centuries, because of the value and meaning of the sculptures.[377] The excavators recorded some information about the sequence and character of the reuse of the stones from the two monuments when they were incorporated into the wall,[378] although certain stones were removed by the contractors without archaeological record.[379] Blagg has noted that it is likely that these fifty-two stones formed around one fifth of the original stones that made up the two monuments.[380] Many of the other stones had presumably been built into neighbouring sections of the riverside wall which had been lost as a result of erosion, collapse and the removal of material.[381]

As Blagg has noted, many of these sculptures were carved with distinctive attributes of deities that allowed them to be identified,[382] suggesting that certain particular stones may have been 'positively selected' for reuse in the construction of the wall. Heads, hands holding objects and distinctive animals and birds associated with particular gods and goddesses are very well represented in the surviving fragments.[383] Although fourteen stones from the Arch had no attributes, six stones were carved with a head or partial head and seven with other parts of the body. Heads were less commonly represented on the six stones from the Screen, although five were carved with features that allowed the divine figures to be identified.

These sculpted stones may have been deliberately selected because of the continued significance of fragments of divine representations in the powerfully symbolic context of the construction or reconstruction of the urban limits. The breaking up of the monuments and their sculptures may have served as a means to create fragments that inherited the spirit of the whole, transferring the carved object from one state to another. The demolition of the Arch and the Screen may therefore have created fragments of stonework that drew upon the spirit of the original monuments. By incorporating the fragmentary figures of powerful gods into an offset course on the inner face of the wall the builders could have been drawing upon aspects of their divine roles. The inclusion of fragments of demolished religious structures may have played a comparable role in the construction of solid and firm foundations. The fragmentary sculptures were often hidden within the body of the wall but may have been associated with the idea of the divinities and the protection of the urban boundaries.

The ritual and symbolic values of the urban circuit may be indicated by other objects. Hall has discussed discoveries of clay moulds connected with the production of counterfeit coins at two sites on the Roman walls.[384] The forging of coins was common during the Roman period throughout the empire, an activity that was uncontrollable, especially during periods of high inflation.[385] Clay coin moulds are common finds in Britain, Gaul and Germany.[386] At the Central Criminal Court site a hoard of coins and coin moulds has been used to help date the construction of the wall.[387] It was deposited within a feature that may have been the stairwell of the internal tower, probably between around AD 215 and 225. Found towards the base of the fill of the tower, the coins included one issued during the reign of Caracalla (AD 211–17) in almost mint condition. Two moulds for forging coins were also found, one for an obverse of a coin of Severus (AD 201–10) and the other for an obverse of a coin of Geta (AD 210–11).[388] Since no slag or other materials associated with metalworking were found in this deposit, the coins were probably forged elsewhere and the materials that made up the hoard were subsequently left in the tower.[389] The fill above the hoard was built up and overlain by soil containing a quantity of pottery and the fragmentary skeletons of at least six dogs.[390] Since dog skeletons were often associated with ritual deposits throughout Londinium, this may indicate the nature of the deposition of the forger's materials.

A group of 814 complete and fragmentary clay moulds for forging coins was excavated from the external ditch of the Roman wall, which also contained human remains, at 85–6 London Wall.[391] The wall at this location was crossed by several tributaries of the upper Walbrook where its construction had caused flooding during the early third century.[392] Several parallel ditches were dug to drain flood water from the area to the north into the wall ditch, which was 5 metres wide and 1.5 metres deep.[393] This ditch may have also functioned as a flood relief channel, diverting flood water eastwards around the urban perimeter.[394] The moulds were for the making of a range of counterfeit coins dating from the reign of Trajan (AD 98–117) to the time of Trebonianus Gallus (AD 251–3).[395] Some of these pre-dated the presumed date for the construction of the walls but the majority dated from AD 194 to 253. Hall has argued that these moulds indicate that coins were being forged in a considerable quantity, since at least sixty-one silver *denarii* and sixteen copper-alloy coins would have been in the possession of the forgers. She has also suggested that this forging may indicate an attempt to increase the numbers of small silver denominations at a time when such coins were in short supply, a recognized method of increasing the supply of currency rather than the perpetration of a criminal act.[396] The clay moulds were found scattered through several contexts within the ditch.[397] Fluctuations in the level of water in the ditch resulted in the accumulation of layers of sediment, and water flowing along the ditch distributed the coin moulds to various locations.[398]

On Bermondsey eyot in the Thames, three coin moulds were found in 1998 in what has been interpreted as an agricultural ditch dating from the early third century.[399] The evidence for Roman occupation on this eyot suggests that it may have been primarily used as agricultural land.[400] The moulds from these three sites were all found in the marginal areas and the industrial activities associated with the production of coins may have imbued these items with ritual associations.

Burying the dead

The evidence for the use of water and tidal flow in funerary 'rites of passage' during the first and second centuries might suggest that the deposition of corpses on the edges of ditches was associated with the transformation of members of the community into the fellowship of the ancestors through the exposure, defleshing and disarticulation of the body.[401] The extent to which corpses were exposed to the air and erosion by water during the third century is not entirely clear. Many of the human cranial remains from sites in the upper Walbrook date from before around AD 200, although a female cranium was found at Moor House in a ditch dating from the third or fourth century, accompanied by the skull of a horse.[402]

The Upper Walbrook Cemetery continued to receive burials during the third century, although in far fewer numbers.[403] The major east–west ditch at this cemetery continued to be used for inhumation burials that were eroded by running water. Other inhumation burials were interred further south and a small group of cremations was also found.[404] The cemetery may have continued to be used into the fourth century although marshy conditions were encroaching.[405]

The discovery of human bones and burial offerings from the ditch of the Roman wall at 85–6 London Wall indicates that human remains continued to be buried and subject to erosion by watercourses in other parts of the upper Walbrook Valley.[406] Finds from this section of the ditch included human bone, leather shoes and nine pots that had accompanied the burials, five of which were complete and contained offerings of chickens and coins. These may have been derived from burials that had been washed out from cemeteries to the north by the flooding of the Walbrook.[407] As the ditch at this point was subject to regularly flooding, the corpses and offerings may actually have been placed on the edges to be washed into this water-filled feature.[408] The coin moulds, human bones and burial offerings do not appear to have been closely associated.[409]

During this century the dead were brought to cemeteries the extent of which may have become more defined, although there is only limited information. The burial grounds to the north of Londinium remained in use. Around 150 graves have been excavated at Spitalfields Market that date from around AD 250 to 400.[410] Many additional graves in this area have been destroyed by the digging of medieval graves and pits. The majority of the burials were inhumations, although a few cremations were uncovered, and grave goods included pottery, glass vessels and animal offerings. Burials also continued to be made in the area of cemetery at Crispin Street and probably at 201 Bishopsgate.[411] In Shoreditch a small cluster of three or four late Roman burials were dug in agricultural land around 300 metres north of the Spitalfields cemetery and just west of Ermine Street.[412]

In Southwark the dead were still buried on the south bank of the Thames and it is possible that there were several discrete burial grounds.[413] To the south a series of burial grounds were laid out and developed from the first to fourth centuries along Watling Street, including the example at 165 Great Dover Street. The buildings at this site were further modified, with the final stages of the development of the two walled cemeteries and the construction of the two temple-mausolea.[414] Inhumation burials that may have been of third-century date included a child buried within the northern walled cemeteries dated to AD 250 to 300.[415] Another burial was made in an unenclosed area of this cemetery probably during the middle of the century. Although Watling Street was maintained into the fourth century, the burial monuments alongside it at Great Dover Street had fallen into disuse and may have been demolished. Three burials uncovered at Harper Road may have been in another part of the same cemetery, although the inhumations were not excavated and the only dating evidence suggests that one was buried during the second century.[416]

At 28–30 Trinity Street excavations have uncovered further information for this extensive cemetery landscape, comprising forty-four inhumation burials, two cremations and large quantities of disarticulated human bone.[417] This cemetery may have been established during the late second century, although the majority of burials dated from the third and fourth centuries.

Two of the ditches that crossed the cemetery were the focus of fragmentation rites. The earlier ditch contained human bone and a later ditch that constituted a major topographic feature of the third-century cemetery was filled with materials throughout the later Roman period,[418] including a very large quantity of disarticulated and semi-articulated human bone and some near complete pots.[419] In one area, the cranial remains of three individuals were associated with a pottery vessel. Human longbones were notable in the fill of this ditch, some of which were found on the shallow slope of its western edge.[420] It is possible that corpses were placed at the edges of these ditches at the urban margins as had been the custom elsewhere in Londinium at earlier periods. The bones found at this site may have been defleshed prior to deposition since they showed little evidence of gnawing by wild animals.[421] There may perhaps have been connections with the methods of burial adopted in the Upper Walbrook Cemetery during the late first to third centuries, where corpses were either buried or placed on the edges and within the drainage channel that flowed into the Walbrook. The remains of some of the burials from this cemetery indicate, however, that many of the dead were not exposed to the elements for any length of time and that some of the bodies were buried complete in wooden coffins.[422]

Although burials of third-century date were not found during the excavations at 52–6 Lant Street, the proximity of second- and fourth-century examples is likely to indicate continued funerary activities.[423] At 1–5 Swan Street a third-century ditch contained pottery and human remains, including a frontal bone and a right femur, and a small fragment of funerary inscription in stone.[424] Probably derived from a nearby cemetery, these objects may have been placed in the ditch in connection with fragmentation rites. Two burials were deposited on the edge of this ditch probably during the fourth century, suggesting that burials were made across the extensive area between Watling Street, Stane Street and the Borough Channel to the north.

In the west of the south island, burial practices began during the later second century and continued into the fourth,[425] although it is unclear how extensively this cemetery area was used at this time. Another possible area of burial has already been noted close to Southwark Cathedral on the north of the north island.[426] Five burials that may date to the third century were found during excavations at Guy's Hospital east of the main road on the north island.[427] A scatter of burials on the Bermondsey eyot may also be of late Roman date.[428] Evidently most burials were made south of the Borough Channel with separate cemeteries established on the boundaries of the settled areas of Southwark.

Few modern excavations have been undertaken on the mortuary terrains to the west of Londinium. Twenty inhumations at the St Bartholomew's site probably dated to the third and fourth centuries.[429] Some of the corpses were interred in timber coffins and five were accompanied by grave goods, three with a coin. One woman was buried with jewellery and a miniature bronze bell; scientific analysis of lead and strontium stable isotopes from her tooth enamel suggested that she had had been born in Britain and perhaps in Londinium.[430] A further burial area at 24–30 West Smithfield, 18–20 Cock Lane and 1–4 Giltspur Street has been located.[431] On the west side of the Fleet river, an area of inhumation and cremation burials dating from the second and third centuries has been excavated at Atlantic House.[432]

Some of the best information for late Roman cemeteries is provided by extensive excavations to the east.[433] Burials continued in the areas of the 'eastern cemetery' established during the early Roman period and were not much affected by the building of the wall. The construction of the wall during the later second or early third century may have resulted in the blocking of the 'cemetery road' so that the burials were probably accessed from Londinium by passing through the gateway at Aldgate, although it is possible that a postern gate was constructed through the wall.

Burials were also made outside the immediate area of the walls to the east. Around 5 kilometres east of Londinium, where the London–Colchester road crosses the Lea river, a series of cemeteries have been identified at Old Ford associated with another settlement in close proximity to Londinium.[434] Cremations and inhumations were made in six distinct burial areas, including some examples that may date from the second century, although most were deposited during the third and fourth centuries.[435] Traces of buildings have been uncovered close to the crossing of the road over the river, indicating that an extensive settlement may have existed here to supply Londinium with agricultural goods.

Summary

It is evident that Londinium continued to prosper from the scale and character of the urban defences, the range of temple buildings and the religious dedications that were made throughout Roman London. The population may have reduced since there is less evidence for domestic buildings of third-century date than for the early second century. One of the main problems with assessing the late Roman history of Londinium is the differential preservation of archaeological deposits. Earlier deposits are more commonly waterlogged and less severely truncated by later activity. Building techniques may also have changed in the later Roman period. As a result, a case has been made that London retained a high population during late Roman times. The many excavated sites that have produced pits and wells of this date might suggest that the extent of occupation and the general density of buildings had not declined radically during the third century. The impression that the urban landscape was dominated by substantial stone houses may also result from the nature of the survival of the late Roman archaeological deposits. It is evident that substantial and well-appointed stone dwellings characterized third-century Londinium, although excavations have demonstrated that timber-and-earth buildings continued to be constructed alongside stone houses.

Late Roman Londinium remained a centre for manufacturing and many people will have been involved in its processes. The metalwork, bone and leather goods produced at these places may have been used largely to supply the population of Londinium and it is not very evident whether trade through the port remained significant. Perhaps the official roles of Roman London took over from the trading significance of earlier times. The large numbers of wealthy occupants also means that there was a considerable population of slaves and retainers to support the privileged. Many slaves will have lived with the wealthy families inside the opulent late-Roman houses, but clients, tenants, freedmen and most slaves will have lived elsewhere in Londinium and in its surrounds. At the Courage Brewery site industrial premises were built next to more elaborate stone houses, possibly symbolizing the relative status of industrial and commercial workers and of those who owned them. At Drapers' Gardens the timber houses in a marginal location may have been the property of wealthy individuals living elsewhere in Londinium. Excavations are providing a more balanced picture of the range of buildings which provide a glimpse at the inequalities of provincial society.

The religious and ritual landscapes continued to develop and much of the religious sculpture from London derives from third-century contexts. Several new temple sites were established and others continued to prosper. The sculptures from Baynard's Castle indicate that, on occasions, temples were restored and then demolished. Temples were often situated close to the margins where boundary practices involving the fragmenting of human corpses continued in some areas at the edge of the urban landscape.

9

Endings and Beginnings

Out of the spent and unconsidered Earth,
The Cities rise again.
RUDYARD KIPLING 1906: 139

Introduction

The fourth century has often been described as the period of Londinium's decline, as many of the houses and public buildings were abandoned.[1] This process has usually been regarded as culminating in the total abandonment of the walled urban area and the Southwark suburb at the beginning of the fifth century. The concept of decline and fall has dominated studies of the later Roman Empire since the late eighteenth century.[2] The study of the urban centres of Britannia has been deeply affected by this intellectual model,[3] although new accounts of the later phases of Londinium have begun to challenge this.[4] The emperors and generals who visited during the fourth century confirm Roman London's important administrative and cultural role. More recent archaeological work has suggested that Londinium's role as a significant urban centre may have continued beyond the end of the Roman period.

During the late third or early fourth centuries the two provinces *Britannia Superior* and *Britannia Inferior* were subdivided into two. Anthony Birley has considered that this may have occurred during the political disruptions of the second half of the third century and there were clearly four provinces by the time the Verona List (*Laterculus Veronensis*) was complied between AD 303 and 314 which named them as *Prima, Secunda, Maxima Caesariensis* and *Flavia Caesariensis*.[5] Each was represented at the ecclesiastical council held at Arles in AD 314 which was attended by delegations from the capital of each province including Restitutus who was referred to as a bishop (*episcopus*) at Londinium.[6] London was probably the capital of the province of *Maxima Caesariensis*. The largest urban centre in Britannia, Londinium was the seat of the *vicarius*, a senior official with responsibility for all four provinces,[7] and where the staff and households of imperial officials were based.[8] The mint established under Carausius continued to produce coins until AD 324, further reflecting the economic importance of Roman London.[9]

When compared with important Roman administrative centres on the continent, Simon Esmonde Cleary has remarked that the administrative roles of Londinium should have ensured a high level of prosperity and activity.[10] The strategic value of Londinium was crucially important to emperors and their advisors. In AD 360 the commander Flavius Lupicinus planned to use

London as a base for military operations during the reign of the emperor Julian.[11] In AD 367–8 the emperor Valentinian sent the general Theodosius to regain control of Britain at a time of significant unrest.[12] Ammianus Marcellinus' account of Theodosius' activities records that 'Lundinium' was an old town that later generations had called 'Augusta'.[13] Theodosius may have over-wintered in Londinium to prepare for the successful campaign that led to the recovery of Britannia in AD 368. The name 'Augusta' might have had some official relevance in indicating the importance and status of late Roman London, although it is uncertain which emperor awarded this title.[14] In the legend on coins minted at Londinium during the early fourth century the name was abbreviated to 'L'. The mint was briefly revived under Magnus Maximus in AD 383–8 and some of the coins from this period show the abbreviation 'AVG', suggesting that the title 'Augusta' was current at this time.[15] The early fifth-century Roman document the *Notitia Dignitatum* recorded military dispositions and information on the late Roman administration of the provinces of Britain.[16] The reference to an official in charge of the treasuries at Augusta in this document may suggest that Londinium retained its earlier role as the financial centre of its province or even of the entire diocese of Britannia.[17]

Gerrard has mapped two classes of late Roman finds across Londinium: coins dating to the House of Valentinian and Theodosius (AD 364–402) and three types of pottery that are considered as indicating late Roman occupation.[18] The distribution of these finds suggests that the walled area, the north island in Southwark and, possibly, southern Southwark remained intensively occupied until the early fifth century.[19] Evidence from excavations at several cemeteries indicates that people were still buried in these areas during the late fourth century and for some time into the fifth century. The walled circuit could have provided a safe place during these troubled times.

It is uncertain when the walled area was abandoned. The production of pottery and other manufactured artefacts that formed the basis of market exchange had largely ceased in Britannia during the late fourth and early fifth centuries and coins had ceased to circulate. Life may have continued throughout Londinium for a while, with the population maintaining their buildings, reusing artefacts and occasionally depositing them with their dead. Although Gerrard has argued that the walled area was abandoned during the first half of the fifth century,[20] some of the other towns of Britannia may have continued to be occupied well into the fifth century and beyond. Although there is very little evidence to indicate that Londinium's walled area was still inhabited, results from recent excavations in the hinterland have suggested that occupation continued into at least the fifth century.

Public buildings and infrastructure

Few towns in Britannia have produced evidence for the construction of public buildings during the fourth century.[21] Many earlier buildings were abandoned, although walled circuits continued to be maintained and supplemented. The vitality of fourth-century Londinium was expressed by the walls, the continued use of many of its public buildings and by the construction of a monumental structure of unknown purpose at Colchester House (see Fig. 9.1).

Buildings old and new

The main roads continued to be maintained at this time. Crossing the Thames, it has been suggested that the late first-century bridge had timber decking supported on piers of stone and

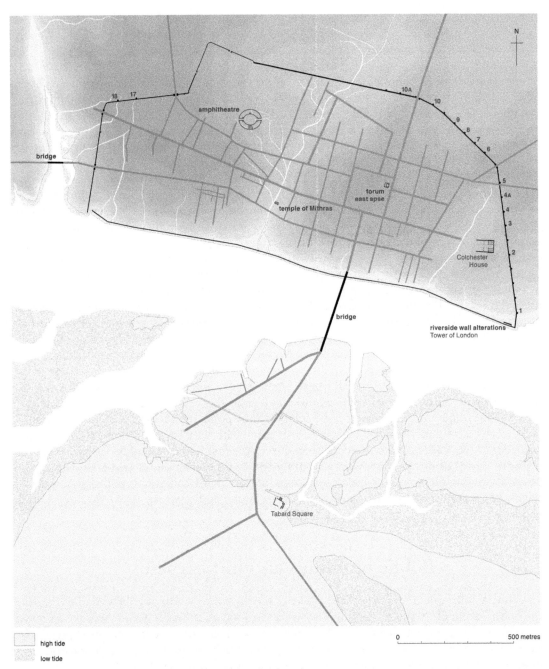

FIG. 9.1 Public buildings and infrastructure in the fourth century.

tile courses, simpler to maintain than a bridge that was entirely built in stone.[22] In his study of the coins from the site of the bridge, Michael Rhodes has observed that there was a substantial decline in the frequency of coin loss from around AD 330, possibly indicating that the bridge had been swept away by the river.[23] There was a particular absence of Valentinian coins, although a few coins were deposited close to the bridge well into the fourth century, including issues of Honorius (AD 395–423). One possibility is that the tradition of depositing coins in the river while crossing the bridge had largely ceased during the mid-fourth century. The superstructure may therefore have been maintained until the final collapse of the civic authority, possibly during the late fourth or early fifth century.

The Theodosian Code recorded that bridge building was a public duty citizens were expected to undertake and this bridge could have been maintained into the fifth century due to the strategic importance of the river crossing.[24] The alignment of the Late Saxon and medieval roads on both banks of the Thames is similar to that of the main north–south Roman road, possibly indicating that the bridge continued to be used and repaired during the centuries after the end of Roman rule.[25] The bridge would, however, not have been constantly maintained nor regularly rebuilt during the fifth and sixth centuries when there is very little evidence for occupation within the walled circuit.[26] During the ninth century the surviving piers of the Roman bridge may have been reused to support a new timber superstructure.[27]

There is little evidence to indicate when the forum and basilica were abandoned and their stone removed, although this probably occurred during the late third or early fourth centuries.[28] The forum may have been demolished by the early fourth century and sections of later walling in the area where it formerly stood could indicate that the area was reoccupied.[29] The chronology of the late phases of the basilica has been dated to the late third century and the building was probably demolished by the early fourth century,[30] although the elaborately decorated eastern apse and the adjoining antechamber may have remained substantially intact during late Roman times.[31] Standing in isolation on the top of the hill, this building may have continued to be associated with ideas of urban power and authority.[32] Trevor Brigham has also suggested that a second part of the basilica beneath Gracechurch Street which has been identified as a possible shrine was retained at least for a while.[33] The apparent demolition of most of the basilica and forum need not indicate that marketing, meetings and ceremonies no longer took place there during the fourth century.[34]

Some limited evidence has been found for activities continuing at other public or official buildings. Previous interpretations of these buildings have tended to state that they were simply abandoned and demolished during the late Roman period and have not considered the possibility that particular places and structures may have retained meanings derived from their earlier histories.[35] The continued significance of the surviving earthworks and ruins of buildings during late Roman and post-Roman times could help to explain the activities that took place at these sites, including occupation and burial. During the late third century the stone amphitheatre had been partially rebuilt and some alterations were made to the structure during the early fourth century, including modifications to the arena wall, the resurfacing of the arena on at least two occasions, the provision of new drains in the arena and eastern entrance, and alterations to the banking.[36] The coins from the latest arena surface date to around AD 340.[37] A single-roomed timber building was constructed to replace earlier structures just outside the eastern entranceway.[38] Significant objects found in contexts dated to the late third and early fourth centuries provide some understanding of the rituals practised in the amphitheatre. Two of the three curses found at the site were deposited at this time, while the third was found in a late second- to early third-century context.[39] Two were deposited in drains, one referring to an offering made to the goddess 'Deana' (presumably Diana) relating to the theft of a hat or hood and neck band or scarf,[40] and another records two non-Roman personal names.

The excavator of the amphitheatre has suggested that the intermittent robbing of stone from the structure may have begun around AD 355.[41] The rubble on the arena floor was presumably a result of this activity, although some building material from elsewhere had also been added to these dumps, indicating that the amphitheatre had been abandoned as a place for large-scale display.[42] Dumped deposits that sealed the remains of the robbed eastern entrance included a large number of mid-fourth-century coins.[43]

A series of archaeological features were cut into the late Roman phases of the amphitheatre, including postholes, drains and pits.[44] Some of the postholes may have been connected with the robbing of stone from the arena wall that could have been used in building projects, perhaps to construct the bastions on the walls.[45] The large amount of coins dating to the mid-fourth century suggests that economic activity continued nearby for a while,[46] although the rarity of later fourth-century coins may indicate that this arena had finally been abandoned.[47] Bateman has mentioned that the arena area would have been uneven, with areas of upstanding wall, robbing pits and surface water, and the environmental evidence from the late deposits has suggested that it reverted to a damp environment that may have ended the use of the amphitheatre as a public structure.

The skull of a bear, probably a brown bear, was recovered from the fill of a revetted drain dated to the late fourth century at Drapers' Gardens in the upper Walbrook Valley.[48] Kevin Rielly has suggested that the bear's head may have been a keepsake or trophy that had been de-fleshed, perhaps retaining the skin.[49] Three other bear bones have been found in Roman deposits in London, one from Courage Brewery, one from Tabard Square and a possible fragment from the amphitheatre.[50] Rielly has suggested that the bones were derived from animals that were being kept for entertainment. It is known that bears from northern Britain (Caledonia) were exported to Rome for entertainments in the arena and the bones indicate that comparable events were held in Londinium. The late context of the skull from Drapers' Gardens suggests that it may either have been a trophy, or that bear-baiting continued into the latest phases of Roman London. The robbing of stonework of the amphitheatre and the dumping of building material from the AD 350s need not necessarily indicate that the associations of the amphitheatre were immediately forgotten, since it had been an important element in the urban infrastructure for almost three centuries. Perhaps the waterlogged and rubble-strewn arena was viewed as an appropriate setting for the hunting of a Caledonian bear.

Three burials of young individuals were found on the eastern side of the disused amphitheatre, including a single burial in the northern part of the entrance and two in the bank.[51] Radiocarbon dates have suggested that these burials dated from the late fourth or early fifth centuries, although no datable finds were found. Similar to those found at amphitheatres in Corinium (Cirencester) and Durnovaria (Dorchester, Dorset), these burials have sometimes been interpreted as those of Christians due to the association of amphitheatres with martyrdom.[52]

The information from the temple of Mithras and from the Tabard Square temple indicates that traditional gods were still worshipped well into the fourth century. Christianity was presumably developed alongside earlier practices of worship. The temple of Mithras was rebuilt during the early fourth century, with the removal of the colonnades to create a more open floor plan, and earlier cult statues were buried in at least one pit cut into the floor.[53] It is possible that two new altars were installed at the west end, but traces of only one have been found. These alterations to the internal layout have been interpreted by Shepherd and Henig as indicating a change in the religion practised from the worship of Mithras to the cult of Bacchus.[54] Shepherd has suggested that a recess created in the face of the raised platform in the apse of the Mithraeum during the early fourth-century alterations might have resulted from the removal of the small marble relief depicting Mithras slaughtering the bull.[55] The six pieces of statuary were found in and around one or more pits in 1954, including heads of the gods Mithras, Minerva and Serapis, two hands of Mithras and the Mercury group.[56] If the heads were attached to bodies, it would not have been possible to display all of the statues inside the Mithraeum at the same time and some were probably brought to the temple especially for burial.

Haynes has suggested, however, that the placing of the sculptures in pits was not necessarily a simple or even a single event and that this did not indicate the cessation of the worship of Mithras.[57] The deposit of fragments of cult statues and inscribed stones in the pits and in floor layers during the early fourth century may have been connected with the joint worship of Mithras and Bacchus rather than with the ending of one cult and the beginning of another.[58] Since the three sculptures of Bacchus were carved during the second and third centuries, they may have formed part of a large collection of statues, some of which were buried in pits in the floor of the temple during the early fourth century. A statuette of Bacchus with his retinue found in a fourth-century context at the Mithraeum was probably carved not much later than AD 250.[59] Two fragments from marble statuettes, including the lower back, upper legs and genitalia of a male god, possibly Bacchus, may have been carved during the second century,[60] although they were deposited in fourth-century contexts. One of the fragmentary statues of Bacchus came from a late context overlying the 'narthex' to the east of the temple.[61] The other was found almost 200 metres to the north-west of the temple in a trench excavated by Grimes. This excavation also revealed a stone platform of a possible late Roman building and poorly preserved traces of timber buildings,[62] possibly a shrine.[63] The survival of the genitals of two of the statues of Bacchus and the similarity of the fragments also appears deliberate.[64]

Further alterations were made to this temple after the early fourth century, although the open floor was retained and at least four new floors were laid. Although there were no coins dating later than the mid-fourth century,[65] a few fragments of pottery found close to the apse of the temple may date to the later century.[66] The building was gradually abandoned and the lack of evidence for the robbing of its stone suggests that it was left to fall into ruin until it was eventually buried.[67]

At Tabard Square in Southwark the temple site was rebuilt on a smaller scale and was more clearly defined during this century. A new precinct was laid out containing a substantial building (see Fig. 9.2).[68] This had two wings connected by a corridor with a timber staircase that probably gave access to an upper floor (see Fig. 9.3).[69] Many late Roman stone houses in Londinium featured at least one room with underfloor heating, although there was no evidence in the Tabard Square building for a hypocaust.[70] This building may have provided guest accommodation for visitors to the temple. The ceremonies that drew crowds of people to this temple may have taken place during the summer months when no heating was required for guests, although it is also possible that it was a temple with an unconventional plan.[71] The southern temple was abandoned and demolished, although the northern temple probably remained in use.

An inscription recording the name of the man who had dedicated the northern temple building at Tabard Square had been carefully buried in a pit within the enclosure of the late-Roman temple in the fourth century (see Fig. 7.12).[72] The pit's fill also contained a small assemblage of pottery dated to around AD 350 to 400, probably deposited when the northern temple building was disused.[73] The worship of Mars Camulus at Tabard Square continued until

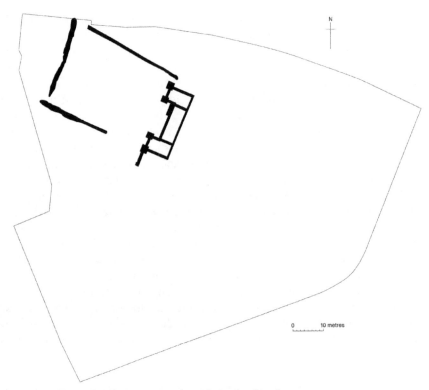

FIG. 9.2 The temple at Tabard Square, Southwark, in the fourth century.

the late fourth century, since the dedicatory slab was buried with considerable care. Dougie Killock has noted that the removal of the inscription, presumably from a context inside the temple where it had been displayed for over 200 years, may not indicate that the temple was being abandoned.

David Sankey has directed the excavation of the north part of a massive basilica or aisled building at Colchester House, located on a small hill in the south-east of the walled area, constructed during the mid-fourth century.[74] This building survived as fragmentary remains but it had substantial walls and a concrete floor and there was a well within its central aisle.[75] A few fragments of marble may indicate internal decoration and small quantities of window glass were found. Finds of stratified pottery have dated the construction of the building to after around AD 350.[76] Sankey originally suggested that this building might have been a state *horreum* (granary) or a cathedral, indicative of the high status of Londinium during the mid-fourth century.[77] He has observed that the ground plan is very similar to the fourth-century cathedral of St Tecla in Mediolanum (Milan) when this city acted as an imperial capital. It has been considered unlikely that the London building was a cathedral,[78] although the position of the well in the central aisle is comparable with that in the baptistery of St Tecla.[79]

Of the 509 Roman coins found at this site, 135 were probably originally deposited within a pottery jar in the backfill of a well while the rest were recovered as a result of sieving a few test pits that were excavated to sample a 'dark earth' deposit that overlay the building, suggesting

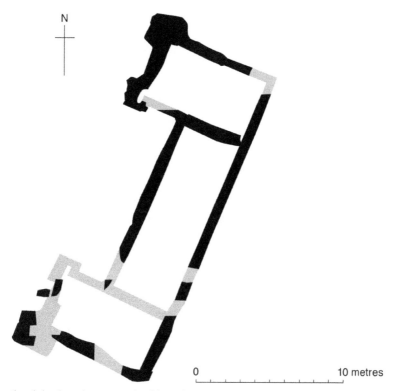

N

0   10 metres

FIG. 9.3 Details of the fourth-century building that may be a temple at Tabard Square.

that these coins represent a small fraction of the total deposited at this site.[80] Many of the coins found with the jar dated to between around AD 355 and 363, although a few coins were of an earlier date. The pot with the coins was found in the top of the fill of the well where they were associated with demolition debris.[81] The large number of coins may indicate that this was a place of worship of a traditional god rather than the location of a Christian church.[82] Gerrard has suggested that, if this building was a granary, it was connected with the storage of grain for export to the continent raised through the *annona* (tax in kind), as has been recorded during the reign of the emperor Julian (AD 361–3).[83]

Although many coins of the mid to late fourth century were found at Colchester House, there was a particularly large number dating from around AD 348 to 364.[84] Forty-two of the coins were of a particularly late date, between AD 378 and 402, including issues of Magnus Maximus, Flavius Victor and Theodosius I.[85] Gerrard has noted that large numbers of coins dating from AD 388 to 402 have been found at other sites and that this indicates that some parts of Londinium continued to receive coins until around the date that has usually been considered as marking the 'end' of the Roman period in Britain (AD 410).[86] It is unfortunate that this building is difficult to interpret but it does provide a clear indication of the continuing administrative significance of Londinium.

The bathhouse and guesthouse at Shadwell underwent alterations and additions during the late third and early fourth centuries.[87] A substantial timber-and-earth building was constructed to the west of the bathhouse during the late third or early fourth centuries.[88] These buildings appear to have been intensively occupied until the later fourth century and alterations to the bathhouse show that it may have remained in use until around AD 375.[89]

The bastions on the walls

The walls were supplemented during the fourth century with substantial external bastions on the east sections of the landward wall.[90] Bastions were a common feature of the late Roman walls that surrounded forts and towns throughout Britannia and in other regions of the empire.[91] The London bastions have been numbered in sequence, beginning in the south-east along the landward wall.[92] A section on the northern landward wall has no bastions, possibly due to the marshland that had formed beyond the walls in this area of the upper Walbrook Valley. The remainder of the wall had fairly regularly spaced bastions around 50 metres apart. A twelfth-century account described walls and towers along the riverside wall, although no physical evidence of any bastions on this section has survived.[93] Only the eastern bastions have been confidently dated to the late Roman period, partly as a result of the substantial quantities of reused Roman sculpture they incorporated. Many of the western bastions were probably constructed in the medieval period.[94] The eastern group were built to a D-shaped plan, usually with solid bases and often incorporating reused Roman sculptures.[95] The western group were horse-shoe shaped, of hollow construction and with no evidence for the reuse of sculptures.[96]

Two of the eastern bastions have been excavated since 1970 and recorded in some detail, confirming a late Roman construction. The excavation of Bastion 6 by Marsden in 1971 indicated that it survived to 1 metre in height and incorporated large sculptured blocks derived from earlier buildings or burial monuments.[97] The foundation of the bastion had been dug through deposits containing fourth-century finds, and a thick layer of material post-dating construction included fourth-century pottery and bronze coins dating to around AD 364–75.[98] John Maloney's subsequent excavations nearby at Dukes Place uncovered part of what he interpreted as the earlier v-section ditch close to Bastion 6, during which a coin of Constans (AD 341–4) was found from a phase of backfilling that may have been conducted during the late 340s or later. It has been assumed that part of this ditch was deliberately infilled to enable the construction of the bastion in around AD 350.[99] This is the most reliable dating evidence for the eastern group of bastions.[100]

The excavations at 8–10 Crosswall in 1979 and 1980 revealed the foundation of a previously unrecorded bastion, designated as Bastion 4A.[101] The foundations incorporated fragments of a third-century tombstone recording a ten-year-old girl named Marciana. The foundation was rectangular in shape with rounded corners, the base stepped down into the V-shaped profile of the ditch to ensure maximum stability for the bastion. This has been interpreted as indicating that the builders were aware of the presence of the earlier ditch and that the bastion was therefore of Roman date.[102] The imprint of larger stones in the top of the surviving foundation of the bastion suggested that its robbed superstructure was solid and D-shaped in plan.[103] There was no indication in the face of the wall adjoining the foundation that the bastion had been bonded into it, evidence for the later addition of bastions to the walled circuit. A layer sealing the remains of the bastion contained medieval pottery, and the outer edge of the foundation was cut away during the digging of the medieval ditch.[104]

The evidence for the western bastions suggests that many were first built during the medieval period, certainly in the case of Bastions 11A and 15.[105] The use of *ballistae* on defensive walls required the excavation of a broad U-shaped ditch to provide greater defence in depth, although the evidence for such a ditch at London is very limited.[106] The limited evidence from the north-west corner of the defences that a broader U-shaped ditch was dug in late Roman times may indicate that Roman bastions were built on this part of the walled circuit.[107] Evidence for a U-shaped ditch was also found during excavations just north of the Roman gateway at Ludgate,[108] indicating that there may also have been bastions on the western wall. Bastions 17 and 18 may have initially been constructed during the fourth century, although this is far from certain.[109] The medieval construction date of the western bastions may be corroborated by the fact that no Roman sculpture has been found built into their stonework.[110]

The question arises of why only part of the circuit of the walls was reinforced with bastions. Bastions have been interpreted as defensive features of late Roman urban and military walls associated with the use of missile-throwing *ballistae*. An alternative interpretation is that bastions at London, like the walls themselves, were intended as a projection of civic pride,[111] intended to be viewed from ships approaching Londinium as they sailed up the Thames from the sea. It has been suggested that the bastions may have been constructed when Theodosius was present in Londinium in AD 367–8, but there is no entirely definitive dating evidence and it is unclear whether the eastern bastions were built as a single coordinated operation or at different times. Although the eastern bastions may have been constructed during the fourth century, their variability indicates that they could have been the work of different gangs of builders.[112]

A late Roman refurbishment of the walls

Maintenance and alterations to the wall continued until the end of the fourth century. Geoffrey Parnell's excavations at the Tower of London in 1976–9 located the late third-century riverside wall (referred to as 'first riverside wall') and evidence for changes to the south-east corner of the walled circuit towards the end of the fourth century involving the construction of the 'second riverside wall'.[113] The second wall was constructed around 4 metres inland and north of the first wall and parallel to its course.[114] This second wall turned southwards at its eastern end and was butted onto the earlier wall.[115] Although the remains were only partly excavated, Parnell suggested that there might have been a blocked entrance at the point where the two riverside walls met.[116] It is possible that the second wall was constructed to convert the south-east corner of the walled area into a salient which could only be approached by a narrow passageway that gave access to the protected gateway. This arrangement would have required a breach in the first riverside wall to the west to create the outer part of the entrance passage, but without further excavation this cannot be verified. The second riverside wall incorporated some reused material such as architectural fragments, tile and lumps of *opus signinum*.[117] Sculpted stones included a column shaft and part of a possible funerary cornice moulding. The wall was constructed with a layer of intramural timbering comparable with other late Roman fortifications in southern Britain.[118]

The mass of material dumped against the northern face of the second riverside wall contained late fourth-century pottery and coins dating from between AD 321–48 and AD 388–92.[119] Parnell has argued that this material was deposited very soon after the building of the second riverside wall and Merrifield has suggested that it may have served as a ramp allowing people to access the walled area from the riverside by entering through the passageway to the gateway.[120] Parnell's excavations in 1979 examined a section of the second riverside wall further to the west, just east of the Tower of London's Wakefield Tower. This showed that, although of comparable construction to the section excavated in 1976–7, this section had been built in a construction

FIG. 9.4 The silver ingot found inside the south-east corner of the Roman city wall in 1777, on the site later occupied by the Tower of London. It has been stamped 'from the workshop of Honorinus' in Latin and dates from the late fourth to fifth century.

trench.[121] Despite the very small area of the excavation, forty-eight coins were found in deposits cut by this construction trench, the latest of which was an issue of the House of Theodosius I and another of Arcadius (AD 388 or later).[122] This stratigraphic evidence demonstrated conclusively that the second riverside wall must have been constructed after AD 388.[123] Traces of late Roman building activity post-dated the construction of the second riverside wall.[124]

Parnell suggested that this development of a guarded entranceway might have constituted part of a late Roman stronghold built at the south-east corner of Londinium's walled circuit.[125] He has also suggested that the Tower of London might have been built on top of the remains of this stronghold in the eleventh century. Parnell has noted the discovery of a silver ingot in 1777 within the Tower,[126] stamped with the Latin inscription 'from the workshop of Honorinus' (see Fig. 9.4).[127] When this find was originally published the President of the Society of Antiquaries of London, Jeremiah Milles, noted that it was discovered during the digging for the foundation for the Board of Ordnances which broke through 'foundations of ancient buildings'.[128] Milles noted that three gold coins were found 'in the same place', including *solidi* of Arcadius and Honorius. He argued that 'The Tower of London was undoubtedly the capital fortress of the Romans; it was their treasury as well as their mint.'[129] Such officially stamped ingots are usually considered to have been used for the payment of soldiers and officials.[130] This has been used to identify the Tower of London area with the treasury referred to in the *Notitia Dignitatum*.[131]

The earlier stone building just east of the White Tower also continued to be occupied and new floors were laid in the building during the mid to late fourth century.[132]

The possibility that there was a protected gate in the riverside wall at this location may show that there was a strategic need to enable access between the riverside and the south-east area of the walled circuit. This part of Londinium may have had significance at the end of the fourth century, although there is no evidence for a discrete fortification within the walls at this location.[133]

Occupation

It has generally been thought that many people were still living in Londinium during the first half of the fourth century, although there was a sudden decline in population after around AD 350 and Londinium was abandoned entirely by AD 450.[134] It is possible, however, that many houses were still being constructed in timber and earth and the late Roman deposits have often been severely damaged or even entirely removed by later development. Research on pottery and other finds is allowing the extent and location of later occupation to be assessed,[135] and this suggests that that Londinium was far more intensively settled throughout this period than has previously been supposed (Fig. 9.5).[136]

North of the Thames

At 1 Poultry the main east–west road and its side roads remained in use during the early fourth century and three earlier properties were combined.[137] This involved extensive modifications and reconstruction to one of the buildings, retaining its mosaic floor. Another building was substantially rebuilt and its hypocaust altered, demonstrating that the baths remained in use when a mosaic was laid at this time.[138] A third structure was built in between these buildings to join them into a single impressive house. Other buildings were built or occupied at this time in the area of 1 Poultry, although these were often less well preserved. A substantial brick culvert and wall associated with a late Roman structure on the southern side of the main east–west road were constructed around AD 340–6.[139] On Site D, west of 1 Poultry, the recutting of the roadside ditches suggest that the main road was still in use during the third and early fourth centuries, and two buildings may date from the fourth century.[140] The coins found at this site suggest that it continued to be occupied during the later fourth century, although the late deposits were heavily truncated.[141]

Hill and Rowsome have suggested that there may have been a fairly abrupt end to the Roman occupation at 1 Poultry.[142] A coin of AD 379–402 was found in the backfill of the hypocaust in one building which may have been abandoned by the late AD 370s. A well which had been in continuous use since the AD 180s was backfilled with deposits that contained coins dating from around AD 378–83.[143] Hill and Rowsome have argued that by the early fifth century the houses at 1 Poultry were probably no longer occupied.[144] Part of a semi-articulated human skeleton was deposited in the upper fills of the southern culvert of the main east–west road, probably during the late fourth century.[145] This may indicate that the drainage of the road was no longer being maintained, although another gully was subsequently cut just to the north.[146] The skeleton was deposited without the skull and this has been interpreted as indicating the ending of regulated urban life.[147] The tradition of depositing corpses in watercourses and ditches, however, has a long history in Londinium and the removal of the head is reminiscent of earlier practices.[148] Some inhumations were deposited within the area enclosed by the walls during the late Roman

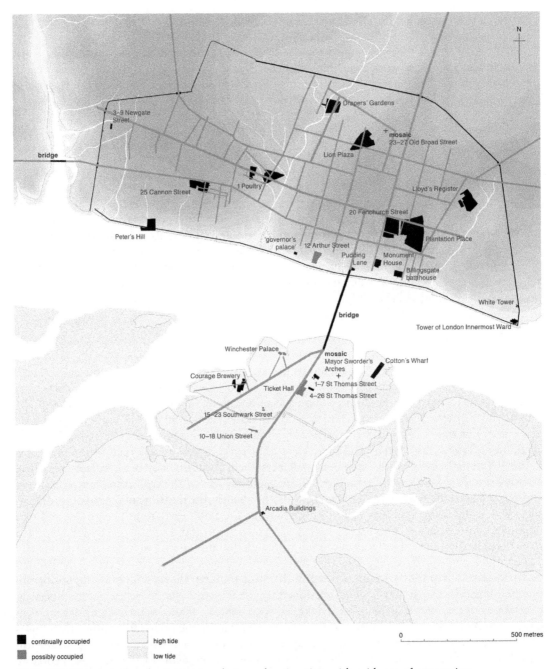

FIG. 9.5 Houses in fourth-century Londinium, showing sites with evidence of occupation.

period and it is not always certain that this indicates that people were no longer living in the vicinity (see below). Occupation at 1 Poultry may have been coming to an end at the time the corpse was placed in the ditch but this is not necessarily the case. Coins of the very latest period of the occupation may not have circulated to all areas of Londinium and the end of the coin sequence at 1 Poultry before around AD 388 need not conclusively indicate that this area was being abandoned prior to the early fifth century.

A late Roman dwelling at Billingsgate continued to be modified and was occupied into the early fifth century.[149] A substantial number of coins were found on the floor of a furnace and the adjacent corridor in the east wing of the building, the latest issues being of Arcadius and Honorius (dating from around AD 395 to 402).[150] Marsden has argued that these coins formed a hoard that had been hidden in a wall that had collapsed after the building was abandoned. The deposit containing the coins sealed earlier layers within the furnace that included ash from its final firing, beneath which was a coin of Theodora (337–41) and a fragment of a Palestinian wine amphora dating from the fourth or early fifth centuries. Marsden has suggested that the building had begun to collapse in the early fifth century and that the vaulted roof of the *frigidarium* in the bathhouse had fallen onto the pink mortar floor.[151]

The pottery has been comprehensively reassessed by Robin Symonds and Roberta Tomber who have dated it to the late fourth to early fifth century.[152] Marsden has referred to a few sherds of handmade pottery which he has dated to the late Roman or sub-Roman period.[153] Marsden has also noted that a small number of fragments of comparable handmade pottery was found during the excavation of the 'governor's palace'. At the south-east of this largely demolished building a hearth of tiles set into an earth floor was overlain by substantial later Roman deposits that included these sherds (see Fig. 5.6).[154] Examples of late Roman amphorae from the eastern Mediterranean were also found in these dumped deposits at the 'governor's palace', indicating the continuation of some trade with the Mediterranean.[155]

The excavations at 1 Poultry, Billingsgate and the 'governor's palace' have revealed that earlier buildings continued to be occupied and modified and it is probable that other stone houses were still being built during the fourth century. To the north of the forum, at 23–7 Old Broad Street, an elaborate late Roman mosaic has been dated to later than AD 350 on the basis of its stylistic associations with a mosaic from Halstock in Dorset.[156] Discovered in 1854, the Old Broad Street mosaic may have embellished a pre-existing house or was added in a new residence. Neal and Cosh have suggested that it was laid to floor the dining room (*triclinium*) of a very grand private house that might have belonged to a notable dignitary. They have also suggested that there was not sufficient demand in Londinium to support resident mosaicists at this time and that the Old Broad Street mosaic was laid by a specialist based in south-western Britannia. One of the largest examples from Londinium, this mosaic is larger than those from other townhouses in Britannia and there is only one comparable example from Verulamium. The very fine mosaic from Leadenhall Street that depicts Bacchus riding a tigress has also sometimes been attributed to the fourth century, although this floor may also date to the second or third centuries.[157] The mosaic at 1 Poultry and others at sites south of the Thames all indicate that elaborate houses continued to be constructed and maintained in fourth-century Londinium.

Elsewhere in Londinium, building and occupation continued into the late Roman period. In the west of the urban area, stone-built houses at 25 Cannon Street were occupied well into the fourth century and there was probably some construction work around AD 350.[158] In the west of the walled circuit, there is little evidence of fourth-century occupation around St Paul's, although the stone-built house at 3–9 Newgate Street continued in use.[159] At Paternoster Row, in an area within the wall that had been occupied before and was largely turned over to agricultural use during the late third century, five east–west graves contained burials, some of which were partly cut into the disused surface of a north–south road.[160] One burial contained a coin dated around AD 340–50 found near the skull of the individual. There were also two instances of disarticulated human bone from late Roman contexts, including part of an infant's skull placed in a pit that was truncated by one of the later burials.[161]

To the north of the forum at Lion Plaza, the poorly-preserved third-century house continued to be occupied into the later part of the century.[162] Just to the south-east of the forum, at Plantation Place, the courtyard townhouse continued to be occupied and elaborated (see Fig. 9.6).[163] The latest addition was a substantial stone tower to the south-west of the complex that may have been built after AD 330.[164] The function of this tower is unclear, although it would have been a highly visible feature in the urban landscape.[165] The dates of the pottery and coins from this site may suggest that people were living there until at least the later fourth century.[166] At 20 Fenchurch Street, although the archaeological deposits had been heavily truncated, a substantial cellar indicated the location of a stone house that may not have been abandoned until the late fourth century.[167] In the east periphery of Londinium convincing evidence for intensive occupation throughout the fourth century has been found at Lloyd's Register.[168] The earlier stone buildings continued to be supplemented and modified and the latest activity was the development of an extensive 'dark earth' deposit that covered many of the buildings.[169] The pottery assemblages from the late contexts are broadly comparable to those from the Billingsgate bathhouse, suggesting that occupation may have continued at least to the end of the century.[170]

The site at 60–3 Fenchurch Street may have been abandoned, although coins found in medieval contexts there show that the road was still used.[171] At Baltic House there was little evidence for occupation after the late second to early third centuries, although dumping and the digging of pits and gullies continued.[172] An earlier well was backfilled around AD 300 to 400, and an older juvenile was laid in a grave dug into the backfill of a ditch dated by pottery from the ditch and grave to after around AD 350.[173] It is likely that some former built-up areas had been abandoned before the late fourth century.

Evidence was found for fourth-century activity on the site of the former building complex at the Salvation Army site. At Peter's Hill a building was constructed over the site of the western temple.[174] The new building was constructed around AD 350 over part of the earlier stone foundations. Incorporating in its construction timbering and containing a hearth, the surviving traces of this building showed that it had several floor layers and that it may have been occupied for some time.[175] To the east at 99–101 Queen Victoria Street the earlier foundations of the Period II buildings may have been robbed and a few pits and postholes indicated late occupation or activity.[176] The truncation of late deposits over the entire area at this site could indicate that evidence for late Roman occupation in other areas has been lost.

Behind the riverside wall at Pudding Lane the small inn or house with bathing facilities continued to be occupied and altered during the third and fourth centuries.[177] It appears to have at least partly collapsed during the middle of the fourth century, but some rooms were restored around AD 370. This final phase, which was dated by coins, included a heated room and a small heated bath, demonstrating that the bathing facilities in this building were being maintained.[178] Pits and trenches were being dug elsewhere at Pudding Lane and occupation may have continued in the waterfront warehouse buildings during the late fourth century and possibly later.[179] Late Roman buildings were located at the Tower of London, close to the walls that may have formed a protected entrance through the circuit of the wall on the south-east at Inmost Ward. The house close to the White Tower was also occupied into the fourth century.[180]

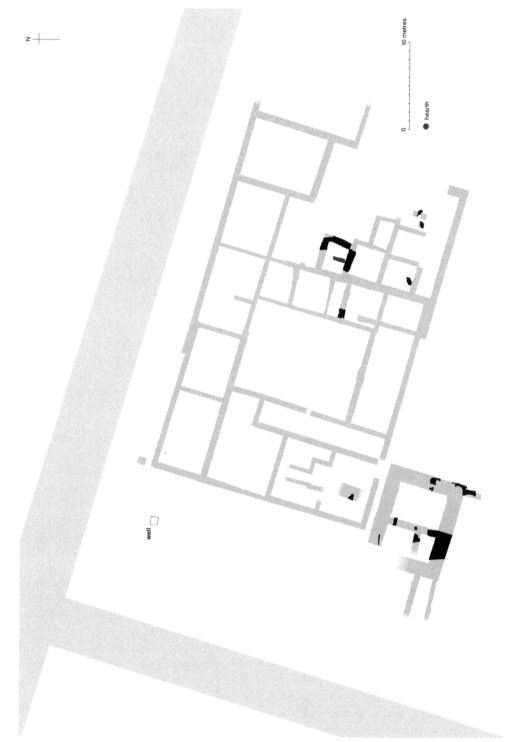

FIG. 9.6 The fourth-century alterations to the earlier house at Plantation Place.

Elsewhere behind the riverside wall, buildings were abandoned before or during the course of the century. At 12 Arthur Street the sequence of high-status buildings came to an end by the late third century and most of the evidence for the latest Roman activity is derived from artefacts found in residual contexts in medieval and post-medieval features.[181] Some late pottery, animal bones and plant remains in three pits probably dating from the third and fourth centuries show that the late Roman buildings on this site could have been truncated.[182] The 'townhouse' at Suffolk House east of the 'governor's palace' may have been demolished during the late third or early fourth century.[183] The earlier building at Monument House probably became disused during the mid to late fourth century.[184] The pottery assemblage from the fill of the culvert beneath this building included bowls of Camulodunum form 306 that may have been placed there as part of a termination rite.[185] Some occupation just south of this building may be dated by a Theodosian coin of AD 378–402.[186]

During this period people continued living in areas at the periphery of Londinium.[187] In the upper Walbrook Valley there is clear evidence for occupation throughout most of this century at Drapers' Gardens.[188] The earlier buildings and properties at this site continued to be maintained and replaced well into the fourth century, although the remains were less well preserved than the earlier deposits as a result of truncation and disturbance.[189] These timber-and-earth buildings were usually formed with deeper construction features, including driven timber piles, pits and wells. The river channel at Drapers' Gardens also continued to be maintained and its sides were revetted to control flooding. Two wells dug in the early fourth century were kept open for some time and occupation continued throughout much of the fourth century, although little evidence of buildings survived. One well was constructed during the AD 330s and may have been infilled around AD 375–8, or possibly later.[190] Gerrard has noted that it was lined with split planks rather than the more usual sawn timber planks.[191] Since the use of split planks is usually associated with rural sites in the Roman period, Gerrard has suggested that the organization of the timber supply to Londinium was failing during the AD 330s. The well contained a hoard of metal vessels and was overlain by dumped deposit.[192] The pottery dates from these excavations suggests that occupation continued into the late fourth century and possibly into the fifth.[193]

Gerrard has noted that an unusual concentration of late Roman pottery, dating to AD 350 or after, has been located in the Spitalfields area.[194] Although this must be partly the result of the number of excavations in this area, there was also a focus on late Roman industrial activity.[195] Information for glassworking and a possible crucible, probably dating from the late third and fourth centuries, was excavated at the Priory and Hospital of St Mary, Spital.[196] The deposit that contained this material was sealed by dumping and cut by a series of pits for rubbish disposal and a large ditched enclosure was also excavated. Mid-fourth-century coins and glassworking waste were found in the pits and the enclosure ditch. Inhumation and cremation burials have been found immediately to the east, indicating an association between burial and industry.

The 'Shadwell Tower' was demolished around AD 365 and features including timber-lined tanks and drains were dug.[197] The latest activity probably dated from the third quarter of the fourth century and no very late Roman deposits were found. There was an inhumation burial, dug in the north-east corner of the 'Tower', after it had been demolished and another burial just outside the building's foundations.[198] These were not accompanied by any objects but are likely to post-date the demolition of the building. After the bathhouse at Shadwell had become disused, a new timber building was constructed to the north and a large building to the west.[199] A late Roman well in the south-west of the site contained three pieces of North African amphorae, indicating that long-distance trading was continuing during the late fourth century, the fills possibly representing a termination deposit.[200] The later Roman deposits from the bathhouse complex contained some unusual coins and other objects owned by wealthy individuals, including a gold earring and part of a gold and bead necklace.[201] The excavators have suggested that occupation at this part of the settlement continued until the end of the century and possibly into the fifth.

The role of Shadwell in the fourth and early fifth centuries is difficult to interpret. That the port may have been relocated downstream to Shadwell during the third century has already been discussed, but there is no clear evidence to support this idea. There was, however, a significant area of late Roman activity and occupation around the bathhouse, which may have been part of a temple site. Gerrard has noted that the ten late Roman pewter ingots found at various times during the nineteenth century on the Thames foreshore at Battersea may have been disturbed by dredging activities during the 1850s related to the construction of new port facilities in the Shadwell basin and moved in materials that were dumped at Battersea.[202] They had ovoid convex bases and were stamped with a chi-rho symbol and the name of the maker, Syagrius or Suagrius.[203] These rare objects attest to Christian worship in the late Roman period, but they may have derived from a hoard or shipwreck and do not necessarily indicate the presence of Christians in Londinium.[204]

Excavations at St Martin-in-the-Fields, well beyond the walled circuit to the west, revealed a tile kiln dating from the very late Roman period, suggesting that industrial activities were closely associated with the burial of the dead.[205] The archaeomagnetic dating of the kiln has established that it was last fired between AD 400 and 450, making this the latest reliably-dated Roman structure from London.[206] Alison Telfer has observed that this industrial-scale kiln with an unusual double-arched flue was producing brick and tile, indicating that there was a demand for these materials in or around Londinium when urban life has usually been supposed to have been in terminal decline. This remarkable discovery may lead to a reassessment of the late Roman and sub-Roman occupation of Londinium, although the distance of the site from the walled circuit suggests that the tile may have been intended for use somewhere in the vicinity of St Martin-in-the-Fields.

South of the Thames

Since many of the later Roman deposits in Southwark have been truncated by later development, the presence of fourth-century pottery in late Roman and post-Roman contexts may help to show where people were living and working during this period.[207] Most of the pottery has been found on the central and west parts of the north island, with a scattering of find spots on the east and alongside the main north–south road on the south island and on the south bank of the Thames. The distribution of this pottery confirms the evidence that buildings across much of the northern part of the north island had been abandoned by the early fourth century, although the main north–south road probably continued in use.

At the Ticket Hall site most of the buildings had been abandoned, although some evidence may have been removed by later truncation.[208] One of the roadside drains of the main north–south road had been robbed of its stones and had been backfilled by a 'dark earth' deposit containing a large number of coins dating from between AD 340 and 378.[209] These have been interpreted as losses from roadside traffic, although they may also suggest that people were living in the vicinity. The only other archaeological feature that was recorded was a pit that contained a substantial quantity of fourth-century pottery, including a few sherds of amphora and twelve coins.[210] The pottery assemblage was broadly comparable to that from the Billingsgate bathhouse and the latest coin dated from AD 379–402,[211] suggesting that some activity continued in this area until very late in the urban sequence.

Just to the north-east of the Ticket Hall site, excavations at 4–26 St Thomas Street have produced evidence for at least two phases of late Roman buildings.[212] During the late third or early fourth century, buildings on this site included two constructed of timber and earth and another with a substantial cellar.[213] The cellar was almost entirely robbed of its stone but had originally been divided into two rooms. These buildings were replaced by a single structure probably constructed after AD 350.[214] Its surviving remains consisted of a very truncated construction slot and evidence for a mosaic or tessellated floor. This building was associated with a well containing pottery that included some of the same wares that dominated the assemblage at the Billingsgate bathhouse.[215] Slightly further north, excavations at 1–7 St Thomas Street have also indicated that third-century stone buildings were occupied into the fourth century.[216] The buildings at this small site may have formed part of a building complex with a hypocaust.[217]

On the east of the north island, at Mayor Sworder's Arches, limited excavation has revealed a large part of a polychrome mosaic which may have been designed by a visiting mosaicist from the south-west.[218] A coin dating from AD 330–41 in the backfill of the robber trench shows that this mosaic was laid in a building of some significance around the middle of the fourth century. At Cotton's Wharf, excavations have suggested that occupation of the earlier stone house continued into the fourth century.[219]

On the west of the north island some occupation continued at certain sites but at a much reduced scale by the second half of the fourth century. At 15–23 Southwark Street, the earlier buildings may have been abandoned by the early part of the century and their stone removed, although pits were dug containing pottery and coins that dated to the late third and fourth centuries.[220] Subsequent excavations close to this location have produced evidence for the dumping of material in around AD 335–41, probably contemporary with the demolition of an earlier building,[221] suggesting that occupation may have continued until around the middle of the fourth century. Inhumation burials were deposited in graves cut into the remains at this site, aligned either north–south or east–west, some dug into the robbed walls of the buildings.[222] Five of these burials contained grave goods.[223] The deposits on this site were at least partly sealed by 'dark earth'.[224] Just south of the 'mansio', around Redcross Way, additional inhumations were dug into dumped deposits intercutting each other.[225]

At Winchester Palace, it has been suggested that the two buildings that have been most fully excavated had been demolished by the early fourth century, but one of the rooms of 'Building 13' probably continued to be occupied.[226] Coins and pottery were recovered from the deposits of 'dark earth' that partially sealed the buildings and Yule has suggested that occupation continued into the final years of the fourth century, although no definitive evidence was located for the nature, character or duration of this activity.[227]

At Courage Brewery, ironworking was continued but on a reduced scale.[228] Buildings were demolished and new timber-and-earth buildings constructed with several hearths that suggested fewer metalworkers were working at this location than during the third century.[229] The excavators have suggested that metalworking ended on this site around the mid-fourth century, although people continued to live there and a large new building was constructed.[230] To the south-east a substantial third-century house was abandoned and its stone removed by around AD 350 and inhumations interred both in and around the surviving remains.[231] The burials were either aligned east–west or north–south and some were dug through the backfilled robber trenches. Three contained chalk or plaster and one was accompanied by a coin that dated from around AD 340.[232] Two new buildings that were constructed just to the north on the former ironworking site around AD 370 could have been occupied until the end of the fourth century.[233] A limited amount of evidence was uncovered for metalworking around AD 380 before 'dark earth' began to accumulate over the abandoned structures.[234] Several very late Roman coins found in this area demonstrate that this was the final part of the Courage Brewery site to be abandoned.[235] The close proximity of burials and occupied buildings suggests that at other sites in Londinium evidence for the digging of graves does not necessarily indicate that occupation had ceased.

Only limited evidence has been found for activity on the south island. At 10–18 Union Street, activity close to the earlier houses and the well continued into the fourth century where a pit contained a coin of Constantius II (c. AD 355–61) and a lead curse with an inscription including the name Martia.[236] On the south bank of the Thames, at the Old Sorting Office, pits and wells dug during the late third and fourth centuries contained no evidence to indicate that the earlier customs of ritual deposition at this site were continued into the late Roman period.[237] Just to the east, at Arcadia Buildings, part of a substantial building excavated west of Watling Street contained fourth-century pottery and there appears to have been a significant amount of later Roman occupation there.[238] Occupation within the area of the temple at Tabard Square may have continued well into the fifth century.[239] Many of the features that have been interpreted as late Roman and early medieval have been dated by the abraded late Roman pottery found with them, and some handmade shell-tempered sherds and grog-tempered wares may date from the fifth century.[240] Three isolated inhumations were found which also probably dated from this period.[241]

Marking the boundaries

It is evident that the burial practices on the periphery were continued and that people were still taking their dead to the same cemeteries. Wells and pits contained deposits which have been linked with ritual activity. These features have been interpreted as containing termination deposits that related to the disuse of areas of occupation or the abandonment of important buildings, a continuation of earlier practices (see Fig. 9.7).

Dumping, pits and wells

At 201–11 Borough High Street on the south island, finds dating from the first half of the fourth century deposited in a well and pits indicates that people were living close by.[242] The well contained considerable quantities of building debris, including pieces of roof tile, chalk blocks, flint nodules and fragments of painted plaster. A sustained campaign of dumping to raise the ground surface continued in the mid-fourth century at Hunt's House on the edge of Guy's Channel on the east side of the south island.[243] This building up may have continued into the fifth century, perhaps in response to the rising of the tide of the Thames. The material that was tipped onto the site included considerable quantities of pottery, building material and animal bone.[244]

A well excavated in 1977 under the floor of Southwark Cathedral crypt was constructed after AD 270 and filled in during the fourth century.[245] It contained a mass of building material and religious sculptures including parts of burial monuments. The primary fill contained the

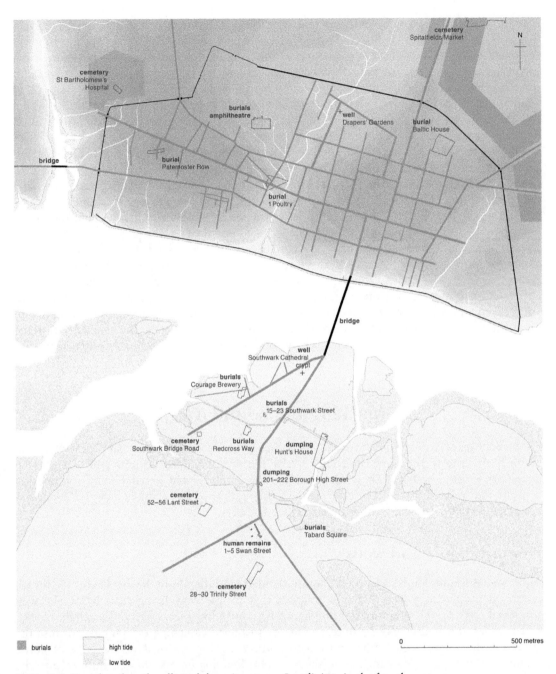

FIG. 9.7 Burials, selected wells and dumping across Londinium in the fourth century.

skeletons of an old dog and young cat,[246] which can be interpreted as a ritual deposit as the remains of dogs were often left in such places. Above this layer the well was filled with large quantities of dumped building debris, including tile, ragstone blocks, mortar chunks and a small amount of painted plaster and some fragments of sculptures, much of which was caked with soot.[247]

Other pits and wells at the margins of Londinium contained significant finds. A substantial pit at Courage Brewery on the north island contained offerings made in connection with continuing occupation and rebuilding at this location.[248] This pit was one of a group of three that pre-dated the construction of what may have been the final building on the site. Four distinct fills contained a large quantity of animal bone, including the skeletons of six dogs, and a complete pottery vessel with the base perforated with five holes.[249] This pit may have been filled on four distinct occasions associated with the construction of the building. It is unclear whether this was a domestic building and the pit could suggest that there was a shrine associated with burials in close proximity.[250]

Another significant feature that may have contained a termination deposit was a well at Drapers' Gardens in the upper Walbrook Valley.[251] Several decades after it was constructed, the well was filled with material that included pottery, animal bone, wood, leather, ironwork and copper-alloy artefacts.[252] A hoard of metal vessels was deposited close to the base and two relatively unworn coins of the House of Valentinian, struck at Arles in the name of Gratian (AD 367–75 and AD 375–8), were also found.[253] These coins may help to date the deposition of the metalwork, although Gerrard has noted that these particular coins continued to circulate for twenty or thirty years. They may have been placed in the well as part of the ritual acts which led to the deposition of the hoard, which could have occurred decades later since some of the metal vessels may date to the fifth century.[254] The metal vessels included utensils such as a copper-alloy bucket, a wine bucket, five bead-rim dishes, the remains of a four-looped zoomorphic hanging bowl and several cauldrons and bowls,[255] items that were produced at different times and in different parts of the empire. Some are likely to have been made in Gaul, others in production centres along the Rhine, and the bucket is likely to have been produced in the eastern Mediterranean.[256] As the hoard includes vessels of different metals, including copper-alloy, iron and pewter, it was not a metalworker's hoard that was dumped in the well but a collection of tableware associated with the preparation, display and consumption of food and drink.[257]

The partial skeleton of a young red deer had been placed above the metal vessels.[258] Deer bones have been found in third-century wells at 10–18 Union Street and 8 Union Street and Gerrard has suggested that they may be the result of animals that had been hunted beyond the walls.[259] He has also noted that the Drapers' Gardens metalwork hoard was found outside and south of a regional pattern of ritual hoarding of metal vessels focused on the Cambridgeshire Fens. Perhaps this act of deposition marked the abandonment of this area of Londinium by a communal 'sacrifice' of precious objects.[260] The excavations at Bloomberg have revealed another well into which four pewter bowls and six cattle skulls were deposited during the late fourth century, possibly as a termination deposit.[261]

At Shadwell, a timber-lined well at the south-west of the site contained a very late Roman pottery assemblage that included three sherds of amphora from North Africa, indicating long-distance trade and suggesting that exotic foodstuffs were being imported until the end of the period at a time when commerce was generally in decline throughout the province.[262] This final backfilling may also have constituted a ritual closing of the well since a large number of complete and almost complete pottery vessels were found. Gerrard has suggested that the preponderance of Oxfordshire fine wares in the upper fills may indicate that feasting was conducted here, perhaps in a similar way to earlier contexts across Londinium.

Rituals on the walls

The most notable feature of the eastern bastions is the incorporation of reused sculpture derived from demolished funerary monuments.[263] John Edward Price produced a remarkably detailed record of the surviving remains of a bastion in Camomile Street (Bastion 10) prior to its destruction in 1876 (see Fig. 9.8).[264] His account indicated that the remains included stones that had been derived from demolished tombs and buildings, and the inner edge of the foundation was defined by a row of coping stones. The reused sculptures had been incorporated into the base layer of the bastion above which a solid structure of Kentish ragstone survived to a height of around 3 metres.[265] The sculptures had been carefully placed in the foundation and were recorded in detailed diagrams of a lower and an upper course of stones.[266] The only sculpture shown in the diagram of the lower course was an eroded colossal head which had been carefully

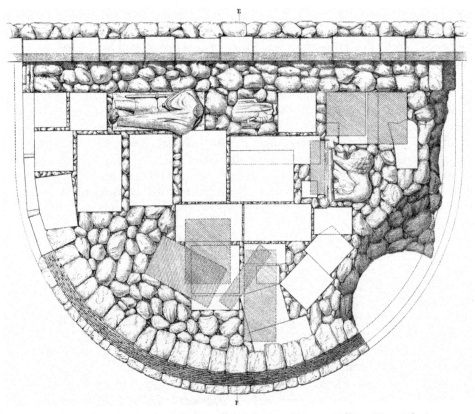

FIG. 9.8 The plan of the stonework of Bastion 10 on the Roman city wall in Camomile Street, recorded in 1876 at 0.68 metres above the base of the bastion. Sculptural fragments had been carefully placed into the core of its foundation. The remains were recorded by Henry Hodge on behalf of the London and Middlesex Archaeological Society.

positioned between several massive slabs close to the middle of the bastion.[267] Toynbee has suggested that this head, positioned face-upwards, might have represented a mid-third-century emperor,[268] although this sculpture has been reinterpreted as part of the funerary monument of an individual who lived in Londinium.[269]

Price provided a detailed plan of the upper course of the foundation that sealed the colossal head that marks the locations of the three other main pieces of sculpture:[270] the Camomile Street legionary soldier, a headless human figure and a lion devouring another animal.[271] The two human figures were placed on their backs facing the sky and the lion was placed on its right side. Price noted that:

If the builders of the bastion had been desirous of saving such precious relics from destruction they could hardly have devised better means for their preservation. The figure of the lion appears to have been most carefully fitted into the position assigned to it, as does the statue of the soldier, which was in three or four pieces.[272]

Price's records indicated that the torso of the figure of the soldier had been broken across the line of the hips into two main pieces which had been placed back together during the building of the bastion, and the head was placed between the feet.[273] It is possible that the torso had broken into several pieces after the statue was placed into the foundation as a result of the weight of the stones from above, but the positioning of the head was intentional and reflects the treatment of some burials in the cemeteries of Londinium.[274] In this burial tradition the heads of corpses were often moved some time after death, and this statue may have represented a dead member of the community and the relocation of his memorial to a new construction could have drawn upon the long-term practices of the manipulation of human remains at the urban boundaries. Other stones from this foundation that survive in modern collections include fluted pilasters, shafts of half-columns, parts of canopies, cornices and door jams.[275]

Records of Bastion 8 indicate that it incorporated Roman sculptures; the base of a circular column, an ornamented shaft and a fragment of an inscribed tombstone survive today.[276] Three fragments of the burial monument of the first-century procurator Julius Classicianus probably derived from the foundation of Bastion 2.[277] Two of these fragments were recorded by Alexander Horace Burkitt when they were revealed in August 1852 at Postern Row, Tower Hill.[278] Burkitt recorded that they were discovered as part of a 'complete quarry of stones, cut in various forms, with mortices at the angles, and belonging to some important building'.[279] These stones included pilasters, capitals, the fragments of the inscription and a large part of a quern stone. Burkitt noted that 'Several portions of these interesting fragments have found shelter in our national collection', including the fragments of Classicianus' tomb.[280] The third fragment of the burial monument was recorded by Frank Cottrill in 1935 as having been placed upside-down and facing outwards in the base layer of the foundation of the north face of Bastion 2.[281]

Bastion 9 at Castle Street and Goring Street was very well preserved when it was revealed in 1884 and the only record is a careful survey probably produced by Henry Hodge. The remains of the solid bastion stood to a height of over 3 metres. It incorporated numerous lengths of shaped stone coping, a cornice and other moulded stones, and parts of a burial inscription and of a frieze carved with swags and running hares.[282] These stones included a fragment derived from a funerary relief and a funerary relief showing a banqueting scene.[283] Evidence for the other eastern bastions is limited. Bastion 3 was very poorly preserved but incorporated a coping stone and other moulded stones.[284]

The incorporation of fragmentary sculptures into later structures need not necessarily indicate the desecration of what they represented or that the fragments had entirely lost their significance. The manner in which the Camomile Street soldier was buried recalls burial practices and suggests that he was treated as a deceased member of the community, while the carved head in the foundation of Bastion 10 may reflect comparable practices associated with human heads. The reuse of other fragments of burial monuments may have drawn upon comparable mortuary rituals.

Burying the dead

Burials dug in the late Roman period in areas where people had been living have long been taken to indicate that the urban area was contracting. There may not, however, have always been a clear boundary between the spaces for the living and those for the dead.[285] It is possible that the increasing practice of burying the dead within Londinium's walls may have resulted from the gradual spread of Christianity. Some of the dead at Courage Brewery were interred close to buildings that may still have been in use into the late fourth century, suggesting that burials could sometimes have been deposited within the boundaries of the settled area. On the Continent, burials were often deposited around late Roman churches within the walls of cities.[286] It has often been assumed that Christianity was spreading in Londinium during the fourth century and that 'pagan' cults were being suppressed.[287] There was a bishop in Londinium in AD 314, although there is little direct evidence of Christianity.[288]

Another difficulty with using burials to establish the shrinking boundaries of Londinium is that many of the late Roman burials are not at all accurately dated.[289] Human burials from 1 Poultry, Paternoster Row, the amphitheatre, Baltic House, Courage Brewery, 15–23 Southwark Street and Redcross Way have been noted above and dating evidence for some of these burials has been discussed. Many of the late Roman burials may date to the early fifth century.[290] Although the production of Roman artefacts found in London is often conventionally ascribed a latest date of around AD 400 to 410, this does not provide an end date for their use in burial and settlement contexts. As the supply of material goods reduced during late Roman times, there appears to have been a concomitant rise in the reuse of old objects in both domestic and burial contexts.

The cemeteries to the east and south continued to be used for burial practices during the fourth century and, quite possibly, beyond. Only a few burials were deposited with artefacts that can be dated to the fourth century in the 'eastern cemetery',[291] although it is possible to date several to this time from the items deposited with the corpse.[292] These burials were made with respect to the layout of existing plots and generally follow similar alignments. It is evident that the building of the bastions on the wall was associated with the robbing of grave stones and burial monuments, including that of the first-century procurator Julius Classicianus, but excavations have shown few signs of disruption to the use of the cemetery.[293] Numerous fragments of stone-built mausolea and monuments in the 'eastern' and 'northern' cemeteries were incorporated into the bastions. Mausolea on the outskirts of Londinium may often have contained sarcophagi. At the north-west corner of Haydon Square, a stone sarcophagus portraying a youthful draped bust, clearly designed to be viewed in a burial chamber, was found in 1853.[294] It is possible that it was buried when a mausoleum was robbed for stone to build one of the bastions.

A male inhumation in Plot 2 of the 'eastern cemetery' was accompanied by an unworn chip-carved belt set and crossbow brooch, while a female inhumation had two distinctive silver brooches and a triangular antler comb.[295] These burials were comparable with other graves in this cemetery in terms of alignment and the position of the burial goods, although they were remarkable because the deceased were dressed with brooches and because of the nature and character of the artefacts themselves.[296] In the excavation report they were interpreted as dating to the later fourth or early fifth centuries,[297] although recent radiocarbon dating has suggested that they were probably interred during the earlier part of the fourth century.[298] These burials form part of a broader late Roman group that has long been interpreted as representing Germanic immigrants in late Roman Britain, but it is generally now considered that such artefacts are more likely to be indicative of the status and official roles of the people who wore them.[299] Gerrard has argued that the chip-carved belt set from the male burial is likely to have been viewed as an article of 'military' dress by his contemporaries.[300] Stable isotope analysis has indicated that this man had probably originated from Londinium.[301] The female with the distinctive brooches and the antler comb appears from the stable isotope analysis to have come from south-western Britain or, more probably, from the continent.[302] In both these cases, particular artefacts need not have been associated with a defined ethnic group.[303] Adopting 'Germanic' dress items appears to have been a cultural choice that allowed people to claim a connection with this identity through either family relationships or roles in the military.[304] Even if the male had cultural or ancestral connections with Germanic peoples, he may well never have travelled outside Britannia.

The cemeteries south of Londinium in Southwark continued to develop. The burials on the west of the south island at Southwark Bridge Road were interred in an area with only limited evidence for earlier settlement and activity, indicated by pitting.[305] The graves were heavily intercut and were not orientated in any particular direction. Pottery urns interred with the dead suggested that they were buried during the fourth century.

The fourth-century burial area at 52–6 Lant Street developed south of the second-century burials, comprising mostly inhumations and two cremations.[306] The inhumations were aligned either parallel to or perpendicular to the two boundary ditches running through the burial area, with many of the burials arranged north-west to south-east. Nine were associated with a chalk-like substance,[307] while twenty-nine were interred with grave goods such as glass and pottery vessels. A detached cluster of graves at the south-west of the site lacked contemporary grave goods but two were associated with sherds of late fourth-century or later date, suggesting that burial at this cemetery continued into the fifth century when pottery was no longer being produced.[308] Three of these burials also contained old damaged pots that had been salvaged for use in later burials,[309] a practice also represented in the 'eastern cemetery',[310] possibly indicating that the south-western part of the cemetery was still being used for burial well into the fifth century. There is, however, no clear method for dating burials that contain no grave offerings or those that contain only reused offerings.[311]

Oxygen stable isotope analysis has suggested that many of the people buried in the Lant Street site had travelled to Britain after they had spent their childhoods in the Mediterranean, while others were probably locals.[312] One of the burials was of a young female of around fourteen years of age who had been interred with particularly unusual grave goods, including a glass vessel, a wooden casket with ivory fittings and a folding knife with a handle carved in the form of a leopard.[313] Work on the cranial morphology of seventeen individuals has also indicated a number may have been of African or Asian ancestry.[314] The analysis has suggested that these incomers from the southern and eastern Mediterranean were buried at this cemetery at 52–6 Lant Street during both the second and the fourth centuries, although there was no continuity of this group as the buried individuals had moved from the Mediterranean area during their lifetimes, suggesting that links were maintained by people living in Londinium with communities far afield for centuries.[315]

East of 52–6 Lant Street two burials were deposited on the south-east edge of the third-century ditch at 1–5 Swan Street.[316] These corpses were placed in very shallow graves,[317] one with a pot of possibly mid-fourth-century date. This is similar to the practices of placing bodies either within or on the side of ditches during the earlier period. The cemetery at 28–30 Trinity Street continued to receive burials during the fourth century. The discovery of late Roman coins and other artefacts has indicated that several bodies were buried during the second half of the century, while two or more of the burials may have dated to the fifth century.[318]

Another migrant from fourth-century London was buried at the northern margins of Londinium. Excavations in 1998–9 at Spitalfields Market, south of the late Roman activity at the medieval Priory and Hospital of St Mary Spital, examined a large group of burials. A stone sarcophagus contained a lead coffin decorated with scallop shells within which were the remains of a woman.[319] She had been around eighteen to twenty-five years of age when she died and lead stable isotope analysis has suggested that she may have spent her childhood in the city of Rome.[320] One of the other male burials from this cemetery had a lead stable isotope ratio consistent with the area around Rome.[321] The woman in the lead coffin was evidently wealthy since she was buried with textile woven with gold thread, a silk damask garment and objects of glass and jet and she was also embalmed.[322] Outside the coffin was found a glass phial which might date after around AD 350.[323] This woman may have belonged to the family of a senior government official serving in Londinium during the late Roman period and was one of several high-status burials on this high ground.[324] Other wealthy individuals were buried close by; an underground chamber contained two skeletons, at least one of which was buried in a stone sarcophagus,[325] while a child was buried with a collection of fine glass vessels.[326]

Burial continued during the late fourth and early fifth centuries to the west of Londinium, for instance at the St Bartholomew's site. The so-called 'Smithfield Buckle' was found to the west of Londinium in the nineteenth century and is broadly comparable to the late Roman 'Germanic' metalwork from the 'eastern cemetery'.[327] Excavations at St Martin-in-the-Fields have provided further information for burial and occupation during the late fourth and early fifth centuries, together with evidence for their continuity into the Early Saxon period.[328] Burials were made during the late Roman period on the slight hill where a building had stood during the first century. Alison Telfer has noted that a man was interred in a limestone sarcophagus orientated south-west to north-east. The radiocarbon dating of his bones suggests that he was buried towards the end of the Roman period.[329] It is thought that an earlier burial had been removed and that this sarcophagus had been reused. Other sarcophagi were found during the eighteenth century in this area. The activity at St Martin-in-the-Fields suggests something rather more substantial than an agricultural settlement since it includes a cemetery and a tile kiln. The cemetery seems too far removed from Londinium to have formed a burial area of the urban population and, presumably, as at Old Ford and Shadwell, it served a community living at a short distance from Londinium.

Early Saxon London

This book will not provide a full assessment of the transition of late Roman Londinium to the Saxon reoccupation, but it is important to briefly address the increasing evidence for continuity between Roman Londinium and the Middle Saxon settlement of Lundenwic (see Fig. 9.9). The

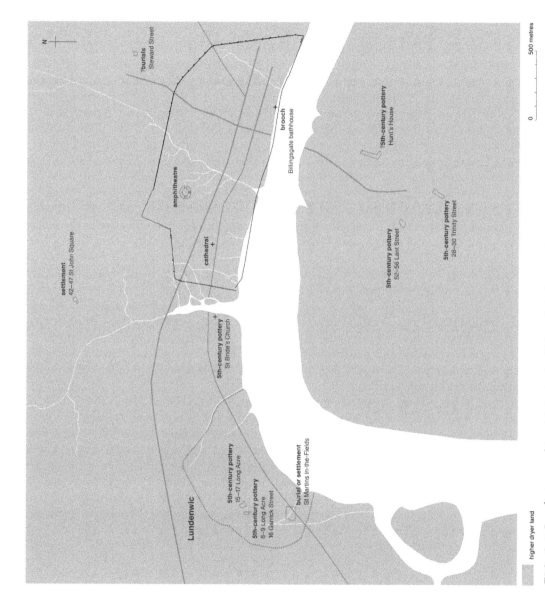

FIG. 9.9 Londinium and its vicinity in the fifth and sixth centuries.

higher dryer land

0   500 metres

N

?burials
Steward Street

brooch

Billingsgate bathhouse

amphitheatre

cathedral

settlement
42–47 St John Square

5th-century pottery
St Bride's Church

Lundenwic

5th-century pottery
15–17 Long Acre

5th-century pottery
8–9 Long Acre
16 Garrick Street

burial or settlement
St Martins in-the-Fields

5th-century pottery
52–56 Lant Street

?5th-century pottery
Hunt's House

5th-century pottery
28–30 Trinity Street

dominant narrative for London during the period from the fifth to the eighth century has suggested that the area within the walled circuit had been abandoned by the beginning of the fifth century and that a new port of trade called Lundenwic developed during the late seventh century 1 kilometre upstream from Londinium.[330] The establishment of the Middle Saxon port of Lundenwic has been interpreted as a royal initiative.[331] The name is first mentioned in a charter of AD 672–4 and documentary sources indicate that trade at Lundenwic was regulated and taxed by the Mercian kings Æthelbald (AD 716–56) and Offa (AD 757–96).[332] Archaeological evidence for the port and the associated settlement has been viewed as supporting this historical information that the port was occupied during the late seventh to late eighth century.[333] The historical narrative indicates that, as a result of Viking raiding, King Alfred reoccupied the walled circuit in AD 886.[334] This historically-derived model for the origins of Lundenwic is now being challenged by new information from archaeological excavation and research that indicates a greater continuity between the occupation of late Roman London and the Middle Saxon port.[335]

Gerrard has reviewed the evidence for the fifth and sixth centuries in London and has concluded that occupation may have continued for some time during the fifth century but that Londinium was largely abandoned by around AD 450.[336] The abandonment of Roman London was presumably a result of the collapse of Roman rule in Britain and also that urban life was heavily dependent on food and other goods imported from outside the boundaries of the urban community. As the political and administrative system disintegrated, the infrastructure of Londinium collapsed. This may have been a lengthy process since imports and coins ceased to be available during the late fourth and early fifth centuries, making it very difficult to assess the latest phases of activity on Roman sites. Further studies of how long pottery, coins and other artefacts remained in use might help to assess the extent to which such items may have been curated during this period.[337] At Calleva, occupation may have continued at least into the fifth century, although the number of distinctively 'Early Saxon' items from the site is very limited.[338] It is not certain how swiftly and dramatically Roman rule may have collapsed across southern Britannia and also the extent to which urban communities might have continued during the early fifth century and possibly later.[339]

A few sites in the walled area of Londinium have produced finds that could date to the fifth and sixth centuries.[340] The 'chaff-tempered' pottery from several sites might be Early Saxon in date, although this fabric may have been made as late as the ninth century.[341] Two Frankish ceramic vessels of probable sixth-century date were found at Gresham Street and Christ's Hospital; another pot from Aldermanbury may be comparable, although it was probably not an import.[342] Roberta Tomber has recorded an amphora from an unknown location in London which is of a type that is usually of post-Roman date.[343] At Billingsgate a Saxon saucer brooch was found on top of the debris of the collapsed roof and was overlain by deposits that derived from the fifth-century collapse of the brick walls of the bathhouse.[344] This brooch does not necessarily indicate that the building continued to be used or occupied. A single sherd of early or middle Saxon pottery from these excavations also indicated later activity in the area of the building.[345]

Some more convincing evidence is now emerging for occupation during the fifth and sixth centuries beyond the walls, particularly to the west. At 42–7 St John's Square, about 400 metres north-west of the Roman wall in the valley of the River Fleet, excavations have uncovered a group of Early Saxon pits containing pottery that has been dated to around AD 450 to 550, indicating that there was domestic settlement at this site with some small-scale industrial activity.[346] At St Bride's Church, on the west bank of the Fleet, the Roman building with the tessellated pavement that may have been constructed during the second or third centuries was overlaid by gravel and building debris that contained late Roman coins and pottery.[347] Included in this deposit were two sherds of handmade pottery that David Williams has interpreted as typical of 'Germanic wares' of the fifth century.[348] An early Roman cemetery was located close to this building and, although it is not certain that this site continued to receive burials during the fourth century,[349] these sherds might indicate that some activities were continued to the west of Londinium. Evidence for burial and occupation during the fourth to sixth centuries has also been found in the area that was later developed as Lundenwic.[350] This was probably mainly open farmland in the Roman period that may have been first occupied during the fifth to seventh centuries.[351] At St Martin-in-the-Fields the tile kiln and burials date from around the time Roman London is thought to have been abandoned. Reworked cemetery soil uncovered during the excavation has produced sherds of pottery dating from the second half of the fourth century and five sherds which have been provisionally dated to around AD 450 to 500.[352] This layer sealed the truncated remains of five inhumations, one of which was oriented north–south and had been buried with a pottery urn that had been placed by the head of the corpse. This largely complete sub-biconical jar with incised decoration may have dated from the fifth century, suggesting the continuation of burials in this late Roman cemetery. Traces of timber-and-earth buildings included one structure that has been dated to the sixth century on the basis of a distinctive glass bead.[353] A group of burials of probable seventh-century date have also been found.

St Martin-in-the-Fields is at the south-west of the Middle Saxon centre of Lundenwic.[354] Telfer has suggested that Lundenwic may have originated at an earlier date than has been suggested by previous work, indicating the continuity between late Roman and Early Saxon London. At 8–9 Long Acre / 16 Garrick Street, excavations have uncovered pits containing pottery that dated from the sixth or early seventh centuries.[355] A small quantity of pottery which is likely to date from the fifth to sixth centuries has also been found at 15–17 Long Acre but this had been redeposited in Middle Saxon features.[356]

There may have been similar activities in this period to the south of the walled circuit. At 52–6 Lant Street five sherds of Saxon pottery that might date from the fifth or sixth century indicate that there was possibly some activity, linked to the recutting of an earlier ditch during either late Roman or early Saxon times.[357] Since only a limited part of the ditch was excavated, the quantity of Saxon pottery recovered may only be a very small fraction of the total deposited.[358] Twenty sherds of pottery of a comparable date were found at 28–30 Trinity Street, although no structures were located.[359] Such finds could indicate small-scale activity or occasional occupation, although future excavation in this area of Southwark may produce more substantial evidence for continued burial or occupation during the fifth century. At Hunt's House there was fifth-century activity including the laying out of enclosures that may have been fields.[360] The associated pottery was mainly residual, although a few sherds were described by the excavators as 'sub-Roman' in character.

At Steward Street, around 500 metres north of the Roman walls, a small burial area to the north of Londinium was intermittently used for burials.[361] Early and later Roman burials were revealed along with two burials that clearly dated from the Middle Saxon period, one of which was buried with a hoard of eighth-century sceattas.[362] All of these individuals were buried with their heads to the west. Although no burials or finds dating from the fifth to seventh centuries were found, the Saxon burials attest to activity on the urban margins of Roman London before the walled circuit was reused.[363] With the information from the St Martin-in-the-Fields excavations in mind, it is possible that burial on the outskirts of Londinium continued during Early Saxon times at Lant Street and Steward Street in the unexcavated areas of these cemeteries.

Although the urban area was abandoned during the fifth century, the walls retained considerable symbolic significance from the former role of Londinium as a major administrative centre and fourth-century bishopric. Bede recorded that in AD 601 Pope Gregory originally intended Augustine to establish his bishopric at London rather than at Canterbury.[364] The cathedral of St Paul's was probably founded in AD 604 in the western part of the walled area of Londinium.[365] The western part of the walled area might also have been occupied during the early seventh century by communities attached to the cathedral, although no evidence for such activity has been located by excavation.[366]

Robert Cowie and Lyn Blackmore have discussed the gradual decay of the Roman buildings and walls during the fifth to seventh century.[367] They have suggested that the partial survival of some stone buildings may have influenced localized activities during the reuse of the remains of Roman London in the ninth century, but that the only feature that had a lasting influence was the walled circuit.[368] By the seventh century, most of the remains of the Roman buildings were hidden beneath a thick layer of naturally formed soil, the so-called 'dark earth'.[369] The street plan of the Late Saxon town did not generally reflect that of Londinium, although the gates and walls were probably reused, perhaps in AD 886 when King Alfred reoccupied the site to found a *burh* (town).[370]

Despite the absence of evidence for direct continuity, the reuse of the walled circuit and areas within may have drawn upon memories that were handed down over generations attributing meanings to the ruins of particular buildings and parts of ruined Londinium. There is an ancient tradition that St Paul's Cathedral may have been built on the site of a Roman temple during the early seventh century.[371] The earthworks of the ruined amphitheatre will also have been visible at this time and Jeremy Haslam has suggested that this may have been a place of public assembly during the Middle Saxon period.[372] The amphitheatre may have been built at a pre-Roman place of assembly and, if people continued to live in close proximity to the walled circuit during the early medieval period, they could have passed down stories about the meaning of this place to their descendants.

Summary

This chapter has built upon recent accounts to emphasize that Londinium remained a highly important urban centre during the fourth century and probably into the fifth century. The practice of commissioning stone inscriptions for the dead had largely ceased in Britannia by the fourth century and there is little information for the population. The evidence from the Lant Street cemetery and Spitalfields indicates the mixed ancestry of at least some of the population. The maintenance of the walls and the construction of the bastions confirms the importance of late Roman Londinium. As the capital of a diocese, London was the base for significant imperial officials. The evidence for stone houses with mosaics to the north and south of the Thames also shows that the community still included wealthy individuals. The temple at Tabard Square, the temple of Mithras and the probable bathhouse at Shadwell were maintained well into the fourth century. Although Londinium appears to have been the seat of a bishop, there is very little evidence for Christianity, and late Roman churches have been difficult to locate throughout Britannia. It is possible that the Colchester House building may have been a cathedral.

The cemeteries around the periphery of Londinium continued to receive burials during the late fourth and early fifth centuries. The very late Roman tile kiln at St Martin-in-the-Fields indicates that there was a demand for building materials at a time when it has been assumed that Roman London was being abandoned. It is possible that this kiln produced tiles for buildings located west of Londinium which have not yet been excavated. Much of the latest evidence for occupation and burial comes from areas at the edge or outside the walled circuit, especially to the west. Perhaps the decaying buildings made the walled area increasingly dangerous and people moved to live in close proximity to their former homes. Settlement and burial may have focused on the area that was to become the Middle Saxon trading settlement of Lundenwic. As Christianity was reintroduced to south-eastern Britain, the establishment of St Paul's Cathedral in the largely abandoned urban centre reflected the continuing significance of Londinium as a former bishopric, as well as a civil and administrative centre.

There is a period of almost 200 years between the apparent abandonment of the walled circuit and the founding of St Paul's Cathedral, a fundamental theme for future research. Londinium was built on the meanings and functions of the landscapes and waterscapes of the pre-Roman period and the post-Roman city was also constructed meaningfully on the ruined Roman remains.

Conclusion:

Beginnings and Endings

We always harbour the illusion that something will have an end-point, that it will then take on a meaning, and will allow us retrospectively to restore its origins and, with this beginning and this end, the play of cause and effect will become possible . . .

JEAN BAUDRILLARD 2003: 61

This book has emphasized the history of the land and waterscapes within which Londinium was set, exploring ideas of continuity and transformation. The emphasis has been mainly upon the material remains and the geography of Roman London.[1] This account therefore has presented a synthesis of relevant material but not a full summary of all the available material sources. The information for some neglected aspects of Londinium has been summarized, as development-led pressures have resulted in an increasing focus on the domestic residences and burials of the population. Many of the 'public buildings' are protected through statutory and planning regulations and modern excavations have tended to be very small scale and aimed at protecting and preserving the buried remains. Certain important themes of urban life have therefore been explored in only a limited way, including the character and chronology of monumental buildings such as the forum-basilica and the walls of Roman London. Other public structures such as the amphitheatre and the Tabard Square temple have been discovered during excavations providing important new insights.

The idea that ritual was embodied in all aspects of human life and death has been emphasized. It is not possible to divide aspects of everyday life – such as building, meeting, producing goods, childbirth and the disposal of the dead – from the ritual beliefs which structured these activities. The narrative has focused upon the people of Londinium and the substantial alterations to waterscapes and landscapes undertaken in order to colonize and occupy the site from the Late Iron Age to the early fifth century AD. There are substantial difficulties in interpreting the character of Londinium from urban landscapes and waterscapes that were in constant transition for 350 years. The significance of the fragmentary picture that has emerged from this discussion may nevertheless be explored thematically.

Beginnings

Although Londinium cannot be identified as deriving from a Late Iron Age *oppidum*, the rites of passage practised in the Thames just upstream of Roman London indicated the significance of this marginal land. Metalwork and human remains recovered during the dredging of the river suggest that waters were used by neighbouring communities for the transformation of their dead into ancestors. The particular significance of the area where Londinium was to develop may have derived from the broadening out of the River Thames at this location, the bifurcation of the channels defining islands and the junction of the Walbrook with the Thames.

There is plentiful information for Iron Age activity on the islands in the Thames around Southwark, although most of the Iron Age metalwork and human cranial remains have been found further west around Battersea and further upstream. Despite the number of excavations, it is unclear what the marginal lands on the Southwark islands were used for during the Middle and Late Iron Age, perhaps because most of the archaeological deposits have been lost as a result of fluvial erosion. There is only very limited evidence for the exposure of corpses on these islands during the Iron Age. Pits and ditches were dug and pottery was deposited by people who visited or lived on the islands, although the high water table and regular flooding may only have allowed seasonal occupation. It is possible that these islands were accessed by bridges or causeways during the Iron Age.

The disarticulated human bones deposited in a stream course in the Upper Walbrook Cemetery indicates that human bodies were exposed to flood waters in the headwaters of the Walbrook. Such headwaters had a special significance during the early Roman period, with activities taking place around ponds in the western headwaters of the Walbrook. The construction of the amphitheatre in this area around AD 70 may have provided a monumental central point for a place where people had been assembling for generations. It is not clear whether any of the other tributaries of the Thames were used to expose corpses. Although a few finds of Iron Age date have been made across the area later developed as Londinium, there is a remarkable absence of evidence for sustained occupation during the Iron Age, especially in Southwark south of the Borough Channel. Boudica's attack on early Roman London in AD 60 may have been influenced by the special importance of the landscapes and waterscapes that were being drained and built upon and the burning of Londinium could have been a ritual act to recreate the earlier marginal and watery landscape dedicated to the dead.

Water and waterscapes

The population of Londinium had an intimate connection with sources of water. The Iron Age activities both in and near the river may have focused on the tidal head of the Thames, the furthest point upstream reached by salt from the sea. Before Roman London was established, the tributaries of the Thames flowed with fresh water and there were marshy conditions in places. The course of the Thames where Londinium was later developed were flushed with salt water as the tide rose and the tidal waters will also have flowed into the lower reaches of the tributaries that drained into the river from the north. Londinium was at the furthest point upriver accessible by sea-going ships and the abandonment of the waterfront facilities during the third century was a result of the falling level of the Thames.

The control and management of water have constituted one of the main themes of this book. This has been well researched as a result of the substantial archaeological work that has examined the course and character of the Thames river. This has indicated that the land across Southwark was gradually raised, the braided courses of the River Thames were canalized and land was slowly reclaimed from the mid-first to the fourth century, considerably modifying the character of the urban areas in Southwark. The waterfront on the north bank of the Thames was successively reinforced to create the main port that was maintained until the middle of the third century. Trade was also conducted along the revetted waterfront in Southwark and buildings have been identified in Southwark that functioned as warehouses. After this time, trading may have taken place at beach markets.

The watery nature of the site of Londinium, the control of water flow to establish land that could be occupied and the construction of wharves to facilitate trade and transport have been considered in some detail. The symbolic role of the Thames and the other water sources was represented by images of water gods and spirits and many ritual activities during the Roman period may have been enacted to placate and seek the support of these divinities. The bridging of the Thames was clearly associated with ritual and religious behaviour represented by the offerings to the water spirits deposited in the river. During early Saxon times Lundenwic also developed to exploit the tidal reach of the Thames, which by this period had extended slightly further upstream.

Extensive archaeological work has been undertaken to explore the location and character of the Walbrook and its context both within and to the north of Londinium. The waters of this river and of its tributaries had a deep ritual and economic significance, with the development of industries, shrines and temples along their courses. Relatively little archaeological work has been undertaken along the Fleet river and other tributaries of the Thames that ran through or close to Londinium. In places, evidence has been found for ponds and springs, some of which were closely connected with ritual and religion. Wells were focal points for the deposition of ritual offerings, possibly indicating that there were shrines or temples in close proximity.

Building

The building up of ground surfaces and continuous additions and alterations to the waterfronts clearly demonstrate that there was a constant demand for the maintenance of dry land. These acts of construction often required offerings to be made to gods and spirits of place. An active programme of the building up of the land surface and margins had begun by the late AD 40s or the early AD 50s. The road system was first established at this time, and subsequently developed to connect the public buildings and properties, with additional side roads and access ways constructed throughout the urban area. That the land was being encultured by these colonization and building operations is a controversial issue in the interpretation of Londinium. Ralph Merrifield has linked the archaeology of Roman London to ideas of ritual and belief and his work has been highly influential, although the central theory has been dismissed by some archaeologists. The evidence to support Merrifield's argument has been provided by the numerous foundation and termination offerings made in different contexts throughout the history of Londinium. Materials that have sometimes been viewed as mundane rubbish may be reinterpreted as ritually-imbued objects that were deposited as offerings to placate spirits of place. This reinterpretation has usually been accepted for material items left in pits and other deposits at temple sites such as the Mithraeum and the Tabard Square temple. Much of the material that archaeologists have recovered from Roman contexts was not merely everyday rubbish. Focusing on the depositional context and the material incorporated within it will help to interpret the meaning of these significant acts.

Although people will have lost personal possessions while living and working in Londinium, the evidence for the deposition of large quantities of materials such as substantially complete pots and valuable metal items in many contexts has been interpreted as an indication that offerings were made to placate spirits and to make physical claims to land. Many of these excavated materials also represent abandoned rubbish, but the occupants of Londinium are unlikely to have distinguished between mundane and ritual activities in the ways that archaeologists have often suggested. Broken and discarded objects could have continued to be imbued with the spirit of the material item present when it was complete and in use. This was not only the case for the fragmented stone sculptures deposited in pits at the temple of Mithras, or built into the riverside wall at Baynard's Castle or into the late Roman bastions, but also for much of the material that was deposited to build up the land and to fill pits and wells. This material was used in this way partly because of ritual beliefs about certain parts of the urban area, building on earlier meanings of the landscape and waterscape that dated back at least to the Iron Age.

The dumping of building materials on a substantial scale on the south island in Southwark may have related to the sorting of materials for reuse in a sparsely settled area. Some of this material may never have been recycled and this could explain the materials found in dumped deposits and in wells. Even the recycling of building materials may, moreover, have been associated with ritual practices. The cycle of use and disuse of a building and its materials were conceived of in particularly special ways. The construction of houses and 'public buildings' constituted part of this symbolic creation of cultural space. These were spiritual and ritual places where the social order of Londinium was generated and manipulated. Houses were associated with cults related to divine spirits and ancestors. Public buildings and houses were the venues for performances that helped to create social distinctions. All these beliefs and actions had ritual dimensions which informed the structures of these buildings, the locations in which they were built and the offerings placed in the foundation and termination deposits often revealed during excavation.

Considering the topography of the urban space, it is possible to identify routes for processions – for example, from the early forum westwards across the Walbrook to the temple zone around the amphitheatre; and from the forum southwards across the Thames bridge to the main islands and the Tabard Square temple. The urban topography may have been created around such routes and the sacred places they connected. Other aspects of urban planning included the location of roads and areas of housing. The available information indicates that there was some degree of planning, with burial and funerary practices usually conducted at the periphery of the urban zone. Certain parts of Londinium appear to have been more heavily occupied and used at different times. It is possible that the area west of the Walbrook was only sparsely occupied after the AD 160s and that the south bank of the Thames in Southwark and the south island may also have been largely unoccupied after the early second century. It is difficult to map the exact extent of occupation and use of the land especially as most archaeological investigation has focused on plotting and interpreting areas that seem to have been intensively used. Future excavations that uncover limited evidence for Roman occupation should try to determine whether this is the result of truncation or whether certain areas were actually largely unoccupied. Extensive garden areas and perhaps sacred groves would have been established within Londinium and the 'dark earth' has indicated that some land may have been cultivated.

Identities

The variable identities of the population have been explored in some detail in this book, particularly their origins and status. There is evidence for incomers from the earliest phase. It is also possible that Britons were living in the urban area in roundhouses during the first century and there is evidence for the working of glass and copper-alloy using Iron Age technologies. These people may have been free members of the British population who were able to exploit the market of the growing urban centre, or they were enslaved Britons who had been settled to develop industries and to assist in the building of the infrastructure. People from elsewhere in Britannia will also have been swiftly assimilated into the urban population and incorporated into the culture and politics of the Roman Empire.

It is mostly men that are represented in the writing tablets. The ninety-two individuals attested at Bloomberg, including Roman citizens, freedmen and slaves, all are male.[2] Their Gallic and Germanic homelands had been incorporated into the Roman Empire during their parents' lifetimes. There is some limited evidence for female slaves, who would have been living in large numbers throughout Londinium, in the form of two writing tablets that record the selling of slaves possibly at a market, possibly in Londinium. Fortunata's family was originally from a *civitas* in northern Gaul but many Britons will also have been enslaved during the conquest and settlement of the province of Britannia. The rebuilding of Londinium during the AD 60s may have involved the labour of enslaved Britons and it has been suggested that the roundhouses at the enclosed site at 10 Gresham Street were the homes of the slave workers who were involved in the reconstruction operations. Many industrial premises were probably dependent on the labour of slaves, and the distinction between more ornate houses and less elaborate premises associated with industrial production at the Courage Brewery ironworking site may have expressed the division between the masters and their slaves. Tenants and small-scale landowners will also have produced industrial goods, for example at sites in the Walbrook Valley. There are, however, few definitive ways that archaeologists can identify slaves and tenants in the residues of the past.[3]

During its history, traders, soldiers and imperial officials were present in Roman London. When the results of the excavation of the 'eastern cemetery' were published in 2000, it was suggested that many of these people probably belonged to an 'indigenous' Romano-British population,[4] although since this time ideas regarding the mobility of people across the empire have changed.[5] Deposits of human bone have now been assessed by aDNA, stable isotope and cranial analyses which have indicated that the population of Londinium was highly mixed in terms of origins and culture. Many of the detailed scientific studies explored in this book have emphasized the provisional nature of their arguments, although this evidence from London is now making a substantial contribution to the interpretation of mobilities.[6]

The ways in which the people buried their dead reflect their discrepant styles of life and death. Cremation was a common funerary practice during the first century and half of the life of Londinium, although there were also inhumation burials. During the third and fourth centuries cremation continued and inhumation became the most usual form of burial. The artefacts buried with these people show their international connections and occasionally perhaps their geographical origins. Inscriptions commemorating the deceased often record the place of origin of the buried individual and attest to the presence in London of people from across the empire. Trading through the port was particularly attractive to merchants from overseas, many of whom were evidently wealthy. A trader commissioned at least one temple building at Tabard Square and a military officer probably commissioned the Mithraeum. Classical texts and richly furnished burials show that wealthy individuals were still present into the fourth century, and perhaps beyond.

New ways of bathing and dining and literacy were adopted by the urban population. Public and private bathhouses were constructed and were popularly used, perhaps by all social groups. The evidence from Shadwell may suggest that public bathing was still practised in the fourth century and private houses also had bathing suites in later Roman times. Tenants and clients may have been able to access bathhouses with the agreement of their masters. The widespread practice of writing is attested by writing tablets and other implements and by graffiti on pots and personal items. Many people involved in trade and industry will have been required to write in Latin, as indicated by the records in the writing tablets found in the Walbrook Valley. The public and private buildings of Roman London were constructed in such a way that status and social position were constantly on display in the houses of the rich and of the poor as well as more formally at the forum and the amphitheatre.

The economic hub of Londinium may well have been the capital of its province for much of the Roman period. The procurators of Britannia may have been based here from AD 61 and the late Roman economic role of London suggests that it had a vital part to play. The governors may also have been based in Londinium from the late first century, although there is no direct evidence that their headquarters was based in London. The 'governor's palace' was a particularly opulent and important building complex. There were elaborate 'palaces' at the Salvation Army site and Winchester Palace that may have been the homes of very wealthy traders or which had a more official function. These buildings have been excavated in small areas and so their information is very incomplete. There are strong indications of the military importance of Roman London in terms of the presence of military men and also the building of the forts at Plantation Place and Cripplegate during the AD 60s and the early second century respectively. The army had an important role and Londinium retained its strategic military significance well into the fourth century. Whether it was the provincial capital may be unimportant since it had a vitally important economic and strategic role at various times.

Boundary practices

A key feature that has emerged from recent excavations is the variety of activities that characterized Londinium's boundaries during its periods of growth and decline. The urban peripheries may not always have been particularly clearly defined prior to the construction of the walled circuit north of the Thames, and south of the river they remained unclear throughout the Roman period. Even after the walls were constructed, boundary practices were continued both at and beyond the urban limits, for example the deposition of coin moulds and the reuse of monumental masonry in the riverside wall and in the bastions of the landward wall.

The walls did not constitute the only physical limit of the urban space. The dead were always expected to be disposed of beyond the margins of settlement. The blurring of the boundaries between the living and dead at the west edge of early Londinium was probably the result of the extension of the urban area to incorporate some cemeteries into the occupied area. To the south of the Thames most burials were deposited in an area where little evidence for occupation has been found, although temple buildings and industrial activities were located there. The exposure of some corpses and the manipulation of their remains may, however, have brought people into regular contact with the disarticulated bones of the dead at the urban margins, especially in the upper Walbrook Valley. During the course of the second to fourth century the cemeteries became further established with a complex range of burial ground developing around the urban margins.

Another boundary practice was the establishment of religious locations at the periphery of Londinium. Some of these cults may have been associated with important deceased members of the urban community. Feasting was also a common activity in marginal urban areas from the AD 60s to at least the third century. Feasts may often have been connected with the commemoration of the dead and with religious practices conducted at shrines and temples. On the margins there usually was a distinction between areas of burial and manufacture, although industrial activities could often have been closely connected with beliefs about spirits and divinities. Substantial industrial activities may naturally have been developed toward the urban peripheries and perhaps the associations between industry and ritual arose from their mutual marginal character.

Ritual activities continued with the establishment of the walls. The deposition of coin moulds in three locations on the urban boundary probably drew upon such ritual connections and the incorporation of sculpted stones in the riverside wall at Baynards Castle and in the late Roman bastions on the eastern landward wall involved highly significant fragments of sculptured divinities to reconstitute these important limits. That burial activities were conducted outside, and later inside, the walled circuit shows that these walls only constituted one element in the tradition of boundary practices. The continued maintenance of this impressive stone construction by the urban authorities until the end of the fourth century demonstrates their special military and symbolic significance.

Endings and new beginnings

Both the origin of Londinium and the ending have previously been considered in too specific terms. The assessment of fourth-century London suggests that it retained a considerable strategic and political significance. There is currently little to indicate that life continued inside the walled area after the first decade of the fifth century, although there is growing information that people continued to live in a cluster of settlements both at and beyond the urban margins in early Saxon times. People may also have continued to live within the walled area into the fifth century – later than has usually been assumed – and activities in the suburbs could indicate that the core of Londinium retained a particular significance. Many archaeologists are now moving away from concepts of decline and fall to explore social continuity during the fifth century and to allow for the considerable disruptions to life that had evidently taken place. Since very little material that clearly dates from the fifth and sixth centuries has been found, people living in the walled area may have curated and used older material items in their daily lives. Alternatively, the crumbling buildings of early fifth-century Londinium may have no longer been occupied until part of the urban area was recolonized when the cathedral of St Paul's was established during the early seventh century. The walled area was then substantially reoccupied during the ninth century.

Life in early medieval London built upon the significance of Roman London. Exploring the continuities and discontinuities between late Roman and Saxon London is an exciting topic which requires further attention, and the possibilities have only been briefly addressed in this book. Beginnings and endings are particularly significant issues and the nature of continuity and change may often prove difficult to comprehend.[7] Research agendas tend to divide up the periods of London's early history, but new directions of research are required that work across the chronological divisions that partly obscure the potential of the study of London's past.

A final point

In setting new agendas for the study of Roman London, we should not abandon the focus of past work on the economic, political and strategic roles of Londinium. The work on small finds, human bones and site stratigraphy has been vital to the arguments developed in this book. The themes summarized above are not intended as a prescriptive list but as indicating some directions in which future research might focus in order to explore the ancient past of Roman London. Acknowledging how different the past was from the city today also draws attention to issues that may appear to be of contemporary significance, such as the multicultural population and the economic and strategic international roles of Londinium.

APPENDIX: SITE CODES AND NAMES FOR EXCAVATIONS DISCUSSED IN THE TEXT

These codes and names have been used to locate sites excavated across London and relate to works undertaken by archaeologists since the 1930s. This list gives site name (brief) and main publication report (I = interim or other fairly limited mention of site, F = final report or detailed report).

Much of this information is derived from the sources quoted, but prime sources are usually included and not secondary mentions of sites. Site codes have sometimes been determined from the Museum of London's site catalogue: www.museumoflondon.org.uk/laarc/catalogue/. GM codes are those for excavations undertaken by the Guildhall Museum, and the Museum of London codes are for subsequent excavations, including those undertaken by the Museum of London and other organizations (cf. Schofield 1998).

Guildhall Museum	Site name	Main publication
GM4	Guildhall Extension Site / Guildhall Library	Guildhall Museum (1968: 4–10) [I]
GM7	1–2 Aldgate / Aldgate, junction with Duke's Place	Guildhall Museum (1969: 20–3) [I]
GM12	12 Arthur Street (Minster House)	Swift (2008: 6–7, 40) [I]
GM25	Site of Bush Lane ('Governor's Palace')	Marsden (1975) [I]
GM29	78–80 Cannon Street ('Governor's Palace')	Marsden (1975) [I]
GM37	110–16 Cheapside (bathhouse)	Marsden (1976) [I]
GM44	8–10 Cooper's Row	Schofield (1998: 46) [I]
GM55	Dukes Place (Bastion 6)	Marsden (1980: 171–2) [I]
GM60	112–14 Fenchurch Street / 17–18 Billiter Street	Schofield (1998: 51) [I]
GM68	17–19 Gracechurch Street	Marsden (1987: 32–3, 106–16) [I]
GM91	101 Queen Victoria Street (Salvation Army site)	Marsden (1993) [I]
GM95	22 Lime Street (forum)	Marsden (1987: 90–2) [I]
GM100	54–8 Lombard Street (forum)	Marsden (1987: 140–7) [I]
GM101	54 Lombard Street (forum)	Marsden (1987: 135–40) [I]

(*continued*)

Guildhall Museum	Site name	Main publication
GM111	Billingsgate bathhouse (Coal Exchange)	Marsden (1980: 151–5, 167, 180, 182–6) [I]
GM121	55–61 Moorgate	Schofield (1998: 72) [I]
GM131	Central Criminal Court, Old Bailey	Guildhall Museum (1969: 4–6); Guildhall Museum (1970: 2–6) [I]
GM136	Paternoster Square	Marsden (1969) [I]
GM142	Aldermary House, 61–2 Queen Street	Wilmott (1982) [I]
GM157	Bucklersbury House	Wilmott (1991) [I]
GM157/GM256	Temple of Mithras	Shepherd (1998) [F]
GM182	Blackfriars ship 1	Marsden (1994: 33–95) [F]
GM210	9–11 Bush Lane ('Governor's Palace')	Marsden (1975) [I]
GM226	Founders' Court, 2 Moorgate	Schofield (1998: 106) [I]
GM240	Huggin Hill (bathhouse)	Marsden (1976: 3–29) [I]
GM248	Regis House, King William Street / Fish Street Hill	Dunning (1945: 53) [I]
GM251	37 Ludgate Hill	Guildhall Museum (1970: 9) [I]
GM297	22 Lime Street, 168–70 Fenchurch Street (forum)	Philp (1977) [I]
GM451	Guy's Hospital boat	Marsden (1994: 97–104) [F]

Museum of London	Site name	Main publication
207BHS72/201BHS75	201–11 Borough High Street	Ferretti and Graham (1978) [F]
MIL72/MLK76	1–6 Milk Street	Roskams (1991b) [F]
CUS73	Old Custom House (waterfront)	Brigham (1990a: 118–25, 140) [F]
106BHS73	106–14 Borough High Street	Schwab (1978) [F]
1SS73	1–5 Swan Street, Great Dover Street	Graham (1978) [F]
64BHS74	64–70 Borough High Street	Graham (1988) [I]
88BHS74	88 Borough High Street	Yule and Hinton (1988) [I]
199BHS74	199 Borough High Street	Schaaf (1988); Hammerson (1988: 245–7) [I]
LD74/LD76	Shadwell 'Tower'	Lakin (2002) [F]
1STS74	1–7 St Thomas Street	Dennis (1978) [F]
NFW74/SM75/FRE78	New Fresh Wharf (waterfront)	Miller, Schofield and Rhodes (1986) [F]
TR74	Billingsgate Buildings	D. Jones (1980) [F]
TW74	Toppings Wharf, Sun Wharf	Sheldon (1974) [F]
8US74	8 Union Street	Marsh (1978) [I]
BC75	Baynard's Castle, Upper Thames Street (city wall)	C. Hill, Millett and Blagg (1980) [F]
GPO75	76–80 Newgate Street	Roskams (1991a) [F]

175BHS76/179BHS89	175–7 and 179–91 Borough High Street	Schaaf (1976) [I]; Cowan and Pringle (2009: 80) [I]
FSE76	160–2 Fenchurch Street (forum)	Boddington and Marsden (1987) [I]
SB76	Silvester Buildings	Seeley and Wardle (2009: 145) [I]
TOL39/THL78b (1976 to 1979)	Tower of London	Parnell (1977; 1978; 1981; 1985) [I]
DUK77	Dukes Place (including Bastion 6)	J. Maloney (1979) [I]
HR77/HR79	Harper Road	Dean and Hammerson (1980); Cotton (2008) [I]
SCC77	Southwark Cathedral crypt	Hammerson (1978) [I]
213BHS77	213 Borough High Street	Cowan et al. (2009: 18, 24) [I]
AB78	Arcadia Buildings	Dean (1980) [I]
THL78b	Tower Hill	Whipp (1980) [F]
WAT78	Watling Court	Perring (1991a) [F]
BAR79	St Bartholomew's Hospital, Medical School	Bentley and Pritchard (1982) [F]
170BHS79	170–94 Borough High Street	Cowan et al. (2009: 14) [I]
HIB79	Hibernia Wharf	Cowan (2009: 178–9); Wardle (2009: 124–9) [I]
ILA79	Miles Lane (Waterfront)	Miller (1982) [I]
XWL79	8–10 Crosswall (Bastion 4A)	J. Maloney (1980) [F]
15SKS80	15–23 Southwark Street ('mansio')	Cowan (1995) [F]
ARC81/SEN91/MCF06	Mariner House (Crossed Friars)	Lerz and Holder (2016) [F]
107BHS81	107–15 Borough High Street	Yule (1982) [I]
223BHS81	223–37 Borough High Street	Cowan et al. (2009: 14, 185–6) [I]
NEW81/ENG84/CLK 86, etc.	St Mary Clerkenwell	Sloane (2012: 10–14) [F]
PDN81	Pudding Lane (Waterfront)	G. Milne (1985) [I]
PET81	Peter's Hill (Salvation Army site)	T. Williams (1993: 57–63) [F]
SWA81	Swan Lane (Waterfront)	Brigham (1990a: 111–17) [F]
GRH82	Guy's Hospital, St Thomas Street	White (2009) [F]
LIB82	119–21 Cannon Street	Schofield (1998: 183) [I]
LUD82	42–6 Ludgate Hill and 1–6 Old Bailey	Rowsome (2014) [I]
SLO82	Sugar Loaf Court, 14 Garlic Hill	Davies, Richardson and Tomber (1994: 232) [I]
SPT82	Central Foundation Girls' School	Thomas, Sloane and Phillpotts (1997: 6) [I]
4STS82	4–26 St Thomas Street	Westman and Pringle (2009: 84–9); Cowan et al. (2009: 157–8) [I]
ACE83	77–9 Gracechurch Street (forum)	Upson and Pye (1987: 117–19) [I]
BWB83	Billingsgate Lorry Park (waterfront)	Brigham (1990a: 100–7) [F]

(continued)

Museum of London	Site name	Main publication
CW83/CWO84/ CHWH83	Cotton's Wharf	Cowan and Pringle (2009: 82–3) [I]
FEN83	5–12 Fenchurch Street, 1 Philpott Lane	Schofield (1998: 193–4); L. Wallace (2014: 91–2) [I]
FW83/FW84	Fennings Wharf	Brigham (2001a) [F]
KEY83	15–35 Copthall Avenue	C. Maloney (1990) [F]
LIM83	25–6 Lime Street	Schofield (1998: 196) [I]
WP83	Winchester Palace	Yule (2005) [F]
BA84/TOB95	Bermondsey Abbey	Sidell et al. (2002: 40–3); Rayner (2009: 38) [I]
COSE84[1]	Courage Brewery (Area C)	Cowan (2003) [F]
COSE84[2]	Courage Brewery (Area A)	Hammer (2003) [F]
LCT84	Leadenhall Court	G. Milne (1992); G. Milne and Wardle (1996) [F]
28PS84[1] (trenches 1, and 3)	28 Park Street (Courage Brewery Area Q)	Cowan (2003) [F]
28PS84[2] (trenches 4 and 5)	28 Park Street (Courage Brewery Area R)	Cowan (2003) [F]
TW84	Toppings Wharf	Brigham (2001a) [F]
CSW85 (trench 2)	Courage Brewery (Area J)	Cowan (2003) [F]
NRT85/SPQ87, etc.	Priory and Hospital of St Mary Spital	Thomas, Sloane and Phillpotts (1997: 11–13) [I]
PCH85	1–3 St Paul's Churchyard, 1–9 Ludgate Hill	Schofield (2011: 29, 336–7) [I]
CUE86	Premier Place, Devonshire Square	Sankey and Connell (2008) [F]
JBL86	Jubilee Gardens	Schofield (1998: 229) [I]
NHA86	9 Northumberland Avenue	Schofield (1998: 232) [I]
SUN86	Sunlight Wharf (Salvation Army site)	T. Williams (1993: 57–62) [I]
ABC87	Abacus House	Schofield (1998: 237–8) [F]
ASQ87	1 America Square	Hunt (2011) [F]
BBH87	Billingsgate bathhouse	Rowsome (1996) [I]
BLM87	85–6 London Wall (Blomfield House)	Schofield (1998: 242–3) [I]
BUC87	DLR Bucklersbury (1 Poultry Site C)	J. Hill and Rowsome (2011) [F]
CG87	Cherry Garden Pier	Girardon and Heathcote (1988: 414) [I]
CO87	Courage Brewery (Area F)	Hammer (2003) [F]
GAG87/GDH85/GYE92/ GYU99	Amphitheatre	Bateman, Cowan and Wroe-Brown (2008) [F]
MFI87	4–12 Monument Street, 17 Fish Street	Schofield (1998: 252) [I]

MGT87	55–61 Moorgate	Keily and Shepherd (2005: 147–8) [I]
MSL87	49–59 Mansell Street etc. (eastern cemetery)	Barber and Bowsher (2000) [F]
RIV87	River Plate House, 7–11 Finsbury Circus	Harward, Powers and Watson (2015) [F]
UTA87	Cannon Street Station south	Schofield (1998: 259) [I]
CO88[1]	Courage Brewery (Area E)	Hammer (2003) [F]
CO88[2]	Courage Brewery (Area D)	Cowan (2003); Hammer (2003) [F]
DMT88	Huggin Hill bathhouse (Dominant House)	Rowsome (1999: 263–73) [I]
ELD88	Liverpool House, 15–17 Eldon Street	Harward, Powers and Watson (2015) [F]
FIB88	12–15 Finsbury Circus	Harward, Powers and Watson (2015) [F]
HOO88	Hooper Street (eastern cemetery)	Barber and Bowsher (2000) [F]
LHY88	DLR Lothbury (1 Poultry Site B)	J. Hill and Rowsome (2011) [F]
LOW88	52–63 London Wall	Redfern and Bonny (2014) [I]
LSO88	Leith House, 47–57 Gresham Street	Schofield (1998: 274) [I]
LYD88	Cannon Street Station north	Schofield (1998: 274–5) [I]
MOH88	Moorgate Hall, 143–71 Moorgate	Schofield (1998: 276) [I]
OBA88	18–25 Old Bailey	Schofield (1998: 277) [I]
SKS88	Skipton Street	Connell (2009: 257); Shepherd and Wardle (2015: 99–100) [I]
TEX88	Thames Exchange site	Parry (1994) [I]
USA88/USB88	10–18 Union Street	Heard (1989) [I]
VAL88	Fleet Valley	Schofield (1998: 283–7) [I]
WIV88	Whittington Avenue	G. Brown and Pye (1992) [I]
ATL89/ATC97	Atlantic House	S. Watson (2003) [F]
AW89	Alaska Works	Cowan et al. (2009: 14); Rayner (2009: 38–9) [I]
120BHS89/124BHS77	120–4 and 124–6 Borough High Street	Dean and Hammerson (1980) [I]; Cowan and Wardle (2009: 107–8) [I]
ETA89	7 Bishopsgate	Sankey (2003) [F]
GHL89/GHD90/GHSC77	Guy's Hospital	L. Wheeler (2009: 73–6) [I]
170GRA89/GRW91	170–6 Grange Road and 41–5 Grange Walk	Heard (1996: 78); Rayner (2009: 38–40) [I]
JON89	42–7 St John's Square, Clerkenwell	Sloane and Malcolm (2004: 20–3) [F]
PEP89	Colchester House	Sankey (1988); Gerrard (2011g) [I]
52SOS89	Courage Brewery (Area M) (52–4 Southwark Street)	Cowan (2003); Hammer (2003) [I]
WES89	24–30 West Smithfield	Schofield (1998: 298–9) [I]

(continued)

Museum of London	Site name	Main publication
CID90	72–5 Cheapside / 83–93 Queen Str. (1 Poultry Site D)	J. Hill and Woodger (1999) [F]; J. Hill and Rowsome (2011) [F]
BSP91	14 Elden Street / 16 Broad Street Place	Harward, Powers and Watson (2015) [F]
ABY91	Abbey Street / Neckinger	Heard (1996: 78) [I]
ROY91	Leroy Street	Cowan and Pringle (2009: 91) [I]
JSS92	Joiner Street (Borough High Street Ticket Hall)	Drummond-Murray and Thompson (2002) [F]
MSA92	Mayor Sworder's Arches	Drummond-Murray and Thompson (2002: 146) [F]
REW92	Redcross Way, traction power substation	Drummond-Murray and Thompson (2002: 145–6) [F]
RWT93/RWG94	Redcross Way ('mansio')	Drummond-Murray and Thompson (2002: 127–39) [F]
SBC92	St Bride's Church	G. Milne (1997) [F]
TOS93	283 Tooley Street	Drummond-Murray, Saxby and Watson (1994: 254–5) [I]
KWS94	Regis House, 39–46 King William Street (waterfront)	Brigham and Watson (1996); Brigham, Watson and Tyres (1996) [I]
NST94	Shelly House	Howe and Lakin (2004) [F]
ONE94	1 Poultry (1 Poultry Site A)	J. Hill and Rowsome (2011) [F]
SUF94	Suffolk House (Governor's House)	Brigham (2001c) [F]
TOY94	271 Tooley Street	Drummond-Murray, Saxby and Watson (1994: 254–5) [I]
BAX95	Baltic House	Howe (2002) [F]
BGH95	Borough High Street Ticket Hall	Drummond-Murray and Thompson (2002) [F]
BPL95	Monument House	Blair and Sankey (2007) [F]
FCC95	Lloyd's Register, 71 Fenchurch Street	Bluer and Brigham (2006) [F]
FEH95	168 Fenchurch Street (forum)	Dunwoodie (2004) [F]
GAH95	Garrard House	Howe and Lakin (2004) [F]
LBE95	London Bridge Station	Drummond-Murray and Thompson (2002: 143) [F]
LBI95	Station Approach	Drummond-Murray and Thompson (2002: 71–7) [F]
MRG95/KHS98	20–8 Moorgate / Northgate House	Seeley and Drummond-Murray (2005) [F]
AES96/PLH97	1–6 Aldersgate	Butler (2002) [F]
CAO96	25 Cannon Street	Elsden (2002) [F]
GDV96	165 Great Dover Street	Mackinder (2000) [F]

MGE96	12–18 Moorgate	Bruce et al. (2010) [F]
ESC97	13–21 Eastcheap	Blair and Sankey (2007) [F]
FER97	Plantation Place	Dunwoodie, Harward and Pitt (2015) [F]
GSM97	10 Gresham Street	Casson, Drummond-Murray and Francis (2014) [F]
HHO97	Hunt's House	Taylor-Wilson (2002) [F]
OBL97	16–17 Old Bailey	Pitt (2006: 27–35) [F]
WOO97	90–2 and 100 Wood Street	Howe and Lakin (2004) [F]
AHS98	87–9 Aldgate High Street	B. Bishop (2000) [I]
BGB98	201 Bishopsgate	Swift (2003) [F]
BYQ98	Bermondsey Square	C. Maloney (1999: 21); Hall (2014: 180) [I]
GCC98	Christ Church Greyfriars (Merrill Lynch Financial C.)	Lyon (2007) [F]
KEW98	King Edward Buildings (Merrill Lynch Financial Centre)	Lyon (2007) [F]
MRL98	Moor House	Butler (2006) [F]
NEG98	3–9 Newgate Street	Pitt (2006: 44–53) [F]
NHG98	25 Gresham Street	Lyon (2005) [F]
OJW98	8–10 Old Jewry	S. Watson (2004) [I]
SRP98	Spitalfields cemetery	Thomas (2004) [I]
SWN98	Old Sorting Office	Beasley (2007) [F]
TEA98	Lion Plaza, 1–8 Old Broad St / 41–3 Threadneedle St	McKenzie (2012) [F]
CPW99/CPQ03/CRZ06/ ASQ87	8–14 Cooper's Row / 1 America Square	Hunt (2011) [F]
CTC99	Courtenay House (Paternoster Square)	S. Watson (2006) [F]
LCR99	15–17 Long Acre	Capon (2006) [I]
LGK99	5–27 Long Lane	Douglas (2008) [F]
MTA99	Southwark Cathedral	Divers et al. (2009: 11–34) [F]
PSU99	Stonemason's Yard Ramp (Paternoster Square)	S. Watson (2006) [F]
GHT00	30 Gresham Street	Blair et al. (2006) [I]; Maloney (2002: 4) [I]
LGC00	8–9 Longacre / 16 Garrick Street	Blackmore, Vince and Cowie (2004) [I]
NGT00	Newgate Triangle (Paternoster Square)	S. Watson (2006) [F]
SLY00	Juxton House (Paternoster Square)	S. Watson (2006) [F]
TLT00	285–91 Tooley Street	Leary (2004) [I]

(*continued*)

Museum of London	Site name	Main publication
AUT01	12 Arthur Street	Swift (2008) [F]
CPN01	Crispin Street	Sudds and Douglas (2015) [F]
EAE01	41 Eastcheap	Pitt (2015) [F]
FNE01	60–3 Fenchurch Street	Birbeck and Schuster (2009) [F]
PNS01	Paternoster Row (Paternoster Square)	S. Watson (2006) [F]
QUV01	99–101 Queen Victoria Street (Salvation Army site)	Bradley and Butler (2008) [F]
SMD01	St Martin-in-the-Fields	Telfer (2010) [I]
THY01	6–8 Tokenhouse Yard	Leary and Butler (2012) [F]
LGM02	211 Long Lane	M. J. Allen et al. (2005); McKinley (2006) [F]
LLS02	Tabard Square	Killock et al. (2015) [F]
TOC02/HGA02	Tobacco Dock / Babe Ruth restaurant, Shadwell	Douglas, Gerrard and Sudds (2011) [F]
BDC03	6 Broad Street Place	Harward, Powers and Watson (2015) [F]
ENS03	16–18 Finsbury Circus / 18–31 Eldon Street	Harward, Powers and Watson (2015) [F]
LTU03	52–6 Lant Street	Ridgeway, Leary and Sudds (2013) [F]
SBK03	56 Southwark Bridge Road	Ridgeway, Leary and Sudds (2013) [F]
USS03	33 Union Street	Gerrard (2009a) [I]
CCP04	Cannon Place	Cowan (2008: 76) [I]
CDP04	120–2 Cheapside	S. Watson (2015a) [F]
OCU04	82–96 Old Kent Road	Thrale (2008) [I]
BAZ05	35 Basinghall Street	Wardle (2015b) [F]
BBB05	Bow Bells House	Howell (2013) [F]
GHM05	14–18 Gresham Street	S. Watson (2015a) [F]
POU05	36–9 Poultry	Pitt and Seeley (2104) [F]
SSZ05	Steward Street, Tower Hamlets	Cass and Preston (2010) [F]
DGT06	Drapers' Gardens	Hawkins (2009) [I]
GHB06	6–12 Basinghall Street and 93–5 Gresham Street	S. Watson (2015b) [F]
GSJ06	54–66 Gresham Street	C. Maloney (2007: 62) [I]
HLW06/SDX07	Holywell Lane / 196–200 Shoreditch High Street	Bull et al. (2011: 20–6) [F]
RKH06	Riverbank House (Waterfront)	Mackinder (2015) [F]
TIY07	28–30 Trinity Street	Killock (2010) [I]

WOZ07	30–7 Walbrook and 97–101 Cannon Street	Booth (2007: 291) [I]
BBI08	Royal College of Art (Battersea)	Stephenson and Edwards (2012) [I]
FEU08	20 Fenchurch Street	Wroe-Brown (2014) [F]
LBN08	25 London Bridge Street	Tomlin (2012: 395–6) [I]
BZY10	Bloomberg	Tomlin (2016) [I]
GYH10	Guy's Hospital (boat)	B. Watson (2012) [I]
HPZ10	Harper Road, Symington House	Edwards (2010) [I]
BVK11	11–15 Borough High Street / 2 London Bridge Street	Fairman and Taylor (2013) [I]
MNR12	24–6 Minories	Booth (2014: 375) [I]

NOTES

Introduction

1 Fulford (2015: 197).

2 Millett (1998: 7); Perring (2000: 120).

3 An archaeological *Research Framework* for Roman London was published in 2002 (Nixon et al. 2002) and its themes have been drawn upon by a very wide-ranging body of research that is included in the volume *Londinium and Beyond* (Clark et al., eds, 2008).

4 For the map, see Museum of London (2011).

5 Rowsome (2008: 32).

6 Gerrard (2011i: 181).

7 Perring ((1991) 2011); G. Milne (1995). Perring's book was republished in 2011 without any updating of the contents and is now seriously dated as a result of the scale of excavation and publication over the past twenty-six years. Other recent attempts at synthesis of information include Rowsome (2008), Perring (2000), Perring (2011a), Perring (2011b), L. Wallace (2014) and Perring (2015).

8 Perring (2015) is a summary of the information that includes maps that show the chronological development of Roman London.

9 Perring (2015): 20–1.

10 Millett (1996: 33); Esmonde Cleary (1999: 398).

11 Millett (2016: 1693).

12 James and Millett (eds, 2001); Millett, Revell and Moore (eds, 2016).

13 Recent works that explore changing perspectives on Roman Britain include Webster (2001), Croxford (2003), Creighton (2006), Mattingly (2006), Eckardt (ed., 2010), Rogers (2011a), Gerrard (2013), A. Gardner (2013), Pearce (2013) and Rogers (2015). Some changing ideas about the Roman Empire are to be found in Hingley (2005), Laurence, Esmonde Cleary and Seers (2011), Mattingly (2011), Pitts and Versluys (eds, 2015), Revell (2016) and Totten and Lafrenz Samuels (eds, 2012).

14 Many accounts place particular emphasis upon identifying whether Londinium had a military or a civil origin. Another topic that has deeply engaged archaeologists has been the status of Roman London from its foundation to the late fourth century. Generally, it is usually argued that Londinium went into terminal decline in the early fourth century, although it is now becoming possible to imagine that there was greater continuity between late Roman Londinium and Middle Saxon Lundenwic than has been appreciated. In addition, numerous authors have addressed the economy and the cemeteries of Roman London. Increasingly, important attempts to rediscover the people of Londinium are being made as a result of the publication of the excavation of cemeteries and areas of occupation, but new aspects still require to be addressed.

15 See D. Bird (1996), D. Bird (2000), D. Bird (2017: 41–2) and Perring (2000: 150–7) for brief assessments of the environs of Londinium.

16 See Historic England (2015).

17 Hingley (2008); Hingley (2012); Rogers (2015).

18 The Roman section of the *Research Framework* for London (Nixon et al. 2002: 29–43) is divided into the following sections: 'Landscape and environment', 'Development (of Roman London)', 'People' and 'Economy'. In this document, 'Beliefs – religion, magic, rationalism and superstition' are addressed under the topic of 'People' (39–40), which serves to separate beliefs from topics such as economy, everyday life and status.

19 Lafrenz Samuels and Totten (2012) explore concepts of place and time.

20 R. Bradley (2005: xiii) has discussed the idea that ritual was not opposed to domesticity during prehistory but often grew out of it, for instance with regard to food production, the building and occupation of houses and the making of artefacts. I adopt a connected approach to explore the embedded nature of ritual in the domestic and political life of Londinium. Merrifield undertook highly important work on the concept of ritual and ritual deposition in Roman London during the 1970s and 1980s (e.g. Merrifield 1997; Merrifield and Hall 2008) and his arguments have been the subject of considerable subsequent discussion (cf. Wilmott 1991; N. Crummy 2008; Rayner, Wardle and Seeley 2011) that is reflected on below.

21 See Rogers (2011a) and Willis (2007b) for attempts to reintegrate ideas of ritual with other aspects of Roman society. See Hingley (2011) for ritual and religion in the Roman Empire. See Beasley (2007) for an important study which has helped to provide a new perspective on the disposal of the dead at the margins of Londinium.

22 Lafrenz Samuels and Totten (2012: 20).

23 We shall see that this contradicts earlier works that have emphasized change and transformation in the development, life and decline of Londinium.

24 Haynes (2000: 95); Fittock (2015).

25 Garwood (2011) has provided a definition of how ritual is differentiated from everyday life, arguing that ritual activities need to be established in particular cultural contexts.

26 R. Bradley (2005: 33–4).

27 The work of Nick Bateman is important here and his papers on Roman London contain thoughtful ideas about the symbolic creation of Londinium's urban space, including the amphitheatre and gladiatorial display (Bateman 2008; Bateman 2009; Bateman, Cowan and Wroe-Brown 2008).

28 Strang (2005: 113). This article includes a cross-cultural discussion of the range of meanings that is drawn from water, which is reflected upon below.

29 See Rhodes (1991), Cotton (1996) and Merrifield and Hall (2008: 127) for ritual deposition in wet contexts in Roman London. Water was also regularly ritualized in Roman society, including evidence for springs and the worship of running water in the city of Rome (Campbell 2012: 13–20). Although the classical textual material drawn upon in Campbell's study is not available for Londinium, the archaeological information provides hints of some potentially comparable activities which are explored below.

30 See Feldman Weiss (2012) for the need for a personal dimension in the study of ancient cities. Holder (2007: 29) was able to identify 235 'Roman Londoners' from a variety of inscriptions. Of particular significance are the 405 stylus writing tablets from the recent excavations at the Bloomberg site, about eighty of which show legible text. Tomlin (2016: 58, 92) has noted that, as a result of the study of these tablets, ninety-two additional persons have now been named, although not all of these people may have been resident in Londinium.

31 See Eckardt (2010a), Kaur (2011), Eckardt (2014), Eckardt, Müldner and Lewis (2014) and Redfern et al. (in press) for ideas about diaspora and multiculturalism in Roman Britain. The evidence from the study of human remains is also addressed in outline in this book. This is derived from methods such as oxygen, lead and strontium stable isotope analysis, aDNA ('ancient DNA') analysis and the analysis of the shape of skulls (for additional detailed discussion, see Shaw et al. 2016: 62–3 and Redfern et al. 2016). See Eckardt (2010b: 111) for the context of the analysis of ancestry in Roman archaeology. See Redfern et al. (2016: 14–15) for the difficulties of using bioarchaeological techniques to assess an individual's ancestry and origins. aDNA analysis is characterized by the sampling of materials derived from contexts not intended for DNA use, such as bones from archaeological excavations (Redfern et al. in press).

32 Shaw et al. (2016: 62–3, 66) have argued that, of the twenty Roman burials from Londinium studied by lead stable isotope analysis, twelve had results consistent with an origin in Londinium or Roman Britain and four may have travelled there from other areas of the empire; the origins of the remaining four were less clear. These skeletal remains were selected to include males and females, individuals from different phases of the settlement and individuals with different burial characteristics (59). Some of the individuals who were sampled for analysis are referred to in this book. Stable isotope analysis generally only gives an indication of where people had spent their early lives and, as a result, some of these individuals may have had parents or ancestors who had moved to Londinium.

33 The illustrations of the individual buildings in this book are intended, where possible, to show the fragmentary nature of the available information by portraying the extent of the uncovered foundations and lengths of conjectural walling.

34 One limitation is that many of the early excavations undertaken across London are yet to be published. Schofield (1998) contains a handy record of some of the unpublished excavation records, and interim reports are included in the *London Archaeologist* and in annual roundups of excavations and discoveries of inscriptions in the journal *Britannia*.

35 See Grimes (1968), Marsden (1996), Sheldon (2000), Sheldon and Haynes (2000), Sloane (2008), Hingley (2008: 175–80), L. Wallace (2014: xiii–xv) and Polm (2016) for accounts of the early discovery of Roman London, the excavations undertaken since the 1940s and displays of Roman London in the city's museums.

36 Hingley (2008: 175–80); Schofield (2011: 10, 33–8, 326).

37 Marsden (1996: 13–14); Sloane (2008: 11–13).

38 Hingley (2008: 279).

39 Marsden (1996: 14–18); Polm (2016: 213–14).

40 Marsden (1996: 17–18); Sloane (2008: 14–15).

41 Hingley (2008: 283).

42 Sloane (2008: 16, 19).

43 Polm (2016: 222–5). Fulford (2007: 360–1) has considered work in London during the late 1920s and 1930s.

44 Sheldon and Haynes (2000: 3).

45 Grimes (1968); Shepherd (2012: 1–10).

46 Sheldon and Haynes (2000: 3). Many of these excavations were organized under the auspices of the Guildhall Museum and the site codes in the list of excavations (see Appendix) were created by this organization.

47 Sheldon and Haynes (2000: 3–7). The Museum of London was founded by Act of Parliament in 1965. For Museum of London site codes established from 1972, see the Appendix.

48 Sheldon and Haynes (2000: 6).

49 L. Wallace (2014: Table 3) has listed the number of sites according to the archaeological units that undertook the excavations: MOLA, Pre-Construct Archaeology, Oxford Archaeology and Wessex Archaeology.

50 Perring (2015: 20) has noted that the London Archaeological Archive Resource Centre recorded a total of 422 excavations on Roman sites in the City of London and Southwark between 1990 and 2008. L. Wallace (2014: xiv) has commented that in 2012 this database recorded 1,599 sites where Roman artefacts and structures had been identified. The site listed in the Appendix of this book includes 234 archaeological interventions, including all the Iron Age, Roman and Anglo-Saxon sites referred to primarily from published sources.

51 See Wallace-Hadrill (1988: 58–9) for difficulties with the use of the concept of 'public' buildings in the Roman Empire.

52 To avoid regular cross-referencing, each chapter deals only with the information for individual sites at that particular time. To address the entire chronological sequence as particular sites requires the use of the index.

53 I have not aimed to obtain unpublished reports except where this appeared particularly important. Excavation reports are published at regular intervals and the information for this volume was collected until May 2017; any later publications have not been consulted.

54 Including mosaics (Neal and Cosh 2009: 397–462), sculpture (Coombe et al. 2015), inscriptions (Holder 2007), ships and boats (Marsden 1994), pipe-clay figurines (Fittock 2015) and glassworking (Shepherd and Wardle 2015: 97–107). The general absence of corpuses of data for classes of material such as pottery, glass, coins and animal bones provides a problem, while classes of material including industry, housing, pottery and coinage remain to be studied synthetically. A number of articles contained general statements about the current state of research, for example Roman pottery (Rayner and Seeley 1998), the ritual use of animals (Sidell and Rielly 1998); coinage (Hammerson 1996) and dendrochronological dating (I. Tyers 2008a). Detailed and up-to-date studies of classes of material are, however, rare. For example, the last substantial survey of early Roman pottery (Davies, Richardson and Tomber 1994) is now seriously dated and although detailed studies have been produced for particular sites and periods of time, an up-to-date corpus is lacking. There is also no synthetic study of Roman coins from Roman London (Hammerson 2011b: 518). In many cases, detailed accounts of animal bones from archaeological sites are confined to unpublished archives (Maltby 2015: 178). Although the cemeteries have seen very extensive recent research, there is no thorough synthesis of the information and such an account would require a substantial monograph (Harward, Powers and Watson 2015: 135). Barber and Hall (2000) provides the most recent summary, while Harward, Powers and Watson (2015: 135–7) contains some interesting ideas. The Roman walls have seen limited recent discussion although their construction and maintenance in late Roman

times indicate their considerable significance. Hall and Shepherd (2008) consider the temples and places of worship.

55   A few such studies include Gerrard (2009a), Gerrard (2011i) and Ridgeway (2014).

56   It is often impossible to closely date archaeological features and it is inevitable that the complex sequence of this extensive and developing urban landscape will be simplified in this present book. It should also be noted that excavators commonly try to distinguish dates within the process of urban creation that was in continuous transformation.

57   Hassall and Tomlin (1986: 445–7); Collingwood and Wright (1991: 92) (RIB 2436.9).

58   Collingwood and Wright (1991: 92).

59   Roger Tomlin (pers. comm.).

60   Collingwood and Wright (1995b: 55) (RIB 2503.127).

61   Roger Tomlin (pers. comm.).

62   Translation from the Latin by Tomlin (2016: 86).

63   The Guildhall Museum site codes are listed in numerical order in the Appendix. The Museum of London codes are listed in chronological order which allows the reader to locate individual sites in the Appendix (for example, BZY10 was an excavation undertaken in 2010). References to 'RIB' in the endnotes refer to the number of the relevant inscription in the compendium of *The Roman Inscriptions of Britain* (for example, RIB. 2443.2).

1   Rites of Passage on the Thames in the Iron Age

1   See Millett (1990) and Creighton (2006) for influential accounts of the development of Roman *civitas* capitals in Britain from *oppida*.

2   Perring ((1991), 2001: 21); Creighton (2006: 95); L. Wallace (2014: 4). Although it has recently been argued that it is probably incorrect to project the boundaries of Roman *civitates* back into the Late Iron Age, which is likely to complicate this picture of well defined tribal territories (Creighton 2006: 95; Moore 2011).

3   Rogers (2011b: 215–16).

4   Merriman (2000: 47–8); Rogers (2011a: 70). Rogers (2011b: 216) has proposed that this landscape was already deeply embedded with meanings and histories at the time of the Roman conquest.

5   Waite and Cotton (2000: 114).

6   Creighton (2006).

7   The pre-Roman name of this site may have been Camulodunon (Potter 2002: 21).

8   The pre-Roman name of the Roman town of Verulamium may have been Verlamion (Potter 2002: 21).

9   Haselgrove et al. (2001: 29–30); J. D. Hill (2007: 30–3).

10   G. Milne (1995: 40).

11   Bowlt (2008).

12   See P. Tyers (1996) and Merriman (2000: 46–7) for the general scarcity of Late Iron Age pottery and coins in the London region.

13   P. Tyers (1996: 139–40); Cotton and Wood (1998: 25–6); Cotton and Green (2005: 144–7).

14   Sidell et al. (2002: 52).

15   J. D. Hill (2007); Moore (2011).

16   Moore (2011).

17   Moore (2011: 352).

18   Tom Moore (pers. comm.).

19   J. D. Hill (2007: 26); Moore (2011: 353).

20   Holder and Jamieson (2003: 26) have recorded 'little evidence' for Iron Age occupation, but this was partly a result of the focus of their work on the walled area of Londinium north of the Thames.

21   Holder and Jamieson (2003: 23–4).

22 For the medieval myths, see Clark (1981), Holder and Jamieson (2003: 23), Marsden (1996: 11) and L. Wallace (2014: 7).

23 See Hingley (2008: 174–5) for a brief commentary on Stow's contribution.

24 Stow (1599: 1).

25 A sculpture of Lud and his sons survives today in the vestry porch of the church of St Dunstan's in the West in Fleet Street and is likely to be derived from this gate. Stow (1599: 4, 32–3, 161) also commented on Ludgate, Billingsgate and the walls of London.

26 Perring (2011a: 249) has recently backed up earlier accounts by restating that Late Iron Age settlement in the London area was scarce. For general statements about settlement around London at this time and some examples of settlements, see Greenwood (1997: 158–69), Merriman (2000: 46–8), Nixon et al. (2002: 27), P. Tyers (1996), Waite and Cotton (2000: 103, 107) and L. Wallace (2014: 4–7).

27 Holder and Jamieson (2003: 25–6).

28 Coates (1998: 214–18). Rivet and Smith (1979: 396–8) have provided sources for the name Londinium, including textual source and inscriptions on stone, coins and a writing tablet, to which the Tabard Square temple inscription (Grew 2008) and the Bloomberg Writing Tablets 6, 18, 24 and 45 (Tomlin 2016: 70, 94, 106, 156) can now be added.

29 Coates (1998: 218).

30 Coates (1998: 218–20). L. Wallace (2014: 7–8) casts doubt on this interpretation, pointing out that the Romans often gave native names to new settlements. It is likely, however, that they borrowed these from names already attributed to features of the landscape by local peoples.

31 The boundaries of the islands shown on Fig. 1.2 are the result of considerable research that has explored the course of the Thames during prehistory and into the historic period.

32 Rogers (2013: 32–9) summarizes the evidence for the streams and rivers of the London area in the immediately pre-Roman period, drawing upon extensive excavation and landscape study undertaken by other researchers, including: T. Williams (2003: 243–4), Lyon (2007: 11–13), Cowan et al. (2009: 10–33) and L. Wheeler (2009). See Morley (2010) for a recent summary of abandoned channels of the Thames around Battersea.

33 Wilkinson and Sidell (2000: 110), Sidell et al. (2002: 32–3) and Thomas (2008: 103) provide summaries of the evidence for the tidal reach of the Thames.

34 Brigham (1990a: 145–9, Fig. 12).

35 Wilkinson and Sidell (2000: 110). The discovery of a Roman ship at County Hall has indicated that the Thames around Thorney Island must have been tidal during the late third century AD (Marsden 1994: 109–21).

36 Wilkinson and Sidell (2000: 110).

37 Rogers (2013: 36).

38 Lyon (2007: 12).

39 See Leary and Butler (2012: 77–8) and T. Taylor (2012) for up-to-date discussions of the Walbrook in prehistory and the Roman period. The lower reaches of the Walbrook are described as a 'river' in this book, although its upper tributaries were no more than streams.

40 Marsh and West (1981: 86–9).

41 Rogers (2013: 37); Dunwoodie, Harward and Pitt (2015: 34).

42 Sidell (2008: 67).

43 J. Hill and Rowsome (2011: 18–19).

44 Brigham (2001c: xi, 13–14).

45 See Sidell (2008: 68) for the swampy conditions and a review of the pollen species.

46 Sidell (2008: 68).

47 Waite and Cotton (2000: 107–8) have reviewed Iron Age settlement in and around central London.

48 Holder and Jamieson (2003: illus. 6).

49 Bell (1998: 58–9); Sidell et al. (2002: 51); T. Brown (2003).

50 R. Bradley (1998: 107–9).

51 Schulting and Bradley (2013: 52–62).

52 R. Bradley and Gordon (1988: 504). Garwood (2011) has discussed the uses that archaeologists have made of the concept of 'rites of passage' which is derived from the work of the French anthropologist Arnold van Gennep.

53 R. Bradley and Gordon (1988: 504–5); Lambrick and Robinson (2009: 288–94). Schulting and Bradley (2013: 45–6) have argued that the practice of placing human remains either alongside or directly into the river was conducted within the same general time frame as the deposition of elaborate metalwork in the river, confirming the idea that such materials were derived from rites of passage. T. Brown (2003: 10) has observed that the liminal spaces of river islands have been used in other times and places for a variety of functions including illegal activities and marriage ceremonies, although the most universal association appears to be with the dead (cf. Harding 2016: 210).

54 Archaeologists addressing cranial remains often use the term 'skull', but this should only be used when the cranium and mandible are both present (Rebecca Redfern pers. comm.).

55 Schulting and Bradley (2013: 30). Armit (2011) has provided a broader consideration of the evidence for the use of human cranial remains in Iron Age Europe which helps to set the information from London in context.

56 Marsh and West (1981); R. Bradley and Gordon (1988: 507–8); Edwards, Weisskopf and Hamilton (2010: 42–4); Schulting and Bradley (2013: 41–2); Redfern and Bonney (2014). The radiocarbon dates are summarized in Schulting and Bradley (2013: Table 6).

57 Schulting and Bradley (2013: 34–40).

58 Schulting and Bradley (2013: 43).

59 See Merriman (2000: 47) and Waite and Cotton (2000: 109–11) for Iron Age metalwork from the Thames. See Rogers (2013: 31) for the significance of the deposition of objects in rivers and wetlands. Finds of metalwork found within the area of Fig. 1.4 have been marked.

60 Dredging operations during the nineteenth century might have led to the redeposition of material on the banks of the Thames and the movement of individual objects (Cotton 1996: 94). In particular, dredging of the area around Shadwell may have caused dumped material to be moved upstream to the area of Battersea and Hammersmith. This is uncertain, however, and there appears to have been a strong tradition of depositing weaponry in, or close to, the Thames around London during the Bronze Age and the Iron Age.

61 T. Allen and Cox (2000); Lambrick and Robinson (2009: 289). Radiocarbon dates have suggested that funerary activities were taking place on these banks between around 1300 and 200 BC.

62 C. Evans (2013: 61). This site is considered further below.

63 C. Evans (2013: 76).

64 Drummond-Murray, Saxby and Watson (1994: 254); Sidell et al. (2002: 33–42).

65 Sidell et al. (2002: 44); M. J. Allen et al. (2005).

66 Sidell (2008: 64–5).

67 Cowan (2003: 11); Cowan et al. (2009: 10).

68 M. J. Allen et al. (2005: 79).

69 Many of these sites and finds have been located using the gazetteer in Sidell et al. (2002: 56–67), updated by information collected from the published works consulted for this book.

70 Franks (1866); Jope (2000: 255).

71 Cuming (1868). I am grateful to Jenny Hall for this reference.

72 Cuming (1868: 312).

73 See Hingley (2009) for the curation and deposition of ancient items in Iron Age and Roman contexts.

74 Cotton and Merriman (1994: 52–3).

75 Cotton and Green (2005: 142–4).

76 Stead (2006: 153, 154 and 173).

77 Dean and Hammerson (1980: 17, 19) (120BHS89/124BHS77). Connell (1999: 251), Cowan et al. (2009: 14) and Rayner (2009: 38) also discuss this burial.

78 Dean and Hammerson (1980: 17–19) have argued that the burial is Late Iron Age, while Heard, Sheldon and Thompson (1990: 610) suggest that it dated to the Middle Iron Age.

79 Dean and Hammerson (1980: 17).

80 Dean and Hammerson (1980: 17).

81 Cowan et al. (2009: Fig. 8).

82 Individual sherds that may pre-date the Roman conquest have been recorded from 201–11 Borough High Street (P. Tyers 1996: 141) (207BHS72/201BHS75) and 170–94 Borough High Street (Cowan et al. 2009: 14; Rayner 2009: 39) (1070BHS79). At 201–11 Borough High Street (207BHS72), a substantial fragment of a decorated hand-made pot from the same context as the possible Late Iron Age sherd is likely to have been Iron Age in date (Hammerson and Murray 1978a: Fig. 33, no. 1; P. Tyers 1996: 141). The sherds from this site were found in the fill of a natural channel which was suspected to be pre-conquest in date (Ferretti and Graham 1978: 57).

83 Cowan (1995: 10–11); Cowan et al. (2009: 14); Rayner (2009: 38) (15SKS80).

84 Swain (1995: 68–70); Rayner (2009: 38).

85 Cowan (1995: 10).

86 Sheldon (1974: 8, 32) (TW74).

87 Sidell et al. (2002: 40–2); Rayner (2009: 38) (BA84/TOB95). Bermondsey eyot was probably joined to the mainland by a narrow bridge of land during the Late Iron Age and early Roman period (Killock et al. 2015: 232).

88 Heard (1996: 78); Rayner (2009: 38–42) (170GRA89/GRW91).

89 Rayner (2009: 40).

90 Abbey Street / Neckinger (Heard 1996: 78) (ABY91); Alaska Works (Cowan et al. 2009: 14; Rayner 2009: 38–40) (AW89); Cherry Garden Pier (Heard 1996: 78; Girardon and Heathcote 1988: 414) (CG87); and 211 Long Lane (M. J. Allen et al. 2005: 74) (LGM02).

91 Drummond-Murray, Saxby and Watson (1994: 254–5) and Leary (2004) provide interim reports on Late Iron Age occupation on Horselydown eyot, including ditches, postholes and stakeholes and pottery at 283 Tooley Street (TOS93), 271 Tooley Street (TOY94) and particularly at 285–91 Tooley Street (TLT00). The discovery of grain in the archaeological features from 285–91 Tooley Street may show that crops were cultivated on this island.

92 Leary (2004: 287).

93 C. Evans (2013: 61, 63).

94 Evans (2013: 75) has noted that the low-lying topography at the Godwin Ridge site suggests that people would have resided for 'very special reasons', possibly for trade, the seasonal procurement of natural products and for ritual activity.

95 Evans (2013: 63–4).

96 See Stead (2006) for Iron Age swords from Britain, including those from Battersea and London. See Stead (1985) for a shield from Battersea. These finds were made beyond the western edge of the area shown on Figs 1.4 and 1.5.

97 Willis (2007a: 121–2) has explored the ritual significance of the area at Sheepen, (part of the *oppidum* of Camulodunum) during the Iron Age and Roman period as a place that was sited immediately above the tidal flow of the River Colne.

98 Cuming (1857: 237–8). Cuming was able to establish that these finds were 'brought to light' as a result of digging the foundations for the new suspension bridge over the Thames, Battersea Bridge.

99 Cuming (1857: 238).

100 See Stead (1985: 9) for the Battersea shield. Stead (2006: 24) and Fitzpatrick (2007: 342–8) have discussed the likely date and parallels for a number of shields from the River Thames and suggested that they date to the fourth to the second early centuries BC.

101 Stead (2006: 154, 161–2, 164, 164–5, 176–7).

102 Morley (2010).

103 See Stephenson and Edwards (2012) for an interim report (BBI08).

104 Bell (1998). There was some evidence for crop production and processing, although it was not clear whether this was a seasonal or permanent settlement (Bell 1998: 58). The excavator suggested that the construction of ditches and dumping of material were intended to raise the ground beside the river (Bell 1998: 58), suggesting that the island was exposed to flood water.

105 Parnell (1985: 5–7); Field (1985).

106 Parnell (1985: 5–7).

107 Parnell (1985: 7).

108 Brigham (2001c: 14). These finds indicate that the concept of 'burial' is inadequate for understanding the full range of the modes of disposing of the dead practised during the Iron Age (see Booth and Madgwick 2016). Many of the activities related to the deposition of Roman-period corpses also involve complex processes.

109 See Harward, Powers and Watson (2015: 14, 124) for 6 Broad Street Place (BDC03).

110 Harward, Powers and Watson (2015: 14, 105–6, Table 28).

111 Harward, Powers and Watson (2015: 14, 105–6, Table 28).

112 Schulting and Bradley (2013: 52–3, Table 6).

113 Human remains from marginal areas of Londinium indicate that corpses were placed in wet contexts such as ditches, pits and wells during the early Roman period. Such contexts were also common locations for the deposition of parts of human bodies during the Iron Age in the Thames Valley (Lambrick and Robinson 2009: 311–12).

114 Butler (2006: 7, 35) (MRL98). Other sherds found in the upper Walbrook Valley are more likely to date to the Late Bronze Age and Early Iron Age. C. Maloney (2005: 3–4) reported Iron Age pottery from 6 Broad Street Place (BDC03) and Schofield (1998: 257) reported a few sherds of Late Iron Age pottery from River Plate House (RIV87), but Harward, Powers and Watson (2015: 14) have argued that all these sherds date to the Late Bronze Age/Early Iron Age.

115 P. Tyers (1996: 140–1).

116 Schofield (1998: 51).

117 Birbeck and Schuster (2009: 2, 11–12) (FNE01).

118 S. Watson (2015a: 7–8) (GHM05). Future excavations will produce additional evidence. At the extensively excavated site at Plantation Place (FER97), for example, a single pit contained a sherd of possible Late Iron Age date (Dunwoodie, Harward and Pitt 2015: xvi, 13), while a coin of Cunobelinus was found in a context dating to the third quarter of the first century AD (Dunwoodie, Harward and Pitt 2015: 66; Bowsher 2015: 214, 215).

119 Sloane (2012: 10–14) (NEW81/ENG84/CLK86/NEW87/SCT87/SNS87).

120 Cowan et al. (2009: 14); Rayner (2009: 39–40) (223BHS81).

121 Killock et al. (2015: 9–11, 231–5) (LLS02). One fragment of human bone was also found in a prehistoric context in palaeosoil at Tabard Square and is recorded in an interim report (Sayer 2009a: 367). Presumably the reference to a disarticulated human bone from a pre-Roman context in the final report (Killock et al. 2015: 255) refers to the same fragment.

122 Gerrard (2015a: 140). Gerrard has noted another Iron Age coin from the excavations at Trinity Street. Potin coins have also been recorded on the north bank of the Thames at Billingsgate Lorry Park and close to London Bridge, presumably in Roman contexts.

123 Cotton and Wood (1998: 25–6).

124 Thomas (2008: 102–4).

125 Hind (1989: 7) provides the translation. The translation of Dio by Cary (1924: 416–19) reads differently. Dio's account of Britain is often thought to be unreliable, since he was writing well over a century after the events he describes (Braund 1996: 144), but he may have had access to contemporary accounts that he incorporated into his narrative.

126 L. Wallace (2014: 8–9) has observed that the Greek word used by Dio ('γεφύρα') might refer to a damn, platform, deck or causeway rather than to a bridge.

127 Brigham (2001b: 28).

128 Lambrick and Robinson (2009: 232–3).

129 L. Wallace (2014: 8–9) has dismissed the idea that the Britons and Romans crossed the Thames at London in AD 43 on the basis of the lack of evidence for a substantial Late Iron Age settlement, but this assumes that important places need to have been intensively settled.

130 Perhaps the first Roman bridge, which may have been constructed in the early AD 50s, commemorated the crossing of the Roman army at this location in AD 43.

131 Cowan et al. (2009: 14–15).

132 See Rogers (2013: 125–8) and Willis (2007a: 121–2) for the significance of the location.

133 Rogers (2008: 50–1); Rogers (2011a: 70–1).

134 Nixon et al. (2002: 27).

135 Mike Fulford (pers. comm.).

136 L. Wallace (2014: 20–1) has observed an internal circularity in earlier ideas about imported pottery and argues that the general absence of *terra rubra*, *terra nigra* and certain southern Gallic samian forms might relate to a low volume of trade at Londinium rather than to an absence of occupation.

137 P. Tyers (1996: 141).

138 Some finds of 'arretine' pottery attributed to London may have been derived from pre-Roman contexts, although they have usually been dismissed as modern imports (see Marsh 1979; Mike Fulford pers. comm.).

139 Mike Fulford (pers. comm.). See Davies, Richardson and Tomber (1994) for the production of Highgate Ware and the assumption that initial production post-dated the Roman invasion.

2 A Place of Trade: Londinium from AD 45 to AD 60

1 A third road connected the east–west road to Colchester.

2 For military interpretations, see Perring ((1991) 2011: 8–10), Yule (2005: 86–7) and Perring (2011a). For civil interpretations, see Millett (1996), Millett (1998) and L. Wallace (2013). Pitts (2014: 133–4) and L. Wallace (2014: 10–20) have summarized the military and civil interpretations for Londinium's origins.

3 There is information for the organization of urban authorities for certain cities across the empire (Revell 2009: 50–3); the information from Britain is very limited (Wacher 1995: 36–40). The supreme judicial and administrative authority of a Roman urban centre was the *ordo*, a council of about 100 *decuriones*, elected from the citizens. There is no evidence for the date of the creation or for the character of the Roman urban council of Londinium, although it may have been formed primarily from traders settled at the city and may also have included retired soldiers.

4 Creighton (2006: 94).

5 See Tomlin (2016: 55–6) for the potential dating of Boudica's uprising to AD 60.

6 Swain and Williams (2008: 39). These authors based this figure on an assessment of the area occupied and the density of housing. This population figure is based on a series of assumptions that are fully documented by these authors.

7 J. Hill and Rowsome (2011: 564).

8 Birley (2005: 45) provides a translation.

9 Wilkes (1996: 28–9) reappraised Francis Haverfield's idea that London had a *conventus civium Romanorum*.

10 Tomlin (2016: 154). The second-century dedicatory inscription from the temple at Tabard Square in Southwark names a Gallic trader resident in Londinium (Tomlin 2006: 50).

11 Pitts (2014: 134).

12 Brigham (1990a: 134–40).

13 Museum of London (2011).

14 Rogers (2011b: 208) has included a brief review.

15 The construction of Waterfront 1 is usually thought to have commenced in AD 52, but may have begun during the late AD 40s since only parts of the structure have been excavated and subjected to tree-ring dating (L. Wallace 2014: 22, 52–3, 76).

16 See Brigham, Watson and Tyres (1996: 32) for an interim report (KWS94).

17 Brigham, Watson and Tyres (1996: 33).

18 Swift (2008: 18–19, 48) (AUT01).

19 Brigham (2001c: 17, 44–5) (SUF94).

20 T. Bradley and Butler (2008: 64–5); Goodburn (2008: 42–4) (QUV01). The Salvation Army International Headquarters is referred to as the 'Salvation Army site' below.

21 L. Wallace (2014: 52–3, Fig. 14).

22 Brigham (2001a: 12–13) (TW84) (see L. Wheeler 2009: 66; L. Wallace 2014: 76). The other works on riverfronts south of the Thames appear not to have commenced until after AD 60 (Rowsome 2008: 26; L. Wheeler 2009: 66–7).

23 Brigham's detailed study of the limited evidence for the early bridge over the Thames argues for three successive bridges built in close proximity to one another across the river from the first and early second centuries (Brigham 2001b: 30, 42–3, 50). Other accounts discuss the arguments for and against the idea of the construction of an early bridge across the Thames around AD 52 and also the limited archaeological information that may support this idea (Brigham, Watson and Tyres 1996: 33; Rayner 2009: 42).

24 Brigham (2001b: 42–3).

25 Brigham (2001b: 50).

26 Westman and Pringle (2009: 53).

27 See Swift (2008: 14–16) (AUT01) for the possible jetty that may have pre-dated Waterfront 1, although the dating evidence was inconclusive. See Douglas (2008: 15–23) for a timber structure on the south bank of the south Island in Southwark at 15–27 Long Lane (LGK99) that may have formed a landing stage for boats and was possibly constructed between AD 50 and 80.

28 L. Wheeler (2009: 69).

29 Rowsome (2008: 25); L. Wallace (2014: 34–41).

30 J. Hill and Rowsome (2011: 256).

31 J. Hill and Rowsome (2011: 258) and I. Tyers (2011: 564) (ONE94).

32 J. Hill and Rowsome (2011: 26, 256–60).

33 J. Hill and Rowsome (2011: 26, 257–8).

34 Bryan, Hill and Watson (2016: 32–4, Fig. 25) (BZY10). Tree-ring analysis has shown that it is not entirely certain that these timber piles pre-dated the Boudican uprising and that the bridge may have post-dated AD 60 (Bryan, Hill and Watson 2016: 34).

35 S. Watson (2013: 242).

36 Dunwoodie, Harward and Pitt (2015: 32–3, Fig. 33).

37 Dunwoodie, Harward and Pitt (2015: 32: Fig. 62).

38 Dunwoodie, Harward and Pitt (2015: 33, Fig. 33). This is termed the 'Colchester road' or the 'Aldgate road'.

39 Dunwoodie, Harward and Pitt (2015: 33).

40 Drummond-Murray and Thompson (2002: 10–13); Cowan et al. (2009: 10–11).

41 Rowsome (2008: 25); Cowan et al. (2009: 167). See Westman and Pringle (2009: 62–4) for the dating of the initial construction of the road, which is derived from pottery evidence.

42 Westman and Pringle (2009: 53); L. Wheeler (2009).

43 Yule (2005: 46), Cowan and Rowsome (2009: 175), Westman and Pringle (2009: 64), Divers et al. (2009: 12–19, 31) and Ridgeway (2009: 125) have reviewed the evidence for this road.

44 Cowan and Rowsome (2009: 175).

45 L. Wallace (2014: 44–6).

46 L. Wallace (2014: 45).

47 For example, Perring ((1991) 2011: 14).

48 Rowsome (2008: 25–6); L. Wallace (2014: 59–61).

49 Several phases of excavations have included work by Marsden in 1969 (Marsden 1987), Philp in 1968–9 (Philp 1977), Boddington in 1976 (Boddington and Marsden 1987) and Dunwoodie in 1995 (Dunwoodie 2004); the respective site codes are GM95, GM297, FSE76 and FEH95. Dunwoodie (2004: Fig. 4) has mapped additional excavations.

50 Philp (1977: 8); Marsden (1987: 21); Dunwoodie (2004: 15, 23); L. Wallace (2014: 89–91).

51 Dunwoodie (2004: 23).

52 Pitts (2014: 144). This may well suggest that the Roman port at Londinium was a transhipment centre for supplies to be transported to Roman military units across Britannia (Mike Fulford pers. comm.).

53 Marsden (1987: 46, 73); Perring ((1991) 2011: 26).

54 Wacher (1995: 223).

55 Many buildings in Londinium were initially built of timber and earth, or from timber and clay, with a sequence from earth-fast to timber-framing construction during the first century (Perring 2002: 32). In this book, a distinction is drawn between timber-and-earth dwellings and stone-built houses which become common in the

later history of Londinium (Perring 2002: 36–41). However, the concept of the stone-built house is also not simple to define since some buildings had stone foundations and timber-and-earth walls above (see Smith et al. 2016: 53). For the complexities of the architectural traditions on individual sites, which are too complex to address in this book, the reader is referred to the excavation reports referenced in the notes to each chapter.

56 Marsden (1987: 20); Dunwoodie (2004: 15–20).

57 Dunwoodie (2004: 20).

58 Marsden (1987: 20); Straker (1987); Dunwoodie (2004: 19, 23).

59 Philip (1977: 15).

60 Wacher (1995: 90); T. Williams (2003: 248).

61 Philp (1977: 15). Dunwoodie (2004: 22–3) has recorded a few further finds in this area.

62 Richardson (2004).

63 Montiel (2008: 178).

64 See L. Wallace (2014: 91–2) for a summary of these unpublished excavations (FEN83), which quotes forthcoming work by Williams to indicate that this building was pre-Boudican. See Schofield (1998: 193–4) for additional information on the building.

65 Cowan and Wardle (2009: 102).

66 L. Wallace (2014: 91).

67 Hingley (1989: 39–45); J. Taylor (2001: 49–51); Perring (2002: 29); Smith et al. (2016: 66–7). Aisled buildings were also common during the Iron Age in continental Europe.

68 See L. Wallace (2014: 92) for the general absence of public buildings in urban centres in Britain and northern Gaul/Germany during the first century.

69 Pringle (2009: 205–6) has discussed the distribution of box-flue tiles on the two main islands in Southwark. She has argued that there was at least one substantial and richly decorated building south of the Thames during the period between AD 50 and 75–80. At Verulamium the bathhouse in Insula XIX is thought to have been one of the first stone structures and may have pre-dated the Boudican uprising (Niblett 2005: 85).

70 Yule (2005: 46–7, 84) (WP83). Small quantities of building stone, including moulded stone, have also been found on two additional sites in Southwark in contexts dating to before AD 60 and may support the idea that there had been at least one stone building south of the river (Drummond-Murray and Thompson 2002: 19–22, 52–3; Cowan et al. 2009: 15; Cowan and Pringle 2009: 82). See Pringle (2006: 126) and Pringle (2007: 205) for the idea that the tiles from these deposits could be pre-Boudican.

71 Pringle (2006: 126) and Pringle (2007: 205) (FER97).

72 In the full publication of the Plantation Place excavations, it has been argued that the distinctive half-flue box tiles from the site were derived from a substantial stone building, possibly a bathhouse, and that they may date to between around AD 50 and 80 (Dunwoodie, Harward and Pitt 2015: 49, 51, 55, 63; Betts 2015: 176). Dunwoodie, Harward and Pitt (2015: 63) have suggested that this material was imported to the site during the building of the fort rampart during the early AD 60s, although the box tiles may have been transported from some distance.

73 Yule (2005: 86) has argued that the construction of the roads, quays and bridge in London during the first century AD would have required military engineering skills. Westman and Pringle (2009: 61) cast doubt, however, on whether the main north–south road was entirely constructed by the Roman army.

74 Hassall (2012) has provided a summary of the evidence for the Roman military in London, and Shepherd (2012: 166–8) lists the military inscriptions from London. None of these inscriptions date to the period prior to AD 60.

75 Wardle and Rayner (2011: 289) have discussed a range of artefacts from 1 Poultry and have argued that this material was dumped rather than lost and is likely to have been intended for recycling. Comparable military material is known from Borough High Street in Southwark (Drummond-Murray and Thompson 2002: 49).

76 Wardle (2015a: Table 6).

77 Wardle (2015a: 159).

78 Kaminski and Sim (2012).

79 Rayner (2009: 43).

80 At Calleva the large-scale planning of the urban core pre-dates the Roman conquest by decades, indicating that people in Late Iron Age Britain built roads and established properties (Fulford and Timby 2000: 564–5). The Roman development of Calleva involved a complete replanning of the Late Iron Age settlement, instituted by the descendants of the original community. At Verulamium the destruction in AD 60 has allowed archaeologists to plan the extent of the settlement and its roads. In the conquest period roads had been laid to the south-west of the river, under the core of the area that would become the urban centre, and by AD 60 this street grid had probably been expanded across a substantial area (Niblett 2005: 52–3, Plans 1 and 2).

81 Pitts (2014: 159–60) has emphasized the very low proportion of 'locally popular' vessels such as butt-beakers and Gallo-Belgic inspired vessels from early deposits across London, suggesting that many of the population were incomers and did not include a large number of Britons or civilian settlers from *Belgica*.

82 Woolf (1998) has discussed the development of cities across Gaul during the early first century.

83 See Holder (2007) for information derived from inscriptions and writing tablets found in London.

84 Bryan, Hill and Watson (2016) have provided some interim results and details of the structures and other finds are included in the interim reports (Jackson et al. 2013; S. Watson 2013) (BZY10).

85 Tomlin (2016) is the first full publication of information from Bloomberg and provides full documentation of the writing tablets.

86 Bryan, Hill and Watson (2016: 32).

87 All these early tablets were made from wood derived from silver fir conifer trees and were reused from the staves of barrels that had been used to import goods to the market. Since silver fir is known to have grown in the central European alpine region, the Pyrenees and the Massif Central of France, the barrels, which are common in Londinium, were probably transported from at least one of these areas to the port (K. Stewart 2016; Goodburn 2016: 8–9).

88 Tomlin (2016: 54).

89 See Tomlin (2016: 122) for Writing Tablet 30 and the transition of the Latin.

90 Tomlin (2016: 54).

91 See Tomlin (2016: 54, 152) for Writing Tablet 44.

92 See Tomlin (2016: 54, 152) for Writing Tablet 44. See Andreau (1999: 47–9, 64–70) for the important role of freedmen as bankers and financiers between the time of Caesar and the early second century (see Tomlin 2016: 155).

93 Tomlin (2016: 154–5).

94 Tomlin (2016: 154).

95 Some of the later tablets record members of the military and imperial officials (Tomlin 2016: 56).

96 Over 500 inscriptions from London have been discussed by Holder (2007), although none can be dated earlier than AD 60.

97 Tomlin and Hassall (2005: 490); S. Watson (2006: 16, 70–1). The full inscription probably translates as 'century of Surus, [the property] of Vitalis, son of Similis' (Tomlin and Hassall 2005: 490).

98 See L. Wallace (2013: 278).

99 Davies, Richardson and Tomber (1994: 29); Symonds (2003: 57); Rayner and Sealey (2008: 184).

100 Symonds (2003: 57).

101 This complex evidence for the treatment of the dead is also paralleled in northern Gaul.

102 Eckardt (2010b) has discussed stable isotope analysis and information about the place of birth of individuals whose skeletons were excavated from cemeteries in Roman Britain.

103 Dean and Hammerson (1980: 20); Cotton (2008); Rayner (2009: 40); L. Wallace (2014: 62) (HR77/HR79).

104 Cotton (2008: 156, 158–9).

105 Redfern et al. (in press).

106 The evidence of aDNA has indicated that this individual had 'a sex development disorder' (Redfern et al. in press).

107 Redfern et al. (in press).

108 Cotton (2008); Redfern et al. (in press).

109 Eckardt (2002).

110 Eckardt (2002: 37–41, 69–71); L. Wallace (2014: 131–2).

111 See Revell (2009: 172–9) and Laurence, Esmonde Cleary and Seers (2011: 214–23) for bathing, status display and Mediterranean-style living in the Roman Empire.

112 Wardle (2008a: 211).

113 See Monteil (2008) and L. Wallace (2014: 123–4) for writing and literacy in Londinium. See Eckardt (2014: 177–8) for literacy as a defining feature of *romanitas*.

114 J. Hill and Rowsome (2011: 30); Tomlin (2011a: 515); Wardle (2011c: 287).

115 J. Williams (2007).

116 See Campbell (2012: 132–40) and Rogers (2013: 7–8) for the sacred nature of water, springs and rivers in the Roman world and the context of acts of propitiation.

117 See Rogers (2013: 46–51, 203–6) for ideas about the scale, extent and significance of the operations of draining and dumping in Londinium throughout the late first and second centuries AD that have helped to inform the perspective developed in this book.

118 J. Hill and Rowsome (2011: 22) (ONE94).

119 J. Hill and Rowsome (2011: 22, 258, Figs 13 and 14).

120 J. Hill and Rowsome (2011: 22). J. Hill and Rowsome also note that plough marks have also been found associated with clearance for road building on other Roman sites in Britain.

121 J. Hill and Rowsome (2011: 22–6, 264–5).

122 J. Hill and Rowsome (2011: 24–6, 26–30, 264–5).

123 J. Evans (2007).

124 Gerrard (2009a: 130) has noted prehistoric ard marks at 33 Union Street on the south island in Southwark (USS03) and has discussed the idea that these represented the symbolic act of bringing virgin land into cultivation.

125 J. Hill and Rowsome (2011: 258).

126 Campbell (2012: 17) has commented on 'the spiritual and mythological combined with the practical management' of the city of Rome's drinking water, and the drainage of land is likely to have been associated with ritual connotations.

127 See Drummond-Murray and Thompson (2002: 19–22) and Wardle (2009: 120–4) for the dumping of cultural material in the first phases of Roman Southwark.

128 See Merrifield and Hall (2008) and Wardell (2011a) for recent discussions.

129 See L. Wallace (2014: 127–8) for special deposits from early Roman London. See Cowan (2003: 85) and Rayner, Wardle and Seeley (2011: 406–7) for offerings made in buildings during the first to third centuries at Courage Brewery in Southwark and at 1 Poultry.

130 See Fulford (2001) for special deposits in Roman pits.

131 See Perring ((1991), 2011: 11–12, 76–7) for Roman London. See Perring (2002: 31–2, 83–110) for building styles in Roman urban centres in Britain.

132 Mattingly (2006: 274). It has often been thought that the less durable timber-and-earth houses were mainly built during the early Roman period (first and second centuries AD), while the stone-built houses that were often installed with underfloor heating and mosaic floors were typical in the third to fourth century (Perring (1991) 2011: 100–3). It will be shown in subsequent chapters that this picture is too simple (cf. Bluer and Brigham 2006: 70).

133 See L. Wallace (2014: 58–9) for pre-Boudican buildings with tiled roofs.

134 See J. Hill and Rowsome (2011: Table 1) for details of seven areas of excavation at and around 1 Poultry, including several sub-sites discussed below: at 1 Poultry (Site A = ONE94) and 'satellite sites' close to 1 Poultry (including Site B = LHY88, Site C = BUC87 and Site D = CID90). See J. Hill and Woodger (1999) for an earlier and fuller publication of the information for Site D (72–3 Cheapside), including some information which has been reinterpreted in J. Hill and Rowsome (2011).

135 See J. Hill and Rowsome (2011: 38, 275–6) for a detailed discussion of the information for the western suburb of Roman London.

136 J. Hill and Rowsome (2011: 26–7, 263, 273–5). See L. Wallace (2014: 49–50) for the scale of dumping across the urban areas of early Londinium.

137 J. Hill and Rowsome (2011: 26–7, 272–84).

138 Perring (2015: 26).

139 See J. Hill and Rowsome (2001: 69–70, 273–5) for the rectangular houses at 1 Poultry (ONE94) and the round building at Site D (CID90). J. Hill and Woodger (1999: 10, 53) have provided additional details for the round building.

140 See Perring (2002: 55–60) and Hall (2005: 125) for 'strip-buildings' in Roman London and other parts of the empire. MacMahon (2005) has observed that many of these were probably shops.

141 J. Hill and Woodger (1999: 10, 53).

142 Hall (2005: 127–8); Cowan and Pringle (2009: 86); L. Wallace (2014: 58).

143 Roskams (1991a: 3–8); Perring (1991b: 101) (GPO75).

144 Roundhouses at 10 Gresham Street and Toppings Wharf / Fennings Wharf will be discussed in subsequent chapters.

145 Allen et al. (2016, 47) have suggested that the gradual change from a predominantly circular to a predominantly rectangular architecture in Roman Britain was linked with a need for architectural differentiation.

146 Perring ((1991) 2011: 15); Willis (2011: 183).

147 Perring (1991b: 101).

148 Hingley (1989); Mattingly (2006: 367).

149 Rayner (2011a). The pottery from 'Building 23' will be discussed in Chapter 3.

150 J. Hill (2011).

151 J. Hill and Rowsome (2011: 64–5, 80).

152 J. Hill and Rowsome (2011: 62).

153 J. Hill and Rowsome (2011: 305).

154 Rayner (2011b: 280).

155 Willis (2011: 178).

156 J. Hill and Rowsome (2011: 183).

157 Rayner (2011b).

158 J. Hill and Rowsome (2011: 264, 291). Van der Veen, Livarda and Hill (2008: 25, 32) have discussed early imports of exotic plant foods to London and have compared the evidence with other sites across Roman Britain.

159 Hammerson (2011a). Hammerson (2011b) has noted that the excavations at 1 Poultry and across Southwark are typified by a high incidence of Claudian coins in contrast to other sites north of the Thames. This may suggest that the core of the urban centre around the forum was not settled until a later date than Southwark and the 1 Poultry area, but this is unclear.

160 Pitt and Seeley (2014: 15–23) (POU05).

161 Bryan, Hill and Watson (2016: 36–7) (BZY10).

162 L. Wallace (2014: 75, Fig. 36) has discussed the area occupied prior to AD 60, arguing that some sites were occupied south of the main east–west road. See Perring (1991a: 29) for burnt deposits at Watling Court (WAT78) that may have been pre-Boudican. At 25 Cannon Street (CAO96) traces of buildings possibly pre-dating AD 60 were uncovered (Elsden 2002: 8–12, 53). This area has not, however, been included within the likely boundaries of pre-Boudican Londinium by Hill and Rowsome (2011: 275–6, Fig. 263), and their observations have been followed here.

163 See S. Watson (2015a: 13–14, 23) for 'Buildings 8 and 9' (CDP04).

164 Five sites were excavated around Paternoster Square and are discussed by S. Watson (2006: 15–26, Fig. 2), including the individual excavations at Courtenay House (CTC99), Stonemason's Yard Ramp (PSU99), Newgate Triangle (NGT00), Juxton House (SLY00) and Paternoster Row (PNS01). Newgate Triangle and Paternoster Square produced evidence for pre-Boudican occupation.

165 S. Watson (2006: 15–26).

166 Symonds (2006: 85–7).

167 G. Brown and Pye (1992) (WIV88).

168 C. Milne, G. Milne and Brigham (1992: 11); G. Milne and Wardle (1996: 29–30) (LCT84).

169 Wroe-Brown (2014: 8–20) (FEU08).

170 Pitt (2015: 151–4) (EAE01).

171 Dunwoodie, Harward and Pitt (2015: 14–38) (FER97).

172 Dunwoodie, Harward and Pitt (2015: 17, 36); M. Bishop (2015). The cuirass may, however, have been derived from the succeeding post-Boudican occupation (Wardle 2015a: 159).

173 Swift (2008: 16–19, 48) (AUT01).

174 Swift (2008: 19).

175 Swift (2008: 48).

176 Brigham, Watson and Tyres (1996: 34) (KWS94).

177 Drummond-Murray and Thompson (2002: 25–39, Fig. 31) (BGH95).

178 See Drummond-Murray and Thompson (2002: 26) for 'Building 2'; see also Cowan and Wardle (2009: 102).

179 See Drummond-Murray and Thompson (2002: 28–9) for 'Building 3'.

180 Drummond-Murray and Thompson (2002: 28).

181 Drummond-Murray and Thompson (2002: 40).

182 Drummond-Murray and Thompson (2002: 40–1); Wardle (2002a: 214, 219–20); Cowan and Wardle (2009: 107)(JSS92).

183 Discussions of the extent of the pre-Boudican Southwark include Drummond-Murray and Thompson (2002: 51–2, Fig. 34), Cowan et al. (2009: 14–15), Rayner (2009: 42–6) and L. Wallace (2014: Fig. 36).

184 Rayner (2009: Table 2).

185 As shown on Drummond-Murray and Thompson (2002: Fig. 43).

186 The analysis of pottery deposits likely to pre-date AD 70, however, may suggest that a rather larger area across the two main islands was settled by AD 60 (Rayner 2009: 46–8, Fig. 25), although an alternative interpretation is given below. The initial evidence for timber-and-earth buildings and copperworking at Arcadia Buildings may also pre-date AD 60, although this is uncertain (Rayner 2009: 48–50).

187 Cowan (2003: 25–6) (52SOS89; COSE84[1]; COSE84[2]; 28PS84[1]; 28PS84[2]; CSW85; CO87; CO88[1]; CO88[2]).

188 Goodman (2007). The sacred boundary (*pomerium*) of the city of Rome, for example, had special significance. The *suovetaurilia*, the sacrifice of three animals dedicated to Mars, involved a procession beginning at the boundary of the city and ending at the Campus Martius where the animals were killed (Whittaker 1994: 21–6). A comparable practice was conducted by the Roman army on the imperial frontiers, as indicated by the inscribed stone formerly incorporated into the Antonine Wall at Bridgeness on the Firth of Forth in Scotland (Whittaker 1994: 23). This particular sacrificial rite was linked to the concept of the expansion of the boundaries of the empire, although comparable sacrifices may have been conducted to define the limits of other cities.

189 The charter of the city of Urso (Osuna, Spain), for example, prohibited the construction of tile kilns within the urban area (Goodman 2007: 17).

190 Perring (2011a: 250–3); Perring (2015: 21–3).

191 Sankey (2003: 3–4) (ETA 89).

192 The excavation by I. Blair in 2006–7 (WOZ07) is currently published in interim reports (cf. Booth 2007: 291).

193 Perring (2011a: 249–53).

194 Booth (2007: 291).

195 In the initial fill of the larger eastern ditch was an assemblage of Late Iron Age pottery, including a large storage jar made in Late Iron Age grog-tempered ware and probably dating to before AD 50 (Perring 2011a: 250).

196 L. Wallace (2013) and L. Wallace (2014: 37, 68–71, Fig. 32) have cast considerable doubt upon the idea that an early Roman fort may be deduced from the random lengths of ditch discussed by Perring. Perring (2015: 22–3) has provided some additional discussion, but further evidence would be required to demonstrate a military role for these sections of ditch.

197 Wilson (2006: 26).

198 L. Wallace (2013).

199 Niblett (2005: 62–3, Fig. 4.72).

200 See Hammer (2003: 168–9) for the metal workshops of Londinium, several of which are discussed in subsequent chapters. See L. Wallace (2014: 114–16) for the extensive evidence for metalworking in pre-Boudican London.

201 Cotton (2008: 152). Montgomery et al. (2010) outline the evidence for increasing concentrations of lead in human bones during the Roman period and the likely negative connotations for human health (cf. Roberts and Cox 2004).

202 Pringle (2009: 191).

203 S. Watson (2006: 76).

204 Davies, Richardson and Tomber (1994: 29–34, 232); Schofield (1998: 187–8); J. Hill and Rowsome (2011: 275); L. Wallace (2014: 119); Rayner (2017: 358–9) (SLO82).

205 Rayner (2011c).

206 Symonds (2003: 55–7).

207 Birbeck and Schuster (2009: 13–15); Seager Smith (2009b: 55, Fig. 42).

208 Toynbee (1971: 50–1) discusses the Roman practice of burial of the dead beyond the boundary of the city (see Cicero *De. leg. ii*: 23, 58).

209 For the application of this rule to Roman London, see J. Maloney (1983: 96), Barber and Hall (2000: 102) and S. Watson (2003: 8).

210 Pearce (2015: 138) has noted that burials on the edges of Roman urban centres are often interspersed with public buildings, occupation, craft, quarrying, farming and rubbish disposal.

211 The highly fragmentary nature of the evidence for burials throughout Roman London may partly explain the complexity of the information reviewed in this book. It will, however, be argued that the right of burial did not always take place within well-defined contexts; many bodies may have been placed where they were exposed to the elements. The term 'burial', therefore, is too simple to explain the variety of rites of passage that were enacted (see Crerar 2016: 387).

212 McKinley (2008: 169–71).

213 Barber and Bowsher (2000: 54–5, 300) have recorded several early inhumation burials across London and have suggested that these may constitute Britons settling in Londinium from areas with an Iron Age inhumation tradition (for instance, Dorset) or from areas of the empire in which inhumation was the predominant burial rite.

214 Ridgeway, Leary and Sudds (2013: 106); Harward, Powers and Watson (2015: 87). Pearce (2013: 18–19) and Pearce (2015: 146) have noted that inhumations can sometimes form a surprisingly high proportion of early Roman burials in cemeteries in Britannia and also in other provinces.

215 Barber and Bowsher (2000: 299–300); Barber and Hall (2000: 103); Connell (2009: 251).

216 McKinley (2000: 267, Table 68) has noted that cremation burials remain common during the late Roman period in London's 'eastern cemetery'.

217 Shepherd (1988: 10–11, 26–9, Fig. 5). These three cemeteries are poorly understood due to the early date at which they were found (RCHM 1928: 31, 153–4; Shepherd 1988: 10–11; Barber and Hall 2000: 107; S. Watson 2006: 68–71).

218 RCHM (1928: 153–4, Fig. 63).

219 RCHM (1928: 154, Fig. 63, plates 56, 59).

220 RCHM (1928: 154); Schofield (2011: 33–6, 326, 330).

221 Shepherd (1988: 11, 28).

222 Shepherd (1988: 28); Coombe et al. (2015: 110–12 (no. 205)); Perna (2015: 131).

223 See Williams and Hobbs (2015: 845) for a discussion of the geochemical analysis of the stone.

224 Perna (2015: 129–30).

225 Coombe et al. (2015: 112); Perna (2015: 131).

226 Perna (2015: 131).

227 RCHM (1928:154); Willams and Hobbs (2015: 443–4).

228 Coombe et al. (2015: 112).

229 Guildhall Museum (1969: 4–6); Marsden (1980: 76–7).

230 Shepherd (1988: 10–11, 26–9, Fig. 5).

231 C. Milne, G. Milne and Brigham (1992: 11–12); G. Milne and Wardle (1996: 29–30) (LCT84).

232 Davies (1992: 66).

233 See Marsden (1980: 24, 208 n. 14), Schofield (1998: 51) and Hunt (2011: 50) for burials at 112–14 Fenchurch Street and 17–18 Billiter Street (GM60).

234 Two un-urned cremation burials were also found at 60–3 Fenchurch Street, although these were undated (Birbeck and Schuster 2009: 11–12).

235 Perring ((1991) 2011: 14).

236 For this practice during the Iron Age, see Lambrick and Robinson (2009: 309–10). For the Roman period, see Esmonde Cleary (2000: 137–8) and Pearce (2013: 102–9). Harding (2016: 41–2) has discussed the evidence for excarnation in Iron Age Britain. This practice may also have been characteristic of Roman activities on the margins of Londinium (Beasley 2007: 61).

237 Birbeck and Schuster (2009: 11–15); McKinley (2009) (FNE01). The features and burials were dated to c. AD 50–60 but may date to after the Boudican uprising.

238 McKinley (2009: 14).

239 McKinley (2009: 13).

240 S. Watson (2006: 19–21, 68–70); Powers (2006) (NGT00).

241 Powers (2006).

242 S. Watson (2006: 22–5).

243 Verulamium has provided some of the fullest information for burials in Late Iron Age and early Roman southern Britain. See Niblett (1999: 20–1, 310–12, 403) and Niblett (2005: 141, Fig. 4.65) for the information from cemeteries at the margin of the first-century settlement and the suggestion that the dead may initially have been exposed in the ditches of the enclosures that defined these cemeteries. Niblett (1999: 403) has suggested that on cemetery sites at Verumlaium and elsewhere, Late Iron Age and early Roman inhumations might constitute the first stages in two-stage funerary rites in which bodies were exposed in the ditches around cemetery enclosures before being retrieved and cremated. She has argued that, after a period of exposure, the partly disarticulated remains may have been cremated and placed in an individual pit within the enclosure.

244 Niblett (1999: 398, 403, 419 n. 3).

245 Carr (2007: 447).

246 Beasley (2007: 61–4) has surveyed the occurrence of fragmentary human remains on Roman sites in Britain that has suggested that parts of human bodies were retained and manipulated.

247 See Ridgeway, Leary and Sudds (2013: 104, 108–9) for the concept of fragmentation rites.

248 Deposition of human remains in a variety of watery places such as waterholes was also common during the Iron Age in the Thames Valley area and elsewhere (Lambrick and Robinson 2009: 311–12).

249 Ferretti and Graham (1978: 65); Watt (1978a) (207BHS72).

250 Ferretti and Graham (1978: 65).

251 Beasley (2007: 26–36, 47–9) (SWN98).

252 Beasley (2007: 30–3).

253 Beasley (2007: 36, 54–5).

254 Beasley (2007: 36, 54–5). Rayner and Seeley (2008: 192) have discussed this topic drawing on additional materials from London.

255 It is notable that the cranial remains at 201–11 Borough High Street was also associated with two complete pots.

256 See Rayner (2011b: 280) for the complex nature of marketing in early Roman London.

257 See Rowsome (2008: 27) and L. Wallace (2014: 59–61) for evidence for the early planning of Roman London.

258 See Hingley (1997a) for the occurrence of regular and irregular street systems at Roman towns in Britain.

3 Boudica and Londinium in AD 60

1 Tomlin (2016: 55–6) has argued that the dating evidence provided by Bloomberg Writing Tablet 45 supports the idea that Boudica's uprising occurred in AD 60 and this dating has been adopted in this book.

2 For recent accounts of the uprising and the burning of London, see Hingley and Unwin (2005) and L. Wallace (2014: 22–6).

3 The translations of these sections from Tacitus' *Annals* have been taken from Grant's translation (see Bibliography).

4 Hingley and Unwin (2005: 63–9).

5 For early observations about the burnt layer in Roman London, see VCH (1909: 5), RCHM (1928: 32), R. E. M. Wheeler (1930: 21), Dunning (1945: 48–52) and Marsden (1980: 32).

6 See L. Wallace (2014: 22–4, 64–5, 77–8, Fig. 36) for a detailed assessment of the 'fire-destruction horizon' which she dates to around AD 50–70 and which has been found on fifty-six sites north and south of the River Thames.

7 Drummond-Murray and Thompson (2002: 40).

8 Marsden (1980: 31).

9 See P. Crummy (1997: 79–83) for the finds sealed by burnt layers at Camulodunum (cf. Hingley and Unwin 2005: 75–7).

10 J. Hill and Rowsome (2011: 73–82, Fig. 269) (ONE94).

11 Rayner (2011a).

12 For the two pottery 'shops' at Colchester, see Hull (1958: 153–6, 198–9), Millett (1987), P. Crummy (1997: 82–3) and Rayner (2011a: 302–3).

13 At Cornhill a room in the long east–west building which may have been a range of shops was stocked with grain either for sale or storage in a granary (Marsden 1987: 20; Straker 1987).

14 Rayner (2011a: 295–6).

15 Rayner (2011a: 295–6).

16 J. Bird (2011a: 300).

17 Davies, Richardson and Tomber (1994: 74, 82).

18 Rayner (2011a: 295).

19 Millett (1987: 104).

20 See L. Wallace (2014: 24–6, 66) for post-depositional activities that are likely to have disturbed these pre-Boudican deposits and associated dating problems.

21 J. Hill and Woodger (1999: 11–12) (CID90).

22 Pitt and Seeley (2014: 17, 20, 23) (POU05). These excavations located a single sherd of Highgate Wood C pottery from the pre-Boudican layers.

23 S. Watson (2015a: 9–10, 23) (CDP04). Watson has also discussed the lack of evidence for early buildings further north at 14–18 Gresham Street (GHM05; previously known as 25 Milk Street and 14–18 Gresham Street).

24 Roskams (1991a: 6) (GPO75).

25 Wroe-Brown (2014: 18–20) (FEU08); Dunwoodie, Harward and Pitt (2015: 35) (FER97); Pitt (2015: 154–7) (EAE01).

26 L. Wallace (2013: 78).

27 S. Watson (2006: 26) (NGT00). Deposits from the burnt buildings included a Highgate Wood C ware jar or bowl that would usually be dated to around AD 70 (S. Watson 2006: 26).

28 Hill and Rowsome (2011: 274) (GSM97).

29 Hingley and Unwin (2005: 89).

30 Casson, Drummond-Murray and Francis (2014: 10–24).

31 Jackson et al. (2013) (BYZ10).

32 Bryan, Hill and Watson (2016: 37).

33 Drummond-Murray and Thompson (2002: 40–8); Rayner (2009: 44–6).

34 Although it is not certain that the bridge had been constructed by this time.

35 Brigham (2001b: 43).

36 Drummond-Murray and Thompson (2002: 46–8) (BGH95).

37 Drummond-Murray and Thompson (2002: 40–1).

38 Drummond-Murray and Thompson (2002: 59). This could explain the presence of pottery in these deposits that should post-date AD 60.

39 Rayner (2009: 46–8, Fig. 25).

40 See Bluer and Brigham (2006: 10, 18) and McKenzie (2012: 4) for examples of sites without burning but with Highgate Wood C ware that have been dated to after AD 60.

41 Plantation Place also produced Highgate Wood C ware from burnt deposits that are supposed to be pre-Boudican (Dunwoodie, Harward and Pitt 2015: 35).

42 Perring (2011a: 258). Hall and Shepherd (2008: 39) have described the association of the cranial remains with the uprising as an old idea and suggested that they were deposited during native ritual practices.

43 Perring (2011a: 259).

44 L. Wallace (2014: 23).

45 Perring (2011a: 258, n. 61).

46 Perring (1991a: 30) (WAT78). The second skull quoted by Perring (2011a: 258) from Walbrook House is not yet published.

47 See Cotton (1996: 88) and Schofield (1998: 183) for interim reports (LIB82).

48 Marsden (1987: 20); Straker (1987) (207BHS72).

49 C. Maloney (1990: 5).

50 Beasley (2007: 60–1).

51 Two other fragments of a bronze statue that possibly portrayed the emperor Claudius have been found at different locations in East Anglia, perhaps taken from Camulodunum during the destruction of this colony in AD 60 (Hingley and Unwin 2005: 80–2).

52 Blair et al. (2006: 8); Bayley et al. (2009); Coombe et al. (2015: 117 (no. 216)) (GHT00).

53 Bayley et al. (2009: 153–5).

54 Bayley et al. (2009: 155).

55 Blair et al. (2006: 8, n. 13).

56 Since the emperor Nero was damned after his death in AD 68 and stone statues of unpopular emperors were often broken up and dumped in sewers and rivers, the bronze arm from 30 Gresham Street may have been from a statue of this emperor (Bayley et al.: 158; cf. P. Stewart 2003: 276). Roger Tomlin (pers. comm.) has pointed out, however, that metal was expensive and worthy of recycling and metal statue fragments from Roman London may indicate wilful damage and looting rather than a specific act of the damnation of a particular emperor.

57 Bayley et al. (2009: 151).

58 Russell and Manley (2013). These authors also suggest that the statue may have formed part of a group produced to commemorate the re-establishment of the province after the revolt and could have been vandalized after Nero's death in AD 68.

59 Aldhouse-Green (2006: 150).

60 Drummond-Murray and Thompson (2002: 61–2, 97) (BGH95).

4 Re-establishing Urban Order from AD 60 to 70

1 Perring ((1991) 2011: 22–3); Rowsome (2008: 27). In contrast, the colony at Camulodunum seems to have been re-established a short time after Boudica's attack (P. Crummy 1997: 85–6).

2 Perring (2011a: 255–60).

3 Collingwood and Wright (1995a: 5–6); Grasby and Tomlin (2002); Birley (2005: 303–4); Coombe et al. (2015: 49 (no. 82)) (RIB 12).

4 Marsden (1980: 41); Hall (1996: 70); Barber and Bowsher (2000: 304). These stones were derived from Bastion 2.

5 Two fragments were found close to the base of the bastion in 1852 and a third was found in 1935 built into the surviving section of foundation (Grasby and Tomlin 2002: 45–50).

6 Grasby and Tomlin (2002: 67).

7 Grasby and Tomlin (2002: 43).

8 Grasby and Tomlin (2002: 43); Henig (2000: 64).

9 Hassall (2000: 53–5); Mattingly (2006: 265); Perring (2011a: 260).

10 Birley (2005: 304).

11 Birley (2005: 304); Mattingly (2006: 112–13).

12 Bryan, Hill and Watson (2016: 37) (BZY10).

13 Tomlin (2016: 55).

14 See Tomlin (2016: 55–6, 156–9) for Writing Tablet 45 (including the translation).

15 Two other writing tablets from Bloomberg recorded the name of Londinium (Tomlin 2016: 29).

16 Tomlin (2016: 55, 158).

17 Tomlin (2016: 158).

18 See Tomlin (2016: 56, 168–9) for Writing Tablet 50. Florentinus may have been acting as a financial agent for his master (cf. Andreau 1999: 64–70; Tomlin 2016: 168). The name of the farm has not survived.

19 See Tomlin (2016: 124–7) for Writing Tablet 31. The writing tablet names 'Aticus', although this was probably a misspelling of 'Atticus'.

20 Tomlin (2016: 56).

21 See Tomlin (2016: 56, 142) for Writing Tablet 39. Although it is notable that the archaeological context suggests that it was deposited later in the first century and it may, perhaps, have related to a later event (Tomlin 2016: 56, 142).

22 See Tomlin (2016: 56, 130–1) for Writing Tablet 33.

23 See Tomlin (2016: 178–81) for Writing Tablet 55.

24 Tomlin (2016: 181).

25 See Tomlin (2016: 164–5) for Writing Tablet 48.

26 Tomlin (2016: 56).

27 Tomlin (2016: 56).

28 Dunwoodie, Harward and Pitt (2015) (FER97), Wilson (2006: 25–7) and Wroe-Brown (2014: 60–1) include earlier discussions.

29 Dunwoodie, Harward and Pitt (2015: 39–62).

30 Dunwoodie, Harward and Pitt (2015: 39, 49–50, 64–6).

31 Dunwoodie, Harward and Pitt (2015: 41–8); Wilson (2006: 25–6, Fig. 1.12). Dunwoodie, Harward and Pitt (2015: 49–50) have discussed parallels for the dating of these works.

32 Dunwoodie, Harward and Pitt (2015: 68–9).

33 Dunwoodie, Harward and Pitt (2015: 50).

34 Dunwoodie, Harward and Pitt (2015: 67–8).

35 Rowsome (2008: 27).

36 Dunwoodie, Harward and Pitt (2015: 66–7, 76–7).

37 Dunwoodie, Harward and Pitt (2015: 45–6, 64).

38 Dunwoodie, Harward and Pitt (2015: 50–4).

39 Dunwoodie, Harward and Pitt (2015: 55).

40 Dunwoodie, Harward and Pitt (2015: 72–3); Wilson (2006: 25).

41 Thompson (2015: 158).

42 Wardle (2015a).

43 Wroe-Brown (2014: 21–8, 60–1) (FEU08).

44 Wroe-Brown (2014: 21–8).

45 Wroe-Brown (2014: 25, 27). This building appears to coincide with part of the line of the supposed north-west corner of the rampart of the 'fort' marked on the excavation plan (compare Wroe-Brown 2014: Fig. 19 with Dunwoodie, Harward and Pitt 2015: Fig. 58).

46 Wroe-Brown (2014: 60–1).

47 Pitt (2015: 154–7) (EAE01).

48 Dunwoodie, Harward and Pitt (2015: 51, 70).

49 Dunwoodie, Harward and Pitt (2015: 72).

50 Dunwoodie, Harward and Pitt (2015: 56–62).

51 Dunwoodie, Harward and Pitt (2015: 62); Wroe-Brown (2014: 60). In AD 85 any surviving remains of the fortification were levelled as part of the urban redevelopment works (Dunwoodie, Harward and Pitt 2015: 62–4).

52 See Brigham (1990a: 134–5) for information on Waterfront 2, while Brigham (1998a: 25–9) has updated this and explored its chronological relationship to 'Waterfront 3'. The location and extent of this Waterfront is shown on the Museum of London map (2011). Waterfront 2 has been excavated in several locations along the north bank of the Thames.

53 Brigham (2001b: 43).

54 Brigham and Watson (1996: 68).

55 See Brigham and Watson (1996), Brigham, Watson and Tyres (1996) and Brigham (1998a: 25–9) for interim discussions (KWS94). The full publication of this important information will inevitably revise the arguments given in the interim reports that are drawn upon here.

56 Brigham, Watson and Tyres (1996: 36).

57 Brigham (1998a: 25).

58 Brigham, Watson and Tyres (1996: 35–6); Brigham (1998a: 25).

59 Brigham (1998a: 25).

60 Brigham, Watson and Tyres (1996: 36); Brigham (2001b: 43, 50).

61 Brigham (1998a: 25, 27); Hassall and Tomlin (1996: 449). Several publications since this important excavation was undertaken have emphasized the likely involvement of the Roman army in the building of the port facilities (e.g. Brigham 2001b: 43, 50; Perring 2011a: 256; Wilson 2006: 26). The military finds from the filling of the quay, however, form part of a much larger assemblage of artefacts and these are likely to have derived from destruction deposits associated with the Boudican uprising (Brigham, Watson and Tyres 1996: 36).

62 G. Milne (2000: 129). Swan (2009: 89–90) has argued that the high proportion of north Gallic pottery imports to London during the late second to early third centuries supports the idea that the *classis Britannica* were involved in the large-scale importation of pottery to the port.

63 T. Williams (2003).

64 Blair et al. (2006) (GHT00).

65 Blair et al. (2006: 8–9).

66 Perring (2011a: 256).

67 Perring (2011a: 256).

68 Blair et al. (2006: 9–17).

69 Blair et al. (2006: 18–28). Additional wells of a comparable scale at the Cheapside bathhouse and 12 Arthur Street date to later in the first century or to the second century AD.

70 Blair et al. (2006: 9).

71 Marsden (1980: 36); Merrifield (1983: 61); Perring ((1991) 2011: 22–3); Rowsome (2008: 27).

72 Rowsome (2008: 27).

73 J. Hill and Rowsome (2011: 306–7).

74 J. Hill and Rowsome (2011: 74–5) (ONE94).

75 J. Hill and Rowsome (2011: 75, 307).

76 J. Hill and Woodger (1999: 16, 53) initially discussed the information from 1 Poultry Site D (72–5 Cheapside) (CID90), suggesting that rebuilding of houses started soon after the Boudican destruction, since one of the stakes under a building ('Building 9'), which was interpreted as a foundation pile, produced a dendrochronological date of AD 62–3. J. Hill and Rowsome (2011: 307) have suggested, however, that this timber derived from a second drainage feature connected with the main east–west road.

77 Pitt and Seeley (2014: 23–6) (POU05).

78 Drummond-Murray and Thompson (2002: 54–9) (BGH95; JSS92).

79 Drummond-Murray and Thompson (2002: 59).

80 Casson, Drummond-Murray and Francis (2014: 10–24) (GSM97). Prior to the completion of the post-excavation work, it was thought that the roundhouses pre-dated the Boudican uprising (J. Hill and Rowsome 2011: 274), but the final report suggests that there was no significant activity here prior to AD 60.

81 Casson, Drummond-Murray and Francis (2014: 10–12). Traces of this ditch were found to the north-east and south-west of the site which was not entirely uncovered by the excavation.

82 Casson, Drummond-Murray and Francis (2014: 22).

83 Casson, Drummond-Murray and Francis (2014: 14–16); Wardle (2014a: 183–4); Foulds (2017: 16).

84 Wardle (2014a: 184).

85 Shepherd and Wardle (2015) have observed that these beads were designed to appeal to 'native' tastes.

86 The blue melon bead is not clearly an Iron Age type (Elizabeth Foulds pers. comm.).

87 Casson, Drummond-Murray and Francis (2014: 22).

88 Dunwoodie, Harward and Pitt (2015: 72). See Revell (2016: 96–100) for the character of Roman slavery and the difficulties of finding evidence for slaves.

89 Casson, Drummond-Murray and Francis (2014: 20, 32).

90 See Pre-Construct Archaeology (2009: 9) and Hawkins (2009: 39–40, 109–12) for interim reports (DGT06).

91 Hawkins (2009: 109–10); Victoria Ridgeway (pers. comm.).

92 Hawkins (2009: 111).

93 Rayner (2009: Table 2).

94 Cowan (1995: 12–15) (15SKS80).

95 Cowan (1995: 32).

96 Cowan (1995: 21); Stevenson (1995: 82–5).

97 Rayner (2009: 46–8, Fig. 25).

98 Dean (1980: 369) (AB78).

99 Cowan and Wardle (2009: 108–9, Figs 85 and 86); Rayner (2009: 40, Fig. 18). Activity here may have commenced prior to the destruction of Londinium in AD 60.

100 Wardle (2015a: 162); Dunwoodie, Harward and Pitt (2015: Fig. 60).

101 See Tomlin (2016: 98).

5 Londinium from AD 70 to AD 120

1 Hassall (2012: 158).

2 Birley (2005: 11–12).

3 Tomlin (2016: 56). This may partly explain the dramatic expansion of its urban area. Fulford (2015: 197) has observed that the rapid development of Londinium during its first hundred years sets it apart from the other towns of Roman Britain.

4 Tomlin (2016: 56).

5 Tomlin (2016: 56).

6 See Tomlin (2016: 56 and 170–1) for Writing Tablet 51.

7 See Tomlin (2016: 56 and 182–3) for Writing Tablet 56.

8 Tomlin (2016: 56).

9 Bowman (1994: 30, 52).

10 Bowman (1994: 22–3); Anthony Birley (pers. comm.).

11 Hassall (2012: 161).

12 M. Bishop (1983); Perring ((1991) 2011: 38–9); Hassall (1996: 21); Shepherd (2012: 166); Coombe et al. (2015: 47–8 (no. 80)); Tomlin (2016: 56).

13 M. Bishop (1983).

14 M. Bishop (1983: 43).

15 Hassall (2012: 159).

16 Collingwood and Wright (1995a: 9); Shepherd (2012: 166); Coombe et al. (2015: 46 (no. 78)) (RIB 19). The dating is not entirely certain.

17 Hassall (2012: 160).

18 Tomlin (2003); Tomlin (2011a: 515–17). Detailed analysis of the wording suggests that this record dated from around AD 75–125 (Tomlin 2003: 46).

19 See Tomlin (2011a: 517) for the translation.

20 Tomlin (2003: 47). Alternatively, Vegetus may have been purchasing this slave for Montanus or for the emperor himself (J. Gardner 2011: 418).

21 Roger Tomlin (pers. comm.)

22 Tomlin (2003: 48, n. 25). Bowman, Thomas and Tomlin (2011: 130–1) have suggested that this Vegetus, after he had been manumitted (freed by his master), was the Cocceius Vegetus who received one of the Vindolanda letters.

23 J. Gardner (2011: 418).

24 Tomlin (2003: 47–8). Revell (2016: 99) has suggested that Fortunata may have been sold in the forum-basilica.

25 Collingwood and Wright (1995a: 10–11); Perring ((1991) 2011: 41–2) (RIB 21). Coombe et al. (2015: 49–50 (no. 83)) have provided revised dating.

26 Coombe et al. (2015: 50).

27 Coombe et al. (2015: 50).

28 Fishwick (1961: 165–6) has reviewed this inscription and has argued that it 'clearly falls short of proof' for the employment of Anencletus in the service of the provincial council (cf. Coombe et al. 2015: 50).

29 Hassall (1996: 20).

30 See Hassall (2000: 53) for the financial role of Londinium.

31 Collingwood and Wright (1992: 13) (RIB 2443.2).

32 There is no database of Roman military equipment from London but Wardle (2015a: 159–62) has included a study of the military metalwork from Plantation Place and a summary of comparable material from elsewhere across Londinium. Dunwoodie, Harward and Pitt (2015: Fig. 60) have shown the distribution of this material. Wroe-Brown (2014: 60–1, Table 13) has summarized finds from 20 Fenchurch Street.

33 See Tomlin (2016: 56, 142).

34 Collingwood and Wright (1990: 11–13).

35 See Hassall (1996: 20–1) and Hassall (2012) for evidence of soldiers and imperial officials. There are several additional military tombstones from London (including RIB 15, 17, 18, 19); some such tombstones are not closely dated while others date to the later history of Londinium (Collingwood and Wright 1995a: 7–9).

36 Collingwood and Wright (1995a: 6–7); Shepherd (2012: 166) (RIB 13).

37 Tomlin, Wright and Hassall (2009: 24); Shepherd (2012: 166) (RIB 3005). Tomlin, Wright and Hassall (2009: 24) argue from the character of the surviving portion of the inscription that this individual may have been a *beneficiarius* rather than a legionary tribune (cf. Shepherd 2012: 166).

38 Collingwood and Wright (1995a: 4); Coombe et al. (2015: 48–9 (no. 81)) (RIB 9).

39 Marsden (1980: 41).

40 Barber and Bowsher (2000: 115, 338–9); Hassall and Tomlin (1989: 327); Tomlin, Wright and Hassall (2009: 23) (RIB 3004). This inscription was found reused as packing in one of the burials (B 627) from the area of the 'eastern cemetery' at Hooper Street (HOO88).

41 Tomlin (2016: 56).

42 Tomlin (2003: 45, 48); J. Gardner (2011: 418).

43 Joshel (2011).

44 Collingwood and Wright (1992: 15); Tomlin (2011a: 49–50) (RIB 2443.7). The translation from the Latin is given by Tomlin.

45 Revell (2016: 2–5) has addressed the marginalization of women, children and the poor in Roman archaeology. The Bloomberg tablets only include the names of men and do nothing to help correct this bias.

46 Including Catullus, Lucius, Valentinus and Maxi[?mus] (Hartley 2005).

47 Monteil (2008: 178–80).

48 J. Hill and Rowsome (2011: 448).

49 Holder (2007: 31).

50 Tomlin (2016: 54).

51 People from northern Gaul and Germania may, however, have used comparable mortuary rites during the Iron Age.

52 Rowsome (1998: 37); Rowsome (2008: 28).

53 See Wallace-Hadrill (1988: 58–9) for the problems with applying ideas about 'public' and 'private' to houses in the Roman Empire. See Bateman (1998: 47) for the problems in applying this distinction to the buildings of London.

54 A mansio was an official inn connected with imperial transport along the roads of the empire.

55 See Revell (2009) for 'public' buildings and status display in Roman urban centres.

56 Wallace-Hadrill (1988: 58–9). For social patronage and clientage in the domestic context across the empire and in Britain, see Ellis (2000: 22–72) and Perring (2002: 209–11).

57 Wallace-Hadrill (1988: 44–5, 52) has linked the quality and decoration of a Roman house to the social standing of its occupants. Hospitality and the large-scale admission of visitors required an opulent house; the domestic architecture of the house reflected an obsession with distinctions of social rank.

58 Excavations across London have, however, explored buildings of differing social status, including those of the poor.

59 Rowsome (1999).

60 DeLaine (1999: 162) and Rowsome (1999: 276–7) have argued that there were fairly few public baths in London during the period before Hadrian and that they were replaced by a large number of smaller baths, often privately owned, during the late Roman period. This may be paralleled in other provinces. There was probably, however, a public bathhouse in the suburban area at Shadwell, east of Londinium, during the third and fourth centuries, indicating that the situation may have been more complex than is sometimes suggested.

61 Rowsome (1999: 275–6) has listed four possible bathhouses that were discovered during antiquarian excavations but that are not dated (cf. Sudds 2011b: 161).

62 Laurence, Esmonde Cleary and Seers (2011: 122–3); Mattingly (2006: 280).

63 The tiles are stamped with acronyms, including 'PPBRILON', 'PPRBR' and 'PRBLON', for which the preferred reading is 'procurator of the province of Britain at London' ('procurator provinciae Britanniae Londini') (Collingwood and Wright 1993: 30–40; Betts 1995; Betts 2015: 67–9; Crowley 2005: 93). They were made during the period from around AD 70–125.

64 Betts (2015: 215, 222); Crowley (2005: 93).

65 Collingwood and Wright (1993: 30); Pringle (2009: Table 37).

66 The bathhouse at Winchester Palace in Southwark may have been constructed by members of the Roman army.

67 Revell (2009: 72) has observed that epigraphic display was largely ignored in Britain and that many of the inscriptions from London relate to its role as the province's administrative centre. There are fewer inscriptions indicating acts of munificence from London than from many cities in the Mediterranean and those that have been found name people who originated from outside the province.

68 A Gallic trader resident in Londinium during the late second century dedicated a temple at Tabard Square. Evidence for the restoration of temples sacred to Juno and Isis during the early third century has been attested by the altars built into the riverside wall at Baynard's Castle. The temple of Isis was restored by a provincial governor, probably as an act of personal munificence rather than as a state-sponsored project. The temple of Mithras may have been dedicated by a legionary soldier during the early third century. The market hall will be discussed later in this chapter.

69 Brigham (2001c: 72).

70 The foundations of the first forum have been uncovered on a number of occasions (GM100; GM101; GM297; FSE76; ACE83) and are discussed in Marsden (1987). See Dunwoodie (2004) for recent work at 168 Fenchurch Street (FEH95).

71 A basilica in the Roman Empire was an official building connected with legal procedures and public meetings.

72 Marsden (1987: 32, Figs 16 and 18).

73 Marsden (1987: 22–32).

74 Marsden (1987: 26).

75 Marsden (1987: 28).

76 Perring ((1991) 2011: 25); Creighton (2006: 103).

77 Marsden (1987: 36–7); Dunwoodie (2004: 29).

78 Dunwoodie (2004: 29).

79 Blair et al. (2006: 8 n. 13).

80 Bayley et al. (2009: 157–8); Coombe et al. (2015: 116–19, 121 (nos 215, 217, 218, 219, 220 and 224)).

81 See Marsden (1987: 32–3, 108–14) for the temple excavated by F. Cottrill at 17–19 Gracechurch Street (GM68).

82 The evidence for the dating of the forum to after AD 71 is provided by a coin minted in that year reportedly from a rubbish pit that also included pottery of this general date and that was cut by the south wall of the first phase of the basilica (Marsden 1987: 73, 119).

83 G. Milne (1992: 4); Perring ((1991) 2011: 25).

84 Niblett (2005: 78–83, 147, Fig. 4.15). The fragmentary inscription (RIB 3123) used to date the initial forum at Verulamium has usually been dated to AD 79, although Tomlin, Wright and Hassall (2009: 131) have suggested that it is likely to date to AD 81. It is not entirely clear, however, whether this inscription came from the first or second phases of the Verulamium forum (Niblett 2005: 83).

85 Fulford and Timby (2000) have discussed the timber phase of the forum at Calleva, while Creighton (2006: 65–8) has suggested that the earliest phase of this substantial timber building could even date to before AD 43.

86 See Dunwoodie (2004: 28–30) for the limited evidence for these alterations from 168 Fenchurch Street (FEH95).

87 C. Milne, G. Milne and Brigham (1992: 17–25); Davies (1992: 68–9).

88 Bateman, Cowan and Wroe-Brown (2008: 19–31) (GAG87/GDH85/GYE92/GYU99).

89 Perring (2011b: 276); Perring (2015: 26). Because of the constraints of the excavated evidence it is unclear that this pond was the most important early feature in this area.

90 Bateman (2009).

91 Bateman, Cowan and Wroe-Brown (2008: 17–19).

92 Bateman, Cowan and Wroe-Brown (2008: 19–31, 97–101).

93 Bateman, Cowan and Wroe-Brown (2008: 101).

94 Bateman, Cowan and Wroe-Brown (2008: 22–3).

95 Bateman, Cowan and Wroe-Brown (2008: 17–18).

96 Bateman, Cowan and Wroe-Brown (2008: 19–22).

97 Bateman, Cowan and Wroe-Brown (2008: 28).

98 Bateman, Cowan and Wroe-Brown (2008: 28–30).

99 Bateman, Cowan and Wroe-Brown (2008: 24–6, Fig. 11).

100 Bateman, Cowan and Wroe-Brown (2008: 24–6).

101 Bateman, Cowan and Wroe-Brown (2008: 17, 35–7, Fig. 21).

102 Bateman, Cowan and Wroe-Brown (2008: 124–7).

103 Wilmott (2009: 154) has argued that the London amphitheatre had a more complex structure than other urban examples since it incorporated an outer retaining wall. The evidence for this in the timber phase and in the succeeding stone phase is, however, fragmentary at best (Bateman, Cowan and Wroe-Brown 2008: 28, 51, 103). Indeed, the structure of the arena and banking does not appear to be distinctly different from other urban amphitheatres. The legionary amphitheatres at Caerleon and Chester are more substantial stone-built structures than those at London and other urban centres.

104 The Roman-period name of this temple complex is not known. This site has traditionally been known in the literature as Frilford (Hingley 1985), but the recent excavation project here has renamed the site after the neighbouring village of Marcham (Kamash, Gosden and Lock 2010).

105 One significant difference between the Marcham theatre and the first phase of the London amphitheatre was that the former had a stone-enclosing wall, but since the excavations at that site did not include the removal of

the arena wall it is quite possible that there was an earlier timber phase as at Londinium. The amphitheatre at Calleva had a timber-and-earth phase dating to around AD 55–75, followed by a stone phase of a slightly different plan (Fulford 1989). The structures at London, Silchester and Marcham may have had comparable initial phases, although the London amphitheatre was larger and was oval rather than circular in plan.

106 At Marcham the spring was incorporated within the arena and a drain was cut to run below the southern bank, passing under a small stone-walled room that may have been a shrine (Kamash, Gosden and Lock 2010: 108). The excavators defined this construction as ritual behaviour linked to the control of the water emanating from the spring and proposed that it was the 'manipulation and control of water that was significant' (Kamash, Gosden and Lock 2010: 115).

107 Kamash, Gosden and Lock (2010: 106, 113, 117).

108 Bateman, Cowan and Wroe-Brown (2008: 16: Fig. 9).

109 Bateman, Cowan and Wroe-Brown (2008: 115).

110 Bateman, Cowan and Wroe-Brown (2008: 42–3).

111 Hufschmid (2009); Hufschmid (2012a). See Berger (2012) for the context.

112 The theatre was constructed just east of a substantial classical temple that was first built during the late first century AD on top of an earlier Gallo-Roman temple site (Hufschmid 2009: 108). This theatre was reconstructed in three main phases between around AD 70–80 and AD 200 (Hufschmid 2009: 109–12). In the first, of which only limited traces survived, a conventional theatre was built with seating facing toward the temple, siting the stage between the spectators and the religious focus. Around AD 110, a more unconventional semi-amphitheatre replaced the theatre on the same site, retaining seating that overlooked the temple, but with an oval arena comparable to an amphitheatre. The small rooms inside the arena wall may suggest that combat with or between animals took place here (Hufschmid 2009: 110). By around AD 200 a more monumentally elaborate theatre had been constructed and a new amphitheatre was built on the city's outskirts (Hufschmid 2009: 110–12, 114–16; Hufschmid 2012b).

113 Hufschmid (2009: 105–6). The same may have been the case at theatres connected with major temples at the cities of Augusta Emerita (Mérida, Spain) and Lepcis Magna (Libya).

114 Nick Bateman (pers. comm.).

115 Bateman (2009: 159).

116 Bateman (2009: 160).

117 Nick Bateman (pers. comm.).

118 Wilmott (2009: 154).

119 Bateman (2009: 160–2).

120 Bateman, Cowan and Wroe-Brown (2008: 5–6).

121 Wardle (2008b: 199).

122 Bateman, Cowan and Wroe-Brown (2008: 116, Fig. 114). See Bateman (2009: 159) for interim observations (GHT00).

123 Bateman, Cowan and Wroe-Brown (2008: 116–17).

124 Bateman (2009: 159).

125 Blair et al. (2006: 8, Fig. 4) (GHT00).

126 Bayley et al. (2009: 153–5).

127 C. Maloney (2002: 4) and Powers (2015a: 136) (GHT00).

128 Casson, Drummond-Murray and Francis (2014: 28–31) (GSM97).

129 See Andrews (2011) and Andrews and Smith (2011: 197) for Springhead. The ancient name of the site, 'Vagniacis', may refer to a 'marshy place'; a Roman religious complex developed at this site on Watling Street around a series of springs forming a shallow pool at the head of the River Ebbsfleet (Rivet and Smith 1979: 485; Andrews and Smith 2011: 193). Activities around these springs during the Late Iron Age and earlier first century were associated with the ritual use of the landscape and the evidence for settlement at this time is limited (Andrews and Smith 2011: 191). More substantial activities commenced close to the spring following the Roman conquest, including the building of roads and a ditched enclosure (Andrews and Smith 2011: 193–5).

130 The main development of the religious architecture at Vagniacis dated from the end of the first to the third century (Andrews and Smith 2011: 195–9). A distinct contrast with Londinium is indicated by the discovery of

around one hundred Iron Age coins at Vagniacis where they were deposited around the spring and the valley side to the east (Andrews and Smith 2011: 193).

131 Futrell (1997: 70–1, 93–110).

132 Esmonde Cleary (2005: 8–14); Carroll (2001: 51–4). Terraces on the hill slope east of the spring and temples at Vagniacis may have fulfilled a comparable purpose (Andrews and Smith 2011: 195–6).

133 Hingley (1985).

134 Haselgrove (ed. 2016: 487) has commented on the topography of the oppidum at Stanwick (North Yorkshire) and the presence of a 'natural amphitheatre', high-status activity and watery terrain associated with a series of territorial earthworks.

135 Human bodies may already have began to be deposited in the area of the upper Walbrook to the north-east of the amphitheatre during the period prior to the construction work in this location.

136 Nick Bateman (pers. comm.).

137 Perring (2011b: 276).

138 Creighton (2006: 124–30).

139 Creighton (2006: 124–30) has suggested that these buildings and the line of communication established between them became the focus for an 'enduring cycle of ritual acts' within Verulamium that served to frame its geography. Later in this urban sequence the complex of spaces and buildings was elaborated by the construction of a temple and theatre on the south bank of the river to the north-west of the forum (Creighton 2006: 127). This was connected by a second route across the river to the Folly Lane burial enclosure that had by this time been developed into a temple site.

140 Creighton (2006: 130–5). Creighton has also suggested that there was an early Roman-period clustering of buildings linked together at Calleva, including the amphitheatre and the temple in the east of the urban area, to which might be added the potentially early bathhouse located close by (Creighton 2006: 135–42).

141 Perring (2011b: 276–7).

142 Perring (2015: 26).

143 Perring (2011a: 256).

144 See Marsden (1976: 30–46) and Rowsome (1999: 273–4) for information derived from the excavation of this bathhouse by Ivor Noël-Hume in 1955–6 (GM37), including the very limited evidence for the dating of its construction and disuse.

145 Rowsome (1999: 273); Blair et al. (2006: 39 n. 48).

146 Rowsome (1999: 274); J. Hill and Rowsome (2011: 372).

147 Marsden (1976: 32).

148 Marsden (1976: 34).

149 Marsden (1976: 37).

150 Marsden (1976: 38), although dating evidence was very scarce (Rowsome 1999: 274).

151 Marsden (1976: 40). This well is discussed more fully by Blair et al. (2006: 36–9) and was comparable in scale to the three wells found at 30 Gresham Street, although its dating is unclear.

152 Rowsome (1999: 274). Marsden (1976: 47) originally suggested that the Cheapside bathhouse was a military structure connected with the Cripplegate fort, but the dating of the latter to after AD 120 (Howe and Lakin 2004: 25–41, 53–9; Shepherd 2012: 51–3, 59–61, 70, 126–33) together with the distance of the bathhouse from the fort does not support this idea.

153 Marsden (1976: 42–5, Fig. 11).

154 Creighton (2006: 124–30) has observed that bathhouses are common at cult centres in Gaul and were associated with ritual bathing and cleansing the body.

155 It used to be thought that a substantial temple complex was constructed on the Thames side just west of the Huggin Hill bathhouse at the Salvation Army site during the late first or early second centuries (Perring (1991) 2011: 60–1; T. Williams 1993: xi). It was also proposed that this temple could have been comparable in size and layout to the major religious complex at Bath (Blagg 1996: 46; Bateman 1998: 49). More recent excavations, however, have indicated that these poorly-known remains are likely not to have been constructed until the AD 160s (T. Bradley and Butler 2008: xi). The considerable difficulties faced by the builders required the construction of culverts and the use of timber piles and it is possible that this delayed the building operations at this location.

156 See Marsden (1975) for a full discussion of the results of excavation during the 1960s and early 1970s which examined the supposed 'palace' (GM25; GM29; GM210). See Cowan (2008: 76) for interim comments on an evaluation at Cannon Place (CCP04). For the neighbouring 'townhouse' at Suffolk House, see below.

157 Guildhall Museum (1969: 10–16); Marsden (1975: 1, 69).

158 Marsden (1975: 12, 100). The goldworking from Marsden's excavations pre-dated the construction of the east wing of the building complex and the goldworkers may have subsequently been moved to a new site to the east at Suffolk House (see below).

159 Brigham (2001c: xi).

160 Perring ((1991) 2011: 30–4); G. Milne (1996).

161 Marsden (1975: 6: 23–4); Perring ((1991) 2011: 30); Brigham (2001c: 47).

162 Brigham (2001c: 2, 46, 47); Cowan (2008: 76); Perring ((1991) 2011: 32–3).

163 See Marsden (1975: 27–32) for the 'Garden-Court', 'Great Pool' and 'Small Pool'.

164 Cowan (2008: 76).

165 Perring (2002: 181–2).

166 Marsden (1975: 36–49, Fig. 1).

167 Marsden (1975: 52, 67, 99, Fig. 44); Brigham (2001c: 2).

168 Neal and Cosh (2009: 408–10) (mosaics 370.12–16).

169 Neal and Cosh (2009: 399).

170 See G. Milne (1996: 50, Fig. 8.2) for interim comments (LYD88 and UTA87). There is considerable uncertainty regarding the location of Waterfront 2, although the publication of these excavations may clarify this.

171 G. Milne (1996: 50, Fig. 8.2).

172 Brigham (2001c: 47); Wacher (1995: 92).

173 Collingwood and Wright (1995a: 3); Haynes (2000: 87); Henig (2000: 64) (RIB 5).

174 Perring ((1991) 2011: 34); G. Milne (1996: 50). The Museum of London's map (2011) has been understandably cautious by labelling this building complex a 'palace or temple podium'.

175 Brigham (2001c: 47; Marsden 1975: 68). These tiles do not, however, necessarily indicate an official purpose for the building (see above).

176 See Marsden (1976: 3–29) for the earlier excavations that took place in 1964 and 1969 (GM240). See Rowsome (1999: 263–73) for a provisional account of work undertaken during 1988–9 (DMT88).

177 Rowsome (1999: 272).

178 Bateman (1998: 48).

179 Rowsome (1999: 263, 268).

180 Rowsome (1999: 263).

181 Rowsome (1999: 270).

182 Rowsome (1999: 272).

183 Niblett (2005: 85); Wacher (1995: 274).

184 Hillam (1985a: 37); Brigham (2001b: 30, 43).

185 G.Milne (1985: 46–9); Brigham (2001b: 43) (PDN81).

186 Brigham (2001b: 43).

187 Brigham (2001b: 30, 44).

188 This involved the removal of the medieval bridge which had been built close to the site of the Roman Bridge 3.

189 Brigham (2001b: 49).

190 See Rogers (2013: 125–8) for the significance of the Roman bridges as crossing points that are neither land nor water. See Braund (1996: 91–4) and Campbell (2012: 67, 128–40, 164–7, 370–8) for the political context of the construction of certain bridges, their roles during acts of conquest and the association of rivers with deities in the Roman world.

191 Rhodes (1991); Brigham (2001b: 34–5). These were found between 1824 and 1841 during the building of London Bridge.

192 Rhodes (1991: 187–90, Fig. 2).

193 Hassall and Tomlin (1987: 360, n. 5). They have taken the name 'Metunus' to represent a 'Vulgar' pronunciation and spelling of 'Neptunus'.

194 Brigham and Watson (1996: 68); G. Milne (1985: 27).

195 Brigham (1998a: 25); Swift (2008: 20–4).

196 Brigham (1998a: 27).

197 Brigham, Watson and Tyres (1996: 36); Brigham (1998a: 27) (KWS94).

198 Brigham, Watson and Tyres (1996: 96–8); Brigham (1998a: 27).

199 Brigham, Watson and Tyres (1996: 96–8); Shepherd and Wardle (2015: 99).

200 Brigham, Watson and Tyres (1996: 38). See Millett and Gowland (2016) for the rituals that accompanied the burial of infants in Roman Britain and the observation that babies and young children were often deposited within or in close proximity to domestic buildings.

201 Brigham and Watson (1996: 64); Brigham (1998a: 27); Hassall and Tomlin (1996: 446–8).

202 See Hingley (2006).

203 G. Milne (1985: 24–9) (PDN81; ILA79).

204 See G. Milne (1985: 29) and Bateman (1985: 73–5) for 'Buildings 1 and 2'.

205 Swift (2008: 20–4, 33) (AUT01).

206 Brigham (2001c: 17–19, 45) (SUF94).

207 Brigham (2001c: 19); Tyers and Boswijk (2001: 120).

208 See T. Bradley and Butler (2008: ix, 12–14, 64–5) for the evidence for the waterfront from 99–101 Queen Victoria Street (Salvation Army International Headquarters) (QUV01).

209 T. Bradley and Butler (2008: 12–14, 64–5).

210 Swift (2008: 33).

211 Miller (1982: 145–6) and G. Milne (1985: 27) have discussed the houses at Miles Lane (ILA79).

212 Brigham and Watson (1996: 64); Brigham (1998a: 29 n. 10) (KWS94).

213 See Willis (2011: 183, Tables 1 and 2) for the frequency of samian pottery at sites across Britannia, including the evidence for Londinium; this indicates that excavated samples from London and Southwark generally display high percentages of samian through the second half of the first century and into the early second century (often over 10 per cent by weight). Willis has attributed this to the high status of Londinium, the culture of its occupants and also the role of the port as an entry point for shipments of samian. The evidence for the importation of this pottery has often been regarded as indicative of Londinium's vital role at this time in the trade of other manufactured items (Fulford 2004: 315).

214 Pritchard (1986: 171–5, Fig. 2).

215 Holder (2007: 23–5).

216 Unfortunately these labels rarely provide information about the produce that they accompanied.

217 See G. Milne (1985: 27, 29, Figs 13 and 14) for 'Building 7' (PDN81).

218 Neal and Cosh (2009: 399, 432–4) (mosaic 370.73); Collingwood and Wright (1992: 92) (RIB 2448.13). The recording made of this inscription in 1887 has confused the name of the donor (Neal and Cosh 2009: 399).

219 G. Milne (1985: 29).

220 See Schofield (1998: 283–4) for interim results of the Fleet Valley project (VAL88) which was undertaken in the late 1980s and early 1990s but has yet to be fully published.

221 Schofield (1998: 284).

222 L. Wheeler (2009: 66–77).

223 Cowan et al. (2009: Figs 5, 7 and 8).

224 See Cowan (2003: 15–20) (28PS84[2]; CWS85; CO88[2]; 52SOS89) and Taylor-Wilson (2002: 7–19) for Hunts House (HHO97) in Guy's Channel.

225 Drummond-Murray and Thompson (2002: 59–60); Cowan and Wardle (2009: 102) (BGH95).

226 Drummond-Murray and Thompson (2002: 59–60).

227 See Dunwoodie, Harward and Pitt (2015: 76–7, Fig. 62) for the most recent discussion of roads, which modifies some of the information shown on the Museum of London map (2011). The road that runs northwards from the

east side of the forum-basilica has been shown on a slightly more northeasterly alignment than on the Museum of London map. The figures in this present book have adopted the general amendments suggested by Dunwoodie to the roads east and north of the forum, although the course of this particular road follows that shown on the Museum of London map. The alignment of this road shown on Dunwoodie's map would not coincide with the assumed location of the gate in the Roman wall at Bishopsgate. This demonstrates the considerable degree of uncertainty regarding the exact location of many of the streets in the urban area of Londinium.

228 Dunwoodie, Harward and Pitt (2015: 77–8).

229 Leary and Butler (2012: 79).

230 Swain and Williams (2008: 39).

231 Swain and Williams have suggested that the population may have peaked in AD 200 to around 30,000.

232 Tomlin (1996); Collingwood and Wright (1992: 20–1) (RIB 2443.19).

233 Tomlin (1996: 215).

234 Perring (2002: 206–8).

235 Perring ((1991) 2011: 11–12, 76–7).

236 Cowan (2003: 81).

237 J. Hill and Rowsome (2011: 83–129, 309, 312–13) (ONE94).

238 J. Hill and Rowsome (2011: 127–61).

239 J. Hill and Rowsome (2011: 161–5).

240 See J. Hill and Rowsome (2011: 316–18) for 'Building 18/48'.

241 See J. Hill and Rowsome (2011: 316–18) for 'Building 18/48'.

242 J. Hill and Rowsome (2011: 317); Goodburn, Goffin and Hill (2011: 428).

243 Dungworth and Stallybrass (2011); Wardle (2011b).

244 J. Hill and Rowsome (2011: 114–21, 322–4); J. Hill, Peacock and Williams (2011: 350–1). See Shaffrey (2015) for a summary of the information for intensive milling practices in Roman Britain which lists five millstones from 1 Poultry.

245 Jackson et al. (2013) (BZY10).

246 Wilmott (1991: 177).

247 J. Hill and Rowsome (2011: 321).

248 C. Maloney (1990: 26); Wilmott (1991: 175–7); Merrifield and Hall (2008).

249 Merrifield (1997); Merrifield and Hall (2008: 126).

250 Wilmott (1991: 170–2); Harward, Powers and Watson (2015: 105). Merrifield and Hall (2008: 126) have suggested that many of the items deposited in and around the Walbrook are derived from the collecting and discard of scrap material by metalworkers when industrial premises were being abandoned in the middle of the second century (cf. Wilmott 1991: 178–80), although this does not necessarily explain the remarkable concentration of items from the long sequences of dumping (Merrifield 1997: 28).

251 J. Hill and Rowsome (2011: 322).

252 Rayner (2011d).

253 Wardle (2011a: 349).

254 N. Crummy (2008: 218–19); Leary and Butler (2012: 84–6); Rogers (2013: 202–3).

255 Leary and Butler (2012: 84–6) have suggested that the deposition of certain items after periods of flooding at 6–8 Tokenhouse Yard (THY01) might have related to rituals associated with water. This interpretation may be more widely applicable to activities throughout the Walbrook Valley and elsewhere across Londinium.

256 Campbell (2012: 128–40).

257 J. Hill and Rowsome (2011: 310, 313, 443).

258 Pitt and Seeley (2014: 26–35) (POU05).

259 S. Watson (2004) (OJW98).

260 See Bryan, Hill and Watson (2016: 37–51) for an interim discussion (BZY10).

261 Bryan, Hill and Watson (2016: 32).

262 Tomlin (2016).

263 The thorough excavation and recording of these deposits have allowed the contexts of these writing tablets to be considered in detail.

264 Bryan, Hill and Watson (2016: 42).

265 Bryan, Hill and Watson (2016: 42–5).

266 Bryan, Hill and Watson (2016: 45–9).

267 Bryan, Hill and Watson (2016: 45).

268 Bryan, Hill and Watson (2016: 51).

269 Bryan, Hill and Watson (2016: 49).

270 Bryan, Hill and Watson (2016: 49).

271 Perring (1991a: 26–9) (WAT78).

272 Perring (1991a: 30).

273 Perring (1991a: 30–41).

274 See Perring (2002: 64–72) for the town houses of Roman Britain.

275 See Perring (1991b: 104) for 'Building D'. The southern parts of this potential courtyard building were not excavated and this may equally possibly have been an elaborate strip-building.

276 Perring (1991a: 30).

277 Perring (2002: 161).

278 Neal and Cosh (2009: 399, 450–1) (mosaics 370.97 and 370.98).

279 Neal and Cosh (2009: 450–1) (mosaic 370.100).

280 Perring (1991b: 104).

281 See Perring (1991a: 30, 36–7) for 'Building F'.

282 Neal and Cosh (2009: 451–2) (mosaic 370.102).

283 Wallace-Hadrill (1988: 46–7), Perring (2002: 209–11) and Hales (2003: 171–2) have discussed opulence, hospitality and patronage in Roman houses.

284 See Perring (1991a: 37–8) for 'Buildings H, K and L'.

285 Perring (1991b: 85–6).

286 Perring (1991a: 41); Perring (1991b: 105). Collingwood and Wright (1990: 11–13) (RIB 2401.5).

287 Perring (1991b: 105).

288 Collingwood and Wright (1990: 12).

289 Elsden (2002: 14–17) (CAO96).

290 Howell (2013: 18) (BBB05).

291 Howell (2013: 18, 28).

292 The impact of later truncation on Roman deposits is fully assessed in Chapter 7.

293 Howell (2013: 28–31).

294 Excavation strategies that have been directed primarily toward the uncovering and publishing of buildings and other structures may have resulted in the extent of undeveloped ground, including gardens, being underestimated within Londinium (Cowan 2008: 75, 80).

295 Cowan (2008: 75). See von Stackelberg (2009: 65–72) for Roman gardens as social and cultural spaces. Many of the more ornate houses of Londinium will have had associated gardens which played a part in enacting emerging identities among the urban elites of the empire.

296 Cowan (2008: 80). One way of considering this issue further would be to study sites in Londinium that have not produced evidence for any intensive Roman occupation.

297 S. Watson (2015a: 13–16) (CDP04).

298 See S. Watson (2015a: 14, Fig. 13) for 'Building 12'. Neal and Cosh (2009: 452–3) have suggested that the building was destroyed in the 'Hadrianic fire' as the mosaic (370.105) had been burned. The full publication of the excavation (S. Watson 2015a: 14) has noted that the surface of this mosaic was burned but does not explicitly connect this to the fire event of the AD 120s–130s.

299 S. Watson (2015a: 16–23, Fig. 19) (GHM05).

300 S. Watson (2015a: 24, 35–6).

301 S. Watson (2015a: 19).

302 S. Watson (2015a: 29–30).

303 Casson, Drummond-Murray and Francis (2014: 25–62) (GSM97).

304 Casson, Drummond-Murray and Francis (2014: 55).

305 Casson, Drummond-Murray and Francis (2014: 80–7).

306 S. Watson (2006: 30–45).

307 S. Watson (2006: 30–2, 39) (NGT00).

308 S. Watson (2006: 31).

309 S. Watson (2006: 39).

310 S. Watson (2006: 33–8, 40–5) (PNS01); (SLY00).

311 S. Watson (2006: 34).

312 Schofield (2011: 29, 336–7) (PCH85).

313 Roskams (1991a: 13–17) (GPO75).

314 See Roskams (1991a: 13–14) for 'Buildings J and K'.

315 Perring (1991b: 102–4).

316 Perring (1991b: 101–5). See Perring (2002: 55–60) for strip-buildings in Londinium and at other urban sites across Britain.

317 Lyon (2007: 16–29) (GCC98; KEW98).

318 Pitt (2006: 6–12, 49) (NEG98); Bentley and Pritchard (1982: 135–6) (BAR79).

319 Shepherd (2012: 146–54).

320 See Howe and Lakin (2004: 15–24, 48–50) and Lyon (2005: 154–8) for this settlement and industry.

321 See Howe and Lakin (2004: 20–1, 24, 49) for occupation including 'Building 3' on the sites at 90–2 and 100 Wood Street (W0097), Shelly House (NST94) and Garrard House (GAH95).

322 Bateman, Cowan and Wroe-Brown (2008: 116).

323 See Merrifield and Hall (2008: Fig. 3.2.1) for the division between the upper and middle Walbrook Valley.

324 Seeley and Drummond-Murray (2005: 5–6).

325 C. Maloney (1990: x); Wilmott (1991: 168–72); Perring ((1991) 2011: 52).

326 See Leary and Butler (2012: 13, 80) for excavated evidence from 6–8 Tokenhouse Yard (THY01), for a substantial flood in around AD 70–120 and for comparable deposits in other parts of the Walbrook Valley.

327 Bateman, Cowan and Wroe-Brown (2008: 116–18); C. Maloney (1990: x, 119–22, 124); T. Williams (2003: 244); Merrifield and Hall (2008: 121, 124); Leary and Butler (2012: 5).

328 Leary and Butler (2012: 80); Wardle and Shepherd (2015: 36).

329 C. Maloney (1990: 26, 44–6).

330 C. Maloney (1990: 120); Leary and Butler (2012: 79).

331 See Pre-Construct Archaeology (2009) and Hawkins (2009: 37–42; 109–13) for interim reports (DGT06).

332 The excavated evidence may suggest that this work began around AD 50–70 (Leary and Butler 2012: 8–14, 79–80) (THY01).

333 Mould (2012).

334 Redfern and Bonney (2014: 216) (LOW88).

335 See Schofield (1998: 242) for an interim report (BLM87).

336 Wardle (2015b: 9–15) (BAZ05).

337 See Keily and Shepherd (2005: 147–8, Fig. 170) for interim information (MGT87).

338 McKenzie (2012: 3–8) (TEA98).

339 C. Milne, G. Milne and Brigham (1992: 13–17); G. Milne and Wardle (1996: 30–52) (LCT84).

340 G. Milne and Wardle (1996: 30–2).

341 G. Milne and Wardle (1996: 32–7); C. Milne, G. Milne and Brigham (1992: 16).

342 C. Milne, G. Milne and Brigham (1992: 13–14).

343 G. Brown and Pye (1992) (WIV88).

344 Dunwoodie, Harward and Pitt (2015: 106).

345 Dunwoodie, Harward and Pitt (2015: 79–81) (FER97).

346 Dunwoodie, Harward and Pitt (2015: 82–102, 107–8).

347 Dunwoodie, Harward and Pitt (2015: 107).

348 Dunwoodie, Harward and Pitt (2015: 99, 107, 108–9).

349 Wroe-Brown (2014: 29–42) (FEU08).

350 Pitt (2015: 158–63) (EAE01).

351 Bluer and Brigham (2006: 10–27) (FCC95).

352 Bluer and Brigham (2006: 13).

353 Bluer and Brigham (2006: 18–27).

354 Birbeck and Schuster (2009: 16–27); Andrews (2009) (FNE01).

355 Lerz and Holder (2016: 139–41) (ARC81/SEN91/MCF06).

356 Blair and Sankey (2007: 54–7) (ESC97).

357 Blair and Sankey (2007: 56).

358 Swift (2008: 24–33) (AUT01).

359 The substantial quantities of building material, painted plaster and small fragments of mosaic that was dumped as infill during the construction of Waterfront 3 are thought to have been derived from these buildings. Swift (2008: 35, 50–3) has discussed the fragments of mosaic. Neal and Cosh (2009: 404) have noted that this fine mosaic (370.1) was broken up for inclusion in the construction of the river frontage.

360 Swift (2008: 35–6).

361 Swift (2008 Ibid.: 27–31); Blair et al. (2006: 28–36). The three wells at 30 Gresham Street, the Cheapside bathhouse and 12 Arthur Street were much more substantial than numerous other Roman wells that have been excavated across London (T. Williams 2003: 244–5).

362 Marsden (1975: 54–60, 72–3).

363 Brigham (2001c) (SUF94).

364 Brigham (2001c: 31–3, 45).

365 Brigham (2001c: 31–3, 45).

366 Dennis and Ward (2001).

367 See Cowan (1995: 15–35) for the complex of buildings at 15–23 Southwark Street that is often titled the 'mansio' (15SKS80). See Drummond-Murray and Thompson (2002: 127–39) for the later excavations at Redcross Way (RWT93) which explored the south-western part of the same building complex.

368 Cowan (1995: 34).

369 Cowan (1995: 32).

370 Goffin (1995: 157–9).

371 Cowan (1995: 32, 35–53).

372 Cowan (1995: 33–4).

373 Cowan (1995: 33).

374 Neal and Cosh (2009: 457).

375 Yule (2005: 26–32).

376 Yule (2005: 49); Goffin (2005: 104–20) (WP83).

377 Yule (2005: 104, 12).

378 Yule (2005: 32–45, 74–5).

379 Yule (2005: 38).

380 See Cowan (2003: 24, 26) for dumped building material at Courage Brewery Area Q (28 Park Street) (28PS84[1]).

381 Cowan (2003: 23).

382 Drummond-Murray and Thompson (2002: 59–90); Cowan and Pringle (2009: 89) (BGH95).

383 See Fairman and Taylor (2013: 126–7) for an interim report (BVK11).

384 Brigham (2001a: 13–24) (TW84) and (FW83/FW84).

385 Brigham (2001a: 13).

386 Drummond-Murray and Thompson (2002: 71–7) (LBI95).

387 Drummond-Murray and Thompson (2002: 71).

388 Cowan et al. (2009: 18, 19). Part of the problem with assessing the occupation of the south island throughout the first to fourth centuries is the comparative absence of excavations across the west of this area (Cowan et al. 2009: Fig. 1). Recent excavations have suggested that there was a cemetery in the western area of this island that may have been established during the second century and used until the fourth.

389 Cowan and Wardle (2009: 107–8, Fig. 84) (120BHS89/124BHS77).

390 Marsh (1978) (8US74); Schwab (1978) (106BHS73); Ferretti and Graham (1978) (207BHS72).

391 Heard (1989) and Cowan et al. (2009: 18, 183–4) (USA88/USB88).

392 Douglas (2008: 23–5) (LGK99).

393 Cowan et al. (2009: 19); Cowan and Pringle (2009: 80) (175BHS76/179BHS89).

394 Wardle (2009: 129–39).

395 Wardle (2009: 129–32).

396 Wardle (2009: 119).

397 Cowan and Pringle (2009: 80); Wardle (2009: 141).

398 See Drummond-Murray, Saxby and Watson (1994: 254–5) for pits, ditches and occupation of Iron Age and early Roman date from sites on Horselydown eyot (TOS93; TOY94). See Leary (2004: 287) for the idea that occupation at 285–91 Tooley Street (TLT00) started in the late Iron Age and may have ceased by the AD 60s or 70s.

399 Heard (1996: 78–80); McKinley (2006: 89); Cowan et al. (2009: 24); L. Wheeler (2009: 77); Cowan and Wardle (2009: 117). Building material has been found at several sites to the west of Bermondsey eyot, although the truncation and reworking of these deposits makes them difficult to interpret (Heard 1996: 78, 80).

400 Killock et al. (2015: 12–18, 238–9) (LLS02).

401 Killock et al. (2015: 19–24, 240).

402 Killock et al. (2015: 240).

403 Cowan et al. (2009: 185) (223BHS81).

404 Wilson (2006: 15–17); Lyon (2007: 31).

405 Esmonde Cleary (2003) has discussed the urban boundaries of towns in Britain and the western provinces and shows that many civil defences are of later second-century date. The character of earlier boundaries around cities and towns has not been very fully researched.

406 Hunt (2011: 48–50, Fig. 6). Perring (2011a: 256–7) has suggested that the potential boundary feature at Drapers' Gardens (DGT06) in the upper Walbrook Valley may have formed part of the same circuit. The interim reports on the Drapers' Gardens excavation (Pre-Construct Archaeology 2009: 9; Hawkins 2009: 109) have suggested that the timber corduroy structure, dated by tree-ring analysis to around AD 62,
may have formed a timber track or an embankment or rampart on the northern edge of Londinium, but it was not in use for long and could pre-date the other sections of the urban boundary identified by Hunt. Other ditches of late first-century date found in London have been referred to by Perring (2011a: 256–7), but these do not necessarily constitute a single line of defensive works. Dunwoodie, Harward and Pitt (2015: 71–2) have discussed other possible defensive ditches across eastern Londinium.

407 The fill of a ditch dug with a v-shaped cross-section at Baltic House (BAX95) contained pottery dating from AD 70–100 (Howe 2002: 6–9). Schofield (1998: 232) has discussed another ditch with an alignment of post pits on its eastern side at 9 Northumberland Avenue (NHA86). Three parallel boundary ditches have been excavated just to the west of the Roman wall at 8–14 Cooper's Row and 1 America Square (Hunt 2011: 48–50, Fig. 5) (CPW99/CPQ03/CRZ06).

408 Hunt (2011: 48–50).

409 Hunt (2011: 50). Watling Street and Stane Street on the south bank of the Thames in Southwark formed a comparable junction at the southern edge of Londinium.

410 Wilson (2006: 3–6).

411 At Verulamium, several ditches enclosed the town during the first and second centuries AD (Niblett 2005: 62–3, Fig. 4.72; Wilson 2006: 17–18). During the mid-second century the urban area was at least partly defined by a ditch known as 'Fosse' that followed an irregular course and may not have been continuous (Wilson 2006: 155–6). There may have been a sequence of ditched circuits that surrounded the town of Calleva during the late first century BC to the late second century AD, some of which were probably discontinuous (Creighton and Fry 2016: 322–7; Fig. 9.9).

412 Hall (2005).

413 Hall (2005).

414 Brigham (1998a: 27).

415 Dunwoodie, Harward and Pitt (2015: 99, 107, 108–9).

416 Drummond-Murray and Thompson (2002: 96–7) (BGH95; JSS92).

417 Drummond-Murray and Thompson (2002: 61–2, 97).

418 See Goodman (2007: 105–12) for the complex relationship between industries and urban peripheries in Roman Gaul.

419 Merrifield (1997: 36–9). See Hingley (1997b) and Scott (2017: 301–2) for the ritual associations of ironworking in Iron Age and Roman society. An assessment of contexts of Roman date may suggest that boundary places for the deposition of iron and other objects were still significant at this time (e.g. Hingley 2006: 227–9).

420 Schofield (2011: 34, 330) has called this 'kiln 1'.

421 Schofield (2011: 34–6, 326) has called this 'kiln 2'. Marsden (1969: 39–40), Shepherd (1988: 28) and Sloane (2008: 11) have also described this kiln which was identified by Conyers in 1677 as a pottery kiln. An illustration of the pottery recovered by Conyers from this kiln has enabled Schofield (2011: 35–6) to suggest that it may have been dumped in the area of the kiln from occupation elsewhere rather than forming a dump of kiln waste.

422 Marsden (1969: 41–4) (GM136).

423 S. Watson (2006: 76).

424 S. Watson (2006: 37–8, 75–6) (SLY00). See Betts (2017) for tile production and supply in early Roman London.

425 S. Watson (2006: 76).

426 Betts (2015: 67–8) (CDP04).

427 One problem with this interpretation is that only a single example of a tile with a procuratorial stamp was found during the excavation of the Cheapside bathhouse (Marsden 1975: 61).

428 Collingwood and Wright (1993: 30); Betts (1995: 221).

429 Hall (2005: 136–7); Seeley and Drummond-Murray (2005: 142–3); Rayner (2017: 350–7).

430 Birbeck and Schuster (2009: 13–15); Seager Smith (2009b: 55, Fig. 42); Rayner (2017: 359, 361) (FNE01). This pottery production may also have commenced prior to AD 60.

431 Seager Smith (2009a; 2009b: 55); Birbeck and Schuster (2009: 37).

432 Seager Smith (2009b: 55–6).

433 Birbeck and Schuster (2009: 17–24).

434 Seeley and Drummond-Murray (2005: 12–48) (MRG95).

435 Seeley and Drummond-Murray (2005: 142).

436 Seeley and Drummond-Murray (2005: 144–5).

437 See Keily and Shepherd (2005: 147–8, Fig. 170) for interim information (MGT87).

438 Heathcote (1988: 386); Schofield (1998: 72, 252–3).

439 Keily and Shepherd (2005: 147). Heathcote (1988: 368) has supported this dating.

440 Keily and Shepherd (2005: 147).

441 Coombe et al. (2015: 36 (no. 60)).

442 Schofield (1998: 72) (GM121).

443 Bateman, Cowan and Wroe-Brown (2008: 42–3); Perez-Sala and Shepherd (2008a); Perez-Sala and Shepherd (2008b).

444 Wardle (2015b: 15–28); Wardle and Shepherd (2015) (BAZ05).

445 Keily and Shepherd (2005: 154–5).

446 Wardle (2015b: 21).

447 Perez-Sala and Shepherd (2008a: 145).

448 See Schofield (1998: 284) for a brief summary of the industrial activity beside the Fleet (VAL88). This site is discussed in more detail by Shepherd and Wardle (2015: 24, 99–100) where it is named 18–25 Old Bailey (OBA88).

449 Perez-Sala and Shepherd (2008a: 145). Shepherd and Wardle (2015: 99–101) have noted, however, that glassworking at 18–25 Old Bailey may have continued throughout the second century.

450 Haynes (2000: 93).

451 The work close to Bucklersbury House (GM 157) was largely undertaken by Ivor Noël-Hume and W. F. Grimes in 1954–5. This included extensive works close to the temple of Mithras which only recovered fragments of the archaeological information as a result of the difficult conditions experienced by the excavators (Wilmott 1991: 18–33; Shepherd 1998: 218–19; Schofield 1998: 87).

452 See Marsden (1991) and Wilmott (1991: 98) for 'feature 8'. Cotton (1996: 89–91), Merrifield (1997: 37–8) and Haynes (2000: 91) have also discussed this site.

453 Marsden (1991: 30).

454 Shepherd (1998: 220–1); Henig (1998: Fig. 247).

455 Courage Brewery had fourteen sub-sites, labelled A to S (Cowan 2003: Table 1; Hammer 2003: Table 1). See Cowan (2003) for the archaeological information and sequence from these sites, and Hammer (2003) for the evidence for industry.

456 See Hammer (2003: 33–44) for the industrial evidence from Areas E and F (COSE84[2]; CO88[1]; CO87).

457 See Cowan and Wardle (2009: 106–7) for Area A.

458 See Cowan (2003: 20–38) for the information for 'Building 5' at Area C (COSE84[1]) that may have included a tessellated floor (Cowan 2003: 23) and the slightly later 'Building 7' at Area C that possibly had window glass (Cowan 2003: 26–30).

459 See Hammer (2003: 35, 38, 42–3) for the foreshore dumps at Area D (CO88[2]) and M (52SOS89) at Courage Brewery.

460 Dean (1980); Cowan and Wardle (2009: 109) (AB78).

461 Henig (1984: 26–32). Goodman (2007: 149–50) has discussed the connection between festivals and urban peripheries in Roman Gaul.

462 Barber and Bowsher (2000: 307–9); S. Watson (2003: 36).

463 The evidence for feasting at the cemetery sites during the later history of Londinium will be considered below.

464 Richardson (2008: 123).

465 Bateman, Cowan and Wroe-Brown (2008: 43).

466 Richardson (2008: 123).

467 Richardson (2008: 123).

468 J. Bird (2008: 135).

469 J. Bird (2008: 135, 139, Fig. 129) (RP172). It appears that these samian vessels may have been deliberately selected to be deposited in this context since many of the figures of gladiators and beasts seem rather complete.

470 See S. Watson (2015b: 188–93) and J. Bird, Thorp and Wardle (2015) for 6–12 Basinghall Street and 93–5 Gresham Street (GHB06).

471 Lyon (2007: 24–9) (GCC98; KEW98).

472 Lyon (2007: 24–5).

473 Lyon (2007: 25).

474 Lyon (2007: 25–9).

475 Lyon (2007: 25).

476 See Bateman (2008: 162) for the potential ritual function of the tazze and the presence of such items and ceramic lamps in cremations. Casson, Drummond-Murray and Francis (2014: 60) have cast some doubt on this idea as the result of the frequent occurrence of tazze in what appear to represent domestic contexts at 10 Gresham Street (GSM97).

477 Lyon (2007: 25, 29); Wardle (2007: 167).

478 Henig (1984: 43) has considered the images on the pediment of the temple at Bath, the relevance of the Medusa mask on Minerva's breastplate and the image of Minerva on the patera from Capheaton (Northumberland).

479 Lyon (2007: 29).

480 Heathcote (1988: 386); Schofield (1998: 252); Davies, Richardson and Tomber (1994: 228); Seeley and Wardle (2009: 150) (MFI87).

481 Schofield (1998: 252).

482 Lyon (2007: 29).

483 Davies, Richardson and Tomber (1994: 229). A coin of Vespasian (AD 69–79) was also found in the well (Heathcote 1988: 386).

484 Wardle (2007: 167).

485 These include a figurine of Minerva from Monument House (MFI87) which presumably came from the well containing evidence for feasting (Wardle 2007: 167). Another fragmentary ceramic figurine of Minerva was recorded in a dumping context at Plantation Place (Dunwoodie, Harward and Pitt 2015: 115, Fig. 109). A bone pin possibly representing Minerva from a third-century building just east of the amphitheatre may also have had watery associations (Wardle 2008b: 192).

486 Schaaf (1988: 113–14) (199BHS74). See Hassall (1988) and Holder (2007: 22–3) for the suggestion that these pots may have derived from communal eating or drinking customs, perhaps at an inn.

487 Holder (2007: 22–3).

488 Hammerson (1998: 245–7).

489 Barber and Bowsher (2000: 8–9).

490 Hall (1996) has discussed the available information for the four distinct cemeteries (west, north, east and south) of Roman London, while Barber and Hall (2000) have updated this information.

491 Harward, Powers and Watson (2015: 134).

492 Bentley (1982); Pritchard (1982); Hall (1996: 58–9); Barber and Hall (2000: 107–8); S. Watson (2003: 8–9, Fig. 6).

493 The extent of the information for settlement and human burial is limited by the extent of the excavated area.

494 See Bentley (1982: 159–62) and Shepherd (1988: 10–11) for assessments of the dates of burials across a large part of the western margins of Londinium from St Paul's to the Smithfield area, including individual burials outside the line of the later wall.

495 Shepherd (1988: 10–11, 26–9, Fig. 5).

496 Guildhall Museum (1969: 4–6); Marsden (1980: 76–7) (GM131).

497 Guildhall Museum (1969: 6). The limited evidence for the cemeteries at St Martins le Grand and St Paul's has been discussed above.

498 Hall (1996: 58–9).

499 J. Maloney (1983: 97, Fig. 92); S. Watson (2003: 7–8, Fig. 6).

500 Simon Esmonde Cleary (2000) has discussed the character of Roman cemeteries across Britain and has suggested that there was a distinction between burial areas in urban contexts and other less clearly defined burial practices more characteristic of small towns and rural settlements. He has argued that the town cemeteries were often well defined and located outside the urban boundaries, while those in small towns sometimes included less formal burials deposited in the backlands of properties.

501 Pitt (2006: 27–31, 49) (OBL97).

502 Pitt (2006: 29).

503 RCHM (1928: 165, Fig. 68); G. Milne and Reynolds (1997: 19–20).

504 G. Milne and Reynolds (1997: 20).

505 See Hall (1996: 64–73), Barber and Hall (2000: 108–10), Swift (2003: 21–3), Butler (2006: 40) and Harward, Powers and Watson (2015: 80) for summaries of information from the 'northern cemetery'.

506 Cass and Preston (2010) (SSZ05).

507 See Thomas, Sloane and Phillpotts (1997: 6, 13) for an interim report on Roman burials from the Central Foundation Girls' School (SPT82) and other sites close by. See Thomas (2004) for interim comments on excavation at Spitalfields (SRP98).

508 This area of Roman burials was excavated in five sub-sites, four of which produced evidence for scattered early burials. See Harward, Powers and Watson (2015: 18–20) for the burials at River Plate House (RIV87), 12–15 Finsbury Circus (FIB88), Liverpool House (ELD88) and 16–18 Finsbury Circus (ENS03). Most of these burials were dated by their stratigraphic position and only a single example was more closely dated by an associated artefact. The excavation report suggests that they all post-dated AD 50–70 (Harward, Powers and Watson 2015: 18).

509 Harward, Powers and Watson (2015: 21, 124).

510 Harward, Powers and Watson (2015: 21).

511 C. Maloney (1990: x).

512 Marsh and West (1981); C. Maloney (1990: 30–1, 124); Redfern and Bonney (2014: Table 1).

513 Hall (1996: 73–4); Barber and Hall (2000: 110–19); Barber and Bowsher (2000: 334–9).

514 See Marsden (1980: 24, 208, n. 14), Schofield (1998: 51) and Hunt (2011: 50) for burials at 112–14 Fenchurch Street and 17–18 Billiter Street (GM60).

515 See J. Maloney (1979) and Schofield (1998: 151) for interim reports (DUK77).

516 J. Maloney (1979: 293).

517 Barber and Bowsher (2000: Table 1) have listed the Museum of London site codes for the twelve individual sites included in the volume on the 'eastern cemetery'. They have discussed the tombstones from the 'eastern cemetery' that are likely to date to the first and second centuries (Barber and Bowsher 2000: 338–9). See Barber and Hall (2000: 110–12) for a summary of information for the 'eastern cemetery' and Barber and Bowsher (2000: 51, 54, 298–9) for the location and date of the 'cemetery road' and the commencement of burials across the southern part of the eastern cemetery during the late first or early second centuries.

518 Barber and Bowsher (2000: 115, 338–9).

519 Dean and Hammerson (1980); Hall (1996: 74–83); Barber and Hall (2000: 104–7); Connell (2009); Ridgeway, Leary and Sudds (2013: 104–6).

520 Seeley and Wardle (2009: 156).

521 Ridgeway, Leary and Sudds (2013: 6–7, 103).

522 Beasley (2007: 36–41, 48) (SWN98).

523 Beasley (2007: 30–3).

524 Beasley (2007: 36–41).

525 Beasley (2007: 23). Another possibility considered below is that the ditches and pits marked the edges of a temple or sacred area.

526 Ridgeway, Leary and Sudds (2013: 9–13) (LTU03).

527 Ridgeway, Leary and Sudds (2013: 9). Information from the 'Upper Walbrook Cemetery' may suggest that the bones from the ditches at Lant Street were eroded by stream water from inhumation burials that were not found during the excavation.

528 Ridgeway, Leary and Sudds (2013: 11).

529 Ridgeway, Leary and Sudds (2013: 104, 108–9).

530 Mackinder (2000: 8–9) (GDV96).

531 Beasley (2007: 59).

532 See Killock (2010: 25–7, 84, 93–4) for an interim report (TIY07).

533 Killock (2010: 84).

534 Seeley and Wardle (2009: 144, Fig. 110) (SKS88).

535 Coombe et al. (2015: 39, 62 (no. 65 and 102)).

536 Redfern and Bonney (2014: 224); Powers (2015a: 131).

537 Ferretti and Graham (1978: 65); Watt (1978a) (207BHS72). These cranial remains may have been deposited in a pre-Boudican context.

538 Perring (1991a: 26, 29, 30) (WAT78).

539 Wilmott (1982: 9, 31, Fig. 11) (GM142).

540 The deposits above the level of the natural soil had been removed which may have included building remains (Wilmott 1982: 1, 16). Although the finds from this well seemed to date it to the late first or early second

centuries, the cranial remains may have been deposited later since it was found in the upper part of the backfill.

541 See Richardson (1983: 277) and Schofield (1998: 183) for interim reports (LIB82).

542 Woodward and Woodward (2004: 77–8); Beasley (2007: 55–6, 62). See Andrews and Smith (2011: 199) for a discussion of dog bones and ritual at the temple site of Springhead (Kent) and elsewhere.

543 Rhodes (1980a: 35); M. Morgan (1980) (TR74). One of these bone fragments came from a late Roman or Saxon layer.

544 M. Morgan (1980).

545 See Marsh and West (1981: 95 (skulls 'E')) and Perring (2000: 147) for interim reports on human remains from Waterfront 2 at Regis House (KWS94). See Marsh and West (1981: 95) for the cranial remains from Upper Thames Street (skull F).

6 'Hadrianic Fires', AD 120s and 130s

1 Casson, Drummond-Murray and Francis (2014: 62).

2 Dunning (1945).

3 Dunning (1945) (GM248). This dating has subsequently been refined to around AD 120–5.

4 Perring and Roskams (1991: 119).

5 J. Hill and Rowsome (2011: 127, 161–5, 354–7); Casson, Drummond-Murray and Francis (2014: 61–2).

6 Dunning (1945: 53); Marsh (1981: 221–4); Brigham, Watson and Tyres (1996: 32).

7 Dunning excavated the materials but only published a short note. Marsh (1981: 221–4) has included a summary of the evidence for the site derived from Dunning's unpublished notes.

8 Brigham and Watson (1996: 64–6).

9 Brigham and Watson (1996: 64–6) (KWS94). Archaeomagnetic dating of two mud brick walls has produced dates suggesting that the fire may have occurred as late as AD 130 (Brigham and Watson 1996: 64). G. Milne (1985: 29) has discussed evidence for other fires in the waterfront area.

10 Swift (2008: 33–6), including some uncertainties about the dating of material from the destruction deposits incorporated in the infill of Waterfront 3 (AUT01).

11 Perring ((1991) 2011: 72–3).

12 See Schofield (1998: 193–4, 196) for interim information (FEN83; LIM83)

13 Perring (1991a: 38, 41) (WAT 78).

14 Perring (1991a: 72–3).

15 Roskams (1991a: 17) (GPO75).

16 See J. Hill and Rowsome (2011: 355–7) (ONE94) for a discussion of the character and date of these burnt deposits, including a detailed assessment of the dating of the ceramics, particularly the stamped samian. This report also compared this material to the ceramics found from earlier excavations that have uncovered burned deposits thought to derive from the Hadrianic fire horizon (J. Hill and Rowsome 2011: 355–7).

17 J. Hill and Rowsome (2011: 127–9, 354–5).

18 J. Hill and Rowsome (2011: 354–5).

19 J. Hill and Rowsome (2011: 161–5).

20 J. Hill and Rowsome (2011: 357) (BUC87).

21 Casson, Drummond-Murray and Francis (2014: 61–2) (GSM97).

22 Casson, Drummond-Murray and Francis (2014: 61–2).

23 S. Watson (2015a: 29–30) (CDP04).

24 S. Watson (2015a: 30).

25 Blair et al. (2006: 18–26) (GHT00).

26 Blair et al. (2006: 20).

27 Blair et al. (2006: 26).

28 Marsden (1976: 34–8); Blair et al. (2006: 39).

29 S. Watson (2006: 46–8, 52–5).

30 S. Watson (2006: 46–8) (PNS01; PSU99).

31 S. Watson (2006: 48) (SLY00).

32 S. Watson (2006: 52–5) (NGT00).

33 Lyon (2007: 29–30, 33) (GCC98; KEW98).

34 Sankey (2003: 4–7) (ETA89).

35 Blair and Sankey (2007: 57) (ESC97).

36 Dunwoodie, Harward and Pitt (2015: 117–18) (FER97).

37 Wroe-Bown (2014: 50) (FEU08).

38 Dunwoodie, Harward and Pitt (2015: 118).

39 Bluer and Brigham (2006: 18, 27), including problems with the dating of this material (FCC95).

40 Bateman, Cowan and Wroe-Brown (2008: 118–19); Howe and Lakin (2004: 50).

41 Rayner (2009: 46, Table 2).

7 Londinium's Peak of Development from AD 125 to AD 200

1 See Perring ((1991) 2011: 57–89) for the fullest recent assessment of Londinium at this time. See Perring (2011a: 262–3) and Perring (2011b) for more recent assessments. The Roman walls were probably constructed around the end of the second century and will be addressed in Chapter 8.

2 Perring ((1991) 2011: 57, 76–8); Perring (2011b); Perring (2015: 32–3). This idea draws upon earlier accounts, including the work of Sheldon (1978: 36–7) and Marsden (1980: 110–17), which suggested a reduction in the extent of building activity across London after around AD 130 or 150.

3 Tomlin (2016: 56, 138–9) has noted that Bloomberg Writing Tablet 37, dated to around AD 65 or 70 to 80, may refer to Londinium as a *civitas* and therefore that it was not a colony or *municipium* at this date.

4 Schofield (1998: 266); Tomlin (2006); Tomlin, Wright and Hassall (2009: 25) (RIB 3006).

5 Tomlin (2006).

6 The writing tablets that have been fully published mostly date to the first century AD.

7 Tomlin, Wright and Hassall (2009: 33–6).

8 Blagg (2000: 62).

9 Shepherd (2012: 166–9) has listed military inscriptions from London, but none of these clearly date from the period covered by this chapter.

10 Tomlin, Wright and Hassall (2009: 30).

11 Holder (2007: 29–31).

12 Barber and Bowsher (2000: 310–11).

13 Eckardt (2010a); Eckardt (2010b); Eckardt (2014: 77–9); Montgomery et al. (2010).

14 Ridgeway, Leary and Sudds (2013: 114–15); Redfern et al. (2016) (LTU03).

15 Redfern et al. (2016: 14).

16 Redfern et al. (2016: 17–19, Table 4). This includes discussion of the provisional character of these identifications.

17 Ridgeway, Leary and Sudds (2013: 109, 114); Rebecca Redfern (pers. comm.). The suggestion of people with African ancestry has been derived from the analysis of grave goods included in a fourth-century burial and also the ancestral analysis of skulls, including first-century examples. See Eckardt (2014: 63–91) for other evidence for people with African ancestry in Roman Britain.

18 Shaw et al. (2016: 65, 66).

19 See Rowsome (1999: 263–73), Schofield (1998: 265–6) and Rogers (2011a: 136) for interim reports and comments (DMT88).

20 A number of excavations have been undertaken on this building complex (see Chapter 3). The north part of the larger second forum-basilica extended further north than the earlier building and has been excavated at Leadenhall Court (G. Milne 1992) (LCT84).

21 Marsden (1987: 39, 74); Perring ((1991) 2011: 58); Brigham (1992a: 81); Laurence, Esmonde Cleary and Seers (2011: 185). Several excavations have been conducted to explore particular parts of the forum and basilica but the information for its plan and chronology is limited due to the small area that has been available and the damage to the Roman deposits by later developments.

22 Marsden (1987: 39); Dunwoodie (2004: 32).

23 Bateman (1998: 50). Laurence, Esmonde Cleary and Seers (2011: 184) have described it as 'colossal'.

24 The forum-basilica complexes at Augst (Switzerland) and Bavai (France), for example, appear to have been far more ornate (Laurence, Esmonde Cleary and Seers 2011: Figs 7.6, 7.9 and 7.10).

25 C. Milne, G. Milne and Brigham (1992: 17–25); Davies (1992: 68–9). See Brigham (1990b: 58–62) and Brigham (1992b: 83–4) for the evidence that the basilica was constructed in several phases and over a protracted period of time.

26 Brigham (1992b: 88–93, Fig. 31).

27 The argument for the late date for the south range of the forum is based primarily upon evidence for differences in the character of the construction of this range from those on the west and east and also upon the idea that the original forum remained in use and was not demolished until the final stages in the completion of the second forum-basilica (Marsden 1987: 39–40, Fig. 27). The subsequent excavations at 168 Fenchurch Street (FEH95) have also indicated that the south wing was constructed in a different manner from the east wing (Dunwoodie 2004: 33).

28 Brigham (1992c: 101–2).

29 Brigham (1990b: 83); Brigham (1992c: 100).

30 Brigham (1992b: 84–5); Brigham (1992c: 92).

31 Brigham (1990b: 92).

32 Brigham (1992c: 98).

33 Dunwoodie (2004: 32).

34 Dunwoodie (2004: 32). These piers may have been a secondary feature of the first forum.

35 The courtyard may have been on a single level or on two different levels (Brigham 1992b: 92). A feature in the centre of the courtyard has been interpreted as a sunken pool (Marsden 1987: 64–5) and a colonnaded east–west walkway (Brigham 1992b: 92).

36 Revell (2009: 70); Laurence, Esmonde Cleary and Seers (2011: 185).

37 Laurence, Esmonde Cleary and Seers (2011: 185–6).

38 Toynbee (1964: 50–1); Coombe et al. (2015: 115–16 (no. 213)).

39 Henig (2000: 63, 67); Opper (2008: 80–2); Coombe et al. (2015: 116).

40 Toynbee (1964: 51).

41 Bayley et al. (2009: 157–9).

42 C. Milne, G. Milne and Brigham (1992: 25).

43 C. Milne, G. Milne and Brigham (1992: 25). See Wacher (1995: 92) for doubts about the idea that these rooms constituted a row of shops opening to the north.

44 Brigham (1990b: 65–73); C. Milne, G. Milne and Brigham (1992: 25–8); Brigham (1992b: 84–7).

45 Brigham (1990b: 71, 73).

46 Marsden (1987: 67).

47 Bateman, Cowan and Wroe-Brown (2008: 39–62, 101–14).

48 The dating evidence has mostly been derived from the finds included in the backfill of features associated with the earlier timber phase (Bateman, Cowan and Wroe-Brown 2008: 51, 54–5, 61).

49 Bateman, Cowan and Wroe-Brown (2008: 125–6).

50 Bateman, Cowan and Wroe-Brown (2008: 113–14).

51 Bateman, Cowan and Wroe-Brown (2008: 46–62).

52 Bateman, Cowan and Wroe-Brown (2008: 48).

53 Bateman, Cowan and Wroe-Brown (2008: 55–7).

54 Bateman, Cowan and Wroe-Brown (2008: 50–1).

55 Bateman, Cowan and Wroe-Brown (2008: 51).

56 Bateman, Cowan and Wroe-Brown (2008: 53–5).

57 Bateman, Cowan and Wroe-Brown (2008: 63–72).

58 Bateman, Cowan and Wroe-Brown (2008: 57–8, 69–72).

59 C. Maloney (2007: 62) (GSJ06). This building appears to have had the usual double square form of a Romano-Celtic temple.

60 Bateman, Cowan and Wroe-Brown (2008: 118).

61 Nick Bateman (pers. comm.).

62 Bateman (2008).

63 It has been suggested that this stone fort might have been preceded by a less substantial fort, possibly built during the AD 90s (Perring (1991) 2010: 39–40; Perring 2000: 126; Mattingly 2006: 265), although the excavations have suggested that this was not the case (Howe and Lakin 2004: xiii, 24; Shepherd and Chettle 2012: 153).

64 Grimes had been investigating areas of the city damaged by bombs during the Second World War in order to explore discrepancies in the course and sequence of the construction of the Roman walls when he located the deeply-buried remains of the fort (Grimes 1968: 15–46).

65 The full publication of the work undertaken by Grimes was delayed by the quantity of analytical work required on the finds and by a lack of funds. These excavations have now been synthesized and published (Shepherd 2012).

66 Guildhall Museum (1968: 7–10).

67 See Howe and Lakin (2004: 25–41, 53–9) for excavations in the fort's southern area between 1992 and 1998. Additional excavations include 25 Gresham Street (Lyon 2005) (NHG98) and at Aldersgate (Butler 2002) (AES96/PLH97).

68 Howe and Lakin (2004: 15–24); Shepherd and Chettle (2012: 144–54).

69 Shepherd and Chettle (2012: 154, 155).

70 Howe and Lakin (2004: 50).

71 Shepherd (2012: 51–3, 59–61, 70, 126–33).

72 See Howe and Lakin (2004: 39, Table 7) for a careful consideration of the available evidence, which has noted that some of the pottery incorporated in fort construction deposits could date from as late as AD 160.

73 See Perring ((1991) 2011: 39–40), Howe and Lakin (2004: 53–9) and Shepherd (2012) for the excavated evidence for various features of the fort.

74 See Guildhall Museum (1968: 8) for this work by Peter Marsden (GM4).

75 See Butler (2002: 45, Fig. 4) for 1–6 Aldersgate (AES96/PLH97).

76 Guildhall Museum (1968: 8); Peter Marsden (pers. comm.).

77 See Shepherd (2012: 79–84, 88–90) for the interval tower and a corner tower from Grimes' excavations. See Lyon (2005: 159, Fig. 3) for the information for a second interval tower south of the fort at 25 Gresham Street (NHG98).

78 See Shepherd (2012: 56–78) for the west gate at Falcon Square, the remains of which are preserved in a basement close to the Museum of London and can be visited by prior arrangement.

79 Howe and Lakin (2004: 25–41, 57–9, Fig. 49).

80 Howe and Lakin (2004: 54).

81 Howe and Lakin (2004: 55).

82 Grimes (1968: 34–5); Peter Marsden (pers. comm.).

83 See Butler (2002: 45–7) for 1–6 Aldersgate (AES96/PLH97).

84 Howe and Lakin (2004: 58); Shepherd and Chettle (2012: 142).

85 Hassall (2012).

86 Philp (1981). The first, supposedly unfinished, fort at Dover was not closely dated but may relate to the first decade of the century (Philp 1981: 91–3). The second fort is more closely dated to around AD 130–40 (Philp 1981: 93).

87 Two fragments of tile with CL BR stamps were found at Winchester Palace in the demolition debris from 'Buildings 13 and 14', while single additional fragments of this type have been excavated at 117 Borough High Street and Hunt's House, Guy's Hospital (Crowley and Betts 1992: 219–20; Crowley 2005: 92–3; Yule 2005: 69, 75; Cowan et al. 2009: 169).

88 Crowley (2005: 93, 94).

89 Crowley and Betts (1992: 219); Marsden (1994: 17); Crowley (2005: 92).

90 G. Milne (2000).

91 The *classis Britannica* was commanded by the provincial governor although the fleet's immediate commander was a *praefectus*, a senior administrative officer (Roger Tomlin pers. comm.).

92 Fischer (2002); Handel (2002).

93 Marsden (1994: 17, Fig. 6).

94 Henig and Ross (1998).

95 Coulston (2000: 82–4, Fig. 5.9). I am very grateful to Roger Tomlin for this suggestion.

96 Coulston (2000: 82, Fig. 5.1).

97 Roger Tomlin (pers. comm.).

98 Shepherd and Chettle (2012: 156–7).

99 Guildhall Museum (1968: 9); Lyon (2005: 163). Much of the extensive deposit of pottery dumped in the eastern ditch, filling a boggy hollow, dated to the late second and third centuries (Guildhall Museum 1968: 9) (GM4). This included a large quantity of animal bone, a large portion of a human skull and three almost complete cooking pots, all of which appeared to have been placed in the ditch around the same time.

100 Howe and Lakin (2004: 46, 52); Lyon (2005: 164); Shepherd and Chettle (2012: 157).

101 Howe and Lakin (2004: 47).

102 Brigham (1990a: 135); Brigham (1998a: 29–30).

103 Brigham (1990a: 135–7, Fig. 13) and Brigham (1998a: 29–30) have defined Waterfronts 3 to 5 (cf. G. Milne 1985: 29–32). Museum of London (2011) has located these successive waterfronts.

104 Marsden (1994: 26).

105 Brigham (1990a: 143). The prime evidence for this suggestion is the location and height of the successive waterfronts. The discovery of the County Hall ship upstream of the Roman wharves, however, suggests that the river was navigable by seagoing ships during the late third century.

106 Brigham (1990a: Fig. 13); Brigham (1998a: 29, n. 10).

107 Brigham (1998a: 30, n. 12); Brigham (2001c: 20–1, 46); Tyers and Boswijk (2001).

108 Swift (2008: 34–5, 57) (AUT01).

109 G. Milne (1985: 29–31).

110 Brigham (1990a: 135–7, Fig. 13); Brigham (1998a: 29–30); G. Milne (1985: 29–32).

111 Brigham (1990a: 127, 136) has reinterpreted the excavations reported in Miller and Schofield (1986a: 31–2) and Miller and Schofield (1986b: 63) for the first phase of waterfront works at New Fresh Wharf (NFW74/SM75/FRE78).

112 Brigham (1990a: 111, 135–6) (SWA81).

113 Mackinder (2015: 7–11) (RKH06).

114 Mackinder (2015: 9).

115 Brigham (1990a: 136–7) has discussed Waterfront 5 and the individual excavations along its line.

116 Miller and Schofield (1986a: 32–5); Miller and Schofield (1986b: 63). The dating evidence has suggested that 'Phase 3' was constructed during the late second or early third century.

117 Rhodes (1986b: 89).

118 G. Milne (1985: 29–31, 133); Bateman (1985: 75).

119 Brigham and Watson (1996: 65–666) (KWS94).

120 Cowan (2003: 46–9); L. Wheeler (2009); Cowan and Wardle (2009: 104–6).

121 L. Wheeler (2009: 66); Cowan et al. (2009: Figs 10 and 11).

122 See Brigham, Woodburn and Tyres (1996) and Cowan (2003: 50–1) for Courage Brewery Area D (CO88[2]).

123 The analysis of the timber has indicated that it had been cut from managed woodland rather than natural wildwood or 'primeval forest' (Goodburn 1996). This has provided clear evidence for the organization and control of the landscape in the vicinity of Londinium, including the coppicing of trees.

124 Cowan and Wardle (2009: 102–4).

125 Esmonde Cleary (1989: 83–5); Perring ((1991) 2011: 84–5); Marsden (1994: 16, 22); Fulford (2004: 315).

126 Fulford (2004: 315) has noted that the primary evidence for changes in patterns of trade has been based on the presence of samian pottery but also that wider forces were at work. The survey of the frequency of samian from sites across Britannia by Willis (2011: 174, Table 1) has included some information that supports the idea of a general reduction in the quantity of samian in some contexts in London dating from the later second century.

127 Rayner and Wardle (2011).

128 Schofield (1986: 15); Richardson (1986) (NFW74/SM75/FRE78). These dumps incorporated in the construction of 'Waterfront 6' may have been deposited during the second quarter of the third century.

129 J. Bird (1986: 139, 142–5).

130 Redknap (2015: 23, 31).

131 See C. Wallace (2006) for the idea that samian may have remained in use in Roman Britain for long periods of time. Wallace has reviewed more recent accounts of the samian from New Fresh Wharf, suggesting that it might have represented a single shipment and also casting doubt on the available information for the dating of Waterfront 6 (C. Wallace 2006: 259–60). This is a useful reminder of the fragility of much of the dating evidence on which the interpretations of Roman London are built.

132 Fulford (2004: 315).

133 Collingwood and Wright (1992: 19); Marsden (1994: 17) (RIB 2443.16).

134 See Marsden (1994: 97–104) for the Guy's Hospital or New Guy's House boat (GM 451).

135 See Booth (2011: 378) and B. Watson (2012) for interim reports (GHY10).

136 Marsden (1994: 103–4).

137 Marsden (1994: 104).

138 L. Wheeler (2009: 73).

139 See Marsden (1994: 33–95) for Blackfriars ship 1 (GM182).

140 Marsden (1994: 91–5).

141 I. Tyers (1994: 204).

142 Marsden (1994: 95).

143 Marsden (1994: 85).

144 Houston (1988: 557).

145 Marsden (1994: 86–8); Peter Marsden (pers. comm.).

146 Marsden (1994: 80–3).

147 Marsden (1994: 49).

148 References are made to the 'Salvation Army site' when discussing the entire building complex. These include observations made during building construction and from limited excavations undertaken in 1840–1, 1924, 1961–2, 1981, 1986, 2001 and 2003. Detailed reports are provided by Marsden (1993) and Schofield (1998: 62) for work in 1961–2 at 101 Queen Victoria Street (GM91); T. Williams (1993: 39–63) for excavations in 1981 at Peter's Hill (PET81) and in 1986 at Sunlight Wharf (SUN86); and T. Bradley and Butler (2008: 18–22, 65–6) for the 2001–3 excavations at 99–101 Queen Street (QUV01).

149 See T. Bradley and Butler (2008: 6–9, Fig. 9) for an up-to-date history of the excavations and also a map showing the locations of the individual excavations.

150 The remains of the Period I buildings were buried under a substantial chalk raft or foundation upon which the Period II structures were constructed during the last decade of the third century.

151 T. Bradley and Butler (2008: xi).

152 T. Bradley and Butler (2008: 16, 66) (QUV01).

153 T. Bradley and Butler (2008: 63).

154 See Marsden (1993) and T. Williams (1993: 7–9) for 101 Queen Victoria Street (GM91). T. Bradley and Butler (2008: 65) have updated these observations.

155 See T. Bradley and Butler (2008: 15–22, 65–72) for 99–101 Queen Victoria Street (QUV01).

156 T. Bradley and Butler (2008: 16, 66); Tyers (2008b: 52).

157 T. Bradley and Butler (2008: 16, 66); Sudds (2008: 39–40).

158 T. Williams (1993: 88–9); Sudds (2006: 36). Some of this material could also have been imported to the site.

159 T. Bradley and Butler (2008: ix, 18–22).

160 T. Bradley and Butler (2008: 65–7).

161 T. Bradley and Butler (2008: 69).

162 Blagg (1980: 126, 180).

163 Killock et al. (2015: 253).

164 T. Bradley and Butler (2008: 70–1). The problem with this interpretation relates to the limited areas that have been excavated at each of these sites.

165 See Yule (2005: 50–77) for the Roman 'palace' at Winchester Palace (WP83). This major complex of buildings replaced earlier buildings on the same site. Yule has discussed the dating evidence for the construction of the buildings (Yule 2005: 74–5, Tables 13 and 18). This has been derived from the presence of black-burnished ware 1 and 2 in the demolition deposits related to the clearing of the site prior to the new building works and also from a consideration of the dating of one scene from the painted wall plaster in one of the rooms (other painted panels were later in date).

166 Yule (2005: 84, 86).

167 See Yule (2005: 52–3, 63–4) for 'Building 12'.

168 See Yule (2005: 52–64) for 'Building 13'. On the basis of the underfloor heating and the distribution of rooms, Yule has suggested that the modified phase for 'Building 13' might have constituted a bathhouse (Yule 2005: 60–1).

169 See Yule (2005: 65–72) for 'Building 14'.

170 Yule (2005: 75).

171 Yule (2005: 52–72).

172 Yule (2005: 57, 61). See MacKenna and Ling (1991) for the wall plaster from 'Building 13' and dating parallels. Goffin (2005: 120–37) has provided a full report on the painted plaster from various phases of this building.

173 Yule (2005: 57).

174 MacKenna and Ling (1991: 170).

175 MacKenna and Ling (1991: 166–8). Yule (2005: 74–5) has followed MacKenna and Ling's suggestions regarding the dating for both phases of decoration, although he has acknowledged the difficulty of dating the paintings at Winchester Palace when the best parallels are in Italy rather than in Britain (see MacKenna and Ling 1991: 168).

176 MacKenna and Ling (1991: 169–70).

177 Yule (2005: 65–72).

178 Yule (2005: 70); Sudds (2011b: 163, Fig. 120).

179 Yule (2005: 70).

180 Yule (2005: 69).

181 Yule (2005: 69–72). Hassall and Tomlin (1985: 317–22); Yule and Rankov (1998: 72–6), updated by Tomlin, Wright and Hassall (2009: 33–6) (RIB 3016 and RIB 3017).

182 Tomlin, Wright and Hassall (2009: 33–6) have argued that there were two inscriptions, one of which had lists of soldiers from at least four cohorts of a legion on two panels, while the second is a fragment that originally included the details of at least four centurions.

183 Yule (2005: 70), drawing on Hassall and Tomlin (1985: 317–22); Yule and Rankov (1998: 72–6). Yule (2005: 69–71, 75) has argued that the list is likely to include a detachment of legionary soldiers involved in the reconstruction of the riverside buildings during the early third century.

184 Tomlin, Wright and Hassall (2009: 35) have observed that the frequency of the nomen (the middle part of a full 'Roman' name) 'Aur(elius)' in the list of soldiers is likely to indicate that it dated from no earlier than the reign of Antoninus Pius (AD 138–61) and that the 'excellent, well-drawn and spacious lettering probably excludes a Severan or third century date'. They also quote parallels for this inscription from across the Roman Empire.

185 Yule (2005: 70).

186 Tomlin, Wright and Hassall (2009: 38, 40) (RIB 3018 and RIB 3019). See also Hassall (2012: 162).

187 Killock et al. (2015: 25–42, 242–9) (LLS02).

188 See Killock et al. (2015: 30–2, 241, 243–8) for Ditch 8.

189 Killock et al. (2015: 30–2).

190 Killock et al. (2015: 31).

191 Killock et al. (2015: 243).

192 Killock et al. (2015: Fig. 2.23).

193 Killock et al. (2015: 35–42). This publication contains a summary of the relative scarcity of dating evidence for the construction of these buildings.

194 Killock et al. (2015: 39, 40, Fig. 2.24).

195 Coombe (2015: 194–6); Coombe et al. (2015: 120 (no. 223)).

196 Coombe (2015: 197–8).

197 Seeley and Wardle (2009: 145, Fig. 113) (SB76).

198 Killock et al. (2015: 66).

199 Hassall and Tomlin (2003: 364, n. 12); Tomlin, Wright and Hassall (2009: 30–1) (RIB 3014).

200 For this translation, see Tomlin, Wright and Hassall (2009: 30).

201 Tomlin (2015: 193).

202 Tomlin, Wright and Hassall (2009: 30–1). Although there were joint rulers after AD 177–80, for instance in 197–211 (Antony Birley pers. comm.).

203 Grew (2008).

204 Tomlin (2014a: 431–2, n. 3); Tomlin (2015: 193–4).

205 Killock et al. (2015: 253).

206 Killock et al. (2015: 248–9, 255–6).

207 Killock et al. (2015: 255).

208 See Tomlin (2012: 395–6) and Perring (2015: 30) for interim reports (LBN08). The dating of the temple is not discussed in these interim reports.

209 Tomlin (2012: 396).

210 See Fairman and Taylor (2013: 56–66, 127–9) for an interim report (BVK11).

211 Killock et al. (2015: 256).

212 Sheldon and Yule (1979); Wallower (2002a); Wallower (2002b); Hall and Shepherd (2008: 38).

213 Henig (2000: 66); Coombe et al. (2015: 33–4 (no. 54)); Tomlin and Hassall (2000: 433, n. 3); Tomlin, Wright and Hassall (2009: 41) (RIB 3024).

214 Andrews et al. (2011).

215 See Heathcote (1989: 52), Perring ((1991) 2011: 81, Fig 37), Schofield (1998: 277, 284), Haynes (2000: 93) and Shepherd and Wardle (2015: 99–100) for interim comments on 18–25 Old Bailey (OBA88).

216 Haynes (2000: 93).

217 Perring ((1991) 2011: 81).

218 See Killock et al. (2015: 253) for some doubts about the identification of this building as a temple.

219 See Haynes (2000: 93) and Hall and Shepherd (2008: 37) for the possible association of octagonal temples in Britain and Gaul with the hunter god, drawing upon the earlier work of Merrifield (1996: 110, Fig. 12.6).

220 Perring ((1991) 2011: 57, 76–8); Perring (2011b; 2015: 32–3).

221 Perring (2011b: 279–80); Perring (2015: 33).

222 See Harper (2015) for the likely impact of this plague on the peoples of the Roman Empire. Simmonds, Márquez-Grant and Loe (2008: 140–1) have provided a summary of the background to this plague and outlined some evidence for this event from Roman Britain. The excavation of the London Road cemetery at Glevum (Gloucester) has given an indication of the potential impact of the 'Antonine Plague' on another urban population (Simmonds, Márquez-Grant and Loe 2008: 140–1). A mass grave containing the remains of a large number of corpses dated by associated finds may indicate an outbreak of the plague.

223 Perring (2011b: 279–80). The Cripplegate fort and the Huggin Hill bathhouse were disused, although there is little evidence for the abandonment of other public buildings. Perring has mentioned temples at Tabard Square in Southwark and the possible temples in the Fleet Valley and at the Salvation Army site.

224 Tomlin (2014b); C.P. Jones (2016).

225 Tomlin (2014b: 201).

226 Rowsome (2008: 30); J. Hill and Rowsome (2011: 358–9).

227 Swain and Williams (2008: 39).

228 Perring and Roskams (1991).

229 Perring and Roskams (1991: 120).

230 Perring ((1991) 2011) has defined the period AD 120–50 as 'The city in its prime' and the period AD 150–200 as 'The city in contraction'. He has argued that Londinium was at its maximum extent by the mid-second century (Perring (1991) 2011: 69), was in apparent decline from around AD 160 (Perring (1991) 2011: 76–8) and that areas on both sides of the Thames were deserted between AD 150 and 200 (Perring (1991) 2011: 77).

231 Perring (1991a: 41–4) (WAT78).

232 Perring (1991a: 43–4). A possible structure ('Building T') was associated with pottery dating to the mid-second century but also with a coin that may have dated from AD 335–41 that was considered to be residual.

233 Roskams (1991a: 18–26) (GPO75).

234 Roskams (1991a: 26). A later reassessment of the pottery from this site has concluded that the sequence of buildings had ended by AD 160 (Davies, Richardson and Tomber 1994: 220–1).

235 Roskams (1991b: 49, Plate 8) (MIL72/MLK76).

236 Neal and Cosh (2009: 431–2) (mosaic 370.72).

237 Roskams (1991b: 49).

238 Yule (1990).

239 Yule (1990). 'Dark earth' in London was first identified and discussed by Kathleen Kenyon in the 1940s.

240 Cowan and Seeley (2009: 164–5).

241 At Winchester Palace (WP83) dark soils are thought to have resulted from gardening practices and they ceased to be accumulated during the late second or third century (Yule 2005: 73–4, 78–81; Macphail 2005).

242 Symonds and Tomber (1994: 59); see Rayner and Seeley (1998: 92).

243 J. Hill and Rowsome (2011: 358–9).

244 Perring ((1991) 2011: 102–3).

245 Bluer and Brigham (2006: 70); see Dunwoodie, Harward and Pitt (2015: 146).

246 Bluer and Brigham (2006: 69–70); Rowsome (2006: 97–8); J. Hill and Rowsome (2011: 359).

247 Perring (2011b: 270–1); Perring (2015: 32–3).

248 Perring (2011b: 270–1).

249 Roskams (1991a: 26, Fig. 23).

250 Fulford, Clarke and Eckardt (2006); Fulford (2012: 259–60). These timber houses do not appear to have been built using techniques that have left a clear footprint, contrasting with the buildings of the first and early second centuries which were often defined by postholes, sleeper-beams or clay walls. One building at Calleva was identified by a rectangular area containing the remains of a hearth, delimited at the edges by pits and wells (Fulford 2012: 259). These excavations uncovered a large area and it was possible to view the timber buildings in plan, while most of the excavations across London have sampled small areas that have often been highly truncated.

251 The extensive area excavations at Drapers' Gardens in the upper Walbrook Valley have revealed the remains of earth-and-timber buildings dating from the third and fourth centuries. These would have been difficult to identify if the excavated areas had been small in extent (James Gerrard pers. comm.).

252 Gerrard (2011i: 183); Mike Fulford (pers. comm.).

253 Howell (2013: 19–31) (BBB05).

254 See Howell (2013: 27, 28, Fig. 16) for 'Building 13'. This dating appears to have been derived from two sherds of central Gaulish samian that have been attributed to AD 120–250 (Howell 2013: 45–6).

255 S. Watson (2006: 48–61).

256 S. Watson (2006: 51–2, 73) (SLY00).

257 S. Watson (2006: 53–4, 75–6) (NGT00).

258 S. Watson (2006: 55–6, 58–61).

259 See S. Watson (2006: 59) for 'Building 29'.

260 S. Watson (2006: 62, 78).

261 S. Watson (2006: 57).

262 Neal and Cosh (2009: 437, 446) (mosaics 370.78, 370.79 and 370.90); these were revealed in the nineteenth century, but have been poorly recorded and are not closely dated (see Schofield 2011: 41).

263 Schofield (2011: 29, 336–7) (PCH85).

264 Lyon (2007: 31–6) (GCC98; KEW98).

265 Lyon (2007: 31).

266 Lyon (2007: 35–6). There may have been some buildings in this extensive area that were not uncovered during the excavation of the small trenches.

267 Norman and Readers (1912: 280, Plate XLVII); Lyon (2007: 45).

268 Bentley and Pritchard (1982: 136) (BAR79).

269 S. Watson (2015a: 30–6, Fig. 30) (CDP04; GHM05).

270 S. Watson (2015a: 30, 34).

271 S. Watson (2015a: 30, 36).

272 S. Watson (2015a: 36).

273 Howe and Lakin (2004: 41–6, 52) (NST94; GAH95).

274 Howe and Lakin (2004: 50); Bateman, Cowan and Wroe-Brown (2008: 120).

275 See Schofield (1998: 274) for an interim report (LSO88).

276 Casson, Drummond-Murray and Francis (2014: 63–104) (GSM97).

277 Casson, Drummond-Murray and Francis (2014: 80–7).

278 Neal and Cosh (2009: 399, 418) (mosaic 370.48).

279 Casson, Drummond-Murray and Francis (2014: 85).

280 Casson, Drummond-Murray and Francis (2014: 99–104).

281 Neal and Cosh (2009: 419); Casson, Drummond-Murray and Francis (2014: 92, Fig. 77) (mosaic 370.49) (ABC87).

282 Schofield (1998: 237).

283 Bateman, Cowan and Wroe-Brown (2008: 118).

284 Bateman, Cowan and Wroe-Brown (2008: 120).

285 Elsden (2002: ix, 19–22, 53–4); J. Hill and Rowsome (2011: 359) (CAO96).

286 Elsden (2002: 54).

287 Elsden (2002: 21).

288 J. Hill and Rowsome (2011: 166–93) (ONE94) have identified two distinct periods (AD 125–70 (period 5, phase 1) and AD 170–220 (period 5, phase 2)) and have included the information for dating and also the truncation of deposits.

289 J. Hill and Rowsome (2011: 166–74).

290 The publication of these important excavations is supported by an excellent assessment of the extent to which information might have been lost as a result of later disturbance of the archaeology.

291 J. Hill and Rowsome (2011: 174–84).

292 J. Hill and Rowsome (2011: 365).

293 J. Hill and Rowsome (2011: 363, 365–66); Goodburn; Goffin and Hill (2011: 416). Timber-and-earth buildings were also built alongside stone houses at later Roman Calleva (Fulford 2012).

294 Pitt and Seeley (2014: 29–35) (POU05).

295 See J. Hill and Rowsome (2011: 367, 369–73) for the two substantial houses ('Building 64' and 'Building 65').

296 J. Hill and Rowsome (2011: 187–90, 367–9) (LHY88); this building has been identified on the Museum of London map (2011) as a late Roman stone building with mosaic floors.

297 J. Hill and Rowsome (2011: 369).

298 See Schofield (1998: 106), J. Hill and Rowsome (2011: 368) and Neal and Cosh (2009: 428–9) (mosaic 370.65) for the building at Founders' Court (GM226).

299 Schofield (1998: 242–3) (BLM87).

300 Leary and Butler (2012: 16–17) (THY01).

301 Leary and Butler (2012: 16–17).

302 Hawkins (2009: 45–57; 113–21) (DGT06).

303 Wilmott (1991: 178–9).

304 Sankey (2003: 9–13, Fig. 6) (ETA89).

305 McKenzie (2012: 8–13, 27) (TEA98).

306 G. Brown and Pye (1992) (WIV88).

307 G. Brown and Pye (1992).

308 Wroe-Brown (2014: 43–50) (FEU08).

309 Wroe-Brown (2014: 50).

310 Dunwoodie, Harward and Pitt (2015: 119–24) (FER97).

311 Dunwoodie, Harward and Pitt (2015: 121, 147).

312 Dunwoodie, Harward and Pitt (2015: 123–4, 148–9).

313 Dunwoodie, Harward and Pitt (2015: 145).

314 Pitt (2015: 163–6) (EAE01).

315 Blair and Sankey (2007: 57–9) (ESC97).

316 Bluer and Brigham (2006: 27–45, 69–70) (FCC95).

317 Bluer and Brigham (2006: 69–70).

318 Bluer and Brigham (2006: 44–5).

319 Bluer and Brigham (2006: 69).

320 Birbeck and Schuster (2009: 24–30, 33–6) (FNE01).

321 Birbeck and Schuster (2009: 36–7); Andrews (2009).

322 Birbeck and Schuster (2009: 32–3).

323 The Museum of London's map (2011) has labelled this area as 'relatively undeveloped area or open ground'.

324 Lerz and Holder (2016: 141–4) (ARC81/SEN91/MCF06).

325 Lerz and Holder (2016: 142–4).

326 Hunt (2011: 49–50) (CPW99/CPQ03/CRZ06/ASQ87).

327 Neal and Cosh (2009: 400, 410) (mosaic 370.22).

328 Howe (2002: 10–20) (BAX95).

329 Howe (2002: 13, 15–16).

330 Although these building materials may have been dumped on the site and derived from elsewhere.

331 Parnell (1985: 8–9).

332 Butcher (1982).

333 Butcher (1982).

334 Parnell (1982: 131).

335 Blair and Sankey (2007: 7–8) (BPL95).

336 G. Milne (1985: Fig. 17a); Bateman and Milne (1985: 138–41, Fig. 81) (PDN81). This report referred to the initial construction of this building in the mid-second century but has not provided details of the dating evidence.

337 G. Milne (1985: Colour Plate 5b).

338 Bateman and Milne (1985: 140).

339 Rowsome (1999: 274–5).

340 Depending on the extent and complexity of the unexcavated part of this building to the east, it may not have been very much narrower or smaller than the third-century bathhouse at Shadwell (Sudds 2011b: Fig. 120).

341 Swift (2008: 35–40) (AUT01).

342 Swift (2008: 40).

343 Brigham (2001c: 34–41, 47) (SUF94). The discussion of the townhouse has indicated that it was built after around AD 120, although a rather later date may be possible (Brigham 2001c: 40).

344 Brigham (2001c: 9, 34–41).

345 See Brigham (2001c: 41–3) for 'Buildings 4 and 5'.

346 Perring (2011b: 272) has used a range of sources to support his claim that there was a decline in settlement and activity across Southwark during the later second century (see Sheldon 1978: 36–7). Cowan et al. (2009: 19, 24–5, Figs 8, 9 and 10) contains a comparison of the known extent of settlement and activity at this time.

347 Cowan et al. (2009: 24); L. Wheeler (2009: 73–6) (GHL89/GHD90/GHSC77; HHO97).

348 See Cowan (1995: 35–53) (15SKS80). Drummond-Murray and Thompson (2002: 127–39) (RWT93) have provided additional information.

349 Drummond-Murray and Thompson (2002: 133, 135, 139).

350 Cowan (1995: 35–53); Crowley (1995: 144–57); Cowan and Pringle (2009: 90).

351 Neal and Cosh (2009: 456–458) (mosaics 371.8–371.12).

352 See Cowan (2003: 38–58) for the general sequence and stone houses in Areas C, M and Q (COSE84[1]; 52SOS89; 28PS84[1]) at Courage Brewery.

353 Brigham (2001a: 22, 24) (TW84; FW83/FW84).

354 Divers et al. (2009: 23–30) (MTA99).

355 Drummond-Murray and Thompson (2002: 96–100); Cowan and Wardle (2009: 107) (BGH95; JSS92).

356 Drummond-Murray and Thompson (2002: 96–7).

357 Drummond-Murray and Thompson (2002: 122–7).

358 Cowan et al. (2009: 19).

359 Graham (1988) (64BHS74).

360 Yule and Hinton (1988) (88BHS74).

361 Heard (1989) and Cowan et al. (2009: 184–5) (USA88/USB88).

362 Cowan et al. (2009: 19) have listed additional sites on the south island with occupation of early second-century date that may have been deserted later in the century, including 107–15 Borough High Street (107BHS81), 106–14 Borough High Street (106BHS73), 201–11 Borough High Street (207BHS72/201BHS75) and 213 Borough High Street (213BHS77).

363 Cowan et al. (2009: 24).

364 Schaaf (1976); Cowan and Pringle (2009: 80, Fig. 64); Wardle (2009: 129–42) (175BHS76/179BHS89).

365 Cowan et al. (2009: 24).

366 Douglas (2008: 23–9) (LGK99).

367 Gerrard (2009a: 131–3) (USS03).

368 Cowan and Pringle (2009: 80).

369 Cowan et al. (2009: 19); Cowan and Pringle (2009: 80).

370 Including the wells at 10–18 Union Street and 107–15 Borough High Street.

371 Yule (1982: 245–6).

372 See Smith and Powell (2010: 155) and Poole (2010) for the quantity of ceramic tiles in a well dating to the third or fourth century at the rural site of Cotswold Community (Gloucestershire/Wiltshire). A quantity of voussoir tiles was found in a well on this low-status farming settlement and such materials were usually used in the

construction of high status buildings. It is possible that this indicates that rubbish was brought from the town of Corinium (Cirencester) to Cotswold Community to be sorted and recycled (Smith and Powell 2010: 155).

373   Cowan et al. (2009: 186) (223BHS81).

374   Cowan et al. (2009: 186–7, Fig. 146) (AB78).

375   Killock et al. (2015: 25–42, 242–9) (LLS02).

376   Killock et al. (2015: 28–30).

377   Neal and Cosh (2009: 399–400).

378   Neal and Cosh (2009: 406 (mosaic 370.7) and (mosaic 370.49)).

379   Seeley and Drummond-Murray (2005) (MRG95).

380   Seeley and Drummond-Murray (2005: 48–74).

381   Seeley and Drummond-Murray (2005: 75).

382   J. Bird (2005) and Seeley and Drummond-Murray (2005: 29–32, 141–2) discuss this pit (A(1066)).

383   Seeley and Drummond-Murray (2005: 141–2).

384   See Rogers (2011b: 218).

385   Keily and Shepherd (2005: 147–8, Fig. 170).

386   Wardle (2015b: 15–28); Wardle and Shepherd (2015) (BAZ05). Glassworking waste weighing over 76 kg was found in large pits which the excavators believe was associated with a workshop.

387   Wardle (2015b: 21).

388   Wardle (2015b: 30–4).

389   C. Maloney (1990: 47–55, Fig. 84) (KEY83).

390   C. Maloney (1990: 67, 124).

391   Groves (1990: 83).

392   Hawkins (2009: 44) (DGT06); Victoria Ridgeway (pers. comm.).

393   Lees, Woodger and Orton (1989); Heathcote (1990: 162–3); Schofield (1998: 273–4); Redfern and Bonney (2014: 216) (LOW88). These buildings may initially have dated from the later first century, although only interim reports have been published.

394   Cowan (2003); Hammer (2003). Hammer (2003: 44–73) has outlined the sequence of metalworking buildings in Areas A, E and F (COSE84[2]; CO88[1]; CO87) and the dumping of metalworking waste on the foreshore.

395   See Hammer (2003: 47–8) for 'Buildings 18 and 19' in Areas E and F.

396   See Hammer (2003: 48) for 'Building 23' on site A.

397   Hammer (2003: 60).

398   Drummond-Murray and Thompson (2002: 96–7) (BGH95; JSS92).

399   Drummond-Murray and Thompson (2002: 97, 110) (1STS74). The well was titled Feature 30. For further discussion of this item, see Dennis (1978: 302–6) and Seeley and Wardle (2009: 155).

400   Dennis (1978: 306); Hammerson and Murray (1978b: 369).

401   See Dennis (1978: 302–6) for the rectangular pits titled 'Features 28 and 29'. These features contained forty-two pots that were either whole or could be largely reconstructed and were interpreted by Dennis as votive in nature.

402   Cowan et al. (2009: 109, 186–7, Fig. 146) (AB78).

403   Hall (1996: 80).

404   Swift (2003: 8–24) (BGB98).

405   Swift (2003: 12–13).

406   See Thomas (2004: 19) for interim comments (SRP98); most of these burials dated to the period from around AD 250–400.

407   Thomas (2004: 15).

408   Sudds and Douglas (2015: 5–21) (CPN01).

409   Sankey and Connell (2008) (CUE86).

410   Edwards, Weisskopf and Hamilton (2010: 46–8) and Harward, Powers and Watson (2015: 127–33) contain careful discussions suggesting that some, if not all, of the human bones in the Walbrook were deposited as a

result of the river erosion of burials. Butler (2006: 40–2) has observed, however, that burial on the edges of watercourses might in itself be part of ritual actions relating to the release of the spirit of the deceased and to rites of passage from the world of the living to that of the dead.

411 For the discovery of human cranial remains in the Walbrook Valley, see Marsh and West (1981), R. Bradley and Gordon (1988), Cotton (1996: 88–9), Merrifield (1997: 34–6), Edwards, Weisskopf and Hamilton (2010) and Harward, Powers and Watson (2015: 7–9, 127–32).

412 Marsh and West (1981); Butler (2006: 40–2); Edwards, Weisskopf and Hamilton (2010); Redfern and Bonney (2014: 222–3); Harward, Powers and Watson (2015: 7–9, 127–32).

413 Marsh and West (1981: 86–9, Figs 1 and 2).

414 Schulting and Bradley (2013: 53).

415 Harward, Powers and Watson (2015: 134); the Upper Walbrook Cemetery included the excavated sites at River Plate House (RIV87), 12–15 Finsbury Circus (FIB88), Liverpool House (ELD88), 14 Eldon Street / 6 Broad Street Place (BSP91) and 16–18 Finsbury Circus (ENS03).

416 Powers (2015a: 131).

417 Redfern and Bonney (2014).

418 Redfern and Bonney (2014: 24–33).

419 As shown on the Museum of London map (2011). An excavation at Jubilee Gardens (JBL86) has located a metalled surface that may indicate the location of this road (Schofield 1998: 229). Lyon (2007: 39) has included additional discussion of the location of an extramural road to the north and east of the walled circuit of late Roman Londinium.

420 Harward, Powers and Watson (2015: 28–9).

421 Harward, Powers and Watson (2015: 25, 27, 28, 32).

422 See Harward, Powers and Watson (2015: 34–54) for the burials from these five sites.

423 Harward, Powers and Watson (2015: 81).

424 Harward, Powers and Watson (2015: 81, 96–8).

425 Harward, Powers and Watson (2015: 51–2, 87).

426 Harward, Powers and Watson (2015: Fig. 16).

427 Harward, Powers and Watson (2015: 38).

428 Harward, Powers and Watson (2015: 39, 124–5).

429 Harward, Powers and Watson (2015: 80).

430 Harward, Powers and Watson (2015: 53).

431 Harward, Powers and Watson (2015: 39–40, 45–9).

432 Harward, Powers and Watson (2015: 48–50).

433 Harward, Powers and Watson (2015: 49).

434 Powers (2015a: 127).

435 Powers (2015a: 127–32).

436 Schofield (1998: 276) (MOH88).

437 Butler (2006) (MRL98).

438 This wetland later became known as Moorfields, a significant feature of medieval London that was finally drained during the sixteenth and seventeenth centuries.

439 Butler (2006: 10–12, 38–44).

440 Butler (2006: 39–40).

441 Dodwell (2006); Armitage (2006).

442 Butler (2006: 35–6).

443 Butler (2006: 40–2).

444 See Lees, Woodger and Orton (1989), Heathcote (1990: 162–3), Schofield (1998: 273–4) and Redfern and Bonney (2014: 216) for interim reports (LOW88).

445 Redfern and Bonney (2014).

446 Redfern and Bonney (2014: 217, Table 1).

447 Redfern and Bonney (2014: 216, Table 1); Redfern et al. (in press).

448 Redfern and Bonney (2014: 217–21).

449 Rebecca Redfern (pers. comm.).

450 Cf. R. Bradley and Gordon (1988: 504–5). Edwards, Weisskopf and Hamilton (2010: 39–40) have suggested, conversely, that female cranial material may be more common than male in the general sample for the Thames and Walbrook.

451 Redfern and Bonney (2014: 224); Powers (2015a: 131).

452 Ferris (2000: 68, 70, 91); Redfern and Bonney (2014: 223).

453 Redfern and Bonney (2014: 222–3).

454 Redfern and Bonney (2014: 222–3).

455 Nick Bateman (pers. comm.). See Kyle (1998: 214–17) for spectacles of death in Rome, which usually took place on the edges of the city and often close to flowing water that enabled the city to be purged of its 'filth and guilt'. The exposing of dead bodies on the edges of rivers provides an alternative explanation for many of the cranial remains from Roman London.

456 The human remains have been discussed by C. Maloney (1990: 30, 31, 34, 44) in the chapter addressing drainage and reclamation and, although the dating evidence from this small excavation area was unclear, the third cranium may have been deposited in the ditch before 'Building A' was constructed.

457 Sayer (2009b); Victoria Ridgeway (pers. comm.).

458 Sayer (2009b: 375).

459 Sayer (2009b: 378–9). An infant burial and the cranial remains of two individuals were also found in a quarry pit associated with the glassworking at 35 Basinghall Street (Wardle 2015b: 23–4; Powers 2015b).

460 Bruce et al. (2010: 77–81) (MGE96).

461 Bruce et al. (2010: 80).

462 Ridgeway (2014: 2).

463 A useful comparison may be made between Roman Southwark and Vagniacis (Springhead). The evidence from Vagniacis has indicated a close connection between religious activity, burial and the ritual use of human remains. Burial places were located on the outskirts of the religious complex at Springhead, comprising one main cemetery and smaller burial grounds which included a walled cemetery with high-status burials (Andrews et al. 2011). Fragments of human bone and burials were found in and around the temples, including those of a large number of newborns (McKinley 2011: Figs 1 and 2).

464 Langthorne (2015: 229–30); Killock et al. (2015: 255); Ridgeway, Leary and Sudds (2013: 106). Forcey (1998) and Creighton (2006: 123–56) have suggested a close connection between elite mortuary behaviour and Romano-Celtic temples in Britain during the first century AD.

465 Langthorne (2015: 230).

466 Langthorne (2015: 229–30).

467 Beasley (2007: 41–5) (SWN98).

468 Beasley (2007: 42–5). The dating of pottery from 'Well 1447' suggested that it was filled in around AD 120–60.

469 Beasley (2007: 42–3).

470 Beasley (2007: 43–4).

471 Beasley (2007).

472 Beasley (2007: 54–5).

473 Andrews (2011: 67–83). One particular shaft was located in the entrance area of the enclosure surrounding the temple. This deep pit was infilled during the later second and early third centuries with deposits that included animal skeletons, a human cranium and other human bones. The skeletons of dogs were particularly well represented and they may have had a significant role in the rituals at this temple (Andrews 2011: 82; Andrews and Smith 2011: 199; McKinley 2011: 5). Several pits in an alignment within the enclosure contained large numbers of dog skeletons, and human burials were found cut into the line of the temple enclosure (Andrews 2011: 71–5, 80).

474 Ridgeway, Leary and Sudds (2013: 12–15, 75–8, 107) (LTU03).

475 Another group of burials dating from the fourth century was located slightly further to the south.

476 Killock (2010: 21–6: 81–5) (TIY07). This interim report contains some detailed information that may suggest the use of ditches to expose the bodies of deceased people.

477 Killock (2010: 23).

478 Killock (2010: 84).

479 Killock (2010: 23–4). This context is referred to as 'Group 67' in the report.

480 Killock (2010: 24).

481 Killock (2010).

482 Killock (2010: 23).

483 Victoria Ridgeway (pers. comm.).

484 Killock (2010: 84–5).

485 Human bones have also been found in third-century ditches at 28–30 Trinity Street and 1–5 Swan Street.

486 Mackinder (2000) (GDV96).

487 Mackinder (2000: 10–13). A *bustum* burial is one where the pyre was constructed over a pit and the burnt remains of the body and grave goods were allowed to fall into the pit. The dating of this burial has been derived from the lamps which have parallels in contexts dating to the late first and second centuries and were unused at the time of burial (Mackinder 2000: 33–7).

488 Mackinder (2000: 12–13, 33–7).

489 Mackinder (2000: 37).

490 Wardle (2000); Mackinder (2000: 10–13, 33–4).

491 Wardle (2000: 28); Bateman (2008: 163).

492 Wardle (2000: 28).

493 Bateman (2008).

494 Collingwood and Wright (1995b: 55); Hall and Shepherd (2008: 31) (RIB 2503.127). Henig (1984: 100–1) has suggested that the jug may have played a role in rites connected with purification by water, which were important in the rites of Isis, and that the flagon may have been carefully deposited in a sealed location when it ceased to be used.

495 Haynes (2000: 89–90).

496 Mackinder (2000: 9–10) has suggested that this building dates from after AD 120, although the dating of the pottery from the associated well may indicate that it was constructed during the late first to early second centuries. This later dating is based on the material derived from the structures that had been replaced by the mausoleum.

497 Mackinder (2000: 14–23, Fig. 12).

498 Mackinder (2000: 14–16).

499 Mackinder (2000).

500 Mackinder (2000: 38). 'Burial 8'. Beasley (2007: 62) has argued that the evidence for the manipulation of this burial may support the information from the excavations at the Old Sorting Office that excarnation was practised on the south margin of Londinium.

501 The moving of skulls after burial has often been interpreted as representing a tradition that developed during the third century, although an earlier origin has been suggested as a result of the evidence from the first-century burial at 60–3 Fenchurch Street (McKinley 2009: 13).

502 Mackinder (2000: 18–19).

503 See Mackinder (2000: 18) for 'Burial 12'.

504 Mackinder (2000: 16–18).

505 Mackinder (2000: 22, 31).

506 Blagg (2000: 62). See Coombe et al. (2015: 70–1 (no. 124)) for further discussion and also a note of a second pine cone finial from the Tabard Square excavations (Coombe et al. 2015: 71 (no. 125)).

507 Blagg (2000: 61–2); Coombe et al. (2015: 37–8 (no. 63a)). Henig (2000: 65–6, 67) has argued that this figure was one of the limestone carvings made by sculptors from the Cotswolds who had settled in London. Other comparable sculptures mentioned by Henig include the hunter god from the well at Southwark Cathedral, those from the so-called 'Screen of Gods' and the Monumental Arch and several examples from the Mithraeum.

508 See Thrale (2008) for an interim report (OCU04). This site was located too far south to be marked on Fig. 7.16.

509 Thrale (2008: 20–2).

510 Cowan and Pringle (2009: 91); Seeley and Wardle (2009: 144; Fig. 111) (ROY91). This site was located too far south to be marked on Fig. 7.16.

511 See Hammerson (1978) for a report of the original discovery of the well in 1977 during work in the crypt of Southwark Cathedral (SCC77). Seeley and Wardle (2009: 144) and Divers et al. (2009: 12) have provided further discussions of the context and significance of these finds.

512 Hall (1996: 76).

513 Alternatively, the building material and sculptures from the well in Southwark Cathedral crypt may have been brought to the site from some distance and from different sites.

514 Hammerson (1978: 209) has observed that the packing of the well contained three mid-third-century coins.

515 Coombe et al. (2015: 43–4 (no. 74)). Two additional figures of the hunter gods from London north of the river include a relief carving on a limestone altar found in 1830 on the site of the Goldsmith's Hall and a statue found in 1849 in Bevis Marks (Merrifield: 1996, 106–7; Coombe et al. 2015: 42–4 (nos 73 and 75)).

516 Coombe et al. (2015: 35 (no. 56)).

517 Merrifield (1996: 107–8).

518 Coombe et al. (2015: 52–4 (no. 87)) have mentioned, however, that it is too small to have been the lid of a funerary ash chest and that it may have been associated with the worship of Cybele.

519 Coombe et al. (2015: 4 (no. 8)).

520 Tomlin, Wright and Hassall (2009: 39) (RIB 3020).

521 Tomlin, Wright and Hassall (2009: 23) (RIB 3015).

522 The river god from the third-century Mithraeum constitutes another example from north of the river.

523 Blagg (2000). The idea that the Thames may have been used for disposing of the dead during the Iron Age and the Walbrook may have served a comparable function during the Roman period provides additional support for this association between water spirits and rites of passage.

524 Campbell (2012: 21).

525 Merrifield (1997: 38–9); Fittock (2015).

526 Barber and Bowsher (2000: 189).

527 A survey in Southwark has recorded seventeen pipe-clay figurines, fifteen of which were of Venus, some found in pits and the fill of ditches and channels (Seeley and Wardle 2009: 145). North of the Thames many broken figures of Venus have been found in and around the Walbrook Valley, suggesting that the goddess was worshipped at domestic shrines along the riverside (Merrifield 1997: 38; Fittock 2015: 119, Fig. 7). Four Venus figurines were found during the excavations at 1 Poultry (Wardle 2011a: 347) and six were recovered at New Fresh Wharf on the waterfront (Jenkins 1986). Pipeclay figurines of Venus were also sometimes placed in graves and three complete examples were found with a burial in the 'eastern cemetery' (Barber and Bowsher 2000: 186–9). Fittock (2015: 123) discusses an additional pipe-clay figurine from a burial context in the 'northern cemetery'. Two pipeclay figurines of Minerva found in earlier wells north of the Thames may also have been associated with a water cult, as may the marble head of this goddess from the Mithraeum.

528 S. Watson (2003: 15–21) (ATL89/ATC97).

529 Bentley and Pritchard (1982: 137–59) (BAR79).

530 See Schofield (1998: 298–9) for an interim report (WES89). Treveil and Watson (2006: 144) have provided a brief review of other discoveries and further excavations in the immediate vicinity of these sites.

531 G. Milne and Reynolds (1997: 21–3) (SBC92).

532 G. Milne and Reynolds (1997); G. Milne (1997: 58).

533 G. Milne (1997: 100).

534 Merrifield (1983: 132–3). Cremation burials have been found to the north in Shoe Lane with pottery vessels that may date from the first and fourth centuries.

535 Pitt (2006: 14–15, 50–3, Fig. 17) (NEG98).

536 Pitt (2006: 53).

537 Pitt (2006: 15).

538 A fragment of a monumental tomb that had been built into Bastion 10 on the late Roman wall was comparable to examples from Cologne and Trier (Coombe et al. 2015: 56–7 (no. 93)). This may have been from a monument comparable to that originally sited at 3–9 Newgate Street (Coombe et al. 2015: 112).

539 Pitt (2006: 53).

540 Coombe et al. (2015: 112).

541 Barber and Bowsher (2000).

542 Barber and Bowsher (2000: 298–333). The twelve individual areas excavated produced 550 inhumation burials and between 92 to 112 cremation burials (Barber and Bowsher 2000: 311–12).

543 The term 'decapitation' for burials in which the head was displaced is not really appropriate since the bodies were not beheaded but the skulls moved after decay had set in. See Barber and Bowsher (2000: 89–91, 240, 317) for one 'decapitated' burial that may have dated from the second century, while the other comparable burials were either undated or were from the third to fourth century.

544 Barber and Bowsher (2000: 90).

545 Barber and Bowsher (2000: 101–4).

546 Mackinder (2000: 21, 26).

547 Barber and Bowsher (2000: 76, 80–1, 309).

548 Ridgeway, Leary and Sudds (2013: 113); S. Watson (2003: 36).

549 Gee (2008). Carroll (2006: 71–4) has discussed the limited evidence for funeral banquets.

550 Barber and Bowsher (2000: 326–7).

551 Barber and Bowsher (2000: 326–7).

552 See Booth (2014: 375) and Wardle (2014b) for interim information (MNR12).

553 Coombe (2015: 124–6 (no. 229)).

554 Coombe (2015: 124).

555 Coombe (2015: 125).

556 Booth (2014: 375).

557 Lakin (2002) (LD74/LD76).

558 Lakin (2002: 10–11).

559 Lakin (2002: 8–10).

560 Lakin has discussed parallels among the mausolea of Britain, and the close proximity of several cremation burials is likely to support this interpretation (Lakin 2002: 26–7), although D. Bird (2008: 98) has argued that this building is unlikely to have been a mausoleum or burial enclosure since it is too large and has unusually wide walls. For further discussion, see below.

561 See Hill and Rowsome (2011: 368–9) for additional substantial stone buildings in London that may have been comparable to those at 10 Gresham Street, DLR Lothbury and 1 Poultry, but some of these sites remain unpublished.

562 Neal and Cosh (2009: 400–1).

8 Third-Century Stability

1 There is no particularly detailed recent account of third-century Londinium on which to draw. Rowsome (2008: 30) and Perring (2015) have provided short summaries. Earlier accounts are now very dated (Marsden 1980: 131–62; Perring (1991) 2011: 90–112).

2 Perring ((1991) 2011: 90).

3 Mattingly (2006: 177). Birley (2005: 208: 333) has argued that the division was at the earliest in AD 212 and at the latest in AD 216.

4 Blagg (1980: 180).

5 Coombe et al. (2015: 8). If the dating of the temple of Mithras is correct, the statue would have had to have been the property of an earlier temple that was later buried in the Mithraeum.

6   Coombe et al. (2015: 8).

7   Coombe et al. (2015: 14–15 (no. 23)).

8   Coombe et al. (2015: 15–16 (no. 24)).

9   Merrifield (1983: 197–8); Birley (2005: 382, 393). The image of Londinium was based upon the city of Trier where the medal was struck.

10 T. Williams (1991); T. Williams (1993: 31–2).

11 Birley (2005: 388–91).

12 Hassall (1980: 195–6). Tomlin, Wright and Hassall (2009: 18–19) have updated this discussion and have provided the translations and interpretations, including some uncertainties (RIB 3001).

13 Tomlin, Wright and Hassall (2009: 18); Birley (2005: 360–1).

14 Hassall (1980: 197–8); Coombe et al. (2015: 41–2 (no. 71)). Tomlin, Wright and Hassall (2009: 20–1) have provided the translations and interpretations, including uncertainties (RIB 3002).

15 Shepherd (1998: 228).

16 Collingwood and Wright (1995a: 5); Shepherd (2012: 167) (RIB 11).

17 Collingwood and Wright (1995a: 8–9); Shepherd (2012: 166–7); Coombe et al. (2015: 46–7 (no. 79)) (RIB 17).

18 This third-century dating has been based on the assumption that soldiers were not able to officially marry prior to AD 197. This is now known to have been based on a misunderstanding of Herodian (Greene 2015: 126–7, n. 11). As a result, these two tombstones are no longer closely dated.

19 J. Bird (1986: 142–5); J. Bird (2002); J. Bird (2011b).

20 Hassall and Tomlin (1982: 396); Tomlin, Wright and Hassall (2009: 21–2); Coombe et al. (2015: 50–1 (no. 84)) (RIB 3003); this fragmentary tombstone was found reused in Bastion 4A.

21 Tomlin, Wright and Hassall (2009: 21).

22 Tomlin, Wright and Hassall (2009: 22).

23 Sankey and Stephenson (1991: 122), Sheldon (2011: 233) and Sheldon (2014) have suggested that the entire circuit of the wall, including the landward wall, was constructed during the second half of the third century. The idea that the wall was built in two stages will, however, be followed here (Perring 2015: 24).

24 J. Maloney (1983: 97).

25 For accounts of the landward wall, see Marsden (1980: 119–27), J. Maloney (1983), Sankey and Stephenson (1991: 118–22), Perring ((1991) 2011: 90–93), Perring (2000: 130–1), Wilson (2006: 6–7) and Sheldon (2011). Lyon (2007: 37–46) has discussed the recent works undertaken on the wall close to the Merrill Lynch Financial Centre and has included an up-to-date review of the information for the wall's structure and dating.

26 Schofield (2000: 227).

27 City walls were often built to symbolize the status of colonies (Pinder 2011: 72–3). Tomlin (2006) has tentatively suggested, as a result of a fragmentary inscription found at the Huggin Hill bathhouse, that Londinium may have been made a colony under Hadrian in AD 122. Wilson (2006: 2–20, 29–32) has argued that the building of the stone wall at Londinium may have been associated with the granting of colonial status to the urban community.

28 Lyon (2007: 40–1).

29 See Wacher (1995: 97, 428–9, n. 79) for the fragility of the available dating evidence. J. Maloney (1983: 103–4) has argued for a date of AD 193 to 197 on the basis that the project may have been instigated by Clodius Albinus when he attempted to claim the empire on the death of Commodus (see Fulford 2002: 68–9). Sankey and Stephenson (1991: 120) have suggested, however, that the wall could have been built at least two decades later.

30 J. Maloney (1983: 104, 115); Lyon (2007: 45–6).

31 Laurence, Esmonde Cleary and Seers (2011: 141–69) have briefly summarized the evidence for the walled circuits of Roman cities in the Western empire and have argued that these were rare across Gaul and North Africa during the first two centuries AD. They have suggested that the presence of stone walls at this time was usually an assertion of urban status.

32 See Wacher (1995: 70–81) for a summary of the evidence for town walls in Britannia. This topic has fallen out of fashion and a thorough reassessment of the information would constitute a significant contribution to Roman studies.

33 Wacher (1995: 75).

34 The fort's south and east walls may not have been demolished at this time.

35 J. Maloney (1983: 98).

36 J. Maloney (1983: 97).

37 Marsden (1980: 126–7). Marsden (1994: 83) has observed that the supplying of this quantity of stone would have required 1,750 voyages from the quarry to Londinium by a ship the size of the Blackfriars Ship 1.

38 Sankey and Stephenson (1991: 119).

39 J. Maloney (1983: 98).

40 Marsden (1980: 122); Lyon (2007: 39).

41 J. Maloney (1983: 97).

42 J. Maloney (1983: 98).

43 Shepherd (2012: 78).

44 J. Maloney (1983: 98, 110).

45 Butler (2002: 47–52) (AES96/PLH97).

46 Norman and Readers (1912: 294–5, Plate LVI); Lyon (2007: 42–3, 45).

47 J. Maloney (1983: 97).

48 Guildhall Museum (1969: 20–3) (GM7); B. Bishop (2000) (AHS98).

49 See Guildhall Museum (1970: 9) (GM251) and Rowsome (2014: 5) for an interim report (LUD82).

50 See Schofield (1998: 284) for a brief description of the evidence (VAL88).

51 J. Maloney (1983: 98).

52 Guildhall Museum (1970: 4–6, Plate B); Marsden (1980: 122, 123, 126); Merrifield (1983: 160, 162, Fig. 35); Schofield (1998: 75) (GM131).

53 Whipp (1980: 53–5) (THL78b); Schofield (1998: 46); Hunt (2011: 54) (GM44); Butler (2002: 48–50) (AES96/PLH97).

54 J. Maloney (1983: 101); Sankey and Stephenson (1991: 120); Lyon (2007: 39–40).

55 Wacher (1995: 75).

56 Merrifield (1983: 159–63); J. Maloney (1983: 101, 104); Sankey and Stephenson (1991: 120); Wilson (2006: 6–7, 14); Lyon (2007: 40–1).

57 See Shepherd (2012: 24, 44, 53–6, 62–4, 78, 96–8) and Shepherd and Chettle (2012: 156–7) for Grimes' work at Windsor Court.

58 Shepherd (2012: 88–9, Figs 73 and 74).

59 Shepherd (2012: 78).

60 Sankey and Stephenson (1991: 120).

61 J. Maloney (1979: 294–7); Dyson and Schofield (1981: 44–5); Schofield (1998: 151) (DUK77).

62 J. Maloney (1979: 295). This excavation has not, however, been fully published and more evidence about the pottery is required before this dating can be confirmed.

63 Butler (2002: 48) (AES96/PLH97).

64 See Schofield (1998: 184–5) and Rowsome (2014) for interim reports (LUD82).

65 Guildhall Museum (1970: 6); Merrifield (1983: 160, 162–3, Fig. 36); Hall (2014: 180). The two 'forger's' hoards are discussed further below.

66 See Schofield (1998: 242–3) for an interim report (BLM87).

67 Brigham (1990a: 138).

68 L. Wheeler (2009: 76).

69 Fulford (2004: 315).

70 See Schofield (1986: 8–19) and Miller and Schofield (1986a: 31–50) for the information for Phase 3 (presumably 'Waterfront 6') at New Fresh Wharf (NFW74/SM75/FRE78). Brigham (1990a: 128–9) has reflected on this information. See Miller and Schofield (1986b: 63–4) and Hillam and Morgan (1986) for the dating evidence.

71 Schofield (1986: 11–20); Miller and Schofield (1986a: 49–50).

72 J. Bird (1986: 142–5).

73 C. Wallace (2006).

74 Parry (1994) (TEX88). This material has never been completely written up and only one dendrochronological date was determined.

75 Parry (1994: 267).

76 Parry (1994: 266).

77 Parry (1994: 267). This might help to explain why this pottery had such a wide range of dates, although not why late second-century samian was dumped within an early third-century wharf.

78 Rhodes (1986a). One such assemblage from Regis House may have been burnt in the 'Hadrianic fire'. Another group of unused samian was found in a second-century pit at the pottery production site at 20–8 Moorgate (J. Bird 2005; Seeley and Drummond-Murray 2005: 29–32, 141–2).

79 Rogers (2011b: 218).

80 See Brigham (1990a: 105–6, 139–140) for the fragmentary evidence for the possible additional third-century works ('Waterfront 7') (BWB83), which is dated through dendrochronology to AD 239–75 (Brigham 1990a: 162). Brigham (1990a: 106, 119, 124) has also discussed the probable rebuilding of the Waterfront at around the same time at New Fresh Wharf (NFW74/SM75/FRE78) and the Old Custom House (CUS73).

81 Brigham (1990a: Fig. 13) has shown Waterfront 7 to lie around the mouth of the Walbrook and the Museum of London map (2011) marks this Waterfront in the same location. Brigham's article did not provide a detailed description of the structure or chronology of this work.

82 Brigham (1990a: 106).

83 Symonds and Tomber (1994: 80).

84 Symonds and Tomber (1994: 81).

85 Symonds and Tomber (1994: 80–1).

86 Symonds and Tomber (1994: 81).

87 Unger (2009). Most of the tile used in late Roman buildings in London was reused, since little tile was produced during the later Roman period (Sudds 2011b: 160–1).

88 J. Bird (1986: 142–5); J. Bird (2002); J. Bird (2011b).

89 Rowsome (2008: 31).

90 Douglas, Gerrard and Sudds (2011: xiii); Gerrard (2011a: 83–6); Gerrard (2011f: 167).

91 Brigham (1990a: 159–60); Gerrard (2011a: 81). Gerrard (2011f: 167) has noted that beach markets occurred along the Thames in the medieval period.

92 Douglas, Gerrard and Sudds (2011) (TOC02/HGA02). These excavations uncovered two distinct areas as Site A to the west and Site B to the east. The bathhouse and winged building were at the eastern site and a succession of other buildings were at the western site.

93 Much of the building material used for the Shadwell 'bathhouse' had been salvaged from an earlier building with a substantial hypocaust (Sudds 2011a; Sudds 2011b: 160–1). This material may have been transported by boat from another riverside site or it might indicate that there had been an earlier bathhouse at Shadwell which has yet to be located.

94 Gerrard (2011d).

95 See Douglas, Gerrard and Sudds (2011: 13–27) and Sudds (2011b) for the layout of the initial bathhouse (Period 3), including some doubts about the function of individual rooms.

96 Douglas, Gerrard and Sudds (2011: 26).

97 Douglas, Gerrard and Sudds (2011: 26–7).

98 Douglas, Gerrard and Sudds (2011: 27–31).

99 Douglas, Gerrard and Sudds (2011: 31).

100 Lakin (2002); Douglas, Gerrard and Sudds (2011: 13); Gerrard (2011f: 165) (LD74/LD76).

101 Gerrard (2011d: 152) has considered a religious interpretation for these buildings and points out potential comparisons with the late Roman temple at Lydney (Gloucestershire), but also that there is no unambiguous evidence to support such an interpretation at Shadwell.

102 Forcey (1998); Creighton (2006: 123–56).

103 A small fragment of an inscription from the buildings interpreted as a bathhouse does not indicate the functions of the buildings (Tomlin 2011b).

104 Wardle (2002b).

105 Gerrard (2011c); Douglas, Gerrard and Sudds (2011: 43–4).

106 Johnson (1975); J. Maloney (1983: 104–5); D. Bird (2008: 98).

107 Gerrard (2011f: 165–6).

108 J. Bird (2002); J. Bird (2011b).

109 As no waterfront or port facilities have been found at Shadwell, Gerrard (2011f: 169) has proposed that the late Roman samian from this site may indicate that a migrant group from Gaul had settled there, just beyond the urban margin of Londinium.

110 Rhodes (1991: 189).

111 Brigham (1990b: 92–3).

112 Brigham (1990b: 75, 77); C. Milne, G. Milne and Brigham (1992: 28–9).

113 Brigham (1992b: 93).

114 Dunwoodie (2004: 34).

115 Rogers (2011a: 78).

116 Davies (1992: 72).

117 Bateman, Cowan and Wroe-Brown (2008: 63–72).

118 Bateman, Cowan and Wroe-Brown (2008: 69–71, 72). Bateman's suggestion about the function of this building ('Building 3') has been derived from its location rather than from the finds made during the excavation.

119 Bateman, Cowan and Wroe-Brown (2008: 71); Wardle (2008b: 192).

120 T. Bradley and Butler (2008: ix, 18–22) (QUV01).

121 Marsden (1975: 75–6). In 'Area 2' of the site.

122 Marsden (1975: 78). In 'Area 6' of the site.

123 Brigham (2001c: 48). Although part of the south-east area may have been occupied during the fourth century (Marsden 1975: 77–8).

124 Yule (2005: 52–72) (WP83).

125 See Yule (2005: 52–63) for 'Building 13'. It is possible that this was part of an additional bathhouse to that comprising the late second-century bath building ('Building 14'), although the excavator preferred the idea that it formed part of the residential suite of a high-quality house or palace, since the building had been developed over a period of time rather than constructed as a planned whole (Yule 2005: 60).

126 MacKenna and Ling (1991: 169–70); Goffin (2005: 125–30).

127 See Yule (2005: 65–72) for 'Building 14'. The fragments of finely-cut marble inscriptions found during the excavations have usually been dated to the third century, but this has now been revised to the late second.

128 Yule (2005: 59, 66, 73–4, 85).

129 Killock et al. (2015: 43–52, 259–62) (LLS02).

130 Killock et al. (2015: 44, 48–9).

131 Killock et al. (2015: 43, 45–7).

132 Killock et al. (2015: 49–50).

133 Killock et al. (2015: 51).

134 See Schofield (1998: 277, 284) for an interim discussion (OBA88; VAL88).

135 Marked on the Museum of London map (2011) as a '4th century AD suburban villa'.

136 See Shepherd (1998) for a full report on Grimes' excavations (GM157/GM256), along with an account of other structures and deposits in the vicinity. See Grimes (1968: 92–117) for an initial report on the excavations.

137 Shepherd (1998: 55–6, 85–6).

138 Shepherd (1998: 221–2).

139 See Clauss (2000) and Beck (2006) for summaries of the character of the worship of Mithras. Clauss (2000: 7) has argued that although Mithraism has usually been supposed to have derived from Persian religious beliefs, attention should be focused on the creativity that gave rise to this mystery cult within the empire. Clauss has also

provided an assessment of the character of this mystery cult and the evidence for the worship of Mithras across the empire.

140 Shepherd (1998: 220–1); Henig (1998: Fig. 247).

141 Collingwood and Wright (1995a: 4); Shepherd (1998: 191) (RIB 8).

142 Shepherd (1998: 232); J. Bird (1996).

143 Shepherd (1998: 220–1, Fig. 247); Henig (1998).

144 Clauss (2000: 43–5).

145 Shepherd (1998: 225–9).

146 Shepherd (1998: 55–6, 85–6).

147 Brigham (1998b).

148 Shepherd (1998: 225–7); Clauss (2000: 42–61).

149 Macready and Sidell (1998: 214); Shepherd (1998: 227).

150 Martens (2004a: 30–41); Martens (2004b).

151 See Shepherd (1998: 165–71) for the evidence for the contexts in which the group of sculptures were found in and around 'Pit A' in 1954. This has been provided by the information recorded about the original excavations: the heads of Mithras and Minerva were found in a shallow pit 'overlying the easternmost column of the northern colonnade' (presumably 'Pit B'). The head of Serapis and the statue of Mercury were found in a pit to the south-east of the one containing the heads of Mithras and Minerva (presumably 'Pit A').

152 Toynbee (1986); Shepherd (1998: 165–74, 182–3, 188–91).

153 These numbers were allocated to single pieces by Toynbee and are used in Chapters 8 and 9.

154 See Toynbee (1986: 21–3, 31–2), Shepherd (1998: 170–1) and Coombe et al. (2015: 7, 42 (nos 14 and 72)) for the sculptures of Mithras (sculpture 1), Minerva (2) and Serapis (3), Mercury (4), a 'colossal hand' of Mithras slaying the bull (5) and a limestone hand and forearm of Mithras (11). Toynbee (1986: 31) has suggested that sculpture 11 was found just outside the temple in the north-west, but Shepherd (1998: 171) has recorded that it came from a layer 'sagging' into the pit in which the head of Minerva was found.

155 Toynbee (1986: 10, 12–13, 17); Coombe et al. (2015: 3, 7, 8 (nos 6, 14 and 16)). Minerva may have been carved in the early second century (Coombe et al. 2015: 3).

156 Toynbee (1986: 57).

157 Toynbee (1986: 5).

158 Croxford (2003) has focused attention on the symbolic and ritual associations of the fragmentation of Roman statues in Britain. He has observed that statue fragments were frequently deposited and has argued that different parts of the body are under- and over-represented in the materials from the province (cf. Chapman 2000). Croxford (2003: 83–4) has observed that, when a statue was deliberately fragmented, some pieces may have been considered to have had more inherent value than others through a process of 'positive selection'. Other less valuable fragments might have been discarded as having less significance through a process of 'negative selection'. The most obvious pattern from this analysis of sculptures throughout Britain was that heads appear to be over-represented among the fragments of sculpture, which might indicate positive selection, while hands and legs are often under-represented (Croxford 2003: 87–8). The hands and heads are often the parts of the statue that provide the evidence of the identity of the figure it portrayed, and positive and negative selection might indicate the fragments of the statues that retained significance.

159 Shepherd (1998: 55–6, 85–6).

160 See Toynbee (1986: 25–30) and Shepherd (1998: 171–4) for the water deity (sculpture 8), a genius (sculpture 9) and the relief of Mithras slaying the bull (sculpture 10).

161 Toynbee (1986: 25–6); Coombe et al. (2015: 3–4 (no. 7)).

162 Toynbee (1986: 28); Coombe et al. (2015: 2 (no. 4)).

163 Shepherd (1998: 172).

164 Toynbee (1986: 30); Coombe et al. (2015: 7 (no. 15)).

165 The exact meaning is unclear (Coombe et al. 2015: 7).

166 Shepherd (1998: 228); see Clauss (2000: 43, 88).

167 Although Coombe et al. (2015: 8) have suggested that the fine marble head of Serapis was possibly from a statue donated by a wealthy patron during Septimius Severus' visit to Londinium, since this emperor identified himself with this deity. If the dating of the temple is correct, the statue would have had to have been the property of an earlier temple that was later buried in the Mithraeum.

168 See Toynbee (1986: 32–4), Shepherd (1998: 182–3) and Coombe et al. (2015: 41 (no. 70)) for sculpture 12. This was found six months after the excavations had finished, around 20 metres south of the temple.

169 See Toynbee (1986: 34–6), Shepherd (1998: 182–3), Hall (1998: 108), Henig (1998: 202) and Coombe et al. (2015: 34–5 (no. 55)) for sculpture 13.

170 Toynbee (1986: 22–5, 39–42); Shepherd (1998: 189–91, 201–2).

171 Toynbee (1986: 59–62); Clauss (2000: 146–67).

172 C. Hill (1980b: 62–6) (BC75). Blagg (1980) has reconstructed the two monuments and these have recently been fully documented and discussed by Coombe et al. (2015: 74–95 (nos 133–65)).

173 Hassall (1980).

174 Blagg (1980: 126).

175 Blagg (1980: 180).

176 Blagg (1980: 126); Coombe et al. (2015: 92).

177 Sheldon and Tyers (1983: 358–61); Hillam and Morgan (1986: 84); Coombe et al. (2015: 74).

178 Blagg (1980: 180). This western section did not have timber in the foundations and was constructed entirely of stone (see below).

179 Coombe et al. (2015: 74).

180 See Blagg (1980: 127–52, 175–81) for details of the stones. See Blagg and Gibson (1980) for the reconstruction of the Arch. Coombe et al. (2015: 74–91, Fig. 2) have included a redrawing of the monument.

181 Blagg (1980: 177).

182 Blagg and Gibson (1980: 153–4).

183 Blagg and Gibson (1980: 154).

184 Blagg (1980: 178–9).

185 Blagg and Gibson (1980: 155).

186 Blagg and Gibson (1980: 155).

187 Blagg (1980: 181–2); Coombe et al. (2015: xxix).

188 Blagg (1980: 157–69, 181–2).

189 Blagg (1980: 169–75). See Coombe et al. (2015: 103–4 (nos 186–7)) for two fragments of a cornice from the Baynard's Castle section of the riverside wall.

190 Blagg (1980: 169–71); Coombe et al. (2015: 45–6 (no. 77)).

191 Tomlin, Wright and Hassall (2009: 18–19) (RIB 3001).

192 C. Hill (1980b: 62; cf. Blagg 1980: 191–3).

193 The Museum of London map (2011) has marked the area immediately to the west and north-west of Baynard's Castle as 'relatively undeveloped area or open ground?'. Several streams ran through this area and excavations have produced only limited information for Roman activity (cf. Schofield 1998).

194 T. Williams (1993: 10).

195 The re-dating of the initial construction of these buildings (Period I) to around the AD 160s and the evidence for the additional building work during the third century fits well with Blagg's tentative argument for the dating for the Arch and Screen (T. Bradley and Butler 2008: 69). This assumes that the fragmentary sculptures were incorporated into the riverside wall during its initial phase rather than in a later rebuilding.

196 T. Williams (1993: 10–11). The building that may have been a temple on the east bank of the Fleet river was demolished during the later third century and could have provided one source for the stones.

197 J. Maloney (1983: 111–15); Perring ((1991) 2011: 106–8); Sankey and Stephenson (1991: 122–3).

198 C. Hill, Millett and Blagg (1980) (BC75).

199 C. Hill (1980a: 30–3).

200 C. Hill (1980b: 57, 61).

201 C. Hill (1980b : 61).

202 Sheldon and Tyers (1983: 358–61). Initially, this section of wall was dated to the fourth century as a result of radiocarbon dating (C. Hill 1980b: 69–71; R. Morgan 1980), but this date was later re-evaluated when the dendrochronological dates became available.

203 See Parnell (1977), Parnell (1978), Parnell (1981), Parnell (1982) and Parnell (1985) for the Tower of London excavations (TOL39/THL78b). The substantial remains of the 'Period II' riverside wall to the north of the 'Period I' wall may have formed a protected entrance built in the late fourth century.

204 Parnell (1985: 12–13).

205 Hillam (1985b: 46).

206 Miller and Schofield (1986a: 50–4); Miller and Schofield (1986b: 64) (NFW74/SM75/FRE78).

207 Miller and Schofield (1986b: 64).

208 Hillam and Morgan (1986: 84).

209 At Peter's Hill (PET81) part of the inner face of the riverside wall was presumably constructed prior to the Period II building complex at the Salvation Army site which has been closely dated to AD 293–4 (T. Williams 1993: 13, 40–1). Mackinder (2015: 9–11) has discussed the recent work on the riverside wall at Three Quays near the Tower of London which has yielded a date of AD 251–87 for the construction of the wall. At Riverbank House (RKH06), part of the riverside wall was uncovered but dating evidence was not obtained since the foundations were not excavated (Mackinder 2015: 9–11).

210 Hillam and Morgan (1986: 84) have noted that these dates do not necessarily imply that all the sections of riverside wall were built simultaneously.

211 See C. Hill (1980a: 38–42) for the complexity of the evidence for part of the western section of the wall which, in itself, may suggest rebuilding above the foundation (cf. Marsden 1980: 174).

212 Coombe et al. (2015: 74).

213 Parnell (1985: 30).

214 Mattingly (2006: 226, Table 6).

215 Brigham (1990a: 143–6); Wilkinson and Sidell (2000: 110).

216 Fulford (2004: 315, 323–4).

217 Brigham (1990a: 143–6); Wilkinson and Sidell (2000: 110).

218 Sidell et al. (2000: 110); Thomas (2008: 103). This ship was found beyond the western extent of the area shown on Fig. 8.1.

219 Marsden (1994: 128–9).

220 Marsden (1994: 109–30, 168–70).

221 Marsden (1994: 109).

222 Marsden (1994: 112–17).

223 Marsden (1994: 124).

224 Marsden (1994: 122–3).

225 I. Tyers (1994: 205).

226 Marsden (1994: 128).

227 T. Williams (1993: 13, 40–1) (PET81).

228 T. Williams (1993: 14–32, 39–56); T. Bradley and Butler (2008: 22–30, 72–9).

229 Blagg (1996: 46); T. Bradley and Butler (2008: 73).

230 These two buildings were discovered on the Salvation Army site at Peter's Hill (T. Williams 1993: 13, 40–1) (PET81) and 99–101 Queen Victoria Street (T. Bradley and Butler 2008: 26–30, 75–8) (QUV01).

231 T. Bradley and Butler (2008: 73) have noted that they may have replaced the temples of Jupiter and Isis indicated by the altars built into the riverside wall at Baynard's Castle. It is not clear, however, that these altars had necessarily come from the Period I buildings at the Salvation Army site.

232 T. Williams (1993: 14–17); T. Bradley and Butler (2008: 25–6). This platform is broadly comparable to the timber pile and half foundation used for the riverside wall, which is thought to have been constructed during the AD 250s to 270s.

233 The analysis of timber piles from Peter's Hill, Sunlight Wharf and 99–101 Queen Victoria Street have indicated that the trees from which they were cut were felled in AD 293 and the spring of AD 294 (Hillam 1993: 96, 9; I. Tyers 2008b: 52–4).

234 T. Williams (1993: 26, 48–51).

235 See Marsden (1993: 64–5) and T. Williams (1993: 58–60) for the excavations at 101 Queen Victoria Street during 1961–2 and in 1986 at Sunlight Wharf.

236 T. Bradley and Butler (2008: 26–30, 75–8). This plinth was first excavated by Marsden in 1961–2.

237 T. Bradley and Butler (2008: 76–8, Fig. 54).

238 T. Williams (1993: 32, 37), T. Bradley and Butler (2008: 79) and Sudds (2008: 40) have discussed the idea that these buildings were never finished.

239 Casey (1994); Fulford (2002: 72–3); Birley (2005: 371–93).

240 Fulford (2008: 44).

241 Antony Birley (per. comm.).

242 T. Williams (1991); T. Williams (1993: 31–2); Casey (1994: 133–4); Fulford (2008: 44). T. Bradley and Butler (2008: 75) have suggested that some of the trees for the timber piles may have been felled during Carausius' reign as part of the initial plan to construct the complex and that Allectus continued the project but died prior to its completion.

243 Birley (2005: 388–91).

244 Casey (1994: 71–85). The mint continued in operation for the next forty years under a succession of emperors.

245 Carausius and Allectus also controlled other mints in Britain and Gaul.

246 Merrifield (1983: 197–8); Birley (2005: 382, 393).

247 Brigham (2001b: 35); Birley (2005: 393).

248 Perring ((1991) 2011: 100–5).

249 Perring ((1991) 2011: 100–3); see Brigham (1990b: 93).

250 Sites that will be considered below with evidence for late Roman timber-and-earth houses include Lloyd's Register, 1 Poultry, Drapers' Gardens and Arcadia Buildings.

251 Sankey (1989: 78).

252 Fulford, Clarke and Eckardt (2006: 8–9, 273–8).

253 J. Hill and Rowsome (2011: 194–211) (ONE94). They interpret two phases: 'period 6, phase 1' (c. AD 220–70) and 'period 6, phase 2' (c. AD 270–300).

254 'Building 64' and 'Building 65'.

255 J. Hill and Rowsome (2011: 370, 373).

256 See J. Hill and Rowsome (2011: 194–9) for 'Building 64'. See Goffin (2011) for the wall plaster.

257 J. Hill and Rowsome (2011: 370–2). The late Roman buildings at Billingsgate and Pudding Lane may have also been private residences with attached bath buildings formed of suites of heated rooms.

258 J. Hill and Rowsome (2011: 205–1). Titled 'Building 61/65'.

259 Neal and Cosh (2009: 437–40); Neal (2011) (mosaics 370.81–2).

260 Neal (2011: 378); J. Hill and Rowsome (2011: 370). 'Building 62' lay between 64 and 65, a modification of an earlier building that may still have been in use at this time (J. Hill and Rowsome 2011: 205).

261 J. Hill and Rowsome (2011: 205, 365, Fig. 190).

262 J. Hill and Rowsome (2011: 363).

263 J. Hill and Rowsome (2011: 231–41, 373).

264 Neal and Cosh (2009: 444–6) (mosaic 370.88).

265 J. Hill and Rowsome (2011: 358, Fig. 209) for DLR Bucklersbury (BUC87).

266 J. Hill and Rowsome (2011: 372).

267 Pitt and Seeley (2014: 35–9) (POU05).

268 J. Hill and Rowsome (2011: 187–90, 367–9) (LHY88).

269 J. Hill and Rowsome (2011: 205–21).

270 Goodburn, Goffin and Hill (2011: 416).

271 Elsden (2002: 19–27, 54) (CAO96).

272 Keily (2002).

273 Casson, Drummond-Murray and Francis (2014: 99–104) (GSM97).

274 Casson, Drummond-Murray and Francis (2014: 104).

275 Casson, Drummond-Murray and Francis (2014:102).

276 Schofield (1998: 237) (ABC87).

277 See Howell (2013: 27, 28, Fig. 16) for 'Building 13' (BBB05).

278 Howell (2013: 28, 30).

279 S. Watson (2015a: 36–9) (CDP04; GHM05).

280 Lyon (2007: 35–6); Roskams (1991a: 26, Fig. 23).

281 S. Watson (2006: 58–9) (NGT00).

282 S. Watson (2006: 59–61) (PNS01).

283 S. Watson (2006: 61) (SLY00).

284 Pitt (2006: 14–18, 53, Fig. 17) (NEG98).

285 See Howe and Lakin (2004: 41–6, 52) for Shelly House and Leith House (NST94; GAH95).

286 Howe and Lakin (2004: 47).

287 C. Maloney (1990: 68) (KEY83) and neighbouring sites.

288 Seeley and Drummond-Murray (2005: 75–82) (MRG95).

289 Leary and Butler (2012: 18–20) (THY01).

290 Hawkins (2009: 52–63, 117–23) (DGT06).

291 Sankey (2003: 13) (ETA89).

292 Neal and Cosh (2009: 407) (mosaic 370.11). It was initially thought that the mosaic was installed in an apsidal room (Sankey 2003: 13), but further consideration of the fragment suggests that it comprised the floor of a rectangular room (Neal and Cosh 2009: 407).

293 McKenzie (2012: 13–20) (TEA98).

294 McKenzie (2012: 13).

295 McKenzie (2012: 13).

296 McKenzie (2012: 422–5) (mosaic 370.56).

297 Dunwoodie, Harward and Pitt (2015: 124–31, 146–8) (FER97).

298 Dunwoodie, Harward and Pitt (2015: 147).

299 Wroe-Brown (2014: 51–7) (FEU08).

300 Wroe-Brown (2014: 54–7).

301 Wroe-Brown (2014: 54–7).

302 Pitt (2015: 167–71) (EAE01).

303 Blair and Sankey (2007: 59–61) (ESC97).

304 Bluer and Brigham (2006: 27–62, 69–70) (FCC95).

305 Bluer and Brigham (2006: 46–62).

306 Birbeck and Schuster (2009: 31–3, 36) (FNE01).

307 Birbeck and Schuster (2009: 36).

308 Lerz and Holder (2016: 141–4) (ARC81/SEN91/MCF06).

309 Howe (2002: 16–20) (BAX95).

310 Howe (2002: 19–20).

311 Butcher (1982).

312 Marsden (1968); Marsden (1980: 151–5) (GM111). This building was excavated by Ivor Noël-Hume in 1951 and by Marsden in 1968–71 (for additional information, see Schofield 1998: 69 and Rowsome 1999: 275). The impressive remains had previously been uncovered in 1848. In 1989–90, conservation work was conducted on the remains (BBH87), which now lie in the basement of a modern building. See Rowsome (1996) for an interim

reassessment of the building, including the sequence of its construction. Rowsome has suggested that the building may have remained in use until the end of the Roman period.

313 Bateman and Milne (1985: 138–41) (PDN81).

314 Rowsome (1996: 418).

315 Rowsome (1996: 418–19). Perring ((1991) 2011: 101) has commented on the dating of the pottery, drawing on the observations of Richardson.

316 Rowsome (1996: 420).

317 Blair and Sankey (2007: 8–16) (BPL95).

318 Blair and Sankey (2007: 9–16).

319 Blair (2007).

320 Roberts and Cox (2004: 249). Latrines have been found throughout Londinium although there is little information for the measures that were taken to dispose of human waste.

321 Blair (2007).

322 Blair and Sankey (2007: 16); Millett and Gowland (2015).

323 Swift (2008: 40–6), including the excavations undertaken by Ivor Noël-Hume at Minster House (GM12) and the more recent work (AUT01).

324 Swift (2008: 40–2). This was titled 'Building 12'.

325 Swift (2008: 43–4). This was titled 'Building 13'. Neal and Cosh (2009: 404–5) (mosaic 370.2).

326 Swift (2008: 44, Fig. 46).

327 Swift (2008: 45).

328 Brigham (2001c: 40, 48–9) (SUF94).

329 Cowan et al. (2009: 25, Fig. 12).

330 Cowan et al. (2009: 25).

331 Cowan (1995: 53–6); Drummond-Murray and Thompson (2002: 139) (15SKS80) and (RWT93/RWG94).

332 See Hammer (2003: 73–112) for Courage Brewery Areas A, E and F (COSE84[2]; CO88[1]; CO87).

333 Hammer (2003: 90–1).

334 Hammer (2003: 155).

335 See Cowan (2003: 61–5, 69–70) for 'Building 37' in Area C (COSE84[1]).

336 Hammer (2003: 155).

337 See Cowan (2003: 68–70, Fig. 65) for other stone third-century houses in Areas A, C, M and Q.

338 Drummond-Murray and Thompson (2002: 122–7) (BGH95).

339 Drummond-Murray and Thompson (2002: 127).

340 Drummond-Murray and Thompson (2002: 123–6).

341 Dennis (1978: 307–11) (1STS74).

342 Drummond-Murray and Thompson (2002: 143) (LBE95).

343 Cowan et al. (2009: 25); Cowan and Pringle (2009: 82–3) (CW83/CWO84/CHWH83).

344 See Heard (1989) and Seeley and Wardle (2009: 150–3, Fig. 150) for 'Building 11' (USA88/USB88). The stone foundation of this building had been robbed.

345 Ferretti and Graham (1978: 68–70) (207BHS72).

346 Douglas (2008: 29–32) (LGK99).

347 Douglas (2008: 32).

348 Cowan and Wardle (2009: 109–10, Fig. 86) (AB78).

349 Westman and Pringle (2009: 57).

350 Gerrard (2009a: 131–3) (USS03).

351 Taylor-Wilson (2002: 22–30) (HHO97).

352 For 175–7 and 179–91 Borough High Street, see Cowan and Pringle (2009: 80) (175BHS76/179BHS89). The three wells were at 8 Union Street, 10–18 Union Street and 107–15 Borough High Street.

353 Rayner and Seeley (2008: 190–3); Seeley and Wardle (2009: 148–56).

354 Heard (1989) (USA88/USB88).

355 Seeley and Wardle (2009: 150). Other activities at this site were not domestic, suggested by fourth-century finds (Seeley and Wardle 2009: 148; Heard 1989).

356 Seeley and Wardle (2009: 150–3). Tazze are often thought to have been used for incense burning (Bateman 2008: 162).

357 Rayner and Seeley (2009: 214–18).

358 Beasley (2007: 55–6, 62).

359 Marsh (1978); Rixson (1978); Seeley and Wardle (2009: 153) (8US74).

360 Marsh (1978: 223).

361 Yule (1982); Seeley and Wardle (2009: 155) (107BHS81).

362 Cowan et al. (2009: 183).

363 Yule (1982: 243).

364 Seeley and Wardle (2009: 153–5).

365 Seeley and Wardle (2009: 155); Symonds (2007); Haynes (2008: 128–30); Symonds (2007: 64).

366 Seeley and Wardle (2009: 153–5).

367 Seeley and Wardle (2009: 155–6).

368 Wardle (2009: 124–9) (HIB79).

369 Wardle (2009: 124).

370 Hall (1996: 76).

371 Cool (2006: 112–14); Liddle, Ainsley and Rielly (2009: 245, Table 54); Gerrard (2011h: 555–6, 566); M. G. Allen (2015: 181–2); Maltby (2015: 185).

372 M. G. Allen (2015: 174).

373 M. G. Allen (2015: 175).

374 Deer bones have also been found at other sites in London. Part of an articulated deer skeleton had been deposited in a late fourth-century well at Drapers' Gardens in the upper Walbrook Valley (Gerrard 2011h: 555–6), while a pit in the 'eastern cemetery' contained the skeletons of an adult horse, a dog and a deer that probably formed a ritual deposit (Barber and Bowsher 2000: 19–20, 319–20). Red deer and roe deer were also present in the animal bone assemblage from Winchester Palace, mainly from early Roman deposits (Rielly 2005: 160, 165). At the Courage Brewery sites deer antler was processed for combs, beads and knife handles (Pipe 2003a: 182; Pipe 2003b).

375 Merrifield (1996).

376 See Pinder (2011), Rogers (2011a: 110–12), Rogers (2015: 150–1) and Rykwert ((1976) 1995: 132–44) for ritual and city boundaries in the Roman world.

377 T. Williams (1993: 24); Rogers (2015: 150–1).

378 Sculpted stones from the Arch were found in areas to the west of the site (Areas II, V and VIII; Blagg 1980: 191), while the stones from the Screen were all found in Area VIII, possibly suggesting that they were transported to the site as a group (Blagg 1980: 192–3). The stones had been built into the wall in two distinct locations. In Areas II and V, sculpted stones had been set in a line along the internal face of the wall, probably at a height of around 5 metres, where they survived because this section had collapsed northwards (C. Hill 1980a: 40, 42, 44; C. Hill 1980b: 62, 64). A line of six carved blocks in Area V, which included the two altars and the relief of the female figures, was a distinctive feature of the wall that had required the controlled lifting of these heavy blocks into place. These six stones were recorded in some detail; some of them were built into the wall with inscriptions and sculptures facing into the fabric (C. Hill 1980a: 44, Plate 10). C. Hill (1980b: 62) has discussed the lifting of these blocks into place. In Area VIII, the sculpted stones were reused as part of the riverside wall's foundation layer (C. Hill 1980a: 51).

379 Blagg (1980: 192).

380 Blagg (1980: 126).

381 C. Hill (1980b: 62).

382 Blagg (1980: 126); Blagg and Gibson (1980: 155).

383 Croxford (2003: 83–8).

384 Hall (2014).

385 Hall (2014: 168).

386 Hall (2014: 169–72).

387 Guildhall Museum (1970: 1–9); Schofield (1998: 75).

388 Guildhall Museum (1970: 6); Hall (2014: 180).

389 Guildhall Museum (1970: 6).

390 Guildhall Museum (1970: 6, Fig. 4).

391 See Sankey and Stephenson (1991: 117, 119, 120–2), Schofield (1998: 242–3) and Hall (2014: 167–78) for interim reports and discussion of the coin moulds (BLM87).

392 Sankey and Stephenson (1991: 120).

393 Schofield (1989: 242).

394 T. Taylor (2012: 98).

395 Hall (2014: 167–78, Table 1).

396 Hall (2014: 182–3).

397 Hall (2014: 167).

398 Hall (2014: 167).

399 Hall (2014: 180); C. Maloney (1999: 21) (BYQ98).

400 Heard (1996: 78–80); McKinley (2006: 89); Cowan et al. (2009: 24); Cowan and Wardle (2009: 117); L. Wheeler (2009: 77).

401 Prominence has been given to these practices of exposure here since the more traditional practices of inhumation and cremation have been fully addressed in other accounts of burial in Roman London.

402 Dodwell (2006) (MRL98).

403 See Harward, Powers and Watson (2015: 55–68) for 16–18 Finsbury Circus / 18–31 Eldon Street. The other areas of the cemetery reviewed in earlier chapters would appear to have been disused by this time.

404 Harward, Powers and Watson (2015: 64–5, 88, 92–3).

405 Harward, Powers and Watson (2015: 66–7).

406 Schofield (1989: 242); Hall (2014: 167).

407 Hall (2014: 167).

408 Presumably the pots containing the burial offerings were not washed very far downstream from the location at which the burials were made.

409 Hall has noted that the building material and human bone lay at the bottom of the ditch and the coin moulds on the sloping side, while the upper layer of the fill contained a mixture of moulds and building material (Hall 2014).

410 See Thomas (2004: 18–29) for interim comments (SRP98).

411 Sudds and Douglas (2015: 5–21) (CPN01); Swift (2003: 20–1) (BGB98).

412 Bull et al. (2011: 23–6) (HLW06/SDX07). These burials were north of the area shown on Fig. 8.15.

413 See Ridgeway, Leary and Sudds (2013: 105–6, Fig. 71) for the extent and character of the Southwark cemeteries, including sites referred to in this chapter.

414 Mackinder (2000: 22–4) (GDV96).

415 Mackinder (2000: 24).

416 See Edwards (2010) for the burials from Harper Road (HPZ10); more recent excavations close by have uncovered additional burials.

417 See Killock (2010: 27–36, 84–6) and Langthorne (2010) for interim assessments (TIY07).

418 Killock (2010: 29–31, 85–6).

419 Killock (2010: 30).

420 Killock (2010).

421 Killock (2010: 31).

422 This full publication of the results of the excavation of this site will potentially provide highly significant information about the continuation of early Roman fragmentation rites into the third and fourth centuries.

423 Ridgeway, Leary and Sudds (2013: 105, Fig. 71) (LTU03). Recent research is suggesting that some of the excavated burials from 52–6 Lant Street may be of third-century date (Redfern et al. in press).

424 Graham (1978); Watt (1978b) (1SS73).

425 See Ridgeway, Leary and Sudds (2013: 7, 104–7) for a summary of some of the unpublished material from 2 America Street. The 56 Southwark Bridge Road cemetery site was a fourth-century extension to this burial area (Ridgeway, Leary and Sudds 2013: 7, 104–7).

426 Hall (1996: 76).

427 Connell (2009: 251); White (2009) (GRH82).

428 Heard (1996: 80–1).

429 Bentley and Pritchard (1982: 137–59) (BAR79).

430 Shaw et al. (2016: 62–3).

431 See Schofield (1998: 298–9) for an interim report (WES89).

432 S. Watson (2003: 15–21) (ATL89/ATC97).

433 Barber and Bowsher (2000: 301–3, 330).

434 G. Brown (2008: 84–7); G. Brown (2012).

435 G. Brown (2012: 34, 47).

9 Endings and Beginnings

1 Previous accounts suggest a gradual decline in London during the late third and fourth centuries, e.g. Perring ((1991) 2011: 106–31), B. Watson (1998: 100) and Perring (2015: 35–8).

2 Rogers and Hingley (2010).

3 Rogers (2011a: 14–26); Gerrard (2011i: 182). Esmonde Cleary (1999: 398) has suggested that the tradition of focusing on urban decline has led to a damaging lack of attention to the late Roman period in London.

4 Sankey (1998); Gerrard (2011g: 85); Gerrard (2011i). Rogers (2011a), Gerrard (2013) and Speed (2014) have made comparable points for the other towns of later Roman Britain.

5 Birley (2005: 397–8) has discussed the evidence for the division into four provinces and the role of London within the province of *Maxima*. Mattingly (2006: 334–5) has reviewed the uncertainties about the exact location and the character of the four provinces.

6 M. Jones (1996: 145, n. 5); Petts (2003: 38).

7 Esmonde Cleary (1989: 82); Hassall (1996: 25).

8 Birley (2005: 403–4).

9 Merrifield (1983: 206, Fig. 50).

10 Edmond Cleary (1989: 82).

11 Birley (2005: 425).

12 See Birley (2005: 430–40) for the text of Ammianus Marcellinus (8. 6–8; 28. 3. 1–3).

13 Birley (2005: 434).

14 Birley (2005: 398, n. 4).

15 Merrifield (1983: 215).

16 The *Notitia Dignitatum* is a problematic document. The basic text may have been complied between around AD 386 and 394, but the information about the western empire clearly underwent revisions until at least AD 419 (Kulikowski 2000: 360). Therefore, the information on Londinium could refer to the AD 380s and 390s. The document's records may also portray a more organized administration in Britain than actually existed at this time (Kulikowski 2000: 359).

17 Rivet and Smith (1979: 225, 260).

18 Gerrard (2011i).

19 Gerrard (2011i: 187–90).

20 Gerrard (2011i: 190).

21 Rogers (2011a).

22 Brigham (2001b: 36–7, 51). This was titled 'Bridge 3'.

23 Rhodes (1991: 190).

24 Brigham (2001b: 51). The Theodosian Code was published by a constitution of 15 February AD 438 and included in the Code were individual imperial enactments dated to 370, 382 and 390 (Anthony Birley pers. comm.).

25 Haslam (2010: 134).

26 Dawson (2011: 6).

27 B. Watson (2001: 52), although the very limited information suggests that the Roman and Saxon bridges were in slightly different locations which may indicate that the latter bridge avoided the remains of its predecessor (B. Watson 2001: 52).

28 See Dunwoodie (2004: 34) for information for activities in the south-east of the forum at 168 Fenchurch Street (FEH95), which may suggest that the main building was demolished by the early fourth century (cf. Rogers 2011a: 78).

29 Brigham (1992b: 94–5). The conditions under which excavations have been undertaken, together with the poor preservation of the deposits, have severely restricted understanding of these final phases. Dunwoodie (2004: 34) has noted that the potential information for later buildings on the site of the demolished forum is far from definitive since it is also possible that the excavated features represented alterations to the structure of the forum itself.

30 See Davies (1992: 72) for the latest pottery and a coin from the floor layers. Brigham (1990b: 82) has observed that the basilica was 'razed following a period of abandonment around the end of the third century'. The evidence for the demolition of most of the superstructure of the basilica relates to the sealing of the entire site by a layer of 'dark earth' that contained fourth-century pottery and early fourth-century coins (Brigham 1990b: 82).

31 Brigham (1990b: 77–9, 93); Brigham (1992b: 94).

32 Rogers (2011a: 78–80).

33 Brigham (1990b: 79); Brigham (1992b: 94–5).

34 Speed (2014: 113).

35 Rogers (2011a: 38–42).

36 Bateman, Cowan and Wroe-Brown (2008: 72–93).

37 Hammerson (2008).

38 Bateman, Cowan and Wroe-Brown (2008: 82, 84).

39 Wardle (2008b: 199); Bateman, Cowan and Wroe-Brown (2008: 131–2).

40 Wardle (2008b: 199).

41 The demolition debris that overlay the arena contained coins dating from around AD 367–75, while coins dated to AD 355 to 365 and 365 to 375 were found in the backfill of trenches that had been cut to remove stone from the arena walls (Bateman, Cowan and Wroe-Brown 2008: 91).

42 Bateman, Cowan and Wroe-Brown (2008: 87–8).

43 Bateman, Cowan and Wroe-Brown (2008: 91).

44 Bateman, Cowan and Wroe-Brown (2008: 92).

45 Bateman, Cowan and Wroe-Brown (2008: 92).

46 See Hammerson (2008) for the coins from the amphitheatre and a comparison of these to those from other areas of Londinium, including Southwark, 1 Poultry and 75 Cheapside.

47 Hammerson (2008).

48 Hawkins (2009: 368).

49 Rielly (2008).

50 Bateman, Cowan and Wroe-Brown (2008: 129) have discussed the example from the amphitheatre.

51 Bateman, Cowan and Wroe-Brown (2008: 91–2).

52 Bateman, Cowan and Wroe-Brown (2008: 93); Speed (2014: 114).

53 Shepherd (1998: 84–97, 227–9) (GM157/GM256).

54 Shepherd (1998: 227–9); Henig (1998: 230).

55 Shepherd (1998: 82, 227–8).

56 Croxford (2003: 90–2).

57 Haynes (2008: 128, 131, 132) has drawn on the work of Schäfer to argue that the worship of Mithras continued in this building during the fourth century, since there may have been a connection between the worship of Mithras and Bacchus.

58 A large fragment of a marble inscription that contains a dedication to Mithras, probably dating to AD 307–8, was found facing upwards on the floors of the fourth-century temple (Collingwood and Wright 1995a: 2; Shepherd 1998: 174–5) (RIB 4). It was placed in the second layer of flooring following the rebuilding of the temple, although it need not indicate a change of religious practice since its deposition could have been for cult purposes.

59 See Toynbee (1986: 39–42) and Shepherd (1998: 189–91) for Toynbee's sculpture 15. Shepherd has recorded that this sculpture came from Floor 8 in the temple (Shepherd 1998: 51, 96). Toynbee (1986: 42) and Coombe et al. (2015: 1 (no. 1)) have discussed the date of the statuette.

60 See Toynbee (1986: 22–5), Shepherd (1998: 188–9, 201–2) and Coombe et al. (2015: 1–2 (nos 2 to 3)) for sculptures 6 and 7.

61 Shepherd (1998: 189).

62 Toynbee (1986: 24–5). Shepherd (1998: 50–1, 201–2) has provided a further description and information on the context.

63 Shepherd (1998: 232).

64 Henig (1998: 230). Ferris (2014: 106) has argued that the portion of the midriff of a pipe-clay figurine of Venus from the Roman fort of Binchester (County Durham) has been carefully mutilated before deposition in a pit. Fittock (2015: 125–9, Fig. 9b) has undertaken fragmentation analysis of the pipe-clay figurines from London and has concluded that the prominence of the torso, body and legs of figurines of Venus may relate to the iconography of the goddess and reflect healing and fertility rituals.

65 Hall and Merrifield (1998).

66 Groves (1998) and Shepherd (1998: 192–3).

67 Shepherd (1998: 229).

68 Killock et al. (2015: 53–60, 263–5) (LLS02).

69 Killock et al. (2015: 54–6, 263–4).

70 Killock et al. (2015: 54).

71 Killock et al. (2015: 264).

72 Killock et al. (2015: 66–7).

73 Killock et al. (2015: 66).

74 See Sankey (1998) for an interim discussion (PEP89). The excavation of this important site has yet to be fully published but a summary of the evidence for the building and the large number of late Roman coins that were recovered has been published by Gerrard (2011g).

75 Gerrard (2011g: 78–80). Petts (2003: 63) has emphasized the highly fragmentary nature of the surviving evidence for this building.

76 Gerrard (2011g: 85).

77 Sankey (1998: 80–1).

78 Esmonde-Cleary (1999: 398) has stated that the idea that this building is a *horreum* or church 'does not convince' but provides no alternative interpretation. Petts (2003: 63–5) has argued that this building clearly resembles the cathedral at St Tecla but that the fragmentary nature of the London building makes interpretation difficult to sustain. Gerrard (2011g: 87–8) has noted that the function of this building is unclear.

79 Petts (2003: 100).

80 Gerrard (2011g: 81, 83–5).

81 Gerrard (2011g: 83).

82 Gerrard (2011g: 87–8) has also noted the discovery of sherds of Camulodunum 306 bowls from deposits sealed below the building, interpreted elsewhere in southern Britain as indicating 'pagan' ritual activity.

83 Gerrard (2011g: 85).

84 Gerrard (2011g: 84).

85 Gerrard (2011g: 85, Table 1).

86 Gerrard (2011g: 85).

87 Douglas, Gerrard and Sudds (2011: 27–58) (TOC02/HGA02).

88 Douglas, Gerrard and Sudds (2011: 41–2).

89 Douglas, Gerrard and Sudds (2011: 55).

90 J. Maloney (1980: 70–4); J. Maloney (1983: 105–11); Marsden (1980: 170–3); Merrifield (1983: 228–35).

91 Pearson (2002: 71–5); Speed (2014: 110).

92 When a new bastion is located it is given the suffix 'A' (hence Bastion 4A).

93 J. Maloney (1980: 72–4).

94 Lyon (2007: 47–52).

95 The evidence that these eastern bastions were solid has been derived from the remains of Bastions
    9 and 10 recorded in the Victorian period (RCHM 1928: 100–3; J. Maloney 1983: 110) and the evidence from
    the excavation of Bastion 4A (below). Coombe et al. (2015: xx) have provided a general discussion of the reused
    stones in these bastions.

96 J. Maloney (1980: 72–4).

97 Marsden (1980: 172); J. Maloney (1979: 295–6, 297); J. Maloney (1983: 105–8) (GM55; DUK77).

98 Marsden (1980: 172).

99 J. Maloney (1979: 295).

100 Maloney's interim report on his excavation has clearly indicated, however, that the dating of Bastion 6 was far
     from conclusive and these excavations have not been published in full.

101 J. Maloney (1980); J. Maloney (1983: 105–8); Merrifield (1983: 231–2) (XWL79).

102 J. Maloney (1980: 70).

103 J. Maloney (1980: 68).

104 J. Maloney (1980: 68).

105 Lyon (2007: 47). Shepherd (2012: 47–9) has updated this discussion for Bastion 11A. Butler (2002: 53) has
     provided further discussion of Bastion 15.

106 J. Maloney (1983: 111). Evidence may have been largely removed by post-Roman recuttings of the ditch (Butler
     2002: 51).

107 Butler (2002: 51).

108 See Rowsome (2014: 5) for the excavation of this ditch at 42–6 Ludgate Hill and 1–6 Old Bailey (LUD82).

109 Lyon (2007: 47–52).

110 The limited information available for a gateway in the wall at Aldersgate suggests that it featured projecting
     towers and may have been constructed at the same time as the bastions (J. Maloney 1983: 110). Butler (2002:
     47) has suggested, however, that this might represent the rebuilding of an earlier gateway constructed as part of
     the original wall.

111 Gerrard (2013: 47–9).

112 J. Maloney (1983: 108).

113 Parnell (1985: 13–22, 30–4) (TOL39/THL78b).

114 Parnell (1985: 13–22).

115 Parnell (1985: 18, Fig. 17).

116 Parnell (1985: 18, Fig. 17).

117 Parnell (1985: 16).

118 Parnell (1985: 16–17).

119 See Parnell (1985: 21) and Curnow (1985) for 'layer 32'.

120 Merrifield (1983: 226).

121 Parnell (1981: 69–70).

122 Parnell (1981: 70).

123 Parnell (1981: 70); Parnell (1985: 30).

124 Parnell (1981: 71–2).

125 Parnell (1981: 69); Parnell (1985: 33).

126 Parnell (1985: 33–4); Collingwood and Wright (1990: 30) (RIB 2402.4).

127 Merrifield (1983: 241–4) has suggested that three additional silver ingots may have come from the Tower of London.

128 Milles (1779: 291).

129 Milles (1779: 295).

130 Collingwood and Wright (1990: 29).

131 Parnell (1985: 33). The ingot and coins may have constituted a silver and gold hoard. See Painter (2015: 76, 78, Table 3) for a broadly comparable and slightly earlier hoard with two silver ingots and coins from a late Roman house in Emona, the Roman city of Ljubljana (Slovenia). Painter has considered that many such late Roman gold and silver hoards were buried at times of political crisis.

132 Butcher (1982: 105).

133 Gerrard (2013: 44) has argued that the idea of a late Roman stronghold in the area of the Tower of London is unlikely since this idea is based on parallels with the urban centres of Gaul where walled circuits only define small parts of these earlier cities.

134 Perring ((1991) 2011: 117, 125, 128).

135 Symonds and Tomber (1994) undertook an important study of late Roman ceramics in London that has helped to draw the attention of pottery specialists to this material. A number of more recent pottery reports have built on this work in examining particular sites. Cowan and Seeley (2009), for example, have assessed a range of ceramics of fourth-century date across Southwark.

136 Gerrard (2011i: 186) has observed that the extent of late Roman occupation is indicated by the frequency of certain forms from the Oxfordshire pottery and particularly by three wares known as 'Porchester D', Calcite gritted ware and Mayen ware.

137 See J. Hill and Rowsome (2011: 211–31, 383–8, 446–7) for 'Buildings 64 and 66' (ONE94).

138 J. Hill and Rowsome (2011: 212–17). See Neal and Cosh (2009: 437–40) and Neal (2011) (mosaic 370.80) for 'Building 64'.

139 See J. Hill and Rowsome (2011: 221–4) for 'Building 72'.

140 J. Hill and Woodger (1999: 23–4) (CID90).

141 Hammerson (2008: 211); Hammerson (2011b). The coins from the sites at and around 1 Poultry indicate that fourth-century currency was reasonably plentiful, especially for the period from AD 340–50 and AD 355–65. At Site D, there was a slightly higher frequency of coins dating from the period of AD 388 than there had been at 1 Poultry, although the numbers of coins may be too small to confirm this.

142 J. Hill and Rowsome (2011: 386, 447).

143 See J. Hill and Rowsome (2011: 386) for the well ('Structure 53').

144 J. Hill and Rowsome (2011: 386). At the 'satellite sites' around 1 Poultry there was some evidence for rebuilding and activity at earlier buildings that continued in some cases until the second half of the fourth century, although not beyond this date (J. Hill and Rowsome 2011: 233–49).

145 J. Hill and Rowsome (2011: 248, 386–8, 447).

146 J. Hill and Rowsome (2011: 386).

147 J. Hill and Rowsome (2011: 447).

148 Cf. Gerrard (2013: 274–5).

149 Marsden (1980: 167, 180, 182–6) (GM111); Rowsome (1996: 418–20) (BBH87).

150 Marsden (1980: 180).

151 Marsden (1980: 185).

152 Symonds and Tomber (1994: 77–80).

153 Marsden (1980: 185, 214, n. 30). Lyne (2015) has identified handmade pottery from this site as derived from a small late Roman pottery industry in the valley of the River Cray near Orpington.

154 See Marsden (1975: 77–8) for 'Area 5'.

155 Merrifield (1983: 250–1).

156 Neal and Cosh (2009: 400–1, 434–7) (mosaic 370.76).

157 Neal and Cosh (2009: 422–5) (mosaic 370.56).

158 Elsden (2002: 22–5) (CAO96).

159 Pitt (2006: 14–18, 53, Fig. 17) (NEG98).

160 S. Watson (2006: 64–7) (PNS01).

161 S. Watson (2006: 64–7).

162 McKenzie (2012: 13–20) (TEA98).

163 Dunwoodie, Harward and Pitt (2015: 124–31, 146–8) (FER97).

164 Dunwoodie, Harward and Pitt (2015: 128–30, 147–8).

165 The third-century house at Lion Plaza had a comparable tower.

166 Dunwoodie, Harward and Pitt (2015: xvi); Thompson (2015: 192–3); Bowsher (2015: 217–18).

167 Wroe-Brown (2014: 54–7) (FEU08).

168 Bluer and Brigham (2006: 57–62, 70) (FCC95).

169 Bluer and Brigham (2006: 56–7).

170 Bluer and Brigham (2006: 61–2); Rowsome (2006: 96).

171 Birbeck and Schuster (2009: 36) (FNE01).

172 Howe (2002: 20–5) (BAX95).

173 Howe (2002: 23, 25).

174 T. Williams (1993: 32, 52–3, 56) (PET81).

175 T. Williams (1993: 32).

176 T. Bradley and Butler (2008: 30, 79) (QUV01).

177 G. Milne (1985: 32–3); Bateman and Milne (1985: 138–41) (PDN81).

178 G. Milne (1985: 32); Bateman and Milne (1985: 140–1).

179 G. Milne (1985: 33).

180 Butcher (1982).

181 Swift (2008: 45–6) (AUT01).

182 Swift (2008: 46).

183 Brigham (2001c: 44, 48–9) (SUF94).

184 Blair and Sankey (2007: 16–17) (BPL95).

185 Symonds (2007).

186 Blair and Sankey (2007: 17).

187 Perring ((1991) 2011: 117).

188 See Hawkins (2009: 57–65, 121–4) for an interim report (DGT06).

189 Hawkins (2009: 123).

190 Hawkins (2009: 59). See Gerrard (2009b), Gerrard (2011h) and Gerrard (2013: 107–9) for details of the well (Well 569) and the hoard it contained.

191 Gerrard (2009b: 165–6).

192 Hawkins (2009: 64–5).

193 Further south in the upper Walbrook Valley, at 6–8 Tokenhouse Yard (THY01), a rectangular pit containing cess deposits from occupation in the vicinity contained a small pottery assemblage dated after around AD 325 (Leary and Butler 2012: 19–20, 83). Other gullies and features in this low-lying area were also thought to date to around the same period, suggesting that occupation continued. At 15–35 Copthall Avenue (KEY83), where an abandoned area of roadside settlement was recolonized during the middle of the fourth century, the ground level had been raised, indicating that drainage was becoming less effective (C. Maloney 1990: 70–7, 122). Further industrial activities in this area may be indicated by pits and traces of buildings.

194 Too far north to be shown on Fig. 9.5.

195 Gerrard (2011i: 189).

196 See Thomas, Sloane and Phillpotts (1997: 11–13) for an interim report (NRT85/SPQ87/NRF88/SIN88/SPQ88/BOG89/SPI91).This is too far north to be shown on Fig. 9.5.

197 Lakin (2002: 19–24) (LD74/LD76). This is too far east to be shown on Fig. 9.5.

198 Lakin (2002: 23–4).

199 Douglas, Gerrard and Sudds (2011: 54–8) (TOC02/HGA02).

200 Douglas, Gerrard and Sudds (2011: 56–7); Gerrard (2011a: 68); Gerrard (2011f: 172); D. Williams (2011: 81).

201 Gerrard (2011b); Gerrard (2011c: 101).

202 Gerrard (2011e); see Cotton (1996: 94).

203 Collingwood and Wright (1990: 68–70) (RIB 2406.1 to 2406.10).

204 Petts (2003: 108–9).

205 Telfer (2010: 53–4). This site was too far west to be shown on Fig. 9.5, although it is marked on Fig. 9.9.

206 Telfer (2010: 53–4).

207 Cowan and Seeley (2009: Fig. 131) have used late Roman pottery to plot the likely extent of fourth-century settlement across Southwark. These observations have been updated by Gerrard (2011i: 190).

208 Drummond-Murray and Thompson (2002: 143–8) (BGH95).

209 Drummond-Murray and Thompson (2002: 143–4).

210 Drummond-Murray and Thompson (2002: 144–6).

211 Drummond-Murray and Thompson (2002: 145).

212 See Cowan and Pringle (2009: 87–89), Cowan and Seeley (2009: 157–8) and Cowan et al. (2009: 179–80) for 4–26 St Thomas Street (4STS82).

213 Cowan and Pringle (2009: 86–9).

214 Cowan and Seeley (2009: 157–8).

215 Cowan and Seeley (2009: 161).

216 Dennis (1978: 307–11) (1STS74).

217 Dennis (1978: 307–11); Cowan and Pringle (2009: 90).

218 Drummond Murray and Thompson (2002: 146); Neal and Cosh (2009: 454–5) (mosaic 371.4) (MSA92).

219 Cowan et al. (2009: 25); Cowan and Pringle (2009: 82–3) (CW83/CWO84/CHWH83). The latest coin in a hoard from this site is Theodosian (AD 378–83; Cowan and Pringle 2009: 166).

220 Cowan (1995: 53–6) (15SKS80).

221 Drummond-Murray and Thompson (2002: 139) (RWG94).

222 Cowan (1995: 56–9).

223 Cowan (1995: 57). One burial had a coin of AD 41–54 that was presumably an heirloom.

224 Cowan (1995: 59–60).

225 Drummond Murray and Thompson (2002: 147–8) (REW92). A coin dating from around AD 270–365 was found in one of these burials, although it was not clearly associated with the corpse. It is possible that these burials might have dated to the nineteenth century (Drummond Murray and Thompson 2002: 148).

226 Yule (2005: 59, 66, 73–4, 85) (WP83).

227 Yule (2005: 85) has defined this as 'squatter occupation' and has noted the evidence for boneworking. See also Macphail (2005).

228 See Hammer (2003: 98–123) for Areas E and F (CO88[1]; CO87).

229 Hammer (2003: 102–3).

230 See Hammer (2003: 105–12) for 'Building 48' on Sites E and F.

231 See Cowan (2003: 70–3, 87–8) for 'Building 37' and the seven inhumations from Courage Brewery Area C (COSE84[1]).

232 Cowan (2003: 72–3).

233 See Cowan (2003: 73) for these buildings in Areas E and F.

234 Cowan (2003: 73–5). Hammer (2003: 117–23).

235 Hammer (2003: 123).

236 Heard (1989: 130) (USA88/USB88). Heard has dated the coin to *c.* AD 355–65, but Anthony Birley has pointed out to me that Constantius II died in AD 361.

237 Beasley (2007: 45–6) (SWN98).

238 Cowan et al. (2009: 57); Cowan and Seeley (2009: 161) (AB78).

239 Killock et al. (2015: 67–70, 265–6).

240 Killock et al. (2015: 69); Gerrard (2015b: 122).

241 Killock et al. (2015: 69–70); Langthorne (2015: 225–9).

242 Ferretti and Graham (1978: 68–70) (207BHS72).

243 Taylor-Wilson (2002: 31–6) (HHO97).

244 Taylor-Wilson (2002: 31–6).

245 Hammerson (1978); Merrifield (1996: 105); Seeley and Wardle (2009: 144, 149) (SCC77).

246 Hammerson (1978: 209).

247 Hammerson (1978: 210).

248 See Hammer (2003: 16, 113–14, 115, 125) for the pit ('Structure 40') and 'Building 52' at Site F (CO87).

249 Hammer (2003: 113–14).

250 Hammer (2003: 113–14).

251 See Gerrard (2009b) and Gerrard (2011h) for 'well 569' (cf. Hawkins 2009).

252 Gerrard (2009b: 163–4); Gerrard (2011h: 552).

253 Gerrard (2009b: 166).

254 Gerrard (2013: 109).

255 Gerrard (2009b).

256 Gerrard (2009b: 178).

257 Gerrard (2009b: 179).

258 Gerrard (2011h: 555–6).

259 Gerrard (2011h: 556).

260 Gerrard (2011h: 568).

261 See Jackson et al. (2013) for an interim report (BZY10).

262 See Gerrard (2011a: 68) and Douglas, Gerrard and Sudds (2009: 57–8) for 'well A[1399]' (TOC02/HGA02).

263 J. Maloney (1983: 108, 110); Merrifield (1983: 229–30).

264 See Price (1880) for a detailed account of Bastion 10.

265 RCHM (1928: 101–3).

266 Price (1880: 25–95, Plates II and II).

267 Price (1880: 80–1, Plate II).

268 Toynbee (1964: 55, Plate VIIa).

269 Coombe et al. (2015: 59 (no. 98)).

270 Price (1880: Plate III).

271 M. Bishop (1983); Toynbee (1964: 113); Coombe et al. (2015: 69 (no. 121)).

272 Price (1880: 27).

273 Price (1880: 27).

274 Coombe et al. (2015: 48).

275 Coombe et al. (2015: 56–8, 63, 99, 105–6 (nos 93, 96, 107, 174, 191–6)) have recorded ten of these fragments.

276 RCHM (1928: 100). See Coombe et al. (2015: 100–1, 107 (nos 180 and 197)) for a column shaft and a dressed block.

277 Grasby and Tomlin (2002: 45–50).

278 Burkitt (1853).

279 Burkitt (1853: 241). Price (1880: 23) has suggested that these substantial quantities of reused stone were derived from the demolished bastion, stating that 'no less than forty cart-loads of sculptured stones were removed . . . and comprised for the most part sepulchral memorials, fragments of tombs, and inscriptions, mouldings of varied patterns, pilasters and capitals, blocks of oolitic stone coated with plaster, on which were described devices and letters in red colour, portions of quern stones, &c., &c.'.

280 Burkitt (1853: 242).

281 Grasby and Tomlin (2002: 45, 47, Figs 5 and 6).

282 RCHM (1928: 100, Plate 32). See Coombe et al. (2015: 70, 96 (nos 123, 166)) for an architectural frieze with a hound chasing a hare and a Corinthian pilaster capital derived from this bastion.

283 Coombe et al. (2015: 54–5 (nos 88 and 89)).

284 Hunt (2011: 55) (ASQ87).

285 Gerrard (2013: 163–4).

286 Nick Bateman (pers. comm.).

287 Lavan (2011) has discussed the complexities of relationships between 'pagan' religions and Christianity during the fourth century and beyond. Mulryan (2011: 52) has argued that indigenous cults may in general have survived longer in Britain than in Gaul and Germany. Goodman (2011: 171) has suggested that Romano-Celtic temples in Britain may have survived longer in the countryside than in the towns, although the evidence for the two London temples suggests that urban temples continued well into the fourth century.

288 See Petts (2003: 62), Hall and Shepherd (2008: 36–7), McCourt (2010: 214) and Schofield (2011: 42–3) for the scarcity of evidence for Christianity in Roman London. See Speed (2014: 105–6, 114–5) for the general lack of evidence for churches in late Roman towns in Britain and the evidence for the survival of temples.

289 Cowan and Seeley (2009: 164).

290 Sankey (1998: 82).

291 One burial contained a coin dating from between AD 388 and 402 (Barber and Bowsher 2000: 210 for Burial 557), indicating that the burial ground remained in use in late Roman times.

292 Barber and Bowsher (2000: 303–7).

293 Barber and Bowsher (2000: 304).

294 Barber and Bowsher (2000: 336–7); Coombe (2015: 52, 126 (no. 86)).

295 See Barber and Bowsher (2000: 183–4, 206–8, 305–6) for Burial 538 (male) and Burial 374 (female) (MSL87). The area of the 'eastern cemetery' was divided into several plots by the excavators.

296 Barber and Bowsher (2000: 305–6).

297 Barber and Bowsher (2000: 305–6).

298 Rebecca Redfern (pers. comm.).

299 Barber and Bowsher (2000: 184, 306).

300 Gerrard (2013: 199, 152–3).

301 Shaw et al. (2016: 63). This individual could, of course, have had cultural or ancestral connections with the Germanic area of the empire.

302 Shaw et al. (2016: 63–4); see Barber and Bowsher (2000: 183–4).

303 Shaw et al. (2016: 65).

304 Shaw et al. (2016: 65); Eckardt, Müldner and Lewis (2014: 537).

305 See Ridgeway, Leary and Sudds (2013: 25–30, 97–102) for these eighteen burials (SBK03).

306 Ridgeway, Leary and Sudds (2013: 16–23) (LTU03).

307 Ridgeway, Leary and Sudds (2013: 19).

308 Gerrard and Lyne (2013: 36).

309 Gerrard and Lyne (2013: 36).

310 Barber and Bowsher (2000: 122–3); see Gerrard and Lyne (2013: 36).

311 Radiocarbon dating is not usually sufficiently accurate to provide anything more than a general idea of the date of an individual body.

312 Ridgeway, Leary and Sudds (2013: 113–15); Redfern et al. (2016: 20).

313 Major (2013: 47); Redfern et al. (2016: 19); Redfern et al. (in press).

314 Ridgeway, Leary and Sudds (2013: 114); Redfern et al. (2016: 14, Table 2).

315 The dating of burials is largely dependent on the grave goods interred with them and it is possible that all these burials of immigrants dated from the fourth century, although the ancestry analysis appears to indicate that some individuals of African descent died during the second and fourth centuries (Ridgeway, Leary and Sudds 2013: 114).

316 Graham (1978: 1–5) (1SS73).

317 Little trace of grave cuts were observed.

318 See Killock (2010: 37–55, 86–9) for an interim report (TIY07).

319 Thomas (2004: 20–6); Montgomery et al. (2010: 217–18) (SRP98).

320 Initial aDNA testing had suggested that this woman might have originated from the southern Mediterranean and, more recently, it has been suggested that she spent her early life in Rome (Montgomery et al. 2010: 217–18). aDNA work is currently underway to provide more reliable information about her origins (Rebecca Redfern pers. comm.).

321 Shaw et al. (2016: 65).

322 Museum of London (1999: 15); Thomas (2004: 25); Brettell et al. (2015: 643).

323 Museum of London (1999: 15); Thomas (2004: 25).

324 Thomas (2004: 27).

325 Thomas (2004: 27). This had been badly disturbed by later activity.

326 Thomas (2004: 27).

327 Marsden (1980: 181); Pritchard (1982: 163); Cowie and Blackmore (2008: 128).

328 See Telfer (2010) for an interim report (SMD01).

329 Telfer (2010: 52).

330 Vince (1991: 411–12); T. Brown (2008); Cowie (2008); Cowie and Blackmore (2008: 126–30); Cowie and Blackmore (2012: xxiii, 100–1, 106).

331 Cowie (2000); Cowie and Blackmore (2008: 6, 137–40); Cowie and Blackmore (2012: 1–3, 108–10).

332 Cowie and Blackmore (2012: 15, 95, Table 5).

333 Cowie and Blackmore (2012: 108, 110).

334 Cowie and Blackmore (2012: 112).

335 Cowie and Blackmore (2012: 106–7).

336 Gerrard (2011i: 192); Cowie and Blackmore (2012: 100–1).

337 Fulford, Clarke and Eckardt (2006: 280–1).

338 Fulford, Clarke and Eckardt (2006: 280–1); Creighton and Fry (2016: 441–3).

339 There is a lively debate about this issue. It has been argued that the Roman town at Viroconium (Wroxeter) was occupied well into the early medieval period, although Lane (2014) has recently argued that this settlement may have been abandoned soon after the collapse of Roman rule.

340 Gerrard (2011i); Cowie and Blackmore (2012: 101, 106–7).

341 Rhodes (1980b: 97) has observed that the excavations of the riverside wall at Baynard's Castle (BC75) had produced five sherds of handmade 'chaff-tempered' pottery. These were associated with late Roman pottery and a single medieval sherd from a dumped deposit that may have pre-dated the collapse of a section of the riverside wall. Rhodes has compared these with a sherd found during Marsden's excavations at Bastion 6 (GM55) in 1971. Vince and Jenner (1991: 48) have noted that one sherd of 'chaff-tempered' pottery was found at New Fresh Wharf (NFW74), although they have also suggested that such fabrics might date from the fifth to the ninth century and as such cannot be taken to indicate only Early Saxon activity.

342 Vince and Jenner (1991: 20, 113–14).

343 Tomber (2003: 107–8). She has noted that as no amphorae of this type have been found in Roman contexts in Britain, this example is unlikely to be a genuine London find.

344 Marsden (1980: 185). Cowie (2008: 50) and Gerrard (2011i: 190) have discussed the date of the brooch.

345 Symonds and Tomber (1994: 62, Table 8).

346 Sloane and Malcolm (2004: 20–3) (JON89).

347 G. Milne and Reynolds (1997: 21–3) (SBC92).

348 Blackmore (1997: 54–6).

349 G. Milne and Reynolds (1997: 20).

350 Telfer (2010: 57–8); Cowie and Blackmore (2012: 106–8).

351 Thomas (2008: 104–5); Malcolm and Bowsher (2003: 14); Cowie and Blackmore (2012: 105).

352 Telfer (2010: 53).

353 Telfer (2010: 55).

354 Telfer (2010: 57–8).

355 Blackmore, Vince and Cowie (2004) (LGC00).

356 Capon (2006: 172) (LCR99).

357 Ridgeway, Leary and Sudds (2013: 24, 115–16) (LTU03). See Jarrett (2013) for the Saxon pottery.

358 Ridgeway, Leary and Sudds (2013: 115); Jarrett (2013).

359 See Killock (2010: 43–4, 55) and Sudds (2010) for interim reports (TIY07).

360 Taylor-Wilson (2002: 36–8) (HHO97).

361 Cass and Preston (2010) (SSZ05).

362 Cass and Preston (2010: 57).

363 Cass and Preston (2010: 70).

364 Cowie and Blackmore (2012: 101).

365 Vince (1991: 412–13); McCourt (2010); Schofield (2011: 44); Cowie and Blackmore (2012: 101). The Saxon cathedral was probably constructed on the site of the later medieval and present-day St Paul's Cathedral.

366 Cowie and Blackmore (2012: 101).

367 Cowie and Blackmore (2012: 101–2, 200–1).

368 Cowie and Blackmore (2012: 201).

369 Cowie and Blackmore (2012: 201).

370 Vince (1990: 90); Haslam (2010).

371 Clark (1996). Petts (2003: 65) has also discussed the possibility that this might have been the site of a late Roman cathedral that was refounded in the seventh century, although he acknowledges the absence of any archaeological evidence.

372 Haslam (2010: 137).

Conclusion

1 It has not been the intention of the present study to include a thorough summary of the Roman artefacts from Londinium or the evidence that has been derived from human skeletons for the health and lifestyle of its inhabitants.

2 Tomlin (2016: 57).

3 Slaves and freedmen are, however, attested on writing tablets from London, including the examples that mention the slave Fortunata and several references to slaves and freedmen from the Bloomberg tablets (Tomlin 2016: 54).

4 Barber and Bowsher (2000: 310–11).

5 Eckardt, Müldner and Lewis (2014).

6 The work of the Museum of London has been fundamental.

7 Hingley (2015).

BIBLIOGRAPHY

Abbreviations

JBAA:	*Journal of the British Archaeological Association*
LA:	*London Archaeologist*
RCHM:	Royal Commission on Historical Monuments (England)
TLMAS:	*Transactions of the London and Middlesex Archaeological Society*

Classical and medieval sources

Dio, Cassius, *Dio's Roman History*, ed. E. Cary (1924), London: William Heinmann.

Geoffrey of Monmouth, *The History of the Kings of Britain*, trans. L. Thorne (1966), London: Penguin.

Tacitus, C., *The Annals of Imperial Rome*, trans. M. Grant (1989), London: Penguin.

Modern sources

Ackroyd, P. (2012), *London Under*, London: Vintage.

Aldhouse-Green, M. (2006), *Boudica Britannia: Rebel, War-leader and Queen*, London: Pearson Longman.

Allen, M. G. (2015), 'Chasing Sylvia's Stag: Placing Deer in the Countryside of Roman Britain', in K. Baker, R. Carden and R. Madgwick (eds), *Deer and People*, 174–86, Oxford: Windgather.

Allen, M. J., R. Scaife, N. Cameron and C. J. Stevens (2005), 'Excavations at 211 Long Lane, Southwark Part 1', *LA* 11, no. 3: 73–81.

Allen, T. and M. Cox (2000), 'Burial in Water "Normal Rite" for 1,000 years', *British Archaeology* 53 (June 2000). Available online: http://www.archaeologyuk.org/ba/ba53/ba53toc.html (accessed 18 August 2015).

Andreau, J. (1999), *Banking and Business in the Roman World*, Cambridge: Cambridge University Press.

Andrews, P. (2009), 'Metalworking Debris', in V. Birbeck and J. Schuster, 86–8.

Andrews, P. (2011), 'Springhead Religious Complex', in P. Andrews et al., 13–134.

Andrews, P., E. Biddulph, A. Hardy and R. Brown (2011), *Settling the Ebbsfleet Valley: High Speed 1 Excavations at Springhead and Northfleet, Kent. The Late Iron Age, Roman, Saxon, and Medieval Landscape, Volume 1: The Sites*, Oxford: Oxford Archaeology.

Andrews, P. and A. Smith (2011), 'Curing Ales and Brewing Ales: The Story of Springhead from the Late Iron Age to the Late Roman period', in P. Andrews et al., 189–248.

Armit, I. (2011), 'Headhunting and Social Power in Iron Age Europe', in T. Moore and X.-L. Armada (eds), *Atlantic Europe in the First Millennium BC: Crossing the Divide*, 590–607, Oxford: Oxford University Press.

Armitage, P. L. (2006), 'Dog Gnawing and Other Marks on the Human Bone', in J. Butler, 27–8.

Barber, B. and D. Bowsher (2000), *The Eastern Cemetery of Roman London: Excavations 1983–1990*, London: Museum of London, MOLAS Monograph 4.

Barber, B. and J. Hall (2000), 'Digging up the People of Roman London: Interpreting Evidence from Roman London's Cemeteries', in I. Haynes, H. Sheldon and L. Hannigan (eds), 102–20.

Bateman, N. C. W. (1985), 'Warehousing in Roman London', in G. Milne, 68–78.

Bateman, N. C. W. (1998), 'Public buildings in Roman London: Some Contrasts', in B. Watson (ed.), 47–57.

Bateman, N. C. W. (2008), 'Death, Women and the Afterlife: Some Thoughts on a Burial in Southwark', in J. Clark et al. (eds), 162–6.

Bateman, N. C. W. (2009), 'What's the Point of London's Amphitheatre? – a Clue from Diana', in T. Wilmott (ed.), 157–64.

Bateman, N. C. W., C. Cowan and R. Wroe-Brown (2008), *London's Roman Amphitheatre: Guildhall Yard, City of London*, London: Museum of London, MOLAS Monograph 35.

Bateman, N. C. W. and G. Milne (1985), 'Building on the Waterfront', in G. Milne, 127–41.

Baudrillard, J. (2003), *Passwords*, London, Verso.

Bayley, J., B. Croxford, M. Henig and B. Watson (2009), 'A Gilt-Bronze Arm from London', *Britannia* 40: 151–62.

Beasley, M. (2007), 'Roman Boundaries, Roads and Ritual: Excavations at the Old Sorting Office, Swan Street, Southwark', *TLMAS* 57 (2006): 23–68.

Beck, R. (2006), *The Religion of the Mithras Cult in the Roman Empire: Mysteries of the Unconquered Sun*, Oxford: Oxford University Press.

Bell, C. (1998), 'An Archaeological Excavation on Land Adjacent to Snowy Fielder Waye, Isleworth, London, Borough of Hounslow, Middlesex', *TLMAS* 47 (1996): 35–60.

Bentley, D. (1982), 'A Roman Cemetery in the Smithfield Area', in D. Bentley and F. Pritchard, 159–63.

Bentley, D. and F. Pritchard (1982), 'The Roman Cemetery at St. Bartholomew's Hospital', *TLMAS* 33: 134–72.

Berger, L. (ed.) (2012), *Führer durch Augusta Raurica*, Basel: Verlag.

Betts, I. M. (1995), 'Procuratorial Tile Stamps From London', *Britannia* 26: 207–29.

Betts, I. M. (2015), 'Building Material', in S. Watson (2015a), 67–70.

Betts, I. M. (2017), 'The Supply of Tile to Roman London', in D. Bird (ed.), 368–83.

Birbeck, V. and J. Schuster (2009), *Living and Working in Roman and Later London: Excavations at 60–63 Fenchurch Street*, Salisbury: Wessex Archaeology, Wessex Archaeology Report 25.

Bird, D. (1996), 'The London Region in the Roman Period', in J. Bird, M. W. C. Hassall and H. Sheldon (eds), 217–32.

Bird, D. (2000), 'The Environs of *Londinium*', in I. Haynes, H. Sheldon and L. Hannigan (eds), 151–74.

Bird, D. (2008), '"The Rest to Some Faint Meaning Make Pretence, but Shadwell Never Deviates into Sense" (Further Speculations about the Shadwell "Tower")', in J. Clark et al. (eds), 96–101.

Bird, D. (2017), 'The Countryside of the South-east in the Roman period', in D. Bird (ed.), 35–54.

Bird, D. (ed.) (2017), *Agriculture & Industry in South-Eastern Roman Britain*, Oxford: Oxbow.

Bird, J. (1986), 'Samian Wares', in L. Miller, J. Schofield and M. Rhodes, 139–85.

Bird, J. (1996), 'Frogs from the Walbrook: A Cult Pot and its Attribution', in J. Bird, M. W. C. Hassall and H. Sheldon (eds), 119–27.

Bird, J. (2002), 'Samian Wares', in D. Lakin, 31–48.

Bird, J. (2005), 'Discussion of Decorated Samian from Pit A[1066]', in F. Seeley and J. Drummond-Murray, 32.

Bird, J. (2008), 'The Decorated Samian', in N. C. W. Bateman, C. Cowan and R. Wroe-Brown, 135–42.

Bird, J. (2011a), 'The Decorated Samian', in J. Hill and P. Rowsome, 299–300.

Bird, J. (2011b), 'The Samian', in A. Douglas, J. Gerrard and B. Sudds, 71–4.

Bird, J., A. Graham, H. Sheldon and P. Townend (eds) (1978), *Southwark Excavations 1972–74*, London: London & Middlesex Archaeological Society/Surrey Archaeological Society, Joint Publication 1.

Bird, J., M. W. C. Hassall and H. Sheldon (eds) (1996), *Interpreting Roman London: Papers in memory of Hugh Chapman*, Oxford: Oxbow.

Bird, J., A. Thorp and A. Wardle (2015), 'Aspects of the Roman Finds Assemblage', in S. Watson (2015b), 196–8.

Birley, A. R. (2005), *The Roman Government of Britain*, Oxford: Oxford University Press.

Bishop, B. (2000), 'A Keyhole through the Gateway: A Watching Brief at Aldgate', *LA* 9, no. 7: 179–84.

Bishop, M. (1983), 'The Camomile Street Soldier Reconsidered', *TLMAS* 34: 31–48.

Bishop, M (2015), 'Roman Armour', in L. Dunwoodie, C. Harward and K. Pitt, 212–14.

Blackmore, L. (1997), 'Stratified Pottery, Fifth to Seventeenth Century', in G. Milne, 54–7.

Blackmore, L., A. Vince and R. Cowie (2004), 'The origins of Lundenwic? Excavations at 8–9 Long Acre/16 Garrick Street, WC2', *LA* 10, no. 11: 301–5.

Blagg, T. F. C. (1980), 'The sculptured stones', in C. Hill, M. Millett and T. Blagg, 125–93.

Blagg, T. F. C. (1996), 'Monumental Architecture in Roman London', in J. Bird, M. W. C. Hassall and H. Sheldon (eds), 43–7.

Blagg, T. F. C. (2000), 'Sculptures and Architectural Fragments', in A. Mackinder, 61–3.

Blagg, T. F. C. and S. Gibson (1980), 'The Reconstruction of the Arch', in C. Hill, M. Millett and T. Blagg, 153–7.

Blair, I. (2007), 'The Function and Significance of the Culvert (S3) and Terraced Building 2 at Monument House', in I. Blair and D. Sankey, 62–3.

Blair, I. and D. Sankey (2007), *A Roman Drainage Culvert, Great Fire Destruction Debris and Other Evidence from Hillside Sites North-east of London Bridge: Excavations at Monument House and 13–21 Eastcheap, City of London*, London: Museum of London Archaeology Services, MOLAS Archaeological Studies 17.

Blair, I., R. Spain, D. Swift, T. Taylor and D. Goodburn (2006), 'Wells and Bucket-Chains: Unforeseen Elements of Water Supply in Early Roman London', *Britannia* 37: 1–52.

Bluer, R. and T. Brigham (2006), *Roman and Later Development East of the Forum and Cornhill: Excavations at Lloyd's Register, 71 Fenchurch Street, City of London*, London: Museum of London, MOLAS Monograph 30.

Boddington, A. and P. Marsden (1987), '160–167 Fenchurch Street', in P. Marsden, 92–101.

Booth, P. (2007), 'Roman Britain in 2006: Greater London', *Britannia* 38: 286–94.

Booth, P. (2011), 'Roman Britain in 2010: Greater London', *Britannia* 42: 374–80.

Booth, P. (2014), 'Roman Britain in 2013: Greater London', *Britannia* 45: 370–9.

Booth, T. J. and R. Madgwick (2016), 'New Evidence for Diverse Secondary Burial Practices in Iron Age Britain', *Journal of Archaeological Science* 67: 12–24.

Bowlt, C. (2008), 'A Possible Extension to Grim's Dyke', in J. Clark et al. (eds), 107–11.

Bowman, A. K. (1994), *Life and Letters on the Roman Frontier: Vindolanda and its People*, London: British Museum Press.

Bowman, A. K., J. D. Thomas and R. S. O. Tomlin (2011), 'The Vindolanda Writing-tablets (Tabulae Vindolandenses IV, Part 2)', *Britannia* 42: 113–44.

Bowsher, J. (2015), 'The coins', in L. Dunwoodie, C. Harward and K. Pitt, 214–39.

Bradley, K. and P. Cartledge (eds) (2011), *The Cambridge World History of Slavery: Volume 1, The Ancient Mediterranean World*, Cambridge: Cambridge University Press.

Bradley, R. (1998), *The Passage of Arms: An Archaeological Analysis of Prehistoric Hoard and Votive Deposits*, 2nd edn, Oxford: Oxbow.

Bradley, R. (2005), *Ritual and Domestic Life in Prehistoric Europe*, London: Routledge.

Bradley, R. and K. Gordon (1988), 'Human Skulls from the River Thames, Their Dating and Significance', *Antiquity* 62: 503–9.

Bradley, T. and J. Butler (2008), *From Temples to Thames Street – 2000 Years of Riverside Development: Archaeological Excavations at the Salvation Army International Headquarters, 99–101 Queen Victoria Street, City of London*, London: Pre-Construct Archaeology, Monograph 7.

Braund, D. (1996), *Ruling Roman Britain*, London: Routledge.

Brettell, R. C., E. M. J. Schotsmans, P. Walton Rogers, N. Reifarth, R. C. Redfern, B. Stern and C. P. Heron (2015), '"Choicest Unguents": Molecular Evidence for the use of Resinous Plant Exudates in late Roman Mortuary Rites in Britain', *Journal of Archaeological Science* 53: 639–48.

Brigham, T. (1990a), 'The Late Roman Waterfront in London', *Britannia* 21: 99–183.

Brigham, T. (1990b), 'A Reassessment of the Second Basilica in London, AD 100–400: Excavations at Leadenhall Court, 1984–86', *Britannia* 21: 53–98.

Brigham, T. (1992a), 'Basilica Studies', in G. Milne (ed.), 106–13.

Brigham, T. (1992b), 'Civic Centre Redevelopment', in G. Milne (ed.), 81–95.

Brigham, T. (1992c), 'Reconstructing the Basilica', in G. Milne (ed.), 96–105.

Brigham, T. (1998a), 'The Port of Roman London', in B. Watson (ed.), 23–34.

Brigham, T. (1998b), 'Appendix 3: New Reconstructions of the Third-century Mithraeum and Fourth-century *Bacchium* or *Sacrarium*', in J. Shepherd, 237–40.

Brigham, T. (2001a), 'The Thames and the Southwark Waterfront in the Roman Period', in B. Watson, T. Brigham and T. Dyson, 12–27.

Brigham, T. (2001b), 'Roman London Bridge', in B. Watson, T. Brigham and T. Dyson, 28–51.

Brigham, T. (2001c), *Roman and Medieval Townhouses on the London Waterfront: Excavations at Governor's House, City of London*, London: Museum of London, MOLAS Monograph 9.

Brigham, T. and B. Watson (1996), 'Current Archaeological Work at Regis House in the City of London (part 2)', *LA* 8, no. 3: 63–9.

Brigham, T., B. Watson and I. Tyers (1996), 'Current Archaeological Work at Regis House in the City of London (part 1)', *LA* 8, no. 2: 31–8.

Brigham, T., D. Woodburn and I. Tyers (1996), 'A Roman Timber Building on the Southwark Waterfront, London', *Archaeological Journal* 152 (1995): 1–72.

Brown, G. (2008), 'Archaeological Evidence for the Roman London to Colchester Road between Aldgate and Harold Hill', in J. Clark et al. (eds), 82–9.

Brown, G. (2012), '"The graveyard draws the living still, but never anymore the dead": 150 Years of Funerary Archaeology in Old Ford, Tower Hamlets', *TLMAS* 62 (2011): 31–68.

Brown, G. and B. Pye (1992), 'Whittington Avenue Excavations: A Summary', in G. Milne (ed.), 135–7.

Brown, T. (2003), 'Divisions of Floodplain Space and Sites on Riverine "islands"', *Journal of Wetland Archaeology* 3: 3–15.

Brown, T. (2008), 'After the Romans: Was there a Saxon Southwark?', in J. Clark et al. (eds), 54–8.

Browne, T. (1658), *Hydriotaphia, urne-buriall, or a Discourse on the Sepulchrall Urnes lately found in Norfolk. Together with The Garden of Cyrus*, London: Henry Brome.

Bruce, G., D. Perring, T. Stevens and M. Melikian (2010), 'Roman and Medieval Activity in the Upper Walbrook Valley: Excavations at 12–18 Moorgate, City of London, EC2, 1997', *TLMAS* 60 (2009): 73–89.

Bryan, J., J. Hill and S. Watson (2016), 'The Archaeological Context', in R. S. O. Tomlin, 31–51.

Bull, R., S. Davis, H. Lewis and C. Phillpotts (2011), *Hollywell Priory and the Development of Shoreditch to c. 1600: Archaeology from the London Overground East London Line*, London: Museum of London, MOLAS Monograph 53.

Burkitt, A. H. (1853), 'On Excavations near the Roman Wall on Tower Hill', *JBAA* 8: 240–2.

Butcher, S. A. (1982), 'Excavation of a Roman Building on the East Side of the White Tower 1956–7', in Parnell, 101–5.

Butler, J. (2002), 'The City Defences at Aldersgate', *TLMAS* 52 (2001): 41–112.

Butler, J. (2006), *Reclaiming the Marsh: Archaeological Excavations at Moor House, City of London*, London: Pre-Construct Archaeology, Monograph 6.

Campbell, B. (2012), *Rivers and the Power of Ancient Rome*, Chapel Hill: University of North Carolina Press.

Capon, L. (2006), 'Saxon Activity at 15–17 Long Acre, City of Westminster', *LA* 11, no. 7: 171–6.

Carr, G. (2007), 'Excarnation to Cremation: Continuity or Change?', in C. Haselgrove and T. Moore (eds), 444–53.

Carroll, M. (2001), *Romans, Celts & Germans: The German Provinces of Rome*, Stroud: Tempus.

Carroll, M. (2006), *Spirits of the Dead: Roman Funerary Commemoration in Western Europe*, Oxford: Oxford University Press.

Casey, P. J. (1994), *Carausius and Allectus: The British Usurpers*, London: Batsford.

Cass, S. and S. Preston (2010), 'Roman and Saxon Burials at Steward Street, Tower Hamlets', *TLMAS* 60 (2009): 53–72.

Casson, L., J. Drummond-Murray and A. Francis (2014), *Romano-British Round Houses to Medieval Parish: Excavations at 10 Gresham Street, City of London, 1999–2002*, London: Museum of London, MOLAS Monograph 67.

Chapman, J. C. (2000), *Fragmentation in Archaeology: People, Places and Broken Objects in the Prehistory of South-eastern Europe*, London: Routledge.

Clark, J. (1981), 'Trinovantium – The Evolution of a Legend', *Journal of Medieval History* 7, no. 2: 135–51.

Clark, J. (1996), 'The Temple of Diana', in J. Bird, M. W. C. Hassall and H. Sheldon (eds), 1–9.

Clark, J. (2008), '"Fanciful Iconography": William Stukeley's maps of Roman(?) London', in J. Clark et al. (eds), 4–10.

Clark, J., J. Cotton, J. Hall, R. Sherris and H. Swain (eds) (2008), *Londinium and Beyond: Essays on Roman London and its Hinterland for Harvey Sheldon*, York: Council for British Archaeology. CBA Research Report 156.

Clauss, M. (2000), *The Roman Cult of Mithras: The God and his Mysteries*, trans. R. Gordon, Edinburgh: Edinburgh University Press.

Coates, R. (1998), 'A New Explanation of the Name of London', *Transactions of the Philological Society* 96, no. 2: 203–29.

Collingwood, R. G. and R. P. Wright (1990), *The Roman Inscriptions of Britain, Volume 2, Fascicule 1*, ed. S. S. Frere, M. Roxan and R. S. O. Tomlin, Gloucester: Allan Sutton.

Collingwood, R. G. and R. P. Wright (1991), *The Roman Inscriptions of Britain, Volume 2, Fascicule 3*, ed. S. S. Frere and R. S. O. Tomlin, Gloucester: Allan Sutton.

Collingwood, R. G. and R. P. Wright (1992), *The Roman Inscriptions of Britain, Volume 2, Fascicule 4*, ed. S. S. Frere and R. S. O. Tomlin, Stroud: Allan Sutton.

Collingwood, R. G. and R. P. Wright (1993), *The Roman Inscriptions of Britain, Volume 2, Fascicule 5*, ed. S. S. Frere and R. S. O. Tomlin, Stroud: Allan Sutton.

Collingwood, R. G. and R. P. Wright (1995a), *The Roman Inscriptions of Britain, Volume 1*, new edn with addenda and corrigenda by R. S. O. Tomlin, Stroud: Allan Sutton.

Collingwood, R. G. and R. P. Wright (1995b), *The Roman Inscriptions of Britain, Volume 2, Fascicule 8*, ed. S. S. Frere and R. S. O. Tomlin, Stroud: Allan Sutton.

Collins, R. and F. McIntosh (eds) (2014), *Life in the Limes: Studies of the Peoples and Objects of the Roman Frontiers*, Oxford: Oxbow.

Connell, B. (2009), 'Human Bone', in C. Cowan et al., 248–57.

Cool, H. (2006), *Eating and Drinking in Roman Britain*, Cambridge: Cambridge University Press.

Coombe, P. (2015), 'Copper-alloy Statuary', in D. Killock et al., 194–8.

Coombe, P., F. Grew, K. Hayward and M. Hennig (2015), *Roman Sculpture from London and the South-east*, Oxford: Oxford University Press, Corpus Signorum Imperii Romani, Great Britain, Volume 1, Fascicule 10.

Cotton, J. (1996), 'A Miniature Chalk Head from the Thames at Battersea and the "Cult of the Head" in Roman London', in J. Bird, M. W. C. Hassall and H. Sheldon (eds), 85–96.

Cotton, J. (2008), 'Harper Road, Southwark: An Early Roman Burial Revisited', in J. Clark et al. (eds), 151–61.

Cotton, J. and A. Green (2005), 'Further Prehistoric Finds from Greater London', *TLMAS* 55 (2004): 119–51.

Cotton, J. and N. Merriman (1994), 'Some Recent Prehistoric Finds from Greater London', *TLMAS* 42 (1991): 33–57.

Cotton, J. and B. Wood (1998), 'Recent Prehistoric Finds from the Thames Foreshore and Beyond in Greater London', *TLMAS* 47 (1996): 1–34.

Coulston, J. (2000), '"Armed and belted men": The Soldiery in Imperial Rome', in J. Coulston and H. Dodge (eds), *Ancient Rome: The Archaeology of the Eternal City*, 76–118, Oxford: Oxbow.

Cowan, C. (1995), 'A possible Mansio in Roman Southwark: Excavations at 15–23 Southwark Street, 1980–86', *TLMAS* 43 (1992): 3–192.

Cowan, C. (2003), *Urban Development in North-west Roman Southwark*, London: Museum of London, MOLAS Monograph 16.

Cowan, C. (2008), 'The Roman Garden in London', in J. Clark et al. (eds), 75–81.

Cowan, C. and S. Pringle (2009), 'The buildings', in C. Cowan et al., 78–90.

Cowan, C. and P. Rowsome (2009), 'Future Research Directions', in C. Cowan et al., 174–7.

Cowan, C. and F. Seeley (2009), 'Contraction and Decline of the Settlement', in C. Cowan et al., 157–66.

Cowan, C., F. Seeley, A. Wardle, A. Westman and L. Wheeler (2009), *Roman Southwark Settlement and Economy: Excavations in Southwark 1973–91*, London: Museum of London, MOLAS Monograph 42.

Cowan, C. and A. Wardle (2009), 'Economy', in C. Cowan et al., 91–118.

Cowie, R. (2000), '*Londinium* to *Lundenwic*: Early and Middle Saxon Archaeology in the London region', in I. Haynes, H. Sheldon and L. Hannigan (eds), 175–205.

Cowie, R. (2008), 'Descent into Darkness: London in the 5th and 6th centuries', in J. Clark et al. (eds), 49–53.

Cowie, R. and L. Blackmore (2008), *Early and Middle Saxon Settlement in the London Region*, London: Museum of London, MOLAS Monograph 41.

Cowie, R. and L. Blackmore (2012), *Lundenwic: Excavations in Middle Saxon London, 1987–2000*, London: Museum of London, MOLAS Monograph 63.

Creighton, J. (2006), *Britannia: The Creation of a Roman Province*, London: Routledge.

Creighton, J. and R. Fry (2016), *Silchester: Changing Visions of a Roman Town*. London: Society for the Promotion of Roman Studies, Britannia Monograph 28.

Crerar, B. (2016). 'Deviancy in Late Romano-British Burial', in M. Millett, L. Revell and A. Moore (eds), 381–405.

Crowley, N. (1995), 'Building Material', in C. Cowan, 144–57.

Crowley, N. (2005), 'Building Materials', in B. Yule, 90–100.

Crowley, N. and I. M. Betts (1992), 'Three "Classis Britannica" Stamps from London', *Britannia* 23: 218–22.

Croxford, B. (2003), 'Iconoclasm in Roman Britain', *Britannia* 34: 81–95.

Crummy, N. (2008), 'Small Toilet Instruments from London', in J. Clark et al. (eds), 212–25.

Crummy, P. (1997), *City of Victory: The Story of Colchester – Britain's First Roman Town*, Colchester: Colchester Archaeological Trust.

Cuming, H. S. (1857), 'On the Discovery of Celtic Crania in the Vicinity of London', *JBAA* 13: 237–40.

Cuming, H. S. (1868), 'On some Gladiatorial Relics', *JBAA* 24: 309–12.

Curnow, P. (1985), 'The Coins', in G. Parnell, 73–4.

Davies, B. (1992), 'An Absolute Chronology', in G. Milne (ed.), 60–72.

Davies, B., B. Richardson and R. Tomber (1994), *A Dated Corpus of Early Roman Pottery from the City of London*, York: Council for British Archaeology, Research Report 98.

Dawson, G. (2011), 'Saxon Defences of Southwark', *LA* 13, no. 1: 3–8.

Dean, M. (1980), 'Excavations at Arcadia Buildings, Southwark', *LA* 3, no. 14: 367–73.

Dean, M. and M. Hammerson (1980), 'Three Inhumation Burials from Southwark', *LA* 4, no. 1: 17–22.

DeLaine, J. (1999), 'Introduction: Baths – The Urban Phenomenon', in J. DeLaine and D. E. Johnston
    (eds), 157–63.

DeLaine, J. and D. E. Johnston (eds) (1999), *Roman Baths and Bathing: Proceedings of the First International
    Conference on Roman Baths Held at Bath, England, 30 March–4th April 1992: Part 2: Design and Context*,
    Portsmouth, RI: Journal of Roman Archaeology, Supplementary Series 37.

Dennis, G. (1978), '1–7 Thomas Street', in J. Bird, M. W. C. Hassall and H. Sheldon (eds), 291–422.

Dennis, M. and M. Ward (2001), 'The Roman Gold Working Evidence', in T. Brigham (2001c), 116–20.

Divers, D., C. Mayo, N. Cohen and C. Jarrett (2009), *A New Millennium at Southwark Cathedral: Investigations into
    the First Two Thousand Years*, London: Pre-Construct Archaeology, Monograph 8.

Dodwell, N. (2006), 'The Human Bone', in J. Butler, 26–7.

Douglas, A. (2008), 'An Excavation at 5–27 Long Lane, London Borough of Southwark', *TLMAS* 58 (2007): 15–52.

Douglas, A., J. Gerrard and B. Sudds (2011), *A Roman Settlement and Bath-house at Shadwell: Excavations at
    Tobacco Dock and Babe Ruth Restaurant, The Highway, London*, London:
    Pre-Construct Archaeology, Monograph 12.

Drummond-Murray, J., D. Saxby and B. Watson (1994), 'Recent Archaeological Work in the Bermondsey District of
    Southwark', *LA* 7, no. 10: 251–7.

Drummond-Murray, J. and P. Thompson (2002), *Settlement in Roman Southwark: Archaeological Excavations
    (1991–8) for The London Underground Limited Jubilee Line Extension Project*, London: Museum of London,
    MOLAS Monograph 12.

Dungworth, D. and H. B. Stallybrass (2011), 'Ironworking', in J. Hill and P. Rowsome, 390.

Dunning, G. C. (1945), 'Two Fires of Roman London', *Antiquaries Journal* 25, no. 1–2: 48–77.

Dunwoodie, L. (2004), *Pre-Boudican and Later Activity on the Site of the Forum: Excavations at 168 Fenchurch
    Street, City of London*, London: Museum of London, MOLAS Archaeological Studies Series 13.

Dunwoodie, L., C. Harward and K. Pitt (2015), *An Early Roman Fort and Urban Development on Londinium's
    Eastern Hill: Excavations at Plantation Place, City of London, 1997–2003*, London: Museum of London,
    MOLAS Archaeological Monograph 65.

Dyson, T. and J. Schofield (1981), 'Excavations in the City of London Second Interim Report, 1974–1978', *TLMAS*
    32: 24–81.

Eckardt, H. (2002), *Illuminating Roman Britain*, Montagnac: Monique Mergoil.

Eckardt, H. (2010a), 'Introduction: Diasporas in the Roman World', in H. Eckardt (ed.), 7–12.

Eckardt, H. (2010b), 'A Long Way from Home: Diaspora Communities in Roman Britain', in H. Eckardt (ed.),
    99–130.

Eckardt, H. (2014), *Objects & Identities: Roman Britain and the North-Western Provinces*, Oxford: Oxford
    University Press.

Eckardt, H. (ed.) (2010), *Roman Diasporas: Archaeological Approaches to Mobility and Diversity in the Roman
    Empire*, Portsmouth, RI: Journal of Roman Archaeology, Supplementary Series 78.

Eckardt, H., G. Müldner and M. Lewis (2014), 'People on the Move in Roman Britain', *World Archaeology* 46, no. 4:
    534–50.

Edwards, C. (2010), *Harper Road, Symington House, London Borough of Southwark: An Archaeological Evaluation
    Report*, London: AOC.

Edwards, Y. H., A. Weisskopf and D. Hamilton (2010), 'Age, Taphonomic History and Mode of Deposition of Human
    Skulls in the River Thames', *TLMAS* 60 (2009): 35–51.

Ellis, S. P. (2000), *Roman Housing*, London: Duckworth.

Elsden, N. J. (2002), *Excavations at 25 Cannon Street, City of London: From the Middle Bronze Age to the Great
    Fire*, London: Museum of London, MOLAS Archaeological Studies Series 5.

Esmonde Cleary, A. S. (1989), *The Ending of Roman Britain*, London: Routledge.

Esmonde Cleary, A. S. (1999), '[Review of] Interpreting Roman London: Papers in Memory of Hugh Chapman . . .',
    Britannia 30: 397–8.

Esmonde Cleary, A. S. (2000), 'Putting the Dead in their Place: Burial Location in Roman Britain', in
    J. Pearce, M. Millett and M. Struck (eds), *Burial, Society and Context in the Roman World*, 127–42, Oxford:
    Oxbow.

Esmonde Cleary, A. S. (2003), 'Civil Defences in the West under the High Empire', in P. Wilson (ed.), 72–85.

Esmonde Cleary, A. S. (2005), 'Beating the Bounds: Ritual and the Articulation of Urban Space in Roman Britain', in
    A. MacMahon and J. Price (eds), 1–17.

Evans, C. (2013), 'Delivering Bodies unto Waters: A Late Bronze Age Mid-Stream Midden Settlement and Iron Age
    Ritual Complex in the Fens', *Antiquaries Journal* 93: 55–79.

Evans, J. G. (2007), 'Styles of Pottery Deposition at a Roman Rural Site in Hampshire', in R. Hingley and S. Willis (eds), *Roman Finds: Context and Theory*, 176–85, Oxford: Oxbow.

Fairman, A. and J. Taylor (2013), *Thameslink Archaeological Assessment 2: Archaeological Excavations at 11–15 Borough High Street and 2 London Bridge Street, London Borough of Southwark: Post-Excavation Assessment*, London and Oxford: Oxford Archaeology/Pre-Construct Archaeology.

Feldman Weiss, C. (2012), 'Bodies in Motion: Civic Ritual and Place-making in Roman Ephesus', in D. M. Totten and K. Lafrenz Samuels (eds), 50–64.

Ferretti, E. and A. H. Graham (1978), '201–211 Borough High Street', in J. Bird, M. W. C. Hassall and H. Sheldon (eds), 53–176.

Ferris, I. (2000), *Enemies of Rome: Barbarians through Roman Eyes*, Stroud: Sutton.

Ferris, I. (2014), 'A Pipeclay Pseudo-Venus Figurine from Binchester Roman Fort, County Durham', in R. Collins and F. McIntosh (eds), 105–8.

Field, D. J. (1985), 'The Prehistoric Pottery', in G. Parnell, 51.

Fischer, T. (2002), 'Neue Grabungen an der Westseite des römischen Flottenlagers Köln–Alteburg', in P. Freeman et al. (eds), 904–12.

Fishwick, D. (1961), 'The Imperial Cult in Roman Britain', *Phoenix* 15, no. 3: 159–73.

Fittock, M. G. (2015), 'Broken Deities: The Pipeclay Figurines from Roman London', *Britannia* 46: 111–34.

Fitzpatrick, A. P. (2007), 'Dancing with Dragons: Fantastic Animals in the Early Celtic Art of Iron Age Britain', in C. Haselgrove and T. Moore (eds), 339–57.

Forcey, C. (1998), 'Whatever Happened to the Heroes? Ancestral Cults and the Enigma of Romano-Celtic Temples', in C. Forcey, J. Hawthorne and R. Witcher (eds), *TRAC 97: Proceedings of the Seventh Annual Theoretical Roman Archaeology Conference, Nottingham 1977*, 87–8, Oxford, Oxbow.

Foulds, E. M. (2017), *Dress and Identity in Iron Age Britain: A Study of Glass Beads and Other Objects of Personal Adornment*, Oxford: Archaeopress.

Franks, A. W. (1866), '. . . a Bronze Helmet . . .', *Proceedings of the Society of Antiquaries of London* 3 (1864–7): 342–4.

Freeman, P., J. Bennett, Z. T. Fiema and B. Hoffmann (eds) (2002), *Limes XVII: Proceedings of the XVIIIth International Congress of Roman Frontier Studies Held in Amman, Jordan (September 2000)*, Oxford: Archaeopress, BAR International Series 1084.

Fulford, M. (1989), *The Silchester Amphitheatre: Excavations of 1979–85*, London: Society for the Promotion of Roman Studies. Britannia Monograph 10.

Fulford, M. (2001), 'Links with the Past: Pervasive "Ritual" Behaviour in Roman Britain', *Britannia* 32: 199–18.

Fulford, M. (2002), 'A Second Start: From the Defeat of Boudica to the Third Century', in P. Salway (ed.), 39–73.

Fulford, M. (2003), 'Julio-Claudian and Early Flavian *Calleva*', in P. Wilson (ed.), 95–104.

Fulford, M (2004), 'Economic Structures', in M. Todd (ed.), 309–26.

Fulford, M. (2007), 'The Grand Excavation Projects of the Twentieth Century', in S. Pearce (ed.), *Visions of Antiquity: The Society of Antiquaries of London, 1707–2007*, 353–82, London: Society of Antiquaries.

Fulford, M. (2008), '*Imperium Galliarum, Imperium Brittanniarum*: Developing New Ideologies and Settling Old Scores', in J. Clark et al. (eds), 41–5.

Fulford, M. (2012), 'Urban Essentials: Perspectives on Change in a Residential *Insula* at Silchester (early 2nd to 5th c. A.D.)', in M. Fulford (ed.) *Silchester and the Study of Romano-British Urbanism*, 257–71, Portsmouth, RI: Journal of Roman Archaeology, Supplementary Series 99.

Fulford, M. (2015), 'Retrospect and Prospect: Advancement of Knowledge, Methodologies and Publication', in M. Fulford and N. Holbrook (eds), 194–211.

Fulford, M., A. Clarke and H. Eckardt (2006), *Life and Labour in Late Roman Silchester: Excavations in Insula IX Since 1997*, London: Society for the Promotion of Roman Studies, Britannia Monograph 22.

Fulford, M. and N. Holbrook (eds) (2015), *The Towns of Roman Britain: The Contribution of Commercial Archaeology Since 1990*, London: Society for the Promotion of Roman Studies, Britannia Monograph No. 27.

Fulford, M. and J. Timby (2000), *Late Iron Age and Roman Silchester: Excavations on the Site of the Forum-basilica 1977, 1980–86*, London: Society for the Promotion of Roman Studies. Britannia Monograph 15.

Futrell, A. (1997), *Blood in the Arena: The Spectacle of Roman Power*, Austin: University of Texas Press.

Gardner, A. (2013), 'Thinking about Roman Imperialism: Postcolonialism, Globalisation and Beyond?', *Britannia* 44: 1–25.

Gardner, J. F. (2011), 'Slavery and Roman law', in K. Bradley and P. Cartledge (eds), 414–37.

Garwood, P. (2011), 'Rites of Passage', in T. Insoll (ed.), 261–84.

Gee, R. (2008), 'From Corpse to Ancestor: The Role of Tombside Dining in the Transformation of the Body in Ancient Rome', in F. Fahlander and T. Oestigaard (eds), *The Materiality of Death: Bodies, Burials, Beliefs*, 59–68, Oxford: Archaeopress, BAR International Series 1768.

Gerrard, J. (2009a), 'Dumps and *Tesserae*: High-status Building Materials from 33 Union Street, Southwark', *LA* 12, no. 5: 130–4.

Gerrard, J. (2009b), 'The Drapers' Garden Hoard: A Preliminary Account', *Britannia* 40: 163–84.

Gerrard, J. (2011a), 'Roman Pottery', in A. Douglas, J. Gerrard and B. Sudds, 61–86.

Gerrard, J. (2011b), 'Roman Coins', in A. Douglas, J. Gerrard and B. Sudds, 86–91.

Gerrard, J. (2011c), 'Romano-British Small Finds', in A. Douglas, J. Gerrard and B. Sudds, 91–103.

Gerrard, J. (2011d), 'Alternative Interpretations of the Bath House', in A. Douglas, J. Gerrard and B. Sudds, 151–2.

Gerrard, J. (2011e), 'The Shadwell Sites and the Thames', in A. Douglas, J. Gerrard and B. Sudds, 164.

Gerrard, J. (2011f), 'Discussion and Conclusions', in A. Douglas, J. Gerrard and B. Sudds, 165–72.

Gerrard, J. (2011g), 'Cathedral or Granary? The Roman Coins from Colchester House, City of London', *TLMAS* 61 (2010): 81–8.

Gerrard, J. (2011h), 'Wells and Belief Systems at the End of Roman Britain: A Case Study from Roman London', in L. Lavan and M. Mulryan (eds), 551–72.

Gerrard, J. (2011i), 'New Light on the End of Roman London', *Archaeological Journal* 168: 181–94.

Gerrard, J. (2013), *The Ruin of Roman Britain*, Cambridge: Cambridge University Press.

Gerrard, J. (2015a), 'Coins', in D. Killock et al., 140–4.

Gerrard, J. (2015b), 'Romano-British Pottery', in D. Killock et al., 113–22.

Gerrard, J. and M. Lyne (2013), 'The Romano-British Pottery', in V. Ridgeway, K. Leary and B. Sudds, 31–6.

Girardon, S. and J. Heathcote (1988), 'Excavation Round-up 1987: Part 2, London Boroughs', *LA* 5, no. 15: 410–16.

Goffin, R. (1995), 'The Wall Plaster', in C. Cowan, 157–64.

Goffin, R. (2005), 'Painted Wall Plaster', in B. Yule, 103–45.

Goffin, R. (2011), 'The Painted Wall Plaster Decoration', in J. Hill and P. Rowsome, 381–3.

Goodburn, D. (1996), 'From Tree to Town', in T. Brigham, 33–59.

Goodburn, D. (2008), 'Timber', in T. Bradley and J. Butler, 41–52.

Goodburn, D. (2016), 'The Manufacturing of Waxed Stylus Writing Tablets in Roman London', in R. S. O. Tomlin, 8–13.

Goodburn, D., R. Goffin and J. Hill (2011), 'Domestic Buildings and Other Structures of Timber', in J. Hill and P. Rowsome, 414–37.

Goodman, P. J. (2007), *The Roman City and its Periphery*, London: Routledge.

Goodman, P. J. (2011), 'Temples in Late Antique Gaul', in L. Lavan and M. Mulryan (eds), 165–93.

Graham, A. (1978), 'Swan Street/Great Dover Street', in J. Bird, M. W. C. Hassall and H. Sheldon (eds), 473–97.

Graham, A. (1988), '64–70 Borough High Street', in P. Hinton (ed.), 55–66.

Grasby, R. D. and R. S. O. Tomlin (2002), 'The Sepulchral Monument of C. Julius Classicianus', *Britannia* 33: 43–76.

Greene, E. (2015), '*Conubium cum Uxoribus*: Wives and Children in the Roman Military Diplomas', *Journal of Roman Archaeology* 28: 125–59.

Greenwood, P. (1997), 'Iron Age London: Some Thoughts on Current Knowledge and Problems 20 years on', *LA* 8, no. 6: 153–61.

Grew, F. (2008), 'Who was Mars Camulus?', in J. Clark et al. (eds), 142–50.

Grimes, W. F. (1968), *The Excavation of Roman and Medieval London*, London: Routledge and Kegan Paul.

Groves, J. (1990), 'Summary Finds Report', in C. Maloney, 82–4.

Groves, J. (1998), 'The Pottery: General Note', in J. Shepherd, 102–8.

Guildhall Museum (1968), 'Archaeological Finds in the City of London 1965–6', *TLMAS* 22, no. 1: 1–17.

Guildhall Museum (1969), 'Archaeological Finds in the City of London 1966–8', *TLMAS* 22, no. 2: 1–26.

Guildhall Museum (1970), 'Archaeological Finds in the City of London 1966–9', *TLMAS* 22, no. 3: 1–9.

Hales, S. (2003), *The Roman House and Social Identity*, Cambridge: Cambridge University Press.

Hall, J. (1996), 'The Cemeteries of Roman London: A Review', in J. Bird, M. W. C. Hassall and H. Sheldon (eds), 57–84.

Hall, J. (1998), 'The Sculptures: General Note', in J. Shepherd, 107–8.

Hall, J. (2005), 'The Shopkeepers and Craft-workers of Roman London', in A. MacMahon and J. Price (eds), 125–44.

Hall, J. (2014), 'With Criminal Intent? Forgers at Work in Roman London', *Britannia* 45: 165–94.

Hall, J. and R. Merrifield (1998), 'The Coins', in J. Shepherd, 99–102.

Hall, J. and J. Shepherd (2008), 'Places of Worship in Roman London and Beyond', in D. Rudling (ed.), *Ritual Landscapes of Roman South-East Britain*, 27–44, Oxford: Heritage Marketing and Publications/Oxbow.

Hammer, F. (2003), *Industry in North-west Roman Southwark: Excavations 1984–8*, London: Museum of London, MOLAS Monograph 17.

Hammerson, J. (1978), 'Excavations under Southwark Cathedral', *LA* 3, no. 8: 206–12.

Hammerson, M. (1988), 'Roman Pottery', in P. Hinton (ed.), 193–294.

Hammerson, M. (1996), 'Problems of Roman Coin Interpretation in Greater London', in J. Bird, M. W. C. Hassall and H. Sheldon (eds), 153–64.

Hammerson, M. (2008), 'Coins', in N. C. W. Bateman, C. Cowan, R. Wroe-Brown, 208–12.

Hammerson, M. (2011a), 'The Claudian Coins', in J. Hill and P. Rowsome, 261–2.

Hammerson, M. (2011b), 'Coins', in J. Hill and P. Rowsome, 518–20.

Hammerson, M. and C. Murray (1978a), 'Other Roman Pottery', in J. Bird, M. W. C. Hassall and H. Sheldon (eds), 102–25.

Hammerson, M. and C. Murray (1978b), 'Other Roman Pottery', in J. Bird, M. W. C. Hassall and H. Sheldon (eds), 337–75.

Hanel, N. (2002), 'Recent Research on the Fortification of the Headquarters of the *classis Germanica*: Cologne-Marienburg (Alteburg)', in P. Freeman et al. (eds), 913–20.

Harding, D. W. (2016), *Death and Burial in Iron Age Britain*, Oxford: Oxford University Press.

Harper, K. (2015), 'Pandemics and the Passage to Late Antiquity: Rethinking the Plague of c. 249–270 described by Cyprian', *Journal of Roman Archaeology* 28: 223–60.

Hartley, K. F. (2005), 'Mortarium Stamps', in Seeley and Drummond-Murray, 96–103.

Harward, C., N. Powers and S. Watson (2015), *The Upper Walbrook Valley Cemetery of Roman London: Excavations at Finsbury Circus, City of London, 1987–2007*, London: Museum of London, MOLAS Monograph 69.

Haselgrove, C. (ed.) (2016), *Cartimandua's Capital? The Late Iron Age Royal Site at Stanwick, North Yorkshire, Fieldwork and Analysis 1981–2100*, York: CBA Research Report 175, Council for British Archaeology.

Haselgrove, C., I. Armit, T. Champion, J. Creighton, A. Gwilt, J. D. Hill, F. Hunter and A. Woodward (2001), *Understanding the British Iron Age: An Agenda for Action*, Salisbury: Wessex Archaeology.

Haselgrove, C. and T. Moore (eds) (2007), *The Late Iron Age in Britain and Beyond*, Oxford: Oxbow.

Haslam, J. (2010), 'The development of London by King Alfred: a reassessment', *TLMAS* 60 (2009): 109–44.

Hassall, M. W. C. (1980), 'The Inscribed Altars', in C. Hill, M. Millett and T. Blagg, 195–8.

Hassall, M. W. C. (1988), 'Roman Graffiti', in P. Hinton (ed.), 365.

Hassall, M. W. C. (1996), 'London as a provincial capital', in J. Bird, M. W. C. Hassall and H. Sheldon (eds), 19–26.

Hassall, M. W. C. (2000), 'London: The Roman City', in I. Haynes, H. Sheldon and L. Hannigan (eds), 52–61.

Hassall, M. W. C. (2012), 'The 2nd-century AD Garrison of Londinium', in J. Shepherd, 158–63.

Hassall, M. W. C. and R. S. O. Tomlin (1982), 'Inscriptions', *Britannia* 13: 396–422.

Hassall, M. W. C. and R. S. O. Tomlin (1985), 'Inscriptions', *Britannia* 16: 317–32.

Hassall, M. W. C. and R. S. O. Tomlin (1986), 'Inscriptions', *Britannia* 17: 428–54.

Hassall, M. W. C. and R. S. O. Tomlin (1987), 'Inscriptions', *Britannia* 18: 360–77.

Hassall, M. W. C. and R. S. O. Tomlin (1989), 'Inscriptions', *Britannia* 20: 327–45.

Hassall, M. W. C. and R. S. O. Tomlin (1996), 'Inscriptions', *Britannia* 27: 439–57.

Hassall, M. W. C. and R. S. O. Tomlin (2003), 'Inscriptions', *Britannia* 34: 361–82.

Hawkins, B. (2009), *An Assessment of an Archaeological Excavation and Watching Brief at Drapers' Gardens, City of London, London EC2*, London: Pre-Construct Archaeology.

Haynes, I. (2000), 'Religion in Roman London', in I. Haynes, H. Sheldon and L. Hannigan (eds), 85–101.

Haynes, I. (2008), 'Sharing Secrets? The Material Culture of Mystery Cults from Londinium, Apulum and Beyond', in J. Clark et al. (eds), 128–33.

Haynes, I., H. Sheldon and L. Hannigan (eds) (2000), *London Underground: The Archaeology of a City*, Oxford: Oxbow.

Heaney, S. (1990), 'Bog Queen', in S. Heaney, *New Selected Poems 1966–1987*, 66–8, London: Faber and Faber.

Heard, K. (1989), 'Excavations at 10–18 Union Street, Southwark', *LA* 6, no. 5: 126–31.

Heard, K. (1996), 'The Hinterland of Roman Southwark, Part 1', *LA* 8, no. 3: 76–82.

Heard, K., H. Sheldon and P. Thompson (1990), 'Mapping Roman Southwark', *Antiquity* 64: 608–19.

Heathcote, J. (1988), 'Excavation Round-up 1987, Part 1: City of London', *LA* 5, no. 14: 382–7.

Heathcote, J. (1989), 'Excavation Round-up 1988, Part 1: City of London', *LA* 6, no. 2: 46–53.

Heathcote, J. (1990), 'Excavation Round-up 1989, Part 1: City of London', *LA* 6, no. 6: 160–7.

Henig, M. (1984), *Religion in Roman Britain*, London: Batsford.

Henig, M. (1998), 'Appendix 1: The Temple as a *Bacchium* or *Sacrarium* in the Fourth Century', in J. Shepherd, 230–2.

Henig, M. (2000), 'Art in Roman London', in I. Haynes, H. Sheldon and L. Hannigan (eds), 62–84.

Henig, M. and A. Ross (1998), 'A Roman Intaglio Depicting a Warship from the Foreshore at King's Reach, Winchester Wharf, Southwark', *Britannia* 29: 325–7.

Hill, C. (1980a), 'The Riverwall Excavations, 1975–6', in C. Hill, M. Millett and T. Blagg, 27–56.

Hill, C. (1980b), 'Discussion', in C. Hill, M. Millett and T. Blagg, 56–76.

Hill, C., M. Millett and T. Blagg (1980), *The Roman Riverside Wall and Monumental Arch in London: Excavations at Baynard's Castle, Upper Thames Street, London 1974–76*, London: London and Middlesex Archaeological Society, Special Paper No. 3.

Hill, J. (2011), 'Building 11: A Possible Tavern', in J. Hill and P. Rowsome, 291–3.

Hill, J., D. Peacock and D. Williams (2011), 'Evidence for Grain Processing and Storage', in J. Hill and P. Rowsome, 349–51.

Hill, J. and P. Rowsome (2011), *Roman London and the Walbrook Stream Crossing: Excavations at 1 Poultry and Vicinity, City of London*, London: Museum of London, MOLAS Monograph 37.

Hill, J. and A. Woodger (1999), *Excavations at 72–75 Cheapside/83–93 Queen Street, City of London*, London: Museum of London, MOLAS Archaeological Studies Series 2.

Hill, J. D. (2007), 'The Dynamics of Social Change in Later Iron Age Eastern and South-eastern England c. 300 BC–AD 43', in C. Haselgrove and T. Moore (eds), 16–40.

Hillam, J. (1985a), 'Dendrochronology', in G. Milne, 36–9.

Hillam, J. (1985b), 'The Dendrochronology', in G. Parnell, 45–7.

Hillam, J. (1993), 'Appendix 1: Tree Ring Dating of Oak Timbers from Peter's Hill and Sunlight Wharf', in J. Williams, 95–9.

Hillam, J. and R. A. Morgan (1986), 'Tree-ring Analysis of the Roman Timbers', in L. Miller, J. Schofield and M. Rhodes, 75–85.

Hind, J. G. F. (1989), 'The Invasion of Britain in A.D. 43 – an Alternative Strategy for Aulus Plautius', *Britannia* 20: 1–21.

Hingley, R. (1985), 'Location, Function and Status: A Romano-British Religious Complex at the Noah's Ark Inn, Frilford (Oxfordshire)', *Oxford Journal of Archaeology* 4: 201–14.

Hingley, R. (1989), *Rural Settlement in Roman Britain*, London: Seaby.

Hingley, R. (1997a), 'Resistance and Domination: Social Change in Roman Britain', in D. Mattingly (ed.), *Dialogues in Roman Imperialism: Power, Discourse and Discrepant Experiences in the Roman Empire*, 81–100, Portsmouth, RI: Journal of Roman Archaeology, Supplementary Series 23.

Hingley, R. (1997b), 'Iron, Ironworking and Regeneration', in A. Gwilt and C. Haselgrove (eds), *Reconstructing Iron Age Societies*, 9–18, Oxford: Oxbow.

Hingley, R. (2005), *Globalizing Roman Culture: Unity, Diversity and Empire*, London: Routledge.

Hingley, R. (2006), 'The Deposition of Iron Objects during the Later Prehistoric and Roman Periods: Contextual Analysis and the Significance of Iron', *Britannia* 37: 213–57.

Hingley, R. (2008), *The Recovery of Roman Britain: 'A colony so fertile'*, Oxford: Oxford University Press.

Hingley, R. (2009), 'Esoteric Knowledge: Ancient Bronze Artefacts from Iron Age Contexts', *Proceedings of the Prehistoric Society* 75: 143–65.

Hingley, R. (2011), 'Rome: Imperial and Local Religions', in T. Insoll (ed.), 745–57.

Hingley, R. (2012), *Hadrian's Wall: A Life*, Oxford: Oxford University Press.

Hingley, R. (2015), 'Post-colonial and Global Rome: The Genealogy of Empire', in M. Pitts and M. J. Versluys (eds), 32–46.

Hingley, R. and C. Unwin (2005), *Boudica: Iron Age Warrior Queen*, London: Hambledon.

Hinton, P. (ed.) (1988), *Excavations in Southwark 1973–76, Lambeth 1973–79*, Warwick: London & Middlesex Archaeological Society/Surrey Archaeological Society, Joint Publication 3.

Historic England (2015), *Building the Future, Transforming our Past: Celebrating Development-led Archaeology in England, 1990–2015*, London: Historic England.

Holder, N. (2007), 'Mapping the Roman Inscriptions of London', *Britannia* 38: 13–34.

Holder, N. and D. Jamieson (2003), 'The Prehistory of the City of London: Myths and Methodologies', *Archaeological Journal* 160: 23–43.

Houston, G. W. (1988), 'Ports in Perspective: Some Comparative Materials on Roman Merchant Ships and Ports', *American Journal of Archaeology* 92, no. 4: 553–64.

Howe, E. (2002), *Roman Defences and Medieval Industry: Excavations at Baltic House, City of London*, London: Museum of London Archaeological Services, MOLAS Monograph 7.

Howe, E. and D. Lakin (2004), *Roman and Medieval Cripplegate, City of London*, London: Museum of London Archaeological Services, MOLAS Monograph 21.

Howell, I. (2013), *Roman and Medieval Development South of Cheapside: Excavations at Bow Bells House, City of London, 2005–6*, London: Museum of London, MOLAS Archaeological Studies Series 26.

Hufschmid, T. (2009), 'Theatres and Amphitheatres at Augst (*Augusta Raurica*), Switzerland', in T. Wilmott (ed.), 105–18.

Hufschmid, T. (2012a), 'Die Theaterbauten von Augst Neun-Türme', in L. Berger (ed.), 79–117.

Hufschmid, T. (2012b), 'Das Amphitheater im Sichelengraben', in L. Berger (ed.), 118–30.

Hull, M. R. (1958), *Roman Colchester*, Oxford: Research Report of the Society of Antiquaries.

Hunt, G. (2011), 'Along the Eastern Defences: Excavations at 8–14 Cooper's Row and 1 America Square in the City of London, EC3', *TLMAS* 61 (2010): 41–80.

Illustrated London News (1869), 'Roman Pavement found in the Poultry, near the Mansion Houses', *Illustrated London News* 54 (1540, 1541), 29 May 1869: 545.

Insoll, T. (ed.) (2011), *The Oxford Handbook of the Archaeology of Ritual and Religion*, Oxford: Oxford University Press.

Jackson, S., S. Watson, A. Wardle and M. Marshall (2013), 'London's Pompeii? The Rise and Fall of a Roman waterfront', *Current Archaeology*, 9 June. Available online: http://www.archaeology.co.uk/articles/londons-pompeii.htm. (accessed 29 June 2016).

James, S. and M. Millett (eds) (2001), *Britons and Romans: Advancing an Archaeological Agenda*, York: Council for British Archaeology. Research Report 125.

Jarrett, C. (2013), 'Saxon Pottery', in V. Ridgeway, K. Leary and B. Sudds, 48–50.

Jenkins, F. (1986), 'Ceramic Figurines', in L. Miller, J. Schofield and M. Rhodes, 205–8.

Johnson, T. (1975), 'A Roman Signal Tower at Shadwell, E1', *TLMAS* 26: 278–80.

Jones, C. P. (2016), 'An Amulet from London and Events surrounding the Antonine Plague', *Journal of Roman Archaeology* 29: 469–72.

Jones, D. M. (1980), *Excavations at Billingsgate Buildings 'Triangle', Lower Thames Street, 1974*, London: Special Paper of the London and Middlesex Archaeological Society, no. 4.

Jones, M. E. (1996), *The End of Roman Britain*, London: Cornell.

Jope, E. M. (2000), *Early Celtic Art in the British Isles*, Oxford: Clarendon Press.

Joshel, S. R. (2011), 'Slavery and Roman Literary Culture', in K. Bradley and P. Cartledge (eds), 214–40.

Kamash, Z., C. Gosden and G. Lock (2010), 'Continuity and Religious Practices in Roman Britain: The Case of the Rural Religious Complex at Marcham/Frilford, Oxfordshire', *Britannia* 41: 95–125.

Kaminski, J. and D. Sim (2012), 'The Production and Deposition of the Thames Coolus Helmet', *TLMAS* 62 (2011): 69–88.

Kaur, R. (2011), '"Ancient cosmopolitanism" and the South Asian Diaspora', *South Asian Diaspora* 3, no. 2: 197–213.

Keily, J. (2002), 'Stone Mould for Decorated Pewter Plates', in N. J. Elsden, 27.

Keily, J. and J. Shepherd (2005), 'Glass Working in the Upper Walbrook Valley', in Seeley and Drummond-Murray, 147–55.

Killock, D. (2010), *Assessment of an Archaeological Excavation at 28–30 Trinity Street, London SE1, London Borough of Southwark*, London: Pre-Construct Archaeology.

Killock, D., J. Shepherd, J. Gerrard, K. Hayward, K. Rielly and V. Ridgeway (2015), *Temples and Suburbs: Excavations at Tabard Square, Southwark*, London: Pre-Construct Archaeology Limited, Monograph 18.

Kipling, R. (1906), 'Cities and Thrones and Powers, in R. Kipling, *Puck of Pook's Hill*, 139, London: Macmillan.

Kulikowski, M. (2000), 'The "Notitia Dignitatum" as a Historical Source', *Historia: Zeitschrift für Alte Geschichte* 49, no. 3: 358–77.

Kyle, D. G. (1998), *Spectacles of Death in Ancient Rome*, London: Routledge.

Lafrenz Samuels, K. and D. M. Totten (2012), 'Roman Place-making: From Archaeological Interpretation to Contemporary Heritage Contexts', in D. M. Totten and K. Lafrenz Samuels (eds), 11–32.

Lakin, D. (2002), *The Roman Tower at Shadwell, London: A Reappraisal*, London: Museum of London, MOLAS Archaeological Studies Series 8.

Lambrick, G. and M. Robinson (2009), *The Thames Through Time: The Archaeology of the Gravel Terraces of the Upper and Middle Thames, The Thames Valley in Later Prehistory, 1500 BC–AD50*, Oxford: Oxford Archaeology Thames Valley Landscapes Monograph 29.

Lane, A. (2014), 'Wroxeter and the End of Roman Britain', *Antiquity* 88: 501–15.

Langthorne, J. Y. (2010), 'Human Bone and Cremated Bone Assessment', in D. Killock, 192–9.

Langthorne, J. Y. (2015), 'Human Bone', in D. Killock et al., 225–30.

Laurence, R., S. Esmonde Cleary and G. Seers (2011), *The City in the Roman West, c. 250 BC–c. AD 250*, Cambridge: Cambridge University Press.

Lavan, L. (2011), 'The End of the Temples: Towards a New Narrative?', in L. Lavan and M. Mulryan (eds), xy–lxv.

Lavan, L. and M. Mulryan (eds) (2011), *The Archaeology of Late Antique 'Paganism'*, Leiden: Brill.

Leary, J. (2004), '285–291 Tooley Street: Further Evidence for Late Iron Age/early Roman Settlement in Bermondsey', *LA* 10, no. 11: 233–88.

Leary, J. and J. Butler (2012), *Roman Archaeology in the Upper Reaches of the Walbrook Valley: Excavations at 6–8 Tokenhouse Yard, London EC2*, London: Pre-Construct Archaeology Limited, Monograph 14.

Lees, D., A. Woodger and C. Orton (1989), 'Excavations in the Walbrook Valley', *LA* 6, no. 5: 115–19.

Lerz, A. and N. Holder (2016), 'Medieval Crossed Friars and its Roman to Post-medieval Landscape: Excavations at Mariner House, in the City of London', *TLMAS* 66 (2015): 137–97.

Leven, J. (2000), *Defending Ancient Springs*, music CD, London: Cooking Vinyl.

Liddle, J., C. Ainsley and K. Rielly (2009), 'Animal bone', in C. Cowan et al., 244–8.

Lyne, M. (2015), 'The End of Roman Pottery Production in England', in J. Gerrard (ed.), *Internet Archaeology* 41 (*Roman-British Pottery in the Fifth Century*). Available online: http://intarch.ac.uk.ezphost.dur.ac.uk/journal/issue41/ (accessed 20 April 2016).

Lyon, J. (2005), 'New work on Cripplegate Fort: Excavations at 25 Gresham Street, 2000–2001', *TLMAS* 55 (2004): 153–82.

Lyon, J. (2007), *Within These Walls: Roman and Medieval Defences North of Newgate at the Merrill Lynch Financial Centre, City of London*, London: Museum of London, MOLAS Monograph 33.

MacKenna, S. A. and R. Ling (1991), 'Wall Paintings from the Winchester Palace Site, Southwark', *Britannia* 22: 159–71.

Mackinder, A. (2000), *A Roman-British Cemetery on Watling Street: Excavations at 165 Great Dover Street, Southwark, London*, London: Museum of London, MOLAS Archaeological Studies Series 4.

Mackinder, A. (2015), *Roman and Medieval Revetments on the Thames Waterfront: Excavations at Riverbank House, City of London, 2006–9*, London: Museum of London, MOLAS Archaeological Studies Series 33.

MacMahon, A. (2005), 'The Shops and Workshops of Roman Britain', in A. MacMahon and J. Price (eds), 48–69.

MacMahon, A. and J. Price (eds) (2005), *Roman Working Lives and Urban Living*, Oxford: Oxbow.

Macphail, R. I. (2005), 'Soil Micromorphology', in B. Yule, 88–90.

Macready, S. and J. Sidell (1998), 'The Animal Bones', in J. Shepherd, 208–15.

Major, H. (2013), 'Metal and Bone Objects', in V. Ridgeway, K. Leary and B. Sudds, 43–8.

Malcolm, G. and D. Bowsher (2003), *Middle Saxon London: Excavations at the Royal Opera House 1989–99*, London: Museum of London, MOLAS Monograph 15.

Maloney, C. (1990), *The Upper Walbrook in the Roman Period*, London: Council for British Archaeology, Research Report 69.

Maloney, C. (1999), 'London Fieldwork and Publication Round-up 1998', *LA* 9 (supplement 1): 1–30.

Maloney, C. (2002), 'Fieldwork Round-up 2001', *LA* 10 (supplement 1): 1–30.

Maloney, C. (2005), 'Fieldwork Round-up 2004', *LA* 11 (supplement 1): 1–22.

Maloney, C. (2007), 'Fieldwork Round-up 2006', *LA* 11 (supplement 3): 56–85.

Maloney, J. (1979), 'Excavations at Dukes Place: The Roman Defences', *LA* 3, no. 11: 292–7.

Maloney, J. (1980), 'The Discovery of Bastion 4A in the City of London and its Implications', *TLMAS* 31: 68–76.

Maloney, J. (1983), 'Recent Work on London's Defences', in J. Maloney and B. Hobley (eds), *Roman Urban Defences in the West*, 96–117, London: Council for British Archaeology, Research Report 51.

Maltby, M. (2015), 'Commercial Archaeology, Zoo Archaeology and the Study of the Romano-British Town', in M. Fulford and N. Holbrook (eds), 175–93.

Marsden, P. (1968), 'Roman House and Bath at Billingsgate', *LA* 1, no. 1: 3–5.

Marsden, P. (1969), 'The Roman Pottery Industry of London', *TLMAS* 22, no. 2: 39–44.

Marsden, P. (1975), 'Excavation of a Roman Palace Site in London, 1961–1972', *TLMAS* 26: 1–102.

Marsden, P. (1976), 'Two Roman Public Baths in London', *TLMAS* 27: 2–70.

Marsden, P. (1980), *Roman London*, London: Thames and Hudson.

Marsden, P. (1987), *The Roman Forum Site in London: Discoveries Before 1985*, London: HMSO.

Marsden, P. (1991), 'Feature 8', in T. Wilmott, 29–30.

Marsden, P. (1993), 'Observations at the Salvation Army Headquarters', in T. Williams, 63–9.

Marsden, P. (1994), *Ships of the Port of London: First to Eleventh Centuries AD*, London: English Heritage, Archaeological Report 3.

Marsden, P. (1996), 'The Beginnings of Archaeology in the City of London', in J. Bird, M. W. C. Hassall and H. Sheldon (eds), 11–18.

Marsh, G. (1978), '8 Union Street', in J. Bird, M. W. C. Hassall and H. Sheldon (eds), 221–32.

Marsh, G. (1979). 'Nineteenth and Twentieth Century Antiquities Dealers and the Arretine Ware from London', *TLMAS* 30: 125–9.

Marsh, G. (1981), 'London's Samian Supply and its Relationship to the Development of the Gallic Samian Industry', in A. C. Anderson and A. S. Anderson (eds), *Roman Pottery Research in Britain and North-West Europe*, 173–238, Oxford: British Archaeological Reports, International Series 123.

Marsh, G. and B. West (1981), 'Skullduggery in Roman London?' *TLMAS* 32: 86–102.

Martens, M. (2004a), 'The *Mithraeum* in Tienen (Belgium): Small Finds and What they can Tell Us', in M. Martens and G. De Boe (eds), *Roman Mithraism: The Evidence of Small Finds*, 25–56, Brussels: Archaeology in Vlaanderen, Monograph 4.

Martens, M. (2004b), 'Re-thinking Sacred "Rubbish": The Ritual Deposits of the Temple of Mithras at Tienen (Belgium)', *Journal of Roman Archaeology* 17: 333–53.

Mattingly, D. (2006), *An Imperial Possession: Britain in the Roman Empire*, London: Penguin.

Mattingly, D. (2011), *Imperialism, Power and Identity: Experiencing the Roman Empire*, Princeton, NJ: Princeton University Press.

Maxfield, V. A. and M. J. Dobson (eds) (1991), *Roman Frontier Studies 1989: Proceedings of the XVth International Congress of Roman Frontier Studies*, Exeter: University of Exeter Press.

McCourt, K. M. (2010), 'An Archaeological Assessment of the Origins of St Paul's Cathedral', *LA* 12, no. 8: 213–18.

McKenzie, M. (2012), 'Roman, Medieval and Later Occupation at Lion Plaza, 1–18 Old Broad Street and 41–53 Threadneedle Street, London, EC2', *TLMAS* 62 (2011): 1–30.

McKinley, J. (2000), 'Cremation Burials', in B. Barber and D. Bowsher, 264–77.

McKinley, J. (2006), 'Excavations at 2011 Long Lane, Southwark Part II; Romano-British Pasture to Post-medieval Tanneries', *LA* 11, no. 4: 87–94.

McKinley, J. (2008), 'In the Heat of the Pyre: Efficiency of Oxidation in Romano–British Cremations – Did it really Matter?', in C. W. Schmidt and S. A. Symes (eds), *The Analysis of Burned Human Remains*, 163–83, Oxford: Elsevier.

McKinley, J. (2009), 'Inhumation Burial in a Ditch', in V. Birbeck and J. Schuster, 13–14.

McKinley, J. (2011), 'Human Bone', in C. Barnett, J. I. McKinley, E. Stafford, J. M. Grimm and C. J. Stevens (eds), *Settling the Ebbsfleet Valley: High Speed 1 Excavations at Springhead and Northfleet, Kent. The Late Iron Age, Roman, Saxon, and Medieval Landscape, Volume 3, Late Iron Age to Roman Human Remains and Environmental Reports*, 1–14, Oxford: Oxford Archaeology.

Merrifield, R. (1983), *London: City of the Romans*, London: Batsford.

Merrifield, R. (1996), 'The London Hunter-god and His Significance in the History of Londinium', in J. Bird, M. W. C. Hassall and H. Sheldon (eds), 105–13.

Merrifield, R. (1997), 'Roman Metalwork from the Walbrook – Rubbish, Ritual or Redundancy?', *TLMAS* 46 (1995): 27–44.

Merrifield, R. and J. Hall (2008), 'In its Depths, What Treasures – the Nature of the Walbrook Stream Valley and the Roman Metalwork found therein', in J. Clark et al. (eds), 121–7.

Merriman, N. (2000), 'Changing Approaches to the First Millennium BC', in I. Haynes, H. Sheldon and L. Hannigan (eds), 35–51.

Miller, L. (1982), 'Miles Lane: The Early Roman Waterfront', *LA* 4, no. 6: 143–7.

Miller, L. and J. Schofield (1986a), 'The Excavations at New Fresh Wharf, 1974–1978', in L. Miller, J. Schofield and M. Rhodes, 25–59.

Miller, L. and J. Schofield (1986b), 'Synthesis and Discussion', in L. Miller, J. Schofield and M. Rhodes, 62–74.

Miller, L., J. Schofield and M. Rhodes (1986), *The Roman Quay at St Magnus House, London: Excavations at New Fresh Wharf, Lower Thames Street, London 1974–78*, London: Museum of London/Middlesex Archaeological Society, Special Paper of the London and Middlesex Archaeological Society No. 8.

Milles, J. (1779), 'Observations on Some Antiquities Found in the Tower of London in the Year 1777', *Archaeologia* 5: 291–305.

Millett, M. (1987), 'Boudicca, the First Colchester Potters' Shop, and the Dating of Neronian Samian', *Britannia* 18: 93–123.

Millett, M. (1990), *The Romanization of Britain*, Cambridge: Cambridge University Press.

Millett, M. (1996), 'Characterizing Roman London', in J. Bird, M. W. C. Hassall and H. Sheldon (eds), 33–7.

Millett, M. (1998), 'Introduction: London as Capital?', in B. Watson (ed.), 7–12.

Millett, M. (2016), 'Review Article: Improving our Understanding of *Londinium*', *Antiquity* 90: 1692–9.

Millett, M. and R. Gowland (2015), 'Infant and Child Burial Rites in Roman Britain: a study from East Yorkshire', *Britannia* 46: 171–89.

Millett, M., L. Revell and A. Moore (eds) (2016), *The Oxford Handbook of Roman Britain*, Oxford: Oxford University Press.

Milne, C., G. Milne and T. Brigham (1992), 'From Fields to Forum: Roman Developments at Leadenhall AD 50–450', in G. Milne (ed.), 9–33.

Milne, G. (1985), *The Port of Roman London*, London: Batsford.

Milne, G. (1992), 'The Patient Discovery of London's Past', in G. Milne (ed.), 1–8.

Milne, G. (1995), *Roman London*, London: Batsford/English Heritage.

Milne, G. (1996), 'A Palace Disproved: Reassessing the Provincial Governor's Presence in 1st-century London', in J. Bird, M. W. C. Hassall and H. Sheldon (eds), 49–55.

Milne, G. (1997), *St Bride's Church London: Archaeological Research 1952–60 and 1992–5*, London: English Heritage, Archaeological Report 11.

Milne, G. (2000), 'A Roman Provincial Fleet: The *Classis Britannica* Reconsidered', in G. J. Oliver, T. J. Cornell and S. Hodkinson (eds), *The Sea in Antiquity*, 127–31, Oxford: British Archaeological Reports, International Series 899.

Milne, G. (ed.) (1992), *From Roman Basilica to Medieval Market: Archaeology in Action in the City of London*, London: HMSO.

Milne, G. and A. Reynolds (1997), 'Archaeology of St Bride's Church', in G. Milne, 19–49.

Milne, G. and A. Wardle (1996), 'Early Roman Development at Leadenhall Court, London and Related Research', *TLMAS* 44 (1993): 23–170.

Monteil, G. (2008), 'The Distribution and Use of Samian Inkwells in Londinium', in J. Clark et al. (eds), 177–83.

Montgomery, J., J. Evans, S. Chenery, V. Pashley and K. Killgrove (2010), '"Gleaming white and deadly": Using Lead to Track Human Exposure and Geographic Origins in the Roman Period in Britain', in H. Eckardt (ed.), 199–226.

Moore, T. (2011), 'Detribalizing the Late Prehistoric Past: Concepts of Tribes in Iron Age and Roman Studies', *Journal of Social Archaeology* 11, no. 3: 334–60.

Morgan, M. (1980), 'Human Bone', in D. M. Jones, 164.

Morgan, R. (1980), 'The Carbon 14 and Dendrochronology', in C. Hill, M. Millett and T. Blagg, 88–94.

Morley, M. (2010), 'The Battersea Channel: A Former Course of the River Thames?', *LA* 12, no. 7: 175–81.

Mould, Q. (2012), 'Leather', in J. Leary and J. Butler, 42–8.

Mulryan, M. (2011), '"Paganism" in Late Antiquity: Regional Studies and Material Culture', in L. Lavan and M. Mulryan (eds), 41–86.

Museum of London (1999), *The Spitalfields Roman*, London: Museum of London.

Museum of London (2000), *The Archaeology of Greater London: An Assessment of Archaeological Evidence for Human Presence in the Area Now Covered by Greater London*, London: Museum of London.

Museum of London (2011), *Londinium: A New Map and Guide to Roman London*, London: Museum of London.

Neal, D. (2011), 'The Mosaic Floors', in J. Hill and P. Rowsome, 378–81.

Neal, D. S. and S. R. Cosh (2009), *Roman Mosaics of Britain: Volume III, South-East Britain, Part 2*, London: Society of Antiquaries of London.

Niblett, R. (1999), *The Excavation of a Ceremonial Site at Folly Lane, Verulamium*, London: Society for the Promotion of Roman Studies, Monograph 14.

Niblett, R. (2005), 'Roman Verulamium', in R. Niblett and I. Thompson (eds), *Alban's Buried Towns: An Assessment of St Albans' Archaeology up to AD 1600*, 41–165, Oxford: Oxbow.

Nixon, T., E. McAdam, R. Tomber and H. Swain (2002), *A Research Framework for London Archaeology 2002*, London: Museum of London.

Norman, P. and F. W. Readers (1912), 'Further Discoveries Relating to Roman London, 1906–12', *Archaeologia* 63: 257–344.

Opper, T. (2008), *Hadrian: Empire and Conflict*, London: British Museum.

Painter, K. S. (2015), 'Emergency or Votive? Two Groups of Late-Roman Gold and Silver Hoards', in J. Naylor and R. Bland (eds), *Hoarding and the Deposition of Metalwork from the Bronze Age to the 20th Century: A British Perspective*, 67–92, Oxford: Archaeopress, BAR British Series 615.

Parnell, G. (1977), 'Excavations at the Tower of London, 1976–7', *LA* 3, no. 4: 97–9.

Parnell, G. (1978), 'An Earlier Roman Riverside Wall at the Tower of London', *LA* 3, no. 7: 171–6.

Parnell, G. (1981), 'Tower of London – Inmost Ward Excavation 1979', *LA* 4, no. 3: 69–73.

Parnell, G. (1982), 'The Excavation of the Roman City Wall at the Tower of London and Tower Hill, 1954–76', *TLMAS* 33: 85–133.

Parnell, G. (1985), 'The Roman and Medieval Defences and the Later Development of the Inmost Ward, Tower of London: Excavations 1955–77', *TLMAS* 36: 1–79.

Parry, J. (1994), 'The Roman Quay at Thames Exchange, London', *LA* 7, no. 10: 263–7.

Pearce, J. (2013), *Contextual Archaeology of Burial Practices: Case Studies from Roman Britain*, Oxford: Archaeopress, BAR British Series 588.

Pearce, J. (2015), 'Urban Exits: Commercial Archaeology and the Study of Death Rituals and the Dead in the Towns of Roman Britain', in M. Fulford and N. Holbrook (eds), 138–66.

Pearson, A. (2002), *The Roman Shore Forts*, Stroud: Tempus.

Perez-Sala, M. and J. Shepherd (2008a), 'The Cullet Dump and Evidence of Glass Working', in N. C. W. Bateman, C. Cowan and R. Wroe-Brown, 142–6.

Perez-Sala, M. and J. Shepherd (2008b), 'The Glass Cullet Assemblage', in N. C. W. Bateman, C. Cowan and R. Wroe-Brown, 202–8.

Perna, S. (2015), 'Roman Coloured Stone Funerary Urns', in P. Coombe et al., 126–31.

Perring, D. ((1991) 2011), *Roman London*, Abingdon: Routledge.

Perring, D. (1991a), 'Watling Court: 39–53 Cannon Street, 11–14 Bow Lane (WAT 78)', in D. Perring and S. Roskams, 26–44.

Perring, D. (1991b), 'The Buildings', in D. Perring and S. Roskams, 67–107.

Perring, D. (2000), 'Londinium and its Hinterland: The Roman Period', in Museum of London, 119–70.

Perring, D. (2002), *The Roman House in Britain*, London: Routledge.

Perring, D. (2011a), 'London's Military Origins', *Journal of Roman Archaeology* 24: 249–66.

Perring, D. (2011b), 'Population Decline and Ritual Landscapes in Antonine London', *Journal of Roman Archaeology* 24: 269–82.

Perring, D. (2015), 'Recent Advances in the Understanding of Roman London', in M. Fulford and N. Holbrook (eds), 20–43.

Perring, D. and S. Roskams (1991), *Early Development of Roman London West of the Walbrook*, London: Museum of London and Council for British Archaeology, CBA Research Report 70.

Petts, D. (2003), *Christianity in Roman Britain*, Stroud: Tempus.

Philp, B. J. (1977), 'The Forum of Roman London: Excavations of 1968–9', *Britannia* 8: 1–64.

Philp, B. J. (1981), *The Excavation of the Roman Forts of the Classis Britannica at Dover, 1970–1977*, Dover: Kent Archaeological Rescue Unit, Kent Monograph Series, Third Research Report.

Pinder, I. (2011), 'Constructing and Deconstructing Roman City Walls: The Role of Urban Enceintes as Physical and Symbolic Boundaries', in D. Mullin (ed.), *Places in Between: The Archaeology of Social, Cultural and Geographical Borders and Borderlands*, 67–79, Oxford: Oxbow.

Pipe, A. (2003a), 'The Animal Bone', in C. Cowan, 175–82.

Pipe, A. (2003b), 'The Evidence for Antlerworking', in F. Hammer, 148–50.

Pitt, K. (2006), *Roman and Medieval Development South of Newgate: Excavations at 3–9 Newgate Street and 16–17 Old Bailey, City of London*, London: Museum of London, MOLAS Archaeological Studies Series 14.

Pitt, K. (2015), 'Excavations at 41 Eastcheap, London EC3', *TLMAS* 65 (2014): 149–83.

Pitt, K. and F. Seeley (2014), 'Excavations at 36–39 Poultry, London EC2', *TLMAS* 64 (2013): 13–56.

Pitts, M. (2014), 'Reconsidering Britain's First Urban Communities', *Journal of Roman Archaeology* 27: 133–73.

Pitts, M. and M. J. Versluys (eds) (2015), *Globalisation and the Roman World: World History, Connectivity and Material Culture*, Cambridge: Cambridge University Press.

Polm, M. (2016), 'Museum Representations of Roman Britain and Roman London: A Post-colonial Perspective', *Britannia* 47: 209–41.

Poole, C. (2010), 'Ceramic Building Material', in K. Powell, A. Smith and G. Laws, 180.

Potter, T. (2002), 'The Transformation of Britain: From 55 BC to AD 61', in P. Salway (ed.), 11–36.

Powell, K., A. Smith and G. Laws (2010), *Evolution of a Farming Community in the Upper Thames Valley: Excavation of a Prehistoric, Roman and Post-Roman Landscape at Cotswold Community, Gloucestershire and*

Wiltshire. Volume 1: Site Narrative and Overview, Oxford: Oxford Archaeology, Thames Valley Monographs No. 31.

Powers, N. (2006), 'Burial Catalogue (period 2)', in S. Watson, 20.

Powers, N. (2015a), 'The Effect of Fluvial Erosion on the Burials', in C. Harward, N. Powers and S. Watson, 127–32.

Powers, N. (2015b), 'The Human Bone', in A. Wardle (2015b), 154–5.

Pre-Construct Archaeology (2009), *Secrets of the Garden: Archaeologists Unearth the Lives of Roman Londoners at Drapers' Gardens*, Brockley: Pre-Construct Archaeology.

Price, J. E. (1880), *On a Bastion of London Wall, or, Excavations in Camomile Street, Bishopsgate*, London: J. B. Nichols and Sons.

Pringle, S. (2006), 'Early Box Flue Tiles from London', *LA* 11, no. 5: 124–9.

Pringle, S. (2007), 'London's Earliest Roman Bath-houses?' *LA* 11, no. 8: 205–9.

Pringle, S. (2009), 'Building Materials', in C. Cowan et al., 187–206.

Pritchard, F. (1982), 'Supporting Finds Evidence', in D. Bentley and F. Pritchard, 163–9.

Pritchard, F. (1986), 'Ornamental Stonework from Roman London', *Britannia* 17: 169–89.

Rayner, L. (2009), 'Origins and Earliest Development of the Settlement', in C. Cowan et al., 38–52.

Rayner, L. (2011a), 'Building 23: A Shop Selling Pottery and Foodstuffs', in J. Hill and P. Rowsome, 294–304.

Rayner, L. (2011b), 'Pottery', in J. Hill and P. Rowsome, 280–4.

Rayner, L. (2011c), 'Comparison of the Early Roman Pottery Assemblage from the Dumps South of Road 1 at 1 Poultry and site D', in J. Hill and P. Rowsome, 265–72.

Rayner, L. (2011d), 'The Pottery from Open Area 45 and Open Area 75', in J. Hill and P. Rowsome, 325–8.

Rayner, L. (2017), 'Clay, Water and Fuel: An Overview of Pottery Production in and around Early Roman London', in D. Bird (ed.), 346–67.

Rayner, L. and F. Seeley (1998), 'Pottery Publications and Research in Roman London', in B. Watson (ed.), 90–4.

Rayner, L. and F. Seeley (2008), 'The Southwark Pottery Type-series: 30 Years On', in J. Clark, J et al. (eds), 184–93.

Rayner, L. and F. Seeley (2009), 'Pottery', in C. Cowan et al., 206–29.

Rayner, L. and A. Wardle (2011), 'Trade and Imports', in J. Hill and P. Rowsome, 402–3.

Rayner, L., A. Wardle and F. Seeley (2011), 'Ritual and Religion', in J. Hill and P. Rowsome, 404–8.

RCHM (1928), *An Inventory of the Historical Monuments in London, Volume III, Roman London*, London: HMSO.

Redfern, R.C. and H. Bonney (2014), 'Headhunting and Amphitheatre Combat in Roman London, England: New Evidence from the Walbrook Valley', *Journal of Archaeological Science* 43: 214–26.

Redfern, R.C., D. R. Gröcke, A. R. Millard, V. Ridgeway, L. Johnson and J. T. Hefner (2016), 'Going South of the River: A Multidisciplinary Analysis of Ancestry, Mobility and Diet in a Population from Roman Southwark, London', *Journal of Archaeological Science* 74: 11–22.

Redfern, R., M. Marshall, K. Eaton and H. N. Pointar (in press), '"Written in Bone": New Discoveries About the Lives of Roman Londoners', *Britannia* 48.

Redknap, M. (2015), 'Observations on Roman Pottery from Pudding Pan and the Thames Estuary and Early Surveys', *Britannia* 46: 15–36.

Revell, L. (2009), *Roman Imperialism and Local Identities*, Cambridge: Cambridge University Press.

Revell, L. (2016), *Ways of Being Roman: Discourses of Identity in the Roman West*, Oxford: Oxbow.

Rhodes, M. (1980a), 'The Finds Reports, Introduction', in D. M. Jones, 34–7.

Rhodes, M. (1980b), 'The Saxon Pottery', in C. Hill, M. Millett and T. Blagg, 97–8.

Rhodes, M. (1986a), 'Dumps of Unused Pottery near London Bridge', in L. Miller, J. Schofield and M. Rhodes, 199–210.

Rhodes, M. (1986b), 'Discussion [The Finds]', in L. Miller, J. Schofield and M. Rhodes, 88–95.

Rhodes, M. (1991), 'The Roman Coinage from London Bridge and the Development of the City and Southwark', *Britannia* 22: 179–90.

Richardson, B. (1983), 'Excavation Round-up', *LA* 4, no. 10: 274–7.

Richardson, B. (1986), 'Pottery', in L. Miller, J. Schofield and M. Rhodes, 96–138.

Richardson, B. (2004), 'Discussion of the Character of the pre-Boudican Pottery Assemblage', in L. Dunwoodie, 38–9.

Richardson, B. (2008), 'An early 2nd-century Ceramic Assemblage', in N. C. W. Bateman, C. Cowan and R. Wroe-Brown, 134–5.

Ridgeway, V. (2009), 'Conclusions', in D. Divers et al., 125–8.

Ridgeway, V. (2014), 'A Ritual Landscape in Roman Southwark? The View from Watling Street and Londinium's Southern Approaches', MLitt diss., Newcastle University.

Ridgeway, V., K. Leary and B. Sudds (2013), *Roman Burials in Southwark: Excavations at 52–56 Lant Street and 56 Southwark Bridge Road, London SE 1*, Cambridge: Pre-Construct Archaeology, Pre-Construct Archaeology Monograph 17.

Rielly, K. (2005), 'Animal Remains', in B. Yule, 158–67.

Rielly, K. (2008), 'The Drapers Gardens Bear', *LA* 11, no. 12: 318.

Rivet, A. L. F. and C. Smith (1979), *The Place-Names of Roman Britain*, London: Batsford.

Rixson, D. (1978), 'Animal Bones', in J. Bird, M. W. C. Hassall and H. Sheldon (eds), 231–2.

Roberts, C. and M. Cox (2004), 'The Human Population: Health and Disease', in M. Todd (ed.), 242–72.

Rogers, A. (2008), 'Religious Place and its Interaction with Urbanism in the Roman Era', *Journal of Social Archaeology* 8, no. 1: 37–62.

Rogers, A. (2011a), *Late Roman Towns in Britain: Rethinking Change and Decline*, Cambridge: Cambridge University Press.

Rogers, A. (2011b), 'Reimagining Roman Ports and Harbours: The Port of Roman London and Waterfront Archaeology', *Oxford Journal of Archaeology* 30, no. 2: 207–25.

Rogers, A. (2013), *Water and Roman Urbanism: Towns, Waterscapes, Land, Transformation and Experience in Roman Britain*, Leiden: Brill.

Rogers, A. (2015), *The Archaeology of Roman Britain: Biography and Identity*, Abingdon: Routledge.

Rogers, A. and R. Hingley (2010), 'Edward Gibbon and Francis Haverfield: The Traditions of Imperial Decline', in M. Bradley (ed.), *Classics & Imperialism in the British Empire*, 189–209, Oxford: Oxford University Press.

Roskams, S. (1991a), 'Newgate Street (GPO75)', in D. Perring and S. Roskams, 3–26.

Roskams, S. (1991b), '1–6 Milk Street (MLK 76), 7–10 Milk Street (MIL 72)', in D. Perring and S. Roskams, 44–51.

Rowsome, P. (1996), 'The Billingsgate Roman House and Bath – Conservation and Assessment', *LA* 7, no. 16: 415–23.

Rowsome, P. (1998), 'The Development of the Town Plan of Early Roman London', in B. Watson (ed.), 35–46.

Rowsome, P. (1999), 'The Huggin Hill Baths and Bathing in London: Barometer of the Town's Changing Circumstances?', in J. DeLaine and D. E. Johnston (eds), 262–77.

Rowsome, P. (2006), 'Conclusions', in R. Bluer and T. Brigham, 96–8.

Rowsome, P. (2008), 'Mapping Roman London: Identifying its Urban Patterns and Interpreting their Meaning', in J. Clark et al. (eds), 25–32.

Rowsome, P. (2014), 'Roman and Medieval Defences North of Ludgate: Excavations at 42–6 Ludgate Hill and 1–6 Old Bailey, London EC4', *LA* 14, no. 1: 3–10.

Russell, M. and H. Manley (2013), 'Finding Nero: Casting a New Light on Romano-British Sculpture', *Internet Archaeology* 32. Available online: http://dx.doi.org/10.11141/ia.32.5 (accessed 5 May 2017).

Rykwert, J. ((1976) 1995), *The Idea of a Town: The Anthropology of Urban Form in Rome, Italy and the Ancient World*, Cambridge, MA: MIT Press.

Salway, P. (ed.) (2002), *The Roman Era: Short Oxford History of the British Isles*, Oxford: Oxford University Press.

Sankey, D. (1998), 'Cathedrals, Granaries, and Urban Vitality in Late Roman London', in B. Watson (ed.), 78–82.

Sankey, D. (2003), 'Roman, Medieval and Later Development at 7 Bishopsgate, London EC2: From a 1st-century Cellared Building to the 17th-century Properties of the Merchant Taylors' Company', *TLMAS* 53 (2002): 1–24.

Sankey, D. and B. Connell (2008), 'Late Roman Burials and Extramural Medieval and Later Development at Premier Place, Devonshire Square, Houndsditch, London EC2', *TLMAS* 58 (2007): 53–77.

Sankey, D. and A. Stephenson (1991), 'Recent Work on London's Defences', in V. A. Maxfield and M. J. Dobson (eds), 117–24.

Sayer, K. (2009a), 'Human Bone Assessment', in D. Killock, *An Assessment of the Archaeological Excavation at Tabard Square, 34–70 Long Lane & 31–47 Tabard Street, London SE1, London Borough of Southwark*, 364–72, London: Pre-Construct Archaeology.

Sayer, K. (2009b), 'Human Bone Assessment', in B. Hawkins, 373–9.

Schaaf, L. (1976), 'Excavations at 175–7 Borough High Street, Southwark', *LA* 3, no. 1: 3–7.

Schaff, L. (1988), '84–6 Borough High Street', in P. Hinton (ed.), 83–132.

Schofield, J. (1986), 'The Discoveries at St Magnus House', in L. Miller, J. Schofield and M. Rhodes, 1–24.

Schofield, J. (1998), *Archaeology in the City of London 1907–91: A Guide to Records of Excavations by the Museum of London*, London: Museum of London, Archaeological Gazetteer Series 1.

Schofield, J. (2000), 'London: Buildings and Defences 1200–1600', in I. Haynes, H. Sheldon and L. Hannigan (eds), 223–38.

Schofield, J. (2011), *St Paul's Cathedral Before Wren*, Swindon: English Heritage.

Schulting, R. J. and R. Bradley (2013), '"Of Human Remains and Weapons in the Neighbourhood of London": New AAM 14C dates on Thames "river skulls" and their European context', *Archaeological Journal* 170, no. 1: 30–77.

Schwab, I. (1978), '106–114 Borough High Street', in J. Bird, M. W. C. Hassall and H. Sheldon (eds), 177–220.

Scott, I. (2017), 'Ironwork and its Production', in D. Bird (ed.), 301–29.

Seager Smith, R. (2009a), 'Pottery from Open Area 2', in Birbeck and Schuster, 15.

Seager Smith, R. (2009b), 'Roman Pottery', in Birbeck and Schuster, 53–61.

Seeley, F. and J. Drummond-Murray (2005), *Roman Pottery Production in the Walbrook Valley: Excavations at 20–28 Moorgate, City of London, 1998–2000*, London: Museum of London Archaeological Services, MOLAS Monograph 25.

Seeley, F. and A. Wardle (2009), 'Religion and Ritual', in C. Cowan et al., 143–56.

Shaffrey, R. (2015), 'Intensive Milling Practices in the Romano-British Landscape of Southern England: Using Newly Established Criteria for Distinguishing Millstones from Rotary Querns', *Britannia* 46: 55–92.

Shaw, H., J. Montgomery, R. Redfern, R. Gowland and J. Evans (2016), 'Identifying Migrants in Roman London Using Lead and Strontium Stable Isotopes', *Journal of Archaeological Science* 66: 57–68.

Sheldon, H. (1974), 'Excavations at Toppings and Sun Wharves, Southwark, 1970–1972', *TLMAS* 25: 1–116.

Sheldon, H. (1978), 'The 1972–74 Excavations: Their Contribution to Southwark's History', in J. Bird, M. W. C. Hassall and H. Sheldon (eds), 11–49.

Sheldon, H. (2000), 'Roman Southwark', in I. Haynes, H. Sheldon and L. Hannigan (eds), 121–48.

Sheldon, H. (2011), 'Enclosing *Londinium*: The Roman Landward and Riverside Walls', *TLMAS* 61 (2010): 227–35.

Sheldon, H. (2014), 'Roman *Londinium's* Walls,' *TLMAS* 64 (2013): 284–6.

Sheldon, H. and I. Haynes (2000), 'Introduction: Twenty-five Years of London Archaeology', in I. Haynes, H. Sheldon and L. Hannigan (eds), 1–8.

Sheldon, H. and I. Tyers (1983), 'Recent Dendrochronological Work in Southwark and its Implications', *LA* 4, no. 13: 355–61.

Sheldon, H. and B. Yule (1979), 'Excavations in Greenwich Park 1978–79', *LA* 3, no. 12: 311–17.

Shepherd, J. (1988), 'The Roman Occupation in the Area of Paternoster Square, City of London', *TLMAS* 39: 1–30.

Shepherd, J. (1998), *The Temple of Mithras London: Excavations by W F Grimes and A Williams at the Walbrook*, London: English Heritage, Archaeological Report 12.

Shepherd, J. (2012), *The Discovery of the Roman Fort at Cripplegate, City of London: Excavations by W F Grimes 1947–68*, London: Museum of London Archaeology, MOLAS.

Shepherd, J. and S. Chettle (2012), 'The Cripplegate Fort and Londinium', in J. Shepherd, 142–63.

Shepherd, J. and A. Wardle (2015), 'The Basinghall Glass in Context', in A. Wardle (2015b), 91–107.

Sidell, J. (2008), 'Londinium's Landscape', in J. Clark et al. (eds), 62–8.

Sidell, J., J. Cotton, L. Rayner and L. Wheeler (2002), *The Prehistory and Topography of Southwark and Lambeth*, London: Museum of London, MOLAS Monograph 14.

Sidell, J. and K. Rielly (1998), 'New Evidence for Ritual Use of Animals in Roman London', in B. Watson (ed.), 95–9.

Sidell, J., K. Wilkinson, R. Scaife and N. Cameron (2000), *The Holocene Evolution of the London Thames: Archaeological Excavations for the London Underground Limited Jubilee Line Extension Project*, London: Museum of London, MOLAS Monograph 5.

Simmonds, A., N. Márquez-Grant and L. Loe (2008), *Life and Death in a Roman City: Excavation of a Roman Cemetery with a Mass Grave at 120–122 London Road, Gloucester*, Oxford: Oxford Archaeology.

Sloane, B. (2008), 'Images of Empire: Illustrating the Fabric of Roman London', in J. Clark et al. (eds), 11–24.

Sloane, B. (2012), *The Augustan Nunnery of St Mary Clerkenwell, London: Excavations 1974–96*, London: Museum of London, MOLAS Monograph 57.

Sloane, B. and G. Malcolm (2004), *Excavations at the Priory of the Order of the Hospital of St John of Jerusalem, Clerkenwell, London*, London: Museum of London, MOLAS Monograph 20.

Smith, A., M. Allen, T. Brindle and M. Fulford (2016), *The Rural Settlement of Roman Britain*, London: Society for the Promotion of Roman Studies, Britannia Monograph 29.

Smith, A. and K. Powell (2010), 'In the Shadow of Corinium – The Later Iron Age to Late Roman Period', in K. Powell, A. Smith and G. Laws, 99–166.

Smith, C. R. (1842), 'Observations on Roman Remains Recently Found in London', *Archaeologia* 29: 145–66.

Speed, G. (2014), *Towns in the Dark? Urban Transformations from Late Roman Britain to Anglo-Saxon England*, Oxford: Archaeopress.

Stead, I. M. (1985), *The Battersea Shield*, London: British Museum.

Stead, I. M. (2006), *British Iron Age Swords and Scabbards*, London: British Museum.

Stephenson, A. and C. Edwards (2012), 'The Royal College of Arts Site, Battersea Bridge Road, from the Iron Age to Modern Times', *LA* 13, no. 6: 162–7.

Stevenson, J. (1995), 'Copper Alloy Objects', in C. Cowan, 82–97.

Stewart, K. (2016), 'Identifying the Wooden Tablets to Species', in R. S. O. Tomlin, 6.

Stewart, P. (2003), *Statues in Roman Society: Representations and Responses*, Oxford: Oxford University Press.

Stow, J. (1599), *A Survay of London: Contayning the Originall, Antiquity, Increase, Moderne estate, and Description of that Citie*, London: John Wolfe.

Straker, V. (1987), 'Carbonised Cereal Grain from First Century London', in P. Marsden, 151–3.

Strang, V. (2005), 'Common Senses: Water, Sensory Experiences and the Generation of Meaning', *Journal of Material Culture* 10, no. 1: 92–120.

Sudds, B. (2008), 'Ceramic and Stone Building Material and Structural Remains', in T. Bradley and J. Butler, 34–40.

Sudds, B. (2010), 'Post-Roman Pottery Assessment', in D. Killock, 146–52.

Sudds, B. (2011a), 'Building Materials', in A. Douglas, J. Gerrard and B. Sudds, 103–18.

Sudds, B. (2011b), 'Reconstruction of the Bath House', in A. Douglas, J. Gerrard and B. Sudds, 153–64.

Sudds, B. and A. Douglas (2015), 'Excavations at Crispin Street, Spitalfields: From Roman Cemetery to Post-Medieval Artillery Ground', *TLMAS* 65 (2014): 1–50.

Swain, H. (1995), 'Prehistoric Pottery', in C. Cowan, 67–70.

Swain, H. and T. Williams (2008), 'The Population of Roman London', in J. Clark et al. (eds), 33–40.

Swan, V. (2009), *Ethnicity, Conquest and Recruitment: Two Case Studies from the Northern Military Provinces*, Portsmouth, RI: Journal of Roman Archaeology, Supplementary Series 72.

Swift, D. (2003), *Roman Burials, Medieval Tenements and Suburban Growth: 201 Bishopsgate, City of London*, London: Museum of London, MOLAS Archaeological Studies Series 10.

Swift, D. (2008), *Roman Waterfront Development at 12 Arthur Street, City of London*, London: Museum of London, MOLAS Archaeological Studies Series 19.

Symonds, R. P. (2003), 'Romano-British Amphorae', *Journal of Roman Pottery Studies* 10: 50–9.

Symonds, R. P. (2006), 'The Pottery', in S. Watson, 81–6.

Symonds, R. P. (2007), 'The Importance of the Camulodunum Form 306 bowl', in I. Blair and D. Sankey, 63–5.

Symonds, R. P. and R. S. Tomber (1994), 'Late Roman London: An Assessment of the Ceramic Evidence from the City of London', *TLMAS* 42 (1991): 59–99.

Taylor, J. (2001), 'Rural society in Roman Britain', in S. James and M. Millett (eds), 46–59.

Taylor, T. (2012), 'A study of the River Walbrook through Roman London', *LA* 13, no. 4: 95–9.

Taylor-Wilson, R. (2002), *Excavations at Hunt's House, Guy's Hospital, London Borough of Southwark*, London: Pre-Construct Archaeology, Monograph 1.

Telfer, A. (2010), 'New Evidence for the Transition from the Late Roman to the Saxon Period at St Martin-in-the-Fields, London', in M. Henig and N. Ramsay (eds), *Intersections: The Archaeology and History of Christianity in England, 400–1200*, 49–58, Oxford: Archaeopress, BAR British Series 505.

Thomas, C. (2004), *Life and Death in London's East End: 2000 Years at Spitalfields*, London: Museum of London.

Thomas, C. (2008), 'Roman Westminster: Fact or Fiction?', in J. Clark et al. (eds), 102–6.

Thomas, C., B. Sloane and C. Phillpotts (1997), *Excavations at the Priory and Hospital of St Mary Spital, London*, London: Museum of London, MOLAS Monograph 1.

Thompson, C. S. (2015), 'Military Aspects of the Ceramic Assemblage', in L. Dunwoodie, C. Harward and K. Pitt, 154–9.

Thrale, P. (2008), 'Roman Stone Building, Ditches and Burials along Watling Street', *LA* 12, no. 1: 19–22.

Todd, M. (ed.) (2004), *A Companion to Roman Britain*, Blackwell Companions to British History, Oxford: Blackwell.

Tomber, R. (2003), 'Two Unusual Amphora Types from the Museum of London', *Journal of Roman Pottery Studies* 10: 107–8.

Tomlin, R. S. O. (1996), 'A Five-Acre Wood in Roman Kent', in J. Bird, M. W. C. Hassall and H. Sheldon (eds), 209–15.

Tomlin, R. S. O. (2003), '"The Girl in Question": A New Text from Roman London', *Britannia* 34: 41–51.

Tomlin, R. S. O. (2006), 'Was Roman London ever a *Colonia*? The Written Evidence', in R. J. A. Wilson (ed.), 49–64.

Tomlin, R. S. O. (2011a), 'Stylus Writing Tablets', in J. Hill and P. Rowsome, 514–17.

Tomlin, R. S. O. (2011b), 'Inscription', in A. Douglas, J. Gerrard and B. Sudds, 118.

Tomlin, R. S. O. (2012), 'Inscriptions', *Britannia* 43: 395–421.

Tomlin, R. S. O. (2014a), 'Inscriptions', *Britannia* 45: 431–62.

Tomlin, R. S. O. (2014b), '"Drive away the cloud of Plague": A Greek Amulet from Roman London', in R. Collins and F. McIntosh (eds), 197–205.

Tomlin, R. S. O. (2015), 'Inscriptions', in D. Killock et al., 192–4.

Tomlin, R. S. O. (2016), *Roman London's First Voices: Writing Tablets from the Bloomberg Excavations, 2010–14*, London: Museum of London, MOLAS Monograph 72.

Tomlin, R. S. O. and M. W. C. Hassall (2000), 'Inscriptions', *Britannia* 31: 432–49.

Tomlin, R. S. O. and M. W. C. Hassall (2005), 'Inscriptions', *Britannia* 36: 473–97.

Tomlin, R. S. O., R. P. Wright and M. W. C. Hassall (2009), *The Roman Inscriptions of Britain, Volume III: Inscriptions on Stone Found or Notified Between 1 January 1955 and 31 December 2006*, Oxford: Oxbow.

Totten, D. M and K. Lafrenz Samuels (eds) (2012), *Making Roman Places, Past and Present*, Portsmouth, RI: Journal of Roman Archaeology, Supplementary Series 89.

Toynbee, J. M. C. (1964), *Art in Britain Under the Romans*, Oxford: Oxford University Press.

Toynbee, J. M. C. (1971), *Death and Burial in the Roman World*, London: Thames and Hudson.

Toynbee, J. M. C. (1986), *The Roman Art Treasures from the Temple of Mithras*, London: London and Middlesex Archaeological Society, Special Paper 7.

Treveil, P. and B. Watson (2006), 'Roman, Medieval and Post-medieval Activity at West Smithfield: Recent Work at 8–22 Smithfield Street and 30–38 Hosier Lane, City of London', *LA* 11, no. 6: 143–50.

Tyers, I. (1994), 'Appendix 6 Dendrochronology of Roman and Early Medieval Ships', in P. Marsden, 201–9.

Tyers, I. (2008a), 'A Gazetteer of Tree-ring Dates from Roman London', in J. Clark et al. (eds), 69–74.

Tyers, I. (2008b), 'Dendrochronology', in T. Bradley and J. Butler, 52–4.

Tyers, I. (2011), 'Tree-ring Analysis', in J. Hill and P. Rowsome, 562–7.

Tyers, I. and G. Boswijk (2001), 'The Dendrochronological Dating', in T. Brigham, 120–1.

Tyers, P. A. (1996), 'Late Iron Age and Early Roman Pottery Traditions of the London Region', in J. Bird, M. W. C. Hassall and H. Sheldon (eds), 139–45.

Unger, S. (2009), 'Red or Yellow? The Changing Colour of Roman London's Roof-line', *LA* 12, no. 4: 107–13.

Upson, A. and B. Pye (1987), '79 Gracechurch Street', in P. Marsden, 117–19.

van der Veen, M., A. Livarda and A. Hill (2008), 'New Plant Foods in Roman Britain – Dispersal and Social Access', *Environmental Archaeology* 13, no. 1: 11–36.

VCH (1909), *The Victorian History of London, including London within the Bars, Westminster & Southwark*, ed. W. Page, London: Constable.

Vince, A. (1990), *Saxon London: An Archaeological Investigation*, London: Seaby.

Vince, A. (1991), 'The Development of Saxon London', in A. Vince (ed.), 409–35.

Vince, A. (ed.) (1991), *Aspects of Saxo-Norman London: 2, Finds and Environmental Evidence*, London: London and Middlesex Archaeological Society, Special Paper 12.

Vince, A. and A. Jenner (1991), 'The Saxon and Early Medieval Pottery of London', in A. Vince (ed.), 19–119.

von Stackelberg, K. T. (2009), *The Roman Garden: Space, Sense and Society*, London: Routledge.

Wacher, J. (1995), *The Towns of Roman Britain*, London: Batsford.

Waite, G. and J. Cotton (2000), 'The Iron Age', in Museum of London, 101–17.

Wallace, C. (2006), 'Long-Lived Samian?', *Britannia* 37: 256–72.

Wallace, L. M. (2013), 'The Foundation of Roman London: Examining the Claudian Fort Hypothesis', *Oxford Journal of Archaeology* 32, no. 3: 275–91.

Wallace, L. M. (2014), *The Origins of Roman London*, Cambridge: Cambridge University Press.

Wallace-Hadrill, A. (1988), 'The Social Structure of the Roman House', *Papers of the British School at Rome* 56: 43–97.

Wallower, B. (2002a), 'Roman Temple Complex in Greenwich Park? Part 1', *LA* 10, no. 2: 46–54.

Wallower, B. (2002b), 'Roman Temple Complex in Greenwich Park? Part 2', *LA* 10, no. 3: 76–81.

Wardle, A. (2000), 'Funerary Rites, Burial Practices and Beliefs', in A. Mackinder, 27–30.

Wardle, A. (2002a), 'The Accessioned Finds', in J. Drummond-Murray and P. Thompson, 212–31.

Wardle, A. (2002b), 'Accessioned Finds', in D. Lakin, 51–3.

Wardle, A. (2007), 'Roman Accessioned Finds', in J. Lyon, 167–9.

Wardle, A. (2008a), '*Bene Lava*: Bathing in Roman London', in J. Clark et al. (eds), 201–11.

Wardle, A. (2008b), 'Accessioned Finds', in N. C. W. Bateman, C. Cowan and R. Wroe-Brown, 191–200.

Wardle, A. (2009), 'Delving into the Dumps', in C. Cowan et al., 118–43.

Wardle, A. (2011a), 'Finds from the Wallbrook Deposits', in J. Hill and P. Rowsome, 329–49.

Wardle, A. (2011b), 'Non-ferrous Metalworking', in J. Hill and P. Rowsome, 390–2.

Wardle, A. (2011c), 'The Accessioned Finds', in J. Hill and P. Rowsome, 284–9.

Wardle, A. (2014a), 'Roman Vessel Glass and Glass Working', in L. Casson, J. Drummond-Murray and A. Francis, 178–86.

Wardle, A. (2014b), 'The Minories Eagle', *TLMAS* 64 (2013): 297–8.

Wardle, A. (2015a), 'Military Aspects of the Accessioned Finds Assemblage', in L. Dunwoodie, C. Harward and K. Pitt, 159–62.

Wardle, A. (2015b), *Glass working on the Margins of Roman London: Excavations at 35 Basinghall Street, City of London, 2005*, London: Museum of London, MOLAS Monograph 70.

Wardle, A. and L. Rayner (2011), 'Evidence for a Military Presence', in J. Hill and P. Rowsome, 289–90.

Wardle, A. and J. Shepherd (2015), 'Working in the Margins: The Glass-working Waste from Basinghall Street', in A. Wardle (2015b), 36–74.

Watson, B. (1998), '"Dark Earth" and Urban Decline in Late Roman London', in B. Watson (ed.), 100–6.

Watson, B. (2001), 'The Late Saxon Bridgehead', in B. Watson, T. Brigham and T. Dyson, 52–60.

Watson, B. (2012), 'The Guy's Hospital Roman Boat Fifty Years On', *LA* 13, no. 5: 119–25.

Watson, B. (ed.) (1998), *Roman London: Recent Archaeological Work, Including Papers Given at a Seminar Held at The Museum of London on 16 November, 1996*, Portsmouth, RI: Journal of Roman Archaeology, Supplementary Series 24.

Watson, B., T. Brigham and T. Dyson (2001), *London Bridge: 2000 Years of a River Crossing*, London: Museum of London, MOLAS Monograph 8.

Watson, S. (2003), *An Excavation in the Western Cemetery of Roman London: Atlantic House, City of London*, London: Museum of London, MOLAS Archaeological Studies Series 7.

Watson, S. (2004), 'Roman and Medieval Occupation at 8–10 Old Jewry, City of London', *LA* 10, no. 10: 264–70.

Watson, S. (2006), *Developments on Roman London's Western Hill: Excavations at Paternoster Square, City of London*, London: Museum of London, MOLAS Monograph 32.

Watson, S. (2013), 'The Bloomberg Bonanza', *LA* 13, no. 9: 242–3.

Watson, S. (2015a), *Urban Development in the North-west of Londinium: Excavations at 120–122 Cheapside and 14–18 Gresham Street, City of London, 2005–7*, London: Museum of London, MOLAS Archaeological Studies Series 32.

Watson, S. (2015b), 'Excavations at 6–12 Basinghall Street and 93–95 Gresham Street, City of London EC2', *TLMAS* 65 (2014): 185–219.

Watt, R. J. (1978a), 'The Human Bones', in J. Bird, M. W. C. Hassall and H. Sheldon (eds), 175–6.

Watt, R. J. (1978b), 'Other Human Bones', in J. Bird, M. W. C. Hassall and H. Sheldon (eds), 497.

Webster, J. (2001), 'Creolizing the Roman Provinces', *American Journal of Archaeology* 105: 209–25.

Westman, A. and S. Pringle (2009), 'Infrastructure: Roads and the Layout of the Settlement', in C. Cowan et al., 52–66.

Wheeler, L. (2009), 'Infrastructure: Waterfronts, Land reclamation, Drainage and Water Supply', in C. Cowan et al., 66–77.

Wheeler, R. E. M. (1930), *London in Roman Times*, London: Museum of London.

Whipp, D. (1980), 'Excavations at Tower Hill 1978', *TLMAS* 31: 47–67.

White, W. (2009), 'Site 38: Guy's Hospital, St Thomas Street (GHR82)', in Cowan et al., 252–4.

Whittaker, C. R. (1994), *Frontiers of the Roman Empire: A Social and Economic Study*, London: Johns Hopkins University.

Wilkes, J. (1996), 'The Status of Londinium', in J. Bird, M. W. C. Hassall and H. Sheldon (eds), 27–31.

Wilkinson, K. and J. Sidell (2000), 'Late Glacial and Holocene Development of the London Thames', in J. Sidell et al., 103–10.

Williams, D. (2011), 'The Amphorae', in A. Douglas, J. Gerrard and B. Sudds, 78–81.

Williams, D. and R. Hobbs (2015), 'An Unusual Roman Stone Cinerary Urn From London', in P. Pensabene and E. Gasparini (eds), *Interdisciplinary Studies on Ancient Stone X*, 843–49, Rome: L'Erma di Bretschneider.

Williams, J. (2007), 'New Light on Latin in Pre-Conquest Britain', *Britannia* 38: 1–11.

Williams, T. (1991), 'Allectus's Building Campaign in London: Implications for the Development of the Saxon Shore', in V. A. Maxfield and M. J. Dobson (eds), 132–41.

Williams, T. (1993), *Public Buildings in the South-west Quarter of Roman London: The Archaeology of Roman London Volume 3*, London: Museum of London and the Council for British Archaeology, CBA Research Report 88.

Williams, T. (2003), 'Water and the Roman City: Life in Roman London', in P. Wilson (ed.), 242–50.

Willis, S. (2007a), 'Sea, Coast, Estuary, Land, and Culture in Iron Age Britain', in C. Haselgrove and T. Moore (eds), 107–29.

Willis, S. (2007b), 'Roman Towns, Roman Landscapes: The Cultural Terrain of Town and Country in the Roman period', in A. Fleming and R. Hingley (eds), *Prehistoric and Roman Landscapes: Landscape History After Hoskins*, 143–64, Macclesfield: Windgather.

Willis, S. (2011), 'Samian Ware and Society in Roman Britain and Beyond', *Britannia* 42: 167–242.

Willmott, T. (1982), 'Excavation at Queen's Street, City of London, 1953 and 1960, and Roman Timber-lined Wells in London', *TLMAS* 33: 1–78.

Wilmott, T. (1991), *Excavations in the Middle Wallbrook Valley, City of London, 1927–1960*, Over Wallop: London and Middlesex Archaeological Society, Special Papers 13.

Wilmott, T. (2009), 'Function and Community: Some Thoughts on the Amphitheatres of Roman Britain', in T. Wilmott (ed.), 141–56.

Wilmott, T. (ed.) (2009), *Roman Amphitheatres and Spectacula: A 21st-century Perspective*, Oxford: Archaeopress, BAR, International Series 1946.

Wilson, P. (ed.) (2003), *The Archaeology of Roman Towns*, Oxford: Oxbow.

Wilson, R. J. A. (2006), 'Urban Defences and Civic Status in Early Roman Britain', in R. J. A. Wilson (ed.), 1–48.

Wilson, R. J. A. (ed.) (2006), *Romanitas: Essays on Roman Archaeology in Honour of Sheppard Frere on the Occasion of his Ninetieth Birthday*, Oxford: Oxbow.

Windle, B. (1897), *Life in Early Britain*, London: David Nutt.

Woodward, P. and A. Woodward (2004), 'Dedicating the Town: Urban Foundation Deposits in Roman Britain', *World Archaeology* 36, no. 1: 68–86.

Woolf, G. (1998), *Becoming Roman*, Cambridge: Cambridge University Press.

Wroe-Brown, R. (2014), *Roman Occupation South-east of the Forum: Excavations at 20 Fenchurch Street, City of London, 2008–9*, London: Museum of London, MOLAS Archaeological Studies Series 31.

Yule, B. (1982), 'A Third Century Well Group, and the Later Roman Settlement in Southwark', *LA* 4, no. 9: 243–9.

Yule, B. (1990), 'The "Dark Earth" and Late Roman London', *Antiquity* 64: 620–8.

Yule, B. (2005), *A Prestigious Roman Building Complex on the Southwark Waterfront: Excavations at Winchester Palace, London, 1983–90*, London: Museum of London, MOLAS Monograph 23.

Yule, B. and P. Hinton (1988), '88 Borough High Street', in P. Hinton (ed.), 71–81.

Yule, B. and N. B. Rankov (1998), 'Legionary Soldiers in 3rd-c. Southwark', in B. Watson (ed.), 67–77.

INDEX